SOCIAL DIMENSIONS OF CANADIAN SPORT AND PHYSICAL ACTIVITY

Edited by

JANE CROSSMAN
Lakehead University

JAY SCHERER
University of Alberta

Toronto

Acquisitions Editor: Matthew Christian
Marketing Manager: Lisa Gillis
Program Manager: Madhu Ranadive
Project Manager: Susan Johnson
Developmental Editor: Christine Langone
Production Services: Kailash Jadli, iEnergizer Aptara, Inc.
Permissions Project Manager: Kathryn O'Handley
Photo Permissions Research: Krystyna Sperka Borgen
Text Permissions Research: Varoon Deo-Singh
Cover Designer: Bill Gillis, iEnergizer Aptara, Inc.
Cover Image: Steve Kingsman/Dreamstime

Credits and acknowledgments for material borrowed from other sources and reproduced, with permission, in this textbook appear on the appropriate page within the text.

If you purchased this book outside the United States or Canada, you should be aware that it has been imported without the approval of the publisher or the author.

Library and Archives Canada Cataloguing in Publication

Crossman, Jane, author
    Social dimensions of Canadian sport and physical activity / Jane Crossman,
Lakehead University, Jay Scherer, University of Alberta.
Includes bibliographical references and index.
ISBN 978-0-13-344446-9 (pbk.)
    1. Sports—Social aspects—Canada. I. Scherer, Jay, author II. Title.
GV706.5.C76 2014   306.4'830971   C2014-905540-4

3   16

ISBN 978-0-13-344446-9

This book is dedicated to Paulene, Heather and Emma.

Contents

Preface

Many of our students who study the social dimensions of sport and physical activity inevitably bring their own perceptions of what these popular practices are all about. Yet, in many instances, after completing one or two sociocultural and historical courses, their perceptions change quite remarkably. For example, students learn that the opportunities to participate in sport aren't equitable; that the control of sport is in the hands of a minority, many of whom are white males of affluence; that racism in sport still exists today even though it may not be readily apparent when watching a contest on television or reading about it online; that powerful economic and political forces shape what sport is today and what it might look like in the future; and that the mass media act as a filter of what we see and how we see it.

Although *Social Dimensions of Canadian Sport and Physical Activity* has a deliberately distinctly Canadian focus, we live in a world that has never been more interconnected. Indeed, what happens in the world of sport *outside* our borders influences sport *inside* our borders. Canadians have, historically, embraced a wide range of local sport and athletic heroes, in addition to consuming copious amounts of sports content from our American neighbours via the mass media. Today, more and more Canadians follow not only the major leagues of North American sport, but teams and leagues from around the world, including the most popular European soccer leagues. For generations, meanwhile, immigrants have been bringing their sports and their ways of doing physical activity to Canada. As such, we are not simply a carbon copy of another country or an amalgamation of countries. We are uniquely Canadian and, over time, we have shaped our own cultural ideologies and our own ways of interpreting and playing sport, sometimes in competing and contradictory ways.

THE CONTENT OF THE TEXT

Social Dimensions of Canadian Sport and Physical Activity contains 15 chapters. Because the chapter sequence has been purposely coordinated, we recommend that the chapters be read consecutively. However, since their content is so distinctive, it is possible to read the chapters in an altered order. Each chapter concludes with relevant Critical Thinking Questions, Suggested Readings, and References.

In the first chapter, Drs. Jane Crossman and Jay Scherer provide an introductory foundation for understanding the social dimensions of sport and physical activity from a Canadian perspective. They describe how pervasive sport is in Canadian society and outline terms that will be used throughout the text, such as *sociological imagination*, *agency*, *social structures*, *power*, *ideology*, and *hegemony*.

In the second chapter, Dr. Ian Ritchie presents a rich overview of sociological theories that set the foundation for understanding the social world, and more specifically for our purposes the world of sport. Since it is impossible to present a complete inventory of the myriad sociological theories, he focuses on four major ones: Durkheim's *functionalism*, Marx's *conflict theory*, Mead's *symbolic interactionism*, and *critical social theories* (cultural, feminist, and critical race studies).

In Chapter 3, Dr. Don Morrow condenses Canadian sport history from the 15th century to the present day. He highlights the people who have influenced our sport history (First Nations, French, British), as well as the existing social conditions, power relations, and developments that have had such a profound effect on shaping the development of sport in Canada. Highlighted are industrial and technological changes, the evolution of sporting equipment, transitions to commercial mass sport, and the impact of the entrepreneurial spirit.

Dr. Rob Beamish, author of Chapter 4, addresses the inequalities of condition and opportunity that exist in sport today. Theories of social inequality are outlined as well as current patterns of class and sport. He points out that in Canada we endorse an unequal, performance-based rewards system. Success is linked, for example, to proximity to facilities, gender, social class, and physical ability.

In Chapter 5, Drs. Victoria Paraschak and Susan Tirone explore issues of racial and ethnic discrimination in Canadian sport. They point out that sport provides opportunities to feel pride in one's own cultural heritage. Unfortunately, the system is structured so that some individuals—that is, those of white European heritage—feel more pride than others. Poverty and access are key components that prevent ethnic minority people from fully participating in sport in Canada. The need to create equal opportunities in sport for all Canadian people (e.g., through race-structured sport systems) is a fundamental message in this chapter.

In Chapter 6, Dr. Mary Louise Adams helps us understand the current issues relevant to gender, sexuality, and sport and poses the question: Is sport really a male thing? Adams does not shy away from controversial topics such as separate events for men and women, sex testing in sport, and sport typing (certain sports are "male only"). Issues for athletes who are transgender, transsexual, gay, or lesbian are also discussed.

In Chapter 7, Drs. Ralph Wheeler, Jay Scherer, and Jane Crossman outline the current sport system in Canada for children and youth, including school, community, and private agencies. Critical issues and concerns related to organized sport for children and youth are described and include reasons for the high rate of dropout, ethical issues, sport specialization, risk of injury, parental interference, and coaches' influence. Solutions to remedy the problems posed are offered.

Chapter 8 by Dr. Jason Laurendeau focuses on sport deviance. He describes how deviance is conceptualized and differentiates deviance on and off the field of play. He covers timely topics such as drug use in sport and risk sports and points out that deviance arises out of an overly enthusiastic adoption of a set of expectations that characterizes particular activities.

Dr. Stacy Lorenz, author of Chapter 9, addresses the fact that sport is replete with violence. Theories of violence are explained along with a historical overview of how violence in sport has grown in our society. Who encourages sport violence is a question he broaches to help the reader better understand contemporary trends in sport violence committed by both players and fans. He also discusses gender and gender relations as they relate to violence.

In Chapter 10, Drs. Tim Fletcher and Duane Bratt consider the relationship between sport and educational institutions in Canada. They describe the nature and purposes of physical education in the public school system and how the curriculum has evolved. The challenges and issues inherent in Canadian interuniversity sport are outlined and include gender equity, athletic scholarships, doping, hazing, challenging the NCAA, alumni funding, and academic achievement.

In Chapter 11, Dr. Jay Scherer explains the influence, extent, and power the media have in shaping what we know and how we think. He outlines the historical development of the televised sports-media complex in Canada and points out that sports media are replete with symbols of nationalism and militarism and other gender and racial ideologies. Sport journalism and new media technologies that will change how we view and interpret sport are also included.

Dr. Jean Harvey, in Chapter 12, focuses on the marriage between politics and sport. He provides a historical overview and reasons for the Canadian government's intervention in sport. The author outlines current federal sport policies that include programs such as the Athlete Assistance Program, Hosting Program, and the Children's Fitness Tax Credit. Also included is the controversial topic of funding for high-performance sport versus mass participation sport.

Chapter 13, written by Dr. Brad Humphreys and Professor Moshe Lander, delves into the ever-changing and multifaceted business of sport. They cover the structure and functioning of professional leagues such as the NHL, CFL, MLB, NBA, NFL, and MLS. Under the auspice of these cartels, they address a host of issues such as the costs and revenues to the owners, reserve clauses, free agency, collective bargaining agreements, work stoppages, payroll caps, ticket pricing, revenue sharing, and facility subsides. A discussion about the costs to bid on and subsequently host the Olympic Games concludes this chapter. Students with an interest in the economic side of professional sport will find this chapter a fascinating read.

In the penultimate chapter, Dr. David Whitson lends a keen eye to how globalization affects sport along cultural, political, and economic lines. He discusses both the upside and downside to globalization, homing in on the power of transnational corporations and the global sports labour market. He points out that, thanks to electronic media, professional sport is now marketed and consumed around the globe in fascinating and contradictory ways.

Dr. Brian Wilson frames the final chapter on the future of sport on four overarching categories that have been associated with major social changes: governance, globalization, technology, and the environment. He makes 11 predictions based on the social trends from the above four categories and describes ways to use research and theory to inform intervention.

On behalf of all the contributors, we hope you enjoy reading this book—and furthermore that it provides you with a sound basis for understanding the social dimensions of sport and physical activity from a uniquely Canadian perspective.

Jane Crossman and Jay Scherer

SUPPLEMENTS

Test Item File (978-0-13-344160-4)   The Test Item File includes chapter-relevant questions to help instructors create quizzes, exams, homework, and practice handouts. There are approximately 400 questions in multiple-choice format that address factual, applied, and conceptual material from the textbook. It is available from the Pearson online catalogue to instructors who adopt the textbook at http://catalogue.pearsoned.ca.

CourseSmart for Instructors (978-0-13-344158-1) CourseSmart goes beyond traditional expectations—providing instant, online access to the textbooks and course materials you need at a lower cost for students. And even as students save money, you can save time and hassle with a digital eTextbook that allows you to search for the most relevant content at the very moment you need it. Whether it's evaluating textbooks or creating lecture notes to help students with difficult concepts, CourseSmart can make life a little easier. See how when you visit www.coursesmart.com/instructors.

CourseSmart for Students (978-0-13-344158-1) CourseSmart goes beyond traditional expectations—providing instant, online access to the textbooks and course materials you need at an average savings of 60%. With instant access from any computer and the ability to search your text, you'll find the content you need quickly, no matter where you are. And with online tools like highlighting and note taking, you can save time and study efficiently. See all the benefits at www.coursesmart.com/students.

Pearson Custom Library For enrolments of at least 25 students, you can create your own textbook by choosing the chapters that best suit your own course needs. To begin building your custom text, visit www.pearsoncustomlibrary.com. You may also work with a dedicated Pearson Custom Editor to create your ideal text—publishing your own original content or mixing and matching Pearson content. Contact your local Pearson representative to get started.

peerScholar Firmly grounded in published research, peerScholar is a powerful online pedagogical tool that helps develop students' critical and creative thinking skills through creation, evaluation, and reflection. Working in stages, students begin by submitting written assignments. peerScholar then circulates their work for others to review, a process that can be anonymous or not, depending on instructors' preferences. Students immediately receive peer feedback and evaluations, reinforcing their learning and driving development of higher-order thinking skills. Students can then re-submit revised work, again depending on instructors' preferences.

Contact your Pearson representative to learn more about peerScholar and the research behind it.

Acknowledgments

The completion of this text would not have been possible had it not been for the willingness of the contributors to share their expertise. To each of them we extend our sincere gratitude and we trust that readers will appreciate their knowledge, insights, and wisdom.

The authors and contributors greatly appreciate the advice and guidance of our colleagues in their review of the text and the manuscript:

Marc Belanger, *Vanier College*
Graham Fletcher, *University of the Fraser Valley*
Susan L. Forbes, *Lakehead University*
Peggy Gallant, *St. Francis Xavier University*
Fred Mason, *University of New Brunswick*
Barbara Ruttenberg, *Concordia University*
Susan M. M. Todd, *Langara College*

Also, we thank Pearson for their willingness to publish this first edition. Specific thanks go to Matthew Christian, Pearson's acquisitions editor who kick-started this project; Christine Langone, our ever-cooperative and motivating developmental editor; and Leanne Rancourt, our thorough, attention-to-detail copy editor.

We are grateful for the ever-present support of our families in Canada and New Zealand, without whom this book simply would not have been possible.

Jane would like to thank Dr. Brent Rushall for his mentorship and cheerleading through her career and Dr. John Vincent, her research partner, who, through his deft research and writing skills elevated the quality of their published papers. She extends special gratitude to Paulene McGowan for her feedback and constant encouragement.

Jay would like to thank those individuals who have generously shared valuable pedagogical insights and teaching philosophies with him over the years, including: Dave Whitson, Lisa McDermott, Judy Davidson, Steve Jackson, Brian Wilson, and, especially, Vicky Paraschak.

Jane Crossman and Jay Scherer

Contributors

EDITORS

Dr. Jane Crossman is a Professor Emerita at Lakehead University where she held several administrative positions throughout her career including Chair and Graduate Coordinator of the School of Kinesiology. She taught graduate and undergraduate courses in sport sociology, research methods, and mental training. Jane's research, which pertains to the newspaper coverage of sporting events and the psychosocial dimensions of sports injuries, has been published in a number of scholarly journals. She has edited three books: *Coping with Sports Injuries: Psychological Strategies for Rehabilitation* (2001) and *Canadian Sport Sociology*, Editions 1 (2003) and 2 (2007). Jane contributed a chapter to the book *The Sport Scientist's Research Adventures* in which she gave insights into the challenges and gratification of being a researcher. Jane is on the editorial board of the *Journal of Sport Behavior* and regularly reviews for a number of journals and texts in the fields of sport sociology, sport psychology, and research methods. During sabbaticals, Jane has been a Visiting Professor at the Universities of Exeter and Brighton (UK), the University of Otago (New Zealand), Victoria University (Australia), and the University of Ulster (Northern Ireland). Jane enjoys exercising a border collie, golfing, and fiction and nonfiction writing.

Dr. Jay Scherer is an Associate Professor in the Faculty of Physical Education and Recreation at the University of Alberta where he has taught sociology of sport courses since 2005. His primary research interests include cultural studies of sport and leisure; globalization, sport and public policy; and sport and the media. Jay's research has been published in a number of scholarly journals, and his most recent book (with David Rowe) is *Sport, Public Broadcasting, and Cultural Citizenship: Signal Lost?* (2013). Outside of the office, Jay enjoys cycling, running, and cross-country skiing. He is an avid fiction reader and a long-suffering fan of the Toronto Blue Jays and the Edmonton Oilers.

CONTRIBUTORS

Dr. Mary Louise Adams is a Professor in the School of Kinesiology and Health Studies and the Department of Sociology at Queen's University where she teaches courses on sport and culture, the sociology of fitness, and contemporary issues in sexuality. She is the author of *Artistic Impressions: Figure Skating, Masculinity and the Limits of Sport* (2011) and *The Trouble with Normal: Postwar Youth and the Making of Heterosexuality* (1997). She writes on issues related to the history of sexuality, queer and feminist social movements, and on gender and sexuality in sport and physical activity. She has recently started work on two new projects: an oral history with feminist sport activists on the legacies of feminism in contemporary women's sport and a historical cultural study of the meanings of walking.

Dr. Rob Beamish holds a joint appointment in the Department of Sociology and the School of Kinesiology and Health at Queen's University. During that time, in addition to his teaching and research responsibilities, he has served as the Associate Dean (Studies) and two terms as the Head of the Department of Sociology. Dr. Beamish's research centres on high-performance sport as a form of work and specific issues related to work, labour, and classical social theory. In addition to numerous articles, book chapters, and encyclopedia entries related to social theory and sport sociology in general, and the use of performance-enhancing substances in particular, he is the author of several books, including *Marx, Method and the Division of Labor: Fastest, Highest, Strongest: The Critique of High-Performance Sport* (with Ian Ritchie); *The Promise of Sociology: The Classical Tradition and Contemporary Sociological Thinking;* and *Steroids: A New Look at Performance-Enhancing Drugs*.

Dr. Duane Bratt is a Professor of Political Science and Chair of the Department of Policy Studies at Mount Royal University. He teaches public policy and international politics. While his primary research interests are in nuclear energy and Canadian foreign policy, he also writes on sport policy. This includes a recent research project that led to the inclusion of physical literacy standards in Alberta's daycare accreditation standards. As a sport practitioner, he is the National Resource Person and Chair of the LTAD committee for the Canadian Lacrosse Association.

Dr. Tim Fletcher is an Assistant Professor in the Department of Kinesiology at Brock University. His teaching and research interests are in physical education pedagogy and teacher education. In particular, his research focuses on ways in which teachers understand the connections between their teaching identities, practices, and student learning. Much of his recent work has used self-study methodology, including the co-edited text *Self-Study of Physical Education: The Interplay of Scholarship and Practice* (forthcoming 2014) with Alan Ovens from the University of Auckland in New Zealand. In 2014 he was awarded a Young Scholar Award from the International Association for Physical Education in Higher Education (AIESEP).

Dr. Jean Harvey is a Professor at the School of Human Kinetics at the University of Ottawa. He is also the founding director of the Research Centre for Sport in Canadian Society. His main areas of research are sport policy in Canada and abroad as well as sport in the context of globalization. Jean has published extensively both in French and in English in multiple refereed journals. He is also the co-editor with Lucie Thibault of *Sport Policy in Canada* (2013) and co-author of *Sport and Social Movements* (2013).

Dr. Brad Humphreys is a Professor in the College of Business and Economics, Department of Economics at West Virginia University. He holds a PhD in economics from Johns Hopkins University. He previously held positions at the University of Illinois at Urbana-Champaign and the University of Alberta. His research on the economics of gambling, the economics and financing of professional sports, and the economics of higher education has been published in academic journals in economics and policy analysis. He has published more than 80 papers in peer-reviewed journals in economics and public policy. He twice testified before the United States Congress on the economic impact of professional sports teams and facilities. His current research projects include an assessment of the informational efficiency of sports betting markets, an examination of the effect of new sports facilities on urban residential construction projects, an assessment of the causal relationship between recreational gambling and health outcomes, and an evaluation of the value Canadians place on Olympic gold medals.

Professor Moshe Lander is a Lecturer at Concordia University. He holds a Masters in Applied European Languages and is a PhD candidate in Economics. He is an award-winning teacher, having spent most of the last two decades teaching economics, statistics, mathematics, and finance at postsecondary institutions in Alberta, Ontario, and Quebec. Moshe is known on campus as much for his unique presentation skills and his appearance as he is for his extremely dry wit and linguistic dexterity. Though he spends much of his time in the classroom teaching, Moshe loves to spend his down time either at his picturesque summer retreat in Hapolonia or in Flin Flon, Manitoba, watching the annual migration of fake tootie birds.

Dr. Jason Laurendeau is an Associate Professor in the Department of Sociology at the University of Lethbridge. He received an undergraduate degree in Kinesiology, and Masters and PhD degrees in Sociology from the University of Calgary. His research and teaching interests include deviance and social control, sport and embodiment, gender, risk, fatherhood, and autoethnography. His work has appeared in a number of scholarly journals, including *Deviant Behavior, Sociological Perspectives, Sociology of Sport Journal, Journal of Sport and Social Issues*, and *Emotion, Space and Society*. Jason enjoys a number of sport and leisure pursuits, including cross-country skiing, hiking, backcountry camping, cycling, and swimming. He is also active in his local community and an avid traveller. He dedicates this chapter to the memory of Rosco.

Dr. Stacy L. Lorenz is an Associate Professor in Physical Education and History at the University of Alberta, Augustana Campus. He completed a bachelor's degree in History at Augustana University College, a master's in History at the University of Western Ontario, and a PhD in History at the University of Alberta. He teaches in the areas of sport history, sociocultural aspects of sport and physical activity, sport and social issues, and sport and popular culture. He also coached the men's basketball team at Augustana for eight years. Stacy's research interests include newspaper coverage of sport, media experiences of sport, sport and local and national identities, violence and masculinity, and hockey and Canadian culture. He has written several book chapters and published articles in such journals as *Canadian Journal of History of Sport, Journal of Sport History, Sport History Review, Journal of Canadian Studies*, and *Journal of Sport & Social Issues*. He has also written a number of newspaper articles about issues related to sport, society, and culture.

Dr. Don Morrow is a Professor of Kinesiology at Western University. His academic teaching and research interest areas are Canadian sport history, sport literature, body culture and concepts of exercise history, integrative health/medicine, and health promotion. He is the author of eight textbooks, including the most recent third edition of *Sport in Canada: A History* (2013) and numerous academic journal articles, an award-winning teacher, a past-president of the North American Society for Sport History, and an elected Fellow of the American Academy Kinesiology and Physical Education.

Dr. Victoria Paraschak is a Professor of Kinesiology at the University of Windsor where she teaches sociology of sport, government and sport, social construction of leisure, and outdoor recreation. She received a bachelor's degree from McMaster University in 1977, a master's from the University of Windsor in 1978, and a PhD from the University of Alberta in 1983. The primary focus of her research is Aboriginal peoples in sport and in physical cultural practices more broadly. In 1999 she took a year's leave to work with seven different Northwest Territories sport and recreation organizations and establish a direction for the new millennium. She looked at the creation of health services for the Canada Games held in Whitehorse, Yukon, in February 2007, examining the interfaces between sport and public health perspectives on such services as part of a health services legacy for these Games. Her work focuses on power relations, social construction, and the creation, reproduction, or reshaping of cultural practices through the duality of structure. She is currently expanding on that framework to incorporate a strengths perspective, which includes fostering practices of hope that enable individuals to work together to achieve broader collective goals.

Dr. Ian Ritchie is Associate Professor in the Department of Kinesiology at Brock University. Ian received his PhD in Sociology from Bowling Green State University, Ohio, where he studied classical and contemporary sociological theory. He teaches courses in sport sociology and sociology of the modern Olympic Games. Ian's research interests include performance-enhancing drug use in sport and the history of anti-doping rules, media, gender, and various aspects of the Olympic Games. In addition to several chapters in edited volumes, he co-authored (with Rob Beamish) the book *Fastest, Highest, Strongest: A Critique of High-Performance Sport* (2006) and is currently writing a manuscript on the history of the modern Olympic Games. A former Canadian varsity rower and coach, Ian now enjoys long distance trail and marathon running, golfing, cycling, curling, and various outdoor travel-related activities such as hiking and camping. Ian lives in Fenwick, Ontario, with his wife and three children.

Dr. Susan Tirone is the Associate Director of the College of Sustainability at Dalhousie University. Her administrative duties involve overseeing the Environment, Sustainability and Society program, a multi-disciplinary undergraduate program with an enrolment of over 600 students each year, and she is the academic leader of the RBC Sustainability Leadership Certificate program offered by the College of Sustainability. She co-teaches a problem-based learning course in the College, drawing upon current and topical sustainability issues in the local community to inform discussions about how people in their various roles as employers, volunteers, consumers, and engaged citizens contend with the sustainability problems we face. Susan is interested in how communities sustain their populations by welcoming new and diverse groups of immigrants. She focuses her studies on the formal and informal social support networks that facilitate a welcoming environment for new immigrants. Some of her research has delved into how sport organizations contribute to welcoming new immigrants to communities in Canada. She is cross-appointed in the Faculty of Health Professions at Dalhousie University where she has taught since 2001.

Dr. Ralph Wheeler is an Associate Professor in the School of Human Kinetics and Recreation at Memorial University. He received his PhD from the University of Alberta in 1998. His research and teaching interests include pedagogy of teaching and curriculum studies. Ralph was a successful varsity and club swim coach and his CIS teams went undefeated in Atlantic University Sport competition for four years and was ranked as high as fifth in the CIS national team rankings. He also served as provincial coordinator for the National Coaching Certification Program. Ralph has served on many provincial and national committees promoting physical education and sport, and in 2006 he was awarded the Certificate of Honour from the Provincial Physical Education Council for his outstanding contribution to the profession. A passionate fly fisherman, he has been known to "disappear" for weeks into the Labrador wilderness in pursuit of the king of sport fish—the Atlantic salmon.

Dr. David Whitson is a Professor Emeritus in the Department of Political Science at the University of Alberta. He is co-author of *Game Planners: Transforming Canada's Sport System* (with Donald Macintosh), *Hockey Night in Canada: Sport, Identities, and Cultural Politics* (with Richard Gruneau), and *Writing Off the Rural West: Globalization, Governments, and the Transformation of Rural Communities* (with Roger Epp), as well as numerous articles on global events and the globalization of sport and culture. In retirement, he continues to enjoy cycling and skiing and watching the world of sport.

Dr. Brian Wilson is a sociologist and Professor in the School of Kinesiology at the University of British Columbia. He is author of *Sport & Peace: A Sociological Perspective* (2012) and *Fight, Flight or Chill: Subcultures, Youth and Rave into the Twenty-First Century* (2006) as well as articles on sport, social inequality, environmental issues, media, social movements, and youth culture. His most recent work focuses on how the sport of running is used for peace promotion in Kenya and on responses to golf-related environmental concerns.

Chapter 1

Perspectives on the Social Dimensions of Sport and Physical Activity in Canada

Jane Crossman and Jay Scherer

Take a few moments to think about the importance of sport and physical activity in your life.

Sport provides opportunities for socialization for Canadians.
Mark Spowart/Alamy

Blend Images – Pete Saloutos/Brand X Pictures/Getty Images

For thousands of students enrolled in kinesiology, human kinetics, and physical education programs across the country, the practices of sport and physical activity are so pervasive that they are widely taken for granted as a part of the rhythm of their own lives and also indelible elements of the fabric of Canadian society. For many of us, our earliest childhood memories include our first athletic experiences in organized sport settings or informal experiences at the playground or in school. Moreover, sport is a popular and pleasurable everyday topic of conversation among ordinary Canadians of all ages and is widely regarded as a common sense social lubricant. We habitually discuss the chances of our favourite National Hockey League (NHL) team making the playoffs, the performance of our fantasy football team, the latest scandal rocking the sports world, how the high school soccer team is performing, or the latest tweet by a sports personality.

Sport is intimately connected to the most significant social institutions of Canadian society (e.g., the media, the education system, and various levels of government). Canadians are inundated with images and stories of sports and athletes that now air on an unprecedented number of specialty sport channels (such as TSN and Sportsnet) that are part of the BCE and Rogers telecommunications empires. Students will be well aware that the Internet has a never-ending reservoir of sports-specific sites offering live feeds, recent and past game results and statistics, and continual insider information about teams and players. Online fantasy leagues, meanwhile, allow millions of sports fans to control the destiny of "their" teams and chosen players at their convenience. Most city newspapers still devote an entire section to sports (in print and online), knowing that a significant percentage of readers purchase or subscribe to newspapers for the sports coverage alone—a fact not lost on advertisers in search of sizable and predictable audiences. Following Sidney Crosby's overtime gold-medal-winning goal for the Canadian men's hockey team at the 2010 Winter Olympic Games in Vancouver—a game watched by 26.5 million Canadians—Bell Canada wireless and wireline networks carried the most calls and text messages in its history. In sum, sport is an extremely popular social phenomenon that has exploded in visibility and popularity in the last 30 years.

Of course, we aren't merely a nation that follows sports. Many parents devote huge amounts of time, energy, and money so that their children can participate in organized sport. Provinces, mindful of the declining fitness levels and soaring obesity rates of children and youth, are taking a hard look at extending the number of hours per week devoted to physical education. Canadian colleges and universities offer a wide range of intramural and interschool sports for both women and men. Some baby boomers now reaching retirement age are spending significant amounts of their leisure time actively involved in their favourite sport or physical activity. The number of sporting activities and leisure pursuits available to Canadians has expanded radically over the past 50 years. We have approximately 2,500 arenas, 1,300 curling rinks, and more than 2,300 golf courses. The 2013 Goodlife Fitness Toronto Marathon saw roughly 12,000 people cross the finish line. Many of these activities are more than sports played for the fun of friendly competition—they're also popular social and cultural events.

In addition, many groups that have historically been left out of the sport equation are now finding more opportunities to participate. For example, the 2014 Winter Paralympic Games in Sochi, Russia, had 585 competitors from 45 countries. The 2014 North American Indigenous

Games held in Regina, Saskatchewan, had 6,000 competitors. Cleveland, Ohio, home of the 2014 Gay Games, welcomed more than 10,000 athletes from more than 65 countries. Unprecedented numbers of girls and women now participate in a host of sporting activities they were once excluded from—especially sports that traditionally emphasized aspects of physicality for boys and men, like wrestling. Still, while there is no doubt that the opportunities to "do sport" have expanded across Canada, there remain significant and enduring issues of inequality between men and women, rich and poor, and along racial and ethnic lines that continue to structure sporting experiences for Canadians in different ways. For example, according to the latest research paper on sport participation rates released by Canadian Heritage (2013):

1. Sport participation rates across the country continue to decline.
2. The gender gap in sport participation has increased, and men are more likely to participate in sport than women.
3. Sport participation rates decrease as Canadians get older, yet the participation rates of young Canadians are declining faster than that of older Canadians.
4. Higher income earners are more likely to participate in sport than less affluent Canadians, and household income decisively influences children's participation in sport.
5. Sport participation of non-Anglophones is declining, and established immigrants participate in sport less than recent immigrants.

There are other obvious disparities as well. For example, female athletes are still regularly marginalized and under-represented by the media and society at large. Furthermore, in 2013 women comprised only 21 of 101 active members of the International Olympic Committee (IOC), and in 2011 women held only 15% of head coaching positions in Canadian Interuniversity Sport (CIS). Yet, while all of these observations are important and point to the fact that interest and participation in sport and physical activity are related to a number of standard sociological variables (gender, race, social class, age, geographic location, education levels, etc.), they do little to address the wider sociological significance of these seemingly obvious facts. Instead, it is more fruitful to ask, as Hall, Slack, Smith, and Whitson (1991) did over two decades ago, are patterns of male and female participation in sport products of social structures that favour and empower men in innumerable ways? What is it about the class structure of Canadian society that perpetuates unequal class relations and unequal access to sport participation? Why do older Canadians continue to struggle to gain access to various sports facilities? These questions and many others

> connect the study of sport to the study of change and resistance in relations between dominant and subordinate groups in society. When these questions are asked, and when research uncovers interesting lines of analysis and further investigation, we show that to study sport sociology is not just of interest to a few fans but something that is important to the understanding of Canadian society. (Hall et al., 1991, p. 20)

In this respect, while sport continues to offer a host of opportunities and pleasurable experiences, including fun and relaxation for millions of Canadians, we would be naive to believe that the world of sport is devoid of the problems, social issues, and unequal power relations present in our society. Moreover, sport regularly makes the headlines for all the wrong reasons: Discriminatory practices, exploitation of athletes, labour disputes, drug

Christine Sinclair, captain of the 2012 bronze-medal-winning Olympic soccer team and the 2012 Canadian Athlete of the Year.
Carlos Osorio/ZUMA Press/Newscom

use, sexual abuse and assault, gambling, and the habitual glorification of violence which are byproducts of an industry focused on promoting a hypermasculine spectacle for profit. Indeed, it seems as the rationalization of sport continues to increase, moral conduct decreases while other ways of imagining sport are obscured.

The sociological analysis of sport and physical activity provides students with the opportunity to ask thought-provoking questions using "concepts and theories that emphasize social as opposed to individual causes and that point toward structural solutions to problems identified in sport" (Hall et al., 1991, pp. 11–12). For example:

- Why has participation in sport historically been stratified by age, gender, race, and socioeconomic status?

- Why is a power and performance model of sport privileged over alternative ways of playing and doing sport?

- Will leagues with high rates of concussions and other injuries (e.g., the Canadian and National Football Leagues) still exist in two decades?

- Why do so many cities invest significant amounts of public funds in "world-class" sports arenas and stadiums?

- Why do countries spend billions of dollars to host the Olympic Games?

- Should the Canadian government invest in high-performance sport (e.g., the Own the Podium program) at the expense of programs that could increase mass participation?

- Why do gay men hesitate to come out in professional sports environments?

Crucially, in raising these types of difficult questions and political issues, "the sociology of sport is going beyond a concern with phenomena within sport. It is seeking to demonstrate the significance of sport to some of the central problems of sociology: the explanation of structures of class, gender, and racial inequality, as well as the processes through which social change is achieved and circumscribed" (Hall et al., 1991, p. 12).

Thus, the chapters in this text will emphasize that sport is not simply a reflection or mirror of society but, as Jean Harvey (2000) (author of Chapter 12) notes, "a world in its own right, with its own life and its own contradictions" (p. 19). It is also important to recognize, though, that as sport is *shaped by the social world around us, so it actively shapes the social world.* As we shall see throughout this textbook, while sport is a social practice that is shaped by broader power relations that benefit some individuals and groups more than others, it also enables individuals and groups with varying resources to reproduce current practices or resist them.

On this latter note, students often walk into their first sociology of sport and physical activity course with preconceived ideas about the world of sport and how it works. For example, because of the predominance of black athletes in certain sports, we may believe that racism no longer exists in sport, or that black athletes are "naturally gifted." Or, thanks to our regular exposure to hockey, we may have come to accept that fighting is simply "part of the game." Still, even our most accepted beliefs and normalized values need to be held up for critical reflection and analysis, while all of the sports that we play and enjoy—and the institutions that they are connected to—need to be recognized as social and historical products that have been made and remade by Canadians over the course of many decades against the backdrop of a range of cultural struggles. Students of sport sociology need to look critically at sport to better describe, explain, and improve it, but also to engage in broader processes of social change and transformation. At its very root, then, the sociological study of sport is a fundamentally creative and exhilarating practice that can reveal new insights and lines of analysis that contribute to the understanding of contemporary Canadian society.

SOCIOLOGY AS A SOCIAL SCIENCE

Sociology is one of the social sciences, along with economics, anthropology, political science, and psychology. It is "the disciplined study of human social behaviour, especially the investigation of the origins, classifications, institutions, and development of human society on a global level" (Henslin, Glenday, Pupo, & Duffy, 2014, p. 5). Sociologists are interested in social interactions that take place between humans, groups, and societies. They examine the ways in which social structures, power relations, and institutions (e.g., family, social class) enable and constrain individuals and groups; they are concerned with the social rules and ideologies that not only bind people together, but also separate them.

Yet as the English sociologist Anthony Giddens (1987) noted, it must also be emphasized that "sociology cannot be a neutral intellectual endeavor" (p. viii). Rather, it is a critical examination of the contemporary social situation with the underlying goal not only to *understand* social phenomena but to *improve* society. Because sociology is concerned with our behaviour as social beings, subdisciplines have emerged that are broad in scope and diverse in nature. One of those subdisciplines is called *sport sociology*.

Sport sociology examines the relationship between sport and society and studies sport as an ever-present part of social and cultural life. Sport sociologists study humans/agents involved in sport (e.g., athletes, coaches, fans, team owners), the institutions and social structures that affect their sport experiences (e.g., education, media, economics, politics), and the processes that occur in conjunction with sport (e.g., social stratification and mobility, deviance, violence, inequality). Some of the aims of the sociology of sport include:

- to examine critically the role, function, and meaning of sport in the lives of people and the societies they form;
- to describe and explain the emergence and diffusion of sport over time and across different societies;
- to identify the processes of socialization into, through, and out of modern sport;
- to investigate the values and norms of dominant, emergent, and residual cultures and subcultures in sport;
- to explore how the exercise of power and the stratified nature of societies place limits and possibilities on people's involvement and success in sport as performers, officials, spectators, workers, or consumers;
- to examine the way in which sport responds to social changes in the larger society; and
- to contribute both to the knowledge base of sociology more generally and also to the formation of policy that seeks to ensure that global sport processes are less wasteful of lives and resources. (ISSA, 2005)

Sport sociologists are also concerned with the links between the structure of organized sport and dominant cultural ideologies such as class, race, sexuality, and nationalism. Indeed, one of the main roles of sociologists is to "disentangle the complex relationships between individuals and their social world" (Naiman, 2012, p. 2). We challenge long-held myths and common sense assumptions about the world of sport and, by doing so, seek to make it better for all those involved.

An overview of what sport sociologists actually *do* is listed below:

1. **Serve as experts** to government agencies, public enquiries, and commissions in areas such as drugs, violence, and health education, thus contributing to their reports.

2. **Act as advocates** for athlete's rights and responsibilities by providing research for groups who seek to challenge inequalities of gender, class, ethnicity, age, and disability, particularly with respect to access, resources, and status.

3. **Promote human development** as opposed to performance efficiency models within physical education and sport science.

4. **Encourage better use of human and environmental resources**, thus ensuring that there is a sporting future for generations to come. (ISSA, 2005)

It's important to emphasize, then, that sport sociologists look for extrinsic or structural and historical explanations to explain social behaviour and social issues. On the other hand, psychologists examine intrinsic explanations to explain individual behaviour. However, is it enough to consider intrinsic factors and personal choices by athletes to explain the systemic use of, for example, performance-enhancing drugs in many professional sports? Or do we need to consider a host of structural issues and, indeed, the increasing rationalization of high-performance and professional sport in relation to values of competition and the significant financial rewards (sponsorship and salaries) on offer to contemporary athletes as decisive factors that contribute to these patterns? Alternatively, why should we consider banning performance-enhancing drugs at these levels if their use is endemic (i.e., is it cheating if everyone is doing it)? Finally, why are the debates associated with drug use in sport so heavily moralized when the use of other performance-enhancing drugs is normalized in other occupations and industries and actively encouraged and promoted in relation to other aspects our personal lives? Students will be well aware, for example, that other performance enhancers (i.e., Viagra and Cialis) are habitually promoted during popular sports broadcasts to reach male audiences.

Because we seek to both understand and denaturalize longstanding assumptions and beliefs, in addition to engaging in political dialogue and debate on how to improve contemporary sporting practices and cultures in Canadian society, the sociology of sport is a complex, controversial, and often challenging pursuit. Moreover, sport sociologists pose difficult questions about social problems and issues that are not always answered. It is, however, a fascinating endeavour—so much so that it can foster stimulating discussion on a wide range of topics and ideas.

In so doing, the chapters in this text will regularly ask you to reflect on your own sporting experiences and, indeed, hold up your own *practical consciousness* for critical reflection. By practical consciousness we mean your accepted beliefs—all of the things about sport and Canadian society that you may be tacitly aware of without, at times, being able to give them direct expression or explanation. Your practical consciousness is shaped by your experiences of "doing," "consuming," and "interacting" with various social structures, institutions, and ideologies; these are the experiences that frame the possibilities you can imagine in sport and beyond. However, your practical consciousness is far from simply reflective of dominant interests and beliefs—it is also subject to ongoing refinement (hence, practical), especially as you encounter new experiences, ideas, and information. As such, practical consciousness is never static. Actions and experiences supporting practical consciousness strengthen it, while new actions and experiences can challenge our assumptions and make us question various "truths" about what we once took for granted.

For example, a "power and performance" model based on competition, domination of opponents, rationalized rules, and scorekeeping by adults is widely understood as a common sense and normal way for children and youth to play sport in the eyes of many administrators, coaches, and parents, who themselves often grew up playing similarly structured sports. Indeed, your own practical consciousness may have been reinforced over years of engaging in these types of sporting experiences that have now simply come to seem natural (and, of course, regularly pleasurable, thrilling, and fun). Still, is this the only way that youth sport can be structured? Or, are there alternative ways of structuring sport according to different values and principles? Before revisiting these ideas, though, let's first briefly consider the origin of the sociology of sport and some of the issues associated with defining sport.

ORIGINS OF SPORT SOCIOLOGY

The academic study of sport sociology is relatively new, and scientific research in the field only emerged in the 1960s. From 1965 to 1969, Kenyon and McPherson (1973) of the University of Wisconsin published a series of articles devoted to the sociology of sport, positioning it "firmly within the positivistic perspective of science" (Sage, 1997, p. 326). In the late 1960s the annual meetings of the American Alliance for Health, Physical Education and Recreation included a session devoted to the sociology of sport (Dance was added to this organization's title in 1979). In 1976, this same association founded the Sociology of Sport Academy with the purpose of coordinating and promoting the study of sport sociology (Sage, 1997).

The 1960s and 1970s constituted an important time for the development of the study of sport sociology. During that time there was much unrest in North America, particularly with regard to the involvement of the United States in the Vietnam War as well as the civil rights movement. For example, in 1968, during the medal presentation at the Summer Olympic Games in Mexico City, two black athletes, John Carlos and Tommie Smith, made a gloved black power salute, thereby using the global visibility provided by the Olympic Games as a vehicle to broadcast their anger with the plight of black Americans and unequal race relations in the United States. This resistant gesture was symbolic of the imbalance of societal power that prevailed not only for black Americans, but also for other minority groups. Sport was no exception. Sport sociologists understood that it was no longer enough to simply describe and celebrate sport and various athletic accomplishments; instead, they needed to examine and explain how various social institutions transform sport and, likewise, how sport can be used to transform broader social structures against the backdrop of a range of cultural struggles, pressing political debates, and social movements.

Within this context, an organized society for the study of sport sociology (which later became the North American Society for the Sociology of Sport [NASSS]) emerged after a Big Ten Symposium in 1978. The mission statement of the NASSS was "to promote, stimulate, and encourage the sociological study of play, games, sport and contemporary physical culture." In 1980, the first NASSS conference took place in Denver, and subsequently several Canadian cities have hosted this annual gathering. NASSS publishes a peer-reviewed journal entitled the *Sociology of Sport Journal*. An international umbrella group called the International Sociology of Sport Association (ISSA) was founded in 1965. The ISSA holds annual conferences and publishes a peer-reviewed journal entitled the *International Review for the Sociology of Sport*. Other international journals in which sport sociologists commonly publish include the *Journal of Sport and Social Issues, International Journal of Sport Communication, Sport and Society, Leisure Studies,* and *Qualitative Research in Sport, Exercise and Health*. Some sociology and sport management journals also publish articles with a sport sociology theme.

Therefore, while there are a host of various national and international organizations associated with the sociology of sport, it is vital for students to understand sport within the context of Canadian society while also making connections to continental and, indeed, global patterns and forms of social organization. The organization of Canadian society has many similarities with the United States; however, there are also significant differences between the countries. Canadian history is, of course, substantially different from that of the United States, and there are unique social relations (between Anglophones and Francophones, Aboriginal and Euro-Canadians, etc.) that point to these enduring distinctions. Canadians also have competing visions of the roles and structures of government, vastly different commitments to the provision of social services including universal healthcare, a longstanding history of public broadcasting by the Canadian Broadcasting Corporation and Radio-Canada, and, at times, radically different visions of foreign policy.

It should be no surprise, then, that significant aspects of the organization and structure of Canadian sport are different compared to sport in the United States and, indeed, other parts of the world. Of course, as Jay Scherer and David Whitson note in Chapters 11 and 14, Canadians have always followed the North American major leagues in significant numbers (in addition to NCAA football and basketball). As well, we are more interconnected with the rest of the world than ever before. In 2014, for example, we watched Germany win the FIFA World Cup in Rio de Janeiro with 32 nations qualifying; Martin Kaymer (Germany) and Michelle Wie (United States) win the US Open Golf Championships; and Novak Djokovic (Serbia) and Petra Kvitová (Czech Republic) win the singles events at Wimbledon. So to claim that Canadian sport is a unique entity thriving on its own without any external influences would be naive and inaccurate.

There are, however, undeniably unique elements in Canadian life and culture, and sport continues to play a significant role in providing a range of symbolic meanings and values that are important to Canadians and are part of the ongoing story that we tell ourselves about who we are and what it means to be Canadian. For example, winter sports are often thought of as distinctly Canadian cultural forms, especially sports like hockey, curling and, perhaps to a lesser extent, cross-country and alpine skiing and snowboarding. In many neighbourhoods across the country the boards go up for outdoor ice rinks, and when the weather gets cold enough surfaces and backyards are flooded to make rinks for thousands of Canadians to play shinny on. Sport has, moreover, the capacity to represent our communities and indeed our nation on the world stage. In the 2010 Winter Olympic Games in Vancouver, Canada won the most gold medals ($N = 14$) of the 82 nations competing and was third overall in medal count. Both the women's and men's hockey teams won gold over their US rivals, and Sidney Crosby's sudden-death overtime winning goal, referred to by the *Globe and Mail* newspaper as "The Shot Heard Around the World"

Alexandre Bilodeau, Canadian freestyle skier, was the first Canadian to win an Olympic gold medal on home soil in 2010. He won a second gold medal at the 2014 Sochi Olympic Games.
Cameron Spencer/Getty Images

(March 1, 2010, p. A3) became an indelible Canadian memory and provided a new generation of Canadians with their own "Paul Henderson moment" (*Globe and Mail*, March 2, 2010, p. 4), a reference to the iconic 1972 Summit Series between Canada and the Soviet Union. These victories (and others, like Alexandre Bilodeau's gold medal in the men's moguls—the first gold medal for Canada at an Olympic Games held in our country) have been "mythologized" in Canadian culture as part of the story of who we are and what we value as a country. Similar feats and stories were experienced in the 2014 Sochi Olympic Games when Canada won gold medals in men's and women's hockey and curling, women's moguls, freestyle skiing, bobsleigh, and men's speed skating, to name a few.

The sheer popularity and visibility of these sporting events and physical activities that bring together more groups of Canadians than other aspects of culture suggests that they are important features of everyday life in Canada and contribute to a distinctive Canadian cultural identity. Still, even our most cherished identities and normalized sporting practices such as the national sport of hockey are far from simply natural extensions of the Canadian environment, while even the definition of *sport* has been widely debated and contested.

DEFINING SPORT: POWER AT PLAY

The meaning of the word *sport* has evolved over time, and until recently sport has simply been understood as an activity that requires *physical exertion*. For the purposes of this textbook, sport shall be defined as any formally organized, competitive activity that involves vigorous physical exertion or the execution of complex physical skills with rules enforced by a regulatory body.

An examination of the components of this definition is worthwhile. First, in order for the activity to be *competitive* the organizational and technical aspects must become important, including equipment and systematic training protocols. Second, the *rules* of the activity must become standardized and formalized by a regulatory body that oversees rule enforcement. "What we are talking about, in short, is the institutionalization of sport and the rationalization of both sports training and the sports organizations that sponsor training, and under whose auspices competition occurs" (Hall et al., 1991, p. 14).

Nonetheless, even these broad, general ideas do not necessarily provide a neat solution to what "counts" as sport. For example, are chess boxing (an 11-round match consisting of alternate rounds of boxing and "blitz" chess sessions) or competitive rock-paper-scissors contests sporting events? The World Chess Boxing Organization and the World Rock Paper Scissors Society may think so; others may not. Also consider the made-for-TV coverage of the World Series of Poker. In his article "Sport or Not a Sport? Pot Is Split on Poker," Mike Dodd (2006) considers this question. ESPN (the E standing for Entertainment) never called poker a sport. Certainly, a mental component is required to play poker, but is there a physical component? Some poker players, such as Doyle Brunson, age 72, argue that there is because of the length of tournaments: "The last tournament I won, I played 18 hours one day, 16 hours the next day and 16 hours the last day. That's pretty tough" (Dodd, 2006, p. 13C). On the other hand, some athletes might object to the use of the words *poker* and *sport* in the same sentence. Bryan Clay, the 2004 Olympic silver medallist in the decathlon, feels that "the word athlete and the word sport are getting so watered down" (Dodd, 2006, p. 13C) Even though the IOC hasn't recognized poker, it does recognize another card game: contract bridge.

Instead of focusing on the endless (but often enjoyable!) debates and discussions over the definition of sport, it is more productive to consider some of the ideas associated with the concept of social construction and how both organized sport and informal ways of playing have emerged over the course of many years. In so doing, we will focus not only on formal practices associated with sport, but also on the less formalized aspects of physical activity that are important for millions of Canadians. By informal sport, we mean physical activities that are self-initiated with no fixed start or stop times. Informal sport has no tangible outcomes such as prizes or ribbons, and victory and reward are not dominant features in this form of activity (e.g., children getting together after dinner to play a game of pickup baseball, playing a game of tennis with a roommate, going for a round of golf with three friends, rock climbing, or windsurfing). Here we are interested in the social significance not only of prominent forms of sport in Canadian culture (e.g., NHL hockey and the CFL), but also of games of pickup basketball, shinny, the beer leagues of old-timer hockey, softball, and all of the other informal activities that are important and popular parts of Canadian culture and everyday life.

Sport (formal and informal) is *socially constructed,* as are all of the meanings about social life that shape the world in which we live. That is, sport has been invented and reinvented by generations of men and women for a wide range of purposes. Sport also shapes and is shaped by the social world around us, and because sport is a social construct it can be changed and given different forms and meanings over time and from place to place (i.e., it can be socially *reconstructed)*. Indeed, it scarcely needs saying that a certain activity that is considered to be a sport in one culture or subculture may simply not be considered a sport in another culture or another era. In other words, the debates about defining sport "are less important than studying the social relations and distributions of political and economic resources that have meant that some games and physical pursuits have become institutionalized features of Canadian life while others have not" (Hall et al., 1991, p. 15).

Together, all of these ideas point toward the importance of embracing a critical sociological outlook that emphasizes the role of social construction in all of our lives; human beings live in webs of meaning that they themselves have spun. Indeed, even our most naturalized social relations (money, democracy, the legal system, etc.) and taken-for-granted identities need to be understood as historical and cultural constructs that are constantly changing as we interact with each other and with social structures. In this respect, we will focus on making historical and comparative connections to illuminate how various sports and their related meanings change, but also illustrating the significance of sport and human agency in processes of broader sociohistorical reproduction and transformation.

WAYS OF LOOKING AT SOCIAL PHENOMENA

In the study of sociology, there are different ways of looking at social phenomena: micro, macro, and global. The three levels of social structure are not necessarily in opposition to each other. Rather, they are ways of looking at social phenomena from different perspectives.

1. *Microstructures* are intimate, face-to-face social interactions with, for example, friends, family, work colleagues, teachers, and coaches and how they influence society. These are small groups such as a curling foursome, bowling team, or the board of a children's soccer league. People participate in microstructures for personal

reasons and because they "tend to be emotionally deep and enduring" (Brym, 2014). An example of a microstructure is a child from a single-parent family who looks to his softball coach for guidance in dealing with a problem he is experiencing at home.

2. *Macrostructures* are larger than microstructures and represent social relations that occur outside a person's inner circle. In this text, we will be concerned primarily with macrostructures, focusing on the relationship of sport to institutions such as education, politics, and the media. Inequities in sport as a result of sex, race, ethnicity, and socioeconomic status will be the focus in other chapters.

3. *Global structures*, which are larger than macrostructures, are relations between nations, cultures, and societies. As a result of advancements in transportation and communication, sport has globalized. Even though the world's population is growing at an alarming rate, as a result of advancements in transportation and communication our world has, in fact, shrunk. Today, the Internet has made communication of everything sport-related instantaneous, and teams and their fans can travel quickly to competitor's venues thanks to more rapid modes of transportation.

Examining social phenomena from a global perspective can be socially important. In light of the 2013 building collapse of a clothing factory in Bangladesh that killed 1,127 workers and left 2,500 others injured, there is increased concern about the practices of sporting goods companies that outsource the manufacture of clothing and sporting goods and employ cheap labour in developing countries. Sociologists, and more specifically those who study social dimensions of sport, have not only studied the events that led up to this disaster but also offered solutions so that it will hopefully never happen again. Chapter 14 of this text deals with how globalization has changed the world of sport in the 21st century.

It is important to remember that all of these structures can be studied relationally and need to be understood as historical products that have been made and remade by generations of men and women who are themselves the products of those very structures.

The Sociological Imagination

In 1961, American sociologist C. Wright Mills coined the phrase *sociological imagination*, which is the ability to go beyond a person's immediate life issues and troubles and connect them to society's broader characteristics, including macro- and global structures. In other words, what seems to be a personal concern, upon social analysis, is actually a broader social and public issue. For example, if a child cannot participate in hockey because his or her family cannot afford the increasing costs of registration, equipment, and transportation required to play in organized hockey leagues, this is clearly a personal trouble and private matter. However, the root cause of the family's private problem could be a downturn in the economy where both or one of his parents has been laid off from work resulting in a reduced household income. The costs associated with the structure of highly professionalized minor hockey leagues would be prohibitive for his family and many others, thus pointing to a much broader public issue associated with income inequality and the class structure of Canadian society.

Three kinds of sensitivities are associated with sociological imagination: historical, comparative, and critical. *Historical sensitivity* is an awareness that brings even the smallest details of personal experience into the larger frame of history. It is also an awareness that to truly understand the sporting present, we must also understand the past. With the de-emphasis of history in our educational system, the importance of a historical perspective has been marginalized across Canada over the course of the past two decades. Clearly, a lack of full appreciation of Canadian history leaves us vulnerable to simply repeating the mistakes of the past. However, by neglecting our history and an analysis that stresses the reality of sociohistorical change, we also risk accepting present "realities" and social relations as natural as opposed to social and historical constructs that have been continually made and remade by generations of men and women against the backdrop of a range of cultural and ideological struggles.

The importance of having historical sensitivity is, of course, one of the main reasons why this text includes a comprehensive chapter about sport history (Chapter 3). In her account of the Edmonton Grads—the women's basketball team that, between 1915 and 1940, played over 400 games and lost only 20—Ann Hall (2007) outlines the historical development of women's basketball in Canada against the backdrop of debates over gender-based rules and broader changes to Canadian society. The Grads played games around the world (often to remarkable crowds) and became, in many ways, unlikely ambassadors for the city of Edmonton. Still, many Canadians may be unaware of the importance of the team, and when most people think of the "City of Champions," Edmonton's nickname, the teams that they likely think of are the city's professional sports franchises—the Edmonton Oilers and the Edmonton Eskimos. Indeed, for many Canadians it is simply impossible to imagine a contemporary female professional team (or league) like the Edmonton Grads that would have levels of visibility and financial remuneration on par with the world of male professional sports. In other words, we may simply take for granted that the current structure of professional sport is distinctly gendered.

Comparative sensitivity is learning about how sport has been socially constructed according to different meanings and forms in various cultures. Not only do we learn about other cultures, but as a result of comparative sensitivity we come to appreciate and respect diversity and the range of ways that sport and physical activity have been institutionalized and socially constructed around the world. Indeed, one of the many values of attending university is that students live and study with people from other cultures and, hopefully, develop an appreciation of cultures other than their own. Sometimes North Americans take a myopic view of the world, particularly those who haven't had the opportunity to travel and experience different cultures. We can often adopt the attitude that "our way is the best way" or "our sports are the only ones that matter." Worthy of note, in this respect, is that in North American major league baseball, the championship competition is called the "World Series" even though teams from only two countries vie for the title. Or we may simply understand the North American versions of gridiron football as the only way of playing a sport that has numerous codes (associations of football/soccer, rugby unions, rugby leagues, etc.) and has been institutionalized in dramatically different forms in various cultures around the world. A comparative awareness, like historical sensitivity, simply grants us the perspective to be open to new ideas and possibilities and encourages us to recognize, once again, that there is nothing natural about sport or social relations in Canadian society.

Finally, *critical sensitivity* is a willingness to think and act critically. Certainly there is much to celebrate about sport: cross-country skiing on perfect snow, achieving a personal best time, the team you support winning the championship. However, our job as sport sociologists is to examine sport from a critical and analytical perspective so that improvement is realized and social relations are transformed.

Students of the social dimensions of sport and physical activity should develop a sociological imagination so that they can understand how their personal problems link to broader public issues that arise largely from power imbalances in our social structure. This sociological imagination gives students the opportunity to think critically about sport and how change occurs in Canadian society in relation to the concepts of structure, agency, power, and hegemony.

Social Structure

Social structures are the patterned relationships that connect different parts of society to one another (from individuals to the entire society of economic structures, political structures, structures of gender and race/ethnicity, and structures of sexual relations).

Social structures set powerful limits and boundaries within which we live our lives that often appear to be quite "natural"—they become limits and boundaries when individuals and groups give meaning to them and interact with them. Structures, in this sense, can facilitate or restrict the capacity of individuals or groups (either consciously or unconsciously) to act. Importantly, structures are also transformed when we interact with them; that is, our actions are enabled and constrained by structures and those actions can, in turn, reproduce and maintain those structures or transform and produce new structures via social change.

Finally, social structures are often categorized as *rules* and *resources*. By rules we mean both the internal assumptions and ideologies embraced by men and women as common sense and the external laws, regulations, and policies that set limits and possibilities with respect to how we can act in our social lives. Resources, meanwhile, are divided into three main components: financial (money), material (equipment, property, etc.), and human (other agents).

Agency and Power

Agency is the ability of individuals and groups to act independently in a goal-directed manner and to pursue their own "free" choices. Sociology, in this respect, "involves an attempt to understand the degree to which human agents, whether individual or collective, are constrained to think and act in the ways they do" (Gruneau, 1999, p. 1). *Power* is "the capacity of a person or group of persons to employ resources of different types in order to secure outcomes" (Gruneau, 1988, p. 22). In this sense, power can be understood as a level of control or prestige of one group over another as an exercise of agency, or "the ability of an individual or group to carry out its will even when opposed by others" (Naiman, 2012, p. 6). Power, of course, implies the existence of power relations and inevitably resistance. Groups and individuals differ in terms of power with respect to access to resources (financial, material, and human) and to benefits derived from rules (internal and external). In Canada and indeed around the world, the Occupy Movement drew our attention to unequal power relations along the lines of social class and the growing gap between the wealthiest 1% of Canadians and the influence they wield at political and economic levels and the other 99% in our country. The Idle No More movement, meanwhile, cast a critical spotlight on the continuation of unequal power relations between Euro-Canadians and Aboriginal peoples and the historical significance of colonization in Canada. Despite significant gains by the women's movement, feminists continue to draw our attention to the unequal power relations between men and women, including the underrepresentation of women in positions of economic, political, religious, and military power.

We want to follow Rick Gruneau (1988, p. 22) by suggesting that there are at least "three notable measures of the 'power' of different social groups" that need to be fully considered in the sociological analysis of sport. They are the capacity to

1. structure sport in preferred ways and to "institutionalize" these preferences in sports rules and organizations,

2. establish selective sports traditions, and

3. define the range of "legitimate" practices and meanings associated with dominant sports practices.

It's important to emphasize, again, that sport is a social practice shaped by broader power relations and that it benefits some individuals and groups more than others. Indeed, to have power and achieve a result or social change, one needs access to a range of resources and favourable rules.

For example, consider the debate over the exclusion of women's ski jumping at the 2010 Winter Olympic Games in Vancouver. In 2006, the IOC rejected an application by the International Ski Federation to include women's ski jumping at the 2010 Olympic Games. The IOC claimed that women's ski jumping was not yet fully established and did not deserve to be an Olympic event. In response to this decision, a group of 15 female ski jumpers took legal action against the Vancouver Organizing Committee (VANOC) on the grounds that a publicly funded sporting competition that included male ski jumping but excluded female jumpers was in violation of the Canadian Charter of Rights and Freedoms. The women argued that ski jumping was not a new event and that VANOC's decision was simply representative of a long pattern of discrimination against female athletes (e.g., a women's marathon was not added until the 1984 Olympics in Los Angeles; up until then female athletes were deemed to be too frail to participate in such a strenuous event). While admitting that the decision was discriminatory, the judge ruled that the IOC (and not VANOC) had exclusive control over the decision, and thus VANOC could not be held accountable. Moreover, the decision acknowledged that because the IOC exists as an international nongovernmental organization, it was not subject to the constitutional laws of Canada. As a result, the women lost their case (and further appeals) and were prohibited from participating in Vancouver.

Hegemony

Finally, an overriding theme throughout this textbook is *hegemony*, which comes from the Greek word *Hegemonia* meaning leadership. The Italian political theorist Antonio Gramsci developed the theory of hegemony (which will be outlined in more detail in the next chapter) to draw attention to some of the effects of dominant ideologies and ideas in the maintenance (or challenging) of various power relations in society. By ideology, we mean a framework of beliefs that guides behaviour. In particular, Gramsci was interested in understanding how various societies with obvious unequal power relations and inequalities (class, race, gender, etc.) were consensually held together. For Gramsci, the ability of dominant individuals and groups (with more power and resources) to establish ideological systems of meanings and values that justified those various inequalities as "common sense" was a vital step in the maintenance of their positions of moral and intellectual leadership.

Gramci's ideas about hegemony, for example, force us to consider all of the ways in which our daily experiences in sport and beyond become a part of our everyday practical consciousness, "a common sense that offers us 'normal' aspirations and ways of feeling, as well as orthodox ideas" (Hall et al., 1991, p. 45). Historically, the "common sense" belief that sport was by its very nature a masculine endeavour restricted the opportunities of girls and women (and, by extension, boys and men) to participate in various physical activities. Indeed, to this day a particular vision of masculinity based on aggression, violence, and emotional stoicism, what the Australian sociologist R.A. Connell (1990, 2005) has called hegemonic masculinity, is culturally exalted in competitive sport and in broader Canadian society. It is a dominant vision of masculinity that many boys and men consent to as something that is entirely "natural" and "self-evident," even while hegemonic masculinity is being perpetually challenged, reinforced, and reconstructed in relation to other forms of masculinity and femininity. Thus, the value in Gramsci's approach is that it politicizes our analysis about culture and sport in Canadian society and forces us to recognize that what we understand as our practical consciousness "cannot really be understood without reference to social structures within which particular cultural practices are privileged, and particular vocabularies or motives are presented not just as right but as natural" (Hall et al., 1991, p. 45).

Conclusions

Over 50 years ago, in his classic text *Beyond a Boundary* (1963), the renowned Afro-Trinidadian historian and social theorist C. L. R. James posed a powerful question about the sport of cricket in the West Indies: "What do they know of cricket if all they know is cricket?" James was interested in examining West Indian national culture and society (education, family, class, race, and colonialism) through cricket, the sport's history, and his own life as a cricketer and commentator on the sport. Reflecting on his own experiences in the sport, and using his own sociological imagination, James simply recognized in hindsight that "Cricket had plunged me into politics long before I was aware of it." Indeed, for James the sport of cricket—its salience, discipline, representational power, and contested meanings—played a decisive role in the broader anti-colonial struggle of an emergent West Indian society on the brink of independence.

Like James, the practices of sport and physical activity have plunged Canadians from across the country into a wide range of historical and contemporary political struggles, perhaps long before being fully conscious of those power relations and social structures. And, like James, sociology of sport students in Canada can pose a similar question, albeit in a radically different context, that speaks precisely to the importance of the sociological imagination as a way of thinking and method of sociological analysis: "What do we know of hockey if all we know is hockey?"

Many sociologists paint a rather gloomy picture of sport in Canadian society, especially in light of enduring inequalities and a wide range of social issues, and certainly it would be naive and irresponsible to ignore the range of issues that need to be addressed and mended in various sports across Canada. Still, it's important to recognize that sport provides millions of Canadians with pleasurable, exhilarating, and enjoyable ways of spending time and powerful understandings of community. Equally important, even though involvement in sport and physical activity has many imbalances and injustices, Canadians from across the country are involved daily in a complex dance of reproducing and resisting a host of social structures and power relations, and are subsequently transforming not only sport and physical activity but Canadian society itself. The good news to leave you with at this chapter's end is that some of the problems that exist are being addressed through an awareness of their existence and a willingness to find solutions. The processes of personal and social transformation starts here with you, the student of sociological dimensions of sport and physical activity.

Critical Thinking Questions

1. Discuss the reasons why a course in the sociology of sport and physical activity should be part of an undergraduate curriculum in a kinesiology/human kinetics/physical education/sport science program.

2. How does sport sociology differ from sport psychology?

3. Provide examples of the three notable measures of the "power" of different social groups that need to be fully considered in the sociological analysis of sport.

4. Discuss what is meant by the phrase "sport (formal and informal) is socially constructed."

5. a. Using your sociological imagination, how was a personal issue—the exclusion of women's ski jumping—intimately connected to a host of public issues of social structure in Canadian society and beyond?

    b. How did those structures facilitate and restrict the agency of the women ski jumpers? Use each of the three measures of power in your answer.

    c. What resources did the women need to challenge both VANOC's and the IOC's rules?

    d. What rules worked in their favour? Which ones did not?

    e. What role did gender ideology play in this debate?

Suggested Readings

Giddens, A., & Sutton, P.W. (2013). *Sociology*. London, UK: Polity Press.

Gruneau, R. (1999). *Class, sports, and social development*. Champaign, IL: Human Kinetics.

Gruneau, R., & Whitson, D. (1993). *Hockey night in Canada: Sports, identities, and cultural politics*. Toronto, ON: Garamond Press.

Mills, C.W. (1961). *The sociological imagination*. New York, NY: Grove Press.

Naiman, J. (2012). *How societies work*. Halifax, NS: Fernwood.

Whitson, D., & Gruneau, R. (2006). *Artificial ice: Hockey, culture, and commerce*. Peterborough, ON: Broadview Press.

Zirin, D. (2013). *Game over: How politics has turned the sports world upside down*. New York, NY: The New Press.

References

Brym, R. J. (2014). *We the people: Society in question*. Toronto, ON: Nelson.

Canadian Heritage. (2013). *Sport participation 2010: Research paper*. Retrieved from http://publications. gc.ca/collections/collection_2014/pc-ch/CH24-1-2014-eng.pdf.

Connell, R. W. (1990). An iron man: The body and some contradictions of hegemonic masculinity. In. M.A. Messner & D.F. Sabo (Eds.), *Sport, men, and the gender order: Critical feminist perspectives* (pp. 83–114). Champaign, IL: Human Kinetics.

Connell, R. W. (2005). *Masculinities* (2nd ed.). Berkeley, CA: University of California Press.

Dodd, M. (2006, April 30). Sport or not a sport? Pot is split on poker. *USA Today*, p. 13C.

Giddens, A. (1987). *Social theory and modern sociology*. Palo Alto, CA: Stanford University Press.

Gruneau, R. (1988). Modernization and hegemony: Two views on sport and social development. In J. Harvey & H. Cantelon (Eds.), *Not just a game: Essays in Canadian sport sociology* (pp. 9–32). Ottawa, ON: University of Ottawa Press.

Gruneau, R. (1999). *Class, sports, and social development*. Champaign, IL: Human Kinetics.

Hall, A. (2007). Cultural struggle and resistance: Gender, history, and Canadian sport. In K. Young & P. White (Eds.), *Sport and gender in Canada*, (pp. 56–74). Toronto, ON: Oxford University Press.

Hall, A., Slack, T., Smith, G., & Whitson, D. (1991). *Sport in Canadian society*. Toronto, ON: McClelland & Stewart.

Harvey, J. (2000). What's in a game? In P. Donnelly (Ed.), *Taking sport seriously*. Toronto, ON: Thompson Educational Publishing.

Henslin, J. M., Glenday, D., Pupo, N., & Duffy, A. (2014). *Sociology: A down to earth approach* (6th Canadian ed.). Toronto, ON: Pearson Canada.

ISSA (International Sociology of Sport Association). (2005). About ISSA. Retrieved from issa. otago.ac.nz/about.html.

James, C. L. R. (1963). *Beyond a Boundary*. London: Stanley Paul & Co.

Kenyon, G., & McPherson, B. (1973). Becoming involved in physical activity and sport: A process of socialization. In G. L. Rarick (Ed.), *Physical activity: Human growth and development*. New York, NY: Academic Press.

Mills, C. W. (1961). *The sociological imagination*. New York, NY: Grove Press.

Naiman, J. (2012). *How societies work: Class, power, and change*. Halifax, NS: Fernwood.

Sage, G.H. (1997). Physical education, sociology, and sociology of sport: Points of intersection. *Sociology of Sport Journal, 14*, 317–339.

Chapter 2
Sociological Theories of Sport

Ian Ritchie

Sociological theory is the foundation of the discipline of sociology in general and its particular understanding of sport and physical activity in sport sociology. This chapter introduces four major theoretical perspectives: structural functionalism, conflict theory, symbolic interactionism, and critical social theories. The theories offer competing perspectives but at the same time occasionally complement one another in their attempts to answer questions about the nature of social and cultural life. Examples from the study of sport and physical activity demonstrate that the perspectives often raise serious challenges to many common assumptions about sport.

A young girl working in a cotton mill in the early 20th century in the United States. Child labour was one of many hardships the first sociologists attempted to understand during the early days of the Industrial Revolution.
Library of Congress Prints and Photographs Division[LC-DIG-nclc-01336]

UNDERSTANDING SOCIOLOGICAL THEORY: GENERAL THEMES AND HISTORICAL CONTEXTS

Lying at the foundation of sociology is theory. Theory is the central tool that sociologists use to understand the human world around us in general, and more specifically for sport sociologists, the role that sport and physical culture play within that world.

In simple terms, sociological theory is a proposition or set of propositions about the nature of the social world and people's roles or active engagement in that world. However, theory is in many ways not so different from the fact that people "theorize" about the world around them all the time, in the sense that they ponder various aspects of social and cultural life, or perhaps just think about the conduct of other people around them in their everyday lives.

"Theory," then, is a continuation of something that is universal to human beings: Their attempt to explain the social world around them to themselves and to gain a better understanding of their personal lives in turn. For example, *myths* have always played an important role in human cultures in that they explain to people the nature of their role in the greater scheme of things. But even our most cherished and taken-for-granted myths, social anthropologists remind us, and contrary to the literal meaning of the term itself, are really stories that are based not only on fictionalized or exaggerated accounts, but also on factual ones. We can find an example of this by looking no further than Canada today, in that the sport of hockey provides a fictionalized or exaggerated account of the country and its history, even though hockey's mythology often refers to real people and real events, such as great wins or great players (Gruneau & Whitson, 1993).

However, what sets serious theory apart from everyday ideas about the world is the fact that sociological theories must ultimately be accountable—they must prove themselves through a process of verification with the facts of the social world. In other words, they must withstand the test of systematic verification, whether in the form of facts and statistics or simply careful and systematic observations about certain aspects of social life. Good sociological theory withstands the test of time through constant refinement and rigorous debate, and it must be provable through careful observation and systematic verification.

Sometimes the results are contrary to common perceptions or "common sense." When the term *common sense* is used, it typically means that someone is using sound and practical judgment. However, here the term is meant in the more literal meaning; that is, that there are often ideas that people—perhaps many people—have in common. Albert Einstein, though, once said that "Common sense is the collection of prejudices acquired by age 18," which points to the problem with this kind of sense—it is quite often wrong. We accumulate ideas through various sources as we grow, Einstein suggests, but that does not mean those accumulated sets of ideas are accurate or a true reflection of the world around us.

So one of the first points about sociological theory to keep in mind is that it does not always support common sense notions about the nature of the social world. A simple yet profoundly important example comes from sport. One myth that has been perpetuated over time is that sport is, to use a familiar expression, as "old as the hills." In other words, people have always practised "sport" in the same way over time. As an important corollary to this, many believe that the Olympic Games—likely the most important and influential example of organized sport in modern times—was based on the model of ancient Greece when it was revived by the Frenchman Pierre de Coubertin in the 19th century. However, solid historical evidence, informed by theory, has shown that sport in ancient Greece had *far* more differences than it did similarities to sport today. For example, the ancient Greeks adopted a "winner takes all" approach that far outweighed our own today. In ancient Greece, extremely violent acts in wrestling were commonplace and victorious athletes—despite, and often in fact *because* of their violence—were held up as almost the equivalent to gods themselves (Public Broadcasting Service, 2004). Canadian sport historian Bruce Kidd (1984) points out that "the modern handshake would have seemed an act of cowardice" because of the dramatically different approach the ancients took to their sport (p. 76).

Besides the challenges that sociological theories and the discipline of sociology as a whole often bring to some common understandings of sport, there are a few other important points to keep in mind before considering the theories themselves. First, the theoretical perspectives offer not only an interpretation of social conditions at present, they also offer interpretations of history. Events in history are interpreted according to the tenets of the particular theory, or in other words, theory will guide the manner in which events of the past are viewed. History is not thought of as a *static* accumulation of facts but rather a *dynamic* set of events, and the interpretation of events or what "facts" are considered important is guided by theory. Also, each of the theoretical perspectives encourages us to think about and evaluate social conditions as they currently are by putting those conditions into historical context. In other words, we can learn a lot about the way things are today by looking back and placing events in their proper historical context. You will find that many of the authors of chapters in this text remind us of important elements of Canadian sport history so that we might better understand current issues.

The discipline of sociology itself should be thought of in this historical context. While the events that lay the foundation of sociology are many and complex, two stand out. The first event was a series of *democratic revolutions* that led to the emergence of democratic institutions and various forms of government; the revolutions in France and the United States in the late 18th century are the most important examples. These changes brought about the idea that governments are responsible to people and that people as citizens can actively play a role in the affairs of the state. Sociology emerged in part to consider these changes and to contemplate the newly envisioned role of democratic institutions and people's relationship to those institutions. The second, more important, event was the *Industrial Revolution*. So important was the development of industrial society to the emergence of sociology that the discipline in its earliest days was more or less defined as the study of the causes and consequences of the Industrial Revolution, which dramatically changed the way in which goods were produced and people laboured. But it also brought new social problems: mass exoduses of people from rural settings to urban centres, miserable and often dangerous working and living conditions, new forms of crime, vast inequalities between the rich and the poor, and a general sense of alienation or disaffection caused by the dramatic changes in people's lives.

Out of these two historical contexts, sociology emerged to consider two main questions or issues. The first was the *issue of social problems*. In light of the hardships wrought by the Industrial Revolution and the full emergence of capitalism, the earliest sociologists were concerned with how to create a social order that could resolve some of the fundamental problems: food production and distribution in growing cities, lack of clean water, poor hygienic living conditions, the physical hardships from long hours of strenuous work in factories, child labour, vast inequalities between the rich and poor, and so forth. These issues, of course, continue to plague us today to varying degrees.

The second issue pertains to *community, authority, and tradition*. As peasants were lifted from their land to work in cities as labourers, as small manufacturers were replaced by big companies, as urban living quickly replaced rural life, questions arose as to how to maintain and develop authority structures in the new social order, how to provide people with a sense of community in light of rapid changes, and how to answer questions regarding the loss of rural and religious traditions as society became more secularized. How should the new social order be organized and established? What was the role of individual citizens in relation to newly emerging state-run institutions and forms of government? What social bonds would unite people in newly emerging urban communities? These were some of the important questions the first sociologists attempted to answer. Again, these questions continue to be asked and sociologists continue to try to answer them, even if some of the issues of community, authority, and tradition have changed, especially in the context of globalization (see Chapter 14).

The theories we are about to consider should not be thought of as static, but instead in a constant dynamic state in which debate and refinement have led and will continue to lead to their change and evolution. The temptation at first in reading accounts of theories is to look for the one that is "right"; however, that search will likely be futile because theories that have attempted to make all-encompassing universal claims usually fall short in one way or another. Instead, each theory should be thought of as having certain strengths that help explain certain elements of the social world, but also weaknesses or areas it does not consider.

Importantly, sociological theories all have in common a political motivation to understand the nature of the social world around us to make it better for everyone. This motivation dates back to the historical foundations of the discipline itself and the first questions and issues it addressed, as discussed earlier. One of the natural consequences of this political motivation is that the theories often point to the many problems that exist in the social world. This *critical* element of the theories should in no way overshadow sociology's recognition of the many ways in which sport and physical culture more generally can play an active and positive role in human life. Identifying problems, however, is a necessary step in making the positive aspects of physical activity and sport available for as many people as possible.

Finally, the theories discussed here do not by any means represent a complete inventory of sociological theories. The discipline offers a dizzying array of perspectives, and they continue to grow. However, what follows provides a concise summary of major perspectives that have guided thinking in sociology's past and continue to guide thinking currently, that have laid the foundation of sociological inquiries in sport and physical activity, and that will put into context the various topics in the chapters that follow. The theories presented here are also very general and, in most cases, there is a diversity of more specific perspectives that fall within each. As such, they should be thought of as general guidelines as opposed to theoretical "formulae" into which sport can simply be plugged. Having said that, all sections will quite naturally include a discussion of the application of theories to sport using both general examples but also ones specific to Canada.

SOCIAL FACTS: ÉMILE DURKHEIM AND STRUCTURAL FUNCTIONALISM

The foundations of *structural functionalism*—often referred to synonymously as *functionalism*—are very old and can be traced to elements of ancient Greek thought and, much more recently, British social philosophy (McQuarie, 1995, pp. 1–2). Charles Darwin's theory of evolution had an important influence on the theory, and the earliest functionalist theorists equated social processes with biological or organic ones, claiming that society operates according to principles similar to that of animal life and the manner in which that life develops and evolves.

The most important and influential figure to develop and more fully express these basic functionalist tenets was Émile Durkheim (1858–1917). While active in French politics and social life generally, Durkheim's most noted accomplishments were realized in his active reforms of French education, and he is generally recognized as the "father" of French sociology. During his lifetime, the new discipline of sociology was not generally respected in higher academics, and Durkheim should be credited with working to gain its respect. Many identify Durkheim as being the single most important early founder of the discipline (see Beamish, 2010, pp. 123–166; Loy & Booth, 2002, pp. 41–43).

The essential elements of Durkheim's theories on social life can be seen in what many consider to be his most important work, *Suicide: A Study in Sociology*, published in 1897. *Suicide*, a classic of social science research, gives us not only Durkheim's sociological view of the act of suicide, but ultimately an indication of his more general account of sociology, as the subtitle of the book suggests.

Durkheim makes what appears to be the counterintuitive claim that the act of suicide is much more than just a personal act of agency by an individual. Suicide is, instead, a social act and in fact operates according to social laws. Durkheim referred to any human activities of this sort as *social facts*, by which he meant any phenomena that operated according to social rules or laws independent of any one individual. His notion of social facts was the basis for Durkheim's more general vision of how human social life should be studied. As he clearly states, "[s]ociological method as we practice it rests wholly on the basic principle that social facts must be studied as things, that is, as realities external to the individual" (Durkheim, 1951, pp. 37–38).

This point of view sets Durkheim dramatically apart from common ideas about suicide, particularly in his own day. He challenged two major ways of thinking about the act of suicide in the late 19th century: individual psychological views about the motivations of the suicide victim, and Christian religious thinking that thought of the act as a sin against God.

Durkheim collected a remarkable inventory of statistics on suicide rates across Europe. After collecting his data, Durkheim observed that suicide rates followed identifiable social patterns. For example, men committed suicide at significantly higher rates than women, Protestants more than Catholics, unmarried people more than married people, and wealthy people, interestingly, more than poorer people. Durkheim recognized a common theme: Levels of social *integration* across categories of people significantly impact the chances of a particular individual committing suicide or not.

By social integration, Durkheim meant common ties or bonds that hold people together and give them a common outlook and a feeling of solidarity. As stated clearly in his own terms: "suicide varies inversely with the degree of integration of the social groups of which the individual forms a part" (Durkheim, 1951, p. 209). Thus, for example, while men and those who are wealthy might achieve greater autonomy and independence, such personal "gains" may come at a cost of reduced integration and social bonds, and thus a greater chance of suicide.

Durkheim and other functionalist theorists who followed him in the 20th century expanded upon this essential notion of the role of social integration to develop a much more general and complex theory of society. In general, structural functionalism views society as a *complex system in which all of the different elements of its structure work to promote stability and solidarity within that system*. The essential elements of the theory's view of society can be seen in the two terms in the name of the theory. First, society has a *structure*, which means it has a stable and persistent pattern of elements, including institutions, patterns of interpersonal behaviour, and values and norms. In terms of *function*, all elements function or contribute to the overall stability of the structure of society (Parsons, 1961).

For understanding sport, functionalism has been important in terms of considering several vital functions sport serves to wider society. Also, the theory was dominant in the discipline of sociology when the specific subdiscipline of sport sociology was first developing in the 1960s and 1970s. According to the structural functionalist analysis, sport functions to develop group bonds, to encourage a sense of community, and to integrate people into society's dominant values. Sport also acts as a significant agent of socialization and helps children in particular develop solid social skills. In addition, sport functions as positive entertainment and as an "escape valve" from some of the more laborious aspects of everyday life. Finally, it is often argued that sport functions to deter youth and others from deviant and antisocial behaviour (Loy & Booth, 2000, 2002).

Following Durkheim, Alan Ingham (2004) refers to public sporting events as *serialized civic rituals*—in other words, sport acts as quasi-religious events in which ideals of communities become represented and reaffirmed. "Regardless of whether *our* team is winning or losing," Ingham says, "the faithful seem compelled by an abstract force, larger than themselves, to go and worship at the shrine" (p. 27). Sport, in other words, acts symbolically to represent what is important for communities and ties the people in them together. We don't have to look further than the ritualistic manner in which fans of the Toronto Maple Leafs and Montreal Canadiens worship at their respective "shrines" to understand Ingham's point.

In one of the more intriguing recent applications of functionalism to sport, authors Simon Kuper and Stefan Szymanski in their book *Soccernomics* claim that soccer actually helps curb suicide rates. Building directly on Durkheim's *Suicide*, the authors cite statistics from several countries to demonstrate that during periods of intense international competitions like the World Cup, national suicide rates drop. The authors surmise that intense feelings of "belongingness," often with attendant strong nationalistic associations, enhances *social cohesion* and the strong common bonds necessary for social life. Interestingly, supporting a point made by Ingham above, Kuper and Szymanski also point out that winning is not a necessary outcome for suicide rates to improve; win or lose, it's the manner in which the intense feelings generated in rooting for the team "pulls people together" that matters (Kuper & Szymanski, 2009, pp. 253–266).

In Canada, we can think of the many ways in which sport plays a crucial role in the construction of a common sense of nationhood. Athletes supported under Sport Canada serve as both a means to enhance nationalism and a common identity, while simultaneously acting as international ambassadors. Following Ben Johnson's world-record medal performance at the World Track and Field Championships in Rome in 1987, Minister of State for Fitness and Amateur Sport Otto Jelinek said (ironically, in retrospect) that "Ben Johnson, doing what he's doing for Canadians in Rome, is probably worth more than a dozen delegations of high-powered diplomats" (Beamish & Borowy, 1988, p. 11). And, of course, many Canadians can vividly recall the outpouring of nationalism following Sydney Crosby's final goal to give Canada the gold medal at the 2010 Olympic Winter Games in Vancouver.

While it dominated sociology by the mid-20th century and influenced the first research on sport in the 1960s and 1970s, structural functionalism then declined in influence because of several flaws. Crucially, the theory was criticized for what was seen as its inherent conservatism.

In particular, structural functionalism suggests that all elements of society are viewed as necessary and good for the simple fact that they exist to reinforce the overall structure of the system as a whole. But surely not all elements of social systems are justified—it is questionable how poverty, violence, crime, institutionalized racism or sexism, and many other social problems can be thought of as positive elements in a social system.

The low point for functionalism came when Kingsley Davis and Wilbert Moore (1945) argued that class inequalities are inevitable components of social systems and play important, even positive, functional roles. Their proof was based on their observation that class stratification has existed in all social systems and, they argued, it was simply necessary to reward those who spend time and effort training and working in jobs that are more important for society as a whole with greater compensation in the form of status or wealth. Critics pointed out that even if there was some truth in this claim, it by no means justified the often huge inequalities or discrepancies in terms of status or pay. The most successful and highly paid professional athletes come to mind right away: While they may provide great entertainment, it is difficult to justify their multimillion-dollar salaries given their questionable utility or usefulness to society otherwise. The Davis–Moore thesis drew the proverbial line in the sand in debates about sociological theory. Statements such as theirs eventually led to the downfall of functionalist theory and the rise of competing perspectives that attempted to account for the existence of social problems and inequalities in much more realistic ways.

CLASS AND GOAL-RATIONAL ACTION: KARL MARX, MAX WEBER, AND CONFLICT THEORY

Like structural functionalism, some of the central tenets of modern conflict sociology are very old and can be traced back to ancient times. However, the theory's more modern form owes itself to the work of Karl Marx (1818–1883) (McQuarie, 1995). Marx was born in Trier in the Rhineland (in what is now Germany), and in his earliest years as a student he became interested in the study of law and philosophy before turning his attention later to journalism, political activism, and writing social and political critiques. His radical politics and involvement in workers' organizations were partly the cause for his migration—sometimes forced—from Germany to France and eventually England (Beamish, 2002).

Marx sought to develop a social theory that understood the emerging capitalist world around him and, at the same time, actively help create social conditions that would be more egalitarian and democratic. Marx's political commitment was due to a large degree to the harsh conditions of life, discussed earlier, encountered by a majority of people in the emerging industrial society. His famous words "[t]he philosophers have only *interpreted* the world, in various ways; the point, however, is to *change* it" (Marx, 1972, p. 109) remain a clear and decisive reflection of his political commitment.

The unique characteristics about Marx's analysis of society and what lay at the foundation of his ideas were threefold: first, his recognition that *economic* conditions formed the base or foundation of social life more generally; second, his ability to synthesize and expand his observations regarding the basic economic conditions of social life into a more general theory regarding the nature of social, cultural, and individual life; and third, his observations regarding the important role *social conflict* played in social and cultural life and the history of societies.

The idea that economic conditions lay the foundation for social life is really at the core of Marx's theory. Marx observed that throughout history different economic forms shaped social systems and, in turn, people's lives within those systems. He referred to these forms as the *modes of production*. Within each mode of production—and Marx studied many in human history, including ancient society, feudalism, and capitalism—Marx also observed that classes emerged based on their ability to wrest control over economic resources and the means of producing goods. This, Marx observed, had led to a state of *conflict* between the respective groups in each case. The opening lines of *The Communist Manifesto*, one of the most important political documents in modern history, state this clearly:

> The history of all hitherto existing society is the history of class struggles. Freeman and slave, patrician and plebeian, lord and serf, guildmaster and journeyman, in a word, oppressor and oppressed, stood in constant opposition to one another, carried on an uninterrupted, now hidden, now open fight, a fight that each time ended, either in a revolutionary reconstitution of society at large, or in the common ruin of the contending classes. (Marx & Engels, 1948, p. 9)

While Marx was interested in various modes of production throughout history and the conflicts that emerged from them, the *capitalist* mode of production drew the lion's share of his attention and work. In his most important work, *Capital*, published in 1867, Marx attempted to explain in scientific terms the manner in which the capitalist mode of production worked (Marx, 1977). His central insight is that capitalism, in its unyielding drive to create profit, produces two separate classes: capitalists who realize the profits and surpluses from the system, and workers who do not. However, the strength of the capitalist mode of production—one unlike other modes of production—is that workers *appear* to be acting freely and of their own choice. But Marx claimed that workers do not in fact realize their full potential because their labour is *alienated* labour; that is, labour that ultimately benefits those who profit from it. As Marx states clearly: "work is *external* to the worker . . . consequently, he does not fulfill himself in his work but denies himself. . . . His work is not voluntary but imposed, *forced labour*. It is not the satisfaction of a need, but only a *means* for satisfying other needs" (Marx, 1963, pp. 124–125). Marx's dual insights regarding the production of the class system within the capitalist mode of production and the alienation of the worker would many years later be central to both Marxist and conflict-based analyses of sport.

We will return shortly to the influence of Marx on *conflict theory*; however, a second major influence comes from a theorist who many consider to be the third "great figure" (besides Durkheim and Marx) in the foundation of sociology—Max Weber (1864–1920). Weber is today associated with the discipline of sociology; however, because the discipline was in its infancy during his time, Weber was formally associated with it only near the end of his life. His training came in law and economics, and he taught in several universities in Germany in those disciplines; however, his knowledge base was derived from several other disciplines, including philosophy and history. As sport sociologists Hart Cantelon and Alan Ingham (2002)—both of whom were deeply influenced by Weber's work—put simply, "Weber was a superior thinker" (p. 64).

Just like we can get a glimpse of their respective theoretical positions by understanding Durkheim's *Suicide* or Marx's *The Communist Manifesto* and *Capital*, so too through what is arguably his most important work, *The Protestant Ethic and The Spirit of Capitalism*, we can start to understand Weber's insights. Well versed on the varied ways in which religion had impacted different societies at different periods in time, Weber made the specific claim in *The Protestant Ethic* that a value system that emerged in the 17th century in Protestant sects in the United States led to a dominant, and ultimately successful, form of capitalism. While Protestantism and the capitalist economy had been emerging in other locations around the globe, Weber claimed that the Puritans in the American northeast developed a specific value system out of the original teachings of 16th-century Protestant reformer John Calvin, who had preached, among other things, of God's all-knowing ways. Being all-knowing, Calvin claimed, God predestined certain dutiful followers to be chosen to go to heaven. However, followers could not ever be certain of their ultimate acceptance into God's grace, so the best they could do was search for signs.

The belief in predestination was the foundation of the Puritan sects' value system, one that was conducive to the development of capitalism, Weber argued. The Puritans particular interpretation of predestination, one that manifested itself in terms of their everyday activities and beliefs, was that followers must prove their loyalty to God by leading an *ascetic* lifestyle; in other words, loyal followers demonstrated their acceptance into God's grace by leading lives of duty, hard work, and abstaining from worldly pleasures such as alcohol consumption, gambling, "pleasures of the flesh" and, interestingly, material goods. The connection between the belief in the necessity to lead an ascetic life and the economy came in the form of the "calling" (Beamish, 2010, pp. 191–194). The calling was the development of personal fulfillment through the commitment of one's life to work and, importantly, the reuse of material rewards, including direct financial ones, back toward the work in a rational and disciplined way. Wealth accumulated based on one's hard work could not be used toward worldly possessions for their own sake, because of course that would have contradicted the essential belief in the importance of leading an ascetic life. It could, however, be put back into the calling and the disciplined hard work of the believer. As Weber explains in an important section of *The Protestant Ethic*:

> the religious valuation of restless, continuous work in a worldly calling, as the highest means to asceticism, and at the same time the surest and most evident proof of rebirth and genuine faith, must have been the most powerful conceivable lever for the expansion of that attitude toward life which we have here called the spirit of capitalism. (Weber, 1958, p. 172)

Over time, the emphasis on hard, rationalized work became common even if, as Weber points out, the original religious source of that value system disappeared.

Two things are important about Weber's theory regarding the development of modern capitalism. First, it is important to note the difference between Weber and Marx in terms of their respective interpretations of the development of capitalism. Unlike Marx, who emphasized the structure of the economy, Weber put an emphasis on the important role that *ideas* (religious ones in this case) play in human affairs and in human history. Second, and more importantly with respect to the understanding of modern sport, Weber believed that ascetic Puritanism and the economic value system that emerged out of the 17th century ultimately led to a greater emphasis on what he termed "goal-rational action," or human action involving the most calculated (rational) means toward achieving a particular end (goal) (Beamish, 2010, pp. 175–179; Cantelon & Ingham, 2002, p. 65). We see this sort of action every day in our lives, as people make calculated decisions toward satisfying personal and professional objectives. At one level it is an approach that we might simply pass off as "making sense"; in other words, we might ask ourselves why anyone would conduct themselves differently. But for Weber goal-rational action can entrap people into a limited way of thinking and leading their lives.

We have to look no further than the realm of sport to find examples of goal-rational action. High-performance athletes—the ones the general public tends to look up to as the epitome of athleticism and what sport is supposed to "be about"—undertake daily, weekly, monthly, and year-by-year training regimens in which virtually every movement and workout is carefully calculated in relation to the other ones to achieve ultimate, long-term goals, such as winning Olympic gold. But in placing such great emphasis on goal-rational action, other possibilities for sport, such as emphasizing the play element in physical movement and the sheer joy and liberation that "uninhibited" movement can provide—movement we often see in children's spontaneous play—get pushed to the side. We will return to other implications of Weber's work momentarily.

Both Marx's insights into the role of class conflict and Weber's into the role that religious ideas played in the development of capitalism formed the base of *conflict theory* more generally, although Marx is really the more important figure. The central difference between Marx's analysis and the one of conflict theory is that the latter developed a much broader and encompassing definition of conflict, especially as the theory was adopted in US sociology in the post–World War II era (McQuarie, 1995). Conflict was recognized as being much more ubiquitous in society, beyond the conflicts between the capitalists and

The German Democratic Republic enters the stadium of its rival Federal Republic of Germany during the 1972 Summer Olympic Games in Munich. Nothing accelerated the emphasis on what Weber referred to as "goal-rational action" as much as the Cold War. Today, many of the features of Canada's high-performance sport system are essentially the same as (former) East Germany's.
AP Images

working classes as Marx saw them. Examples include conflicts between workers and middle managers in industrial settings, between authority figures and subordinates in many different bureaucratic organizational contexts, or between political elites and citizens or secondary-level government members in totalitarian political regimes, under socialist–communism, or for that matter in liberal–democratic societies.

Some overarching questions or issues flow from Marx's and Weber's central insights and the more general conflict model that followed from them. First, how does sport contribute to or reinforce class and other power structures in society? While it may not be "common sense" for many of us to think of sport as reinforcing class inequalities or other forms of power, sport has in fact played an important role in Canada's history in this regard (Gruneau, 1983). In his landmark book *The Struggle for Canadian Sport,* for example, Bruce Kidd (1996a) demonstrates that the active political power struggles between various groups during the period between the two World Wars created the foundation for some of the most important elements of the Canadian sport landscape. One for-profit business cartel, the National Hockey League (NHL), was particularly successful in setting the agenda for Canadian sport. However, Kidd demonstrates that this did not come without a cost: the handful of owners—all men—were successful, but their success came at the expense of other vibrant sporting traditions, including a successful women's organization under the direction of the Women's Amateur Athletic Federation.

Also, amateur leaders, who in general supported middle- to upper-class sporting clubs and the elite men who made up their membership, actively used sport to control working-class people. This fact is perhaps best embodied in the statement by amateur leader Henry Roxborough in *Maclean's* magazine in 1926: "A nation that loves sport cannot revolt" (cited in Kidd, 1996a, p. 50). In other words, sport was used as an active diversion to keep workers "in line" so they would not challenge the authority of bosses and politicians who supported the interests of bosses in turn: "[s]ocial obedience, labour discipline, and company loyalty could be inculcated amid the joys and excitement of a well-played game" (Kidd, 1996a, p. 50). Interestingly, attempts to control workers' lives were met with resistance: a vibrant workers' sport movement during the 1920s and 1930s used sport as a means to fight for workers' rights. We will return to this example later in the chapter; however, for now it is important to recognize the fact that conflict based on class differences helped shape the organization and define the *meaning* of sport in Canada (see Chapter 3).

A second issue that arises from conflict theory is the manner in which conflict and change occur within sporting organizations and practices. Donald MacIntosh's and David Whitson's *The Game Planners: Transforming Canada's Sport System* (1990) is a classic example of this. The authors demonstrate that during the development of the government-run and-funded sport system from the 1960s to the late 1980s, particular political objectives combined with an emerging cadre of sport "professionals" determined the direction of the sport system to meet their own interests and agendas. As a result, despite the fact that the first legislation supporting government involvement in sport in 1961 called for support for sport at both the high-performance level and the everyday grassroots level, the former has completely overshadowed the latter because high-performance sport satisfied the political and professional objectives of those within the system. One major and, as the authors argue, unfortunate consequence is there has been very little support for grassroots efforts to support mass recreation and sport at the local level. A second consequence flowing from Weber's account of goal-rational action is that, as the federal sport system developed, physical education programs changed to reflect the need to produce performances at the national and international levels:

> In the model of "professionality" that now dominates Canadian physical education, the young sport scientist or sport manager is encouraged to see his or her job as the production of performance . . . and is seldom seriously introduced to the social and political questions that surround the concentration of resources on elite sport. (MacIntosh & Whitson, 1990, p. 120)

Macintosh's and Whitson's analysis continues to have direct relevance today. Interestingly, as there has been increased support for the federal high-performance sport system over time, participation rates and activity levels of Canadian youth have shrunk.

The third issue stems both from Marx's idea about the alienation of the worker in the capitalist mode of production and Weber's analysis of goal-rational action. Some conflict theorists have claimed that sport has produced an alienated experience that overemphasizes the unquestioned rational approach. In *Sport: A Prison of Measured Time*, French social and political theorist Jean-Marie Brohm (1978) gives a classic condemnation of sport and, in particular, the Olympic Games. Sport, Brohm claims, is an institutional form through which capitalist class inequalities are reproduced and excessive attention to work has become an unquestioned ideal. Athletes pay excessive attention to the details of time (thus the subtitle of the book) and the command of space at the exclusion of other forms of physical activity that might be more liberating and fulfilling. Expressed in his own no uncertain terms, Brohm claims that "sport is the *ideology of the body/machine*—the body turned into a robot, alienated by capitalist labour" (p. 77).

Rob Beamish (author of Chapter 4 on social stratification) has also expressed the dynamic of sport's potential combined with the problem of limiting that potential under alienating conditions:

> If sporting activity is so rich with creative potential—so robust with opportunities for individuals to explore their own limits and the limitations of human physical performance—the loss of control of the product can have devastating consequences for the creative potential of physical activity. . . . rather than realising the full productive potential of the athlete, sport stands against the athlete and builds the power of the market's influence over sport while restricting the expressive potential of the athletes themselves. (Beamish, 2002, p. 37)

Beamish elsewhere has pointed out that the gradual commodification of virtually every aspect of high-level professional and commercial sport comes with consequences, as athletes and sport itself become valued only if they become sellable. Interestingly, Frenchman Pierre de Coubertin, when he started the modern Olympic Games, had as part of his goal to use the Olympic movement as a social platform to overcome what he saw as a creeping "crass materialism" in late 19th-century European society. This was one of the reasons that for the first 80 years of the existence of the Olympic Games the IOC defended the amateur rule in its Charter, restricting payment of any kind to athletes and perpetuating an ideal of Olympic sportsmen as being "true" and "pure." The amateur rule, however, was abandoned, and Beamish argues that in some ways this is unfortunate because Coubertin's vision was one in which sport would overcome the more vulgar aspects of the materialistic world in favour of something better: "beauty, creativity and transcendental freedom" (Beamish, 2009, p. 88).

It was mentioned at the beginning of this chapter that all sociological theories used to study sport have a political motivation. The legacy of Marx's and Weber's ideas and conflict theory as a whole is the identification of inequalities and the manner in which they influence the experience of sport and the promise of an unalienated full expression of physical movement for as many people as possible. However, one of the problems sociologists have identified with conflict sociology's perspective is the fact that it tends to favour broad sweeping social structures and institutions, economic ones in particular, instead of the people who exist within those structures and institutions. The ability of people to influence the social world around them—their volition or *agency*, in other words—disappears. But of course real people do have agency and the ability to influence both their own lives and the nature of institutional structures around them. And so it is to the next theories that we turn for a greater consideration of the everyday experiences of human beings.

UNDERSTANDING EVERYDAY EXPERIENCES: GEORGE HERBERT MEAD AND SYMBOLIC INTERACTIONISM

Symbolic interactionism is part of a much bigger tradition in sociology called *microsociology*, which in general studies and attempts to understand the real-life behaviours of people in society. Microsociological approaches are generally critical of *macrosociology* or "grand theories"—such as structural functionalism and conflict theories—because of their overemphasis on sweeping structural processes at the expense of understanding how *people* understand the world around them and interact.

The most important individual in terms of the development of symbolic interactionism was George Herbert Mead (1863–1931). Mead's *Mind, Self, and Society* was first published in 1934 a few years after his death based on a collection of notes taken by students who took and were enthralled by his courses. The book is considered a classic in sociology (Mead, 1962; see also Donnelly, 2002, pp. 83–85; McQuarie, 1995, pp. 188–190).

Mead claimed that macrosociological theories grossly underestimated the role of human thought and volitional action. In particular they did not account for the *symbolic* nature of human thought and the ability of humans to interpret and give meaning to the world around them through language. They also did no justice to the *social context* or the role of *social interaction* in determining human behaviour. These two fundamental insights are the foundation of Mead's thinking and, combined, the source of the perspective that would eventually become known as *symbolic interactionism*, coined by one of Mead's students, Herbert Blumer.

At the heart of Mead's theory is the manner in which humans develop a sense of *self*. When the term is used in everyday language it is usually meant in a purely individual sense, as in "myself." However, Mead pointed out that the self is a dynamic, not a static thing. In other words, we do not simply *have* a self; rather, we continually *develop* a sense of self over time—it is an ongoing process. Mead spent much time explaining the development of the self in children as they grew, pointing out that children grow through a series of stages, each of which gives them a greater sense of themselves as individuals and at the same time a greater sense of others' perspectives and how they *think* others view them (Mead, 1962).

The latter point regarding the image others have of a person gets to the core of a second important point Mead made about the self. Mead described two components of the self, which he called the *I* and the *Me*. While the terms are very simple, the ideas they represent are much more profound. The I for Mead is the internal component of our self—the part of the self that is subjectively experienced and initiates a person's actions in the world. This is the part of the self we associate with our internal feelings, motivations, and general purpose in life. The Me, however, is the image we have of ourselves that comes from outside of ourselves—how others view us and how we believe or think others view us. While the I is the subjective experience of the self, the Me is the objective experience. In Mead's own words:

> The "I" is the response of the organism to the attitudes of the others; the "me" is the organized set of attitudes of others which one himself assumes. The attitudes of the others constitutes the organized "me," and then one reacts toward that as an "I." (Mead, 1962, p. 175)

For Mead, the two parts can be separated at the conceptual level, but not at the real-life level as they are actually experienced; we constantly live through and with both the I and the Me. But what is important in making the conceptual break for Mead lies at the heart of his theory and its impact on sociology: The Me component of the self is created from the wider social world, meaning our very sense of *ourselves* is, in essence, at one and the same time, part of a social identity.

Intuitively, we can think of what Mead is trying to suggest by thinking about our own day-to-day experiences. For example, we have all seen people who are self-conscious about the way they are dressed, to the extent that they frequently look at themselves to make sure whatever pieces of clothing they are wearing on a given day are appropriate. They may also fix their hair, or perhaps carry their bodies in particular ways to appear a certain way. The feeling that people have when they go through this process represents perfectly Mead's notions of the self as it is composed of the I and the Me. The person's identity and sense of him or herself is "wrapped up," so to speak, in the presentation of self through physical appearance. But who is doing the "looking" here? Certainly, it's an internal process, in the sense that the person asks "How do I look?" But of course the second part of the process—perhaps the more important one—is external. The imaginary mirror that the person is holding up, which generates the external image the person has of him or herself, is the social world itself. The social world is looking in and has become a part of the person's personality or sense of self as he or she learns how to dress and look a certain way, and how to carry or "comport" him or herself in a certain way. This, in essence, is the Me component of the self Mead is describing. The important part of Mead's analysis is that the self, human identity, and even the very act of being conscious of oneself is *social*. Mead's original insights and the development of symbolic interactionist perspectives have led to a collection of methods for understanding the meaning that people bring to their own lives and actions, the lives and actions of others around them, and the complex interaction between people's everyday lives and the wider social structure (Beal, 2002).

For sports studies, two major themes have emerged. The first is the study of *socialization* and the processes through which people are both socialized into sport, and socialized through sport. Socialization *into* sport means the active process of learning sport's rules, codes, values, and norms. Socialization *through* sport, on the other hand, refers to the lessons that are learned from sport that have some application to wider society. While much of the research in socialization has concentrated, not surprisingly, on children's sport (see Chapter 7), it should be pointed out that socialization is a life-long process. One example of this is the development of mid-life sports identities, such as is gained through any one of the many adult Masters sport organizations and competitions. Also, sociologists are only just beginning to understand the experience of sport and physical movement for older adults.

The second theme is sport *subcultures*. Here, research has attempted to understand the process through which subcultural groups form their own unique language, belief system, normative structure, and general inner-group identity. Some so-called alternative sports, such as surfing, rock climbing, extreme sports, skateboarding, ultimate Frisbee, and others provide interesting and accessible contexts to understand the process through which members develop subcultural identities. However, members of all longstanding traditional sports develop their own unique language, belief system, and identity as well.

For example, in his book *Men at Play: A Working Understanding of Professional Hockey*, Michael Robidoux demonstrates how hockey reproduces dominant notions of "manliness" or of what it means to be "properly" masculine through the everyday interactions with other players and coaches, alongside the rough and sometimes violent aspects of the game. Far from what many consider to be the common sense idea that masculinity emerges from within players, that it is just "how they are," Robidoux points out that social factors such as day-to-day rituals play important roles in *producing* masculinity: "initiation rituals are not only symbolic representations of the player's transformation on entering professional hockey, they are also a means of divesting the young player of undesirable (that is, unmanly) qualities so as to ensure his new status within the group" (Robidoux, 2001, p. 189).

Microsociological perspectives have a bright future because researchers have only just scratched the surface in terms of understanding people's experiences in sport and in the development of sporting identities. But Robidoux's work demonstrates one of its general flaws. In his account of how masculinity is produced in professional hockey, Robidoux also points out that masculine codes of conduct and everyday rituals accomplish something important in terms of power relations in hockey. Specifically, men have been taught to "not rock the boat"; that to be a man within the practical day-to-day confines of professional hockey means, ironically, being subservient to coaches and owners. Ultimately, Robidoux points out that "manliness" is linked to power and money, because the status that is achieved in the sport ultimately benefits those who profit, namely owners. While a few players achieve great wealth, the vast majority do not (see also Parcels, 2011). Robidoux's work reminds us that to fully understand the social experience of being a hockey player, one must understand the everyday experience alongside the social factors that influence power relations, or in this case players being treated as a commodity in the system of hockey production. While studies emanating from the theoretical traditions of symbolic interactionism have not always considered these elements of power, more recent critical theories in sociology have.

CRITICAL SOCIAL THEORIES: CULTURAL, FEMINIST, AND CRITICAL RACE STUDIES

Critical social theories are first of all a number of theories that have more recently been developed in the sociology of sport. As such, they should be thought of as "works in progress." If any generalization about these theories can be made, it is that they are a combination, reflection, and development of two of the theories mentioned to this point: conflict theory and symbolic interactionism. Power and inequality tend to be continuing concerns, but generally critical theories differ from conflict theory in two major respects. First, it is not assumed that people are simply subservient, passive "dupes." As discussed briefly in the previous section, people and groups have *agency*, meaning they can control, at least to some degree, the conditions of the world around them, even in the face of power relations that might try to limit them. Humans actively and often imaginatively interpret and give meaning to the world and in doing so challenge dominant ways of seeing things. People can challenge power relations to evoke change and to make sense of their lives while they are doing so. Second, these theories tend to expand notions of power and authority beyond that of conflict theory, in particular to an understanding of gender and sexual relations on the one hand and race relations on the other. Also, as we will see, the work of theorist Michel Foucault has been important, and his notion of power was very different from the one developed out of conflict sociology.

Three major strands can be identified within these new and emerging theoretical perspectives. The first is cultural studies, which itself has emanated from a number of theoretical strands. The second and third critical social theories are gender and feminist studies and critical race studies, respectively.

While *cultural studies* itself encompasses a growing and diverse body of work, certain historical predecessors denote common elements. One important inspiration for the development of cultural studies was Antonio Gramsci (1891–1937), an Italian social and political theorist and activist who was arrested in 1926 because of his involvement in the Central Committee of the Italian Communist Party. Gramsci was particularly interested in the manner in which power and control are maintained in capitalist economies under liberal–democratic forms of government, both of which were still in relatively early phases and under contestation from alternate forms of economic planning and political structures in Gramsci's day. Gramsci used the term *hegemony* to describe how this process happens. Instead of direct physical control, Gramsci believed that the power of dominant classes is maintained through a process of developing consent among the populace. This can occur in a *structural sense* in that groups at different levels of social organization make compromises with ruling classes, such as is the case when labour organizations concede to wage or salary increases, or when volunteer organizations compensate for social inequalities by fundraising.

But consent also occurs through a second manner, when the ideas that benefit the ruling classes are accepted and become *common sense* in the minds of people. For Gramsci, the process is an ongoing one in which consensus of the people always has to be won over. As cultural studies theorists Jennifer Hargreaves and Ian McDonald (2000) explain:

> In Gramsci's formula, it is not simply a matter of class control, but an unstable process which requires the winning of consent from subordinate groups. It is, then, never "complete" or fixed, but rather diverse and always changing. (p. 50)

While people rarely think of sport as playing a "hegemonic" role in reinforcing social power relations, there is no question that it has done so in Canada's history. Interestingly, this was more fully recognized years ago when social and political organizations used sport much more directly for ideological purposes than they typically do today. In the 1920s and 1930s, the Workers' Sports Association of Canada fully realized that amateur organizers would happily use sport as a means to appease the working classes (Kidd, 1996a). Earlier in this chapter the example of amateur sport leader Henry Roxborough's comment in

Maclean's magazine in 1926 that "A nation that loves sport cannot revolt" was cited. However, his position could not have been more politically opposite to one from a workers' rights paper the following year:

> The whole capitalist class profits by a system that keeps workers excitedly interested in trivial matters remote from true concerns . . . The brain-numbing narcotic of the sporting page is perhaps more deadly to the average worker than the more active poison of the editorial page. (cited in Kidd, 1996a, pp. 50, 167)

In these words we see the dual parts of power at play as cultural theorists see it; sport is used both as a means of social control but at the same time the workers' rights paper demonstrates that a certain degree of agency, or in this case resistance, is possible. Workers in fact formed their own Workers' Olympic Games movement that at its peak in the early 1930s was in many ways more successful than the "regular" Olympics, attracting thousands of spectators and participants while simultaneously expanding opportunities to more women, children, and those "past their prime" (Kidd, 1996a, p. 155).

A second influence on cultural studies was the creation of the Centre for Contemporary Cultural Studies (CCCS) in Birmingham, England, in 1964. While the Centre started as a means to study the history of the English working class, cultural studies as it became defined at the Centre developed over time and spread internationally to include both the culture and structure of class in many other countries and the influence of people's experiences with popular forms of culture, including sport, and how those experiences intersect with power and class (Hargreaves & McDonald, 2000). Importantly, one of the central goals of the CCCS was to take all elements of culture seriously. Traditionally, *culture* had been defined and implicitly recognized to be "high" culture, meaning "refined" arts and the strict reserve of those who could appreciate them (painting, music, literature, and so forth). However, the CCCS expanded this definition to include elements of "mass" culture—popular music, television and other media programming, and myriad other elements of popular life, including sport. Taking on this expanded definition, Canadian authors Hall, Slack, Smith, and Whitson defined culture as the "symbolic forms and the everyday practices through which people express and experience meaning" (Hall, Slack, Smith, & Whitson, 1991, p. 31). The authors' definition reminds us that it is important to consider both popular commercial- and media-based sport forms alongside the day-to-day physical activities in people's lives that give them meaning—both are important in understanding the role sport plays in people's lives and both "are profoundly affected by (and in turn affect) ongoing structures of power and inequality" (Hall et al., 1991, pp. 45–46).

Finally, the work of French philosopher and historian Michel Foucault (1926–1984) has had an immense impact on many sport sociologists working within the cultural studies framework. Foucault's work is complex and deserves greater attention for anyone interested in understanding modern sport today. However, two facets of human life Foucault emphasized, and the interrelationship between the two, gives us insight into his more general theories: *power* and the *body* (Maguire, 2002). First, it is useful to think about Foucault's conception of power in terms of what it is not. For him, power is not something that one person or a group of people have over another person or group of people; this is a standard way in which many people think about power. Instead, for Foucault power is something that is *exercised* between people or groups. Although it may appear to be a strange term to use to describe this relationship, to exercise power means simply that one person or group provides possibilities for the actions of others. For example, coaches often tell athletes not only how to perform at their best in their respective sport in a technical and physical sense, but also in a social sense—how the athletes ought to "behave" on the bench, during after-practice times, and so forth. Here, we have a Foucauldian form of power because the coach is directing (but not necessarily ordering) the athletes, and the athletes are in turn (presumably) accepting the direction. Both parties participate in the power relationship, even though both parties do not have a relationship based on overt coercion, physical or otherwise. In her excellent summary of Foucault's work, Jennifer Maguire (2002) uses the example of the advice coaches often give to "get a lot of sleep" before competitions:

> [T]he coach can convince the athletes that it is in their own interests to do as she suggests. The relation is not repressive in that the athletes ideally have the option of refusing or resisting the coach's influence. Moreover, the relation is *productive*, generating the ideal of (and a self-identity as) a "committed athlete." (pp. 295–296)

Two immediate things flow from this seemingly simple example. First, the power relationship here is just that—a relationship. Even though some have the ability to control the actions of others, others must ultimately accept the direction and lead some aspect of their lives accordingly for power as Foucault defined it to exist. Second, power is not seen by the athlete (necessarily) as negative. The athlete may willingly participate in the direction of the coach, and in this sense power is "positive."

But there is a significantly greater issue related to Foucault's work that lies behind this everyday example. In his work, Foucault outlined the histories of many institutions that came to influence people's behaviour in modern times. These now-famous historical studies included the history of modern prison systems, liberal–democratic political governments, mental hospitals and the study of psychiatry, medical hospitals and the study of medicine, understandings of human sexuality, and other institutions and approaches to understanding human life as well. Throughout, Foucault emphasized that generalized forms of power developed between institutions, forms of knowledge, and people's lives. In this process, Foucault claimed that people came to define themselves in relation to the manner in which institutions and forms of knowledge production treated, studied, and ultimately directed them. Foucault's point is that power pervades people's lives in myriad ways.

Another example highlights this point. Many reading this text will define themselves as a university "student." In one sense, the purpose of a university education is to learn knowledge and skills, and for many it is to create greater opportunities for future careers and (hopefully) higher financial compensation. But consider the following questions: How much of your day-to-day routine is determined by the academic and nonacademic schedule of the university? In turn, how is your routine organized? Assuming you experience at least some of your education through a lecture format, in what ways do you experience the lecture? What do you *do* while the lecture is going on? Are you generally quiet and attentive? Do you argue or take issue with what professors teach you? How many hours during the week do you *sit* in a lecture hall or in front of a desk while studying? Now consider the following set of questions: Imagine full-time work *after* university life is over. What do most full-time jobs entail in terms of day-to-day routine? For how many hours will you be required to sit in front of a desk in most (although certainly not all) jobs? How many jobs require employees to follow and accept directions from higher-ups? The point of these questions, perhaps not surprisingly, is to think about universities and the institution of education more generally, as a form of power in which students are directed, often with full compliance and acceptance, to act in specific ways that are conducive to being compliant *subjects* in modern society. The act of *being* a student is one of countless examples of the operation of power.

The second major concept introduced earlier—the *body*—is one Foucault addressed constantly in his work. The institutions and forms of knowledge directing people in modern times, Foucault pointed out, were often directing (or exercising power through) the body, in terms of how it should be studied, understood, and ultimately how people in turn should conduct themselves. For the study of sport Foucault's work is important because the examples in which forms of power are linked to the body are endless. We can think of the many private or public directives that encourage people to be healthy citizens and employees, such as ParticipACTION in Canada; the regulation of high-performance athletes lives through their day-to-day training regimens and the coaches, trainers, physical therapists, psychologists, and so forth that help them attain their goals; or the many ways in which every day exercise regimens encourage people to achieve certain body ideals or standardized levels of health.

A second strand within critical social theories is *feminist studies*. Shona Thompson (2002) has expressed feminism's main social and political objectives in clear terms:

> Fundamentally, feminism champions the belief that women have rights to all the benefits and privileges of social life equally with men. For the purposes of those concerned with sport, this means that girls and women have the right to choose to participate in sport and physical activity without constraint, prejudice or coercion, to expect their participation to be respected and taken seriously, and to be as equally valued and rewarded as sportsmen. (p. 106)

Feminist-inspired histories of sport in Canada have identified the important role that gender relations and ideas about both women and men have played in the country's sporting traditions. A landmark book is Helen Lenskyj's *Out of Bounds: Women, Sport & Sexuality*, published in 1986. The year is important because Lenskyj's book was published at a time when there were very few published works on the history of or social issues related to women's sport, a reflection on the fact that the disciplines of sociology and history were dominated by men who as a rule pushed women's issues to the side.

A more recent example in feminist-inspired studies is Ann Hall's *The Girl and the Game: A History of Women's Sport in Canada* (2002), likely the most complete historical account of women's sport in Canada ever written. Interestingly, Hall's opening line of the book, "The history of modern sport is a history of cultural struggle" (p. 1) replicates, but with significant differences, the opening sentence of *The Communist Manifesto:* "The history of all hitherto existing society is the history of class struggle" (Marx & Engels, 1948, p. 9). Hall's opening line reflects, first, the central difference between feminism and conflict theories—the recognition by the former that power operates at levels conflict theory, in its classical theoretical form, had not envisioned; second, the "struggle" in Hall's sentence reflects a position common in critical social theories in general—that resistance is possible and power is never complete. While male power and privilege certainly played an important role in women's sport historically, Hall recounts in her text the various ways in which women—and sometimes men—resisted that power and privilege to create opportunities:

> Women's long history of confronting a male preserve like sport illustrates the "double movement of containment and resistance" that characterizes cultural struggles among dominant and subordinate groups. (Hall, 2002, p. 2)

An interesting and important example from history verifies Hall's point. During the 1920s a Frenchwoman named Alice Milliat was fighting for greater recognition of women in sport. Realizing that the Olympic Games, the biggest sporting event at the time, was exclusively run by men and almost exclusively for male participants, Milliat decided to take matters into her own hands and organized the Fédération Sportive Féminine Internationale in 1921 and subsequently the first Women's Olympic Games in Paris in 1922. While only a one-day event, it was considered a success, so Milliat continued the women's Olympic movement; the second Games in 1926 included participants from 10 countries, and some started to make comparisons with the "other" Olympic Games. With the prestige of the women's movement increasing, the IOC threatened Milliat over the use of the term "Olympic," claiming it legally as its own. Recognizing that the IOC ran the most visible sporting event in the world, Milliat negotiated a settlement whereby she would change her event name to Women's World Games in exchange for the inclusion of 10 track and field events in the IOC's Games. The IOC agreed but then reneged on their promise and included only five events in the 1928 Summer Games in Amsterdam. However, while Milliat's bargain was in some ways unsuccessful, it also gave women the opportunity to showcase their skills and athletic prowess on the international stage for the first time. Milliat's story, in other words, is a perfect example of resistance (Milliat) alongside containment (IOC) that reflects so much of women's sport history (Hall, 2007).

Feminist theory continues to inspire studies of the various ways in which sex, gender, and sexuality influence sporting experiences ; these are discussed in more detail by Mary Louise Adams in Chapter 6.

Myrtle Cook of Canada wins her heat in the 100-metre dash at the 1928 Summer Olympic Games in Amsterdam. If it were not for the fact that Frenchwoman Alice Milliat fought the male-controlled International Olympic Committee to have more women's events in the Olympic Games, Cook and other Canadian female athletes would never have competed.
Underwood & Underwood/Corbis

A final strand within critical social theories is *critical race studies*. The discipline of sociology of sport has been largely negligent in understanding the important role of ethnicity, ideas about race, and racism in sport, at least until recently. Critical race studies have emerged in the attempt to overcome this gap by pointing out the important role race relations and racism have played in shaping sporting traditions in Canadian history and how they continue to shape it today.

Generally, critical theorists of race are interested in three things: first, the manner in which sport and physical movement play important roles in the development of ethnic cultural beliefs and heritage; second, the manner in which certain ethnic traditions in Canada have been privileged at the expense of others; and finally, the manner in which ideas about "race" have been naturalized or reinforced through sport. All of these themes are discussed in more detail in Chapter 5 by authors Victoria Paraschak and Susan Tirone.

One of the important themes taken up by critical race theory—one that has only just begun to be analyzed in relation to sport—is the manner in which ideas about what "Canada" is and what constitutes a "true Canadian" are themselves imbued with assumptions about race. Sociologist Himani Bannerji (2000) has challenged the notion of "Canadianness" by suggesting that it contains within it assumptions about race. The country's colonial history has led to a certain dominant image of "Canadianness," but these dominant notions have been based on specific historical conditions and cultural traditions in which certain groups have been privileged in the development of the image while others have been erased from the picture. In Bannerji's words,

> Official multiculturalism, mainstream political thought and the news media in Canada all rely comfortably on the notion of a nation and its state both called Canada, with legitimate subjects called Canadians. . . . There is an assumption that this Canada is a singular entity, a moral, cultural and political essence. . . . And yet, when we scrutinize this Canada, what do we see? The answer to this question depends on which side of the nation we inhabit. For those who see it as a homogenous cultural/political entity . . . Canada is unproblematic. For others . . . who have been dispossessed in one sense or another, the answer is quite different. (pp. 104–105)

An example in Canada's history is the "two solitudes" account of the English and French in Canada which, while certainly an important and real part of Canada's history and one that continues to influence the country's social and political life, is also an account of Canada's history that has erased Canada's Aboriginal peoples from the historical picture. Interestingly, in justifying funding for a new federal sport system in a campaign speech he made in 1968, Pierre Trudeau claimed that sport could be used effectively to promote nationalism and ease tensions between the French and the English (MacIntosh, Bedecki, & Franks, 1987; MacIntosh & Whitson, 1990). However, the sport "system" that was developed effectively ignored the many and varied sporting traditions of people who were dispossessed, including Aboriginal sport (Morrow & Wamsley, 2013, pp. 246–247).

Some important Aboriginal sporting events today represent resistance against the traditional manner in which "sports and physical activity have been used as assimilative tools, wielded to civilize Canada's Aboriginal peoples" (Morrow & Wamsley, 2013, p. 247). The North American Indigenous Games, first held in Edmonton in 1990, is a regularly held multisport event that attracts thousands of participants and spectators. The objective of the

Games is competition, but more importantly, "[t]o improve the quality of life for Indigenous People by supporting self-determined sports and cultural activities which encourage equal access to participation in the social/cultural/spiritual fabric of the community . . . and which respects Indigenous distinctiveness" (North American Indigenous Games, 2013).

Similarly, the Arctic Winter Games, first held in Yellowknife in 1970, is a circumpolar event attracting northern participants and spectators from all over the world. The Arctic Winter Games includes competitions of both southern and northern Inuit-based activities, including one- and two-foot high kick, Alaskan high kick, sledge jump, arm and head pull, and others. Athletic competitions coincide with cultural exhibitions and exchanges to promote athletic development alongside northern cultural independence, distinctiveness, and exchange (Arctic Winter Games, 2013).

Conclusions

It should be kept in mind that sociological theory is an ongoing and developing process. Part of the purpose of this chapter has been to demonstrate that sociological theories themselves have long heritages and in many cases intersect in terms of perspectives on the social and cultural world. Perhaps the most important thing to keep in mind as you read the chapters that follow and as you consider the myriad perspectives on the themes presented is the ultimate political goals of sociological theory and, in turn, the developing discipline of sociology of sport: to make the world the best one possible, one in which sport and physical activity can play important and significant roles in the enrichment of people's lives.

Critical Thinking Questions

1. This chapter demonstrated that sociology views history itself as a *dynamic* process. What examples can you think of in which having knowledge about some aspect of Canadian sport history has enabled you to understand an issue or controversy in the present?

2. The discipline of sociology emerged out of the problems and issues generated by the emergence of democratic institutions and the Industrial Revolution. What problems or issues still exist today that are similar to the ones the first sociologists were concerned with?

3. Put yourself in the shoes of a Marxist thinker. How would you consider the following topics: the Canadian federal government's funding of elite athletes, Nike Corporation's third-world labour practices, and public access to facilities and resources for sport and recreation?

4. What examples can you think of in which the "Me" part of the individual character (as defined by George Herbert Mead) is reinforced in sport? In other words, think of examples in which the external social environment leads to individuals taking on a certain sports character or identity.

5. In what ways do gender and sexuality continue to play an important role in Canadian sport today in terms of both empowering but also limiting experiences in sport?

Suggested Readings

Beamish, R. (2010). *The promise of sociology: The classical tradition and contemporary sociological thinking.* Toronto, ON: University of Toronto Press.

Coakley, J., & Donnelly, P. (Eds.). (1999). *Inside sports.* London, UK: Routledge.

Coakley, J., & Dunning, E. (Eds.). (2000). *Handbook of sports studies.* Thousand Oaks, CA; Sage Publications. (See especially Chapters 1–5.)

Giulianotti, R. (Ed.). (2004). *Sport and modern social theorists.* New York, NY: Palgrave Macmillan.

Gruneau, R. (1999). *Class, sports, and social development.* Champaign, IL: Human Kinetics.

Hall, M.A. (1996). *Feminism and sporting bodies.* Champaign, IL: Human Kinetics.

Maguire, J., & Young, K. (Eds.). (2002). *Theory, sport & society.* Amsterdam: JAI.

References

Arctic Winter Games. (2013). Retrieved from http://www.arcticwintergames.org.

Bannerji, H. (2000). *The dark side of the nation: Essays on multiculturalism, nationalism and gender.* Toronto, ON: Canadian Scholars Press.

Beal, B. (2002). Symbolic interactionism and cultural studies: Doing critical ethnography. In J. Maguire & K. Young (Eds.), *Theory, sport & society* (pp. 353–373). Amsterdam: JAI.

Beamish, R. (2002). Karl Marx's enduring legacy for the sociology of sport. In J. Maguire & K. Young (Eds.), *Theory, sport & society* (pp. 25–39). Amsterdam: JAI.

Beamish, R. (2009). Marxism, alienation and Coubertin's Olympic project. In B. Carrington & I. McDonald (Eds.), *Marxism, cultural studies & sport* (pp. 88–105). London, UK: Routledge.

Beamish, R. (2010). *The promise of sociology: The classical tradition and contemporary sociological thinking.* Toronto, ON: University of Toronto Press.

Beamish, R., & Borowy, J. (1988). *Q. What do you do for a living? A. I'm an athlete.* Kingston, ON: The Sport Research Group.

Brohm J.-M. (1978). *Sport: A prison of measured time.* London, UK: Ink Links.

Cantelon, C., & Ingham, A. G. (2002). Max Weber and the sociology of sport. In J. Maguire & K. Young (Eds.), *Theory, sport & society* (pp. 63–81). Amsterdam: JAI.

Davis, K., & Moore, W.E. (1945). Some principles of stratification. *American Sociological Review, 10,* 242–249.

Donnelly, P. (2002). George Herbert Mead and an interpretive sociology of sport. In J. Maguire & K. Young (Eds.), *Theory, sport & society* (pp. 83–102). Amsterdam: JAI.

Durkheim, E. (1951). *Suicide: A study in sociology.* New York, NY: The Free Press.

Gruneau, R. (1983). *Class, sport, and social development.* Amherst, MA: University of Massachusetts Press.

Gruneau, R. & Whitson, D. (1993). *Hockey night in Canada: Sport, identities and cultural politics.* Peterborough, ON: Broadview Press.

Hall, A. (2002). *The girl and the game: A history of women's sport in Canada.* Peterborough, ON: Broadview Press.

Hall, A. (2007). Cultural struggle and resistance: Gender, history, and Canadian sport. In K. Young & P. White (Eds.), *Sport and gender in Canada,* (pp. 56–74). Toronto, ON: Oxford University Press.

Hall, A., Slack, T., Smith, G., & Whitson, D. (1991). *Sport in Canadian society.* Toronto, ON: McClelland & Stewart.

Hargreaves, J., & McDonald, I. (2000). Cultural studies and the sociology of sport. In J. Coakley & E. Dunning (Eds.), *Handbook of sport studies* (pp. 48–60). London: Sage.

Ingham, A.G. (2004). The sportification process: A biographical analysis framed by the work of Marx, Weber, Durkheim and Freud. In R. Giulianotti (Ed.), *Sport and modern social theorists* (pp. 11–32). London: Palgrave Macmillan.

Kidd, B. (1984). The myth of the ancient Games. In A. Tomlinson & G. Whannel (Eds.), *Five ring circus: Money, power and politics at the Olympic Games* (pp. 71–83). London and Sydney: Pluto Press.

Kidd, B. (1996a). *The struggle for Canadian sport.* Toronto, ON: University of Toronto Press.

Kuper, S., & Szymanski, S. (2009). *Soccernomics: Why England Loses, Why Germany and Brazil win, and why the US, Japan, Australia, Turkey—and even Iraq—are destined to become the kings of the world's most popular sport.* New York, NY: Nation Books.

Lenskyj, H. (1986). *Out of bounds: Women, sport and sexuality.* Toronto, ON: Women's Press.

Loy, W. J., & Booth, D. (2000). Functionalism, sport and society. In J. Coakley & E. Dunning (Eds.), *Handbook of sport studies* (pp. 8–27). London: Sage.

Loy, W. J., & Booth, D. (2002). Émile Durkheim, structural functionalism and the sociology of sport. In J. Maguire & K. Young (Eds.), *Theory, sport & society* (pp. 41–62). Amsterdam: JAI.

MacIntosh, D., Bedecki, T., & Franks, C.E.S. (1987). *Sport and politics in Canada: Federal government involvement since 1961.* Montreal, QC: McGill-Queen's University Press.

MacIntosh, D., & Whitson, D. (1990). *The game planners: Transforming Canada's sport system.* Montreal, QC: McGill-Queen's University Press.

Maguire, J. S. (2002). Michel Foucault: Sport, power, technologies and governmentality. In J. Maguire & K. Young (Eds.), *Theory, sport & society* (pp. 293–314). Amsterdam: JAI.

Marx, K. (1963). Economic and philosophical manuscripts. In T.B. Bottomore (Ed.), *Karl Marx: Early writings.* New York, NY: McGraw-Hill.

Marx, K. (1972). Thesis on Feuerbach. In R.C. Tucker (Ed.), *The Marx-Engels reader* (pp. 107–9). New York, NY: W.W. Norton & Company.

Marx, K. (1977). *Capital: Vol. I.* New York, NY: Vintage Books.

Marx, K., & Engels, F. (1948). *The communist manifesto.* New York, NY: International Publishers.

McQuarie, D. (Ed.). (1995). *Readings in contemporary sociological theory: From modernity to postmodernity.* Englewood Cliffs, NJ: Prentice Hall.

Mead, G. H. (1962). *Mind, self, & society from the standpoint of a behaviorist.* Chicago, IL: The University of Chicago Press.

Morrow, D., & Wamsley, K.B. (2013). *Sport in Canada: A history.* Toronto, ON: Oxford University Press.

North American Indigenous Games. (2013). Retrieved from http://www.naigcouncil.com/index.php.

Parcels, J. (2011). Straight facts about making it in pro hockey. In P. Donnelly (Ed.), *Taking sport seriously: Social issues in Canadian sport* (pp. 207–211). Toronto, ON: Thompson Educational Publishing.

Parsons, T. (1961). An outline of the social system. In T. Parsons, E. Shils, K.D. Naegele, & J.R. Pitts (Eds.), *Theories of society: Foundations of modern sociological theory: Vol. I* (pp. 30–79). New York, NY: The Free Press of Glencoe.

Public Broadcasting Service. (2004). *The real Olympics: A history of the ancient and modern Olympics Games.* Alexandria, VA: PBS Home Video.

Robidoux, M.A. (2001). *Men at play: A working understanding of professional hockey.* Montreal, QC: McGill-Queen's University Press.

Thompson, S. T. (2002). Sport, gender, feminism. In J. Maguire & K. Young (Eds.), *Theory, sport & society* (pp. 105–127). Amsterdam: JAI.

Weber, M. (1958). *The protestant ethic and the spirit of capitalism.* New York, NY: Charles Scribner's Sons.

Chapter 3
Canadian Sport in Historical Perspective

Don Morrow

As he did in his 2001 honorary doctorate acceptance speech at Western University, Canadian Olympic backstroke-swimmer Mark Tewksbury often tells the story about his experience on the world stage of sport at the 1992 Barcelona Olympic Games. Tewksbury trained hard for most of his life to become a superb athlete who won a silver medal in his event at the 1988 Seoul Olympic Games. He continued to work on his skills and compete internationally for the next four years. In Barcelona, he swam his way through the heats into the semi-finals and earned a place in the men's Olympic backstroke finals. As he sat alone in his room before his event, he found himself thinking about his competitors, mentally noting their achievements, when they had beaten him in past events, their records—in short, he created in his mind all the reasons he would not win. Suddenly, he realized what he was doing: He was engaging in what psychologists call negative self-talk—he was compiling a list of reasons and excuses for not winning. As his awareness of his adverse self-handicapping grew, he started to shift his perspective and reflected on his hard work, his dedication, his skill, his fitness, the years

Curling on the St. Lawrence River, Montreal, Quebec, 1878
Bygone Collection/Alamy

he devoted and sacrificed to his sport. What he came up with were three inspirational words in the frame of a question: *"Why not me?"* Armoured with this more aspirational, inspirational, and accurate self-belief, Mark won the gold medal and in the process set a new Olympic record.

Mark Tewksbury's story is as inspirational and typical of many stories about Canadian athletes over time. We have a rich and fascinating history of sport. It is the intention of this chapter to provide a historical or cultural–historical context that is essential to understanding and analyzing the social constructs and issues in contemporary Canadian sport from a sociological perspective. Human behaviour has continuity to it; socially constructed traditions, historical customs, norms, and cultural and personal values combine to impact behavioural choices and actions over time. At the same time, sport is quite literally an arena in which important cultural struggles and political issues—ones connected to gender, sexuality, social class, and race/ethnicity—play out and mirror or contribute to our culture.

Past, present, and future are all connected in important and inextricable ways. Thus, it is exceedingly difficult to comprehend, for example, contemporary racial, social class, and gender issues (the three dominant social struggles in Canadian sport over time) or sexuality in sport (see Chapter 6) without historical context and perspective. For example, with respect to gender issues and sexuality in sport, consider another Mark Tewksbury example. In a chapter entitled "Bam" from his 2006 autobiography, Tewksbury described the series of stunning events that occurred when he came out as a gay man shortly after his Olympic triumph. While his family, for the most part, was supportive, the media, his agents, and society in general wanted him to stay "in the closet" and not speak of "this" again. It left Mark feeling "terribly and utterly alone." Another example of the power of social constructs within and outside of the institutions of sport was the 2013 anti-gay legislation passed by the Russian government regarding athletes participating at the 2014 Sochi Winter Olympic Games. This incident, along with the Tewksbury example, serves to underscore just how much social issues like sexuality permeate and may even be magnified in the world of sport, impacting athletes from all countries, including Canada.

DOING HISTORY

The term and connotations of the word *history* merit discussion, because there is considerable difference between *the past* and *history*. In everyday terminology, the word *history* is used to talk about anything that happened in the past. For example, when referring to a known sporting championship that was won 10 years ago, we might say "That's history." On the contrary, it's not history—that championship is a *fact*. Facts (and dates) are important tools in the historian's repertoire, but they are not to be equated with history. A list of facts or dates of events is just a list, it's not history. In one sense, history might be perceived as everything that happened in the past. Unequivocally, that's true; equally true is the fact that we can never know everything that happened in the past. Consider your own life. If you were to sit down and make a list of everything—every single event—that has happened to you since the day you were born, would it be complete? Would it be accurate? Upon whose memory would you rely? When you finished, would you have anything more than a compilation of facts that is more akin to a grocery list than to something meaningful and revealing about your life? And whatever list of events (no matter how complete) you compiled, would it by itself convey who you are, how you feel, what is important to you? Not likely. By extension, then, history can never be *the* record of human events simply because we only have a fragment of records and facts about past events. Events in the past must be interpreted to be made meaningful, and that interpretation is the work of the historian.

In reality, history is a method of inquiry about the past. In other words, history is what historians *do*, or history is what a historian articulates about her subject matter. Famed French philosopher Voltaire satirically claimed, "History is after all nothing but a pack of tricks which we play upon the dead" (Durant, 1926, p. 241). In the same vein, we might say that while some historians might feel they are reconstructing the past when they write history, often they are creating a representation of that past simply because of the difficulties of knowing everything that happened concerning an event or a situation or group of people. Historians ask questions about the past to *do* history, and inquiry is the basis of all science and social science. Historians often have the advantage of knowing past people's futures; their disadvantage is that they cannot ask questions directly to those people. Instead, historians rely on extant evidence, especially *primary* evidence—diaries, records, newspapers, census data, photographs, drawings—as the basis for formulating questions about events that happened in the past. We might ask what the formative factors were leading up to the 1972 hockey Summit Series between Canada and the USSR. Or we might ask what the nature of Canadian press coverage was of those games. Both are valid questions asked by the historian, but neither question will reveal everything that happened during that hockey series. Even though it is often the case that historians wish for more abundant evidence, it is really the clear articulation of historical questions that determine the nature and the quality of the history that historians do.

Finally, it is important to consider objectivity and perspective in doing history. There are historians and traditional, historical schools of thought that claim historians can be completely objective and reveal events exactly as those events happened without any interference from the historians' values, biases, or beliefs. In basic science, researchers try to eliminate bias by manipulating a single variable for examination, structuring control groups in experiments, introducing randomization in subject selection, and so forth. It is difficult to imagine that one historian can eliminate all of his or her biases. What might be more important is for historians to acknowledge their assumptions and biases and perspectives. As you learned in Chapter 2, researchers use theoretical frameworks to explain human behaviour—theory informs their perspective. For example, Marxist historians often use the concepts inherent in class reproduction to analyze historical events. Our past in Canadian sport abounds with examples of social class privilege and exclusion (Metcalfe, 1987). Thus, certain rules in sport might have served to preserve social class distinctions. Using a Marxist framework for analysis allows the historian to explain behaviour from that perspective. Other historians take a more narrative approach to doing history; the very word *hi-story* does contain the notion of a story. This is not to suggest that history is fiction; rather, it underscores that one historian's version or interpretation of a series of events might be different than any other historian's analysis of the same events. It depends on the questions the historian asks of the data and the perspective used by the historian.

This chapter will provide a perspective on some of the trends and issues in the development of Canadian sport over time, mostly prior to 1960, the point in time when federal government involvement in sport became paramount and pervasive (Chapters 12, 13, and 14 deal with some of the resultant economic, political, international, and social issues). In considerable measure, this analysis will follow the framework and perspective inherent in the author's recent, larger work, *Sport in Canada: A History* (Morrow & Wamsley, 2013). Readers might wish to refer to that book along with others listed in the Suggested Readings located at the end of this chapter. More importantly, you are encouraged to read critically: Look for my biases as a historian, and ask questions about what you read since reading any text meaningfully involves engaging with the material. In essence, the analysis used in this chapter will be more issue oriented and thematic. Instead of tracing events linearly, certain issues, especially as they relate to social constructs such as race, gender, and social class, will be amplified or explained in different contexts—that is, more a spiralling of events and issues.

SPORTING TRADITIONS IN EARLY CANADA

First Nations Games and Contests

By the 15th century, when European conquests of North America took place, sport in Europe was already an activity that carried great value systems, traditions, and customs. Significantly, the impulse to play games and sports seems timeless. The form and functions of sport before the 15th century seem consistent: Sport was a male preserve—women were virtually excluded from games and sporting contests in Western civilization; the forms of sport were mostly related to war-like activities; upper classes dictated the forms and functions of sport; codes of behaviour were endemic and varied from amateurism to professionalism to chivalry; festivals and spectacles and celebrations were often key motivators for sport; beauty, excellence, discipline, and victory were widely evidenced; and finally, it is clear that organization was a key variable in competitive sport, from funeral games to Olympic Games to Roman spectacles to medieval tournaments and jousts. Prior to European contact, the First Nations were the earliest players of games and contests in Canada.

Aboriginal culture for some 10,000 years before contact was a nomadic one. Groups such as the Algonquians or the Iroquois and subgroups such as the Mohawk, Neutral, Cree, and Ojibwa travelled to be home, not to get home, and they relied on the resources the land provided and demanded of them. That lifestyle required certain skills and attributes such as strength, endurance, and resistance to pain; these, in turn, were values that were reflected in Aboriginal cultural practices like wrestling, physical contests (arm pull, finger pull, even testicle pull), and greeting games that required little equipment. When subgroups gathered together, it was always an occasion for games and contests wherein gambling with material goods added both excitement and a means to redistribute tools, food, and other elements. Blanket toss, moose-skin ball, pole push, running contests, and early forms of lacrosse called either *baggataway* or *tewaarathon* (depending on the particular group) were all events that were connected to the land, ways of life, and the skills of survival. Celebration was a paramount virtue in these contests as was the spiritual significance attached—for example, a game of *tewaarathon* might be conducted to commemorate the bountiful harvest. These were the physical contests, games and traditions that existed as Europeans infiltrated the area now known as Canada beginning in the late 16th and early 17th centuries.

French Conquests

Multiple agendas brought Europeans to this continent. The quest for colonization, presumed riches of gold and other precious metals, a missionary zeal to instill Christianity in every corner of the earth, the allure of a northwest passage to the East, and the discovery of abundant fish (e.g., the Grand Banks) and animal fur (primarily the beaver) all served as magnetic attractions to the New World. The darkness of the Middle Ages gave way to the progressiveness and idealism of the European Renaissance, an era characterized as the "rebirth" of civilization reminiscent of classical Greece. Scientific discoveries such as the printing press and medical innovations went part and parcel with a literary renaissance that was most notably embodied by Shakespeare. Artists such as Leonardo da Vinci and Michelangelo revolutionized notions about beauty and the science of the body. And it was this set of ideals and idealism that permeated the minds of those who set out in conquest of new lands like Canada.

The areas of Canada that were inhabited first by Europeans were the extreme Maritime coasts closest to the Grand Banks, the vast fur trading lands of central and northern Canada, and a major cluster of settlements that became known as New France (later Lower Canada and subsequently Quebec). New France was founded by French explorer Samuel de Champlain in the early 17th century. Early towns established at what became Québec City and Montreal were vibrant communities for the seigneurial or feudal land development/settlement system that was created to foster economic growth along the Saint Lawrence River. Over the course of most of the 17th and the first half of the 18th centuries, the *habitants*, or French peasantry, worked the long, narrow strips of land and raised families while the fur traders, voyageurs, and the Jesuit missionaries fostered the fur trade and the predominantly Catholic religious institutions. Indeed, it is from the *Jesuit Relations*, a set of documents written by Jesuit missionaries and sent back to France as propaganda to induce emigration to New France, that we are able to discern the rich social fabric of this era.

Comparable to the pastimes of ancient and medieval cultures, the form and function of physical activities were those related to survival (Metcalfe, 1970). Thus, the *habitants* engaged in games and contests of running, wrestling, horseracing, snowshoeing, sleighing, and canoeing, as well as balls and dances (the latter much despised by the clerics for their presumed sinful nature). The physical prowess of the *coureurs de bois* (runners of the woods) came to be feared and revered. These men developed into "masculine identities closely linked to the physical demands of their labour: strong, swift, and enduring, combined with fierce independence and a lack of deference to the authority of French administrators" (Morrow & Wamsley, 2005, p. 17).

British Traditions

At the end of the Seven Years War between the British and the French in 1763, the British assumed control of what was then called British North America (BNA). While the French were allowed to retain their culture, religion, customs, and ways of life, Aboriginal groups lost control and ownership of massive tracts of land. The British poured troops and resources into BNA and brought their institutions of justice, religion (primarily Anglican), and social class structures and governance to the Maritime areas of Nova Scotia and New Brunswick and primarily to Upper Canada (now Ontario). The "British" were a composite of people of English, Irish, and Scottish descent who were reinforced later in the 18th century by United Empire Loyalists or British sympathizers living in the United States who came to live in BNA following the defeat of the British in the American War of Independence. We know from various acts of legislation against gambling, liquor production and consumption, Sabbath Day activity restrictions, and hunting or gaming laws along with the necessity to license billiard tables that these activities and practices formed an important part of the lifestyles of early British North Americans.

A great deal more is known about the classic "pioneer" period of BNA, the years between the Rebellions of Upper and Lower Canada in the 1830s and the time of Confederation in 1867. Massive immigration from the United Kingdom, which changed the population from approximately 750,000 in 1821 to over 2 million at mid-century, reflected an economic prosperity that, in turn, was accompanied by a social stability conducive to games and recreation. For example, circuses brought amusement to small towns, and weddings and their accompanying *chivarees* or mock serenades were occasions for physical contests and games. So too were work bees in rural BNA, when neighbours gathered to raise a barn, make quilts, or harvest crops, all followed by dancing, contests like wrestling and games of chance, and of course drinking (liquor sold for 25 cents per gallon). Taverns were ubiquitous along the highways of early Canada. By their very presence and fostered atmosphere of conviviality, taverns served as social and activity centres for the citizenry, including members of the urban underclass. In fact, the very first sporting club for which we have a written record, the Montreal Curling Club, was formed at Gillis Tavern in 1807 (Lindsay, 1969). Travellers' accounts inform us that hunting and fishing were popular pastimes (obviously derived from subsistence needs) among both upper and lower social classes even though the forms of these activities varied by social class (Gillespie, 2002). By contrast, the 1845 Statutes of Upper Canada list a host of activities that legislators sought to prohibit among the lower classes on Sunday:

> And be it enacted, That if any such Merchant, Tradesman, Artificer, Mechanic, Workman, Labourer, or other person whatsoever, shall . . . purchase any wares, merchandizes, goods, chattels, or personal property, or any real estate whatsoever, on the Lord's Day, commonly called Sunday . . . or shall play at skittles, ball, foot-ball, racket, or any other noisy game, or shall gamble with dice or otherwise, or shall run races on foot, or on horseback, or in carriages, or vehicles of any sort on that day, or if any person or persons shall go out fishing, or hunting or shooting, or in quest of, or shall take, kill, or destroy any deer or other game, or any wild animal, bird, or wild fowl, or fish, except as next hereinafter mentioned, or shall use any dog, fishing rod, gun, rifle, or other machine, or shall set any net or trap for the above mentioned purposes on that day . . . shall pay a fine or penalty not exceeding ten pounds, nor less than five shillings, current money of this Province, for each offence, together with the costs and charges attending the proceedings and conviction. (Lindsay, 1969, p. 353)

What is interesting is that such enactments likely reveal the prevalence of these amusements and games rather than any termination of such activities. In essence, Sabbath restrictions were measures implemented by the governing classes to control what were deemed to be unruly activities of the lower classes. By the middle of the 19th century, the cultural practices of subordinate groups were viewed as a growing social problem, especially where drinking and gambling "vices" on the part of the subordinate groups were involved.

Horseracing and the Garrisons

Prior to Confederation, the single sporting activity that crossed all social classes in interest and in direct or vicarious participation was horseracing. Some background information is necessary to understand the prevalence of this activity. The military presence in North America was continuous and widespread; every town was a garrison or military post with troops stationed there. Since military engagements were infrequent, officers and nonofficers had considerable time at their disposal. Commissioned officers, for the most part, were upper- and middle-class gentlemen from Britain who had received their early education at such elite British public schools (equivalent to Canadian private schools) as Eton, Chester, Harrow, and Rugby. Major pedagogical reforms wrought by such educators as Dr. Thomas Arnold, headmaster at Rugby School, advocated school systems of self-governance, hierarchal organization from senior to junior years, prefects, and "houses" or residences that became the social units of the schools. Boys organized themselves into teams for games and activities like hare and hounds (a chase game involving cross-country running), rugby, cricket, football (soccer), and boxing amidst the prevailing Anglican religious culture fostered within the schools. By the time of Dr. Arnold's tenure at Rugby, all boys were expected to be both good students and active participants in games and sport. Moreover, the schools and their gaming activities carried an ideological value system, a code of sporting honour that extolled the virtues of team play, loyalty to one's house, and fair play—in short, a set of gendered and classed values that came to be recognized as "*muscular Christianity*." Nowhere is this value system better portrayed or dispersed than in one of the most popular novels of the 19th century, *Tom Brown's School Days* by Thomas Hughes (1904, originally published in 1857), a tale of Rugby boys and their sporting exploits and attendant values during Arnold's administration at that school. Graduates from the British public schools often became government, civic, and military leaders. Many of the latter served as officers in British North America and carried with them the sporting practices and values promoted in the British public schools. So significant was their impact on early Canadian sport that one researcher stated unequivocally "The paramount influence [on the development of sport] for more than a century after the Conquest was derived from the sporting examples set by the British army garrison [officers]" (Lindsay, 1970, p. 33).

Imbued with this British public school sporting tradition, these officers brought their administrative training and expertise, the opportunity afforded by very little active conflict, and their inclinations toward a variety of sports and games, not the least of which was horseracing. The officers supplied the horses, built the racing tracks and venues, purchased the prizes, and provided officials for equestrian events. To all social classes, horserace meetings were spectacles for amusement, competition, and gambling. For example, an 1843 equestrian steeplechase competition in London, Ontario, attracted some 10,000 people. Royal patronage was granted to many of the equestrian events. However, the social and economic impact of the equine contests was dramatic. Tent cities were spawned for the races, and town commercial and farming activities halted for the events where gambling, brawls, and crime were common. In response, the garrison officers tried moving the events further into the country to discourage the "great unwashed" from attending the events, but they still came. One prominent Canadian city, Halifax, was such a magnet for horserace competitions and their attendant social consequences that around mid-century city officials cancelled and disallowed all horseracing competitions for more than a decade.

While horseracing was the most universally popular of the garrison officer leadership initiatives in sport, there were also other activities promoted by these men. Fox hunting, cricket matches, tandem and sleighing clubs, skating events, and track and field competitions were among the sports and activities fostered by the garrison officers. Evidence for the dependency on the military for the conduct and participation in these pastimes and sports is highlighted by their great decline when British troops were withdrawn during the Crimean War in Europe during the 1850s. With the perceived and real threats of the American Civil War during the 1860s, British militia poured back into BNA and the newspapers of that era show dramatic increases, especially in cricket and horseracing.

In spite of the initiatives of the British garrison officers, it must be pointed out that by Confederation there was a distinct social class and a gendered order to sport. For example, within the military regular militia men were court-martialled for habitual drunkenness; it was the officers who enjoyed sport participation, not the lower ranks. Also, while women worked extremely hard in the home and on the land and demonstrated tremendous physical prowess, "increasingly, social institutions including government, church, school, and private organizations such as men's clubs promoted idealized femininities tied to notions of dependency, domesticity, chastity, and relative weakness—in contradistinction to the daily experiences of most women" (Morrow & Wamsley, 2013). It is abundantly clear from this examination of sporting evolution from ancient cultures through to the mid-19th century that in Western societies, sport was largely the preserve of the male elite citizenry. Quite simply, the roots of sporting practices seem to be tied indivisibly, timelessly, and universally to men and to socially constructed notions of manliness.

INDUSTRIALIZATION AND TECHNOLOGICAL CHANGES

Within BNA or Canada, up until the middle of the 19th century, sporting practices were dependent on individual initiatives and existing social institutions such as the work bee, the tavern, and the managerial resourcefulness of the garrison officers. The transition to modern "organized" sport was very much a product of the Industrial Revolution and the concomitant technological changes that characterized the second half of the 19th century. Coalitions of interests such as those of the Scots and the Montreal middle class developed strong sporting organizations while the process of industrialization altered society in general. In broad terms, *industrialization* characterizes a period of social and economic change that transforms a society from an agrarian to an industrial one; industrialization is part of the process of modernization, wherein social and economic development are closely related to technological innovation. In Canada, as elsewhere, sweeping changes in methods of transportation and communication combined with advances in sporting equipment and facilities catalyzed this process of organizational sophistication in sport, sporting practices, and the availability of sport to wider segments of society. By examining these innovations using a cross-section of sports during the 19th century, the rate, direction, and magnitude of sporting change can be explained and understood.

Transportation modes up to the early 19th century were often cumbersome and relatively slow. One could walk, snowshoe, canoe, or ride on horseback, carriage, or sleigh—all methods of conveyance that required time to travel. For sport, this dependency on leisure time limited most sport participation to the elite. Furthermore, it reflected and contributed to the social nature of early sporting clubs. Instead of a primary athletic motive, clubs like the Montreal Curling Club were formed and developed mainly for social interests, not athletic.

It was the introduction of steam to watercraft that led directly to changes in sporting foci and practices. Steamers and steamboats in the second half of the 19th century were a form of recreation in themselves; often, bands were on board, steamship companies offered excursions, and rival company boats even raced each other to get to destinations. More specifically, these companies offered prizes for sporting competitions, reduced rates to attend cycling and baseball events, and often allowed ferryboats and other steamers to serve as grandstands for rowing events. Certainly, these changes had an accelerative and promotional effect on a variety of sports. When steam was applied to the tracked vehicles used in mining, railway companies quickly developed that form of transportation.

In 1850, there existed some 160 kilometres of railway track in Canada. Government grants induced railway companies to connect towns and cities that were within 100 kilometres of each other. Thus, areas such as southern Ontario, parts of Quebec, and the Maritimes were served rapidly by these transit links. By 1900, some 30,000 kilometres of railway lines linked Canada coast to coast. One of the railway's primary impacts on society was a dramatic reduction in travel time. Whereas it took some three days to travel by stagecoach from Toronto to Montreal early in the 19th century, travel from Toronto to Port Moody, British Columbia, took only five days by train at the end of the century. So great was the time reduction factor that a Canadian, Sir Sandford Fleming, invented the concept of creating time zones for different areas of the world.

For sport, the impact of the railway was almost immediate and widespread. Primarily, railway transportation permitted more people to engage in sport simply because of the time and convenience factors. More profoundly, a universal impact on sport was the potential crystallization of a fundamental concept in organized sport—regularity. Baseball, lacrosse, rowing, and track and field competitions could actually be scheduled well in advance of the events to the extent that a whole new concept—leagues—could be structured prior to a sporting season. Furthermore, multi-club events were possible. For example, 32 teams used rail connections to attend a bonspiel (a curling tournament) during the 1860s. International sporting tours, such as the visit of a British cricket team during the 1870s, were enjoyed because of railway passage. "Spur lines," or short, specially made temporary tracks split off from main lines, were often built to serve as grandstands, especially in winter for events such as the very popular (in terms of competitor and spectator allure) snowshoe races of the 1870s and 1880s.

Emergent methods and means of communication paralleled methods of transport. Mail delivery, for example, took days and weeks; until mid-century, the receiver paid the postage and the bulk of BNA mail went through England. Sports and games could be arranged by letter, or by word of mouth, or by setting out a challenge from one club to another in the press. In the latter regard, the number of newspapers in the country increased from 200 to 1,200 from 1840 to 1900. Sport was irregularly covered for most of this period; the sport pages were more a product of the 20th century. And there was a time lag in reporting sporting contests, such that news of an event in Nova Scotia might take some time to appear in the Ontario press and vice versa. When the telegraph was invented in the 1850s, communication was revolutionized. When the Atlantic telegraph cable was completed in 1866, it meant that news in 1867 of the Saint John, New Brunswick, four-oared rowing crew's success at the World Championships in Paris, France (that team is known as the Paris Crew) was instantly transmitted to Canadians. A byproduct of such accelerated coverage of sporting events combined with league schedules very likely meant reciprocal effects in creating and sustaining fan interest in a variety of sport at the local, provincial, national, and international levels.

Sporting Equipment Evolution

Socially and economically, the 1850s were prosperous years of growth for Canada. In addition, Canada experienced a 37% increase in population between 1851 and 1861, a clear reflection of the country's affluence and its allure to primarily British immigrants. Prosperity and population increases usually have positive effects on sport, and they certainly did in this case. One of the mass trends in sport and recreation, a virtual skating mania "from Gaspé to Sarnia," was reflected in the media across Canada during the 1860s. A symbiotic part of the zeal for skating was the impact of technology on sporting equipment, in this case, skates. For example, interest and demand meant increased production of skates. More patents were taken out regarding improvements in blades and boots, accessibility increased, and costs were quickly reduced.

Another direct impact of technology on equipment manufacture, production, and distribution was uniformity or standardization. As lacrosse sticks, baseball bats, rowing shells, and track and field equipment were mass produced, participants benefited from better-quality and more standard equipment. Whereas early competitors in, for example, the hammer throwing event at a Caledonian track and field competition in Cape Breton might have had to create and sign an "article of agreement" about the size and weight of the hammers to be thrown, standardization meant that all competitors could use the same equipment. The implications for the sophistication of sporting organization are obvious.

There are myriad specific sport transitions brought about by technological change, not all of which can be described in this chapter. Cost reduction is one general change that had wide-reaching repercussions for sport diffusion to the middle and lower classes. Cricket, a popular sport among the British elite, remained a relatively expensive sport for most of the 19th century—bats, balls, and pads were often sold in jewellery stores. One cricket bat cost anywhere from $6 to $9, whereas by 1900 one could purchase a lacrosse stick for less than 50 cents. Similarly, facilities for sport were crucial to sport dispersion and interest. Baseball and lacrosse fields demanded relatively little cost to create and maintain, whereas golf courses (which did not appear until the mid-1870s) were expensive propositions that kept golf an upper-class sport. Skating rinks and curling areas could be cleared on local rivers or, within cities, fire departments often built outdoor rinks and toboggan runs. Very few indoor facilities for sport existed during the late 19th century, but those that did for hockey, skating, and curling increased their respective sport participation and interest, especially when gas lighting allowed play to extend into the evenings, thereby providing broader opportunities to the working class (Jobling, 1970).

Perhaps one of the most intriguing, socially impacting, and recreationally fascinating pieces of equipment developed during the 19th century was the bicycle. Its derivation stems from France and England when hobbyhorses (wooden-framed, two-wheeled vehicles with no pedals and no steering, more like a wooden horse on wheels than a bicycle), bicycle precursors, were used by gardeners to traverse their estate grounds. By mid-century, bicycles

Replica of an old penny farthing bicycle.
unclepepin/Shutterstock

were of the penny farthing variety, which had a 120-centimetre front wheel over which the rider perched on a springless seat and a diminutive back wheel of some 30 centimetres.

The first of these machines to reach Canada likely arrived sometime in the early 1870s. In spite of their height, how uncomfortable they were to ride, poor roads for riding, and their expense (at least $100), the public fascination with bicycles was remarkable. Over the next 30 years, mass marketing and innovations in design lead to pneumatic tires, equal-sized wheels (dubbed "safeties" by the mid-1880s), and all manner of accoutrements, such as lights, horns, spring seats, and greatly reduced costs. Riders, often representing bicycle clubs, raced on the penny farthings and on the safeties. However, much like skating, the real impact of the bicycle was in its widespread use for transportation and recreation across social classes and across gender lines and social conventions. Many historians credit the bicycle for offering one of the first means of recreational pastimes and for catalyzing dress reform for women (Hall, 2002). Specific developments of women's participation in sports are discussed later in the chapter.

Montreal: The Cradle of Organized Sport

Another component of industrialization was the phenomenon of *urbanization*, or the tendency of people to settle in clusters of towns and cities. Organized sport is very much an urban-related and urban-facilitated social behaviour. In many respects, as a result of the twin processes of industrialization and urbanization, most people had more money and time to compete in sport. Leaders and leadership in Canadian sport development came from the largest cities, in particular the city of Montreal. Without question, Montreal was the commercial hub of Canada; it was the nexus for timber, fur trading, shipping, and railway companies and it fostered such giants of national industry as the Molson, Redpath, and McGill tycoons. This centrality of economic and industrial prowess was mirrored in sport such that Montreal is often hailed as the "cradle" of organized sport in Canada. Just in terms of fostering certain sports, entrepreneurs in this city were responsible for founding, defining, developing, and institutionalizing such sports as snowshoeing, ice hockey, figure skating, speed skating, lacrosse (the non-Native version), cycling, and football. Each of these sports carries its own unique story of evolution. However, for the purposes of this chapter, what is important to understand about Montreal's vanguard role in organizing Canadian sport is the formation of the Montreal Amateur Athletic Association (MAAA) in 1881.

A trio of clubs with strong membership and established practices—the Montreal Snow Shoe Club, the Montreal Lacrosse Club, and the Montreal Bicycle Club—bought the Montreal Gymnasium in the core downtown area of the city as a home for the conglomeration of clubs called the MAAA. The oldest of these three clubs, the Montreal Snow Shoe Club (formed in 1843), played an instrumental role in fostering snowshoe events, races, long-distance tramps or outings, charity events, drama productions, social events of dinners and dancing (men with men), and generally championed the manly virtues of being a snowshoe participant (Becket, 1881). Club members and executives brought a wealth of managerial experience to the MAAA. Its sister organization, the Montreal Lacrosse Club, which had a lot of crossover members, was regarded as one of the premier competitive lacrosse clubs in Canada. And of course the Montreal Bicycle Club was symbolic of escalating social interests in the bicycle. The MAAA's original stated purpose was practical and unambitious: "the promotion of physical and mental culture among, and the providing of rational amusements and recreation for, its members" (Morrow, 1981, p. 26). However, the MAAA assumed a position of national sport leadership out of all proportion to its stated purpose.

By the 1890s, the MAAA membership numbered some 2,500 men with the three founding clubs plus football, toboggan, and skating clubs; departments in billiards, shooting, gymnastics, and bowling; and connected clubs in drama, chess, hockey, fencing, and boxing. What was uniquely important about the MAAA was that, for the most part, its members (including its club executives) were middle-class businessmen with considerable professional and managerial skills. With the financial and membership stability of the association itself, these businessmen used their administrative acumen to foster excellence in sport (the MAAA hockey team, to provide only one example, won the first two Stanley Cup championships in the early 1890s) and to found and promote no less than 11 national sport governing bodies such as the Canadian Wheelmen's Association (for cycling), the National Lacrosse Association, and the Canadian Amateur Hockey Federation.

In short, executives within the MAAA wielded tremendous power in the development of organized sport in Canada. Nowhere was this more pronounced or more profoundly felt than in fostering and normalizing the ideological code of amateurism as the guiding principle for Canadian sporting development until late in the 20th century.

AMATEUR IDEALISM

It is clear that organized sport, historically, has been the preserve of elite males and that sporting practices usually carried a gentlemanly code of conduct and proper way of playing—at least proper to those men of the middle classes who made the rules for sport. In Canada, as we have noted, the earliest organized sporting clubs were social first and athletic second in their *raison d'être* and it was the upper class, like the garrison officers, who were the main participants. With the stark and rapid changes accompanying industrialization, sport had the potential to become more democratized, providing opportunities for women and more social classes to participate.

Amateurism has to be one of the most unique tenets in governing any human behaviour; as a principle, it is a concept cemented to exclusion—who will *not* be allowed to compete in what sports. For example, in the mid-1830s in Canada, a thriving horseracing club in Newark, Ontario, published a "rule" that "no black man shall be allowed to compete under any pretext whatsoever" (Cosentino, 1975); we can only speculate about the reasons for this rule. However, in another sport, snowshoeing, there were standardized lists of race cards enumerating the events from shorter to longer distances. For these prestigious races in Montreal, it was common to include an event for First Nations athletes. The prestige event was the "open" two-mile race that was understood to be closed to "Indians." In the early 1870s, two Aboriginal men lined up for the start of an open event. Considerable controversy ensued, the result of which was thereafter to list the open event as "Open (Indians barred)." Clearly, there was a strong element of racism just as there had been in the late 1860s when a black rower, William Berry, was excluded from the Toronto Bay Rowing Regatta. The real issue was control, or control over the perceived "proper" sporting participants. Canada's first amateur definition, which was established by the Montreal Pedestrian Club in 1873, encapsulates this issue:

> An amateur is one who has never competed in any open competition or for public money, or for admission money, or with professionals for a prize, public money or admission money, nor has ever, at any period of his life taught or assisted in the pursuit of Athletic exercises as a means of livelihood *or is a labourer or an Indian*. (Morrow, 1986, p. 174 [emphasis added])

Part of the issue of amateurism was discrimination; not just negatively, in the sense of racial discrimination, but also in the notion of equality of competition. In some sports, such as rowing, lacrosse, and track and field, the quality of the sport was so high and the emphasis on winning so dominant that some competitors did compete for money or they competed under aliases to get a valuable prize. Some athletes were able to acquire fame and monetary gain, then spend more time training in the quest for victory, prestige, and material reward. For those competitors unable or unwilling to follow suit, it meant inequality of competition, somewhat akin to the whole issue of steroid use in contemporary sport, if steroids are examined solely from the issue of equality of competition. Until well into the 20th century, for the most part, to be labelled a "professional" in sport was to be tarnished as someone who would lie, cheat, or fix outcomes—in short, do anything for victory. This is why sport governing bodies like the Canadian *Amateur* Association of Oarsmen and the Montreal *Amateur* Athletic Association took it upon themselves to use the notion of amateurism as a method to police their perceptions of inequality, be they social, racial, or pecuniary.

For the middle-class businessmen of the esteemed and influential MAAA, amateurism became and was promoted as *the* common sense guiding value system in competitive organized sport. So adamant were these men about the significance of this principle that they created the Canadian Amateur Athletic Association (CAAA) in 1884 to be the national custodian of the amateur code. In some iteration or another, the CAAA stayed in continuous existence until the mid-1970s, heavily bolstered by the international prestige attached to the modern Olympic Games whose administrators revered the same amateur ideal.

Transitions to Commercial Mass Sport

In almost every respect, the whole concept of amateurism is very much an elitist, socially exclusionary mechanism instituted to preserve the status quo of the male upper and upper-middle classes in sport. Policing the ideal was like trying to herd cats or grasp mercury in one's hand. Nevertheless, this fossil-like principle became the dominant ethos of sport in Canada. By the turn of the 20th century, in popular team sports alone, multiple levels of sporting competition existed in baseball, lacrosse, and ice hockey. Winning major trophies in these sports became the central focus of sport, larger and more spectator-friendly facilities were built, the athletic quality of competition improved, and so forth.

At the same time, the Canadian economy and landscape were changing. Federal government initiatives translated into 2.5 million new immigrants coming into Canada between 1900 and 1920, many of them to the newly opened and established provinces in the West. Wheat became one of our central exports, the softwood forests of northern Ontario supplied major European markets, and mining of precious minerals in that same region meant boom times for small communities in the north. In the latter regard, it was the smaller communities of Kirkland Lake, Timmins, Renfrew, Sault Ste. Marie, and so on that first promoted a commercial, professional basis for ice hockey by using mining money to pay the best players to live in these communities and play hockey for the local teams. Newspapers catered to and promoted the proliferation and interest in sports with the creation of sport pages. Railway connections expanded to cater to the wheat, wood, and mineral markets. Movie houses opened, women's suffrage was granted (1918) after a long struggle by suffragettes, and labour unions were formed out of the impetus of the violent 1919 Winnipeg General Strike. World War I further solidified British loyalties (and in so doing created an even deeper rift between French and English Canadians with the issue of military conscription), and also stimulated the economy. All these changes underscore the prevailing current of commercial growth and prosperity in Canadian society. The same was true in sport; however, although the iron-clad rule of amateurism reigned supreme among sport governing bodies, this ideal was soon contested.

Entrepreneurial Interests

By 1905, high-level team sports received the most notoriety in the press and in public perception. Concomitant with the commercial trends in society, in lacrosse, ice hockey, track and field, and football there was an "outbreak" of professionals (the equivalent of paid or nonamateur-abiding practitioners) and unsavoury "professional" behaviours (such as playing under an alias to get around amateur regulations). So great was the professional stigma that even to play against a professional athlete on another team could result in the amateur athlete's suspension from competitive sport. For so-called major teams in lacrosse and hockey, whole teams were often suspended. At the same time, to win league championships teams and clubs proclaiming their amateur affiliation used job offers and secret payments to recruit the best players. Ironically, it was the MAAA organization that made a bold suggestion to permit amateurs to play with and against professionals as long as everyone knew who the actual professional players were. What resulted was an almost three-year protracted war among those factions who wanted to remain purely amateur and the MAAA-induced group who wanted more open competition (Morrow, 1986). In the end, amateurism as an ideological ideal prevailed while growing interests and parallel value systems embedded in the 1908 London Olympic Games aided this resolution of the conflict in Canada.

And yet the preservation of the ideal was often nominal even by amateur moguls. For example, consider the case of one consummate amateur athlete, race-walker George Goulding. His racing career spanned some 10 years beginning in 1906. By the time he retired from racing, he held world records in almost every distance from 1 to 10 miles. His technique was flawless; not once was he even accused of "lifting" in a sport where judges would lie on the ground to inspect race-walkers who technically might be running, not walking. While Goulding never accepted anything more than travel expenses for his events, his magnetic attraction for spectators was such that holding matched races featuring his name would attract thousands of paying fans, even to the point of filling Madison Square Gardens in New York City. Clearly, sport venue operators made money from his prowess, and amateur officials often went to great lengths to equalize the competition by handicapping Goulding's starting time to let his competitors gain an advantage or by holding races that had only Goulding and one other major rival, even though the latter was clearly contrary to the rules and ideals of amateurism since it isolated the top athletes only for a competition (Morrow & Leyshon, 1987).

What the Goulding case and many other examples from individual and team sports show is that the quest for excellence in organized sport almost demanded some other method of promotion than the restrictive blanket of amateurism. What transpired was that entrepreneurs envisioned a commercial basis for high-quality sport, especially for team sports. Thus, for example, hockey was developed at every level of amateur play in strictly amateur leagues. And, at the same time, openly professional hockey leagues developed in southern and northern Ontario such that by 1910, the National Hockey Association (the forerunner to the NHL) was formed with contractual obligations that carried rules about how long a player was bound by the contract to play with one team. Lacrosse and baseball did the same thing, although the permanency of the success of these two professional sports in Canada was not the same as hockey. Whereas an athlete like George Goulding had no choice or opportunity to make money from his talent, some 10 years later Lionel Conacher, a Toronto-born athlete who was voted Canada's best all-round athlete of the first half-century, was able to capitalize on his athletic abilities. Conacher excelled in baseball, lacrosse, football, wrestling, boxing, and hockey. It was the professional opportunity in hockey that enabled him to "turn pro" and make his livelihood from earning money in sport. In fact, up until 1937 when he retired from pro hockey, he was a semi-professional or professional in all six of his chosen sports (Morrow, 1979).

The Hero/Star in Sport

One of the important byproducts of the burgeoning development of and interest in high-level sporting competition was the notion of Canadian stars or heroes—athletic luminaries in sport. Both Goulding and Conacher were well known in their sporting times. Sport heroes provide windows or texts through which we can see how communities eulogize and celebrate their stars. Individual sport stories, like myths, provide basic images and metaphors that inform the perceptions, memories, and even aspirations of a society. And we can never minimize the impact one individual can have on the rate, magnitude, and direction of change in sport. A case in point is Dr. Geroge W. Beers, the Montreal dentist and "flaming lacrosse evangelist." Beers codified the first set of rules for his sport and set up a convention to establish its national sport governing body, both in 1867. He also showcased lacrosse to England, the birthplace of modern organized sport, by leading two successful international tours in 1876 and 1883, the latter sponsored in part by the federal Department of Agriculture as an immigration-promoting initiative (Morrow, 1982). Because of Beers's incredible lacrosse salesmanship, for more than a century lacrosse was thought to have been formally declared our national sport (it never was during his lifetime, but both hockey, as our winter sport, and lacrosse, as our summer sport, were given that sanction in the mid-1990s). Certainly, there were other factors in the development and dispersion of lacrosse, but Beers is a striking example of a visionary who provided single leadership in sport (Lindsay, 1972).

Although Beers played lacrosse as a goaltender, he was not the kind of classic sport hero who dominated his sport as an athlete. It is interesting that perhaps the first such hero in Canadian sport was working class, of Irish descent, and an avowed professional oarsman, Ned Hanlan. World champion from 1880–1884, Hanlan absolutely captivated the sporting public during his era. Although smaller in stature than many of his competitors, Hanlan mastered the use of the sliding seat in rowing to the extent that he virtually controlled the pace of his events. His exploits are too numerous to mention here, but what is important is that it was Hanlan's skill combined with his business acumen that worked to solidify his heroic status to a public that was clearly awed by him. Even in the United States, for one single event on the Potomac River, both Houses of Congress adjourned to join some 100,000 spectators for just one of his races, and that was prior to his world champion achievement. He was an anomaly in terms of his professional status; however, his skill and domination of the sport, abetted by the proclivity toward gambling on his events, elevated him above normal standards and conventions (Cosentino, 1974). Moreover, even when he went on tour and competed in Australia after losing his world title he was still so widely acclaimed that on two separate trips he was the major drawing card (Brown, 1980). Hanlan was the consummate hero: male, highly skilled, charismatic, and unabashedly adored internationally. Culturally, sport stars are products of their times and environments. In French Canada, Louis Cyr, hailed during the late 19th to early 20th centuries as the "world's strongest man," embodied the revered physical prowess ennobled by French Canadians (Weider, 1976).

Women Sports Heroes   What also intersects heroic status is gender. We have learned how much sport is a male preserve. Socially, for most of the period under historical examination, women were marginalized socially, politically, and physically. To a considerable extent, women's bodies were under the rule of medical men who somehow understood the "apparent" fragility of the female body and the attendant tendencies toward "hysteria" of the mind. It was indeed the adoption and adaptation of the bicycle during the 1890s that almost literally emancipated women to become more active physically. Drop-frame safety bicycles led to the invention of bloomers and split skirts, thereby greatly facilitating movement for women. There are sporadic records of women participating in all manner of sports, from pedestrianism to ice hockey, by the start of World War I.

Perhaps the most famous and significant influence on Canadian women's participation in sport was the Edmonton Commercial Graduates basketball team, dubbed simply the Edmonton Grads. From 1915–1940 this team excelled at their sport. Coached the entire

The Edmonton Grads, 1922.
Dr. Don Morrow

time by high school teacher J. Percy Page (who eventually became Alberta's lieutenant governor), the Grads won some 93% of over 400 highly competitive games against local, provincial, national, international, and Olympic (exhibition) teams. With a farm team feeder system, tremendous civic boosterism, and the managerial skills of Page, the team was amateur in practice but had all the hallmarks of a skilled, professional team. However, the gendered order of society dictated that they had to be ladies first and athletes second. For example, Page insisted that all players had to remain single, no smoking or drinking was permitted, chaperones were required for all team events, players had to dress off the court as "proper" young women, and fair play was both valued and mandated (Macdonald, 1976). In short, women athletes, if judged by this remarkably successful team, had to live a gendered standard of behaviour that was not expected of men in sport.

Individual women athletes had similar expectations and assumptions placed upon them by society. When Ethel Catherwood, a member of Canada's track and field team in the 1928 Olympic Games, competed in and won a gold medal in the high jump, it was her beauty that captured media attention, not her athletic prowess. Catherwood, a native of Saskatchewan, was proclaimed the "Saskatoon Lily" owing to her perceived good looks. Similarly, Barbara Ann Scott, world and Olympic champion figure skater of the late 1940s, was revered for her good looks—her athletic talent was a distant second. Although voted Canada's best athlete and therefore winner of our prestigious Lou Marsh Award in three separate years, Scott received the greatest share of her media coverage in Canada in the women's section of the press, not on the sport pages. Instead of her athletic skill, reporters focused on her skating outfits. In many ways, Barbara Ann Scott was created by the media to be petite, feminine, blonde, pretty, a darling on skates, the valentine of Canada (she won one world championship in February near Valentine's Day), and Canada's fairy princess (Morrow, 1987). And perhaps owing to the post-war conservatism of her era, it was an image that worked. Handcrafted toy Barbara Ann Scott dolls were treasured by girls and women during the 1950s and are prized artifacts that sell for $350 to $500 today on eBay and craigslist.

The "Matchless Six," Canadian women's Olympic track and field team arriving in Toronto, 1928.
Dr. Don Morrow

State Sport

If one were to choose a symbol to represent the dominant trend in Canadian sport between 1900 and 1960, it would likely be the dollar sign. Entrepreneurial, commercial, and professional interests and opportunities in sport were rampant. This is not to say that these interests and opportunities were not contested. The Workers' Sports Association of Canada (WSA), for example, was formed as a national federation in the mid-1920s. The WSA encouraged all manner of sports for the working class and advocated against mega-sport entities such as the International Olympic Committee. Moreover, the WSA called for the abolition of amateurism and a unionization of professional and Olympic athletes in an open effort to bring social class equality to sport.

Another important thread in Canadian sport development during the 20th century was government involvement in sport, recreation, and fitness. Understandably, the 1867 British North America Act was silent on sport. The federal government's earliest involvement in sport was its immigration-directed investment in the 1883 lacrosse tour to Great Britain (mentioned earlier) and its sponsorship of Canadian involvement in international rifle competitions such as The Bisley, also in Great Britain. Direct federal intervention came first in the form of the 1911 Strathcona Trust, an act to encourage physical and military training in the Canadian public education system. The trust was operated by the Department of Militia in the schools and had the decided effect of embedding military drill and physical training in the curriculum, thereby leaving sport as an extracurricular event for more than half a century.

During the Great Depression, provincial governments in the Western provinces reached a cost-sharing agreement with the federal government to support recreation and sports programs for the public. This important dual-funding precedent (known as the Sport-Rec Movement) lead to a similar arrangement for the passage of the National Physical Fitness Act (NPFA) in 1943. The NPFA was the direct result of war rejection figures due to a lack of physical fitness. In objectives, the act was ambitious in that one of its fourfold goals was to encourage physical activity among all Canadians via a $250,000 per capita cost-sharing scheme with the provincial governments. The most significant results of the NPFA were the establishment of physical education degree training programs in three different provinces and the establishment of a National Advisory Council on Physical Fitness. In 1954, the NPFA was repealed without one dissenting vote in the House of Commons. However, the die of state intervention was cast by these early acts.

During the Cold War of the 1950s, sporting success, particularly in the modern Olympic Games, became a symbol for national political prowess among world super powers. Canadian Olympic achievements were relatively abundant during the first half-century of the Games. For example, the Canadian women's track and field team outperformed all other women's teams in the 1928 Amsterdam Games. At the same Olympiad, Vancouver's Percy Williams won the coveted 100- and 200-metre sprinting events. However, it was Canada's sheer dominance in Winter Olympic ice hockey from 1920 to 1948 that was our country's trademark. In the three quadrennial festivals beginning in 1952, Canada "failed" to win its coveted first place in the international arena. These events and others inspired the federal government to pass the 1961 Fitness and Amateur Sport Act (FASA).

This significant piece of legislation cemented state-supported and -administered elite-level sport through to the end of the 20th century. Managed within the Ministry of National Health and Welfare, the FASA was aimed directly at improvements and victories in national and international sporting competitions. Experts from diverse fields advised the government through a national advisory council. The FASA had considerable impact. Its agents established the Canada Games, set up coaching leadership and training programs, initiated provincial cost-sharing programs to set up elite sporting facilities, founded bursary programs for athletes, and poured money into world hockey team developments and competitions. Clearly, the government's target was gold medal production in important international competitions such as the Olympic Games and the various Canada versus the Soviet Union hockey series of the 1970s. The "fitness" component of the FASA seemed hollow by comparison. However, in 1971, after an intensive study of Canadian fitness levels, the federal government created Particip-ACTION, a not-for-profit, national-level fitness campaign aimed at improving the personal fitness levels of every Canadian. Still, world-class sport prestige was the vision that propelled massive government support for the 1976 Montreal Olympic Games and the 1988 Calgary Winter Olympic Games. The much-touted 1998 federal Mills Report (regarding the state of sports in Canada just before the turn of the century) underscored the economic, social, and cultural impact that international sporting prowess brings to our nation (Morrow & Wamsley, 2013).

Conclusions

Whole histories have been written on the evolution of single sports, individual athletes, teams, particular events, sporting clubs, and so forth. In this chapter, we have merely touched on some of the stories, events, trends, issues, themes, and processes of sport's contested development. The ideological connections between values held in the context of sport from ancient to modern times are quite stark. Fair play, male dominance, social class control, amateurism, professionalism, policies of social exclusion, spectatorship, technology, urbanization, and gender orders have all shaped the form and function of sport over time.

Critical Thinking Questions

1. What are some of the important considerations historical researchers must consider?
2. What other policies of exclusion, other than amateurism, are there in sport?
3. How did social class and social stratification impact sport in Canada over time?
4. What were some of the gender issues prevalent in Canadian sport evolution?
5. How did technological changes transform sport in Canada?
6. How and why did Montreal become such a pervasive force in organized sport?
7. How do heroes impact sport and sport behaviours?
8. What examples do we have of a gender order in Canadian sport, and in what ways did that order manifest itself?

Suggested Readings

Cosentino, F. (1978). *Ned Hanlan* (The Canadians Series). Toronto, ON: Fitzhenry and Whiteside.
Hall, M. A. (2002). *The girl and the game: A history of women's sport in Canada*. Peterborough, ON: Broadview Press.
Melançon, B. (2009). *The Rocket: A cultural history of Maurice Richard*. Vancouver, BC: Greystone Press.
Morrow, D., & Wamsley, K. G. (2013). *Sport in Canada: A History* (3rd ed.). Toronto, ON: Oxford University Press. (This work contains a complete, extensive bibliography of Canadian sports history.)
Weider, B. (1976). *The strongest man in history: Louis Cyr*. Toronto, ON: Mitchell Press.

References

Becket, H. W. (1882). *The Montreal snow shoe club: Its history and record*. Montreal, QC: Becket Brothers.
Brown, A. (1980). Edward Hanlan: The world sculling champion visits Australia. *Canadian Journal of History of Sport and Physical Education, 11*, 1–44.
Cosentino, F. (1974). Ned Hanlan—Canada's premier oarsman: A case study of nineteenth-century professionalism. *Ontario History, 66*, 241–250.
Cosentino, F. (1975). A history of the concept of professionalism in Canadian sport. *Canadian Journal of History of Sport and Physical Education, 6*, 75–81.
Durant, W. (1926). *The story of philosophy*. New York, NY: Simon and Schuster.
Gillespie, G. (2002). *The imperial embrace: British sportsmen and the appropriation of landscape in nineteenth-century Canada*. Unpublished doctoral dissertation, University of Western Ontario, London, ON.
Hall, M. A. (2002). *The girl and the game: A history of women's sport in Canada*. Peterborough, ON: Broadview Press.
Hughes, T. (1904). *Tom Brown's school days by an old boy*. New York, NY: Hurst and Company.
Jobling, I. (1970). *Sport in nineteenth-century Canada: The effects of technological changes on its development*. Unpublished doctoral dissertation, University of Alberta, Edmonton, AB.
Lindsay, P. L. (1969). *A history of sport in Canada, 1807–1867*. Unpublished doctoral dissertation, University of Alberta, Edmonton, AB.

Lindsay, P. L. (1970). The impact of military garrisons on the development of sport in British North America. *Canadian Journal of History of Sport and Physical Education, 1*, 33–44.

Lindsay, P. L. (1972). George Beers and the national game concept: A behavioural approach. In *Proceedings of the Second Canadian Symposium on the History of Sport and Physical Education* (pp. 27–44). Edmonton, AB.

Macdonald, C. (1976). The Edmonton Grads, Canada's most successful team: A history and analysis of their success. Unpublished master's thesis, University of Windsor, Windsor, ON.

Metcalfe, A. (1970). The form and function of physical activity in New France, 1534–1759. *Canadian Journal of History of Sport and Physical Education, 1*, 45–64.

Metcalfe, A. (1987). *Canada learns to play: The emergence of organized sport, 1807–1914.* Toronto, ON: McClelland & Stewart.

Morrow, D. (1979). Lionel Pretoria Conacher. *Journal of Sport History, 6*, 5–37.

Morrow, D. (1981). The powerhouse of Canadian sport: The Montreal Amateur Athletic Association, inception to 1909. *Journal of Sport History, 8*, 20–39.

Morrow, D. (1982). The Canadian image abroad: The great lacrosse tours of 1876 and 1883. In *Proceedings of the Fifth Canadian Symposium on the History of Sport and Physical Education* (pp. 11–23). London, ON.

Morrow, D. (1986). A case study in amateur conflict: The athletic war in Canada, 1906–1908. *British Journal of Sports History, 3*, 183–190.

Morrow, D. (1987). Sweetheart sport: Barbara Ann Scott and the post–World War Two image of the female athlete in Canada. *Canadian Journal of History of Sport and Physical Education, 18*, 36–54.

Morrow, D., & Leyshon, G. (1987). George Goulding: A case study in sporting excellence. *Canadian Journal of History of Sport and Physical Education, 18*, 26–51.

Morrow, D., & Wamsley, K. G. (2005). *Sport in Canada: A history.* Toronto, ON: Oxford University Press.

Morrow, D., & Wamsley, K. G. (2013). *Sport in Canada: A history* (3rd ed.). Toronto, ON: Oxford University Press.

Weider, B. (1976). *The strongest man in history: Louis Cyr.* Toronto, ON: Mitchell Press.

Chapter 4
Sport and Social Stratification

Rob Beamish

Levels of economic inequality have expanded across the country.
Dosfotos/PYMCA/Alamy

Unable to split the defence, Sidney Crosby's long shot was steered into the corner by US goalie Ryan Miller. Beating defenceman Brian Rafalski to the puck, Crosby started up the boards before cycling it down to Jarome Iginla who had gone to the corner. As Ryan Suter moved on Iginla, Crosby saw an opening to the net. "Iggy," he called, and in a split second the puck was on and off Crosby's stick going "5-hole" through Miller—gold medal Canada!

In an instant, Crosby's 2010 "golden goal" replaced Paul Henderson's 1972 Canada–Soviet hockey series "goal of the century" as the pinnacle of Canadian sporting achievement. And for good reason—the goal not only gave an overtime victory to Canada against their American rivals in the final event of the 2010 Winter Olympic Games where feelings of nationalist pride were higher than ever, it also established a new Olympic record for gold medals at the Winter Games. Still, other feats compete to rank as the greatest moment in Canadian sport:

- Donovan Bailey's 1996 Atlanta Olympic Games' gold-medal victory in the 100 metres, which also set a world record, put Canada at the top of the sprinting world, a position consolidated by the Canadian men's 4 × 100-metre relay victory, defeating the highly favoured US relay team "right in their own backyard."

- Between 1915 and 1940, the Edmonton Grads dominated women's basketball internationally. A sporting dynasty without equal, the Grads won 502 of the 522 games they played during their 25-year reign; they won 17 consecutive world championships and four Olympic gold medals.

- The Canadian women's hockey team has demonstrated a similar dominance. The first-ever Women's World Championship was held in 1990, and since then the team has won 10 world titles, 3 Olympic gold medals, 1 Olympic silver medal, and 12 3 Nations/4 Nations Cups.

- Finally, as victory was stolen from the Canadian women's soccer team in the semifinal match at the 2012 London Olympic Games by a questionable call, another heroic legend was woven into the fabric of Canadian history, culture, and sport. Like the Edmonton Grads and the women's hockey team, the national soccer team's successes serve as an inspiration to millions of Canadians—young and old, male and female, and people of all abilities and racialized or ethnic backgrounds.

Greatness in sport centres on victorious struggle because the fundamental objective to formalized competitive sport in the modern era is to place first. And although less competitive forms of sport exist that are not committed to differentiation, ranking, and the unequal allocation of rewards, the essence of almost all high-profile sports—the Special Olympics is an exception—is the pursuit of victory and the associated creation of a stratified system of reward and prestige. At the same time, however, fairness—equality of competitive conditions, which is ensured by the specific rules of the sport—is also sacrosanct.

The co-presence of those opposites—equality in competition and inequality of outcome—seems contradictory, but in sport as well as in all other discussions of social stratification, the presence of those two conditions is of pivotal importance. Furthermore, grasping the full extent of their complex interrelationship is central to a sociological understanding of sport and social stratification.

SPORT AND SOCIAL STRATIFICATION: SOME PRELIMINARY TERMS

Conceptually and ideally, the stratification system found in sport is a particular type: Sport is viewed as a *meritocracy*. A meritocracy is a hierarchical ranking and reward system in which an individual's demonstrated performance determines where she or he will be situated in the existing hierarchy. Sport is often viewed as the most genuine of meritocracies because all competitors face the same rules and compete on a "level playing field." It truly appears that those who make the most of their ability—through personal dedication to long-term preparation, sacrifice, and concerted, concentrated effort during the event—are the victors. The winners justifiably receive the greatest rewards in a meritocratic system. In fact, sport advocates maintain that among sport's most outstanding and socially significant qualities are its meritocratic structure and the model it holds out for other social institutions to emulate.

However, before sport or a specific competitive sport system can be genuinely meritocratic, it must possess two fundamental equalities: *equality of opportunity* and *equality of condition*. Equality of opportunity is the more straightforward of the two and is self-explanatory.

To ensure that a sport system is truly meritocratic and that the very best rise to the top based on their demonstrated merit, every potential participant must have the opportunity to take part; that is, this chance to take part must be equally available to everyone. If barriers impede any individual's opportunity to try to take part in the competition—whether it is due to one's class, sex (with the exception of sex-specific competitions), gender, sexuality, race, ethnicity, physical or cognitive ability, or geographical location, for example—then the system cannot and will not be genuinely meritocratic. Denying an opportunity to any person means that the full talent pool has not been assessed and that the person or persons excluded may well be better than whoever places first in the limited pool of contestants. The immediate assumption of many Canadians is that everyone has the opportunity to compete in any and all sports in Canada. However, upon reflection most realize that this is simply not the case. A number of variables, such as the availability of teams, clubs, or leagues; the necessary facilities; access to the proper equipment; and the ability to get to the locale where the sport is played, prevent many Canadians from having an equal opportunity to play all sports.

Equality of condition is a more complex concept and also harder to ensure. In its simplest terms, equality of condition means that every person taking part in a competitive event does so under the same conditions. Laying the foundation for Canada's high-performance sport system in *A Proposed Sports Policy for Canadians*, the late John Munro, then Minister of Health and Welfare, recognized the importance of equality of condition:

> We must face the fact that it's only fair, just as a dash in a track and field meet is only fair, that everyone has the same starting line, and the same distance to run. Unfortunately, in terms of facilities, coaching, promotion and programming, the sports scene today resembles a track on which some people have twenty-five yards to run, some fifty, some one-hundred, and some as much as a mile or more. (Munro, 1970, pp. 4–5)

The unequal conditions Munro noted are among the easiest to eliminate even though, despite Sport Canada's efforts over almost half a century, significant inequities in facilities, qualified coaches, promotion, and athlete development programs still plague the meritocratic ambitions of sports leaders in Canada (see Chapter 12). Sadly, far more entrenched inequalities of condition also endure, and they are becoming increasingly prohibitive barriers to all attempts to create a truly meritocratic sport system in Canada. These latter factors, along with those Munro identified, remain problematic because of the existing system of structural inequality in Canada as a whole.

To properly address the relationship between sport and stratification in Canada, one must examine organized competitive sport within the larger context of the prevailing conditions of Canadian social inequality and draw upon the major theoretical insights that sociologists have developed regarding social inequality. Because Chapters 5, 6, and 10 present detailed accounts of how race, ethnicity, sex, gender, and education influence equality of opportunity and condition, this chapter will focus on how the economy and social class structure Canada's stratification system, in general, and within sport in particular. In addition, beginning with a focus on the economy and class is appropriate from a chronological perspective because the earliest sociological studies of social inequality emphasized class and economic change far more than race, ethnicity, sex, gender, or education. Once the classical position on class is understood and the developments introduced by more contemporary theorists are also incorporated into the discussion, one can then weave in factors other than class that influence an individual's life chances. To begin, what is the current profile of economic stratification in Canada?

SOCIAL INEQUALITY: THE CANADIAN PROFILE

The Occupy Movement of 2011–2012 turned the profile of social inequality in the United States and Canada into a prime-time media issue for good reason. Patterns of social inequality in both countries show a growing divergence between the rich and the poor—strikingly captured in "the top 1%" epithet. All rhetoric aside, over the past 30 years, the richest group of Canadians has increased their share of the total national income while middle-income and the poorest groups have lost some of theirs. This is true even though the incomes of the poorest Canadians have risen marginally (see Conference Board of Canada, 2012; Fortin, Green, Lemieux, Milligan, & Riddell, 2012; Hunter, Sanchez, & Douglas, 2012; Yalnizyan, 2010).

The standard measure of income inequality is the Gini index. The index ranges from 0 to 1; a Gini index of 0 means that every person has exactly the same income, and an index of 1 means that one person has all of the income. The higher the Gini index number, the greater the level of inequality. Figure 4.1 shows the Gini index for market income (earnings from employment or self-employment, investment income, and private retirement income) and the index for disposable income (after-tax income plus the government transfers to lower-income Canadians).

The graphs illustrate two notable points. First, the Gini index for market income is higher than it is for disposable income. The market income index rises from 0.37 in 1980 to 0.44 in 2007, showing a trend toward greater inequality in Canada (both of those years were the peak of economic booms; Fortin et al., 2012). Second, the graph shows that despite progressive taxes and transfers to poorer Canadians, the Gini index has risen over the past 20 years. In the late 1970s and throughout most of the 1980s, inequality in disposable income fell from 0.3 in 1976 to a low of 0.281 in 1989 (Conference Board of Canada, 2012). However, during the 1990s the Gini index for disposable income grew to more than 0.3 and remained relatively constant at 0.32 during the first decade of the 21st century.

The growing disparity in income between the top 1% and the rest of Canadian income earners has coincided with a significant change in economic policies within Canada and the rest of the Western world. The shift from Keynesian-inspired economic

Figure 4.1 Canadian Inequality Trends

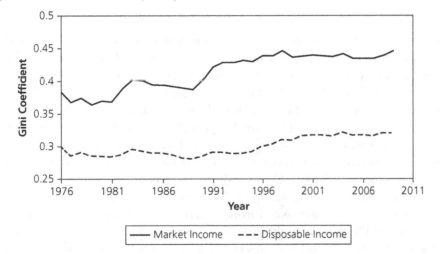

Source: Fortin, N., Green, D., Lemieux, T., Milligan, K., & Riddell, C. 2012. Canadian inequality: Recent developments and policy options. Canadian Public Policy, 38, 121–45., (fig1, p123). Reprinted by permission.

policies, which supported government involvement in the economy and the provision of numerous social services, to monetarist-inspired policies in which the government is less involved in regulating the economy and more and more social services are removed from public sector responsibility and put in the hands of private sector, profit-driven corporations (Harvey, 2007; Keynes, 1936; Von Mises, 1934; Whitson, 2011).

The withdrawal of the government from its regulatory and service roles is often called *neoliberalism*—a new liberalism that Harvey (2007) describes as follows:

> Neoliberalism is in the first instance a theory of political economic practices that proposes that human well-being can best be advanced by liberating individual entrepreneurial freedoms and skills within an institutional framework characterized by strong private property rights, free markets, and free trade. The role of the state is to create and preserve an institutional framework appropriate to such practices. . . . State interventions in markets (once created) must be kept to a bare minimum because, according to the theory, the state cannot possibly possess enough information to second-guess market signals (prices) and because powerful interest groups will inevitably distort and bias state intervention (particularly in democracies) for their own benefit. (p. 2)

While neoliberal policies create the overall context for the growing disparity of income and wealth in Canada, there are other particular factors stemming from neoliberalism's impact around the globe and the increasing interdependency of various markets globally (i.e., the process of *globalization* discussed in Chapter 14).

Alongside the Gini index, another way to express income inequality is to divide all income earners into five groupings of equal size (or quintiles) and see what proportion of the nation's total income falls to each (if all incomes were equal, 20% of the national income would fall to each quintile). In 1980, the top quintile of Canadian income earners received 45% of the nation's total income. In 2007, Canadians in the upper quintile received more than half of the total income (52%) (Fortin et al., 2012). No matter what technique is used to measure income inequality, there is clearly a growing disparity between the rich and the poor in Canada.

The Top 1%

Because of the Occupy Movement's actions, media attention was drawn to the top 1%. There are a number of points to note about this elite 1% within Canada. First, who constitutes this group? In 2007, the year for which the most recent data are available, the richest 1% of Canadians consisted of about 246,000 individuals with a minimum income of $169,000 and an average income of $404,000 (Yalnizyn, 2010). The top 1% is predominantly male (82.7%) and between the ages of 35 and 64 (79% of the upper 1% versus 54.5% of the population as a whole). This group is better educated than most Canadians (58.1% have a bachelor's degree or higher versus 19% of all Canadians). They also work long hours (52% work more than 50 hours a week versus 18.6% of all Canadians); they hold positions in senior management (14.1% versus 0.9%), in management (19.1% versus 6.1%), as health care professionals (11.6% versus 2.0%), or in business and finance (7.1% versus 1.8%) (see Fortin et al., 2012).

How the top 1% becomes wealthy has also changed. Prior to the 1930s, high levels of wealth stemmed from assets such as stocks, bonds, and property, but the Conference Board of Canada (2012) indicates that "[t]he phenomenal growth in incomes of the super-rich is not

Figure 4.2 Share of Total Income in Canada, Richest 1%

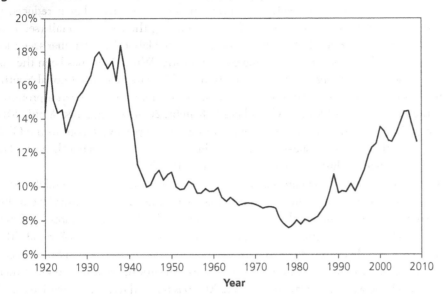

Source: Fortin, N., Green, D., Lemieux, T., Milligan, K., & Riddell, C. 2012. Canadian inequality: Recent developments and policy options. Canadian Public Policy, 38, 121–45. (fig4, p127). Reprinted by permission.

due to the assets they own." Krugman (2009) agrees; the majority of multi-millionaires' incomes is salary and bonuses: "Even at the very top, the highest 0.01 percent of the population—the richest one in ten thousand—almost half of their income comes in the form of compensation" (p. 130). The same trend exists in the United States and Western Europe.

Figure 4.2 shows the share of all incomes that the top 1%'s earnings represent. Among the graph's most striking features is the growing share of total income that the top 1% accrues beginning in 1980. In the late 1970s, the top 1% had incomes that were about eight times larger than all other Canadians; by 2010 that share had almost doubled to 14 times that of all other Canadians. This level of income disparity has not existed since the Great Depression of 1929 when the top 1% captured 18% of total income. The parallel between the economic downfall of 1929 and the present, along with the economic crises of recent years, indicates why economists and sociologists are so concerned with growing income disparity in the West.

Factors Contributing to Economic Inequality

Most of the wage-gap disparity occurred during the economic recessions in the 1980s and 1990s, but the effects differed among workers—younger workers suffered more than established ones (Boudarbat, Lemieux, & Riddell, 2010). During the two recessions, entrants to the labour market could not find jobs or they secured positions at low entrance-level salaries. In the intervening years, those young workers were unable to achieve the incomes they would have reached with higher starting salaries. These lower salaries explain some of the growing disparity in incomes, and the future is not promising. As older workers retire from the workforce and younger workers' salaries lag behind traditional income trajectories, the wage gap between the top 1% and the rest of Canada's workforce will widen further.

Technology has also played a role in the gap's growth. The increasing use of computers and specialized knowledge skills pushed up the wages for high-demand, well-educated workers, but it also allowed firms to outsource production to low-wage countries. This may have benefited consumers through lower prices in some instances, but it reduced the demand for low and unskilled labour in Canada, allowing their wages to fall (see Fortin et al., 2012; Goldin & Katz, 2008). The use of "outsourced labour" is a familiar scenario to anyone interested in sport or the sporting goods industry. While Nike has been the main focus, the use of sweatshops and the exploitation of child labour in the Global South to produce sporting goods at lower costs and higher profit margins has been a prominent media theme since the 1990s (see Greenberg & Knight, 2004; Kaufman & Wolff, 2010). For many Canadians, the impact of the exploitation of inexpensive labour in the Global South is more than a moral issue—it represents the loss of not just jobs but the virtual collapse of the garment industry in North America (see Brooks, 2007).

The increasing use of computers in all areas of the economy eliminates middle-income jobs as technology reduces them to routine tasks that do not require sophisticated skills. This scenario occurs to different degrees throughout Canada, the United States, the United Kingdom, and Germany (Fortin et al., 2012; Goos & Manning, 2007; Green & Sand, 2011). The impact has not been as extreme in Canada as it has been in the United States because there is a higher participation rate in postsecondary education, creating a pool of highly skilled "knowledge workers," a group Florida (2002) has referred to as the "creative class."

Three other factors affecting economic inequality are the minimum wage, the declining unionization of the workforce, and the increasingly widespread use of temporary workers. The minimum wage tends to set the floor for incomes in a country. As a result, European countries with higher minimum wages relative to the average wage do not show the same income disparities as Canada and the United States. Autor, Manning, and Smith (2010) show that there has been a sizable decline in the real value of the minimum wage in the United States since the 1980s, which contributed significantly to the growing inequality identified by the Occupy Movement. In contrast, Fortin and colleagues (2012) indicate that increases in the minimum wage in virtually every Canadian province collectively prevented the great wage disparity that is found in the United States from occurring in Canada.

The impact of unions on wages is somewhat mixed. On the one hand, union wages are higher than those of nonunionized workers. This reinforces a growing inequality in the Canadian income structure. At the same time, however, unions tend to raise the wages of the lowest-paid unionized workers, thus creating greater income equality. Card, Lemieux, and Riddell's (2004) analysis of the relationship between unions and wage inequality in Canada, the United States, and the United Kingdom during the 1970s, 1980s, and 1990s show that unionization declined the most in the United Kingdom and the least in Canada. Wage inequality grew in all three countries, with the largest growth occurring in the United Kingdom and the smallest in Canada. These researchers attribute about 15% of the growth in Canadian inequality to declining unionization rates. More than 20% of the rising inequality in the United States and the United Kingdom is attributable to the greater losses in union membership in those countries.

Since the recession of 2008, temporary work has grown at more than three times the rate of permanent work (14.2% versus 3.8%) (Statistics Canada, 2013a). Between May 2008 and 2012, of the 354,000 new positions created in the Canadian economy 79% were temporary jobs. Temporary workers receive, on average, 46% less pay than those in permanent positions. While the nature and scope of temporary work varies considerably, it seems that temporary, precarious employment is becoming a permanent feature of the Canadian economy. Without the benefit of secure, year-round employment and income, this change has also contributed to Canada's widening income gap (Grabell, 2013; Statistics Canada, 2009). The impact this has on young Canadians' opportunities to take part in sport is quite obvious—families faced with precarious employment have to conserve resources wherever possible, and this turns activities and purchases such as school and community sport registrations and equipment into "fringe luxuries" that are replaced by cheaper forms of passive, home entertainment.

The impact of technological change, outsourcing of production, declining unionization, and the growing use of temporary workers have all contributed to, and will continue to exacerbate, the divide between the rich and the poor in Canada, the United States, the United Kingdom, and Western Europe. Young workers with little education and few marketable skills are most affected by these factors. At the same time, however, those in middle or lower-middle occupational categories have also experienced a decline in income, which has contributed to the increasing polarization of rich and poor in Canada and other developed nations.

On the basis of the above, it is clear that although one might maintain that the principles of classical liberalism should lead to a genuine meritocracy and that this is the best way to allocate resources and rewards in a society, the stratification system in Canada is not a pure meritocracy and it is not a continuous, hierarchical system. In reality, there is a growing divergence between those at the top of the economic structure and those at the bottom, with the middle layers shrinking in size.

STRATIFICATION IN CANADIAN SPORT: EARLY STUDIES

Surprisingly, the patterns of sport participation among Canadians have not received as much empirical analysis as one might assume given the importance of sport participation for young Canadians in particular. Nevertheless, several studies have examined the relationship between athletes' socioeconomic status (SES—a composite indicator of family income, education, and occupation in the paid labour force) and the types and level of sport participation. Each study has shown the same pattern of inequitable involvement despite federal and provincial governments' attempts to eliminate economic inequality as a major factor that excludes many young Canadians from participating in sport and rising within the sport pyramid.

Gruneau's (1972) groundbreaking study of Canada Games athletes showed that the competitors were drawn heavily from families where parents held professional and high-level white-collar positions, while those whose parents were involved in blue-collar and primary industrial occupations were significantly under-represented. The Canada Games athletes were also disproportionately drawn from families with higher incomes and educational achievement. Using Blishen scores that indicated a composite SES ranking, Gruneau found that 37% of the athletes came from the top three Blishen categories, while only 17% of the Canadian labour force ranked there (Blishen scores were one of the most widely used and generally accepted composite rankings of socioeconomic status that sociologists employed in their studies of stratification patterns in Canada during the 1960s through to the 1980s). Only 29% of the athletes came from the two lowest categories, although 63% of the Canadian labour force ranked in those categories.

Kenyon's (1977) study of elite track and field athletes and McPherson's (1977) study of hockey players found similar patterns. Kenyon found that, with 63% of the track and field athletes coming from families ranking in the top three Blishen categories and only

29% coming from families in the bottom two, track and field was more exclusive than the sport system as a whole. McPherson's data on elite hockey players were comparable to Gruneau's—22% of the players' parents were located in the top three Blishen categories.

Beamish's (1990) study focused on national team athletes in 1986. He demonstrated that despite more than 15 years of federal government support for high-performance sport and a number of strategies to reduce the impact of family background on athletic participation, patterns of significant exclusion still existed among Canada's top athletes. Close to half of Canada's national team athletes (44%) came from families in the top 20% of Canadian income earners; only 10% came from the bottom 20% of income earners. Canada's best athletes were drawn from families with fathers in managerial positions at almost two and a half times the expected rate, and those whose fathers were employed in the professional and technical sectors of the economy were more than double their proportional representation. At the other end of the workforce, athletes with parents in farming, logging, mining, crafts, production, and unskilled labour were significantly under-represented. The data on Blishen scores showed that since Gruneau's study, Canada's national teams had become more exclusive—68% of the athletes came from families in the top three Blishen categories. White and Curtis (1990), using a completely different data set, found similar patterns of representation.

On behalf of Sport Canada, EKOS Research Associates (1992) performed a comprehensive study of Canada's high-performance athletes. One of the key areas of concern was the sociodemographic profile of Canada's national team athletes. Sport Canada wanted to know whether factors such as sex, language, education, and economic status affected accessibility to the sport system. The results of this exhaustive study were the same as those mentioned by earlier researchers. EKOS found that there was an over-representation of Anglophones among Canada's best athletes. Canada's athletes did not come from "average" Canadian families. Forty-one percent of the athletes' fathers and 30% of their mothers had university-level educations (compared to 14% in the Canadian population as a whole). Like Beamish (1990), EKOS found that athletes came disproportionately from families with parents employed in professional, managerial, or administrative positions. Most importantly, EKOS concluded that the various funding and support programs in Canada's high-performance sport system had not reduced or eliminated inequalities of socioeconomic condition as a major factor in determining who would rise to the top of the Canadian high-performance sport pyramid.

None of these results were or are particularly surprising. All of the empirical studies before, during, and after these early studies have shown that one's position within the overall social structure significantly influences the extent and nature of sport involvement. Drawing his conclusion from more than a dozen studies between 1973 and his own, Wilson (2002) noted that research has "repeatedly shown that indicators of social class are positive predictors of sport involvement" (p. 5). Similarly, in their comprehensive review article of sport study, Washington and Karen (2001) emphasized that "From our perspective, social class is a key component of our understanding of sports" (p. 190).

The impact of class seems at first glance to be minimal, but the overall result is significant. Part of the reason for the shift to neoliberal policies was the apparent overextension of public services leading to crises at almost every level of government (see Whitson, 2011). As a result, whether it was at the federal, provincial, or local level, public service agencies had to reduce their costs. One solution was the reduction of services and the other was to introduce user fees. Once those fees are set in place, however, they are rarely removed; instead they increase, creating a growing barrier to lower SES families' participation in sport and recreation.

Not every Canadian has access to long-track speed skating training facilities.
Paul Kitagaki Jr./ZUMA Press, Inc./Alamy

School boards, faced with some of the same fiscal constraints in addition to increased demands to meet provincially established standards on standardized academic performance tests, reduced time for physical education to spend more time on the core academic subjects. Those small changes not only reduced (and sometimes eliminated) the amount of time that children spend in sport and physical activity on a daily basis, they also limited the opportunities for some children to discover different sports and activities—activity forms where they might thrive. For some lower SES Canadians, school sport and community recreation programs are often the only physical activity opportunities in which they can take part. When those options are reduced or eliminated, children from lower SES groups are denied the opportunity to discover their physical skills and athletic talents.

Health, recreation, and welfare were once at the centre of federal, provincial, and municipal governments' mandates as public goods. In the neoliberal era, sport and recreation are no longer viewed as essential services for all Canadians; they have become individuals' pursuits that consumers are expected to initiate and fund themselves and, although some sports seem to cost very little, even the smallest cost can be prohibitive to many Canadian families.

CLASS AND SOCIAL INEQUALITY: EARLY THEORIES

The studies that have focused on sport and social inequality based on data exploring the relationship between sport participation and income, or the more complex cluster of factors represented by SES, have drawn their inspiration from a rich scholarly tradition where class—people's relationship to what Karl Marx ([1859] 1911) called "the social relations of production"—is viewed as the most significant structural factor determining an individual's life chances. Although the study of class began with early political economists, and Marx ([1852] 1934) indicated that he did not discover "the existence of classes in modern society nor yet the struggle between them" (p. 56), the idea of class and class analysis is most closely associated with his name.

Karl Marx

In a section that Friedrich Engels placed at the end of *Capital, Volume 3* (a work left unfinished by Marx at his death), Marx ([1894] 1909) began to answer the questions, "What constitutes a class? What makes wage labourers, capitalists, and landlords constitute the three great social classes [of modern society, resting upon the capitalist mode of production]?" (p. 1031). Unfortunately, the fragment breaks off before Marx develops the answer fully. However, Marx wrote enough about classes in other pieces to make his position on the fundamental aspects of class clear and give insight into why class and class analysis have remained so influential in the study of social stratification.

For Marx, there were three fundamental aspects to class. The first is the "objective" or structural aspect of class, which determines where individuals stand within the economic structure of society and, more importantly, within the power structure of a social formation. Analyzing the dynamics of class conflict in France in the 1840s and 1850s, Marx ([1852] 1935) noted that "millions of families live under economic conditions of existence" that separate and distinguish them from—often placing them in "hostile contrast" with—other classes (p. 109). The identification of a class based on the role that "a mass of individuals performs within the social division of labour" is referred to as a "class in itself" (Marx, [1852] 1935; see also Cohen, 1980; Dos Santos, 1970; Draper, 1978).

The second aspect of class concerns its "subjective" aspect—the role class consciousness plays in the constitution of a class. In *The Poverty of Philosophy*, Marx ([1847] 1936) noted that in the transition from feudalism to capitalism, economic circumstances had "transformed the mass of the people of the country into workers" (p. 145). "The domination of capital has created for this mass a common situation, common interests," he continued. "This mass is thus already a class as against capital, but not yet for itself." It is only in the struggle against capital that "this mass becomes united, and constitutes itself as a class for itself." Through the realization of their common circumstances and the presence of a class opposing their interests—the formation of common interests—*and* by engaging in a struggle against the opposing class, a class in itself becomes a "class for itself"—that is, a class that recognizes and struggles for its own interests (see also Marx & Engels, [1845] 1939).

Once the separate individuals become part of a class for itself, then Marx and Engels ([1845] 1939) emphasized, "the class in its turn achieves an independent existence over against the individuals" so that the individuals now see their interests in class terms rather than individualistic ones (p. 49). This represents the third aspect of class for Marx—the idea of class solidarity. Marx maintained that the mass of individuals within a class that is in and for itself no longer think and act autonomously of one another—they act as members of their class (e.g., as members of the working class). Classes, not autonomous individuals, now become the major agents in the drama of history, and it is classes that are stratified and conflict with each other.

There were very sound reasons why people like Adam Smith, David Ricardo, James Mill, and John Stuart Mill, as well as Marx and Engels, identified the three great classes (wage labourers, capitalists, and landlords) as the major elements in the social stratification of Europe as feudalism gave way to industrial capitalism. All of the major social changes they witnessed appeared to be shaped by the spread and growing power of industrial capitalism. Class visibly shaped an individual's life chances, and the working and living conditions of the working class led to the formation of an identifiable class consciousness and the struggles of the working class against the capitalist class (see Engels [1845] 1950; Thompson, 1963). Nevertheless, by the end of the 19th and beginning of the 20th centuries, as capitalist economies became more stable, it became obvious to ensuing sociologists that class position alone did not completely determine an individual's life chances. The formation of a class for itself, with a largely unified conception of its needs, was a phenomenon of the past and not the present or foreseeable future (see Dahrendorf, 1959; Giddens, 1973).

Max Weber

Max Weber is regarded as the theorist who did the most to develop class analysis at the turn of the 20th century in view of the changes that had become institutionalized within capitalist societies (Dahrendorf, 1959; Giddens, 1973). Weber (1968) introduced four major conceptual developments that furthered the study of class and class-based societies: a) the use of the term *community* to locate the bases and exercise of power, b) the view that classes were more fragmented than Marx had suggested, c) the impact of "status groups" (*Stände*) and how they incompletely overlapped with class, and d) the emphasis of the role of political parties and how they influenced class power. Each of these changes merits some elaboration.

Like Marx, Weber's interest in class stemmed from questions of power, which he defined as the ability of an individual or a group to achieve his, her, or their objectives even when resisted by others. To identify where power was exercised, Weber's first conceptual development was his notion of *community*, although the term was quite encompassing— the nation, a province, a city, or what we conventionally think of as "a community" were included in Weber's sense of the term. The key point is that power is exercised within and among an identifiable group of people.

For Weber, there were three fundamental bases of power within a community: class, status, and political party. These are the first complexities that Weber introduced into the notion of class and class analysis. Power is exercised in an identifiable sphere of action, which Weber designated as a community, and power is not related simply to class—it is related to the interaction of class, status, and the formal political process.

Classes, Weber wrote, "are not communities; they merely represent possible, and frequent, bases for social action" (1968, p. 927). He argued that class exists when a number of people share the same life chances because of the particular way they gain their livelihoods—effectively as employers or employees. As a result, Weber, like Marx, began with a twofold conception of class: "'Property' and 'lack of property' are, therefore, the basic categories of all class situations" (p. 927).

Marx, it should be noted, was well aware of divided interests within classes (see, for example, Marx, [1852] 1934). It was later Marxists who often reduced his ideas to the provocative phrasing of *The Communist Manifesto* and presented his theory of class struggle as a dualistic opposition. In response to those interpretations, Weber recaptured the complexity of Marx's actual position on class analysis. But Weber also moved beyond Marx. Weber's second conceptual development was his explicit identification of a far more manifold conception of class than Marx.

Within the categories of employers and employees, Weber noted that one's class position also depended on the type of property the employer had and was using to advance his or her capital and the type of work that the employee undertook. On the employers' side, Weber indicated some of the differences that existed within their class position. The ownership of "dwellings; workshops; warehouses; stores; agriculturally usable land in large or small-holdings" would produce different class positions. Similarly, the ownership of "mines; cattle; men (slaves)" or the control of "mobile instruments of production, or capital goods of all sorts, especially money or objects that can easily be exchanged for money" all created distinctions that differentiated the class situation of employers (Weber, 1968, p. 928). Employees, Weber noted, are also highly differentiated on the basis of the skills and services they bring to the market. Based on his conception of greater diversity in the objective dimensions of class, Weber regarded the development of a shared class consciousness with much greater skepticism than Marx did.

The third change Weber (1968) introduced is the concept and significance of status groups (*Stände*) within a community. Weber noted that groups of individuals within a community come together or form associations based on shared lifestyles or views of life. Even though there was some overlap between class situations and status groups, it was not complete. In addition, Weber indicated that groups enjoying high status could exercise elements of power that were not necessarily equivalent to their actual economic or class position.

Weber was well aware of the significance of how political parties could wield power in the modern period, and this was his fourth conceptual development in the analysis of class and class-based societies. Although he was unaware of Antonio Gramsci's use of the term *hegemony* (see Chapters 1 and 2) to describe the same process Weber had in mind, Weber also believed that individuals and groups could exercise considerable political power without necessarily holding high status positions or inordinate economic power. By situating themselves in positions where they could shape people's perceptions of what is fair and just—by projecting their particular ideas as a form of common sense—political parties, drawing upon the massive resources of the state, could quietly and unobtrusively present a particular worldview as normal, natural, and inevitable.

In short, Weber's conception of social stratification was much more multidimensional than Marx's and significantly more so than the simplified positions many Marxists at the turn of the 20th century offered. Weber's multidimensional conception of stratification was also a major source of inspiration and theoretical guidance for the early studies of sport and social stratification. Nevertheless, contemporary sociologists have continued to refine the theory of class in response to the further consolidation and growing complexity of a capitalist society as well as a growing awareness of how factors other than class influence individuals' life chances and positions within the social structure.

CLASS AND SOCIAL INEQUALITY: CONTEMPORARY THEORIES

Although a number of sociologists have developed theories of social inequality that analysts have employed in recent studies of sport and social stratification, two of the most significant and influential are those of Anthony Giddens and Pierre Bourdieu. While differing in several respects, Giddens' and Bourdieu's ideas complement each other in important ways.

Giddens and Bourdieu draw generously from Marx and Weber in their conceptions of social inequality. As a result, class remains central to their understanding of inequality, but their conceptions of class are also part of systematically developed sociological theories. One of the main features of their work, which shapes their analyses of social stratification, is an integrated conception of "human agency" and "social structure" for Giddens (1979; 1984), or "subjectivism" and "objectivism" for Bourdieu (1973; 1989).

Anthony Giddens

On social action, Giddens (1984) argues that "[t]he basic domain of study of the social sciences, is neither the experiences of the individual actor, nor the existence of any form of social totality, but social practices ordered across space and time" (p. 2). Social action must be seen as "a *continuous flow of conduct*, rather than treating purposes, reasons, etc., as somehow aggregated together" (Giddens, 1979, p. 2, emphasis added). As a result, Giddens does not start with either the social structure or the human agent. His theory of structuration centres on "the recursive nature of human activities"—that is, the recurring (or reoccurring) nature of human action. Most social action is repetitive and it is through these recurring activities that we produce and largely reproduce social action (see Giddens, 1984).

Turning to the notion of social structure, Giddens (1976; 1979; 1984) uses language theory to reconceptualize one of sociology's key terms—*structure*. Giddens emphasizes that structures in social action are not "things," like the girders of a building or the heart, lungs, muscles, and so on of an organism (as structural–functionalist analogies suggest). Instead, structures are resources (just like the English langugage is a resource that people use to communicate) and rules (to communicate meaningfully, people must follow the rules of the English language) that are drawn upon and simultaneously created and re-created as individuals carry out their recursive social practices. Like language, structures—or resources and rules—simultaneously enable and constrain. The English language and its various rules enable communication, but these rules also constrain what can be communicated and how it is communicated. Giddens terms this "the duality of structure."

Giddens' idea is actually quite familiar to students who study sport and those who participate in sport. A game of hockey cannot take place until the players agree on the rules that they will follow—are we playing "real hockey rules," or are slap shots and perhaps even "raises" not allowed? Rules give the game structure—they let us know what is expected and allow us to participate and predict what others will do. The rules adopted for a game enable it to take place, but they also constrain what is and is not permitted.

The recursive nature of social action is also clearly evident in sport. NHL games across North America are virtually the same although, depending on the particular skills and strengths of the teams playing and the officials enforcing the rules, each game is not identical. Similarly, outdoor shinny games across Canada are equally as recursive—they are all virtually the same with slight variations in local rules even though "the rules of shinny" are not written anywhere and are simply passed on from player to player and generation to generation.

Giddens (1984) draws attention to an important contrast between the rules that fundamentally, or intensively, influence our actions versus those that are more superficial. He notes that the former are informal rules that are tacitly (almost unconsciously) understood by human agents and are not associated with any formal punishments if they are broken. Giddens contrasts these unwritten rules with the clearly formalized rules that have explicitly stated punishments if they are broken. The tacit, informal rules are the ones that teammates, for example, follow in the flow of a game or in their interactions within the locker room, while the formal rules are the actual, written, and enforced rules of the game or specified team regulations.

Surprisingly perhaps, the tacit, informal, and weakly sanctioned rules predominate in the recursive nature of all types of social action, including sport, rather than the clearly formalized, articulated rules and their sanctions (the relationship is the opposite of what one expects). One only has to think about the "unwritten codes" that predominate in sports—how some plays or infractions are accepted as "simply part of the game" while others cross an unofficial line and are deplored by everyone (e.g., running up the score on a much weaker opponent, continuing to celebrate goals when the score becomes lopsided, or intentionally injuring an opposing player). Giddens (1973) uses all of the ideas noted above to develop his own theory in his book *The Class Structure of the Advanced Societies*. Before examining Giddens' theory of class and how it applies to sport, Bourdieu's work merits attention.

Pierre Bourdieu

Characterizing his work as a "constructivist structuralism" and a "structuralist constructivism," Bourdieu's (1989) two key concepts integrating human agency (subjectivism) and social structure (objectivism) are *habitus* and field. Bourdieu argues that social action stems from two completely interrelated points of origin: the subjective side, consisting of "schemes of perception, thought, and action," which constitute what Bourdieu calls *habitus*, and the objective side, which are the social structures/spaces Bourdieu calls "fields" within which groups (which, he notes, are "ordinarily call[ed] classes") act (p. 14).

The idea of a field is a metaphor that students of sport can relate to instantly. A field is a hierarchically arranged, delimited "space" where individuals with different abilities and skills (different forms of capital—economic, social, and cultural) compete for positions within the hierarchy (Bourdieu [1983] 1986; 1993; Bourdieu & Wacquant, 1992). The network or configuration of positions define the field and distribute different types of power (or capital), the profits at stake, and the demands made upon the players/actors in the field. All one has to do is think of a football or soccer field and the players spread out on it with each one using his or her distinct skills, fulfilling specific assignments based on their particular position, to outperform their counterparts so that their team triumphs in the end. Social fields, like the fields of sport, are delimited, structured spaces where players, occupying particular positions, compete to gain personal distinction and to distinguish themselves from others (see Bourdieu, 2000).

Habitus is one of Bourdieu's most complex terms. It refers to a system of dispositions representing a practical sense of how to conduct one's actions—how one is "disposed" (inclined, influenced, predisposed, prompted, settled) to act. Like athletes, individuals, based on years of experience, develop an automatic, unconscious knowledge of how to play the game (carry on in any given social situation). That sense is durable because it is deeply embodied in each social agent becoming part of who they are and may be transposed to a variety of situations (Bourdieu, ([1972] 1977; [1980] 1990). For Bourdieu ([1980] 1990), *habitus* is "structured structures predisposed to function as structuring structures" (p. 53). In other words, *habitus* is one's learned, embodied (automatic) response to the actions of another person in the field. A person's response, like that of a competitive athlete, is not normally thought through—it is drawn from an unconscious, automatic reservoir of knowledge that has been learned and acquired in the past (one simply knows what to do—it is "recipe knowledge"). Following that tacit knowledge of what to do, individuals also reproduce the structured nature of social action. Thus, because social action occurs in a field of actions, *habitus* and the field tend to orchestrate, coordinate, and guide people's actions as they unfold, allowing each person to anticipate others' actions, predict potential outcomes, and largely reproduce social action (what Giddens calls *recursive practices*).

Think for a moment of Sidney Crosby's 2010 "golden goal" described at the beginning of this chapter. Every player involved in that play executed, automatically, what coaches had taught and what they had practised innumerable times in their hockey lives—from novice players all the way to their professional careers. While each player could tell you after the fact what he did and why, the whole play unfolded without any conscious calculation—it all seemed instinctual. But Bourdieu would say it was a perfect example of embodied knowledge, or *habitus*, enacted within a particular social field as required by the players in each position in that field. The reason those players were there, and not others, is because through competition and the development of their cultural capital—their particular skills, reaction time, and knowledge of the game—those were the best players competing for the top spot on the Olympic podium just as other players compete for the top spot in industry, the educational system, the world of art, and so on.

Class Analysis under Giddens and Bourdieu

Both Giddens and Bourdieu recognize the importance of power in social action, and they explicitly address its multifaceted character. They both emphasize that the market is intrinsically a structure of power, but rather than viewing class position solely through the ownership of property, capital, or certain commodities, they conceptualize power as the ability to access and employ various capacities (see Bourdieu [1980] 1990; Bourdieu & Wacquant, 1992; Giddens, 1973). This allows each of them to weave a more complex notion of power through their theories of social inequality, social dynamics, and social change.

Giddens' overall theory of structuration provides the basis for him to maintain the importance of class analysis in sociology while also accounting for other factors in the overall stratification of advanced societies. Like Marx and Weber, Giddens (1973) regards class as a basis for social power and an outcome of the ownership or nonownership of productive resources. In and through their economic, political, and social activities, individuals in capitalist societies recursively reproduce a class structure. Furthermore, in terms of the distribution of power, "property ownership remains of primary importance within the economic order" (Giddens, 1973, pp. 271–272). Moreover, the real ability to own the types of property that generate profit and drive the economy is limited—there are boundaries that, although not impossible in all instances to surmount, tend to recursively (re)produce the class structure.

Second, Giddens (1973) agrees with Weber that divisions within classes can be quite numerous and complex: "Class divisions cannot be drawn like lines on a map, and the extent to which class structuration occurs depends upon the interaction of various sets of factors" (Giddens, 1973, p. 273). But, Giddens emphasizes, "this is *not* the same as saying that class is a 'multidimensional' phenomenon which can be analysed as an aggregate of several hierarchical 'dimensions', as is sometimes claimed by certain of those (mis)interpreters of Weber who identify 'class' and 'stratification'" (p. 273). Class structuration,

Giddens notes "is most strongly developed at three levels, separating the upper, middle and working classes" (p. 273).

Finally, and of most significance, Giddens' notions of the duality of structure and the manner in which formal and informal rules both enable and constrain the recursive social actions that constitute people's daily lives allow Giddens to draw nonclass factors into the analysis of social inequality while keeping them distinct from the impact of class in (re)producing systems of stratification. Gender, racialization, (dis)ability, age, and sexuality, for example, are intertwined with class in the social practices ordered across space and time that constitute social action as a whole. Gender, racialization, (dis)ability, and sexuality must be taken into account in analyzing social action, but not in the same manner that class factors must be accounted for. The unique impact of these nonclass factors should be distinguished from the impact of class because their integration in recursive social practices is different than the rules and resources pertinent to class.

Bourdieu's theory of class builds almost directly from Weber's enhancement of Marx's work. Like Weber and Marx, a class structure exists for Bourdieu—that is, a hierarchical field within which an individual's *habitus* is formed and simultaneously operates—even though individuals in the contemporary period may not all feel that they are embedded in a class structure and sociologists must identify it.

> One must construct the *objective class*, the set of agents who are placed in homogeneous conditions of existence imposing homogenous conditionings and producing homogeneous systems of dispositions capable of generating similar practices; and who possess a set of common properties, objectified properties, sometimes legally guaranteed (as possession of goods and power) or properties embodied as class habitus. (Bourdieu, [1979] 1984, p. 101)

Bourdieu identifies the objective position of classes on the basis of the volume of capital—"the set of actually usable resources"—a group possesses ([1979] 1984, p. 114). He identifies three major forms of capital: economic (money and productive property), social (social and institutionalized networks, group memberships, etc.), and cultural (types of knowledge, cultural goods such as books, or in an institutionalized form as educational qualifications, etc.) (Bourdieu, [1979] 1984; [1983] 1986). These latter two, but social capital in particular, allow Bourdieu to use the notion of class *habitus* to draw together, in a manner that goes beyond Weber, the (inter)relationship of class and status groups (*Stände*) (see Bourdieu, 1966). Social networks, knowledge, and tastes create "communities" in the Weberian sense of the term, and they also create and stem from class *habituses* that will overlap significantly but not necessarily fully with economic capital. The volume of capital possessed and the ability to transpose it from one form to another as needed in different situations creates identifiable class groupings in the contemporary world. It is these particular class groupings, as the next section will indicate, that determine the nature and extent to which particular individuals will engage in sport and physical activity as well as the types of sport and activities they will choose.

Two main points are clear from the above discussion. First, class sounds like and seems to be a simple concept but it proves to be extremely complex, and to understand the impact of class on sport and recreational opportunities and participation, the full complexity of the concept needs to be used. Second, whether one uses Marx's, Weber's,

Giddens', Bourdieu's, or one's own integrated conception drawing upon two or more of these theorists, there are three key elements that one must keep in mind:

1. Class involves an "objective" dimension—one that takes into account where different groupings of individuals are located within an increasingly complex social structure. Those objective conditions play a significant role in determining those individuals' opportunities to take part in social life and the conditions under which they will be involved.

2. Class involves a "subjective" dimension that takes into account that individuals living under similar conditions within the social structure will share a particular, general understanding of who they are and what their life chances are like. Their worldview will not be identical, but it will be close enough that their actions will tend to be very similar.

3. Finally, it is the integration of those objective and subjective dimensions of class that is crucial for understanding how one's social location impacts his or her behavior as a member of a class. This is why sociologists today tend to draw more from Giddens or Bourdieu than they do from Marx or Weber. Giddens and Bourdieu, each in his own way, has tried to explain the nature of the objective dimensions of class in the complex, advanced societies of today; the manner in which those objective conditions create subjective understandings of the social world and the potential opportunity structure; and how the objective and subjective dimensions of class impact each other.

CLASS AND SPORT: CURRENT PATTERNS OF ENGAGEMENT

The most recent comprehensive reports on class and sport participation are from an analysis done by the Conference Board of Canada of Statistics Canada's 2004 National Household Survey on Participation in Sport (Bloom, Grant, & Watt, 2005); Ifedi's (2008) study of Statistics Canada data on sport participation; Hernandez, Berger, Brissette, O'Reilly, Parent, and Séguin's (2008) longitudinal analysis of sport participation in Canada using Statistics Canada's General Social Survey data from 1992 to 2005; and a report released by Canadian Heritage (2013) that also draws from Statistics Canada's General Social Survey data for 2010. When the results of all these studies and reports are combined with the most recent information available through Statistics Canada (2013b), the impact of class on sport participation is clearly evident.

The Bloom, Grant, and Watt (2005) report begins in an upbeat manner, noting that more than 8 million Canadians took part in sport in 2004—"about half the entire population of Canada . . . including 55 per cent of adults" (p. 1). But a few paragraphs later, the study notes that between 1992 and 2004, the percentage of Canadians aged 16 or older actively involved in sport fell from 45% to 31%. Ifedi's (2008) report indicates that a year later the participation rate had dropped to 28%, and the Canadian Heritage (2013) report shows that in 2010 only 7.2 million, or 26%, of Canadians aged 15 years and older were involved in sport.

Hernandez and colleagues (2008) also document, in detail, the declining involvement of Canadians in sport. For example, they indicate that the rate of participation among Canadians aged 15 to 19 fell from 75% in 1992 to 58% in 2005. The decrease for Canadians aged 20 to 24 fell from 62% to 42%, and for Canadians aged 25 to 29 the decrease was from 55% to 35%. The most recent data show further declines in participation. Canadian Heritage (2013) reports that in 2005, 58% of Canadians aged 15 to 19 were involved in sport, but that fell to 54% in 2010. There was a similar decline (from 42% to 37%) for Canadians aged 20 to 24, a 2% drop to 29% and 23%, respectively, for Canadians aged 25 to 34 and 35 to 54, and a 1% drop to 17% for the 55 and older age group.

Examining the data on sport involvement in 2005 and 2010 more closely reveals a further concern. If the total time spent in sport is averaged across all Canadians, then in 2005, on average, Canadians spent 30 minutes a day playing sports (Statistics Canada, 2013b). When one focuses solely on those who actually took part in sport and average their time across all active participants, then those Canadians spent, on average, two hours a day involved with sport. By 2010, however, although the time spent on sport averaged across all Canadians had not changed, the time spent averaged across the actual sport participants had dropped to under an hour a day (Canadian Heritage, 2013). In other words, even those taking part in sport were spending less time on sporting activities per day in 2010 than was the case in 2005.

Probing further, all of the studies show a direct relationship between class and sport participation. Consistent with Bourdieu's idea of "economic capital" and Giddens's conception of "allocative resources," Bloom, Grant, and Watt (2005) indicate the extent to which sport participation is tied to class. They point out that 55% of Canadians in households with annual incomes above $100,000 are involved in sport, with participation rates of 46% and 42%, respectively, for families with annual household income between $80,000–$99,999 and $60,000–$79,999. The participation rate drops to 36% for families with annual income between $40,000–$59,999 and another 10% where incomes are between $20,000–$39,999. Less than 22% of Canadians in families with incomes less than $20,000 participate in sport.

The participation rates shown in the Canadian Heritage (2013) report are even more striking. In 2010, only 7% of individuals living in families with household incomes below $20,000 per year participated in sport. In the $20,000–$29,999 range, only 15% of Canadians are involved in sport. Under one in five Canadians living in households with incomes of $30,000–$49,999 take part in sport, rising to one in four in families with household incomes of $50,000–$79,999. One-third of individuals in households with incomes higher than $80,000 engage regularly in sport. All of these rates of participation are lower than just five years earlier.

The vast majority of Canadians involved in sport today began that association in childhood. Sport participation among youths and adults requires particular types of cultural capital and embodied knowledge, to use Bourdieu's terms, so early childhood involvement in sport is critical to an ongoing involvement through the life cycle. The Canadian Heritage (2013) report demonstrates the impact of class on children's involvement in sport: "The lower the household income, the less likely it is that children will participate in sport and the higher the household income the more likely it is that children will participate in sport" (p. 38). In 2010, less than two-thirds (58%) of the children in families with household incomes under $40,000 took part in sport, while almost three in four (72%) children in households with incomes between $40,000–$79,999 played sports and 85% of children in families earning $80,000 or more took part in organized sport. From Giddens' perspective, the class basis of early childhood sport participation allows children from upper-income homes to develop the tacit knowledge necessary to easily participate in a variety of physical activities, whereas children from lower-income homes do not have the opportunity to internalize the informal rules and resources needed to engage, unobtrusively, in various forms of sport.

Most elite athletes come from affluent families.
Monkey Business/Fotolia

The Escalating Cost of Sport

While Canadians are becoming less involved in sport and active forms of leisure, they are spending more to participate. The average, active Canadian family spent just under $2,000 in 2004 on sport, which was one-third more than eight years earlier (Bloom, Grant, & Watt, 2005). This represents a significant increase since 1996 when the money spent on sport participation amounted to 0.9% of Canada's gross domestic product compared to 1.22% in 2004 (Bloom, Grant & Watt, 2005). Although there are no systematic, scholarly studies documenting the rising cost of sport involvement, journalists in various media continually lament the problem. Hockey, Canada's national winter sport, is growing in popularity among girls and is the most high-profile instance of the impact of increased costs, class position, and rates of participation.

Equipment costs for hockey can be prohibitive—especially in the important, early, formative years of athletic participation where children are also growing rapidly and outgrow equipment quickly (sometimes within a single season)—especially if parents buy what is thought of as top-of-the-line equipment. Even a parent who follows the sage advice of investing in a good, well-fitted helmet and good-quality skates while saving on shin, shoulder, and elbow pads, pants, mouth and neck guards, gloves, socks, sweaters, and sticks will still incur "startup costs" between $300 and $600 in most instances. And this is for the forwards and defencemen—the costs for goalies are even higher. In the youngest age groups, associations or teams supply goalie equipment for house league players, but the road to "rep hockey" becomes increasingly expensive as players have to purchase their own pads, mask, stick, gloves, and chest and arm pads. To get a sense of the cost, a junior goalie "combo set"—leg pads and gloves—will cost almost $400 new.

But it is not equipment costs alone that make hockey an increasingly class-based sport; it is the "hockey system" (the field in Bourdieu's terms), which consists of hockey leagues and players from house league (the lowest level) up through "select," "A," "AA," and "AAA" in the minor hockey system. The field sorts and filters out players as they move from "initiation" to novice, minor and major atom, minor and major pee wee, minor and major bantam, minor

The cost of sport is prohibitive for many Canadian families.
SHAUN BISSON/THE OBSERVER/QMI AGENCY

midget, and then junior (or major midget for those not good enough to make the jump to junior). Costs that include equipment, team registration fees, travel, accommodation, hockey schools, specific training programs, and off-season hockey programs—that is, the costs of successfully making one's way toward the top of the field—can be considerable with the odds of a financial return very slim. Parcels's (2002) study of the cohort of boys born in 1975 and playing hockey in Ontario showed that of 22,000 registered players, only 132 made it to leagues that feed the NHL and a mere *seven* made it to "The Show"—that is, 0.03% of the cohort made it to the NHL (see also Total Sports Management, 2013). The sorting/competitive process is partly about skills but it is also centres on resources (allocative and distributive resources in Giddens' terms, economic, symbolic, and cultural capital in Bourdieu's terms).

Fees for house league hockey tend to range from $350 to $700 per player; playing a step higher in an A or AA rep program will cost between $1,000 and $2,000; AAA team fees range from $2,500 to $5,000 per season (Rutherford, 2009). None of these fees include transportation costs, snacks, meals, hotel accommodation for tournaments, and extra tournament entry fees—or, as is the case in some jurisdictions, the admission fee a parent must pay to watch his or her child's games ($6 in the Greater Toronto Hockey League—see Gillmor, 2013). A Royal Bank of Canada (2011) survey found that, on average, Canadian families pay $1,500 per year per child to play hockey. For those who had not kept their child in hockey, cost was cited as the major reason.

Gillmor (2013) writes that although hockey is still thought of as a blue-collar sport, that is no longer true. "Even the middle class has trouble keeping up with the costs. At the highest level, it has become a rich man's game." The best players, one AAA coach in the Greater Toronto Hockey League points out, are from high SES families. "They don't necessarily have a lot of drive, they're just incredibly skilled. And they're afforded the opportunity to have the best instructors, and that is their advantage. Their advantage is that they have money" (cited in Gillmor, 2013). That sentiment is shared by league administrators across Canada. "The one-income family kid is not playing hockey, generally speaking," according to Jack Casey, the president of St. John's Minor Hockey Association. "They can't afford it. That's the bottom line" (cited in Rutherford, 2009). "Most of the parents of kids who play hockey, and particularly the kid who plays all-star hockey," he continues, "the parents are all professional people, they're doing very well. They have to be doing well."

Murray Costello, the retired president of Hockey Canada, has echoed the point that cost is a leading factor in declining hockey registrations. "Hockey is becoming an opportunity only for the people who can pay their way in" (cited in MacGregor, 2012). Bloom, Grant, and Watt (2005) are equally blunt about the role of income and cost in sports participation: "People with higher incomes are much more likely to participate in sport than people who earn less" (p. 4).

Sports like soccer and basketball are less expensive, although depending on the brand, shoes can cost a considerable amount and all the extras from transportation, snacks, and tournament costs quickly add up even for house league players. These costs provide some insight into why economic circumstances influence the conditions under which a child competes with others for the prized spots at the top of the sport pyramid.

Canadian Heritage (2013) underscores the intersection of class, cost, and sport participation when it identifies the 10 most popular sports in Canada for Canadians age 15 and older. Golf is first, followed by hockey, soccer, baseball, volleyball, basketball, downhill skiing, cycling, swimming, and badminton. Of these, golf, hockey, downhill skiing, and cycling carry significant economic costs. They also lead into a discussion of Giddens' and Bourdieu's theories of social stratification and how factors other than income lead to inequitable rates of participation in sport among different identifiable groupings of Canadians. Clearly money is a major factor, but gender, ethnic background, physical ability, and the impact of racialization also influence where people will become involved, how intensively they will participate, and the long-term goals they will establish for that particular activity. All of these factors, whether one thinks in terms of *habitus* and field or the recursive practices that are associated with the duality of structure, impact who takes part in sport and who strives for the top of the high-performance pyramid.

Conclusions

Prior to Alexandre Bilodeau's emotional gold-medal performance in the moguls at the 2010 Vancouver Winter Olympics, Canada was the only country that had failed to win a gold medal while hosting the Olympics. When the IOC granted the 2010 Games to Vancouver, the Canadian Olympic Committee (COC), Sport Canada, and some select commercial sponsors committed themselves to improving Canada's performances at the Games. The third-place finish at the 2006 Torino Olympics (24 medals, 7 gold) was an improvement over the last three winter Olympiads—fifth in 2002 (17 medals, 6 gold), fourth in 1998 (15 medals, 6 gold), and sixth in 1994 (13 medals, 3 gold). And it was a dramatic improvement over recent summer Olympic rankings—21st in 2004 (12 medals, 3 gold), 21st in 2000 (14 medals, 3 gold), and 11th in 1996 (22 medals, 3 gold). To establish Canada as a world leader in high-performance sport, the COC launched Own the Podium, a program that explicitly committed the COC and Canada's athletes to the pursuit of gold. Own the Podium, the COC emphasized, is a "technical program designed to help Canada become the number one nation in terms of medals won at the 2010 Olympic Winter Games, and to place in the top three countries overall at the 2010 Paralympic Winter Games" (Vancouver 2010, 2006).

A great deal of Canada's success at the 2010 Games, where Canada set a Winter Games record of 14 gold medals along with 7 silver and 5 bronze, was attributed to Own the Podium. The program was a dramatic change in philosophy within the Canadian Olympic movement because the pursuit of gold became an overt objective—reaching the top of the sport meritocracy was a stated goal. The new approach would generate a new level of accountability for the funds Sport Canada and the COC invested in high-performance sport.

Own the Podium targeted particular sports where Canada had been successful, providing financial support for athletes who had demonstrated podium potential. That "hot house" approach did not, however, produce the same level of success in London two years later. Rosannagh MacLennan's trampoline victory was Canada's only gold, and the overall medal total of 18 placed Canada 13th—below the COC's objective of 12th.

To enjoy long-term success in international sport, the base of the Canadian sport pyramid must be broadened. But as levels of sport involvement drop, the base will shrink rather than expand. Moreover, declining sport involvement is not a problem that programs like Own the Podium or Sport Canada funding could ever solve. The "hollowing out" or shrinking of the middle class in Canada changes the profile of a number of Canadian institutions, including sport in general and high-performance sport in particular. Rebuilding the middle of the Canadian income and class structure can only come about through a revitalization of the Canadian economy as a whole, although even a revitalized economy will not eliminate the problematic realities of inequality of condition for aspiring athletes in the bottom of the Canadian class structure. The intimate and problematic relationship between sport participation and social class may mean that golden moments like Sidney Crosby's gold-winning goal will become increasingly rare.

Critical Thinking Questions

1. Do you think that Canada is a class-based society? Why or why not?
2. How much money have you spent taking part in sporting activities in the past 12 months?
3. Has the cost of sport or sporting equipment ever affected your participation in sport?
4. What is a meritocracy? Is the Canadian sport system a meritocracy?
5. What is meant by the term *equality of opportunity*, and what factors in Canada prevent a true equality of opportunity in sport?
6. What is meant by the term *equality of condition*, and what factors in Canada prevent a true equality of condition in sport?
7. What are the main features of Canada's current income structure?
8. What are the main features of Karl Marx's theory of class?
9. How did Max Weber's theory of class build on Marx's theory, and what are the main differences between the two theories?
10. What are the main features of Anthony Giddens' theory of class?
11. What are the main features of Pierre Bourdieu's theory of class?
12. What types of cultural and economic capital do you have to draw upon that influence your participation in sport?
13. How does class influence rates of sport participation in Canada?
14. How might Canada's current class structure prevent Canada from fielding the best Olympic teams possible despite government programs like Own the Podium, which are designed to enhance Canadian performances in international events?

Suggested Readings

Gruneau, R. (1999). *Class, sports, and social development*. Champaign, IL: Human Kinetics.

Lemel, Y., & Noll, H. (Eds.). (2002). *Changing structures of inequality: A comparative perspective*. Montreal, QC: McGill–Queen's University Press.

Osmani, S. (2001). On inequality. In J. Blau (Ed.), *The Blackwell companion to sociology* (pp. 143–160). Oxford, UK: Blackwell.

References

Autor, D., Manning, A., & Smith, C. L. (2010). The contribution of the minimum wage to U.S. wage inequality over three decades: A reassessment. *Finance and Economics Discussion Series*. Washington, DC: Federal Reserve Board. Retrieved from http://www.federalreserve.gov/pubs/feds/2010/201060/201060pap.pdf.

Beamish, R. (1990). The persistence of inequality: An analysis of participation among Canada's high-performance athletes. *International Review for the Sociology of Sport, 25*, 143–155.

Bloom, M., Grant, M., & Watt, D. (2005). *Strengthening Canada: The socio-economic benefits of sport participation in Canada*. Conference Board of Canada. Retrieved from http://www.conference-board.ca/e-library/abstract.aspx?did=1340.

Boudarbat, B., Lemieux, T., & Riddell, W. (2010). The evolution of the returns to human capital in Canada, 1980–2005. *Canadian Public Policy, 36*, 63–89.

Bourdieu, P. (1966). Condition de classe et position de classe. *Archives Européennes de Sociologie, 7*, 201–223.

Bourdieu, P. ([1972] 1977). *Outline of a theory of practice*. Cambridge, UK: Cambridge University Press.

Bourdieu, P. (1973). The three forms of theoretical knowledge. *Social Science Information, 12*, 53–80.

Bourdieu, P. ([1979] 1984). *Distinction: A social critique of the judgement of taste*. Cambridge, MA: Harvard University Press.

Bourdieu, P. ([1980] 1990). *The logic of practice*. Stanford, CA: Stanford University Press.

Bourdieu, P. ([1983] 1986). The forms of capital. In J. Richardson (Ed.), *Handbook of theory and research for the sociology of education*, (pp. 241–258). New York, NY: Greenwood Press.

Bourdieu, P. (1989). Social space and symbolic power. *Sociological Theory, 7*, 14–25.

Bourdieu, P. (1993). *Sociology in question*. London, UK: Sage Publications.

Bourdieu, P. (2000) *Pascalian meditations*. Stanford, CA: Stanford University Press.

Bourdieu, P., & Wacquant, L. (1992). *An invitation to reflexive sociology*. Chicago, IL: University of Chicago Press.

Brooks, E. (2007). *Unraveling the garment industry: Transnational organizing and women's work*. Minneapolis, MN: University of Minnesota Press.

Canadian Heritage. (2013). *Sport participation 2010: Research paper*. Retrieved from http://publications.gc.ca/pub?id=434212&sl=0

Card, D., Lemieux, T., & Riddell, C. (2004). Unionization and wage inequality: A comparative study of the US, UK and Canada. *Journal of Labor Research, 25*, 519–559.

Cohen, G. (1980). *Karl Marx's theory of history: A defence*. Oxford, UK: Clarendon Press.

Conference Board of Canada. (2012). *Canadian income inequality: Is Canada becoming more unequal?* Retrieved from http://www.conferenceboard.ca/hcp/hot-topics/caninequality.aspx.

Dahrendorf, R. (1959). *Class and class conflict in industrial society*. Stanford CA: Stanford University Press.

Dos Santos, T. (1970). The concept of social classes. *Science and Society, 34*, 166–193.

Draper, H. (1978). *Karl Marx's theory of revolution: The politics of social classes*. New York, NY: Monthly Review Press.

EKOS Research Associates. (1992). *The status of the high-performance athlete in Canada: Final report*. Ottawa, ON: Sport Canada Directorate, Fitness and Amateur Sport.

Engels, F. ([1845] 1950). *Condition of the working class in England in 1844*. London, UK: G. Allen and Unwin.

Florida, R. (2002). *The rise of the creative class: And how it's transforming work, leisure, community, and everyday life*. New York, NY: Basic Books.

Fortin, N., Green, D., Lemieux, T., Milligan, K., & Riddell, C. (2012). Canadian inequality: Recent developments and policy options. *Canadian Public Policy, 38*, 121–145.

Giddens, A. (1973). *The class structure of the advanced societies*. London, UK: Hutchinson.

Giddens, A. (1976). Functionalism: Après la lutte. *Social Research, 43*, 325–366.

Giddens, A. (1979). *Central problems in social theory*. London, UK: The Macmillan Press.

Giddens, A. (1984). *The constitution of society*. Berkeley, CA: University of California Press.

Gillmor, D. (2013). Is minor hockey worth it? *Toronto Star*. Retrieved from http://www.thestar.com/news/insight/2013/01/11/is_minor_hockey_worth_it.html.

Goldin, C., & Katz, L. (2008). *The race between education and technology*. Cambridge, MA: Harvard University Press.

Goos, M., & Manning, A. (2007). Lousy and lovely jobs: The rising polarization of work in Britain. *Review of Economics and Statistics, 89*, 118–133.

Grabell, M. (2013). How the temp workers who power America's corporate giants are getting crushed. *Financial Post*. Retrieved from http://business.financialpost.com/2013/07/05/how-the-temp-workers-who-power-americas-corporate-giants-are-getting-crushed.

Green, D., & Sand, B. (2011). *Has the Canadian labour market polarized?* Ottawa, ON: Human Resources and Skills Development Canada.

Greenberg, J. & Knight, G. (2004). Framing sweatshops: Nike, global production, and the American news media. *Communication and Critical/Cultural Studies, 1*, 151–175.

Gruneau, R. (1972). *An analysis of Canada Games' Athletes, 1971*. Unpublished master's thesis, University of Calgary, Calgary, AB.

Harvey, D. (2007). *A brief history of neoliberalism*. Oxford, UK: Oxford University Press.

Hernandez, T., Berger, I., Brissette, C., O'Reilly, N., Parent, M., & Séguin, B. (2008). Sport participation in Canada: A longitudinal cohort analysis. Presented at the Administrative Sciences Association of Canada Annual Conference, Halifax. Retrieved from http://ojs.acadiau.ca/index.php/ASAC/article/view/919/802.

Hunter, G., Sanchez, M., & Douglas, F. (2012). Incomes of the one per cent (and everyone else) in Canada. *Poverty Papers 5*. Regina, SK: Social Policy Research Unit, University of Regina.

Ifedi, F. (2008). *Sport participation in Canada, 2005*. Ottawa, ON: Statistics Canada, Culture, Tourism and the Centre for Educational Statistics.

Kaufman, P. & Wolff, E. (2010). Playing and protesting: Sport as a vehicle for social change. *Journal of Sport and Social Issues, 34*, 154–175.

Kenyon, G. (1977). Factors influencing the attainment of elite track status in track and field. *Post-Olympic Conference Proceedings*. Ottawa, ON: Coaching Association of Canada.

Keynes, J. (1936). *The general theory of employment, interest and money*. New York, NY: Harcourt, Brace.

Krugman, P. (2009). *The conscience of a liberal*. New York, NY: W. W. Norton & Company.

MacGregor, R. (2012). Increasingly high cost of hockey is making the game an elitist sport. *Globe and Mail*. Retrieved from http://www.theglobeandmail.com/sports/hockey/increasingly-high-cost-of-hockey-is-making-the-game-an-elitist-sport/article5864491/.

Marx, K. ([1847] 1936). *The poverty of philosophy*. London, UK: Martin Lawrence Limited.

Marx, K. ([1852]) 1934). Marx to Weydemeyer. In *Karl Marx and Friedrich Engels correspondence 1846–1895*, Marx-Engels-Lenin Institute (Ed.), (pp. 55–58). London, UK: Martin Lawrence Ltd.

Marx, K. ([1852] 1935). *The eighteenth brumaire of Louis Bonaparte*. New York, NY: International Publishers.

Marx, K. ([1859] 1911). *A contribution to the critique of political economy*. Chicago, IL: Charles H. Kerr & Company Co-operative.

Marx, K. ([1894] 1909). *Capital, vol. 3*. Chicago, IL: Charles H. Kerr & Company Co-operative.

Marx, K. & Engels, F. ([1845] 1939). *The German ideology*. New York, NY: International Publishers.

McPherson, B. (1977). Factors influencing the attainment of elite hockey status. *Post-Olympic Conference Proceedings*. Ottawa, ON: Coaching Association of Canada.

Munro, J. (1970). *A proposed sports policy for Canadians*. Ottawa: Ministry of Health and Welfare.

Parcels, J. (2002). Chances of making it in pro hockey. Retrieved from http://www.cumberlandminorhockey.ca/to_the_nhl/chances.htm.

Royal Bank of Canada. (2011). RBC survey: 82 per cent of Canadian hockey households believe more support needed from corporate Canada. Press release. Retrieved from http://www.rbc.com/newsroom/2011/1206-grant-hockey.html.

Rutherford, K. (2009). Is the cost keeping kids out of minor hockey? Absolutely, players and parents say. *CBC Sports*. Retrieved from http://www.cbc.ca/sports/hockey/ourgame/story/2009/01/16/hockey-costs-too-much.html.

Statistics Canada. (2009). *The Canadian labour market at a glance*. Retrieved from http://www.statcan.gc.ca/pub/71-222-x/71-222-x2008001-eng.pdf.

Statistics Canada. (2013a). Labour force survey estimates. Retrieved from http://www5.statcan.gc.ca/cansim/pick-choisir?lang=eng&p2=33&id=2820080.

Statistics Canada. (2013b). Time spent on various activities. Retrieved from http://www.statcan.gc.ca/tables-tableaux/sum-som/l01/cst01/famil36a-eng.htm.

Thompson, E. P. (1963). *The making of the English working class*. London, UK: V. Gollancz.

Total Sports Management. (2013). So, you want to play pro hockey! Retrieved from http://www.totalsportsmgmt.com/pro-hockey.

Vancouver 2010. (2006). *Own the Podium—2010*. Retrieved from http://www.vancouver2010.com/en/WinterGames/OwnPodium.

Von Mises, L. (1934). *The theory of money and credit*. London, UK: J. Cape.

Washington, R. & Karen, D. (2001). Sport and society. *Annual Review of Sociology, 27*, 187–212.

Weber, M. (1968). *Economy and society*. New York, NY: Bedminster Press.

White, P., & Curtis, J. (1990). Participation in competitive sport among Anglophones and Francophones in Canada: Testing competing hypotheses. *International Review for the Sociology of Sport, 25*, 125–143.

Whitson, D. (2011). Changing notions of public goods: Paying for public recreation. Paper presented at the 2011 National Recreation Summit, October 23–26, Lake Louise, AB. Retrieved from http://lin.ca/sites/default/files/attachments/Whitson_Dave%5B1%5D.pdf.

Wilson, T. (2002). The paradox of social class and sports involvement. *International Review for the Sociology of Sport, 37*, 5–16.

Yalnizyan, A. (2010). *The rise of Canada's richest 1%*. Ottawa, ON: Canadian Centre for Policy Alternatives. Retrieved from http://www.policyalternatives.ca/publications/reports/risecanadas-richest-1.

Daniel Igali waves our national flag at the 2000 Sydney Olympic Games after winning Canada's first-ever gold medal in freestyle wrestling.
Reuters

We all have individual characteristics that differentiate us from or connect us to others. Hair colour, gender, height, skin colour, ethnicity, and eye colour are a few examples of such characteristics. Think of how you would describe yourself for a minute. When we thought about this question, Vicky described herself as female, brown haired, hazel eyed, 5'4", urban Canadian, and white. Susan described her physical attributes in a similar way, but she lives in a rural community. Yet as each of us live out or "do" our lives, those individual characteristics are continually reshaped by our experiences. For example, Vicky recollects how some children have considered her tall, while adults often claim that she is short. Her eye colour varies with what she wears, and her ethnicity has been shaped by years in the Canadian north and the specific cultural practices she learned there and continues to do. She is also often quizzed about her race, because of her research into First Nations peoples. Susan notes that her studies of Canadian immigrants and children in those immigrant families help her to reflect on what is meaningful in her own life, having been raised within a large extended Italian Canadian family. So while, when asked, we can each describe our individual characteristics, that description changes over time and from the perspectives of others. We continuously construct the ways we see ourselves, and that involves the social world in which we live. Our individual characteristics are much less definitive than we might at first think.

Some of these characteristics take on a particular social significance in our society. While eye colour remains unimportant at a social level, characteristics such as ethnicity and skin colour—or race—have become socially constructed markers of difference. Persistent patterns of unequal treatment have developed around them, in North American society and in sport. Individuals assigned those characteristics get identified as part of a group that shares traits differentiating it from others. Our sense of ourselves is thus constructed in relation to groups we believe are similar to or different from us.

We know ourselves and our culture in part through our bodies. For example, as we "do" physical activities, such as sports, we shape, reinforce, or challenge the understanding we—and others—hold about our racial and ethnic identities. Students in a physical education class learning basketball all perform the same activities, but the ways those movements reinforce or challenge each individual's sense of his or her own race and ethnicity influences the meaning assigned to those movements and the enjoyment felt or not felt within the class. After school, an Asian youth may head to a program where she participates with others from her ethnic background in activities tied to her cultural roots. Through this process, she reinforces the importance of her ethnic identity in a manner that was not possible in her earlier gym class on basketball. A black male student practising with the school basketball team at the end of the day feels confirmed as a talented athlete as he emulates the playing styles of his favourite NBA players. Another student heads home to spend time with her family, having no interest in afterschool athletics. Day after day, these students continue to know themselves and to represent themselves to others through their involvement or noninvolvement in physical activities.

This chapter explores the relationships among movement, race, and ethnicity in Canada. It builds on two assumptions. First, we believe that movement opportunities in Canada, such as sport, potentially provide the opportunity for all individuals to generate a feeling of pride in their cultural heritage. However, the sport system has been structured so that some individuals—specifically white Canadians of European descent—are privileged to feel racial and ethnic pride more so than others, although these hegemonic patterns (like all social relations) are slowly changing. Second, we encourage our readers to enter into a reflective process through which they can better understand how ethnicity and race are constructed in our society and in sport. By doing so, they can more knowledgeably shape their own identities while honouring the individual identities desired by others—prerequisites for shifting existing hegemonic, unequal ethnic and racial relations and creating an inclusive, multicultural sport system in Canada.

ETHNICITY AND SPORT IN CANADA

The Concept of Ethnicity

Sport is one of the most popular leisure activities Canadians enjoy. Whether we enjoy sport as spectators, as recreational participants, or as elite athletes, Canadians are extremely interested and invested in sports. Our ethnic identity shapes and is shaped by our sport participation. Ethnicity refers to the values, beliefs, and behaviours we share in common with a subcultural group to which we most closely identify based on common country of origin, language, religion, or cultural traditions (Hutchison, 1988). Ethnicity takes into account our religious practices, our clothing, our accents and language, the food we eat, and what we value as a result of our cultural heritage. Ethnicity, like race, has social significance in our society. To understand ethnicity and sport we need to know about ethnicity in general and how one's ethnic identity may influence decisions and preferences around sport participation. We also benefit from knowing about past trends and theory developed to explain trends or beliefs about ethnicity.

Everyone can be linked to at least one ethnic group, whether it is one of the dominant European, white, English- or French-speaking groups, or one of the more than 200 other ethnic groups known to exist in this country (Statistics Canada, 2011). The scope of Canada's extraordinary national diversity was evident in the 2011 National Household Survey (NHS) when more than 20% of the population reported being foreign born and 19.1% of Canadians identified themselves as visible minorities (Statistics Canada, 2013c). Thanks to unprecedented levels of immigration, especially in Canadian "arrival cities" (Saunders, 2010), 13 ethnic groups surpassed the 1 million mark in Canada (Statistics Canada, 2011). As new immigrants arrive in Canada from non-Western countries and as the number of people who identify with diverse racial and ethnic groups grows, ethnic diversity in sport is one of the many parts of social life that is changing.

Diversity Theories

With the passing of the Multiculturalism Act of 1988, Canada officially declared its support for cultural freedom of minority peoples. The term *cultural pluralism*, first introduced in 1915 by Horace Kallen, refers to the approach our country takes with regard to receiving and welcoming immigrants. It means that in Canada, we support newcomers in preserving their cultural identity if they choose to do so (Glazer, 1970). Our approach differs from that of our neighbours to the south. In the United States, immigrants are expected to shed their unique cultural practices, adopt new ones based on the values and beliefs of the host country, and as a result of this process of assimilation contribute toward building a better nation. This second approach is commonly referred to as the *melting pot* perspective (Glazer, 1970). Cultural pluralism, on the other hand, recognizes that for many newcomers meaningful experience incorporates "'stubborn chunks' of cultural practice and preference, and is more like a chowder than a melting pot" (Bhabha, 1994, p. 219). Some aspects of life, of course, do change with immersion in the host culture. But other cultural "chunks" remain intact and provide the basis on which some minority people create cultures "in between" that of the dominant majority and the cultures known to the migrants in their homeland (Bhabha, 1994; Hollingshead, 1998).

As a result of our legislation, Canadians officially support physical cultural practices like sport, dance, music, and religious expressions that are meaningful to people of all minority cultural groups and are meaningful to the experience of leisure. However, Claude Denis (1997) challenges this description of Canada, instead labelling it a "whitestream" society because it has been primarily structured on the basis of European white experiences. In keeping with Denis's hegemonic framing of the nature of ethnic and race relations in

Canada, academics and practitioners have only recently begun to explore the meaning of leisure from the perspective of immigrant groups, as well as ethnic minority physical activity practices and the challenges they face related to discrimination, racism, and indifference from dominant group Canadians in mainstream sport.

In spite of Canada's policy of multiculturalism, many immigrants and those who identify as racial and ethnic minority people strive to take on characteristics of their host culture to improve the likelihood that they will "fit in." *Assimilation* is the term used when immigrants adopt the culture of the dominant group (Li, 1990). The underlying assumption of assimilation theory is that ethnically distinct cultural traditions are detrimental to one's ability to fit in and that it is not desirable to be different. This assimilationist approach, which reproduces existing hegemonic social relations, is problematic because it normalizes mainstream cultural practices as the "appropriate" behaviour for all. As well, as new immigrant groups arrive in places like Canada, looking and sounding different from dominant groups, it is not always possible to fit in and become like the majority since race, culture, and behavioural diversity sets newcomers apart. In our discussion, "dominant" refers to those people in Canada who hold the power to make decisions and to exert control over others.

Terminology used in this discussion is worth explanation. We use the word *minority* when referring to people who identify with non-European-white groups and individuals. We realize the problematic nature of this term, since most the world's population is non-European-white. However, in Canada most people identify as European-white, and since terms like *minority racial and ethnic groups* tend to be commonly used in Canada we continue to use these terms.

In trying to understand the behaviour of ethnic minority people, researchers have relied primarily on two theoretical perspectives: *marginality theory* and *ethnicity theory*. Marginality theory suggests that the differences in participation in dominant cultural activities are due to the poverty experienced by many minority racial and ethnic people, which is a function of the discrimination they face in accessing training and education as well as jobs. Therefore, under-participation in activities like sport is thought to be due to their marginalization in society. This perspective helps explain why some minority group Canadians do not choose the same sports as the dominant majority population. However, it falls short when applied to those immigrants and ethnic minority people who are not poor and who have somewhat different sport participation patterns, such as South Asian Canadians who play field hockey, cricket, and other sports that are not popular among dominant group Canadians but are growing in popularity among people who identify with Canada's ethnic populations (Tirone & Pedlar, 2000). For example, the popularity of cricket is on the rise across Canada, and in 2012 Cricket Canada is reported to have proposed that a cricket stadium be built in Toronto (*Maclean's*, 2012).

Ethnicity theory is based on Washburne's (1978) thesis that differences in leisure between dominant and minority populations are the result of variations in the value systems and social norms of the minority groups. This approach suggests that ethnic subgroups interact with dominant cultural groups for school, jobs, commerce, and when needs cannot be met within the subgroup. However, many ethnic minority people maintain their distinct cultural traditions and pass them along to their children and subsequent generations. Using this approach, researchers compare behaviours such as sport participation patterns of ethnic minority people to the leisure experience of dominant group members. Problematic here is that the leisure of the white, Eurocentric majority is held as the norm and minority people are considered as "others" for the sake of comparisons, similar to the "whitestream," hegemonic approach mentioned earlier. This approach fails to explore the unique opportunities for leisure evident in minority cultural groups as a result of their cultural heritage.

We have found that "whitestream sport" is a useful concept for analyzing race and ethnic relations in Canadian sport because it emphasizes that the existing hegemonic sport system is primarily structured by and most effective for individuals who align with white, European values. Additionally, marginality theory identifies that poverty plays a role in limiting access to mainstream sport for some minority ethnic groups. Finally, ethnicity theory emphasizes that the differing value systems of immigrant Canadians can lead to different preferences for sport or different ways of organizing and playing mainstream sports. The pattern of immigration trends in Canada helps to explain how whitestream Canadian society has been created, and also how it is challenged by increasingly diverse minority group Canadians.

Immigration Trends

In the early part of the 20th century, Canada's economic, industrial, agricultural, and commercial growth and development was fuelled by many waves of immigrants seeking a better life than what was available in their countries of origin. Canada recruited its first large wave of immigrants from Great Britain, Europe, and the United States. However, changes to immigration patterns occurred in the last decades of the 20th century and first years of the 21st century when migration flows shifted. New waves of immigrants tended to move from "east" to "west" (i.e., from former Soviet Union and Eastern bloc countries to the United States, Canada, and Israel), and from countries of the "south" to countries of the "north" (such as from South Asia to Canada) (Chiswick & Miller, 2002). The immigrants of the new millennium often look and sound different from the dominant groups, and their distinctiveness in terms of skin colour, language, clothing, religion, and other cultural practices has often resulted in their marginalization.

To learn the language skills necessary for job attainment and to achieve a sense of belonging, immigrant groups may initially cluster into concentrated areas of similar immigrants or ethnic enclaves. Here they find important sources of social support, whether that be in employment opportunities, leisure such as sport participation, education, or shelter (Chiswick & Miller, 2002; Rosenberg, 2003). Ethnic enclaves and institutionally complete ethnic communities have been well established in Canada since the earliest minority group settlers arrived here (Breton, 1964). Communities considered to have high levels of institutional completeness are those in which a range of social supports and relevant services are available to minority people, and often these are delivered within well-established ethnic enclaves. This is what happened in the case of early Jewish, Italian, and German immigrants who formed small communities or enclaves in some of the major Canadian cities. Within the enclaves, people were able to access culturally and ethnically relevant social services, familiar food, and familiar religious and cultural traditions, all delivered in the language of their homeland and by people with common ethnic roots. For example, late 19th- and early 20th-century Jewish immigrants to Toronto settled primarily in the district known as St. John's Ward, where they experienced abysmal housing conditions but had the benefit of social supports such as language, religion, food, music, and other cultural goods that were familiar to them and which facilitated their settlement

(Rosenberg, 2003). Sport organizations operated by ethnic community associations provided youth important opportunities for affirming membership within their own ethnic group and for drawing together people from diverse ethnic groups around common sport interests (Rosenberg, 2003). Those who enter a host community without the help of friends and family members from their country of origin may find they have no alternative but to try to assimilate quickly into the dominant society, although that process is likely to be extraordinarily challenging (Chiswick & Miller, 2002).

We note that among second- and third-generation immigrants there does not seem to be the same degree of interest in living within an enclave. This may be attributed to the high level of educational accomplishments of the children of many groups of immigrants, which is particularly evident in studies of children of immigrants from China, South Asia, and other Asian groups. However, difficulties in achieving job mobility are evident among Afro-Caribbean blacks and some other minorities relative to their educational achievements (Reitz, Zhang, & Hawkins, 2011).

The available information from the 2011 census does not distinguish between those who report a single ethnicity and those who report multiple ethnic identities, which masks our ability to clearly understand the complexity of ethnic identity in Canada. This identification with more than one ethnic minority group, sometimes referred to as *hybridity* or *part cultures* (Bhabha, 1994), is a growing trend that will undoubtedly affect the participation of Canadians in cultural activities and sporting events in years to come. For example, Dallaire's studies of youth participants in the Francophone Games in Alberta, Ontario, and New Brunswick found that the youth tended to identify themselves as having hybrid identities or a "melange of francophoneness and anglophoneness" (Dallaire & Denis, 2005, p. 143). These youth, like the South Asian youth in Tirone and Pedlar's study (2000), construct and reconstruct their identities, drawing upon their inherited traditions and upon the cultural traditions of the dominant group in which they are immersed for much of their school and social lives. While francophone youth in Dallaire's studies participated in the same sports as are offered at the Olympics, other minority youth drew upon the traditional sports they learned from their minority community. As minority youth "do" sports such as field hockey and cricket, common among youth in South Asia, and sports like dragonboat racing and martial arts that originated within minority communities, dominant group youth are also able to access these nontraditional sports, thereby changing the nature of some sport participation in Canada.

Not all immigrants and ethnic minority people choose to live in places where other minorities like themselves also live. Chiswick and Miller (2002) explain the value of immersion into the dominant society where ethnic minority people gain exposure and social capital necessary for career development and economic success. Young immigrants and children of ethnic minority families are often immersed in or at least familiarized with dominant cultural practices because they usually attend schools with peers from a vast range of ethnic and racial backgrounds. Schools therefore provide opportunities for learning the values and beliefs of diverse peers and for learning the priorities of the institutions with which minorities are expected to conform. Sport is very much a part of the Canadian school system; for many ethnic minority youth, school is often the place where they first encounter sport participation.

Immigration trends in recent decades are quite different from those of the past 150 years. This change is evident in data collected for the 2011 census, in which 6.2 million people, or 19.1% of the national population, identified themselves as members of a visible minority group. This represents an increase from the 2006 census and is attributed to the large numbers of new immigrants from non-European countries. The three largest visible minority groups in Canada are South Asians, Chinese, and blacks, followed by Filipinos, Latin Americans, Arabs, South East Asians, West Asians, Koreans, and Japanese (Statistics Canada, 2013c). As more and more newcomers and visible minorities become immersed in Canadian society, their sport traditions and preferences will likely continue to have an impact on how sport is experienced in this country.

Ethnic Minority People and Sport in Canada

Since many of the early 20th-century white settler groups were not British or French, they brought with them a number of sports that were not familiar to dominant group Canadians as part of their distinct traditional cultural practices. For example, Estonians, Finlanders, and people from the former Czechoslovakia introduced modern and rhythmic gymnastics to Canada after World War II, and Southeast Asians have made popular a number of their traditional sports such as tai chi and karate (Burnet & Palmer, 1988). In those early days, sports clubs and teams were sponsored by some ethnic communities and churches to engage the youth of the community in meaningful activity and to shelter participants from discriminatory practices of dominant sport and recreation associations (Kidd, 1996b; McBride, 1975). Exclusionary practices of dominant group sports associations gave rise to sports teams and clubs sponsored by workers' movements and political organizations whose membership was composed of minority ethnic workers. These included sports teams supported by Canadian communists in the 1920s and 1930s (Kidd, 1996b).

Ethnic sport associations remain a valued part of institutionally complete Canadian ethnic communities. These associations provide important opportunities for youth to experience sport and leisure activities similar to those of dominant group peers within organizations that their parents support. In a study of children of immigrants from South Asia, Tirone and Pedlar (2000) learned that during school years prior to university, South Asian clubs and associations were an important venue for sport and physical activity for many of the youth. Several participants in that longitudinal study, which began in 1996, described how they and their families participated in sports such as badminton and volleyball with other South Asian families who rented public gymnasia space exclusively for use by their group (Tirone & Pedlar, 2000). Stodolska and Jackson (1998) describe a similar pattern of sports provision and participation in Polish Canadian ethnic clubs.

Sport and recreation participation is beneficial for new immigrant youth, providing opportunities for social integration with other youth in their neighbourhoods. It is the source of both embedded and autonomous social capital. *Embedded social capital* refers to the connection between people based on trust and common values, which serves to unite people within an enclave or ethnic group. *Autonomous social capital* is the trust and respect that can develop between people of diverse backgrounds and that leads to opportunities for people from an enclave to interact outside of their homogeneous group (Woolcock, 1998). While high levels of embedded social capital mean people within a homogeneous group are well connected to one another, those connections may not provide group members with information and connections they desire to be recognized and to prosper outside of the enclave. Autonomous social capital is useful when people want to interact and be recognized for their skills and potential outside of an enclave.

There are several reasons why ethnic sport associations have continued to exist. Sports teams, music, cuisine, language, and other cultural traditions are an expression of group identity (Burnet & Palmer, 1988). These ethnic sport organizations also provide a supportive environment. For example, worker sport associations and ethnic clubs provided sport and physical activities for early immigrants who were ridiculed and excluded from mainstream sport associations (Kidd, 1996b). More recently, sport associations like those sponsored by Canadian South Asian cultural associations provide youth with the benefits of sport participation as well as opportunities to meet other South Asian youth their own age in competitive environments their parents support (Tirone, 2000). Ethnic sport associations thus serve to protect participants from the harassment some people experience in mainstream sport.

The popularity of ethnic sports is no more evident than in the sport of soccer. Harney (cited in Burnet & Palmer, 1988) describes participation of ethnic groups in soccer in Toronto in the 1970s. His account describes the 78 teams in the Toronto District Soccer League at that time, more than three-quarters of which displayed ethnic emblems or the names of various countries as team names, such as First Portuguese, Croatia, Serbia White Eagle, Hungaria, and Heidelberg. In the winter of 2005–2006, this multicultural approach was linked to hockey for the first time. An inaugural Canadian Multicultural Hockey Championship was held, where 16 teams of Toronto-area players competed for their "home country," such as Russia, Finland, Serbia, Japan, China, Korea, Native Canadians, Poland, Greece, and Italy. This tournament launched the new Toronto-based Canadian Multicultural Hockey League (Lewi, 2006). Participation has grown over the years to the point where there were three divisions in the 2013–2014 championship tournament: Culture Cup (women), Heritage, and Premier.

Early ethnic sport associations have, historically, valued competitive success as well as positive group identity. Ethnic sports teams that displayed ethnic insignia often recruited players based on ability and not ethnicity. Seeking the most skilled players, ethnic sports clubs often accepted players of diverse ethnic backgrounds—as was the case when Finnish Canadians, recognized for their skills, were encouraged to take up Canadian sports (Kidd, 1996b). Ethnic minority athletes have been and continue to be a source of pride for their ethnic group. Participation in sports by ethnic minority athletes provides them with opportunities to engage in and experience the values of other cultures, including those of dominant group members.

Ethnicity, Poverty, and Access to Sport

While few Canadians would argue against the health and social benefits of most sport participation, especially for children, we have not been able to ensure the participation of all children in healthy physical activity and sport. Poverty has long been known to prevent many Canadian youth from participating in organized sports, and often children in poor families have little or no access to unorganized sports and recreation (Frisby et al., 2005; White & McTeer, 2012). Recent immigrants experience poverty at higher rates than Canadian-born workers, and the wage gap between these two groups in the years between 1980 and 2005 increased steadily (Statistics Canada, 2009). In 2003, 80% of new immigrants reported that they found work in Canada during the first two years of residency in this country, but only 42% of them found work in the fields in which they had trained, and many of these people work at jobs that provide little more than subsistence wages (Statistics Canada, 2003). A study of poverty among Torontonians indicates one-third of the immigrant families in Toronto in 2001 lived in higher-poverty neighbourhoods, and that number represents an increase of

400% between 1981 and 2001 (United Way of Greater Toronto, 2004). The same study reports that visible minorities were eight times more likely to live in poverty than they were in 1981. Far fewer children in low-income families participate in sport compared with children in high-income families (Frisby et al., 2005). Ethnic minority youth in low-income families can also face additional limitations because of parental priorities that emphasize academic pursuits and discourage participation in sports (Rosenberg, 2003; Tirone & Pedlar, 2000).

Discrimination

Another barrier to sport participation that affects some ethnic minority Canadians is discrimination, both situational and systemic. In a study of leisure and recreation of teenagers who were the children of South Asian immigrants, racism and indifference were noted as reasons why some youth stopped participating in sports (Tirone, 2000). That group explained how, when faced with overt racism or situations in which they were criticized or ridiculed because of skin colour, clothing, or religious practices, no one in a position of authority attempted to intervene in the situation. In another study of new immigrants to the Halifax area, a young university student who emigrated from the Middle East explained that he felt discrimination played a part in why he was not able to play soccer for his high school team. He had been an accomplished soccer player in his homeland prior to emigration, and when he arrived in Halifax as a high school student he attempted to try out for the school soccer team but was told that all positions were filled and he was not given a chance to demonstrate

Box 5.1

Immigrants and Sport

New immigrants and other Canadians who identify with diverse ethnic, racial, and religious groups benefit from involvement in sport, leisure, and recreation in many ways. For example, sport and recreation provide opportunities for newly arrived immigrants to meet their neighbours and peers at school, to learn and practise English or French, and to engage in activity that contributes to their physically active and healthy lifestyles. Susan Tirone's studies of immigrants and their children illustrate some interesting and unique patterns of sport involvement of immigrants. For example, in a study she conducted with co-researcher Lori Livingston in Halifax in 2007, they learned about immigrants who are involved in recreation and elite-level sports and coaching. In that study it was evident that immigrants from diverse ethnic, racial, and religious groups engage in sports as part of their leisure, as a means to gain acceptance and a sense of belonging in their communities, and in some cases as a source of income for those who immigrate to be professional coaches (Livingston, Tirone, Miller, & Smith, 2008; Tirone, Livingston, Miller, & Smith, 2010).

Tirone's longitudinal study of leisure in the lives of children of immigrants from India, Pakistan, and Bangladesh reveals the difficulties and tremendous advantages young South Asians encountered as they pursued sport, recreation, and leisure. For the youth in that study, it was evident that sport has the potential to facilitate inclusion for some young people while it is the source of exclusion and discrimination for others, as we explain in this chapter. Sport and leisure may also be a tremendous opportunity for young people to explore the traditional cultural practices of the ethnic groups they identify with and to introduce these traditions to their non–South Asian friends.

Tirone's work illustrates that young people who develop a level of comfort in situations where they interact with people of many different cultures, religions, and with people of varying races are well positioned for careers and other civic roles in which they will need to interact across cultures. Sport is an ideal venue in which young people can develop an understanding of and appreciation for cultural diversity (Tirone, 2010; Tirone & Pedlar, 2000).

his skills. He satisfied his love for the game by volunteering as a coach for youth soccer, and upon entering university was recruited to play varsity soccer (Tirone, 2005).

Ethnic identity has thus shaped and been shaped by sport participation in Canada. While participants from diverse ethnic and racial backgrounds can benefit from their involvement in sport, leisure, and recreation (see Box 5.1), barriers to sport participation based on ethnic identity are often compounded by racism. The next section explores ways that racial identity shapes and has been shaped by sport participation.

RACE AND SPORT IN CANADA
The Concept of Race

Unlike the concept of *ethnicity*, *race* is a term used to establish socially constructed distinctions between groups of people based on their genetic heritage. These distinctions, marked by skin colour, take on social significance because of differences assigned to members of these groups. For example, we could look at a group of people and assume that some are white, black, Aboriginal, or Asian. It is, however, the belief that the colour of their skin indicates immutable differences between them that makes race a socially significant category in our society. We might look to white people for leadership, black people for athletic talent, Aboriginal peoples for environmental guidance, and Asian Canadians for academic excellence. By assuming that race automatically gives individuals an advantage in some areas more so than others, we are reproducing race-based understandings of human behaviour.

Skin colour has taken on social meanings in North America that hegemonically privilege white people over others. A hierarchy of privilege/discrimination has thus been created—commonly referred to as *racism*. Carl James explains it this way:

> *Racism* . . . is an uncritical acceptance of a negative social definition of a group identified by physical features such as skin colour. People justify their racist attitudes and perceptions by associating perceived differences between groups with the presence (or absence) of certain biological characteristics and social abilities. (James, 1996, p. 26)

Racial classification systems and ideas about race emerged in the 16th and 17th centuries while Europeans were exploring and claiming imperial dominion over different parts of the world. As they encountered people who appeared and acted differently, these strangers were placed in an evolutionary hierarchy. Those most similar to the European explorers were judged to be the most evolved and civilized, and whiteness became the norm by which others were judged. The exploitation of people from other "races" thus became hegemonically justified on the basis of their presumed inferiority relative to Europeans.

Social Darwinism extended Charles Darwin's theory of natural selection into the social realm. This theory provided British and American social theorists with a scientific tool for determining the superiority of some races over others, and thus with a justification for endorsing racial inequality (Booth & Tatz, 2000). The presence of slavery in Canada, beginning in 1628 (Spence, 1999), and the colonization and legislative regulation of First Nations within North America reinforced the subservient position of blacks and Aboriginal peoples relative to Canadians of European descent in similar ways. This race logic eventually became institutionalized as a racial ideology involving "skin colour with other traits including intelligence, character, and physical characteristics and skills" (Coakley & Donnelly, 2009, p. 262).

Identification by race is not, however, a straightforward process. What did it take, for example, for someone to be considered white, black, Aboriginal, or Asian, and what were the consequences? The social constructedness of this process can be seen in the ways that race was defined for and applied to different groups in Canada. For example, historically, just "one drop of black blood" identified individuals as black, even though they may have had white ancestors. This was even put into legislation in some cases. For example, in Virginia in 1924 "the Racial Integrity Act said that 'if a child has one drop of negro blood . . . it cannot be counted as white.'" (Trembanis, 2008, note 7, p. 283)

In contrast to this, the British North America Act, which constituted Canada as a country in 1867, identified "Indians" as a race apart from other Canadians and placed them under federal jurisdiction. The Indian Act of 1876, which controlled almost every feature of Aboriginal social life, served to separate them further from other Canadians on the basis of race. Treaties were the third factor regulating Aboriginal life. Here again, the underlying premise was that Aboriginal peoples had an "uncivilized nature" that must be altered before they could enjoy full civil rights. Everyday practices, like performing traditional dances, were outlawed. It was not until 1960 that First Nations, as a race, could vote federally in Canada (Paraschak, 1997).

Chinese migrants were treated differently yet again. They were forced to pay a head tax to enter Canada beginning in 1885, and in 1902 a Royal Commission on Chinese and Japanese Immigration concluded that Asians were "unfit for full citizenship . . . obnoxious to a free community and dangerous to the state" (Wickberg, 1988, p. 416). Chinese and East Indian Canadians were not given the right to vote until 1947.

In contrast to these examples, being white in North American society has remained relatively unmarked. White people rarely have to think of themselves in racial terms—they are privileged by race. They have access to opportunities in society without having to worry that their race will be a barrier. However, they may be treated differently because of their ethnic background. For example, on *Hockey Night in Canada* Don Cherry often comments on the differences among—and suitability of—professional hockey players who are Francophone, Anglophone, or European, even though all these athletes would be considered "white" by race (Langford, 2004).

Tiger Woods, a prominent professional golfer of mixed black, Asian, Aboriginal, and white heritage, brought the complexity of defining individuals by race to public notice in 1997. After his successful first year on the tour, and his win at the Masters Tournament specifically, the press heralded him as a successful black golfer. Tiger, however, eventually clarified publicly that he had developed a different racial description for himself as a youth, based on his actual background. He called himself a *Cablinasian*, to reflect his CAucasian, BLack, INdian, and ASIAN genetic heritage. In this way, he highlighted two important points: Racial labels can be assigned to people without those labels being accurate, and the way individuals view themselves may be quite different from the racial category assigned to them by others.

Racial Patterns in Canadian Sport

Canada has an early history of discrimination by race in amateur sport. Cosentino (1998) argues that while *class* formed the basis of amateurism in England, in Canada *race* also became a powerful definer of who could compete. This was evident as early as 1835, when black jockeys were banned from competing at the Niagara Turf Club. The first big regatta in Nova Scotia, in 1826, offered prizes "for first and second class boats and a canoe race for

Indians . . . which was considered the most entertaining . . . [and] remained part of the Nova Scotian scene until at least 1896" (Young, 1988, pp. 87–88). In 1880, Aboriginal players were excluded from competing in amateur competitions for lacrosse—a game that had originated in Aboriginal culture! A special league for black hockey players titled "The Colored Hockey League" was formed in Halifax in 1900, becoming the seventh league in that city— and the first one overtly defined by race (Young, 1988, p. 31). As late as 1913, the Amateur Athletic Association of Canada opted to ban blacks from competing in Canadian amateur boxing championships, since "Competition of whites and coloured men is not working out to the increased growth of sport" (Amateur Athletic Union of Canada, quoted in Cosentino, 1998, p. 13). Even the first definition of an amateur in Canada, created by the Montreal Pedestrian Club in 1873, noted that no "labourer or Indian" could be given that designation.

This pattern of exclusion by race is discussed by Robert Pitter (2006) in relation to hockey, which he sees as part of broader systemic racism in Canadian sport. He details the long history of both Aboriginal and black participants in hockey, along with the delay of their entrance into the National Hockey League (NHL) until 1953 for Aboriginals, when player Fred Sasakamoose joined the league, and 1958 for black players, when Willie O'Ree joined. Racist treatment followed these athletes into the NHL as well. "Aboriginal players depict a Canadian hockey subculture in which racist behaviours are endemic, ranging from routine use of the nickname 'Chief' to pointedly demeaning and hostile treatment" (Pitter, 2006, p. 130). Black players also faced racial taunts and actions within hockey. For example, P. K. Subban of the Montreal Canadiens, who is black, was the target of racist tweets on social media after he scored the winning overtime goal against the Boston Bruins in the 2014 playoffs (Associated Press, 2014). Other players, like Herb Carnegie (1919–2012), were simply banned from playing in the NHL because of the colour of their skin.

The racist mistreatment and exclusion of people of colour from sport can be understood, in part, as ethnocentric distortion (Paraschak, 1989), which further extends hegemonic expectations within Canadian sport by race. When whitestream cultural practices are naturalized as the "norm," select sporting practices of individuals become reframed by those in positions of power as different, less desired, and thus not worthy of support. Aboriginal athlete Tom Longboat, for example, was one of Canada's most successful marathoners in the decade prior to World War I. Despite his many successes, he was accused by his managers and in the media of not training consistently or rigorously enough. Bruce Kidd (1983) ably identifies and debunks the ethnocentric bias embedded in those comments. He analyzes Longboat's training regimen and shows that it was different from, but not inferior to, common training practices of that time period.

In a similar manner, a government review of the Native Sport and Recreation Program in 1977, five years after its inception, criticized Aboriginal recreation organizers for including inappropriate "cultural" activities. While occasional nonsport activities "such as pow wows, music festivals and native cultural traditions workshops" (Paraschak, 1995, p. 4) occurred, the vast majority of activities were Euro-Canadian in orientation but offered within an all-Aboriginal context. Thus, "it is likely that the concerns of government were primarily based on the structure adopted for sport competitions rather than the activities played" (Paraschak, 1995, p. 5). The non-whitestream structuring of such activities, along with the refusal by the National Indian Sports Council to "assimilate" into the National Sport and Recreation Centre, undercut this program's legitimacy within whitestream Sport Canada expectations because these actions did not align with Eurocentric expectations tied to sport. In effect, the actions of Aboriginal organizers were distorted by Euro-Canadian bureaucrats who suggested that their activities were not legitimate because they did not fit within whitestream, Eurocentric understandings of sport.

Despite the presence of these racist underpinnings in sport, Canada has also been a country where black athletes have, at times, found acceptance more readily than in the United States. Jackie Robinson broke the longstanding colour barrier in Major League Baseball by playing for the Brooklyn Dodgers in 1947. However, the president of the Dodgers, Branch Rickey, actually signed Robinson in October 1945 to play professionally for the minor league Montreal Royals. While Robinson played for Montreal that first year, he experienced intense racism during games in the United States. In Montreal, however, he had great fan support:

> Robinson's play made him a beloved sports figure in Montreal. Children hounded him for autographs, while adults poured into the ballpark to see him steal bases and score runs. As a Montreal sportswriter noted, "For Jackie Robinson and the city of Montreal, it was love at first sight." (Scott, 1987, p. 37)

Three decades later, Warren Moon was able to play professional football as a black quarterback in Canada when that opportunity was not available in the United States. At this point in National Football League (NFL) history, there had only been three black quarterbacks in the starting role: Fritz Pollard (1920), James Harris (1969–1977), and Joe Gilliam (1974) (*Burnaby Now*, 2013). Researchers (e.g., Best, 1987; Leonard, 1987) have demonstrated in a number of sports, including professional football, that during this time decision makers appeared, in accordance with racist ideological beliefs, to be positionally segregating or "stacking" blacks in the athletic running positions because they were supposedly "natural" athletes, while only whites were "stacked" in central, leadership positions, such as quarterback, centre, and middle linebacker, simply because they were assumed to have the ability and intellect to fill such positions.

Warren Moon's treatment by the NFL aligned with this racist belief. After being selected as the 1978 Rose Bowl Most Valuable Player in his role as quarterback, Moon was completely overlooked by the NFL in its 1978 US college draft. As a result, he came to play with the Edmonton Eskimos in the Canadian Football League and won five Grey Cups with them. In 1984 he became the highest-paid player in football when he joined the Houston Oilers of the National Football League (Mullick, 2002), and in 2006 he became the first black quarterback inducted into the Pro Football Hall of Fame.

These examples demonstrate different ways that race has been given social meaning in Canadian sport. Such meanings are indicative of broader societal race relations. Frideres (1988), writing on racism in Canadian society, noted that "Racism in Canada from 1800 to 1945 was reflected in restrictive immigration policies and practices regarding non-white immigrants, particularly the Chinese, Blacks and Jews, and by the treatment of native peoples" (p. 1816). Racist sport practices during this time period would thus have reinforced and been shaped by broader understandings of race. Canadian attempts to address racial inequity through legislation coalesced in the 1982 Canadian Charter of Rights and Freedoms, where equality rights in the public domain were entrenched in Section 15:

Equality Rights

15. (1) Every individual is equal before and under the law and has the right to the equal protection and equal benefit of the law without discrimination and, in particular,

without discrimination based on race, national or ethnic origin, colour, religion, sex, age or mental or physical disability.

(2) Subsection (1) does not preclude any law, program or activity that has as its object the amelioration of conditions of disadvantaged individuals or groups including those that are disadvantaged because of race, national or ethnic origin, colour, religion, sex, age or mental or physical disability.

Human rights commissions have also provided a legal avenue for addressing racial inequities in Canada. Participants and administrators who wish to make sport a more welcoming—and legislatively aligned—place for all can benefit by understanding the social construction of race and racism in sport.

Race and Ethnic Relations

In society, individuals always act in relation to others. The possibilities within which we live are thus formed through the "social relations" that exist between individuals and groups. Through social relations, rules are (re)produced concerning how things work and how resources can be distributed. They thus become "power relations," because those rules always provide for or privilege some people over others. Race and ethnic relations are a particular type of power relation—they privilege individuals on the basis of race or ethnicity. As noted in Chapter 1, power is "the capacity of a person or group of persons to employ resources of different types in order to secure outcomes" (Gruneau, 1988, p. 22).

Rayane Benatti is a 9-year-old Quebec girl sent off the pitch in Gatineau for wearing a hijab in July 2012. She was told that she could not play in the tournament at a local park because her headscarf was a safety hazard.
Bruno Schlumberger/Ottawa Citizen. Reprinted by permission.

It was also noted that there are three measures of power in sport: the ability to structure sport, to establish sport traditions, and to define legitimate meanings and practices associated with dominant sport practices. These measures of power, differently shaped by race and at times by ethnicity, can be seen when looking at mainstream sport and at race-structured sporting opportunities such as all-Aboriginal sport competitions.

Whitestream Sport

As was mentioned earlier, Claude Denis (1997) uses the term *whitestream society* "to indicate that Canadian society, while principally structured on the basis of the European, 'white,' experience, is far from being simply 'white' in socio-demographic, economic and cultural terms" (p. 13). Extending his term, the rules of mainstream, or "whitestream," sport have been primarily shaped by individuals of white European heritage in ways that privilege their traditions, practices, meanings, and sport structures. This is an example of *institutionalized racism*, since the structure of the system, if followed, will always produce outcomes that discriminate against those who are not white—it will privilege white people of European heritage over others.

Differential treatment of individuals by race has occurred in whitestream sport in various ways. For example, the ability of George Beers in 1860 to create and then institutionalize lacrosse rules in a manner that he found meaningful, as opposed to the ways the game was played by Aboriginal Canadians, demonstrates his privilege by race over the originators of the game of lacrosse (Cosentino, 1998, p. 15). As well, during this time period black and Aboriginal athletes were banned from competing against white Canadians in a wide variety of sports. If they did compete, descriptors such as "Indian" or "coloured" were added after their name to indicate that they were different from, and subservient to, white competitors.

When overt discrimination was eliminated in sport, other more subtle forms of racism remained. The organization of sport privileged those activities that were played in international competitions, including the Olympics and world championships. The federal government criteria for funding sports reflected this; physical activities that fell outside the whitestream model were not seen as legitimate and were denied federal funding. For example, the Northern Games Society, which has organized yearly Inuit and Dene traditional games festivals in the Northwest Territories since 1970, was informed by letter in 1977 that their federal sport funding would be stopped. The letter pointed out that the Games activities, which had their origin in Aboriginal cultures, were not deemed to be "legitimate sport" according to the parameters of the funding agency. Aboriginal organizers argued that their traditional activities were also sports, but they had less power over defining "legitimate" sports, and thus lost their funding (Paraschak, 1997).

Another drawback to whitestream sport in Canada is the sense of discomfort that is experienced by many marginalized peoples in mainstream sport experiences. Both individual and institutionalized racism in hockey were detailed in a 1991 TSN documentary, *Hockey: A White Man's Game?* Ted Nolan, an Aboriginal NHL player, spoke of the racism he faced from his teammates as a teenager and the isolation he felt as a result. Other Aboriginal players spoke about the racial slurs they endured while playing. And they spoke about the structure of hockey in Canada, which took them far away from their families and support systems, and how that structure made it more difficult for them to succeed in light of their own cultural practices. Since Aboriginal players were not able to structure sport in preferred ways, they found it difficult to feel part of or to succeed in professional hockey.

Robidoux (2012) extends and updates this analysis through his examination of First Nations men's hockey in Canada. He explores disruptions in hockey practices that point to "border thinking," which entails the perceptions formed by individuals along the borders between mainstream and culturally distinct local practices. Robidoux documents ways that Aboriginal cultural values are being proactively expressed through hockey in First Nations settings under Aboriginal control, rather than merely reproducing Euro-Canadian understandings of the sport, supporting his argument that hockey is "a key site for cultural enunciation, not cultural capitulation." (p. 5) Pitter (2006), in his discussion of Aboriginal and black hockey players in and outside of the NHL, affirms that we need to reassert "the accomplishments of non-whites in hockey, as well as the obstacles they have had to struggle against" (p. 135) to address the current distortion in our knowledge about the history of hockey in Canada. This includes non-white groups such as the Chinese, who are one of the largest visible minorities in Canada yet are largely absent from the NHL. He does mention the few Asian players who have played in the NHL, including Larry Kwong, who played one game in 1948 for the New York Rangers, as well as more recent athletes such as Paul Kariya, Jamie Storr, and Manny Malhotra.

Mary Louise Adams (2006) points out one way that successful black hockey players are made invisible in terms of race. She writes about how, in the 2004 Stanley Cup finals, Jarome Iginla, the black team captain of the Calgary Flames, was profiled in the *Globe and Mail* with a photo headlined "Canada's Captain, Canada's Team." Adams points out that here was an opportunity to "shift hockey's limited racial narratives and, by association, maybe shift notions of Canadianness a little bit too" (p. 75) by acknowledging the ways that "Canada's Captain," being black, represents the changing face of an increasingly multicultural country. Yet the newspaper article made no reference to race, except for a comment in the sidebar by Iginla about having grown up as the only black hockey player on his team. This newspaper article thus reinforced, she argued, that hockey contributes to whiteness in the Canadian imaginary: "[T]he neglect of race seems naively hopeful, reflecting the beliefs that race doesn't matter in sport's meritocracy, that race is not an important Canadian issue" (Adams, 2006, p. 75). This approach to erasing visible minorities' contributions, which could otherwise generate a more multicultural understanding of the sporting landscape in Canada, aligns uncomfortably with the way that Ben Johnson was portrayed in the media as an outstanding Canadian athlete when he won gold at the 1984 Olympics, yet was reframed as a Jamaican Canadian once he was found to have taken steroids and stripped of his medal.

Another reason why some Aboriginal people feel uncomfortable in whitestream sport is the tradition of using Indian mascots for sports teams. This issue is laid out clearly in a 1997 documentary on American Indian mascots in sport titled *In Whose Honor?* (Rosenstein, 1997). Through looking at one case study—Chief Illiniwek, the mascot for the University of Illinois—the documentary points out the devastating impact this stereotypic Indian mascot had on Aboriginal children and the efforts required to try to eliminate it. Relevant to our discussion on whitestream sport are the accounts of how the Indian mascot was created by white students at the university, how the actions of Chief Illiniwek are portrayed as "authentic" even though they are constructed by the performer and often degrade Native traditions, and the comments by white alumni and administrators about the importance of the Chief as part of "their" traditions. More recently, ongoing legal efforts by anti-mascot protesters to have the Washington Redskins lose its trademark protection were bolstered by a "letter from 10 members of [the United States]

Congress who want the name changed because it is offensive to many Native Americans" (Canadian Press, 2013). However, this letter was unable to sway NFL Commissioner Roger Goodell, who feels the team's name is a "unifying force that stands for strength, courage, pride and respect . . . [fostering] fan pride in the team's heritage" (Canadian Press, 2013). A subsequent letter, signed by 49 US senators, was sent in May 2014 urging Goodell to change the Washington Redskins's name because "it is a racist slur and the time is ripe to replace it," thereby sending a clear message "that racism and bigotry have no place in professional sports" (*Windsor Star*, 2014, p. B5).

Patterns of differential treatment based on race have been documented in various professional sports. The Centre for the Study of Sport in Society at Northeastern University (now called the Institute for Diversity and Ethics in Sport), for example, has provided a Racial and Gender Report Card since 2001 that reports on progress in the elimination of discrimination, both among the players and in the administration of sport within the various professional and university men's and women's sports leagues operating in North America:

> The Racial and Gender Report Card (RGRC) is the definitive assessment of hiring practices of women and people of color in most of the leading professional and amateur sports and sporting organizations in the United States. The report considers the composition—assessed by racial and gender makeup—of players, coaches and front office/ athletic department employees in our country's leading sports organizations, including the National Basketball Association (NBA), National Football League (NFL), Major League Baseball (MLB), Major League Soccer (MLS) and Women's National Basketball Association (WNBA), as well as in collegiate athletic departments. (Institute for Diversity and Ethics in Sport, n.d.)

On occasion, efforts have been taken directly by professional sports leagues to address the under-representation of minorities in administrative positions in professional sport. This under-representation is one legacy of the racial ideology that saw people of colour as unfit for leadership and thinking positions. For example, the Rooney Rule, implemented by the NFL in 2003, was one attempt to address the lack of visible minority coaches in the league. At that time, about 65% of players were black, but only about 6% of teams had minority coaches. The controversial rule stipulated that NFL teams must interview at least one minority candidate for head coaching and senior management positions. While this rule led to an increase in minority coaches in the NFL, it only required that a minority candidate be interviewed, which made it a superficially symbolic action at times when the team management already knew who they would be hiring as their next coach. In 2012, for example, no minorities were hired to fill eight coaching and seven general manager positions.

In 2014, NBA Commissioner Adam Silver was applauded for taking a strong public stance against the racist behaviours of Donald Sterling, owner of the Los Angeles Clippers. Sterling was recorded on April 25, 2014, "scold[ing] his mistress for bringing African-Americans to games, namely [Magic] Johnson" (Jenkins, 2014, pp. 70–71). NBA players, the general public, and sponsors were all outraged at his racist comments. Silver announced on April 29 that Donald Sterling was banned for life from associating with the Clippers organization or any NBA activities. He was also fined $2.5 million, the maximum amount allowed under the NBA constitution, with those funds going to organizations dedicated to anti-discrimination and tolerance efforts. Silver added that he would also encourage the board of governors to force Sterling to sell the team. He finished by saying, "We stand together in condemning Mr. Sterling's views. They simply have no place in the NBA" (TMZ Sports, 2014). Silver's rapid and punitive actions against Sterling's racist comments and previous behaviours were praised widely in the media as an appropriate way to address racism in professional sport (Jenkins, 2014).

In Canadian amateur soccer, there has recently been controversy over the banning by the Quebec Soccer Federation of youth wearing turbans because they are "unsafe." The director general of the provincial organization, when asked about its decision, commented that "if Sikh kids want to play soccer while wearing a turban there's an easy solution: they can play in their own yard . . . the reason to maintain the ban is for player safety reasons. . . . When asked how many injuries have been linked to turbans [the director general] said there are none" (Associated Press, 2013). Outrage was expressed across the country, including protests by soccer players on one team whose members all donned turbans to play. The Canadian Soccer Association suspended the Quebec Federation for refusing to overturn this decision. The Fédération Internationale de Football Association (FIFA) then addressed the issue. In its ruling, FIFA specifically addressed Canada and said that men's head coverings were permitted as long as they met safety standards and complied with rules such as being the same colour as uniforms. The rule applied "in all areas and on all levels of the Canadian football community," FIFA said (Peritz, 2013). The Quebec Soccer Federation subsequently revoked its decision to align with the FIFA rule clarification.

Whitestream sport, then, provides varying opportunities for athletes depending on their race. This differential treatment can be overt, such as racial slurs that make participation uncomfortable for those groups. But discriminatory treatment is also, at times, built into the existing system of sport. In Canada, for example, the discriminatory treatment of French Canadians in the NHL has been explored in terms of salary discrimination, entry discrimination, under-representation at certain positions (or "stacking"), and under-representation on certain teams. For example, Longley (2000) completed a study that looked at all French Canadians playing in English Canada or the United States on NHL teams from 1943 to 1998. His analysis identified an under-representation of French Canadian players on English Canadian versus US teams. After discounting many other explanations, Longley provides support for the thesis that French–English tensions may lead English Canadian teams to discriminate against French Canadian players. This explanation was strengthened when the degree of under-representation on English Canadian teams was shown to be greater during seasons when sovereignist political threats in Quebec were highest. This research demonstrates that ethnicity, as well as race, affects sporting opportunities. Marginalized groups have thus had to look elsewhere for alternative sport opportunities—or to create some themselves.

Doing Race, Doing Racism

Race as a socially constructed idea becomes naturalized (i.e., accepted as "truth") as individuals, on a daily basis, behave as if it were true. West and Zimmerman (1991), in their discussion on "doing gender," point out that this process involves individuals behaving in appropriately masculine or feminine ways, "but it is a situated doing, carried out in the virtual or real presence of others who are presumed to be oriented to its production" (p. 14). Applying this concept to race, "doing race" means that individuals act in relation to each other in ways that confirm their socially constructed beliefs about race. It is through the acting out, the "doing" of race on a day-by-day basis, both in terms of our own race and the race we assign to others, that we maintain a society where race has social meaning and consequences.

Stereotypes—rigid beliefs about the characteristics of a racial group—take on importance as we live or "do" them into existence by operating as if they were true. Spence (1999), in his study of black male athletes in a Canadian high school, heard from these youth that their teachers encouraged them athletically but not academically. This treatment fits with the stereotype that blacks as a race are athletically more and academically less gifted than whites. As these athletes worked hard on athletic competence and gained status through their success, they had less time to give to academics, and thus their actions reinforced the stereotype. All the while, they and their teachers were "doing racism." This pattern was furthered as black youth identified other black youth who focused on academics as "acting white" or "selling out" (Spence, 1999, p. 92) Through such labelling, the youth were undercutting their peers' efforts at academic success, thus further reproducing the stereotype that they were innately racially gifted in athletics and unsuited for academics.

"Doing race" can also be carried out in ways that offer positive race-connected meanings to members of a group, providing them with a form of cultural expression that is uniquely their own. Majors (1990), for example, identified "cool pose" as a creative way that black men express their masculinity in a society where opportunities are limited and racism is institutionalized. Wilson (1999) describes the expression of cool pose in sport:

> Sport, particularly basketball, are sites where young Black males symbolically oppose the dominant White group and create [a positive race-connected] identity by developing both a flamboyant on-court language (now popularly known as "trash talking") and a repertoire of spectacular "playground" moves and high-flying dunks. (p. 232)

While this way of "doing race" was initially generated by black male youth, Wilson also discusses ways that this style has been incorporated by sport marketers to sell to a mass audience, and in particular to sell the Toronto Raptors basketball team. These advertising messages, he argues, undercut the resistant symbolic message that cool pose provides black males, while potentially reinforcing stereotypic black male images to Canadian audiences. In this instance, sport marketers were "doing racism."

Race-Structured Sport Systems

Opportunities for sport created by and for racial groups outside mainstream society have a long history in Canada. When Aboriginal or black athletes were banned from whitestream sports, they often countered with the creation of their own leagues and competitions, limited to participants from a specified racial background. This provided organizers with the opportunity to assign their own meaning to sport and to develop traditions in keeping with Aboriginal, black, or Asian cultural understandings. And it created opportunities for marginalized groups to play sports when they did not have that chance in the mainstream sport system.

An example of a race-structured sporting event would be the North American Indigenous Games, first held in 1990 in Edmonton. These international Games, restricted to those of verifiable Aboriginal ancestry, "stress fun and participation while encouraging our youth to strive for excellence" (Aboriginal Sports/Recreation Association of BC, 1995). The Games include only mainstream sports, because the intent is to provide a stepping-stone to national- and international-level sport competitions; however, the cultural program showcases various traditional games and dances as well. The 2002 Games in Winnipeg had more than 6,000 participants celebrating Aboriginal culture as well as competing in sporting events organized by Aboriginal sports organizations. The Games have been held at sites in Canada (five times) and the United States (two times); the summer 2014 Games are scheduled for Regina, Saskatchewan.

Through this event, Aboriginal sportspeople experience more "power" in sport than is found in the whitestream system—they are in charge of its structure, its practices and meanings, and the traditions they will continue into the future. Unfortunately, these race-structured opportunities rarely qualify for the kinds of financial and material rewards given to "legitimate" whitestream sport, although the Canadian government has acknowledged

---

Box 5.2

A Strengths-Based Examination of Aboriginal Peoples' Physical Activity Practices in Canada

Examinations of Aboriginal peoples' practices related to physical activity in Canada often begin by talking about the problems or barriers they face. This approach is called the *deficit perspective* because it keeps the focus on what is not working well and looks to experts to fix the problems. The *strengths-based perspective*, which comes out of social work, counters the deficit perspective because all analyses start by looking at what is being done well—the strengths of the group in question. Resources are then identified in their environment that can be drawn upon to further those strengths. Experts become only one resource among many who work with the group so that their hopes for the future may be realized.

One strengths-based analysis, drawing on national survey data, government policies and reports, and research findings, identified four potential strengths tied to Aboriginal cultural practices. (Paraschak & Thompson, 2013):

1. A holistic orientation toward the way physical activity is carried out, stressing an integration of the physical, mental, emotional, and spiritual (see Lavallee's 2007 examination of the traditional medicine wheel and physical activity). This holistic orientation also views all types of physical activity as one concept, rather than separating out sport, recreation, active living, and physical education.

2. The strong emphasis on family and community as part of physical activity practices.

3. The third strength, two-eyed seeing, is originally a concept from Canadian Mi'kmaq Elder Albert Marshall, who recommends drawing on both traditional and Western

knowledge to provide the best solutions to any issue. In terms of physical activity, this can be seen in the engagement by Aboriginal participants in mainstream and all-Aboriginal sport systems, and in mainstream (Euro-Canadian-based) and traditional (Aboriginal based) forms of physical activity.

4. The commitment to self-determination in their approach to physical activity, which has led to the creation of all-Aboriginal events like the North American Indigenous Games and to the insertion of Aboriginal practices into mainstream sporting events, such as prayers to the creator before the start of an event, or a holistic orientation toward coaching, as explained in the *Aboriginal Coaching Manual*, which is a unit of the 3M National Coaching Certification Program.

These strengths provide a strong foundation upon which Aboriginal organizers can build to produce more effective opportunities for their participants. And in keeping with a two-eyed seeing approach, perhaps non-Aboriginal peoples can look at these strengths and incorporate them into mainstream sporting practices where appropriate to enhance the experience of non-Aboriginal participants as well. Incorporating these strengths into the mainstream sport system would contribute toward the 2012 Canadian Sport Policy vision, which is "A dynamic and innovative culture that promotes and celebrates participation and excellence in sport" and would help to further the policy's value of inclusion (Canadian Heritage, 2012, p. 5).

the presence of the all-Aboriginal sport system in Canada through federal policy and funding, as outlined in the 2002 (but not the 2012) Canadian Sport Policy and Sport Canada's Policy on Aboriginal Peoples' Participation in Sport from 2005.

People sometimes attach the term *reverse racism* to describe situations where normally privileged individuals—usually white people—are excluded from opportunities on the basis of race. For example, non-Aboriginal people cannot compete in the North American Indigenous Games, even though Aboriginal athletes can theoretically compete in mainstream sporting events. As directed by Section 15(2) of the Charter of Rights and Freedoms, however, efforts to address "the conditions of disadvantaged individuals or groups including those that are disadvantaged because of race" are seen as a necessary part of providing equality rights, because such efforts are required to help correct the imbalance created by unequal privilege in the first place.

This section on racism in sport has documented the individual and institutionalized racism present in whitestream sport in Canada. Race has been, and remains, an indicator or "marker" that provides meaning in our everyday sporting practices. In order to ensure that all Canadians, regardless of race, have opportunities to find meaningful participation in sport, race-structured sporting opportunities are currently needed to ensure that the sport system in Canada provides broadly for the needs of all Canadians. Until whitestream sport broadens even further and becomes truly inclusive, alternative race-structured opportunities should be celebrated and supported as part of the Canadian sport system. In this way, the institution of sport becomes a more welcoming practice reflective of the cultural meanings and traditions of all Canadians, regardless of race.

Conclusions

Race and ethnicity are aspects of our heritage that take on social meaning in Canadian society. These constructed meanings become naturalized each time we "do" them in accordance with the dominant beliefs around us. White people of European descent in Canada have been the most privileged in sport, with those from other racial backgrounds often discriminated against both overtly and through systemic racism. Whitestream hegemonic sport has emerged, legitimizing select activities such as Olympic sports and marginalizing other activities that do not fit within such understandings. Segregated sporting opportunities have likewise emerged, enabling organizers and participants from marginalized groups to structure their own experiences in sport in ways that foster pride in their cultural heritage, while giving the athletes opportunities to play that are not available otherwise. Legitimizing these sporting opportunities, and the alternative ethnic practices preferred by immigrants and their descendants, takes us one step further toward creating a sport system that is representative of all individuals in Canada.

A racial incident in hockey in 2011 reminds us that racism is still present in Canadian sport. In September, a banana peel was thrown onto the ice by a spectator during the shootout after a tied preseason NHL game in London, Ontario, which landed near Wayne Simmonds, a black hockey player originally from Toronto. Simmonds was able to score after the incident, but said that he was shocked: "I don't know if it had anything to do with the fact I'm black . . . I certainly hope not. When you're black you kind of expect [racist] things. You learn to deal with it" (Canadian Press, 2011). The spectator eventually pleaded guilty and was fined $200, but "[p]olice said there wasn't enough evidence to charge him with a hate crime, and his attorney told the court his client wasn't aware that tossing a banana at a black athlete could be seen as racist and hateful" (Weir, 2012).

In this case, one of our most successful Canadian athletes was inhibited from enjoying pride in his black heritage and skills because of racist behaviours by others in sport. We need to reflect on incidents such as this that still happen in Canada. To begin to resolve the issue, we need a clear definition of racism and discrimination that everyone associated with sport can understand, along with clearly articulated ideas about how everyone should respond when these things happen. Our outrage at such occurrences helps to ensure that we are promoting an inclusive sport system that enables all individuals to foster pride in their ethnic and racial identity. Our silence, on the other hand, reproduces a sport system where particular individuals—those who are privileged by white skin and European heritage—too often benefit while the rest of Canadians do not.

The social construction of race and ethnicity as integral aspects of sport, and of leisure more broadly, needs to be recognized if we are to find ways to decrease discrimination based on these factors. At the same time, the positive ways that our cultural identities can be shaped by movement need to be facilitated equally for all, regardless of race or ethnicity. As we look to others from different cultural backgrounds to see how they know themselves through movement, we will expand the ways that we can potentially know ourselves. In this way, we can help to shape as well as be shaped by the social meanings assigned to race and ethnicity in Canadian sport. And we will be more ready to help create equitable opportunities for all people trying to access meaningful sport in Canada by providing activities that honour the racial and ethnic differences between participants rather than erasing them.

Critical Thinking Questions

1. Explore the sporting interests of minority group residents, including Aboriginal, Inuit, Métis, black, and other minority ethnic groups, in the community in which you live or study. Prepare a table that outlines the various sports, the groups interested in each sport, and the values connected to each sport.

2. If you encounter children from a minority ethnic family—identifiable from their distinct clothing and accents—what are some of the questions you might ask them to determine if there are factors that may prevent or restrict their participation in sport or physical activity? If you determine that they do indeed have special needs, how might you facilitate their involvement in sport or physical activity?

3. What are two ways that a coach, teacher, or sports administrator might respond to an incident of overt racism, such as name calling directed at a teenager in a basketball program?

4. How do you "do race" in your life? In sport?

5. Write about an incident where the social meanings attached to race influenced your life by either privileging you or providing a barrier to opportunities you wished to experience.

6. Write a code of conduct for sport that would align with the Canadian Charter of Rights and Freedoms.

7. How do race-structured sporting events address discrimination in mainstream sport?

8. Outline examples of how sporting performances can provide opportunities for decreasing racial distinctions and for increasing racial distinctions.

9. How do we account for the ethnic diversity evident in the LPGA (Ladies Professional Golf Association) tour, where seven out of the ten top women golfers are Asian?

Suggested Readings

Forsyth, J., & Giles, A. R. (Eds.) (2013). *Aboriginal peoples and sport in Canada: Historical foundations and contemporary issues*. Vancouver, BC: UBC Press.

Joseph, J., Darnell, S., & Nakamura, Y. (Eds.). (2012). *Race and sport in Canada: Intersecting inequalities*. Toronto, ON: Canadian Scholars' Press.

Paraschak, V., & Thompson, K. (2013). Finding strength(s): Insights on Aboriginal physical cultural practices in Canada. *Sport in Society: Cultures, Commerce, Media, Politics, 17*(8), 1046–1060.

Robidoux, M. (2012). *Stickhandling through the margins: First Nations hockey in Canada*. Toronto, ON: University of Toronto Press.

Tirone, S. (2010). Multiculturalism and leisure policy: Enhancing the delivery of leisure services and supports for immigrants and minority Canadians. In S. Arai, D. Reid, & H. Mair (Eds.), *Decentring work: Critical perspectives on leisure, development and social change* (pp. 149–174). Calgary, AB: University of Calgary Press.

References

Aboriginal Sports/Recreation Association of BC. (1995, October). Media release on the 1997 North American Indigenous Games planned for Victoria, BC.

Adams, M. L. (2006). The game of whose lives? Gender, race, and entitlement in Canada's "national" game. In D. Whitson & R. Gruneau (Eds.), *Artificial ice: Hockey, culture and commerce* (pp. 71–84). Peterborough, ON: Broadview Press.

Associated Press. (2013, June 3). Quebec soccer leaders cite safety on turban bans. *Washington Times*. Accessed from http://www.washingtontimes.com/news/2013/jun/3/quebec-soccer-leaders-cite-safety-on-turban-bans.

Associated Press. (2014, May 2). Canadiens' P. K. Subban target of racist tweets. *CBC Sports*. Retrieved from http://www.cbc.ca/sports/hockey/nhl/canadiens-p-k-subban-target-of-racist-tweets-1.2629997.

Best, C. (1987). Experience and career length in professional football: The effect of positional segregation. *Sociology of Sport Journal, 4*(4), 410–420.

Bhabha, H. K. (1994). *The location of culture*. London, UK: Routledge.

Booth, D., & Tatz, C. (2000). *One-eyed: A view of Australian sport*. New South Wales, AU: Allen & Unwin.

Breton, R. (1964). Institutional completeness of ethnic communities and personal relations of immigrants. *American Journal of Sociology, 70*, 193–205.

Burnaby Now. (2013, November 20). STM grad named just third CFL Canadian MVP. Accessed from http://www.burnabynow.com/sports/photo-galleries/stm-grad-named-just-third-cfl-canadian-mvp-1.708508.

Burnet, J. R., & Palmer, H. (1988). *"Coming Canadians": An introduction to a history of Canada's people*. Toronto, ON: McLelland & Stewart in association with the Multiculturalism Program,

Department of the Secretary of State and the Canadian Government Publishing Centre, Supply and Services, Canada.

Canadian Heritage. (2012). Canadian Sport Policy 2012. Retrieved from http://sirc.ca/CSPRenewal/documents/CSP2012_EN.pdf.

Canadian Press. (2011, September 23). NHL says banana-throwing incident in pre-season game is "stupid and ignorant." *The Hockey News*. Retrieved from http://www.thehockeynews.com/articles/41885-NHL-says-bananathrowing-incident-in-preseason-game-is-stupid-and-ignorant.html.

Canadian Press. (2013, June 13). NFL commissioner Goodell defends Redskins nickname, answers letter from members of Congress. *Huffington Post*. Accessed from http://www.huffingtonpost.ca/2013/06/12/nfl-commissioner-goodell-_n_3430152.html.

Chiswick, B. R., & Miller, P. W. (2002). Do enclaves matter in immigrant adjustment? *Discussion paper 449*. Bonn, Germany: Institute for the Study of Labor.

Coakley, J., & Donnelly, P. (2009). *Sports in society: Issues and controversies* (2nd Canadian ed.). Toronto, ON: McGraw-Hill Ryerson.

Cosentino, F. (1998). *Afros, Aboriginals and amateur sport in pre-World War I Canada. Canada's Ethnic Group Series*, Booklet No. 26. Ottawa, ON: The Canadian Historical Society.

Dallaire, C., & Denis, C. (2005). Asymmetric hybridities: Youths at Francophone Games in Canada. *Canadian Journal of Sociology, 30*(2), 143–169.

Denis, C. (1997). *We are not you: First Nations and Canadian modernity*. Peterborough, ON: Broadview Press.

Frideres, J. S. (1988). Racism. In *The Canadian Encyclopedia* (2nd ed., Vol III, p. 1816). Edmonton, AB: Hurtig Publishers.

Frisby, W., Alexander, T., Taylor, J., Tirone, S., Watson, C., Harvey, J., & Laplante. (2005). *Bridging the recreation divide: Listening to youth and parents from low income families across Canada*. Ottawa, ON: Canadian Parks and Recreation Association.

Glazer, N. (1970). Ethnic groups in America: From national culture to ideology. In M. Kurokawa (Ed.), *Minority responses* (pp. 74–86). New York, NY: Random House.

Gruneau, R. (1988). Modernization or hegemony: Two views on sport and social development. In J. Harvey & H. Cantelon (Eds.), *Not just a game: Essays in Canadian sport sociology* (pp. 9–32) Ottawa, ON: University of Ottawa Press.

Hollingshead, K. (1998). Tourism, hybridity, and ambiguity: The relevance of Bhabha's "third space" cultures. *Journal of Leisure Research, 30*(1), 121–156.

Hutchison, R. (1988). A critique of race, ethnicity, and social class in recent leisure-related research. *Journal of Leisure Research, 20*(1), 10–30.

Institute for Diversity and Ethics in Sport. (n.d.). The Racial and Gender Report Card. Retrieved from http://www.tidesport.org/racialgenderreportcard.html.

James, C. (Ed.). (1996). *Perspectives on racism and the human services sector: A case for change*. Toronto, ON: University of Toronto Press.

Jenkins, L. (2014, May 26). All of us, not least Donald Sterling, now know this: Adam Silver, Commissioner, is his own man. *Sports Illustrated, 120*(2).

Kidd, B. (1983). In defence of Tom Longboat. *Canadian Journal of History of Sport, 14*(1), 34–63.

Kidd, B. (1996b). Worker sport in the new world: The Canadian story. In A. Kuger & J. Riordan (Eds.), *The story of worker sport* (pp. 143–156). Champaign, IL: Human Kinetics.

Langford, I. (2004, February 10). Cherry's comments: Racially insensitive and nonsensical. *Toronto Observer*. Retrieved from http://observer.thecentre.centennialcollege.ca/opinion/cherry_ian021004.htm.

Lavallee, L. (2007). Physical activity and healing through the medicine wheel. *Social Work Publications and Research*, Paper 2. Retrieved from http://digitalcommons.ryerson.ca/socialwork/2.

Leonard II, W. M. (1987). Stacking in college basketball: A neglected analysis. *Sociology of Sport Journal, 4*(4), 403–409.

Lewi, D. (2006, January 31). Canada's first multicultural hockey league. *Toronto Observer*. Retrieved from http://tobserver.thecentre.centennialcollege.ca/read_articles.asp?article_id=681.

Li, P. S. (1990). Race and ethnicity. In P. S. Li (Ed.), *Race and ethnic relations in Canada* (pp. 3–17). Toronto, ON: Oxford University Press.

Livingston, L. A., Tirone, S. C., Miller, A. J., & Smith, E. L. (2008). Participation in coaching by Canadian immigrants: Individual accommodations and sport system receptivity. *International Journal of Sports Science & Coaching*, 3, 403–415.

Longley, N. (2000). The underrepresentation of French Canadians on English Canadian NHL teams: Evidence from 1943 to 1998. *Journal of Sports Economics 1*(3): 236–256.

Maclean's. (2012, August 14). Field of dreams: Cricket stadium proposed for Toronto. Retrieved from http://www2.macleans.ca/2012/08/14/field-of-dreams-cricket-stadium-proposed-for-toronto/.

Majors, R. (1990). Cool pose: Black masculinity and sports. In M. Messner & D. Sabo (Eds.), *Sport, men, and the gender order: Critical feminist perspectives* (pp. 109–114). Champaign, IL: Human Kinetics Press.

McBride, P. (1975). *Culture clash: Immigrants and reformers, 1880–1920*. San Francisco, CA: R & E Associates.

Mullick, R. (2002, February). Warren Moon. *CFL Legends*. The Official Site of the Canadian Football League. Retrieved from http://www.cfl.ca/CFLLegends/moon.html.

Paraschak, V. (1989). Native sport history: Pitfalls and promise. *Canadian Journal of History of Sport*, 20(1), 57–68.

Paraschak, V. (1995). The Native Sport and Recreation Program, 1972–1981: Patterns of resistance, patterns of reproduction. *Canadian Journal of History of Sport*, 26(2), 1–18.

Paraschak, V. (1997). Variations in race relations: Sporting events for Native peoples in Canada. *Sociology of Sport Journal*, 14(1), 1–21.

Paraschak, V., & Thompson, K. (2013). Finding strength(s): Insights on Aboriginal physical cultural practices in Canada. *Sport in Society: Cultures, Commerce, Media, Politics*, 17(8), 1046–1060.

Pitter, R. (2006). Racialization and hockey in Canada: From personal troubles to a Canadian challenge. In D. Whitson & R. Gruneau (Eds.), *Artificial ice: Hockey, culture and commerce* (pp. 123–139). Peterborough, ON: Broadview Press.

Peritz, I. (2013, June 14). FIFA authorizes wearing of turbans at all levels of Canadian soccer. *Globe and Mail*. Accessed from http://www.theglobeandmail.com/sports/soccer/fifa-authorizes-wearing-of-turbans-at-all-levels-of-canadian-soccer/article12550476/.

Reitz, J., Zhang, H., & Hawkins, N. (2011). Comparisons of the success of racial minority immigrant offspring successes in the United States, Canada and Australia. *Social Science Research, 40*, 1051–1066.

Robidoux, M. (2012). *Stickhandling through the margins: First Nations hockey in Canada*. Toronto, ON; University of Toronto Press.

Rosenberg, D. (2003). Athletics in the Ward and beyond: Neighborhoods, Jews, and sport in Toronto, 1900–1939. In R. C. Wilcox, D. L. Andrews, R. Pitter, & R. L. Irwin, (Eds.), *Sporting dystopias: The making and meanings of urban sport cultures* (pp. 137–152). Albany, NY: State University of New York Press.

Rosenstein, J. (Producer). (1997). *In whose honor? America Indian mascots in sports*. New Jersey: New Day Films.

Saunders, D. (2010). *Arrival city: The final migration and out next world*. Toronto, ON: Alfred A Knopf.

Scott, R. (1987). *Jackie Robinson: Baseball great*. New York, NY: Chelsea House Publishers.

Spence, C. (1999). *The skin I'm in: Racism, sports and education*. Halifax, NS: Fernwood.

Statistics Canada. (2003). 2001 Census, Analysis series: Canada's ethnocultural portrait: The changing mosaic. Retrieved from http://www12.statcan.ca/english/census01/products/analytic/companion/etoimm/canada.cfm.

Statistics Canada. (2009). Earnings and incomes of Canadians over the past quarter century, 2006 Census highlights. Retrieved from http://www12.statcan.gc.ca/census-recensement.

Statistics Canada. (2011). Analytical document: Immigration and ethnocultural diversity in Canada. National Household Survey, 2011. Retrieved from http://www12.statcan.gc.ca/nhs-enm/2011/as-sa/99-010-x/99-010-x2011001-eng.cfm.

Statistics Canada. (2013c). 2011 National Household Survey: Immigration, place of birth, citizenship, ethnic origin, visible minorities, language and religion. *The Daily*, May 8, 2013.

Stodolska, M., & Jackson, E. L. (1998). Discrimination in leisure and work experienced by a white ethnic minority group. *Journal of Leisure Research, 30*(1), 23–46.

Tirone, S. (2000). Racism, indifference and the leisure experiences of South Asian Canadian teens. *Leisure: The Journal of the Canadian Association of Leisure Studies, 24*(1), 89–114.

Tirone, S. (2005). The challenges and opportunities faced by migrants and minorities in their leisure: An international perspective. Paper presented at the 10th International Metropolis Conference, Toronto, ON.

Tirone, S. (2010). Multiculturalism and leisure policy: Enhancing the delivery of leisure services and supports for immigrants and minority Canadians. In S. Arai, D. Reid, & H. Mair (Eds.), *Decentring work: Critical perspectives on leisure, development and social change* (pp. 149–174). Calgary, AB: University of Calgary Press.

Tirone, S., Livingston, L. A., Miller, A. J., & Smith, E. L. (2010). Including immigrants in elite and recreational sports: The experiences of athletes, sport providers and immigrants. *Leisure, 34*(4), 403–420.

Tirone, S., & Pedlar, A. (2000). Understanding the leisure experience of a minority ethnic group: South Asian teens and young adults in Canada. *Society and Leisure, 23*(1), 145–169.

TMZ Sports. (2014, April 29). Donald Sterling banned for life. Retrieved from http://www.tmz.com/2014/04/29/nba-commish-adam-silver-deciding-donald-sterling-fate-livestream-l-a-clippers/.

Trembanis, S. (2008). Research note: Defining "Aboriginal" in a historical and sporting context. *Journal of Sport History, 35*(2), 279–283.

United Way of Greater Toronto. (2004). *Poverty by postal code: The geography of neighbourhood poverty 1981–2001*. Prepared jointly by the United Way and Canadian Council on Social Development.

Washburne, R. F. (1978). Black underparticipation in wildland recreation: Alternative explanations. *Leisure Sciences, 1*, 175–189.

Weir, T. (2012, January 9). Hockey fan fined $200 for throwing banana at black player. *USA Today*. Retrieved from http://content.usatoday.com/communities/gameon/post/2012/01/hockey-fan-fined-200-for-throwing-banana-at-black-player/1#.UpaN6OKMmHs.

West, C., & Zimmerman, D. (1991). Doing gender. In J. Lorber & S. Farrell (Eds), *The social construction of gender* (pp. 13–37). London, UK: Sage Publications.

White, P., & McTeer, W. (2012) Socioeconomic status and sport participation at different developmental stages during childhood and youth: Multivariate analyses using Canadian national survey data. *Sociology of Sport Journal, 29*(2), 186–209.

Wickberg, E. B. (1988). Chinese. In *The Canadian Encyclopedia* (2nd ed., Vol. I, pp. 415–417). Edmonton, AB: Hurtig Publishers.

Wilson, B. (1999). 'Cool pose' incorporated: The marketing of black masculinity in Canadian NBA coverage. In P. White & K. Young (Eds.), *Sport and gender in Canada* (pp. 232–253). Toronto, ON: Oxford University Press.

Windsor Star. (2014, May 23). Senate wants Redskins renamed, p. B5.

Woolcock, M. (1998). Social capital and economic development: Toward a theoretical synthesis and policy framework. *Theory and Society 27*, 151–208.

Young, A. J. (1988). *Beyond heroes: A sport history of Nova Scotia: Vol. 2*. Hantsport, NS: Lancelot Press.

Chapter 6
Sex, Gender, and Sexuality
Mary Louise Adams

In the 1970s and 1980s feminists worked hard to encourage government agencies, schools, and sport organizations to expand opportunities for girls and women to play sports. Over the past several decades the numbers of girls and women participating in a whole range of sports has grown exponentially and now, for many Canadian girls, sport is a taken-for-granted part of their childhoods, as it has been for many boys for generations.

bikeriderlondon/Shutterstock

For people interested in sex, gender, and sexuality, sport provides seemingly endless opportunities to think about norms and stereotypes, equality and discrimination. From ongoing debates over fighting in the NHL to the launch of the Lingerie Football League in Hamilton, Ontario, issues related to gender and sexuality seem to be unavoidable features of contemporary sports. Sport has long been lauded as a fine vehicle for turning boys into men, which can sometimes make it an awkward institution for women and, indeed, for many boys and men. Sport has also been derided for celebrating hypermasculine behaviours that lead to excessive and violent aggression, risk-taking, and the development of sexist and homophobic attitudes. It has been promoted as a source of empowerment for women and girls and criticized as an inequitable institution in which female athletes don't get their fair share of resources or respect.

In sport sociology, a widely shared view is that there is nothing inherently good or bad about sports themselves, and this is certainly the case with respect to gender and sexuality. As an institution, sport can reinforce the existing organization of gender and sexuality in our culture or it can challenge it. Historically, in Canada and elsewhere, it has done both, with different effects for people of differing physical abilities, ages, nationalities, or racial, ethnic, or class backgrounds. In this chapter I will introduce the main theoretical concepts and frames that sociologists have used to examine issues related to gender and sexuality in sport. I will question the popular assumption that sport is (really!) a male sphere before looking at women's participation in sport in Canada and how it is that sport has come to be a relatively commonplace experience for some Canadian girls and women. The chapter also examines issues related to sexuality and issues of concern to transgendered, transsexual, lesbian, and gay athletes. The purpose of the chapter is not to provide a survey of current issues but to offer conceptual tools that will help you make sense of the issues you encounter in other texts or in your own experiences of sport.

CLARIFYING OUR TERMS

Sex and *gender* are the key concepts in this chapter. While these two terms are often used interchangeably in everyday speech, sociologists find it useful to distinguish between them. *Sex* is a classificatory scheme that is intended to divide humans into groups on the basis of their reproductive capacities. For the most part, people are assigned to one of two groups according to the shape of their genitals or to the presence or absence of certain secondary sex characteristics like beards or breasts. In our culture there are two generally recognized sexes: female and male. While anthropological research suggests that all human societies have classified people by sex, not all societies have classified them into the simple two-category binary system that is the dominant system in most contemporary Western industrial societies (Nanda, 2000).

What makes sex important sociologically is its centrality to the way we understand other people. Sex is one of the first things that registers for us when we encounter someone new. Was that person who just walked by a woman or a man? When we are unable to classify a person's sex it can feel unsettling. How, for instance, should we refer to someone when we do not know their sex? English, like many (but not all) languages, has no room for ambiguity around sex; it is impolite to refer to another human as "it." To speak about or even think of someone, we need to choose the correct pronoun—she or he—according to the binary classification of sex. The assumption that the world is divided into two distinct kinds of people is built directly into the rules of the language and is, therefore, fundamental to the way we see and think about the people around us. Sport is one of many institutions that contribute to the maintenance of this binary system.

Of course, as anyone reading this book will know, mainstream Western cultures do not simply divide bodies into male and female categories, they also saddle the different categories of bodies with different expectations regarding appearance and behaviour. These expectations reflect a belief that not just male and female bodies but male and female people are essentially different from each other—physically, psychologically, and socially. Sex refers to bodies; *gender* refers to the cultural expectations about behaviour, attitudes, and appearance that are imposed on people. Male bodies are supposed to demonstrate masculine traits; female bodies are supposed to be feminine. Stereotyped notions of what counts as appropriately masculine or appropriately feminine often serve as the basis for norms against which people's behaviour is judged and regulated. We see evidence of such judgment when a boy is teased or ridiculed by his friends or his family for wanting to pursue so-called girls' activities like ballet. We see the effects of the judgment when boys keep their desire for such activities to themselves.

Increasingly, it is becoming clear that the expected tidy equation between bodies and genders does not work for everyone. The term *transsexual* refers to people who feel that their sex and their gender do not correspond as social conventions dictate. So a child with a male body might grow up with a very strong sense of being a girl. Or a child with a female body might grow up hoping to become a man and not a woman. Some transsexual people choose to take hormones and have surgery to change their physical sex to align with their own knowledge of their gender identity. Other transsexual people eschew medical intervention to set their own path through the expectations and attitudes of a culture that is heavily invested in having bodies and genders properly lined up. A third group of people describe themselves as *transgendered*. This could mean that they do not identify specifically with masculinity or femininity, or that they understand their gender to be fluid rather than fixed in one category. Some transgender people try to develop a range of masculine and feminine styles of behaviour, while others try to live outside standard gender categories altogether. Later in this chapter, I will address the issues faced by transgender and transsexual people in sport.

The assumed tight links between sex and gender have implications in all aspects of life, but they are particularly strong in the areas of sexual identity, sexual attraction, and sexual behaviour. The conventional equations are that male body = masculine person = attraction to women, and that female body = feminine person = attraction to men. And so people who express non-normative versions of gender, like male figure skaters or ice dancers, are often assumed to be gay. And while there are many gay people who reject conventional gender norms, not all gay people do. Similarly, not all heterosexual people accept them. The conflation of gender and sexual orientation, as we will see, has contributed to the acceptance and celebration of hypermasculine behaviour in some men's sporting cultures and to the reluctance some women have shown to participate in so-called masculine sports. Historically, the conflation of gender and sexual orientation has also had an impact on women's sport participation, as we will see below.

Over the past three decades, Canadians have been witness to significant changes in the relationship between lesbian and gay communities and mainstream culture. The most important of these were the major victories in the 1980s when courts and human rights commissions extended human rights protection to prohibit discrimination on the grounds of sexual orientation. The 2005 Supreme Court decision that opened the door to lesbian and gay marriage also marks a huge shift in public attitudes to lesbian and gay people and the willingness of government agencies to reflect it.

Despite these achievements, Canadian cultures are still largely organized around the assumption that everyone is heterosexual until proven otherwise. *Heteronormativity* is an awkward but useful term that marks the fact that social institutions—like education, law, media, popular music, or sport—privilege and value heterosexuality more than other forms of sexual identity or expression. The term captures the key fact that heterosexuality is more valued not just because it seems to be more common, but because it is considered more normal. By corollary, other sexual orientations or identities are seen, at best, as not quite normal and, at worst, as deviant. *Homophobia* is a more frequently used term that means, quite literally, the fear of homosexuals; it is a product of a heteronormative culture.

SOCIAL CONSTRUCTION: A FRAMEWORK FOR THINKING ABOUT GENDER NORMS

Where do gender norms come from? Some might argue that their roots lie in biology. The notion that men play more contact sports than women do because men's bodies produce more testosterone is an example of this kind of argument. While sociologists do not discount the fact that there are differences between male and female bodies, they do question the extent to which these physical differences are the grounds for cultural and social behaviours. Sociologists would call the testosterone-leads-to-contact-sports argument a kind of *biological determinism*. In other words, it is an argument that explains human social behaviour as a product of human biology. Because such arguments reduce complex phenomena (the fact that more men than women play tackle football) to the effects of a single biological cause, sociologists consider them to be reductionist. The preferred social science perspective is a theoretical framework called *social constructionism*.

In studies of gender, social constructionism came to prominence as a critique of biological determinism. It emerged as a means of explaining the tremendous cross-cultural and historical variations in what counts as "normal" masculine or "normal" feminine behaviour. If gendered behaviours were primarily determined by biology, would we not expect that masculinity and femininity would look fairly similar across time and place? The history of sport provides very good evidence for the fact that they do not. A century ago, in the expanding industrial societies of North America and Europe, it was widely believed that women's biology made them incapable of participating in vigorous sports. This position was developed by white, middle- and upper-class professionals such as physicians, teachers, and ministers and was directed toward women of similar background and social position. It is not, therefore, surprising that white, middle- and upper-class women did not, for the most part, engage in vigorous sport at that time. Given their lack of experience with hard labour or other physically demanding activities, they may not have believed that they were capable of doing so. And yet clear evidence of women's strength and physical competence was easily available to those same women and to the professionals who advised them in the hard physical work done by their own female domestic servants. In short, what was considered "natural" for women in the 19th century varied between classes and racial groups, as it varies with what is seen as "natural" for women today. Canadian girls and women now play a broad range of sports in numbers that would have been unimaginable to earlier generations. Did female biology change over the past century to make this possible? Of course not. What changed were the dominant social and cultural norms around how physical women and girls should be, what their bodies should look like, the kinds of clothes they should wear, and how they should move. Dominant norms reflect the values and interests of powerful groups in society. Here, the white, middle-class norm that suggested women should not be physically strong or competent would have positioned working-class women who were strong and competent as unnatural and inferior.

As a theoretical perspective, social constructionism reminds us that what is considered natural and normal in one place or time might be viewed and experienced as abnormal in another. It keeps us mindful that human behaviour is variable, and it also provides assurance that the way gender is arranged now does not have to be forever set in stone. Things can and will change. For people who are concerned about gender-based and other inequalities, the *possibility* of change can motivate efforts to make change. Many sport scholars who study gender do so with the goal of promoting changes in sport that will feed gender equality in the broader society.

IS SPORT REALLY A MALE THING?

"Sport is a male preserve" is one of the most often-repeated statements in sport sociology. As you saw in Chapter 3, the history of sport has indeed been a history that highlights men and masculinity. A report published by the International Olympic Committee (IOC) described the ancient Olympics in Greece as a "male-only extravaganza" (International Olympic Committee, 2009, p. 3). When modern sporting institutions were developed in Europe and North America in the 19th century, these too were designed by and for men. There were no events for women in the first modern Olympic Games in 1896. Pierre de Coubertin, the founder of the modern Olympics, saw women's roles as spectators and not as competitors.

Coubertin, a French aristocrat, imported his ideas about sport from England. According to historian James Walvin, the type of 19th-century sports that Coubertin so admired had emerged as part of the "cult of manliness" that pervaded boys' private schools in the mid-1800s (Walvin, 1987). In the Victorian era, manliness "stood for neo-Spartan virility as exemplified by stoicism, hardiness, and endurance" (Mangan & Walvin, 1987, p. 1). Educators promoted athletic competition to foster these qualities in boys. In this sense, sport developed as a moral and pedagogical tool of imperialism. Upper-class boys were being educated so that they could govern colonies throughout the British Empire, and sport was meant to teach them about leadership, team play, and courage. For the working-class boys who would one day have to follow their orders, sport was meant to promote the discipline, obedience, and deference to authority that was required by expanding capitalist economies and military service. In both cases, sport was called upon to help turn particular kinds of boys into particular kinds of men—in other words, to prepare boys for the station determined by their class. This was the model of sport that was exported to Canada and other British colonies around the world.

Over the past century and a half, many people have continued to understand sport as a device to toughen up young men and to see athleticism as a central component of virility. Some sociologists of sport argue that sport plays a key role in the construction of *hegemonic masculinity*, which is a term that was introduced and developed by sociologist R. W. Connell. Hegemonic masculinity is one of the many possible images or models of masculinity that circulate in a specific historical or cultural context. It is a dominant and "idealized form of masculinity" (Connell, 1990, p. 83) that has achieved broad public acceptance and operates as "common sense," serving to define what men *should* be like. In the process of becoming the dominant ideal, hegemonic masculinity sidelines other ways of being a man; it sits at the top of the hierarchy of gender identities available to people in male bodies. Connell says that the ideal helps to secure patriarchal power and, more specifically, to perpetuate the subordination of women and the marginalization of gay men. The particular features of the ideal can and do change to maintain acceptance. In today's capitalist consumer economy the ideal emphasizes physical strength, toughness, occupational success, and competitiveness. Sport offers a vehicle through which the ideal is both produced and promoted, with male athletes serving to embody and display the ideal in practice. As Connell writes, "To be culturally exalted, the pattern of masculinity must have exemplars who are celebrated as heroes" (Connell, 1990, p. 94). Men who play on professional sport teams have both the cultural visibility and personal attributes to fulfill this role. The status that accrues to male professional athletes in North American cultures is a product of the hegemonic masculine ideal and helps to legitimize it.

Connell has argued that "sport has come to be the leading definer of masculinity in mass culture" (1995, p. 54). Men and boys who are unable or unwilling to develop their athleticism lose access to a key marker of masculinity (Gill, Henwood, & Maclean, 2005). Researchers in the sociology of education have shown that elementary and high school students understand this, and they use athleticism as protection against gender-based and homophobic bullying. In a study with British elementary schoolchildren, Emma Renold found that some boys who were high-achieving students, and thus at risk of being seen as feminine by their peers, used sport strategically as a way to protect their masculine reputations (Renold, 2001). In her ethnographic study of masculinity in two California high schools, sociologist C. J. Pascoe referred to what she calls "jock insurance." Pascoe found that athleticism allowed some boys to expose "more 'feminine' parts of their identities without being labeled a 'fag.'" Boys told her that their status was, in part, determined by how they were able to position themselves relative to the "jocks" who occupied the top rungs of their school's social hierarchy (Pascoe, 2003).

And what about boys who don't like to or who are unable to play sports or who choose to play sports that are considered to be 'feminine'? Too often they are at risk of

Canada has produced a long line of Men's World Figure Skating Champions, like Patrick Chan, pictured here. Yet strict gender norms in our culture mean that despite such excellent role models, figure skating is not a popular sport for young Canadian boys.
Aleksander V. Chernykh/PhotoXpress/ZUMA Press, Inc./Alamy

being marginalized as "wimps" or "sissies." It is not a coincidence that girls outnumber boys at my local skating club by a ratio of about 10:1. There is both misogyny (hatred of women) and homophobia at work here, as there is when old-school coaches admonish their male athletes not to play like girls (Daniels, 2005). Similar attitudes emerge in the ongoing debates over fighting in hockey. In 2009, *Hockey Night in Canada* commentator Mike Milbury used the term "pansification" to describe what would happen to hockey should fighting be banned. His comment led to complaints that the Canadian Broadcasting Corporation was permitting homophobic speech. Helen Kennedy, executive director of the lesbian and gay advocacy group EGALE, argued that the term "pansy" is generally used "in a derogatory fashion to bully young, effeminate, gay men" (*CBC Sports*, 2002).

Sport researchers have shown that the particular tough-guy (hegemonic) masculinity that is prized by sports personalities like Don Cherry and that is produced in high-profile men's contact team sports has had troubling consequences for the men and boys who aspire to it for themselves. The fear of being called out as a "wuss" is one of the reasons some male athletes play while injured, engage in violence on the field, take drugs to bulk up, and go along with offensive and sometimes abusive, misogynous, and homophobic hazing rituals (Johnson & Holman, 2004; White & Young, 2007). There are many other versions of masculinity available in sport, for example in cross-country skiing or diving or triathlon, but these do not receive the recognition or the rewards that accrue to athletes in the hypermasculine professional sports such as football and hockey that garner the most attention in the media, and therefore have a big influence in popular culture.

Female Athletes in Sport Media

To consider the maleness of present-day sport from a different direction, one can look to see how female athletes are represented in sport media. Many mornings, as I flip through the *Globe and Mail*, I can find no coverage of women's sports at all. The sports sections of daily newspapers are dominated by stories about the big four North American professional male sports leagues, which are the exclusive preserve of men. Television has similar abysmally low rates of coverage of women's sport (see Chapter 11). While very little recent research has been done on sport media in Canada, a report from a longitudinal study that has been tracking the coverage of women's sport on local television news programs in Los Angeles and on the ESPN highlights show *SportsCenter* demonstrates that coverage of women's sport (in non-Olympic periods) has actually declined over the past 20 years, despite the expansion of women's professional leagues and women's participation in a wider range of sports. On the television news programs that were part of the study, and on SportsCenter, coverage of women's sport now accounts for just 1.3 to 1.6% of the total content (Cooky, Messner, & Hextrum, 2013).

As sociologist Margaret Carlisle Duncan has written, the treatment of women athletes in the media is both "ambivalent and derogatory" (Duncan, 2006, p. 247). She argues that studies in various countries show that female athletes are sexualized in images and text, that their accomplishments are trivialized and obscured, and that they are often framed by storylines having little to do with their athletic skills (Duncan, 2006). In a study of Canadian and US newspaper coverage of the women's and men's gold medal contenders in hockey at the 2010 Olympic Games, John Vincent and Jane Crossman present an example of such findings. They found that the coverage infantalized and trivialized women players, undermined their athleticism, and conveyed the impression that the men's game was the one that really counted (Vincent & Crossman, 2012).

Sports reporters routinely mention women's appearance and their romantic and family lives as a means of imposing a heteronormative frame over narratives that might otherwise threaten conventional assumptions about sex and gender. So, for instance, it has not been uncommon for news stories about Canadian hockey player Hayley Wickenheiser, arguably the best female player in history, to make frequent references to her "adopted son Noah" and to her responsibilities as a mother. Certainly it is important to recognize that athletes have lives that extend beyond their sports. However, it would be a rare story about a male hockey player that would spend any time at all wondering about how he juggles his sport and his parenting.

The assumption that sport is, at its core, a male preserve has meant that women have long had to struggle for resources, recognition, and respect as athletes and for their participation in sport to be seen as ordinary. Historically, the equation that conflates sex, gender, and sexual orientation has made sport a difficult choice for many women. Popular assumptions that sport is (really) a masculine pursuit have meant that female athletes have often been seen as mannish and, therefore, as lesbians (Cahn, 1994; Lenskyj, 1986). The fear of being perceived as too masculine or as a lesbian has kept many women—both lesbians and heterosexuals—from choosing to play sports traditionally defined as male. In earlier time periods this fear kept some women and girls out of sport entirely. While the worst effects of this kind of homophobia and gender policing have diminished in recent decades, women's sport is still not completely clear of anxiety around the relationship of athleticism and gender. It is no coincidence that entire teams of women all keep their hair long enough to wear in ponytails. While there is nothing wrong with ponytails, the fact that almost all female athletes seem to be "choosing" them, suggests that homophobia and heteronormativity may well be at work.

SEX AND GENDER DIFFERENCES IN SPORT

One of the many reasons why sport is such an interesting topic of study for those of us interested in gender relations is because it is a highly valued and pervasive cultural institution in which sex and gender differences are, especially at the highest levels, fundamental. Indeed, sport without sex difference is almost inconceivable.

The most powerful means of fostering and maintaining sex and gender difference in sport is the routine segregation of the sexes. Sex segregation operates in sport in two primary ways. First, with exceptions for young children and some intramural or fun leagues, almost all sports have separate events for women and men; female and male athletes almost never compete against each other. Second, there are still some sports that are popularly understood to be more appropriate for one sex than for the other. The sociological term for this is *sport typing*. The CFL or the NFL are good examples here, as are the aesthetic sports (rhythmic gymnastics, synchronized swimming, figure skating, artistic gymnastics, and diving). Gender distinctions are also fostered in sport by the fact that many events have different rules for men and women.

In this section I discuss the two different ways of maintaining sex segregation in sport and two issues that are directly related to sex segregation: sex testing and the inclusion of transgender and transsexual athletes. I will then move on to talk about gender-based rules in sport and lesbian and gay issues in sport.

Separate Events for Men and Women

So why do sport organizations organize separate events for male and female athletes? Most would say that they do so because it ensures fairness for women, given the fact that, on average, men are physically bigger and stronger than women. But if the issue is primarily a matter of size and strength, why does one see sex segregation in sports where men's size and strength give them no advantage? Let's take the shooting event of Olympic skeet (trap shooting) as an example. Introduced in 1968, it was a mixed-sex competition at the Olympics. In 1992, a woman, Zhang Shan of China, won the gold medal. At the Games that followed, in 1996, women were not permitted to compete. A separate women's event was established in 2000. These new sex-segregated events have different rules. Men get five rounds of 25 targets while women get three. In a sport where strength and size make no difference to performance, what was the reason for separating the men from the women? And what was the reason for giving women fewer rounds?

Ski jumping raises similar questions. The preferred body shape for ski jumpers is small and light. Male ski jumpers often weigh less than 130 pounds; there is certainly no argument in favour of men's size in this sport. And yet, not only are male and female athletes separated in ski jumping, women have had to fight to get to compete at all. The International Ski Federation did not recognize women's events until 1998. While men competed in ski jumping at the first Winter Olympics in 1924, women's first Olympic appearance was in Sochi, Russia, in 2014. The fact that women's events have finally made it on to the Olympic schedule is a result of court challenges and extensive lobbying by female ski jumpers and their advocates.

The ski jumping example allows us to see the exclusionary ideological processes that have constrained women's participation in sport. In the years leading up to the 2010 Vancouver Olympic Games, the record holder on the 95-metre jump at Whistler Olympic Park was an American woman named Lindsey Van. And yet, because there was no women's competition in ski jumping at the Games, Van did not get to defend her record. If sporting competitions are supposed to be about extending the limits of human performance, shouldn't the record holder have been able to compete at the Olympics? Should Van not have had a chance to compete against the two men who were her rivals for the record?

In an article on women's ski jumping, sport scholars Jason Laurendeau and Carly Adams put the Olympic controversy into historical context. They noted that in 19th-century Scandinavia, women and men both participated in ski jumping at a local level, often in the same competitions (Laurendeau & Adams, 2010). But as the sport became more structured, with governing bodies and codified rules, officials began to promote ski jumping as "natural" for men but too dangerous for women. (Would a man's bones be less likely to break during a fall?) On the advice of medical experts, officials banned women from competition, and thus ski jumping became a so-called masculine sport—a turn of events that precluded the possibility of a man having to lose to a woman in competition. At the start of the 20th century, the "best" way to ski jump was in a male body. And so it remained until recently when women jumpers finally exerted enough pressure on the International Ski Federation and the IOC to be able to compete at the same level as men (Women's Ski Jumping USA, n.d.).

So, in a society where gender rights advocates have been working for years to eliminate gender segregation in the professions, in education, and in politics, sport presents us with high-profile events that have strict divisions between women and men. The point here is *not* that there are no physical differences between women and men that might need to be accommodated to make some sports fair (although some sociologists (Kane, 1995) have suggested that we would do better to organize events in terms of weight or other sport-specific markers rather than sex, as they do in wrestling). The point is that the continual referencing of gender differences gives them a lot more weight than they would have had otherwise, or than they need to have in a society in which women and men participate equally in the domestic and private spheres in physical, intellectual, and emotional work.

Sex Testing in Sport

One of the striking consequences of the segregation of the sexes in sport is the practice in major competitions like the Olympics of testing female athletes to verify their sex. This is not a practice to which male athletes are subject. The ostensible point is to keep men from competing unfairly against "real" women, although no sex test has ever caught a man masquerading as a female athlete. In the 1960s, the International Association of Athletics Federations (IAAF), which governs track and field, required women competitors to undergo a visual physical inspection by three gynecologists, a practice that athletes found humiliating and degrading (Donnelly & Donnelly, 2013). In 1968, the IAAF and the IOC introduced chromosome tests.

The problem with any "sex test" is that there is no exact standard by which one can determine exactly who is and who is not a woman. Humans do not divide neatly into the subclasses of male and female. Upon which criteria would one determine who belongs in which category? Genitalia? The rate of sexual indeterminacy has been estimated to be between 1 in 1,500 and 1 in 2,000 births (Intersex Society of North America, n.d.). Hormones? Both male and female bodies produce so-called male and female hormones, and there is no absolute level or ratio that separates one sex from the other. Chromosomes? Even the IOC eventually admitted that these are unreliable. After considerable public outcry, the IOC and other major sports organizations abandoned the practice of across-the-board "gender verification" (their term) (Genel, 2001). Yet they continue to test particular athletes, as was the case in 2008 at the Beijing Olympic Games and in 2009 with the horrific treatment of the South African world champion 800-metre runner Caster Semenya, who was subjected to extensive testing by the IAAF and to humiliating treatment in the media after officials and other competitors accused her of not being a "real" woman.

Many women's organizations and sports organizations, including the Canadian Centre for Ethics in Sport (CCES), argue strongly that sex verification testing should be abolished. While the tests may originally have been designed to search out men, they now serve primarily to identify athletes who are *intersex*, that is, who have congenital variations that lead to nontypical physical characteristics related to sex. At the 2006 Asian Games, Indian runner Santhi Soundarajan was stripped of a silver medal and pushed out of sport after a test showed that she had atypical chromosomes for a woman. A report put out by the CCES argues that "the overall evidence from genetics and science support[s] dismantling the structures of suspicion towards athletes with variations of sex development. Even as our knowledge continues to grow, the pivotal point is to transition sport policies and attitudes from gender verification to gender inclusion" (Canadian Centre for Ethics in Sport, 2012, p. 8).

Transgender and Transsexual Athletes in Sex-Segregated Sport

Gender inclusion is another important issue that pertains directly to the segregation of the sexes in sport. Misunderstanding and discriminatory attitudes around gender variation have made sport a difficult space for many transgender and transsexual people. In sport, the almost universal categorization of participants by sex has led to constraints for transgender people who may resist being categorized, and for transsexual people who may categorize themselves differently than sport officials do. The main issue from the perspective of transgender and transsexual athletes is to ensure that they can participate in sport in the sex category with which they identify. The main issue for sport organizations is whether male-to-female transsexuals who have had sex reassignment surgery and who take female hormones have an unfair advantage in women's competitions; medical evidence makes it clear that they do not (Canadian Centre for Sport Ethics, 2012).

In 2004, the IOC adopted rules, referred to as the Stockholm Consensus, that permit the participation of fully transitioned transsexual athletes (athletes who have "changed sex" legally and surgically and who have been taking hormones for at least two years). This is a fairly narrow medical approach to gender diversity, which privileges athletes from countries where the surgery is both available and recognized and does little for trans people who are not able to access or who are not interested in medical interventions. Very few Canadian sport organizations have adopted policies to address the inclusion of trans athletes. The Canadian Collegiate Athletic Association (CCAA) is an exception. The CCAA policy requires transsexuals to show documentation of one year of hormone therapy; it does not require trans athletes to have had surgery. Other organizations at community and intramural levels have been trying to determine open policies that do not

Trans woman Michelle Dumaresq is a competitive downhill mountain bike racer. In the past decade some sport organizations have begun to develop policies to accommodate transsexual athletes.
Marina Dodis

assume that all transsexual people should have medical intervention and that permit transgender and transsexual people to maintain their privacy (Travers & Deri, 2010). Particularly at lower levels of sport, policies are needed to make sure that no one is denied an opportunity to participate because they do not identify with binary sex categories. Even small steps can demonstrate the intent to be inclusive. The Vancouver Board of Parks and Recreation, for instance, holds a regular trans-friendly All-Bodies Swim, an event that can attract more than 100 swimmers (McKinnon, 2013).

As more trans people "come out" at younger ages, their inclusion in sport may force a rethinking of the current default organization of sport along lines of sex. Do all sports at all levels really need to separate male and female bodies? If sex segregation is intended to promote fairness in sport, how must our notions of fairness change when we think about the accessibility of sport to people who do not conform to normative categories of sex or gender?

The other issue for transgender and transsexual athletes is safety. As numerous studies have shown, trans people experience high levels of harassment and violence on the street, in their families, at school, and at work. Sport organizations need to make sure that policies related to locker-room behaviour, travel arrangements, and uniforms provide a comfortable environment for all players regardless of gender identity (Taylor et al., 2011). In Ontario, the Human Rights Code was amended in 2012 to include gender identity as a prohibited ground for discrimination. Should sport organizations fail to address trans issues, it is only a matter of time before someone lodges a formal complaint.

Sport Typing

Sport typing is the notion that some sports are better suited for girls and women and others are better suited for boys and men. It is a particularly powerful means of communicating ideas about sex differences (Kane & Snyder, 1989). Given the history of sport as a sphere of activity dominated by men, it is not surprising that the list of sports traditionally considered appropriate for men is much longer than the list considered appropriate for women, or that included on the male list are those sports most valued in the culture. Not only does this lopsided categorization of sport by sex support a particular understanding of women's (lesser) place in the broader society, it has, historically, also constituted a tremendously effective practical barrier to the sport participation of women and girls. Thus, women's sport advocates have been especially concerned with expanding women's access to the male list. Much less energy has been spent trying to get men to play those sports on the female list.

Ideas about which sports are appropriate for which sex are historically and culturally specific. In its early days, for instance, figure skating, which is now seen by some people as a so-called feminine sport, was almost exclusively an activity of upper-class men (Adams, 2011). Synchronized swimming is another "feminine" sport that originally included men (Bean, 2005). In the present day, field hockey is seen primarily as a women's sport in Canada, while it is popular for both sexes in Asia and Europe. Such differences make clear that sports are socially constructed activities that are given meaning by people in accordance with their social and cultural contexts. As we have seen previously, these contexts are shaped not just by ideas about sex and gender, but also ideas about class and race. Dominant norms of middle-class, white, masculinity, which are based on control and power, do not really include space for men to wear sequined costumes or to move their bodies to music in public. Such behaviour would not reflect the status or power of this group.

People who pursue "inappropriate" sports often face obstacles: questions about their gender identities and sexual orientation; harassment; and belittlement of their achievements. Yet, while increasing numbers of girls and women participate in so-called men's sports, there has been no comparable change in the numbers of men and boys who take up so-called women's sports. In a study of elementary and high school students, Brenda Riemer and Michelle Visio found that the list of sports commonly played by girls is expanding to include so-called masculine sports, but the researchers saw no parallel effort to get boys to participate in "feminine" sports (Riemer & Visio, 2003). Simply put, boys and men face higher gender barriers around their sport choices than do girls and women, and they suffer considerable consequences when they transgress them.

The typing of sport by sex has helped to obscure the fact that all athletes, male or female, in "masculine" or "feminine" sports, require a complex set of skills—power, strength, flexibility, speed, and intelligence. The segregation of women's athletic aspirations and their allegedly sex-specific athletic skills, along with the fact that women were kept from playing men's games, has meant that male athletes have been able to compete free of challenges to their own claims of athletic superiority. Physical activities, as we know, do not fall from the sky fully formed as sports—neither do they emerge fully formed as men's sports or women's sports. There is nothing inherent in forms of movement that makes them masculine or feminine. Gendered adjectives are applied to sports and to other aspects of human behaviour in accordance with the culturally specific definitions of masculinity and femininity that circulate at particular times. And, most important, these definitions change. When we fail to make this simple point, we risk naturalizing the categories and limiting people's ability to see past them.

Gender-Based Rules in Sport

Gender is a system of differences. If masculinity and femininity were to overlap too much, gender would cease to make sense as a way of classifying people. Sport helps to construct the space that holds masculinity and femininity apart. First, as we have seen, male and female athletes rarely compete against each other. Second, they may well compete in sports that are sex-typed. Finally, female and male athletes are often required to play by sex-specific rules. In gymnastics, women and men perform on different apparatus and women perform their floor exercises to music while men do not. In golf, men's tees are further from the green. In hockey, women are not allowed to body check, nor are they allowed to fight; they must also wear full visors at all levels. Physiological explanations are almost always given as justifications for such gender-specific rules. But physiology cannot explain why some physical differences are emphasized and not others, or why these differences are assumed to be worth promoting in the first place. They also can't explain the different uniform requirements for women and men, as we see, for instance, in beach volleyball. Sociologists argue that the practice of treating male and female athletes differently and drawing strict and visible boundaries between them helps to prop up ideologies that constitute women and men as not just different but as unequal.

What are the specific messages in these gender-specific rules? Often they tell us that women are weaker than men: Women hockey players can't take hits, women cross-country skiers can't ski as far as men. Judith Lorber (1994) writes that when we believe there are big differences between women and men, then that is what we will see. In sport, gender-specific rules reflect such beliefs. And then, in the performance of the sports, the beliefs are put into practice. So gender differences *are* what we see—women don't run as far as men do! And once having seen them, they come to be what we look for. Sports could be organized differently. Indeed, sport could be an excellent vehicle for demonstrating the similarities between female and male bodies and the overlapping feminine and masculine traits that all people are capable of expressing. It's the potential of sport to challenge dominant understandings of sex and gender that has made sport an issue of concern for feminists and their supporters in the general effort to achieve greater gender equity in society.

Lesbian and Gay Issues

It is an understatement to say that sport has not always provided the most welcoming environment for lesbian and gay athletes. As we have already seen, given hetero-norms of femininity, women who excel at sport, especially in events that were once reserved for men, have often been presumed to be gay. The assumption that women's teams are full of lesbians has led to parents keeping their daughters from certain sports, to a heavy emphasis on visible markers of femininity (e.g., hair ribbons and makeup) among some women athletes, and to a reluctance on the part of some lesbian players and coaches to come out (Demers, 2006). In 2007, Rene Portland, the women's basketball coach at Pennsylvania State University resigned after many complaints and a lawsuit about her open refusal to allow lesbians on her team. Portland's homophobia is among the most famous and blatant examples of the kind of attitude that has clouded women's sport over the past century (Mosbacher & Yacker, 2008).

The influence of homophobia on men's sport is different than it is on women's sport. The homophobia that is part and parcel of the hypermasculinity that some male athletes aspire to has led to a lot of pain in all-male sport spaces, from the casual but pernicious homophobia of the locker room to the sexual violence that is part of some hazing rituals. In 2005, the McGill University football season was cancelled after veteran players subjected rookies to humiliating and sexually abusive acts (CBC Sports, 2005). In what kind of world does one foster "team spirit" by sexually assaulting a teammate with a broomstick?

In the mainstream sport media, lesbian and gay issues are largely reduced to the question of who is going to come out next, particularly in the context of professional men's sport. While it is true that a high-profile gay player could perhaps shift attitudes among sport fans and other players, the real work in addressing homophobia has to happen at every level of sport, and it has to focus on creating a climate in which athletes of all sexual orientations can feel comfortable.

Such efforts are already underway with straight–gay alliances in some community and university sport programs, including those at Memorial University and McMaster University, and in well-publicized organizations like the You Can Play Project that has close ties to the NHL. These anti-homophobia initiatives are about eliminating discriminatory attitudes from sport and about making arenas and playing fields safe places for lesbian and gay players. You Can Play is very much focused on teams and athletes—its slogan is "If you can play, you can play." In other words, if you are going to help us win, we don't care if you are gay or straight. While this is not the most inclusive position that the organization could have taken, it is definitely a start in terms of shifting the dialogue in environments like the hockey team dressing room. The message needs to be that men can be good, tough, competent athletes while at the same time rejecting the kind of ideas that make homophobic insults, misogynous treatment of women, or violent hazing of teammates seem okay. That said, the end point of anti-homophobia and gender inclusive work in sport needs to extend well beyond the playing field. The effects of hypermasculinity and homophobia in sport are not just a problem for gay athletes—they also shape attitudes that have far-reaching effects outside of sport. What kind of work needs to be done in sport to interrupt the conflation of athleticism and hypermasculinity, to make it seem completely unremarkable that a little boy might want to take ballet?

FEMINISM AND WOMEN'S SPORT

Few readers of this book would see anything unusual in women or girls playing soccer. Indeed, one might expect that many of the women reading this book have played soccer themselves, given that soccer has one of the highest female participation rates of any sport in Canada—42% of registered soccer players are female (Canadian Soccer Association, 2012). The fact that women's soccer is now unremarkable reflects huge changes in the gendering of sport over the past few decades. These changes would not have been possible without feminism.

In the 1970s, 1980s, and 1990s, the number of girls and women involved in sport grew very quickly, as did the number of sports they played. In the mid-1980s, fewer than

Canadian wrestler Carol Huynh won a gold medal at the Beijing Olympic Games in 2008 and a bronze medal at the London Olympic Games in 2012. The fact that girls and women now have access to sports like wrestling, which were once seen as only suitable for men, is to a great extent a product of the widespread social change brought about by feminism over the past half century.
Daiju Kitamura/AFLO SPORT/Mark Eite/Aflo Co. Ltd/Alamy

6,000 women and girls were registered to play hockey in Canada (Hall, 2002); by 2012, there were more than 87,000 (Hockey Canada, 2013). Girls and women now routinely compete in a range of sports, including those that were once thought to be appropriate only for men: rugby, wrestling, boxing, water polo, long distance running, and others. The presence of significant numbers of girls and women in mainstream sporting venues is one of the most visible results of the women's rights movements that emerged in Canada in the 1960s.

Feminism, also known as the women's movement or the women's liberation movement, is an international social, political, and cultural movement that has as a primary goal the resolution of inequities related to sex and gender and the elimination of discrimination against women and girls. Feminist theorist bell hooks has a clear and simple definition of feminism: "Feminism is a movement to end sexism, sexist exploitation, and oppression" (hooks, 2000, p. viii). hooks makes the point that the feminist project is much bigger than simply working for equality between the sexes, because women are not just oppressed due to their gender. Thus feminism is a movement that must address oppression on many levels. hooks writes that the aim of feminism "is not to benefit solely any specific group of women, any particular race or class of women. It does not privilege women over men. It has the power to transform in a meaningful way all our lives" (hooks, 1984, p. 26). For hooks, the goal of feminist activism and feminist thought is a world without oppression and domination. In this sense we can think of feminism as a broad-based movement for social justice.

The term *sexism* refers to discrimination or prejudice based on sex. The term *oppression* refers more generally to a condition of injustice and to uses of power that limit freedom and prevent equality. Oppression is an effect of dominance—that is, of one group trying to establish supremacy and privilege over another. To be oppressed, writes philosopher Marilyn Frye (1983), is to be subject to a network of restrictive forces and barriers that exist at micro- and macroscopic levels. Restrictions on women's ability to engage freely in all kinds of physical activity have impeded women's equitable participation in sport and are part of the kind of network that Frye is talking about.

One key aspect of feminist thought and politics is the understanding that the privileges and oppressions related to sex and gender do not work independently of other systems of oppression and inequality such as, for instance, race and class. Women and men from different ethnic, racial, and class backgrounds, indigenous peoples, or people who live with a disability are all positioned differently in relation to gender. Women with a disability experience different gendered constraints in terms of their access to sports and other athletic resources than do women who do not live with a disability.

Feminist theorists argue for the importance of what is called an *intersectional analysis* or approach to understanding oppression and privilege—to understanding the effects of power in people's lives (Birrell & McDonald, 2000). An intersectional analysis tries to understand how different categories of identity and different structures of power, such as ableism (the privileging of bodies that have not been labelled as disabled), racism, sexism, and class, are intertwined. None of us, for instance, whether we are members of racialized groups or whether we are white, experiences our gender separately from our race. The two categories combine to shape who we are and how we are seen and treated in the world. By using an intersectional analysis to look at an institution like sport, for example, one would not assume that working-class and middle-class women would face similar constraints in terms of opportunities to play, or that a predominantly white team environment would necessarily have the same meaning for a woman of colour as it does for her white teammates.

To adopt an intersectional approach in research or in advocacy work is to acknowledge that our own experiences are not universal and that our society produces more than one form of inequality. It also helps us to be mindful not to obscure the experiences of marginalized groups with the perspectives of those groups that are more dominant.

The Transformation of Women's Sport

American historian Susan Cahn has argued that two main factors shifted understandings of women's sport and helped to open up athletic opportunities for women and girls. The first was the feminist movement of the 1960s and 1970s, and the second was the fitness boom of the 1970s and 1980s (Cahn, 1995), which continues to this day as evidenced by the proliferation of Zumba classes and lululemon stores. The fitness boom was both a popular health movement and a commercialized effort to construct women as a new market for running shoes, sports apparel, exercise videos, and the increasing number of private gyms that emerged over the last decades of the 20th century. In many ways the fitness boom was a capitalist appropriation of feminist ideas about empowerment and women's bodily integrity. While feminists hoped that women would get active so they could benefit from feelings of confidence and physical competence, the marketers who drove the fitness boom wanted women to buy things. Nevertheless, corporate efforts put images of active women into circulation and also helped to normalize the idea that women could be strong and competitive.

Feminists have addressed sport from several perspectives. At the risk of making an overly simple distinction, some feminists have been primarily concerned with the obvious gender inequities in sport and the fact that women did not have equal opportunities to play (Hall & Richardson, 1982). Their goal was to expand women's access to existing sport structures. Other feminists have been more concerned with the ideological effects of sport and the way that an inequitable sport system perpetuated notions about women's frailty (Theberge, 1987). They hoped to shift women's consciousness of their own physical capabilities and also shift broader social views of women's roles in society. Of course many women have been concerned with both sets of issues and have worked hard to demonstrate the links between gender ideologies and participation rates for women in sport.

Over the past three decades, feminists have engaged in research and have designed programs and materials to promote sport for women and girls, to influence policy, and to get women into coaching and other leadership positions in sports organizations. Feminist organizations like the Canadian Association for the Advancement of Women and Sport lobbied Sport Canada to produce a formal policy on women's sport, which it did for the first time in 1986 (Sport Canada, 1986). Feminists launched court cases (so girls could play on boys' teams) and took complaints to human rights commissions (so they could get access to facilities and resources). They argued for changes to physical education curricula and challenged media representations of female athletes. The fact that women's sport looks different today than it did when I was growing up in the early 1970s is a direct result of the efforts that feminists and their supporters put into making sport more equitable. But even in terms of participation, we have not yet achieved gender equity in sport.

A study of interuniversity sport in Canada has shown that in 2012–2013 the numbers of female and male varsity teams across the country was almost equal (482 for women and 483 for men). There were 8,034 roster positions for women and 10,577 for men. Thus, 43% of university athletes were women. But women make up 56% of all university students, and so women remain disadvantaged by the current varsity sport system. For every 100 male students in Canada there were 2.8 chances to be on a varsity team; for every 100 female students there were 1.7 chances. The inequities are even more pronounced in terms of coaching opportunities. In the past two years the number of female coaches in the CIS has dropped from 19% to 17% of the total (Donnelly, Norman, & Kidd, 2013).

At the Olympic level, a gender equality audit of the 2012 London Games noted lingering inequalities in terms of sex and gender, despite the fact that it was the first Games in which there were women competing in every sport. There were 6,068 men competitors and 4,835 women, men were able to compete in 30 more medal events than women, and 48% of events had different maximum numbers of competitors in women's and men's events or different rules for male and female athletes. Authors Peter Donnelly and Michelle Donnelly note that there have been significant improvements at the Olympics over the past two decades, and yet they argue that there is still much to be done—and this even before considering other important questions about funding, sponsorship, and representations of athletes in the media (Donnelly & Donnelly, 2013).

And what of sport at the nonelite levels? Despite significant increases in the participation of women and girls over the past 40 years, it is still the case that men participate regularly in sport at about twice the rate that women do. Figures taken from Statistics Canada's General Social Survey show that in 2010, only about 35% of men and about 16% of women 15 years of age or older participated regularly in sport (Canadian Heritage, 2013). The gap between men's participation rates and women's participation rates has actually been growing wider since 1992, when it was 14%; in 2010 it was 19%. Men's participation rate in 2010 was much the same as it had been at the time of the previous survey in 2005; women's participation rate, by contrast, had decreased by 4%, primarily because of a 13% drop for young women between the ages of 15 and 19 and a 14% drop for women between 20 and 24 years of age (Canadian Heritage, 2013).

What these figures tell us is that sport is a regular leisure-time activity for only a minority of Canadians, that women participate at significantly lower rates than men, and that those rates are dropping. Statistics Canada figures also show that participation rates decrease steadily with age and that people with higher levels of education and higher incomes participate more. People with household incomes of more than $80,000 had a rate of sport participation that was approximately *five times* higher than the participation rates for people with household incomes of less than $20,000 (Canadian Heritage, 2013). Men in both the highest and the lowest income categories had participation rates twice as high as the women in the same categories, but the rates for women in the highest category (20.7%) were twice as high as for the men in the lowest (10.1%).

The statistics related to income and education, which can be a way of marking socioeconomic class, make a lot of sense. Sport is a leisure-time activity that requires time and money, and these are not available equally to all people in Canadian society. The statistics related to sex are more difficult to explain. Statistics Canada notes that people say they do not participate in sport for reasons of time and interest. For women, sport has to compete with childcare and domestic responsibilities, which, research shows, are still not evenly divided between men and women in heterosexual nuclear families (Lindsay, 2008). With the lingering effects of the economic recession, women's time may actually be in shorter supply than it was even 10 years ago. The report also suggests that the decline in women's interest in sport might reflect women's commitment to fitness activities like walking and yoga and the growth in leisure-time fitness activity for both men and women, with 52% of the population engaging regularly in such activities, and participation rates for men and women being fairly similar (Canadian Heritage, 2013).

While fitness activities are definitely beneficial, there is something particular about sport that the feminist advocates of the 1970s and 1980s had wanted women and girls to experience: the challenge of competition, the drive to set records, the experience of being on a team, the intensity of focus, the chance to perform publicly. None of these is exclusive to sport, and each of them can be problematic, but when these factors come together in the right way, they can bring a pleasure and satisfaction that is unique to sport as a form of cultural expression. Feminists promoted sport as a way of giving women access to its joys and pleasures. They also wanted to circumvent some of the body image issues that are related to the commercialization of fitness practices. It's not that sport is free of body image problems but, unlike many fitness endeavours, body image is not the point of the exercise.

Conclusions

This chapter has outlined a conceptual frame for doing your own analyses of gender issues in sport. The concepts that I have introduced in the chapter can help us to see how notions of gender and sexuality are actually playing out in sport. Sport sociologists use these concepts to make sense of a whole range of issues, including representations of gender and sexuality in sport media, fan cultures and spectatorship, sexual harassment and violence in sport, cross-cultural differences in gendered sporting experiences, fundraising calendars that feature photos of nude athletes, the special relationship between gender and nationalism that emerges during the Olympics, racialized stereotypes of both male and female athletes, and the impact of motherhood on women in sport. Many sport scholars also investigate and promote activism and other work to eliminate discrimination in sport and to produce sporting experiences that promote social justice. A recent example of this kind of activity would be the efforts to support a young soccer player in Quebec who was prohibited from playing because she was wearing a hijab (Muslim Women in Sports, 2013).

As I said at the beginning of this chapter, gender is fundamental to the organization of contemporary sport at all but the least competitive levels. And sport presents seemingly endless opportunities for us to reflect on how gender works in contemporary Canadian society. The analytic tools presented here will allow you to analyze the issues that you find important and to do your own assessment of the construction of gender and sexuality in sport—at both the broad social level and in relation to your own experience—and to think of ways to make it more inclusive and more equitable.

Critical Thinking Questions

1. Are there gender-specific rules in the sports you play? How does the presence or absence of such rules affect the gender reputation of the sport?

2. Why do you think women and girls participate in a broader range of sports than men and boys do? Why are there so few males in, for instance, figure skating?

3. What do you think of the no-checking rule in women's hockey? Do you feel it is related to gender stereotypes? Is this rule simply an interesting variation in hockey? Or does it say something important about larger cultural views of men and women?

4. In what ways has your own athletic history been shaped by gender norms? How have race, class, and ability been relevant to this process?

5. Statistics Canada figures show a sharp decline in sport participation for young women. What kind of research project could you design to learn why young women's levels of participation are falling? What assumptions would ground your study? What data would you need to collect?

6. How could sport be made more inclusive for transgender and transsexual athletes? Are you aware of any such efforts in your own community? How would such efforts change sport generally?

7. This chapter has argued that to understand gender in sport we need to consider the relationship between gender and other categories like race and class. Find an example of a sport story in the media that demonstrates how this kind of analysis could be more helpful than an analysis of gender alone.

8. Recently, many sport organizations have initiated efforts to challenge homophobia in sport. Have any such efforts been launched at your school? If so, what do you think the outcome will be? If not, do you think one could be started? What do you think would help such initiatives be successful?

Suggested Readings

Adams, M. L. (2011). *Artistic impressions: Figure skating, masculinity and the limits of sport.* Toronto, ON: University of Toronto Press.

Bridel, W., & Martyn C. (2011). If Canada is a team, do we all get playing time? Considering sport, sporting masculinity and Canadian national identity. In J. A. Laker (Ed.), *Canadian perspectives on men and masculinities: An interdisciplinary reader* (pp. 184–200). Toronto, ON: Oxford University Press.

Hall, M. A. (2002). *The girl in the game: A history of women's sport in Canada.* Peterborough, ON: Broadview Press.

Kidd, B. (2013). Sport and masculinity. *Sport in Society, 16,* 553–564.

References

Adams, M. L. (2011). *Artistic impressions: Figure skating, masculinity, and the limits of sport.* Toronto, ON: University of Toronto Press.

Bean, D. P. (2005). *Synchronized swimming: An American history.* Jefferson, NC: McFarland.

Birrell, S., & McDonald, M. G. (Eds.). (2000). *Reading sport: Critical essays on power and representation.* Richmond, VA: Northeastern University Press.

Canadian Centre for Ethics in Sport. (2012). *Sport in transition: Making sport in Canada more responsible for gender inclusivity.* Ottawa, ON: Author.

Canadian Heritage. (2013). *Sport participation 2010: Research paper.* Retrieved from http://publications.gc.ca/collections/collection_2014/pc-ch/CH24-1-2014-eng.pdf.

Canadian Soccer Association. (2012). *Canadian Soccer Association's annual report: Capturing the moment.* Ottawa, ON: Author.

Cahn, S. K. (1995). *Coming on strong: Gender and sexuality in twentieth-century women's sport*. Boston, MA: Harvard University Press.

CBC Sports. (2005, October 18). McGill scraps football season over hazing. Retrieved from http://www.cbc.ca/sports/football/mcgill-scraps-football-season-over-hazing-1.553792.

CBC Sports. (2009, January 31). Ron MacLean, gay-rights advocate debate the 'P'-word. Retrieved from http://www.cbc.ca/sports/hockey/ron-maclean-gay-rights-advocate-debate-the-p-word-1.853760.

Connell, R. W. (1990). An iron man: The body and some contradictions of hegemonic masculinity. In M. A. Messner & D. F. Sabo (Eds.), *Sport, men and the gender order: Critical feminist perspectives* (pp. 83–95). Champaign, IL: Human Kinetics.

Connell, R. W. (1995). *Masculinities*. Berkley, CA: University of California Press.

Cooky, C., Messner, M. A., & Hextrum, R. H. (2013). Women play sport, but not on TV: A longitudinal study of televised news media. *Communication & Sport, 1*(3), 1–28

Daniels, D. B. (2005). You throw like a girl: Sport and misogyny on the silver screen. *Film & History: An Interdisciplinary Journal of Film and Television Studies, 35*(1), 29–38.

Demers, G. (2006). Homophobia in sport—Fact of life, taboo subject. *Canadian Journal for Women in Coaching, 6*(2). Retrieved from http://www.coach.ca/april-2006-vol-6-no-2-p132855.

Donnelly, P., & Donnelly, M. K. (2013). *The London 2012 Olympics: A gender equality audit*. Toronto, ON: Centre for Sport Policy Studies.

Donnelly, P., Norman, M., & Kidd, B. (2013). *Gender equity in Canadian interuniversity sport: A biennial report (No. 2)*. Toronto, ON: Centre for Sport Policy Studies.

Duncan, M. C. (2006). Gender warriors in sports: Women in the media. In A. A. Raney and J. Bryant (Eds.), *Handbook of Sports and Media* (pp. 231–252). New York, NY: Routledge.

Frye, M. (1983). *The politics of reality*. Trumansburg, NY: The Crossing Press.

Genel, M. (2000). Gender verification no more? *Medscape Women's Health, 5*(3), E2. Retrieved from http://ai.eecs.umich.edu/people/conway/TS/OlympicGenderTesting.html.

Gill, R., Henwood, K., & McLean, C. (2005). Body projects and the regulation of normative masculinity. *Body & society, 11*(1), 37–62.

Hall, A. (2002). *The girl and the game: A history of women's sports in Canada*. Toronto, ON: University of Toronto Press.

Hall, A. & Richardson, D. A. (1982). *Fair ball: Towards sex equality in Canadian sport*. Ottawa, ON: Canadian Advisory Council on the Status of Women.

Hockey Canada. (2013). *2013 Annual Report*. Ottawa, ON: Author. Retrieved from http://www.hockeycanada.ca/en-ca/Corporate/About/Basics/Downloads.

hooks, b. (1984) *Feminist theory: From the margin to the center*. Boston, MA: South End Press.

hooks, b. (2000). *Feminism is for everybody: Passionate politics*. Boston, MA: South End Press.

International Olympic Committee. (2009). *Women and sport: The current situation*. Retrieved from http://www.wcse2011.qa/wp-content/uploads/2011/05/Women-and-Sport-The-Current-Situation-2009-10-eng-.pdf.

Intersex Society of North America. (n.d.). *How common is intersex?* Retrieved from http://www.isna.org/faq/frequency.

Johnson, J., & Holman, M. J. (2004). *Making the team: Inside the world of sport initiations and hazing*. Toronto, ON: Canadian Scholars Press.

Kane, M. J. (1995). Resistance/transformation of the oppositional binary: Exposing sport as a continuum. *Journal of Sport and Social Issues, 19*(2), 191–218.

Kane, M. J., & Snyder, E. (1989). Sport typing: The social "containment" of women in sport. *Arena Review, 13*(2), 77–96.

Laurendeau, J., & Adams, C. (2010). 'Jumping like a girl': Discursive silences, exclusionary practices and the controversy over women's ski jumping. *Sport in Society, 13*(3), 431–447.

Lenskyj, H. (1986). *Out of bounds: Women, sport and sexuality*. Toronto, ON: Women's Press.

Lindsay, C. (2008). *Are women spending more time on unpaid domestic work than men in Canada?* Statistics Canada Catalogue no. 89-630-X. Ottawa, ON: Statistics Canada.

Lorber, J. (1994). *Paradoxes of gender*. New Haven, MA: Yale University Press.

Mangan, J. A., & Walvin, J. (1987). Introduction. In J. A. Mangan & J. Walvin (Eds.), *Manliness and morality: Middle class masculinity in Britain and America, 1800–1940* (pp. 1–7). Manchester, UK: Manchester University Press.

McKinnon, A. (2013, May 14). Vancouver Parks Board wants to make its spaces more trans-friendly. *Xtra*. Retrieved from http://dailyxtra.com/vancouver/news/vancouver-parks-board-wants-make-spaces-trans-friendly.

Mosbacher, D., & Yacker, F (Producers/Directors). (2008). *Training Rules* [Documentary film]. United States: WomenVision.

Muslim Women in Sports. (2013, March 10). Quebec Soccer Federation finally allowing hijab on pitch. [Weblog post]. *Muslim Women in Sports*. Retrieved from http://muslimwomeninsports.blogspot.ca/2013/03/quebec-soccer-federation-finally.html.

Nanda, S. (2000). *Gender diversity: Crosscultural variations*. Long Grove, IL: Waveland Press.

Pascoe, C. J. (2003). Multiple masculinities? Teenage boys talk about jocks and gender. *American Behavioral Scientist, 46*(10), 1423–1438.

Renold, E. (2001). Learning the 'hard' way: Boys, hegemonic masculinity and the negotiation of learner identities in the primary school. *British Journal of Sociology of Education, 22*(3), 369–385.

Riemer, B. A., & Visio, M. E. (2003). Gender typing of sports: An investigation of Metheny's classification. *Research Quarterly for Exercise and Sport, 74*(2), 193–204.

Sport Canada. (1986). *Women in sport: A Sport Canada policy*. Ottawa, ON: Author.

Taylor, C., & Tracey, P., with McMinn, T. L., Elliott, T., Beldom, S., Ferry, A., Gross, Z., Paquin, S., & Schachter, K. (2011). *Every class, in every school: The final report on the first national climate survey on homophobia, biphobia, and transphobia in Canadian schools*. Toronto, ON: EGALE Canada Human Rights Trust.

Travers, A., & Deri, J. (2010). Transgender inclusion and the changing face of lesbian softball leagues. *International Review for the Sociology of Sport, 48*(6), 1–20.

Theberge, N. (1987). Sport and women's empowerment. *Women's Studies International Forum, 10*(4), 387–393.

Vincent, J., & Crossman, J. (2012). "Patriots at play": Analysis of newspaper coverage of the gold medal contenders in men's and women's ice hockey at the 2010 Winter Olympic Games. *International Journal of Sport Communication, 5*, 87–108.

Walvin, J. (1987). Symbols of moral superiority: Slavery, sport and the changing world order, 1800–1950. In J. A. Mangan & J. Walvin (Eds.), *Manliness and morality: Middle class masculinity in Britain and America, 1800–1940* (pp. 242–260). Manchester, UK: Manchester University Press.

White, P., & Young, K. (2007). Gender, sport and the injury process. In K. Young & P. White (Eds.), *Sport and gender in Canada* (pp. 259–278). Toronto, ON: Oxford University Press.

Women's Ski Jumping USA. (n.d.), Our Olympic story. Retrieved from http://www.wsjusa.com/olympic-inclusion/.

Chapter 7

Children, Youth, and Parental Involvement in Organized Sport

Ralph E. Wheeler, Jay Scherer, and Jane Crossman

Organized sport provides socialization experiences for children and youth.
Stockbyte/Getty Images

The popularity of organized sports programs for children in North America is a relatively recent phenomenon, the product of postwar prosperity and the development of new ideas and ideologies about both parenthood and childhood. The expansion of formalized sporting opportunities for Canadian children in the postwar era was the result of the growth in investment in various public recreational facilities across the nation (in urban and rural areas), including the construction of new schools with not only gyms and fields but also pools and tracks (Hall, Slack, Smith, & Whitson, 1991). Parents of this generation of young Canadians who had themselves never experienced similar opportunities or had access to such facilities in their own childhoods thus became committed to being involved in the lives of their children and providing their children with unprecedented sport and leisure opportunities. The increasing visibility of the professional major leagues and, indeed, high-performance sport also reaffirmed the popularity of sport for both parents and children and nurtured the realization that sport could be an institution for instilling not only athletic skills in children but important, taken-for-granted social values and customs.

In the decades that followed, minor sports programs, or *youth sport* as they are often referred to, have grown at a phenomenal rate, and in Canadian society today participation in sport is a normal part of the everyday lives of many boys and girls across the country. In fact, nearly 3 million Canadian children and youth between the ages of 5 and 18 participate regularly in a wide range of organized sport programs that provide experiences of fun and community for participants, parents, and organizers. For example, a report released by the Canadian Fitness and Lifestyle Research Institute (CFLRI) (2010), which examined sport participation rates, revealed that upwards of 75% of children and youth participate in some kind of sport activity. In addition, according to parents surveyed, 46% of these children participate in sport activities all year round. Interestingly, soccer, the most popular sport for Canadian children (42% of all children), is one of the most inexpensive.

Youth sports programs in Canada are provided by a number of local, regional, and national organizations that oversee and administer these activities and a range of other resources. These organizations have a mandate to provide children with optimal developmental benefits from their experiences. On this note, Canadian Sport for Life, an initiative of Canadian Sport Centres and Sport Canada, suggests that children commonly play sports for a number of intrinsic and extrinsic reasons:

- to have fun
- to experience thrills
- to be with friends or make new friends
- to do something they are good at
- to feel good about themselves
- to feel accepted
- to improve and learn new skills (Canadian Sport Centres, 2007, p. 5)

Beyond providing children with valuable and fun experiences, proponents of early and continued participation in sport activities point to the significant health and social

Table 7.1 Sport participation for the top 10 most practised sports among children participants

Sport	Percentage of Children Active in the Sport
Soccer	42%
Swimming	24%
Hockey (all types) and Ringette	22%
Basketball	16%
Baseball/Softball	14%
Martial Arts	8%
Volleyball	8%
Gymnastics	8%
Figure Skating	6%
Karate	6%
Skiing	5%
Source: Canadian Heritage, 2013.	

benefits that can be gained through sport participation and physical activity for young Canadians. For example, Lumpkin (2005) suggests that

> people of all ages enjoy playing games, engaging in recreational activities and exercising to maintain good health. Competitive, rule-bound sports provide opportunities to test one's skills against opponents. Through these programs, the all-around development of the individual is enhanced during activity. The purpose of these programs is to optimize quality of life through enjoyable physical activity and sport experiences. (p. 30)

The Canadian Centre for Ethics in Sport (2008), meanwhile, notes that community-based sports promote a number of social values in children and youth:

> There is strong agreement across the country that community sport is among the most positive forces in the lives of young people today, even more than school, friends and peers, religion and the music/entertainment industry. In addition to crediting community sport with being a constructive force in the lives of children and youth, more than 80 percent of Canadians believe that promoting positive values in youth should be a priority for sport in Canada, underlining the importance of getting sport right. (p. 19)

However, despite the evidence supporting the benefits of sport and physical activity for youths and the optimistic statistics cited above, numerous studies have also demonstrated alarmingly low fitness levels among young people in Canada. The report card published by Active Healthy Kids Canada (2013), for example, tracked physical activity levels for 5 years and found that only 13% of Canadian children and youth are meeting daily guidelines. In relation to these low levels of physical activity, Michelle Brownrigg (2008), former CEO of Active Healthy Kids Canada and director of physical activity and equity at the University of Toronto, noted that

> [a]t a younger and younger age, children are becoming dependent on electronic devices as their sources of entertainment and activity. . . . Getting our children active needs to be a collaborative effort. Governments, industry, communities, schools and parents all need to share the responsibility of replacing sedentary time with active play. (p. 1)

Indeed, for many physical educators we are at a tipping point with respect to the question of the health and well-being of young Canadians, and strategies must be implemented at all levels of government and between all agencies to provide well-funded, inclusive, fun, and safe sporting opportunities that are aimed at getting children physically active. Despite the vast body of knowledge that demonstrates the importance of physical activity for Canadians of all ages, the actual percentages of Canadian children and youth who report being involved once a week or more in sports has *decreased* since 1992 (Gruneau, in press). Moreover, while sport participation rates decline as Canadians get older, the participation rates of young Canadians is declining faster than that of older Canadians (Canadian Heritage, 2013). According to information provided by the 1992 and 2005 General Social Surveys, 64% of Canadian children between the ages of 11 and 14 reported participating in some form of sport at least once a week in the previous calendar year, and the most recent data for participation rates for 15–19 years olds are at 54% (Canadian Heritage, 2013). Importantly, children from less-affluent families are increasingly dropping out of sport. Several critics of youth sport have argued that organized sport has simply become too expensive for ordinary and less-affluent Canadian families, especially as children advance through the sport system. Other critics, meanwhile, suggest that the structure of organized sport is too competitive and has been institutionalized according to adult values and a "power and performance model" that may not provide the types of positive, empowering, and enjoyable experiences young Canadians need to keep them physically active and engaged in long-term sport participation and physical activity.

This chapter will review the organizational structure of children's sport in Canada in addition to exploring a number of critical issues and concerns related to contemporary organized sports programs, including some of the factors that structure sport participation for young Canadians. In so doing, we will connect the personal issues of children and their families (e.g., the inability of many Canadian families to afford the increasing costs associated with youth sport) to broader issues of social structure. We will also consider a number of areas relevant to children's sport participation that will serve as a framework for our examination and discussion. These include

- ethics in youth sport and the overemphasis on winning,
- sport specialization limiting children's choices in organized sport,
- children's withdrawal from sport,
- risk of injury,
- parental involvement in children's sports, and
- coaches' influence in children's sport.

We begin, however, with a discussion of processes of socialization.

SOCIALIZATION

For Canadian children and youth, being involved in sport creates ample opportunities for socialization experiences to occur. In fact, many parents enroll their children in various sports activities so that their children learn "appropriate" social values, skills, and accompanying feelings and attitudes that go beyond the benefits of participation in athletic activities (Kremer-Sadlik & Kim, 2007). *Socialization* is "the process of learning and adapting to a given social system . . . and is the means by which a society preserves its norms and perpetuates itself" (Sage & Eitzen, 2013, p. 66). Importantly, socialization is an ongoing and reciprocally interactive process through which children learn and at times resist socially constructed attitudes, knowledge(s), and dominant values of the society in which they are members and the sports that they play. In other words, scholars interested in processes of socialization and youth sport generally focus on *how children are socialized both into and through sport as an active and ongoing process*.

The earliest socialization theories had a distinctly social–psychological flavour that emphasized individual characteristics (physical and psychological) and socializing situations—a child's "unique blend of opportunities and life experiences" (Bryant & McElroy, 1997, p. 33), including key influences and agents such as parents, siblings, peers, coaches, and teachers working in institutions such as schools, churches, and the broader community who exert varying degrees of influence over the child's sport experience (Smith, 2003). Certainly, parents are the predominant socializing agents when it comes to sport involvement (LaVoi & Stellino, 2008; Pugliese & Tinsley, 2007). For example, if parents include their children in their own sporting ventures, they learn not only how to play a particular sport, but they will often develop a lifelong appreciation for it at the same time (Fraser-Thomas & Coté, 2009). Thus, these early positive experiences in sport can be critical in shaping future attitudes and behaviours.

However, these early theories placed significant emphasis on individuals rather than historical and structural issues. Moreover, the process of being socialized into sport is much more complicated than just making a positive connection with influential social agents and institutions; nor is socialization simply a one-way transmission through which children come to uncritically embrace various cultural identities or the values and activities that their parents believe are important. The most recent sociological researchers have attempted to understand how children (and parents) actively make decisions about sport participation and, in turn, how they produce social meanings and cultural identities on an ongoing basis. In so doing, sociologists are interested in making connections between those personal experiences and individual decisions in a much broader cultural context, including various social structures and all of the ideological meanings attached to understandings of class, race, gender, age, and ability/disability. For example, as we will discuss later in this chapter, a decisive relationship exists between social class and sport, including household income and sport participation: the higher the income, the higher the sport participation. But financial resources are only one factor that plays into sport participation; others include education (the higher the education, the higher the probability of sport participation), time, cultural tastes, and various body orientations that are informed by class status and other social determinants such as gender.

Finally, it has long been the mantra of sport enthusiasts that sport provides a forum through which we are socialized and learn "life's lessons" and develop "character," particularly for children and youth. Yet what kind of character is valued and socially constructed by the lessons and values of contemporary, competitive Canadian sport? In whose interest does this definition of character serve, especially when those understandings of character are lauded and held up for emulation? Discipline, hard work, teamwork, dedication to a common cause, and other laudable personal qualities are supposed to be the "natural" outcome of having been involved in competitive sport for young Canadians (historically, of course, these values were distinctly gendered and reserved for boys). Still, sport does not inherently teach children what is good or bad, and we can certainly point to innumerable examples where role models have taught and coached illegal field tactics or have modelled unsportsmanlike conduct.

Nonetheless, what is important to note is that through socialization we learn a wide range of values and historical beliefs to function in various social worlds. "Conversely, it is in society's interests to bring up young men and women to be able and willing to fulfill the demands that will be made on them as adults: as workers, as family members, as citizens" (Hall et al., 1991, p. 189). Yet, as has been noted throughout this text, Canadian sport and society are social constructions, "and the reproduction of a particular social order . . . has to be seen in terms the reproduction of ideas and norms and values that make these relations seem natural and right" (Hall et al., 1991, p. 189). It is in this sense, then, that we need to understand that youth sport—and all of the meanings associated with sport and physical activity for Canadian youth—have always been sites of struggle between various interest groups who make competing claims about how sports should be organized and run. Before tackling some of these issues and debates, though, we briefly outline some of the main institutions that govern and organize sport for young Canadians across the country.

Youth sport provides opportunities for children to learn not just physical skills but social and emotional skills as well.
Dusan Kostic/Fotolia

THE ORGANIZATION OF MINOR SPORT

In the ensuing discussion of sport for children, it should be noted that sport in this chapter will be discussed in the context of those activities that are organized around a structured, competitively based model of sport, such as the type of institutionalized programs seen in minor hockey and gymnastics or age-group swimming. These programs are competitive in nature, have defined rules, and require specific skills and resources; they are also primarily organized and overseen by adults. Other popular recreational-based activities such as bicycling, skateboarding, or street hockey—while having some of the characteristics of organized sport—will not be considered because the primary distinction for our discussion is the competitive model of organized sport.

In Canada, organized sport for many children and youth often begins in the preschool years and is managed and delivered through four main agencies or institutions: publicly funded community sport and recreation organizations, local sports clubs, service agencies and special-interest groups, and school-based sports. These groups offer a wide variety of sport programs and provide diverse experiences through various levels of training and competitive activities. While many of these programs have different rules for participation than adult programs, they typically reflect the characteristics of adult-based sport, including regular training schedules, increasingly professionalized coaching and managerial environments, and lengthy competitive seasons that include playoffs and championships.

Publicly Funded Community Sport and Recreation Organizations

Community-based sport and recreation programs have become extremely popular activities for children in all parts of Canada for a number of reasons. In particular, some activities, such as soccer, are relatively inexpensive, while others are conveniently located and accommodate a wide range of skill levels. It is not unusual, for example, to find both boys and girls playing a variety of sports such as hockey, soccer, baseball, basketball, and tennis as part of community-organized leagues across the country. Coaches, officials, and league organizers, who are responsible for setting up and running all aspects of the program, often include volunteers and, increasingly, paid staff. Programs are typically organized around "house leagues," which may loosely represent local neighbourhood boundaries. Because these programs are publicly supported, registration fees are usually modest and children who register are assigned to teams on a more or less random basis.

The emphasis at this level is on skill development, enjoyment, fun, and participation. House league participants may practise and play one or two times per week. In addition, many programs support "all-star" teams selected from among a pool of talented players in a particular age group or division. At this level, competition takes on a more serious focus, with teams conducting tryouts, running regular training sessions, and competing in both league and tournament competitions. Teams from a community all-star league may also compete for the right to represent their respective communities in regional, provincial, and interprovincial championships. Unlike house leagues, which usually play on weekdays, all-star teams attend practices during the week with competitions generally held on weekends. In this organizational structure, it is not unusual to find children participating simultaneously on both house league and all-star teams.

Local Sports Clubs

While community-based sports programs encourage wide participation and are relatively inexpensive, more and more children are opting to take part in local sports clubs or private associations. One reason for the emergence of local sports clubs is to provide a higher level of professional training and competition not usually available through school and community-based sport. While these two programs may serve to identify talented youngsters, many parents understand that privately run clubs have the potential to develop young, talented athletes to an elite level. Sports programs operating under this model tend to focus on a specific sport and require a far greater time commitment from the participant; these programs are also more costly and, hence, are often the preserve of affluent families.

Many of these programs, for example, are highly structured with scheduled daily training sessions. Because emphasis is on the development of athletic talent and the promotion of competitive prowess, children are often carefully groomed for success at each of the various levels or stages of competition by professional coaches. Private sport clubs operate in both public and privately owned facilities and offer training and competition in such popular individual sports as swimming, gymnastics, figure skating, martial arts, tennis, track and field, cycling, wrestling, and rowing. These clubs also run programs for team sports such as hockey, basketball, and soccer. Operating costs to run these programs may range from several thousand dollars to hundreds of thousands and employ full- and part-time coaches, instructors, and administrators. Club membership fees can range from a modest several hundred dollars annually to registration fees of over $1,000; in addition, participants are often expected to cover their own travel costs to competitions. Examples of young athletes who have recently come through this system and risen to stardom in sport abound—notable are Canadian professional tennis players Milos Raonic and Eugenie Bouchard.

Service Agencies and Special-Interest Groups

Coexisting and often sharing the same facilities with local sports clubs and publicly funded organizations are a number of other nonprofit groups that promote sport activities for children. These include YM/YWCAs, religious organizations, Boys and Girls Clubs of Canada, Scouts Canada and Girl Guides, and privately funded sports groups. As in other organizations that offer sport programs, a wide variety of activities and competitive opportunities exist for participants. A main focus of sport programs among these groups is to use sport as a vehicle to promote their particular set of values and beliefs. For example, children who participate in a church-run program may also be introduced to the underlying values espoused by that particular religion.

School-Based Sports

Sport at the high school level has long been an integral part of Canadian educational institutions. Organized sport at the elementary and junior high school level, however, is a relatively new phenomenon initiated originally by physical educators concerned about the low physical activity and fitness levels among children in this age group. According to a Canadian Fitness and Lifestyle Research Institute (2004) report, fewer than 10% of children receive their sport experiences through school-sponsored programs. Historically, school sport programs were an attempt to address this concern and originally involved sport activities on a more or less informal basis. Today, programs can involve interschool games on a regional level and may be organized around several weekends or run over a two- to three-month season. These programs rely on coaches and officials who are usually volunteers from the school staff or from within the community.

Because of a number of obstacles, elementary school sport has not achieved the potential outcomes envisioned by its early advocates. The absence of adequate resources such as suitable facilities and qualified coaches along with increased user fees and insufficient funding have continued to prevent sport at the elementary school level from having any significant impact on increasing overall student activity levels. Coupled with these developments is the fact that many of the schools that do sponsor sport programs tend to mirror a high school model, which traditionally has catered to only a small percentage of the school's student population. As well, even though costs associated with school sport programs are usually low compared to community-based programs, student participation is limited based on the number of teams sponsored by a particular school. This latter issue has caused many physical educators to consider alternative activities to organized sport, such as adventure and outdoor experiences, fitness pursuits, and other noncompetitive experiences including co-ed and cooperative game activities. An extensive discussion of school-based sports is covered in Chapter 10.

Other Youth Sport Organizations

In Canada, organized sport associations for children exist for a number of reasons. At the school level, sport is tied to educational objectives and is seen as a way to motivate children to become involved in an active lifestyle. Community programs promote sport opportunities for children for similar reasons while keeping costs at a reasonable level for the participant. Increasingly, however, there is a growing trend for children who aspire to become successful athletes to join private clubs that provide opportunities for children to excel at a high level within a particular sport. Because many of these clubs must operate on income generated through membership fees and corporate sponsors, they regularly resemble the practices and structures found in adult sport organizations. Clearly, minor sport organizations have become an integral part of the social fabric of many Canadian communities. With few exceptions, every province that has a sport association responsible for governing and promoting sport will likely have youth programs in place, often starting as early as age five for many children. As Sage and Eitzen (2013) note,

> There is a well-organized outlet for almost every child who has an interest in being involved in sports. Parents can enroll their children in age-group gymnastics and swimming programs at 3 years of age; ice-hockey, soccer, football, t-ball, and a half dozen other sports at age four. Indeed, an early start is considered essential when parents or children have professional or Olympic-level aspirations. (p. 63)

Still, despite the presence of a wide range of programs across the country, Canadian families have uneven access to organized sport, and participation rates are clearly structured according to a number of variables, which we discuss in the next section.

FACTORS DETERMINING CHILDREN'S INVOLVEMENT IN SPORT

Data from Canadian Heritage (2013) noted many of the underlying sociological factors that structure participation rates for children in organized sport in Canada including regional differences, gender and age, community size, parental involvement in sport, and household income. For example, when both parents are involved in sport, there is over a 90% likelihood that their children will also participate in some kind of sport activity. Household income is another determining factor that underscores the class structure of Canadian society and the growing issue of economic inequality. In families with an income of $80,000 or higher, 85% of children were active in sport, whereas 72% of children from households earning between $40,000 and $79,000 were active, and only 58% of children from households earning less than $40,000 were active.

While household income levels continue to structure participation rates for children in sport, other economic factors decisively limit participation opportunities, most notably the ever-increasing costs associated with minor sport. As youth sport has become more formalized and professionalized, the costs to run these programs have escalated to unprecedented levels. As Gruneau (in press) notes,

> Many clubs operate in a climate of substantially heightened expectations from sports participants and parents, as well as from larger regional, provincial and national associations. Attendant to this, most of the larger clubs and associations in Canada now run programs well beyond their traditional sporting season. Ten and eleven month long programs are increasingly common. In addition, many clubs and associations now have substantially larger budgets then even the recent past, requiring higher levels of professionalism and accountability. Sports clubs and associations are also subject to growing demands for higher quality coaching and facilities at all times of the year.

Coupled with these issues is the increased need for volunteers to help run these programs. Consequently, parents with children in these programs find that they are spending more and more time volunteering in their children's sport programs. These developments have made it more difficult to entice some parents to register their children in programs that require them to volunteer huge amounts of their time. As a result, there has been a push to create paid positions to complete activities that were once simply handled by volunteers, including paid coaching, training, and administrative positions. All of these developments, moreover, have escalated expectations among parents and athletes to have state-of-the-art facilities and travel opportunities within the structure of increasingly professionalized clubs. As Gruneau (in press) notes,

> These three trends: the hiring of paid coaches, the contracting out of formerly volunteer administrative activities, and escalating costs necessary to meet perceived new "needs" for training and completion, are developing unevenly in different sports and in different regions across the country, but their impact is subtly reshaping the way many of the larger community sports clubs and associations operate. Along the way, sports participation is pushed continually further away from Canada's lower classes.

Besides the escalation of costs and issues of inequality, Nixon and Frey (1996) suggest that both social background and status factors such as gender, race, and ethnicity are influential in determining sport participation. For example, household composition, access to training and sporting competitions, and the workplace involvement of parents are important determinants of sport participation for young Canadians (Gruneau, in press). As noted below, participation levels for young Canadians are higher in two-parent families than in single-parent families, although the gap in participation by children from dual- and single-parent families tends to be less for boys than for girls. Regional considerations such as where one lives (e.g., in an urban or rural area) may also affect sport involvement based on available opportunities and resources. Families living in dense urban areas are less likely to participate in sport than families who live in lower density suburban areas or smaller towns where the need for a car is much greater (Gruneau, in press). Indeed, for many children living in small rural communities, programs that are available may be more accessible and affordable than for children in larger urban centres with more sport opportunities but with greater associated costs such as higher program and coaching fees, transportation costs, and facility rentals.

In nearly 60% of families where parents are sports participants, children are active; meanwhile, in families where parents are active as sports administrators or coaches and as athletes, over 80% of children are regular sports participants (Gruneau, in press). Clearly, there appears to be a strong socialization effect at work where the organized activities of children mirror the priorities of their parents. Beyond these patterns of socialization, Coakley and Donnelly (2009) suggest that changes associated with family structure and the perceptions parents have about the role sport can play in their children's development also have major impacts on participation levels in organized sport. Perhaps one of the biggest changes is the increase in the number of families with both parents working. For working parents, afterschool and summer sport programs offer a safe, adult-supervised environment where children may acquire valuable social and athletic skills. On this latter note, parenting ideology has also changed in terms of what it means today to be a "good parent." In the new millennium, parents are expected to be more accountable for the behaviour and whereabouts of their children (Coakley & Donnelly, 2009). For many middle-class and more affluent parents, then, sport is a highly attractive alternative to having their children "hang out" at the mall or on the street corner.

However, perhaps the biggest push for increasing sport participation for children is the realization that obesity rates among children are at epidemic levels. There is a growing awareness that increasing numbers of Canadian children are leading inactive, unhealthy lifestyles. The Canadian Community Health Survey conducted by Statistics Canada reported that the single largest increase in obesity rates was among youth aged 12 to 17, where the rate tripled from 3% in 1978 to 8% in 2004 (Statistics Canada, 2005). More recent research findings are pointing toward a sustained obesity epidemic. According to a 2008 survey by the Centers for Disease Control (2010), the rate of obesity in children aged 6 to 11 years was more than 19%. Of even greater concern is that the present generation of youth will be the first to have a shorter life expectancy than their parents (Olshansky et al., 2005). As a result, both provincial and federal government agencies are under pressure to address the problem of childhood obesity. Yet coupled with this development is the perception that physical education programs across the country are having little or no influence on changing the long-term fitness and activity levels of children. Particularly disturbing is the tendency for schools, once widely regarded as the public focal point for the overall development of the child, to reduce physical education opportunities for students and to impose user fees as cost recovery strategies. Physical and Health Education Canada (2014) reports that "once physical education becomes an optional subject, enrolment in physical education tends to decrease significantly with the decrease more noticeable for adolescent females than males." Furthermore, "at the secondary level, 20% of parents surveyed across Canada indicated that their adolescent child received no physical education at all and this percentage increases as students advance through secondary grades" (Physical and Health Education Canada, 2014). A consequence of all of these issues is that many parents (especially from more affluent backgrounds) are now looking for other opportunities—including private ones—to enroll their children in organized sport programs.

CONTROVERSIES AND ISSUES IN CHILDREN'S SPORT

As the popularity of children's sport has grown, so too have the scrutiny and the criticism of children's sports programs. Critics have, for example, questioned the merits of organized and highly structured sport participation for children as young as 4 or 5 years of age. Moreover, many of the professionals involved in physical education and sport remain convinced of the need for changes in minor sport if children are to reap the benefits that sport and physical activity have to offer. This section will review a number of the interrelated issues associated with children and youth in minor sport. These include ethics in youth sport and the overemphasis on winning, sport specialization, withdrawal from sport, the risk of injuries, parental interference, and the role that coaches play in youth sport.

Ethics and Fair Play in Youth Sport: Is Winning Everything?

One of the most controversial areas of organized sport for children is the highly competitive nature of some programs and the overemphasis placed on performance and winning. It is not unusual for sport clubs, and in some cases community-based sport programs, to promote the success and track records of their programs as evidence of their single-minded commitment to winning to recruit new members in an effort to boost registration numbers. By highlighting their dedication to excellence and showcasing the previous competitive successes of their athletes and teams, these clubs are able to present a very enticing picture to parents and prospective athletes. Indeed, the emphasis on skill and performance in many youth sport organizations, as noted earlier, has also been accompanied by a professionalization of attitudes that has prioritized winning over other values such as simply playing well, let alone having fun.

After countless hours of practice in preparation for a competition, for a coach or player to suggest that winning isn't important is both naive and unrealistic. Competition represents a way to measure athletic skill or prowess and can be used to express that measure of personal achievement in a healthy way. Yet, if excellence in sport is defined solely as winning or "owning the podium," what lengths might one go to win? Does a single-minded focus on winning become more important than acting within the rules of the game or treating your opponents fairly? If winning is important, how does this affect our definitions of strategy, rule bending, and cheating? Can we remain honest, fair, respectful, and unselfish if the ultimate goal is to win?

These and other questions call for us to consider the ethical dimensions of our behaviour. The erosion of ethical behaviour and high standards of those involved in sport is perhaps one of the most overarching concerns with respect to many of the current issues facing youth sport today. Particularly disturbing for some involved in youth sport is the notion that sport may actually serve to promote moral insensitivity. For instance, coaches sometimes use the argument that "everyone is doing it" to rationalize their rule breaking or the use of questionable and unethical tactics.

On this note, many physical educators have argued that the emphasis in youth sport should not solely be on wining and competition, but should focus on the enhancement of physical, cognitive, and affective development of the participants (American Alliance for Health, Physical Education, Recreation and Dance, 2013). Wuest and Bucher (2003), in a criticism of youth sport, note that these issues are particularly critical for younger children, and that the fun of playing (rather than dominating an opponent) should be emphasized along with the development of a broad range of skills within the sport. In so doing, participation opportunities for many children of all abilities should be provided rather than limiting participation to the gifted few in an exclusionary model of youth sport where the primary focus is winning. As Tutor Bompa (1995) points out, "it is important for us to provide more opportunities for children to learn the fundamentals of sports in a fun, low-stress environment" (p. 26).

Sport organizations throughout the country have, of course, taken a number of steps to improve or maintain ethical standards of fair play, sportsmanship, and the conduct of individuals involved in their programs. Codes of conduct, fair play rules, and coaches' and players' creeds have been developed that attempt to prescribe guidelines to serve as the basis for making reasoned judgments related to sport activities. Most notably, the Canadian Centre for Ethics in Sport has as its mission "to promote ethical conduct in all aspects of sport in Canada, and to build a fair and ethical sport system that embodies respect, fair play, safety and non-violence" (Canadian Centre for Ethics in Sport, 2002, p. 1). In the meantime, a number of provinces have instituted programs aimed at fostering fair play and ethical standards in sport. The fair play programs in Nova Scotia and Ontario are quickly becoming models that other provinces are using to develop their own programs to address the issues related to ethics in sport. Nevertheless, while these efforts should be applauded as a positive step in raising awareness and addressing the situation, we still do not have to look very hard to find examples of cheating, abuse of officials, violations of rules, and outrageous behaviour of parents and coaches to conclude that these disruptive and unethical practices are still widespread.

Sport Specialization

Directly linked to the emphasis on winning and performance for children is the increasing pressure to develop highly skilled and specialized athletes in specific sports. The process for identifying athletic talent in Canada is typically based on a sport model that provides a feeder system designed to progressively target and train athletes for the elite levels. While some sports such as swimming, gymnastics, and figure skating have traditionally been known to start training children as early as 5 and 6 years of age, other sports such as soccer, hockey, and basketball are increasingly following suit. Children who show promise are systematically moved through a series of skill development stages, introduced to more intense competitions, and engaged in longer, more frequent training sessions. Because of the sheer amount of effort, time, and resources involved in this development phase, promising athletes are inevitably urged by a coach or parent to choose one sport in which to specialize. Some parents are persuaded that their child's progress and chances for success at the elite level of the sport will be enhanced if there is year-round commitment to that sport, while the prospect of becoming an age-group champion or the dream of making a national team becomes a powerful enticement for both parents and their children. Parents can be easily lured into the "Tiger Woods phenomenon" and come to believe that an explicit focus on one sport early—similar to Woods who reportedly like the world's best male golfer, who reportedly started putting when he was 3 years old—will give their son or daughter a better chance to "make it to the big leagues."

Still, early specialization in youth sport is a contentious issue. Some suggest that early specialization of athletic expertise is most beneficial in sports where peak performance occurs in adolescence, such as women's gymnastics and women's figure skating (Deakin & Cobley, 2003; Law, Cote, & Ericsson, 2007). However, other researchers argue that a specialized approach to sport can have negative consequences for the participants and that specialization undermines many of the positive aspects of sport, including isolating children from other social worlds (Jayanthi, 2012). Strict regimentation, routine, and adherence to a long-term training program increasingly influence and shape the experiences of children in organized sports programs according to the values of professional and high-performance sport. Yet the values that emerge from programs based on specialized, competitive success can be in conflict with, and in some cases act to subvert, the avowed ideals of children's sport, including a movement-education approach that provides opportunities for children to experience the joy of physical movement as opposed to objective and highly skilled performance (Siedentop, 2004).

While some parents want to provide their children with the advantage of an early start by supporting a decision to specialize in a particular sport, there is another interrelated dimension to this trend that encourages children (and their parents) to embrace even greater levels of specialization. Some programs are so highly structured that emphasis is placed on children to specialize *in a particular position within that sport*. For example, it is not unusual for children to refer to themselves by their playing position: a soccer player is now a "striker" or a "fullback," and the age-group swimmer is a "butterflyer" or a "freestyler." In so doing, the young athlete comes to view his or her role in the sport from the perspective of the relative status of the position, thus further limiting and detracting from the fundamental purpose of sport for children. Such a deliberate structured approach to improve a child's sport skills places them under enormous physiological and psychological stress as well as potentially robbing them of opportunities for developing important social skills.

Dropout and Withdrawal from Sport

In a competitive sporting environment, the most promising players are often children who physically mature earlier than their peers and consequently have a greater chance for athletic success in their age group. Within this system, the so-called "late bloomers" often become discouraged simply because limited playing time and fewer opportunities are made available to them, leading them to sometimes drop out of sport. On the other hand, it is scarcely surprising that many boys and girls who have progressed through various sport systems and increasingly find sport to be more work than fun also decide to drop out of sport altogether. The process of dropping out of sport was examined as early as 1976 by Donald Bell, who found that athletes, apart from not getting to play, may be "induced" to quit because of a continuing series of degrading or humiliating experiences. For example, "being yelled at, criticized, or ridiculed by coaches, parents, or teammates" are frequently reported as negative experiences that serve to drive children from a particular sport (cited in Nixon & Frey, 1996, p. 91). In a 10-year study on withdrawal from competitive sports, Butcher, Linder and Johns (2002) concluded that simple "lack of enjoyment" was one of the main reasons given for transferring to another sport or for withdrawing from sport altogether. Other factors causing children to leave a sport may be related to performance anxiety, forming new friendships outside the sport, new demands at school, embracing other aspects of teen culture, or simply losing interest in the sport. In fact, "the annual attrition rate in youth sport is 35% and . . . most youth who leave a team do so because their interests shift—to another sport or to a non-sport activity" (Fullinwider, 2006, p. 7). Not surprisingly, pressure on children is a significant influence on dropout rates, and a reported 70% of youth athletes quit organized sport, outside of school programs, by the age of 13 (Engh, 1999; Fullinwider, 2006).

As noted above, an exclusionary, high-performance model serves to weed out less-talented athletes while also making sport less attractive to children as they get older. Minor hockey in Canada serves as a prime example of a sport that promotes and caters to the talented as they

Parents need to understand that pressure to perform early in sport may lead to stress and dropout.
Bigshots/Getty Images

move through various levels of competition. While minor hockey continues to be a popular sport for Canadians, declining registration numbers are a significant concern. An editorial in the *Globe and Mail* cautioned that "kids 8, 9, and 10 years old, kids with no plans of making the NHL, are forced to treat hockey from an early age like a job. It is estimated that seventy-five percent of those kids who start playing hockey at age 5 or 6 have dropped out by the time they hit 15" (cited in Donnelly, 2000, p. 192). Young hockey players who show promise in the sport are being selected at an earlier age for specialized treatment through various talent identification strategies, while those who fail to make travel teams or are not talented enough to play in an all-star league soon find themselves on the sidelines. The same point can be made with respect to talent development in nonteam sports, as evidenced by the high numbers of children who quit or drop out of individual sports such as swimming, gymnastics, and figure skating.

All of these issues raise questions about the demands that are being placed on young athletes and the possibility of burnout in children who pursue sport at a high level. Burnout is the result of "too much participation, success, and pressure at too early an age. The causes may be physical, psychological, or a combination of elements" (Figler & Whitaker, 1991, p. 122). In a series of interviews with age-group champions, Coakley and Donnelly (2009) found that burnout occurred "when young athletes felt they no longer had control over their lives, and could not explore, develop, and nurture identities apart from sports" (p. 87). Children who withdraw from sport at an early age because of burnout come to "devalue the importance of sport to their self-identity and perceive that other activities are more attractive than sport" (Raedeke, 1997, p. 413). Many burnout situations can be avoided; however, coaches and parents need to recognize burnout symptoms and provide programs that protect young athletes from having excessive demands placed on them at such an early age.

Risk of Injury in Children's Organized Sport

A further consequence with respect to specialization in organized sport is that, while it not only limits children's opportunities in other sports and nonsport activities, exclusive participation in one sport activity at an early age can have significant physical and emotional implications for a child. One of the most alarming effects of sport specialization has been the increased risk of overuse injuries. Physiologically, injuries associated with overtraining or improper technique or conditioning are far more frequent when a child engages in a single sport over a long period. The American Academy of Pediatrics recommends that "sporting activities for children should be limited to a maximum of 5 days per week. In addition, athletes should have at least 2–3 months off per year from their particular sport" (Brenner, 2007, p. 1243). Repetitive movements that cause impact or strain to the joints can lead to damage in the fragile growth area of the bone and can impair normal growth patterns or result in permanent disability. A Canadian Paediatric Society (2006) report advised that

> predicting sport readiness involves the evaluation of an individual child's cognitive, social and motor development to determine his or her ability to meet the demands of the sport. Sporting activities should be tailored to the developmental level of the child through simple modifications, such as smaller equipment, frequent changing of positions, shorter games and practices, and by focusing on fun. Children should be encouraged to participate in a variety of activities and avoid early specialization. (pp. 1–2)

Limiting intensive involvement in sports that are physically demanding and providing children with a choice of less strenuous or more skill-oriented activities may help reduce the risk of overuse injuries.

Sport medicine professionals have also started to raise concerns related to the likelihood of head injuries occurring in contact sports. Until recently, severe contact resulting in head injuries during sporting events were classified as concussions only when a player exhibited typical symptoms, such as disorientation or loss of consciousness. Doctors are now cautioning that any blow to the head, even if it does not appear severe enough to cause the classic symptoms of a concussion, can still have long-term health consequences (Koutures, Gregory, & the Council on Sport Medicine and Fitness, 2010). Marchie and Cusimano (2003) concluded from their research on body checking and concussions in hockey that "repeated mild brain injuries in youth and adults occurring over months or years could result in cumulative deficits. The younger developing brain is at an even higher risk of injury" (p. 3). Young athletes in sports such as hockey, football, rugby, or soccer, where contact is permitted, may be exposed to even greater harm than was previously thought. As sport begins to assume a greater place in a child's life, there is the danger that young athletes will continue to train and compete despite undergoing an injury and may in fact avoid reporting injuries for fear of falling behind in their training and possibly losing their place on the team.

The decision to ban checking in boys' hockey at the peewee level by Hockey Canada in 2013 continues to be debated by various interest groups with direct stakes in minor hockey (e.g., the interests of parents for their children, the individuals who run and organize minor hockey across the country, and various physical educators and physicians who want to see changes in the game). Many men who advocate in favour of checking claim that boys learn important physical skills when they are young and, as a result, may avoid being injured as they move up through the various levels. Yet there is often a defensive resistance evident in many of these claims to social changes that are perceived as threats to "normal" gender relations and to traditional understandings of masculinity. However, detractors such as the Canadian Paediatric Society applauded the decision to ban checking at the peewee level, simply noting that "[t]here is evidence to suggest that an athlete who has sustained a concussion is at an increased risk for subsequent head injuries and that such injuries may be cumulative" (Purcell, Canadian Paediatric Society, & Healthy Active Living and Sports Medicine Committee, 2012, p. 4).

Parental Interference

For the majority of parents who enroll their children in competitive, organized sport, their participation is limited to driving to and from practices or games. In between, they are content to sit in the bleachers or along the sidelines and play the role of fan and supporter, encouraging and enthusiastically cheering their children along. On other occasions, they may volunteer in a coaching or officiating capacity. This scene is played out in hundreds of communities across the country each day. These parents are more concerned with supporting their children and making the sport experience fun than in keeping track of their child's playing time or scoring statistics. Most parents who are involved at this level are interested in the redeeming benefits sport has to offer their children and perhaps an expanded social circle themselves.

However, a major concern for both critics and supporters of minor sport has emerged in recent years: overzealous parents who engage in displays of unacceptable and outrageous behaviours before, during, and after their children's sport events. These behaviours include verbal and even physical abuse directed toward opponents and, in some cases, abuse directed at their own children. James Deacon (2001) reported that the bad behaviour of some parents in hockey "is so common it even has its own name—rink rage." He adds that "hostile behavior at youth games is far more pervasive and sometimes violent than it was a generation ago" (p. 22). Reported incidents of abusive parents threatening coaches, assaulting opposing players, and taunting officials appear to have reached epidemic proportions, and regular coverage of these incidents attests to the fact that concerns about parental behaviour in competitive sport remains a serious, ongoing social issue that must be dealt with collectively by all stakeholders of children's sport.

While parents involved in team sports appear to be the most culpable, individual sports are not immune to abusive parental behaviour. Incidents of a pushy parent who attempts to influence judges in gymnastics or a father who becomes enraged when his child is disqualified at a swim meet are reported more frequently in the popular media. Regardless of the sport, attention to this issue strongly supports the claim that parents are taking their children's sport involvement more seriously than ever before. The investigation of parental involvement in their children's sports is not new. Researchers have focused on child–parent/coach relationships in children's sport (Weiss & Fretwell, 2004) and the challenges of being sport parents (Wiersma & Fifer, 2005). Shields and colleagues (2005, 2007), for example, have examined the behaviour of parents during sport events including the presence of derogatory verbal reactions, physical altercations, and poor sport behaviour.

For parents with aspirations or dreams of their child becoming a top-level athlete or making a national team, sport is not simply about playing games or having fun. These parents willingly make significant sacrifices to give their youngsters every chance to succeed in the culture of competitive sport, where winning is often lauded as the only outcome that matters. The possibility of having their child "make it to the top" remains an underlying motive for many parents involved in minor sport despite extremely slim odds. For example, Sage and Eitzen (2013) report that "three in 10,000 or 0.0003 percent of boys playing high school basketball will be drafted by a National Basketball Association team" (p. 285). However, even with these abysmal odds, many parents simply believe their children are destined for a professional career and are often prepared to do whatever it takes to make it happen. This ranges from buying the most expensive equipment and paying exorbitant club fees to relocating the entire family closer to a training facility or sending a young child to live and train elsewhere in the country. Parents are also often expected to commit a great deal of their own time to club-sponsored activities such as fundraising projects or serving on committees. It is not unusual to see parents spending large amounts of time with other parents, either during practices, at games, or on road trips, and developing social bonds with each other. Consequently, a greater sense of prestige may be associated with their child's athletic success. In effect, a parent's "bragging rights" are heavily influenced by their child's success or failure in sport. It comes as no surprise, therefore, that parents feel they have a personal stake in what happens and attempt to exert undue influence over their child's sport experience.

A second reason for increased interference by parents in children's sport may simply be an implicit desire to experience sport vicariously through their children. Parents who may have had unfulfilled athletic experiences in their own youth sometimes unwittingly pressure their children to succeed in an effort to make up for their own lost opportunities. Even the most restrained parent can lose perspective when faced with the dilemma of giving their child "the chance I never had."

Finally, a third reason for parents becoming overly involved in their children's games is the prospect of future financial rewards. The tantalizing possibility of a college scholarship, endorsements, or a professional contract can become more than just wishful thinking for some parents. Following an Olympic Games when a Canadian athlete in a certain sport medals, it is not unusual for registration numbers in that sport to go up. Publicity surrounding these events and the million-dollar endorsements for medal winners can become a powerful, if unrealistic, motivator for some parents.

Yet while much of the literature on parental involvement focuses on the overly involved or "pushy" parent, there are also a number of dangers associated with parental under-involvement. Children may be more likely to quit sport when parents fail to take an active interest in their child's sport involvement. Support and encouragement are needed most at the initial stage of participation (Canadian Centre for Ethics in Sport, 2008), and children need to feel their efforts are appreciated, which is implicit through their parents sharing the sport experience with them. A lack of parental support and involvement may also inadvertently open the door for the development of an unhealthy coach–athlete relationship:

> Where the athlete is distanced from the parent(s), because of a perceived absence of emotional support or because of family conflict or problems, she may turn to her coach or other authority figure to take on the role of substitute or surrogate parent. She may even fantasize that this person is, in fact, her substitute father or mother. (Brackenbridge, 2001, p. 72)

In spite of the negative consequences of parental involvement, parents can do much to positively influence children's sport experience. Parents need to provide supportive and stable family structures while encouraging involvement in sport; they also need to understand and appreciate the child's expectations as opposed to their own or the coach's expectations for the child.

The Role Coaches Play in Youth Sport

While parental involvement in sport has come under heavy criticism in recent years, it is the coach who has perhaps the greatest potential to influence children in minor sport. The youth sport coach is in a position to provide an atmosphere in which children can realize the many positive benefits of sport participation. Whether these benefits exist for the

Coaches play a pivotal role in children's sport experiences.
kali9/E+/Getty Images

participant depends to a large extent on a coach's understanding of the purposes and goals of youth sport. One program that has played a significant role in providing education for coaches in this area is the National Coaching Certification Program (NCCP). Since 1975, coaches in Canada have had the opportunity to receive formal training in coaching through the NCCP. This five-level program, a collaborative venture among the provinces, sports governing associations, and the federal government, is designed to provide fundamental coaching principles and skills in addition to the particular techniques of each sport. To date, thousands of volunteer coaches from every level of sport in Canada have taken advantage of this program. In fact, many local sport organizations now have requirements in place that specify only certified coaches are permitted to coach in their league or program.

However, despite the best efforts of these and other educational programs to ensure qualified coaches, a number of issues and concerns related to coaches continue to plague youth sport. While children lose interest and drop out of sport for a number of reasons, many times their reasons to quit sports were related to their coaches' behaviour. These were often associated with punitive activities by coaches, unrealistic expectations, and harsh and unfair treatment of players (Canadian Centre for Ethics in Sport, 2008, p. 56):

> Coaching abuse can inflict serious harm on a reliant and impressionable youth. Many studies link bullying to a vast array of serious subsequent psychological issues: addiction, depression and suicide, among others. Child athletes are especially vulnerable, since they are looking only to the next level in their sport and are unable to understand the long-term ramifications of their experience. Let us all appreciate the inordinate trust that a youth athlete might place in the hands of what could be a bullying adult coach. (Steffenhagen, 2013)

In the past several years, there have been numerous incidents of youth sport coaches who have resorted to unethical, exploitative, and oppressive practices to produce a winning team or an elite athlete. For example, reports of falsifying birth certificates, using ineligible athletes, tampering with equipment, and flirting with starvation diets are just some of the disturbing stories that have made their way into the headlines in Canada and around the world.

Perhaps the most frightening and repulsive phenomenon related to organized youth sport to emerge in the past decade has been that of sexual harassment and abuse of young athletes. In a 1999 *Sports Illustrated* special report entitled "Who's Coaching Your Kid?" William Nack and Don Yaeger pointed out that "after decades of being ignored, minimized, or hidden away, the molestation of athletes by their coaches is no longer the sporting culture's dirty little secret" (Nack & Yaeger, 1999, p. 43). Their article revealed that "although child molestation is by no means confined to sports, the playing field represents an obvious opportunity for sexual predators." With few background checks carried out and little supervision of coaches, "youth sports are a ready-made resource pool for pedophiles" (p. 43). Kirby and Graves (1996), in the first national level survey of sexual harassment in sport (amongst 1,200 Canadian Olympians), demonstrated that sexual harassment and abuse by authority figures was widespread: 29% of responses acknowledged distressing comments and advances; 22% acknowledged having sexual intercourse with an authority figure; while nearly 9% reported having been previously subjected to a sexual assault by a coach or team authority figure, and most went unreported. Of the athletes who reported assaults, one in five were under 16 of years of age. Nack and Yaeger (1999), in an 18-month review of newspaper stories, found "more than thirty cases of coaches in the U.S. who had been arrested or convicted of sexually abusing children engaged in nine sports from baseball to wrestling" (p. 43). This abhorrent behaviour continues to exist in youth sport. In 2010, an article in

USA *Today* reported that USA Swimming (the governing body for swimming) had been charged with five lawsuits alleging sexual abuse by former swim coaches. Predominately, the perpetrators of these assaults are male coaches while the victims are girls and women.

In Canada, the 1990s painted a disturbing picture of sexual abuse in the national sport of hockey. First, it emerged that three employees of Maple Leaf Gardens (the former home of the Toronto Maple Leafs) ran a pedophile ring from 1969–1988, where dozens of young boys were sexually assaulted. In 1997, Martin Kruze, one of the survivors, came forward and blew the lid off the Maple Leaf Gardens scandal. Kruze committed suicide later in 1997, two days after one offender was sentenced to under two years of jail time. That same year, the scandal of hockey coach Graham James rocked not only the hockey world, but youth sport organizations across the country (see Box 7.1).

According to Donnelly and Sparks (2000), a number of common circumstances relating to the athlete–coach relationship exist in all of these sexual abuse cases. These include various power relations such as being "under the coach's direct control, often lonely and isolated, sometimes 'romantically' attached to the coach, threatened and/or bribed with regard to their future in sport, and generally unable to report what happened to them to their parents, police, or sport administrators" (p. 110). Athletes often do not feel as though they can come forward for a number of reasons, including feelings of shame, fear of rocking the boat (upsetting teammates), fear of being cut or not making a team, fear of getting a coach fired, feeling that nobody will believe their allegations, and for boys and men, fear of the stigma of homosexuality.

Box 7.1

Sexual Assault Cases in Sport

Recent cases of sexual assault by coaches on young athletes have raised a distressing issue for everyone involved in children's sports, and concerned parents everywhere are calling for greater vigilance at all levels of sport.

Several highly publicized cases reinforce this concern. In 1996, Graham James, a charismatic and highly successful coach in junior hockey and winner of the Man of the Year award from the *Hockey News* in 1989, was accused of sexual assault by two of his players (former NHL player Sheldon Kennedy, and another unnamed player). A year later, James pleaded guilty to 350 sexual assaults involving the two players and was sentenced to only two years in prison. In 2010, former NHL player Theoren Fleury filed a criminal complaint with the Winnipeg Police Service against James, causing the Crown to appeal James's initial sentence, which was revised to 5 years in 2013.

In another case, in 2011 former Pennsylvania State University assistant football coach Jerry Sandusky was found guilty of 45 charges of molesting 10 young boys over a 10-year period. The children, all from disadvantaged homes, gave horrifying accounts of the abuse during testimony at trial. Sandusky was sentenced to what is likely to be life behind bars. The abuse case has had far-reaching consequences for the reputation of PSU, its football program, and a number of university coaches and administrators.

Finally, a former hockey coach, after becoming close friends with a family from Etobicoke, Ontario, sexually abused their two sons and their friends. Michael Dimmick, a retired engineer and coach and referee, was sentenced in 2013 to 7 years for indecent assaults that took place in the 1960s and 1970s.

What is clear about all of these cases is that the sexual abuse was committed over a long period of time, sometimes years, by someone in a trusted position. Therefore, to reduce the risk of sexual abuse in children's sport, rigorous background checks are imperative, as is making sure two adults are present whenever children are being coached. Most importantly, we must take steps to educate our children to be aware of the warning signs, and we must create an environment where children are empowered to disclose abuse and, if needed, receive help and support.

In the wake of new revelations of sexual improprieties involving minor league coaches, sport organizations at all levels have come under increasing pressure to take measures to ensure the safety of young athletes. Consequently, Sport Canada, along with a number of national sport organizations, have developed national guidelines for dealing with sexual assault and harassment incidents. An immediate response by many sport organizations across the country to these incidents has been to implement policies that require all coaches to submit to a police background check. Police checks are, for example, mandatory in Britain for every volunteer who works with children (Anderssen, 2010). As well, in an attempt to protect children many sport organizations have instituted a number of safeguards aimed at volunteers, officials, coaches, and the athletes themselves. These are sometimes drawn up into a bill of rights for young athletes or are formulated as fair play codes (Sage & Eitzen, 2013). Unfortunately, these measures may not be enough to keep sexual predators out of sport, particularly in the larger urban centres where thousands of volunteer coaches would need to undergo screening. Police departments that would normally be responsible for reviewing the backgrounds of these coaches simply do not have the time or the resources to do so. Police checks, moreover, only provide evidence of convictions, not accusations of misconduct, charges, or investigations. Chillingly, the president of Volunteer Canada noted that the notorious murderer Paul Bernardo would have passed a police check to coach young children (Anderssen, 2010).

Regardless, several precautions need to be taken on behalf of children in organized sport programs to help safeguard them against sexual exploitation. First, where feasible, organizers should insist on a background check by police. Where this is not practical, volunteer coaches should, as a condition to coach in a league, be required to submit to a check of their conduct, either through an employer or from previous coaching positions. Second, parents need to be aware of the danger signs that might suggest a sexually abusive or harassing relationship, such as a sudden drop in the child's interest in a particular sport, and take steps to protect their children. They should also try to be present at their children's practices and games (because unattended children are seen as easy targets) while being wary of coaches who lavish expensive gifts on players or spend an unusual amount of time with a child (Nack & Yaeger, 1999). Perhaps most importantly, though, parents need to talk to and inform their children about what is considered inappropriate behaviour by a coach and to reassure them about reporting any improprieties that may occur between athletes and coaches. This latter step can be facilitated by the establishment of specific policies and a complaint process known to all athletes including, if possible, an anonymous tip line (Anderssen, 2010).

Conclusions

Throughout this chapter, we have suggested that many of the original objectives of organized sport for children have become obscured or replaced with an overemphasis on elitism, performance, and the pursuit of athletic glory. The current sport system in Canada comprises school, community, and private agencies, and these organizations often promote and maintain an exclusionary model in which young athletes are pressured to succeed by overzealous parents and domineering coaches. As a result of this pressure and interference, more and more children are expressing the view that sports are no longer fun—a trend that is reflected in the fact that nearly 70% of all children in organized sport drop out before they reach the age of 13 (Sage & Eitzen, 2013).

Strategies need to be put in place to address the issues and concerns brought forward in this chapter. First, parents must begin to take a more proactive stance toward changing the culture of youth sport. The drive for excellence must be balanced with a greater regard for the overall development of the child. There should be a focus not just on athletic performance but also on social, emotional, and intellectual development. Second, organizers responsible for providing youth sport programs need to meet the challenges facing sport as a result of these disturbing trends by instituting sound policies on the ethical conduct of those in decision-making positions. As well, the codes of conduct of sport governing bodies should carry penalties that are severe enough to be real deterrents to those who might choose to act in an unethical manner. Finally, coaches need to be made aware of the potential for damage caused by early specialization and overtraining in young athletes and encourage and support involvement in a variety of sport activities rather than placing primary emphasis on exploiting children who show athletic promise.

On this latter note, it may also be useful to follow the salutary advice of noted environmentalist and activist David Suzuki (2012) who suggests a return to informal, outdoor activities:

> We need to make sure our neighbourhoods have green spaces where people can explore their connections with nature. We need to ask teachers and school board representatives to take students outside so that nature becomes a classroom. And we need to stop making the outdoors seem like a scary place for children by helping parents understand that the benefits of playing outside outweigh the risks.

The enduring barriers to sport and physical activity in Canada need to be addressed, and children need to be provided with inclusive, fun, and safe sporting and leisure opportunities including, as Suzuki noted, challenging some of the ideologies that parents hold about their children playing outside. Given that the habits we take into adulthood are often formed during our youth, we have no greater purpose as physical educators in Canada than to take seriously the issues facing youth and children's involvement in sport.

Critical Thinking Questions

1. What has led to the increase in popularity of organized sport for children over the past several decades?
2. What are the dangers associated with early specialization for children in organized sport?
3. Parents and coaches appear to be mainly responsible for putting unrealistic expectations on children who are involved in organized sport. Is this an accurate statement? Are there other people or other factors involved that contribute to the pressure felt by these children?
4. Studies have shown that more than 70% of all children who participate in organized sport drop out by the time they reach the age of 13. What suggestions and changes would you make to the way youth sport is currently structured in Canada to encourage children to remain in sport?
5. As a parent of a child involved in organized sport, what precautions would you take to ensure that your child remains safe from unethical coaches who might seek to exploit him or her?

6. Assuming that you are in charge of organizing a new sport program for children in your community, what steps would you take to ensure all children in the program receive equal participation opportunities?

7. Discuss what the three major stakeholders (parents, sport governing bodies, and coaches) need to do to resolve some of the problems associated with children's sport.

Suggested Readings

Donnelly, P. (2011). *Taking sport seriously: Social issues in Canadian sport* (3rd ed.). Section 3, Children and Sports, Chapters 10–16. Toronto, ON: Thompson Educational Press.

Gruneau, R. (in press). Goodbye Gordie Howe: Sport participation and class inequality in the "pay for play." In D. Taras & C. Wadell (Eds.), *How Canadians communicate V: Sports.* Edmonton, AB: AU Press.

Malloy, D. C., Ross, S., & Zakus, D. H. (2000). *Sport ethics: Concepts and cases in sport and recreation.* Toronto, ON: Thompson Educational Press.

Orlick, T. (2006). Cooperative games and sports: Joyful activities for everyone. Champaign, Il: Human Kinetics.

References

Active Healthy Kids Canada. (2013). Active Kids Report Card. (2013). *Are we driving our kids to unhealthy habits? Report card on physical activity for children and youth.* Retrieved Feb. 2014 from http://www.activehealthykids.ca/2013ReportCard/en/.

American Alliance for Health, Physical Education, Recreation and Dance. (2013). Comprehensive school physical activity programs: Helping all students achieve 60 minutes of physical activity each day. *Journal of Physical Education, Recreation and Dance, 84*(9), 9–15.

Anderssen, E. (2010, April 9). Game-changing sex-abuse cases mean new rules for nation's coaches. *Globe and Mail.* Retrieved from http://www.theglobeandmail.com/news/national/game-changing-sex-abuse-cases-mean-new-rules-for-nations-coaches/article4314402/#dashboard/follows/.

Bompa, T. (1995). *From childhood to champion athlete.* Toronto, ON: Veritas.

Brackenbridge, C. H. (2001). *Spoilsports: Understanding and preventing sexual exploitation in sport.* London, UK: Routledge.

Brenner, J. S. (2007). Overuse injuries, overtraining, and burnout in child and adolescent athletes. *Pediatrics, 119*(6), 1242–1245. doi: 10.1542/peds.2007-0887.

Brownrigg, M. (2008). Canadian children and youth receive failing grade for physical activity levels as screen time replaces active play. Active Healthy Kids Canada. Retrieved from http://www.newswire.ca/en/story/355749/canadian-children-and-youth-receive-failing-grade-for-physical-activity-levels-as-screen-time-replaces-active-play.

Bryant, J. E., & McElroy, M. (1997). *Sociological dynamics of sport and exercise.* Englewood, CO: Morton Publishing Company.

Butcher, J., Linder, K. L., & Johns, D. P. (2002). Withdrawal from competitive youth sport: A retrospective ten-year study. *Journal of Sport Behavior, 25*(2), 145–163.

Canadian Centre for Ethics in Sport. (2002). *Public opinion survey on youth and sport. Final Report.* Retrieved from http://www.cces.ca/files/pdfs/CCES-RPT-2002Survey-E.pdf.

Canadian Centre for Ethics in Sport. (2008). *What sport can do: The true sport report.* Ottawa, ON: True Sport. Retrieved from http://www.truesportpur.ca/files/pdfs/TS_report_EN_webdownload.pdf.

Canadian Fitness and Lifestyle Research Institute. (2004). *2004 Physical activity monitor.* Ottawa, ON: Author.

Canadian Fitness and Lifestyle Research Institute. (2010). *2010 Physical activity monitor: Facts and figures*. Ottawa, ON: Author.

Canadian Heritage. (2013). *Sport participation 2010: Research paper*. Retrieved from http://publications.gc.ca/collections/collection_2014/pc-ch/CH24-1-2014-eng.pdf.

Canadian Paediatric Society. (2006). Sport readiness in children and youth sport. *Pediatric Child Health, 10*(6), 343–344.

Canadian Sport Centres. (2007). *Canadian sport for life: A sport parent's guide*. Ottawa, ON: Author. Retrieved from http://www.fieldhockey.ca/files/LTHD/parents_guide_eng.pdf.

Centers for Disease Control. (2010). *Childhood obesity*. Retrieved from http://www.cdc.gov/Healthy-people/hp2010.htm.

Coakley, J., & Donnelly, P. (2009). Sports and children: Are organized programs worth the effort? (2nd Canadian ed., pp. 110–143). Boston, MA: McGraw-Hill.

Deacon, J. (2001, March 26). Rink rage. *Maclean's*, pp. 21–24.

Deakin, J. M., & Cobley, S. (2003). A search for deliberate practice: An examination of the practice environments in figure skating and volleyball. In J. Starkes & K. A. Ericsson (Eds.), *Expert performance in sport: Recent advances in research on sport expertise* (pp. 115–135). Champaign, IL: Human Kinetics.

Donnelly, P. (2000). *Taking sport seriously: Social issues in Canadian sport*. Toronto, ON: Thompson Publishing, Inc.

Donnelly, P., & Sparks, R. (2000). Child sexual abuse in sport. In P. Donnelly (Ed.), *Taking sport seriously: Social issues in Canadian sport* (pp. 108–111). Toronto, ON: Thompson Educational Press.

Engh, F. (1999). *Why Johnny hates sports*. Garden City Park, NY: Avery Pub.

Figler, S. K., & Whitaker G. (1991). *Sport and play in American life*. Dubuque, IA: Wm. C. Brown.

Fullinwider, R. K. (2006). Sports, youth and character: A critical survey. Circle Working Paper 44, Institute for Philosophy and Public Policy, University of Maryland. Retrieved from http://www.civicyouth.org/PopUps/WorkingPapers/WP44Fullinwider.pdf.

Fraser-Thomas, J., & Coté, J. (2009). Understanding adolescents' positive and negative developmental experiences in sport. *Sports Psychologist, 23*, 3–23.

Gruneau, R. (in press). Goodbye Gordie Howe: Sport participation and class inequality in the "pay for play." In D. Taras & C. Wadell (Eds.), *How Canadians communicate V: Sports*. Edmonton, AB: AU Press.

Hall, A., Slack, T., Smith, G., & Whitson, D. (1991). *Sport in Canadian society*. Toronto, ON: McClelland & Stewart.

Jayanthi, N. (2012). Injury risks of sport specialization and training in junior tennis players: A clinical study. Paper presented at the Society for Tennis and Medicine Science North American Regional Conference, Atlanta, GA.

Kirby, S., & Greaves, L. (1996, July 11–14). *Foul play: Sexual abuse and harassment in sport*. Paper presented to the Pre-Olympic Scientific Congress, Dallas, TX.

Koutures, C. G., Gregory, A. J., & the Council on Sport Medicine and Fitness. (2010). Injuries in youth soccer. *American Academy of Pediatrics, 125*(2), 410–414. doi: 10.1542/peds.2009-3009.

Kremer-Sadlik, T., & Kim, J. L. (2007). Lessons from sports: Children's socialization to values through family interaction during sports activities. *Discourse and Society, 18*(1), 35–52. doi: 10.1177/0957926507069456.

LaVoi, N. M., & Stellino, M. B. (2008). The relation between perceived parent-created sport climate and competitive male youth hockey players' good and poor sport behaviours. *Journal of Psychology, 142*(5), 471–495.

Law, M., Cote. J., & Ericsson, K. A. (2007). Characteristics of expert development in rhythmic gymnastics: A retrospective study. *International Journal of Exercise and Sport Psychology, 5*(1), 82–103. doi: 10.1080/1612197X.2008.9671814.

Lumpkin, A. (2005). *Physical education, exercise science, and sport studies* (5th ed.). Boston, MA: McGraw-Hill.

Marchie, A., & Cusimano, M. (2003). Bodychecking and concussions in ice hockey: Should our youth pay the price? *Canadian Medical Association Journal, 169*(2), 124–128.

Nack, W., & Yaeger, D. (1999, September 13). Who's coaching your kid? The frightening truth about child molestation in youth sports. *Sports Illustrated*, pp. 39–53.

Nixon, H. L., & Frey, J. H. (1996). *A sociology of sport*. Belmont, CA: Wadsworth.

Olshansky, J. S., Passaro, D. J., Ronald, C., Hershow, R., Layden, J., Carnes, B., Brody, J., Hayflick, L., Butler, R., Allison, D., & Ludwig, D. (2005). A potential decline in life expectancy in the United States in the 21st century. *New England Journal of Medicine, 352*(11), 1138–1145.

Pugliese, J., & Tinsley, B. Parental socialization of child and adolescent physical activity: A meta-analysis. *Journal of Family Psychology, 21*(3), 331–343. doi: 10.1037/0893-3200.21.3.331.

Purcell, L. K., Canadian Paediatric Society, & Healthy Active Living and Sports Medicine Committee. (2012). Evaluation and management of children and adolescents with sport-related concussion. *Paediatrics & Child Health, 17*(1), 31.

Physical and Health and Education Canada. (2014). QDPE—The facts. Retrieved from http://www.phecanada.ca/programs/quality-daily-physical-education/facts.

Raedeke, T. D. (1997). Is athlete burnout more than just stress? A sport commitment perspective. *Journal of Sport and Exercise Psychology, 19*, 396–417.

Sage, G. H., & Eitzen, D. S. (2013). *Sociology of North American sport*. Madison, WI: Brown and Benchmark.

Shields, D. L., Bredemeier, B. L., LaVoi, N. M., & Power, C. F. (2005). The sport behavior of youth, parents and coaches: The good, the bad, and the ugly. *Journal of Research on Character Education, 3*(1), 43–59.

Shields, D. L., LaVoi, N. M., Bredemeier, B. L., & Power, C. F. (2007). Predictors of poor sportspersonship in youth sports: An examination of personal attitudes and social influences. *Journal of Sport and Exercise Psychology, 29*(6), 747–762.

Siedentop, D. (2004). *Introduction to physical education, fitness and sport* (5th ed.). Boston, MA: McGraw-Hill.

Smith, A. L. (2003). Peer relationships in physical activity contexts: A road less traveled in youth sport and exercise psychology research. *Psychology of Sport and Exercise, 4*(1). 25–39. Statistics Canada. (2004). Canadian Community Health Survey. Special Surveys Division. *Statistics Canada*.

Statistics Canada. (2005, July 6). Canadian Community Health Survey: Obesity among children and adults. *The Daily*. Retrieved from http://www.statcan.gc.ca/daily-quotidien/050706/dq050706a-eng.htm.

Steffenhagen, J. (2013, May 21). B.C.'s young athletes need protection from abusive coaches. *Vancouver Sun*. Retrieved from http://blogs.vancouversun.com/2013/05/21/b-c-s-young-athletes-need-protection-from-abusive-coaches-opinion/.

Suzuki, D. (2012, September 27). Get your kids away from the screen and into the green. David Suzuki Foundation. Retrieved from http://www.davidsuzuki.org/blogs/science-matters/2012/09/get-your-kids-away-from-the-screen-and-into-the-green/.

Weiss, M. R., & Fretwell, S. D. (2004). The parent-coach/child-athlete relationship in youth sport: Cordial, contentious, or conundrum? *Research Quarterly for Exercise and Sport, 76*(3), 286–305. doi: 10.1080/02701367.2005.10599300.

Wiersma, L. D., & Fifer, A. M. (2005). It's their turn to speak: The joys, challenges and recommendations of youth sport parents. Paper presented at the meeting for the Advancement of Applied Sport Psychology, Vancouver, BC.

Wuest, D. A., & Bucher, C. A. (2003). *Foundations of physical education and sport* (42nd ed.) St. Louis, MI: McGraw-Hill.

Chapter 8
Sport Deviance
Jason Laurendeau

On August 4, 2013, three BASE jumpers[1] gained illegal access into and then parachuted from the top of a 36-storey building under construction on Jasper Avenue in Edmonton, Alberta, landing in the middle of the Victoria Promenade (Klingbeil, 2013). The jump took place at about 9:15 p.m., was witnessed by a number of local residents, and in the weeks that followed became the focus of significant media attention.

Perhaps you anticipate that this chapter will be about stories like the one outlined above, considering questions of why these BASE jumpers (or other participants in sport and leisure pursuits) engage in deviant activities—what makes them decide to do so, the "techniques of rationalization" (Sykes & Matza, 1957) upon which they draw, and so on. These are important questions that will inform this chapter to a certain extent. More centrally, however, we will concern ourselves not with deviance as a "thing" to be explained or understood, but as the outcome of a social process and cultural struggle (Deutschmann, 2002). In other words, what many scholars of (sport and) deviance find sociologically interesting are the ways in which *particular ideas about what constitutes deviance are produced and enforced*. This approach is rooted in C. Wright Mill's touchstone

Ben Johnson's victory in the men's 100-metre sprint in the 1988 Olympic Games, and the drug scandal that followed, remains a touchstone moment in Canadian Olympic and sporting history. AP Photo/Dieter Endlicher articulation of the "sociological imagination," in which he stresses the importance of understanding "personal biography" (in this case, individual decisions to conform or to engage in deviance) in relation to the social and historical locations in which those decisions arise (Mills, 1961).

How deviance is socially constructed and how society responds to deviance both formally and informally are part of the "deviance dance": "the interactions, negotiations, and debates among groups with different perceptions of whether a behaviour or characteristic is deviant and needs to be socially controlled" (Bereska, 2011, p. 23). It is this ideological "dance" that is of principal interest in this chapter. In what follows, I will consider what kinds of people, activities, ways of being, and ways of participating in sport and recreational pursuits come to be understood as "normal," and who and what come to be seen (e.g., by formal social control organizations, by the "general public," and even by the deviants themselves) as abnormal, pathological, immoral, and so on. This approach reminds us to keep squarely in focus questions of power and ideology as we undertake sociological analyses of sport and physical culture, allowing us to "unpack the centre" (Brock, Raby, & Thomas, 2012) with respect to questions of sport and deviance. Indeed, "discourses about 'normal' behaviour . . . are connected to the power relations" (Brock et al., 2012, p. 7). It is important, then, to consider not only "normal" or "deviant" behaviour, but also the power relations within which these distinctions are embedded.

In order to explore the topic of sport and deviance in the ways described above, I first consider how deviance is conceptualized, exploring questions of what *kinds* of approaches to studying deviance characterize this body of work. Second, I consider the question of

Celebrating their gold-medal win at the Vancouver 2010 Olympic Games subjected the Canadian women's hockey team to a degree of public scrutiny not imposed on men in similar circumstances.
Robert Ghement/dpa/STF/picture-alliance/Newscom

"deviance and otherness" and the related notion of deviantized bodies and embodiments as central in framing this chapter. Third, I take up issues of social control, highlighting the sense in which deviance is not only (and perhaps not even most importantly) about the deviant behaviour or identity, but about the ways in which others—from both inside and outside of particular sporting activities—interpret, respond to, and attempt to regulate this conduct. Fourth, I consider a number of specific examples of deviance on and off the field of play, pointing out how they help us shed light on the idea of deviance as dynamic and subject to contestation (e.g., when deviants resist being labelled), and the related notion that the deviance dance is embedded within particular power relations *and serves to produce* power relations. Finally, I take up questions of deviantized sports and sporting identities and draw together the most important threads from the chapter, pointing out opportunities and challenges for sociologists of sport as we continue to consider questions of sport and deviance.

CONCEPTUALIZING DEVIANCE

It is important at the outset to consider how we might conceptualize deviance to set the stage for an exploration of some of the avenues of investigation that sport scholars have considered as well as those that have been less well developed.

There are various sociological and lay approaches to conceptualizing deviance. Underpinning an objectivist standpoint is the "assumption that there is something inherent in a person, behaviour, or characteristic that is necessarily deviant" (Bereska, 2011, p. 5). The aim from this perspective is to *explain* the "person, behaviour, or characteristic in question" (Bereska, 2011, p. 22). However, this framework has been subject to considerable criticism, particularly from analysts working from a more subjectivist position.

Subjectivist analyses conceptualize deviance as a *social construction*, emphasizing that there is nothing that is *inherently* deviant. From this perspective, the "focus becomes the 'deviance dance'—the interactions, negotiations, and debates among groups with different perceptions of whether a behaviour or characteristic is deviant" (Bereska, 2011, p. 23). In other words, deviance is understood not as a thing to be explained, but as an *outcome* of a social process informed by power and involving negotiation and contestation (Deutschmann, 2002). Even within the broad category of subjectivist approaches to studying deviance, however, there are important debates about what precisely should be the focus of our research. For example, certain subjectivist approaches, including those aiming to "humanize" those labelled as deviant, might actually *reproduce* the idea that deviants are different, even perverted, simply by making them the foci of their investigations (Liazos, 1972).

Critiques such as those outlined above advocate much more sustained attention to the groups, institutions, and regulatory agencies that create and apply the labels, and the processes by which these labels come to be understood as "common sense," and hence play important roles in the maintenance and (re)shaping of *hegemony* (see Chapters 1 and 2). From this perspective, it is important to unpack the centre, asking critical questions about those in position to create, modify, and enforce the rules, whether formal or informal, and the particular ideas that are made to seem normal or common sense in applying these rules. What is at stake here is not simply particular definitions of what constitutes deviance, but also broader ideological struggles about such topics as gender, nationalism, race, sexuality, (dis)ability, and health. This is the critical approach taken in this chapter, one that lends itself to a number of important questions about deviance and sport that shift the focus from those approaches outlined above. For example, this approach to studying deviance and sport considers questions such as the following:

1. How do particular actions, identities, and performances come to be understood as deviant?

2. What formal and informal mechanisms of social control are employed in attempts to bring or keep those defined as deviant "in line"?

3. In what ways are current definitions of deviance shaped by power relations in a particular sociohistorical context?

4. How might we understand deviance not simply as *reflective* of particular power relations but as actively involved in *(re)producing* those power relations?

5. How do particular definitions of deviance serve to produce, reproduce, or transform broader systems of social organization such as race, gender, (dis)ability, and sexuality?

6. How are individual subjectivities shaped and constrained by the definitions of deviance that predominate in particular social contexts?

7. How can we understand individual agency (individuals' abilities to make choices that might resist dominant understandings) with respect to the "rules" that govern the particular sporting spaces they occupy?

The notion of "tolerable deviance" (Stebbins, 1996) is a useful framework for understanding sport-related deviance. Sport is "viewed as a separate social world with its own allowable rule violations," exemplifying the process by which a "culturally tolerable deviance violates a normative code but is not interpreted by audiences as a legitimate threat to the collective (or moral) good" (Atkinson & Young, 2008, p. 11). The tolerable deviance framework sheds important light on the extent to which sport is constructed as a space in which deviance is accepted, tolerated, or even celebrated.

A number of the central arguments characterizing this framework are worth highlighting at this time. One approach suggests that there is a hierarchy of social problems, and agents of formal social control (e.g., the police) focus on more serious criminal activities, which in turn influences "moral entrepreneurs" (Atkinson & Young, 2008). According to the internal policing argument, sporting participants and organizers govern themselves, drawing on a deep understanding of the norms and rules in effect in particular sporting spaces to do so. Another way of thinking within this framework is to understand sport as a "social theater in which spectators are deliberately aroused by the tension-balances created through athletic contests," thus reducing the predictability of day-to-day life (Atkinson & Young, 2008, p. 15). From this perspective, because it functions as theatre, sport is understood as an unusual space in which a certain degree of deviance is tolerated, or even encouraged. In addition, some suggest that the "indiscretions of athletes, however common and statistically typical, tend to be perceived as unusual and unrepresentative of sport culture" more broadly (Atkinson & Young, 2008, p. 16). This argument might also be made with respect to other forms of deviance, such as white-collar crime (Sutherland, 1945).

DEVIANCE AND OTHERNESS

Though numerous sport scholars highlight the importance of institutions and practices that serve to privilege some groups and individuals and to marginalize others, few conceptualize this as a question of deviance. And yet, dominant "groups have the power to impose the

Box 8.1

Ben Johnson: A Case Study

The case of Ben Johnson is illustrative of a number of important points discussed at the outset of this chapter. In 1988, Johnson was one of the best-known athletes on the planet. A Canadian sprinter of Jamaican heritage, Johnson exploded onto the sporting scene, establishing himself in relatively short order as a force to be reckoned with in one of the most prestigious sporting events there is: the men's 100-metre sprint. Johnson's dramatic victory in the event at the 1988 Seoul Olympic Games established a new world record and solidified his position as the "fastest man on Earth."

The fame Johnson gained with this victory was surpassed, however, by the fall from grace less than 48 hours later when it was revealed that he had tested positive for a banned anabolic steroid. Johnson was stripped of his gold medal and whisked out of South Korea. In short order, Johnson's case became the central subject in a formal inquiry. The Dubin Inquiry, which cost Canadian taxpayers $3.6 million, "revealed what almost everyone already knew: that Ben Johnson had used steroids and that the use of performance-enhancing drugs was endemic in elite sport" (Jackson & Ponic, 2001, pp. 54–55). The Dubin Inquiry, however, did more than simply recount the facts: "[G]iven its sheer size and significance, the Inquiry served to institutionalize the memory of the Johnson crisis" (Jackson & Ponic, 2001, p. 55).

The Dubin Inquiry is notable in two other respects. First, it "was the first full-scale examination of doping in sport that looked beyond the athlete's guilt [and] attributed partial responsibility for Ben Johnson's doping offence to his coaches, trainers, and other consultants" (Teetzel, 2009,

p. 87). Second, though the inquiry did more than blame an individual athlete for a doping infraction, it still located blame very much at the feet of particular agents, indicting their moral character for "cheating." In so doing, the inquiry failed to critically consider the performance sport paradigm (one that continues to dominate national discussions of sport) that creates the backdrop against which we must consider individual and collective decisions to use performance-enhancing substances (MacIntosh & Whitson, 1990).

In the months and years that followed, Johnson's sprinting career remained in the news as he served a competition ban and then re-entered the competitive field, albeit with less success than he had previously enjoyed. Later he tested positive a second time and received a lifetime competition ban from the International Amateur Athletic Federation (Jackson, 1998).

This particular case needs to be understood and examined in context to appreciate the deviantization process. As the story unfolded, Johnson's identity was "twisted" as he gained fame and later notoriety (Jackson, 1998). Press coverage of Johnson's athletic career reveals that he was initially framed as a "Jamaican" runner who happened to have immigrated to Canada. As he moved up the ranks, however, Johnson's identity underwent a decisive shift and he became, first, a Jamaican Canadian and, later, a Canadian. When he was stripped of his medal in 1988, however, Johnson was almost immediately relegated back to "Jamaican." We must understand that this process was shaped by Canada–US relations, questions of Canadian identity, and contested racial politics in an ostensibly multicultural society (Jackson, 1998).

norms that comprise their culture on all other cultural groups in society, labelling the norms of conflicting cultural groups as 'deviant' and in need of measures of social control" (Bereska, 2011, p. 90). For the purposes of this chapter, we must understand "culture" in both the broadest sense (e.g., it might refer to the cultural patterns such as heteronormativity, the pattern of social relations that construct heterosexuality as the dominant and only *normal* expression of sexual desire), *and* in the more context-specific sense of the cultural norms created and sustained in particular times and places (such as the norms that characterize certain sporting cultures). What is important to appreciate for the purposes of this discussion, then, is the

notion of a deviant "other"—feared, loathed, or both—as the means to maintaining an idealized self. An understanding of "otherness" helps to explain why identities are often characterized by polarization and by the discursive marking of inclusion and exclusion within oppositional classificatory systems: "insiders" and "outsiders," "us" and "them," men and women, black and white, "normal" and "deviant." (Greer & Jewkes, 2005, p. 20)

These systems of classification are produced and reproduced rather than simply *reflected in* the media and other cultural texts (Hall, 2000). These texts include, for example, the mediation of competitions themselves, but also the rules and codes of conduct in circulation in particular sporting spaces, as well as the interpretations and implementations thereof.

Consider the institutionalized racism in recent codes of conduct and practices in the NBA and the NHL (Lorenz & Murray, 2013). In both cases, we see the (racialized) production of particular choices of style (e.g., dress, music, adornment of equipment) as deviant and in need of "correction." This operates to surveil and police and, ultimately, as an endeavour on the part of these leagues and teams to "'tame' . . . the threatening Black bodies under their control" (Lorenz & Murray, 2013, p. 3). In the case of Ray Emery, a Black NHL goaltender with the Ottawa Senators, the "dominant discourse framing media narratives [was] the discourse of 'otherness'" (Lorenz & Murray 2013, p. 13). NBA and NHL officials, of course, argue that these policies and practices are not *about* race, and indeed that they are "colour-blind." It is important to note, however, that "colour-blindness furnishes acceptable ways to reject race-sensitive equity politics and do so while sounding principled" (Levine-Rasky, 2012, p. 102).

Deviantized Bodies and Embodiments

One central line of questioning directly related to the discussion of deviance and otherness is the production of particular bodies and particular embodiments or bodily (in)capacities as "normal" or "deviant." These processes serve to remind us who belongs and who does not in particular sporting spaces. In other words, they construct particular ideas about bodies and bodily (in)actions, ideas that produce and reproduce particular understandings of ourselves and others and legitimize certain social relations (see Chapter 2). In other words, from a Foucauldian perspective these processes are an exercise in power.

In the early 20th century, for example, the International Olympic Committee (IOC) excluded women from certain Olympic events, arguing that their bodies (and in particular their reproductive functions) would be irreparably harmed by such vigorous activity (Laurendeau & Adams, 2010). Moreover, when women's participation *was* sanctioned, it was often closely observed by officials. At the 1928 Games in Amsterdam, for instance, the IOC sanctioned only five track and field events for women. Following some concerns about women collapsing on the track in the event (as did a number of men in their event, it should be noted), the IOC "argued for complete expulsion of women from the Olympic games" (Wamsley & Pfister, 2005, p. 113). Though this did not come to pass, women's athletics were retained in the Olympics "in a limited capacity and under close scrutiny" (Wamsley & Pfister, 2005, p. 113). The IOC has a long history of deviantizing women and policing gender boundaries, perhaps most notably in practices of sex testing (see Chapter 6).

Another way in which we see the deviantization of particular bodies and embodied practices is in the ways that certain body types are revered (and others deviantized) in particular sporting spaces. Consider the example of larger-bodied participants in long-distance running, a sport that tends to be dominated by slighter athletes: The "large or fat running body presents a site where the disciplinary processes are active and where the participants are subjected to extensive surveillance" (Chase, 2008, p. 140). Particular examples of this kind of surveillance and policing must be understood within a broader social and political landscape in which "fatness" is deviantized more broadly (McDermott, 2007).

"Disabled" bodies are also deviantized in numerous ways. For example, the dominant history of the Paralympic Games serves to marginalize, homogenize, and pathologize disability and disabled bodies (Peers, 2009). This history constructs a story of disabled bodies under the care and training of benevolent experts, and in so doing erases the agency of the very people with disabilities who contributed to laying the foundations of the modern Paralympic movement. Similarly, contemporary representations of Paralympic athletes often erase the identities and subjectivities of the athletes themselves, instead fetishizing the technologies (mobility and otherwise) that make athletic excellence possible (Peers, 2009). Perhaps more troubling still is the extent to which the Olympic Games are produced as the *real* Olympics, whereas the Paralympic Games are constructed as a derivative and, arguably, irrelevant version of the "real" event. An advertising slogan at the 1996 Olympic Games, for example ("The Olympics is where heroes are made. The Paralympics is where heroes come.") celebrates Paralympic athletes and constructs them as heroic simply for *being there*, while Olympians are "made into" heroes in and through their training, athletic successes, and personal sacrifices (Peers, 2009). This serves to reproduce the idea that disabled bodies are *not normal*, even *as it celebrates them*.

It is important to remember that individual choices are both situated within, and serve to reproduce, challenge, or transform broader institutions and structures. Former Paralympian Danielle Peers's own negotiations and performances of disability have sometimes served to reproduce the very conditions that marginalize her as disabled (Peers, 2012). To the extent that she (ambivalently) adopted the role of the "supercrip" in her career as a Paralympic basketball player on the Canadian national team, she was complicit in further entrenching a dangerous narrative about disability, one that constructs a tremendously narrow range of possible subjectivities for those with disabilities and emphasizes individual capacities to *overcome* disability rather than questioning the ableist narratives in which we understand disability as something that *must be overcome* (Peers, 2012).

Also important are the surveillance practices competitors are subjected to and how they sometimes take on and reproduce their deviant identities. In a provocative and moving autoethnography, Peers captures the surveillance dimension in a scene that replays itself numerous times throughout her athletic career:

> It is dark here. I am alone, or at least, I feel alone. It feels like years since I have been here: since they have been asking me the same questions; since they have been trying to figure out who, exactly, I am. Am I the innocent victim? The hostile witness? The suspect? The criminal—cheat? I am finally broken down. I give up. I am ready to confess the truth . . . I am just not sure which truth to tell. (Peers, 2012, p. 175)

SOCIAL CONTROL

As noted above, it is imperative that we consider social control efforts and mechanisms as fundamentally related to and even *implicated in the production* of deviance. In other words, deviance is not deviant in and of itself; it becomes defined as deviant by particular people and groups in particular geographical and social locations as part of the deviantization process described above. And this process is not politically or ideologically neutral. Rather, what is being contested is nothing less than what we understand—and treat—as "normal."

In our consideration of social control, it is important at the outset to note that social control efforts might be formal or informal (e.g., codified rules versus commonly understood norms), they might be direct and specific or more general and diffuse (e.g., penalties for specific rule violations versus broader systems of meaning that operate to remind us of what we *should* be doing and not doing and who we should want to be), and they might come from within a particular sporting location or be imposed from beyond that location (e.g., "doping" rules and norms *within* the sport of cycling versus police actions initiated from outside of the sport).

One avenue of investigation that sheds important light on deviance and social control is the question of informal mechanisms of social control in operation *within* sporting spaces. Though large-scale examples of deviance tend to come easily to mind, everyday violations of expectations, and the responses to such forms of deviance, illustrate the notion that deviance is contextual and contested. As Deutschmann (2002, p. 22) points out, in "the sense that every social grouping generates deviant designations and rules for their application, the deviance process is universal. [Even deviant] communities such as biker gangs include their own deviants, who may be expelled if their behaviour is insufficiently in tune with what the group requires." This is not, however, to suggest that the codes in operation in particular sporting spaces are unrelated to broader constructions of deviance. On the contrary, these notions of what constitutes deviance and conformity are part of the broader landscape of ideological struggle that serves to reproduce (and sometimes reshape) the processes by which consent about such topics as risk, gender, and respect for authority is created (see Chapter 2).

Within particular sporting spaces (including spaces that some might think of as inherently deviant), there are expectations and norms (defined and policed by the group or subculture itself) as to *how* one goes about participating in a sporting activity or what it means to be a "real" participant. As part of my research into BASE jumping (refer to page 182 for a description), for example, I learned of a phenomenon known as "BASE ethics." One central component of BASE ethics is the expectation that jumpers visiting an area contact local jumpers prior to jumping off particular objects:

> The seriousness of the expectation to "contact the locals" is highlighted by the case of John Vincent, who, many years ago, traveled to Atlanta and, without contacting the locals, jumped a crane. Previously, a local crew of jumpers had worked out an agreement with the crane operator that he would leave the crane facing a favourable direction for the jumpers (contrary to company guidelines) in return for a quantity of beer that the jumpers would leave for him each time they jumped it. This arrangement had worked well for locals as well as jumpers visiting the Atlanta area, until Vincent's [jump]. Not only did Vincent jump the crane, but he [also] proceeded to publicize the jump. As a result of the ensuing press coverage, the crane came under much tighter security, the construction company initiated an investigation, and the crane operator who had been friendly to local jumpers lost his job. In breaking the "contact the locals" rule, then, Vincent upset local BASE jumpers enough that they were willing to drive several hours to punish him. (Laurendeau, J. (2012). BASE jumping: The ultimate guide. Santa Barbara, CA: ABC-CLIO. , p26. Reprinted by permission of Copyright Clearance Center.)

The punishment to which I refer here is striking. This crew of jumpers showed up at Vincent's residence, forced their way inside, and literally tarred and feathered Vincent. What's more, they videotaped the events in a recording that has since become folklore in the BASE jumping community (Laurendeau, 2012).

Perhaps a more everyday example, however, will help highlight the importance of informal policing that takes place within particular sporting spaces. In an autoethnography interrogating my own sporting practices (Laurendeau, 2013), including those of violence toward myself and others, I describe a high school gridiron football practice from my youth.

> My coach, furious about the 'moves' we were trying in a particular drill, yelled at us to "actually hit someone." Wanting very much to please my coach (and simultaneously fearing him), I complied, nearly causing both a teammate and myself concussions. My coach, pleased at this display, celebrated this act of violence quite publicly. This scenario—one that I suspect mirrors innumerable practices and games in football and elsewhere—brings to light the sense in which we must understand both deviance and conformity *in relation* to agents and practices of social control. In other words, individuals in sporting spaces make particular choices about whether and how to engage in sporting practices but do so within a system that sets limits of various kinds on what choices are available and intelligible. In the scenario described above, my coach acted as the agent of social control, indicting a group of boys and young men for not adhering to the "sport ethic" (Hughes & Coakley, 1991) and, implicitly, for not emulating the "right" kind of masculinity.

This vignette—one that I suspect mirrors innumerable practices and games in football and elsewhere—brings to light the sense in which we must understand both deviance and conformity *in relation to* agents and practices of social control. In other words, individuals in sporting spaces make particular choices about whether and how to engage in sporting practices but do so within a system that sets limits of various kinds on what choices are available and intelligible. In the vignette above, my coach acts as the agent of social control, indicting a group of boys and young men for not adhering to the "sport ethic" (Hughes & Coakley, 1991) and, implicitly, for not emulating the "right" kind of masculinity. I had the choice not to conform, not to practice in a way that made injury likely, perhaps even inevitable. But at that moment, that was certainly not an attractive choice; rather, it was one that I understood well would mark me as weak, indecisive, and a detriment to the team. And so I conformed.

My "choice" to conform in the moment described above constituted an individual response to the situation and the structural conditions in which it was embedded. It also, however, served to reproduce those very conditions, as I did nothing to subvert or challenge the conditions that made hitting my teammate the only culturally intelligible choice in that moment. That is, by capitulating I shored up the (narrow) definition of hegemonic masculinity I was being encouraged to embody at the expense of my own well-being and that of my teammate. The task for scholars of sport and deviance, then, is to explore not only the ways in which particular sporting identities and practices are normalized, but also the strategies employed to resist those definitions.

DEVIANCE ON THE "FIELD OF PLAY"

Much academic and popular attention is devoted to considering examples of deviance *on the field of play* (the course, the ice, etc.). Perhaps the best-known work in this area explores questions of conformity to the "sport ethic" (Hughes & Coakley, 1991). The notion of *positive deviance* emphasizes the idea that deviance is not always rooted in a *failure* to observe the norms in operation in a particular sociocultural location. Rather, we might also understand deviance as arising out of an overly enthusiastic adoption of a set of expectations that characterizes particular activities:

> [A] portion of the deviance (i.e., behavior that is morally condemned and dangerous) among athletes *does not* involve a rejection of norms, or conformity to a set of norms not endorsed in the rest of society. Instead, many problem behaviors are created when athletes *care too much for, accept too completely, and overconform to* what has become the value system of sport itself, including both goals and means. (Hughes & Coakley, 1991, p. 310, emphasis added)

There are four central beliefs that define "what it means to identify oneself as an athlete and to be treated as an athlete by others in the sport" (Hughes & Coakley, 1991, p. 309). Based on these beliefs, athletes "make sacrifices, strive for distinction, accept risks and refuse limits—practices that initially facilitate success but ultimately compromise health" (McEwen & Young, 2011, p. 157). From this perspective, we might think of examples such as the widespread use of performance-enhancing drugs in particular sport and sport cultures (e.g., the "Festina affair" that marred the 1998 Tour de France, where numerous athletes, including all nine members of the Festina cycling team, confessed to doping) or the willingness of athletes to neglect their physical well-being in the search for athletic excellence (e.g., Korey Stringer, a Pro Bowl player for the Minnesota Vikings, who died of heat stroke after continuing to practise in severe heat on August 1, 2001, even after vomiting several times) not as *failures* of athletes to understand and observe the expectations of them in a particular time, place, and space, but as *exemplars* of that (perhaps uncritical) understanding. Newspaper coverage of Stringer's death, for example, indicted Stringer himself, locating "athletes' mentalities" as the "problem" (Braunsdorf, 2001).

Not all on-field deviance, however, exemplifies the notion of positive deviance. Though not as regular a feature of mediated sport coverage or sociological investigation as the examples above, there are also occasional stories about athletes using illegal equipment (e.g., a hockey stick that does not conform to NHL regulations with respect to material, dimensions, or curve) or tactics (such as a baseball pitcher who scuffs the ball in order to artificially create more erratic movement on pitches). And as with all forms of deviance, for every story we hear about there are undoubtedly many that go undetected or are under-reported.

Another important avenue of investigation with respect to on-field deviance is the question of violence (especially, but not exclusively, that which violates the rules of particular sports). The assault by Vancouver Canucks' Todd Bertuzzi against Colorado Avalanche rookie Steve Moore on March 8, 2004, is just one example of this line of inquiry, which the next chapter will address in depth. For our current purposes, though, it is important to highlight that while we might understand Bertuzzi's actions as an individual deviant act, we might also conceptualize it as *an act of social control*, as it was in response to Moore's hit against Canuck Markus Näslund in a game in mid-February of the same year (Kerr, 2006).

It is important that we critically examine the subjective processes by which individual deviants come to engage in deviant activities. However, this kind of analysis might also produce them *as deviant*. In other words, when we make "nuts, sluts and perverts" (Liazos, 1972) the focus of investigation, we suggest that they are in need of explanation. We must, then, critically consider the cultures from within which particular sport ethics arise and in which they are enacted and reproduced (Young, 1993).

Drugs in Sport

The topic of drugs in sport has been, and remains, one that is hotly contested and deeply politicized and ideological. For many students, it is one of the first topics that comes to mind when asked to think about examples of deviance in sport. This is not surprising since there is something of a "moral panic" about the use of performance-enhancing drugs:

> Societies appear to be subject, every now and then, to periods of moral panic. A condition, episode, person or group of persons emerges to become defined as a threat to societal values and interests; its nature is presented in stylized and stereotypical fashion by the mass media. (Cohen, 1972, p. 9)

In many respects, this describes the contemporary debates around drugs in sport. It is also important to note that we can understand moral panics as intimately intertwined with questions of ideology (Hall, Critcher, Jefferson, Clarke, & Robert, 1978). In other words, elites (like the IOC) are sometimes complicit in the construction of moral panics as part of the process of "orchestrating" or "manufacturing" hegemony. These elites are in a position to shape media content, and in so doing reproduce particular understandings of competition and fairness. Again, these understandings impact not only our comprehension of sport, but also the ways we make sense of global labour relations, for instance.

At the outset of a discussion of this phenomenon, however, it is important to reiterate a point made at the outset of this chapter: The kinds of deviance we hear, talk, and write about have a lot to tell us sociologically about why someone might take drug X in their pursuit of athletic excellence. Perhaps nothing could make this clearer than a thought exercise. Take a moment to think about drug use in sport. What comes to mind when you do so? Perhaps, like many, you think of performance-enhancing drugs such as steroids, EPO, or HGH. Or perhaps you envision practices such as blood doping, in which an athlete has blood drawn and later replaced to increase their oxygen-carrying capacity. Or maybe a well-known case of systematic drug use comes to mind, such as the state-sponsored administration of performance-enhancing drugs in the former East Germany (Dimeo, Hunt, & Horbury, 2011). Perhaps you conjure the image of a famous athlete who had a fall from grace after being caught "cheating." Some examples include the Lance Armstrong saga that played out over several years with Armstrong repeatedly denying accusations of drug use and bullying anyone who accused him of wrongdoing; the case of Jose Canseco, a one-time baseball "slugger" who admitted to long-term drug use after retirement; or Lyle Alzado, a former NFL star who died in 1992 of a brain tumour, a condition he alleged was brought on by years of steroid abuse.

The examples cited above expose some important questions about our understandings of "cheating." Why is it, for instance, that the use of steroids to enhance performance is considered cheating, whereas other techniques aimed at improving athletic performance (e.g., artificial hydration or the use of altitude simulation tents to increase oxygen-carrying capacity) are thought of as good training? Similarly, we might ask whether a practice or product should be considered cheating when its use is widespread. Or we might inquire as to why these particular performance-enhancing drugs are demonized, whereas others (e.g., Cialis or Viagra to treat erectile dysfunction) are acceptable for "performance enhancement" in other areas of our lives.

Furthermore, the examples that we tend to hear about and around which we tend to see investigations and government hearings and reports (such as the Mitchell Report tabled on the topic of steroid use in Major League Baseball) capture a narrow slice of drug use in and around sport. For example, the most used and abused drug vis-à-vis sport is not EPO, HGH, or steroids. Rather, sport and alcohol are closely linked, and numerous scholars have considered the complexities of this pairing, including such topics as alcohol use among recreational and competitive athletes, the place of alcohol in sport-related rituals (e.g., hazing), and the "sport-alcohol-finance nexus" (Dunning & Waddington, 2003, p. 355). It is perhaps particularly important to note that there is a lengthy history of debate as to the benefits and drawbacks of alcohol consumption with respect to athletic performance, and it continues to be touted as a method of reducing anxiety in certain sporting contexts (Collins & Vamplew, 2002), making the point that performance-enhancing substances are not *only* those that heighten physiological capacities.

And yet investigations reveal that drug use is a much broader, more insidious "problem" among amateurs and recreational athletes, is culturally revered and encouraged in many sporting spaces, and is tied to broader normalized understandings of "healthy" bodies, masculinity, and femininity, to name but a few systems of stratification (Safai, 2013). Too often neglected in these discussions are the ways in which other (often over-the-counter) drugs are used by athletes at many ages and levels of experience and participation. For example, some athletes trying to "make weight" use laxatives or appetite suppressants (wrestling, gymnastics), while pain killers are regularly used (and sometimes abused) by athletes in their "push to perform at the edge in the name of success" (Safai, 2013, p. 122).

As mentioned above, agents and processes of social control are not simply a *response to* deviance, but are actually *constitutive of* deviance. In other words, particular acts only become deviant in relation to the rules in place and those charged with policing those rules. For example, the World Anti-Doping Agency (WADA), established in 1999, plays an active and central role as a moral compass, functioning to define what constitutes "cheating" with respect to performance-enhancing products and practices and to surveil and police athletes in an effort to eradicate the use of drugs in sport (or, at the very least, weed out the "bad apples" who use them). We might understand WADA as the logical outcome of a process that began in the Cold War era, in which "international sporting events became a heated battleground of competing state ideologies," laying the groundwork for the proliferation of "a number of pharmaceutical products and methods (i.e., blood doping) that could boost athletic performance" (Park, 2005, p. 177).

The 1998 Tour de France served as a flashpoint of sorts. Allegedly, during the scandal-plagued tour, "almost half of the participants withdrew from competition because of the severe doping inspection" (Park, 2005, p. 178). In response, the IOC organized the World Conference on Doping in Sport in early 1999, and with the participation of partners such as the European Union, the World Health Organization, and Interpol, formed the framework for WADA by July of that same year (Park, 2005).

Canadian lawyer (and one-time IOC presidential hopeful) Richard Pound is a central figure in the history of WADA and has been a staunch advocate for a transnational anti-doping agency as a mechanism to ensure that all athletes are able to participate on a "level" playing field. And yet WADA and similar agencies have been the subject of considerable criticism:

WADA does not simply operate to detect who is doped and who is not by conducting drug testing and penalizing doped athletes. Rather, WADA *attempts to govern doping practices through the administration of a series of programs and the deployment of disciplinary mechanisms . . .* seek[ing] to shape athletic conduct by working through [athletes'] desires, aspirations and beliefs. (Park, 2005, p. 179, emphasis added)

Less subtle critiques have also been raised, suggesting that WADA's surveillance and judgment practices, combined with inconsistencies and problems in their testing protocols, violate the basic human rights of all athletes subject to their mandate (Rushall & Jones, 2007).

To the extent that WADA continues to play a leading role in the ideological war on performance-enhancing drugs, we must also appreciate their reach, as other regulatory bodies draw on WADA policies and procedures. In addition, it is imperative to consider the ways competitors (mis)understand broader discussions about the use of performance-enhancing substances (Johnson, Butryn, & Massuci 2013).

Considerations such as those outlined above are particularly important in light of some of the arguments *against* drug testing. These include an oppressive level of surveillance both in and out of competition, erosion of trust between various stakeholders, and perceptions of arbitrary and inconsistent regulations and applications (Waddington, 2010). Perhaps more centrally, however, sociologists are compelled to look at the various and regimented ways in which athletes' training, diet, preparation, and physiological adaptations are managed, measured, and closely monitored in the interests of performance enhancement, and ask "Why are some methods and drugs banned and not others?" (Connor, 2009, p. 327). In other words, the anti-doping movement itself is as sociologically interesting as particular instances or systematic programs of doping. For example, one of the central arguments made by proponents of drug testing is that performance-enhancing drugs are detrimental to athletes' health. And yet,

if the health of athletes is a concern then drugs are a miniscule part of their health "problems." To actually make elite sport healthy we do not need anti-doping codes, we need anti-training codes limiting the type and amount of training an athlete can do. We also need anti-competition codes restricting the number of games/meets/competitions in which an athlete can engage. (Connor, 2009, p. 335)

DEVIANCE OFF THE FIELD OF PLAY

It is imperative that discussions of deviance and deviantization consider not only those examples of deviance that occur on or near sporting spaces themselves, but also those that are directly connected with particular sporting (mega)events, and what light these might shed on the import of these processes to understanding social institutions, practices, and identities.

In the first instance, analyses of some cases of "off the field" deviance focus on specific examples of deviance, such as sports crowd disorder. The aim of work like this is to broaden our understandings of sporting deviance, shifting the focus from participants' behaviours in competition onto those involved in the production of sporting leagues, organizations, and practices, as well more peripheral participants (such as fans). Often, however, the "object of inquiry" is not the deviant behaviour itself but the moral codes at play in particular contexts. These moral codes are made visible by the social control response to the behaviour or circumstances. For example, after the 2011 "hockey riots" in

Vancouver, British Columbia, numerous press outlets, as well as police officials, referred to those involved as "anarchists" and "troublemakers." Another recent example also comes from Vancouver. The 2010 Winter Olympic Games were constructed as being incredibly important to Canada's sporting reputation. If Canada could win a gold medal, this would go some way toward repairing its international sporting reputation as the only nation to have "failed" to win gold on its own soil (in both the Montreal Games in 1976 and the Calgary Games in 1988). In these pressure-packed circumstances, Canadian athletes shone, eventually tallying an impressive haul of 26 medals, 14 of them gold.

Amidst all of this good news, however, one of the biggest stories of the Games was that our women's hockey team, jubilantly celebrating their victory over their long-time US rivals, took to the ice after the game drinking beer and champagne and smoking cigars (Edwards, Jones, & Weaving, 2013). It is noteworthy that the only people in the stands at this time were "a few Canadian and international journalists . . . completing reports and so forth" (Edwards et al., 2013, p. 682). The women's team was said to have tarnished the reputation of women's hockey, the IOC promised an investigation (a promise from which they later backed away), and Hockey Canada issued an apology. What is telling about this example is *not* that this was the response of the press and Olympic officials; what is striking sociologically is that this *particular* celebratory behaviour was vilified; only days earlier, Canadian skeleton athlete Jon Montgomery, after an emotional gold-medal victory, drank from a pitcher of beer *on national television*:

> [Montgomery's celebratory] moment was replayed constantly on Olympic broadcasts and was considered a pivotal moment of the Vancouver Games for Canadians. Even live on television during the interview, Montgomery continued to drink from the pitcher, and became a Canadian iconic figure. (Edwards et al., 2013, p. 688)

It was not the case, then, that the drinking behaviour of the women's hockey team was deviant in and of itself. Rather, this example illustrates the notion that deviance is "relative" (Deutschmann 2002, p. 23); the behaviour was constructed as deviant *in relation to* particular (gendered) expectations about celebratory behaviours. And, in this case, these expectations reveal as much about gender as a system of social organization as about deviance itself. The expectations (made visible through the social control response to the women's celebration) emphasize that "there are ways of being gendered that are 'normal' and ways that are 'deviant'" (Newman, 2012, p. 65) and remind us that "to 'do' gender is not always to live up to normative conceptions of femininity and masculinity; it is to engage in behavior *at the risk of gender assessment*" (West & Zimmerman, 1987, p. 136, emphasis in original).

Moral codes are also made visible by the ways in which the "accused" respond, resisting the "spoiled identity" (Goffman, 1963) that often accompanies serious examples of deviance. In 1991, for example, NBA star Magic Johnson announced that he had been diagnosed with the human immunodeficiency virus, better known as HIV, the precursor to AIDS. This news rocked the NBA, and Johnson's role in the league was called into question. Tellingly, one important component of the fallout of this announcement was Johnson's claim that he had contracted HIV *not* through homosexual intercourse, but because he had engaged in numerous extramarital (and, he insisted, heterosexual) sexual encounters over the years. He thus disavowed one stigmatizing label (that of being "gay") by adopting another (being "virile" and promiscuous), one that comes with a more manageable stigma and serves to reinforce the dominant "logic of containment" around HIV and AIDS (Cole & Denny, 2004).

In the second instance of analyzing "off the field" deviance, we might conceptualize examples of deviance such as protests of Olympic policies, decisions, and practices (any one of which might be understood as an example of deviance) as *symptoms* of more systemic social problems (Rowe, 2012). Consider the deviantization of athletes who use their celebrity status to make political statements. Famous examples of this kind of protest include Muhammad Ali's refusal to report for duty when drafted for the Vietnam War and John Carlos and Tommie Smith's oft-pictured "black power" salute at the 1968 Summer Olympics in Mexico City (Giardina & Newman, 2011). These examples also illustrate the ways in which notions of deviance shift over time as social conditions change and historical circumstances shed new light on dynamic social conditions. Carlos and Smith, for example, were initially vilified over their protest, accused of making a deeply political statement at an ostensibly apolitical Olympic festival (though the IOC's claims that the Olympics are apolitical are tenuous, at best; Smith, 2006). Similarly, Ali faced sanctions for his actions (in the United States, at least) but is now celebrated for his stand against this unpopular conflict.

Perhaps a less well-known example closer to home will serve us well here. In the lead up to the 1988 Olympic Winter Games in Calgary, there were a number of protests by Aboriginal peoples and supporters. For instance, the torch relay

> was criticized for being sponsored by Petro-Canada, as this conglomerate was invading indigenous territories (including Lubicon lands) across Canada . . . Alwyn Morris, gold and bronze kayaking medalist from the 1984 Los Angeles Summer Olympic Games and a member of the Kahnawake, declared his support for the Lubicon in front of the assembled crowd. (O'Bonsawin, 2013, pp. 47–48)

This is by no means the only time that the IOC has come under fire for social issues related to the hosting of Olympic Games, nor even the only time this has happened specifically in relation to Aboriginal people in Canada. The 2010 Games in Vancouver, for example, were protested by a number of groups against the hosting of the Olympics on "stolen native land" (O'Bonsawin, 2010).

DEVIANTIZED SPORTS AND SPORTING IDENTITIES

Much of the discussion above has centred on questions of particular ways of participating in sport and physical activities, ways that come to be defined as deviant. At this point, however, a brief consideration of activities constructed as deviant in and of themselves is in order. As we shall see, in some cases an activity is thought of as deviant regardless of who undertakes it. In others, however, only certain individuals or groups are read as deviant for participating in certain kinds of activities, once again illustrating the extent to which deviantization processes are fluid, malleable, and interwoven with power.

One particular field of activities often constructed as deviant (and yet simultaneously heralded) is so-called "risk sports." In the late 20th century and into the 21st century, voluntary risk-taking has come to be seen "as foolhardy, careless, irresponsible, and even 'deviant', evidence of an individual's ignorance or lack of ability to regulate the self" (Lupton, 1999, p. 148). In their study of newspaper accounts of back-country adventurers who found themselves in need of rescue assistance, Laurendeau and Moroz (2013) highlight that participants in these kinds of activities are often thought to have a "death wish" or are believed to lack a sense of responsibility toward both themselves and others. These newspaper accounts of rescue operations, then, serve both to deviantize the particular participants in question and to remind readers of their own responsibilities with respect to managing their "risk profiles" (Laurendeau & Moroz, 2013).

The point above is also germane to a consideration of how *particular* social actors are deviantized for their participation in sports thought to be characterized by a high degree of danger. A small number of scholars, for example, have considered the ways in which women are deviantized for their participation in "risk sports" while men are more often lionized for their bravery and adventurousness (Laurendeau, 2008). Consider, for example, the case of Alison Hargreaves, an elite mountaineer. When Hargreaves was killed in 1995,

> we saw the morality of risk taking go into overdrive. As a mother of two, Hargreaves had effectively abandoned her children by taking such extraordinary risks. The particular cultural definitions and limitations imposed upon Hargreaves ensured she would never dramatically, if fatally distinguish herself from the crowd as a *climber*, but rather as an errant, unthinking mother. (Palmer, 2004, p. 66)

The following year, however, when Rob Hall died on Mount Everest, the media did not criticize him for "abandoning" his wife and yet-to-be born child (Donnelly, 2004).

The deviantization of such activities and participants therein, however, is not as straightforward as the examples above might seem to suggest: "Sport continues to celebrate risk while it is also troubled by it!" (Donnelly, 2004, p. 54). This ambivalence is strikingly evident in the case of risk sport participants in that they are constructed on the one hand as deeply irresponsible, while on the other hand they are lauded for their willingness to put themselves "in harm's way" for the sake of exploration (consider the idea of a "first ascent" of an elusive peak), spectacular performance (think here of the recent Red Bull Stratos jump, in which Felix Baumgartner set several world records in performing a parachute jump from an estimated altitude of 39,045 metres), or simply for the sake of entertainment (such as the X Games). It is worth reminding ourselves, however, that the celebration (and commodification) of particular individuals or sporting activities *does not necessarily* indicate that they are not deviantized. On the contrary, this very process of marking "extreme" athletes as spectacular is, in certain respects, simply another reminder that they are fundamentally different from "us." So though we celebrate their accomplishments and are often willing to explore "the edge" vicariously through them, we often do so from the comfort and safety of our living rooms, from where we might later say "I told you so" if and when things go wrong (Laurendeau & Moroz, 2013).

Conclusions

In this chapter, I have aimed to highlight the most importance theoretical and substantive lines of inquiry that have underpinned some of the work considering questions of sport and deviance. Perhaps more importantly, though, I have endeavoured to sketch out some ways in which we might broaden what we *mean* by deviance and the kinds of questions we ask in this area. This broadening, I suggest, comes from critiques of the field of deviance studies more generally and emphasizes the importance of both students and researchers appreciating, engaging with, and thinking critically about a broad array of approaches to studying sport, physical culture, and deviance.

What is centrally important in taking this approach to considering questions of deviance, conformity, and social control is that we highlight and interrogate the ways that deviantization processes work in tandem with systems of social organization such as gender, sexuality, (dis)ability, race, and class, to name but a few. That is, considering deviance as relational and as an *outcome* of a process, rather than a phenomenon to explain, allows us to delve into how unequal social relations are produced and maintained by constructing particular ideas about normality and abnormality. Underscoring power in this way allows us to "unpack the centre" to reveal as much, and perhaps more, about who and what are constituted as "normal" as about who is "deviant" and why.

Critical Thinking Questions

1. How is deviance the "outcome of a social process"? In what ways is this connected to questions of power?

2. Why is it important to consider the ways that deviantization processes produce ideas about who and what is "normal" as well as about who and what is "deviant"?

3. In what ways might particular questions about sporting deviance (including those asked by sport scholars) be *part of* the "deviance dance"?

4. What kinds of questions do interpretive scholars ask about sport and deviance, and how do they differ from those that someone working from an objectivist stance might ask?

5. What do we learn by "unpacking the centre" in contemporary examples of deviance and sport?

Suggested Readings

Atkinson, M. (2011). Male athletes and the cult(ure) of thinness in sport. *Deviant Behavior, 32*, 224–256.

Christiansen, A. (2005). The legacy of Festina: Patterns of drug use in European cycling since 1998. *Sport in History, 25*, 497–514.

Davidson, J. (2009). Lesbian erotics at women's hockey: Fans, flashing, and the Booby Orrs. *Journal of Lesbian Studies, 13*, 337–348.

Fitzclarence, L., & Hickey, C. (2001). Real footballers don't eat quiche: Old narratives in new times. *Men and Masculinities, 4*, 118–139.

Murray, S. (2008). Pathologizing "fatness": Medical authority and popular culture. *Sociology of Sport Journal, 25*, 7–21.

Rinehart, R. (2008). ESPN's X games, contests of opposition, resistance, co-option, and negotiation. In M. Atkinson & K. Young (Eds.), *Tribal play: Subcultural journeys through sport* (pp. 175–195). Bingley, UK: JAI Press.

Silva, C., & Howe, D. (2012). The (in)validity of *Supercrip* representation of Paralympian athletes. *Journal of Sport & Social Issues, 36*, 174–194.

Young, K. (2002). Standard deviations: An update on North American sports crowd disorder. *Sociology of Sport Journal, 19*, 237–275.

References

Atkinson, M., & Young, K. (2008). *Deviance and social control in sport*. Champaign, IL: Human Kinetics.

Bereska, T. (2011). *Deviance, conformity, and social control in Canada* (3rd ed.). Toronto, ON: Pearson Canada.

Braunsdorf, D. (2001, August 4). Heatstroke problem lies within athletes' mentality. *Centre Daily Times*, p. 1B.

Brock, D., Raby, R., & Thomas, M. (2012). *Power and everyday practices*. Toronto, ON: Nelson.

Chase, L. (2008). Running big: Clydesdale runners and technologies of the body. *Sociology of Sport Journal, 25*, 130–147.

Cohen, S. (1972). *Folk devils and moral panics: The construction of the Mods and Rockers*. London, UK: MacGibbon and Kee.

Cole, C., & Denny, H. (2004). Visualizing deviance in post-Reagan America: Magic Johnson, AIDS, and the promiscuous world of professional sport. *Critical Sociology, 20*, 123–147.

Collins, T., & Vamplew, W. (2002). *Mud, sweat and beers: A cultural history of sport and alcohol*. Oxford, UK: Berg.

Connor, J. (2009). Towards a sociology of drugs in sport. *Sport in Society, 12*, 327–343.

Deutschmann, L. (2002). *Deviance and social control* (3rd ed.). Toronto, ON: Nelson Thomson.

Dimeo, P., Hunt, T., & Horbury, R. (2012). The individual and the state: A social historical analysis of the East German "doping system." *Sport in History, 31*, 218–237.

Donnelly, P. (2004). Sport and risk culture. In K. Young (Ed.), *Sporting bodies, damaged selves: Sociological studies of sports-related injuries* (pp. 29–57). Oxford, UK: Elsevier.

Dunning, E., & Waddington, I. (2003). Sport as a drug and drugs in sport: Some exploratory comments. *International Review for the Sociology of Sport, 38*, 351–368.

Edwards, L., Jones, C., & Weaving, C. (2013). Celebration on ice: Double standards following the Canadian women's gold medal victory and the 2010 Winter Olympics. *Sport in Society, 16*, 682–698.

Giardina, M., & Newman, J. (2011). The physical and the possible. *Cultural Studies <=> Critical Methodologies, 11*, 392–402.

Goffman, E. (1963). *Stigma: Notes on the management of spoiled identity*. Englewood Cliffs, NJ: Prentice-Hall.

Greer, C., & Jewkes, Y. (2005). Extremes of otherness: Media images of social exclusion. *Social Justice, 32*, 20–31.

Hall, S. (2000). Racist ideologies and the media. In P. Marris & S. Thornham (Eds.), *Media studies: A reader* (pp. 271–282). New York, NY: New York University Press.

Hall, S., Critcher, C., Jefferson, T., Clarke, J., and Robert, B. (1978). *Policing the crisis: Mugging, the state and law and order*. London, UK: Macmillan.

Hughes, R., & Coakley, J. (1991). Positive deviance among athletes: The implications of overconformity to the sport ethic. *Sociology of Sport Journal, 8*, 307–325.

Jackson, S. (1998). A twist of race: Ben Johnson and the Canadian crisis of racial and national identity. *Sociology of Sport Journal, 15*, 21–40.

Jackson, S., & Ponic, P. (2001). Pride and prejudice: Reflecting on sport heroes, national identity, and crisis in Canada. *Culture, Sport, Society, 4*, 43–62.

Johnson, J., Butryn, T., & Masucci, M. (2013). A focus group analysis of the US and Canadian female triathletes' knowledge of doping. *Sport in Society, 16*, 654–671.

Kerr, J. (2006). Examining the Bertuzzi–Moore NHL ice hockey incident: Crossing the line between sanctioned and unsanctioned violence in sport. *Aggression and Violent Behavior, 11*, 315–322.

Klingbeil, C. (2013, August 6). Pearl divers: Skyline stunt at new tower. *Edmonton Journal*, p. A1.

Laurendeau, J. (2008). "Gendered risk regimes": A theoretical consideration of edgework and gender. *Sociology of Sport Journal, 25,* 293–309.

Laurendeau, J. (2011). "If you're reading this, it's because I've died": Masculinity and relational risk in BASE jumping. *Sociology of Sport Journal, 28,* 404–420.

Laurendeau, J. (2012). *BASE jumping: The ultimate guide.* Santa Barbara, CA: ABC-CLIO.

Laurendeau, J., (2013). "Just tape it up for me, ok?": Masculinities, injury and embodied emotion. *Emotion, Space and Society.* doi: 10.1016/j.emospa.2013.03.010.

Laurendeau, J., & Adams, C. (2010). "Jumping like a girl": Discursive silences, exclusionary practices and the controversy over women's ski jumping. *Sport in Society, 13,* 431–447.

Laurendeau, J., & Moroz, S. (2013). Morality in the mountains: Risk, responsibility, and neoliberalism in newspaper accounts of backcountry rescue. *Communication & Sport, 1,* 382–399.

Levine-Rasky, C. (2012). Whiteness: Normalization and the everyday practice of power. In D. Brock, R. Raby, & M. Thomas (Eds.), *Power and everyday practices* (pp. 86–109). Toronto, ON: Nelson.

Liazos, A. (1972). Nuts, sluts, and perverts: The poverty of the sociology of deviance. *Social Problems, 20,* 103–120.

Lorenz, S., & Murray, R. (2013). "Goodbye to the gangstas": The NBA dress code, Ray Emery, and the policing of blackness in basketball and hockey. *Journal of Sport & Social Issues.* doi: 10.1177/0193723513491750.

Lupton, D. (1999). *Risk.* New York, NY: Routledge.

MacIntosh, D., & Whitson, D. (1990). *The game planners: Transforming Canada's sport system.* Montreal, QC: McGill-Queen's University Press.

McDermott, L. (2007). Governmental analysis of children "at risk" in a world of physical activity and obesity epidemics. *Sociology of Sport Journal, 24,* 302–324.

McEwen, K., and Young, K. (2011). Ballet and pain: Reflections on a risk-dance culture. *Qualitative Research in Sport, Exercise and Health, 3,* 152–173.

Mills, C. W. (1961). *The sociological imagination.* New York, NY: Grove Press.

Newman, Z. (2012). Bodies, genders, sexualities: Counting past two. In D. Brock, R. Raby, & M. Thomas (Eds.), *Power and everyday practices* (pp. 61–85). Toronto, ON: Nelson.

O'Bonsawin, C. (2010). 'No Olympics on stolen native land': Contesting Olympic narratives and asserting indigenous rights within the discourse of the 2010 Vancouver Games. *Sport in Society, 13,* 143–156.

O'Bonsawin, C. (2013). Indigenous peoples and Canadian-hosted Olympic Games. In J. Forsyth and A. Giles (Eds.), *Aboriginal peoples and sport in Canada* (pp. 35–63). Vancouver, BC: UBC Press.

Palmer, C. (2004). Death, danger and the selling of risk in adventure sports. In B. Wheaton (Ed.), *Understanding lifestyle sports: Consumption, identity and difference* (pp. 55–69). New York, NY: Routledge.

Park, J. (2005). Doped bodies: The World Anti-Doping Agency and the global culture of surveillance. *Cultural Studies <=> Critical Methodologies, 5,* 174–188.

Peers, D. (2009). (Dis)empowering Paralympic histories: Absent athletes and disabling discourses. *Disability & Society, 24,* 653–665.

Peers, D. (2012). Interrogating disability: The (de)composition of a recovering Paralympian. *Qualitative Research in Sport and Exercise, 4,* 175–188.

Rowe, D. (2012). The bid, the lead-up, the event and the legacy: Global cultural politics and hosting the Olympics. *British Journal of Sociology, 63,* 285–305.

Rushall, B., & Jones, M. (2007). Drugs in sport: A cure worse than the disease? *International Journal of Sports Science & Coaching, 2,* 335–361.

Safai, P. (2013). Sports medicine, health, and the politics of risk. In D. Andrews and B. Carrington (Eds.), *A companion to sport* (pp. 112–128). Oxford, UK: Blackwell.

Smith, M. (2006). Revisiting South Africa and the Olympic movement: The correspondence of Reginald S. Alexander and the International Olympic Committee, 1961–86. *International Journal of the History of Sport, 23,* 1193–1216.

Stebbins, R. (1996). *Tolerable differences: Living with deviance* (2nd ed.). Toronto, ON: McGraw-Hill.

Sutherland, E. (1945). Is "white collar crime" crime? *American Sociological Review, 10,* 132–139.

Sykes, G., & Matza, D. (1957). Techniques of neutralization: A theory of delinquency. *American Sociological Review, 22,* 664–670.

Teetzel, S. (2009). Sharing the blame: Complicity, conspiracy, and collective responsibility in sport. *Acta Universitatis Palackianae Olomucensis. Gymnica, 36,* 85–93.

Waddington, I. (2010). Surveillance and control in sport: A sociologist looks at the WADA whereabouts system. *International Journal of Sport Policy, 2,* 255–274.

Wamsley K., and Pfister, G. (2005). Olympic men and women: The politics of gender in the modern Games. In K. Young & K. Wamsley (Eds.), *Global Olympics* (pp. 103–125). New York, NY: Elsevier.

West, C., & Zimmerman, D. (1987). Doing gender. *Gender & Society, 1,* 125–151.

Young, K. (1993). Violence, risk, and liability in male sports culture. *Sociology of Sport Journal, 10,* 373–396.

Endnotes

1. BASE jumping, considered by some to be a more "extreme" version of skydiving, involves parachuting from fixed objects such as buildings (B), antennae (A), spans (such as bridges; S), and earth (such as cliffs; E). Other fixed objects, such as silos or cranes, fall into a broad "other" category (Laurendeau, 2011).

Chapter 9
Violence

Stacy L. Lorenz

Violent sports have long been the object of public fascination
Cliff Welch/Icon SMI 357/Cliff Welch/Icon SMI/Newscom

Since the development of the first organized athletic spectacles in the ancient world, violence has been a key part of the attraction of sport. Donald Kyle (2007) describes ancient Greek and Roman sport as "visceral, visual, and vulgar" (p. 22). For example, at the ancient Olympic Games and on elaborate tracks throughout the Roman Empire, chariot races could end in dangerous collisions and lethal crashes. The poet Statius observed that "one would think the drivers were pitted in savage war, so furious is their will to win, so ever-present the threat of a gory death" (quoted in Perrottet, 2004, p. 92). The Greek Olympic program featured wrestling, boxing, and a form of no-holds-barred fighting called the *pankration*. Participants in these combat sports expected broken bones, scarred and disfigured faces, and battered heads. Strangling was a legitimate strategy used by *pankratiasts*; one athlete managed to win an Olympic title despite being choked to death because his opponent was in so much pain from a dislocated ankle that he conceded victory first (Kyle, 2007; Perrottet, 2004). Huge crowds gathered at the Colosseum in ancient Rome to watch animal fights and gladiator combats, where death was part of the entertainment package. Across the Roman Empire, exotic beasts were killed in large-scale hunts and public shows. Animals were used to execute deserters, runaway slaves, or criminals. And gladiators duelled—and often died—in violent mass spectacles sponsored by the state and important political leaders (Kyle, 2007).

In modern society, violent sports still command the attention of many fans and spectators. Michael Messner (2002) argues that the centre of sport—the most rewarded and renowned part of the world of sport today—is "defined largely by physical power, aggression, and violence" (p. xviii). The NFL is the most successful sports league in the United States, and it sells a combination of high-speed collisions and hard hits to massive stadium and television audiences. In Canada, the NHL is the dominant sports business—and the only major sports league that does not punish fist fights between players with ejection from the game. Fighting, body checking, and manly displays of toughness are widely regarded as crucial elements of hockey's spectator appeal. Boxing was perhaps the most widely followed sport of the 20th century, although its economic and cultural significance has diminished in recent decades. However, the growth of mixed martial arts (MMA) since the 1990s, particularly the popularity of the Ultimate Fighting Championship (UFC), indicates the ongoing public fascination with combat sports and raises questions about the place of sporting violence in contemporary culture. In addition, gender identities are closely connected to our understandings of violence in sport, both historically and in the present.

THEORIES OF VIOLENCE

The concept of violence in sport is not easy to define. Discussions of sporting violence are often inconsistent and contradictory because it is difficult to distinguish "violent" behaviours from acts that are "aggressive," "rough," "hard," or "physical." In addition, violent actions in sport are not only expected and tolerated, they are frequently celebrated, respected, and admired (Wamsley, 2008). Michael Smith (1983) describes aggression "as any behaviour designed to injure another person, psychologically or physically" (p. 2). Violence can therefore be seen as a more specific form of aggression—it "is behaviour intended to injure another person *physically*" (Smith, 1983, p. 2). Although violent behaviour will potentially cause physical harm or injury, violent actions in sport are often permitted as an acceptable "part of the game" (Smith, 1983, p. 9). John Kerr (2005) notes that in combat sports and contact sports, in particular, highly aggressive, often violent, forms of physical contact are regarded as "intrinsic and sanctioned" elements of play (p. 8).

Smith (1983) attempts to categorize sports violence on a scale of *legitimacy*, as perceived by participants in the sport, the general public, and the legal system. His analysis includes two "relatively legitimate" types of violence—which he calls "brutal body contact" and "borderline violence"—and two "relatively illegitimate" types of violence—described as "quasi-criminal violence" and "criminal violence" (Smith, 1983, pp. 9–23; see also Hall, Slack, Smith, & Whitson, 1991, p. 215; Young, 2002, pp. 209–210). *Brutal body contact* is permitted by the official rules of a particular sport, while "borderline violence" does not conform to the rules, but nevertheless is widely accepted as a legitimate aspect of the sport (Smith, 1983, pp. 9–14). Examples of brutal body contact include tackles in football, punches in boxing or MMA, and the kind of physical play that is permitted in soccer or basketball. Examples of *borderline violence* include fistfights in hockey, "brushback" pitches aimed near a batter's head in baseball, or the pushes and bumps that occur in a pack of distance runners—practices that might be penalized or, in some cases, lead to ejections or suspensions, but which "occur routinely" and usually can be justified within the context of the sport (Smith, 1983, p. 12). In addition, Kevin Young (2002) notes that the "sanctions imposed by sports leagues and administrators for borderline violence have been notoriously light" (p. 210).

On the other hand, *quasi-criminal violence* "violates not only the formal rules of a given sport (and the law of the land), but to a significant degree the informal norms of player conduct" (Smith, 1983, p. 14). In hockey, for instance, "cheap shots," "sucker punches," and in recent years hits from behind into the boards—especially when these actions result in serious injury—would be regarded as quasi-criminal forms of violence (Young, 2000, 2002). Other examples include vicious head butts in soccer, bench-clearing brawls in basketball, or batters charging the pitcher's mound to start fights in baseball. While such acts are more likely to lead to suspensions or fines than *borderline violence*, punishment is not always consistent for those involved in such incidents. In addition, legal authorities may become involved in dealing with this type of violence, although criminal charges for actions occurring during the course of a sporting contest are extremely rare. Civil litigation is more common in these cases (Smith, 1983). Finally, there are incidents of *criminal violence* in which the degree of violence is "so serious and obviously outside the boundaries of what could be considered part of the game that it is handled from the outset by the law" (Smith, 1983, p. 21).

While Smith's categories are useful in attempting to understand sporting violence, the boundaries between these different types of violence are not always clear, and they can change over time. For example, as the long-term consequences of concussions have become more apparent, the NFL and the NHL have come under pressure to make their sports less dangerous for players. Both leagues have made rule changes that are intended to reduce the number of head injuries sustained by participants, making some acts that had previously been regarded as allowable forms of body contact into plays that are now considered borderline, or even quasi-criminal, forms of violence. As a result, actions that have long been considered acceptable within the cultures of football and hockey are increasingly being seen as violations of the written rules and unwritten codes that operate within these sports. And if some of these trends continue, perhaps the standard for what constitutes criminal forms of violence will change as well (Young, 2002).

Two influential ideas put forward to explain violence in society (and, by extension, violence in sport) are the *instinct* theory and the *frustration–aggression* theory (Lorenz, 2002). The classic expression of *instinct* theory is Konrad Lorenz's *On Aggression*, first published in 1966, which examines "the fighting instinct in beast and man which is directed *against* members of the same species" (Lorenz, 2002, p. ix). In this view, violent behaviour is inevitable because it is rooted in human biology and "natural" instinct. Proponents of this theory also suggest that such violent impulses can be released "safely" through *catharsis*—a healthy venting of aggression that reduces the risk of further, more dangerous manifestations of violence. Sport, for instance, can function as a "safety valve" that provides a controlled outlet for potentially harmful, innate, aggressive energies (Gruneau & Whitson, 1993; Lorenz, 2002; Wamsley, 2008).

The *frustration–aggression* hypothesis proposes that individuals act aggressively, and perhaps violently, when they respond to frustration (Dollard, Doob, Millier, Mowrer, & Sears, 1939). According to this model, people release built-up frustration through a form of catharsis in ways that are similar to the dissipation of aggression described by the instinct theory (Dollard et al., 1939; Wamsley, 2008). Sport, for example, is regarded as being cathartic for players and even spectators because it channels frustration into acceptable forms of aggression. However, critics of the instinct theory and the frustration–aggression theory have raised significant questions about the biological and psychological bases of violence, the degree to which frustration alone can account for aggressive behaviour, and the extent to which catharsis permits the safe discharge of violence. On the contrary, there is considerable evidence to suggest that violence can be attributed to sociological and cultural factors, that frustration is only one contributor to aggression, and that catharsis does not lead to the harmless expression of violence (Gruneau & Whitson, 1993; Wamsley, 2008).

A more convincing explanation of violence is the *social learning theory* (Bandura & Walters, 1963). From this perspective, violence isn't simply "natural" or instinctual; it is *learned* through socialization processes and cultural understandings of what is acceptable and unacceptable in particular societies and social contexts. Aggressive behaviour is a product of observation and interaction with others, including peer groups, role models, and community institutions. In sport, for instance, violent behaviours frequently become naturalized and normalized over time as acceptable, ordinary parts of the game. In this view, then, violence in sport is produced by sporting environments that put "people in situations where aggression visibly 'works' and is rewarded and that sanction and even applaud aggressive behaviour" (Gruneau & Whitson, 1993, p. 177). When individuals are placed in positions where they can observe violence, where they are encouraged to be violent, or where they are subjected to violence themselves, they are likely to respond aggressively or violently to a variety of situations (Sage & Eitzen, 2013).

Social learning theory also raises questions about the validity of the catharsis hypothesis. If violence is a learned response, then violent acts are likely to trigger more violence rather than culminating in a safe, cathartic release of aggression. In contrast to catharsis theory, the *violence-begets-violence* thesis (Gruneau & Whitson, 1993; Smith, 1983) suggests that aggressive environments produce aggressive actions, which lead to more violent outcomes. As a result, "sports violence is a socially constructed and learned behaviour that serves to legitimate and foster more violence" (Hall et al., 1991, p. 217). According to this model, sport does not reduce violent tendencies by providing a place for the healthy venting of aggression. For example, former NHL player Ken Dryden (1989) points out that hockey fights may be "therapeutic" by allowing players to purge violent feelings. However, fights are often "inflammatory," as players "create new violent feelings to make further release (more fighting) necessary" (p. 232). In this way, "violence feeds violence, fighting encourages more fighting" and as the culture of hockey tolerates and accepts such acts they are "*learned and repeated*" over time (Dryden, 1989, p. 233).

Sociologists have identified a number of external factors that influence aggressive behaviour in sport. Sporting violence is encouraged by parents, coaches, other players, team owners and league officials, fans, and the mass media. If parents reward or approve of their children's aggression, young players learn that such acts are acceptable (Smith, 1983). For example, a Canadian lacrosse official reported, "I have seen young mothers at tyke and novice games (six to ten years old) screaming at their sons to 'kill' the opposing player" (Smith,

1983, p. 84). Players also need to impress their coaches if they want to maintain their position on a team. Coaches often want players to display toughness and aggression, and they expect players to engage in the type of violence that is necessary to secure victory (Smith, 1983). As former NBA coach Pat Riley stated during a lengthy break between playoff contests, "Several days between games allows a player to become a person. During the playoffs, you don't want players to be people" (Messner, 2002, p. 49). Similarly, players gain respect from their peers by showing courage, demonstrating a willingness to stand up for their teammates, and executing the violent tactics that help the team win (Smith, 1983).

Franchise owners and league commissioners are reluctant to denounce violence because they are confident that it contributes to spectator interest. The NFL, for instance, has packaged and promoted violence since its inception, portraying players as gladiators, linking the game to war, and making aggression into art through its highly successful NFL Films series (Fainaru-Wada & Fainaru, 2013). Although UFC and MMA have modified some of their rules to make fights safer, the success of these sports as live events and pay-per-view television spectacles relies on the promise of vicious, often bloody, combat (Wertheim, 2007). The sports industry markets violence to fans, and people respond by buying tickets, purchasing merchandise, and watching violent sporting events on television. Smith (1983) explains that "the popularity of violent sports . . . has to do with the tension- and excitement-generating character of violence—not 'mindless violence,' as the media are wont to put it, but violence involving genuine drama, or 'action'" (p. 100). Even promoters of soccer, tennis, and squash—not just hockey, football, and lacrosse—have incorporated violent and confrontational images into their commercial advertising (Smith, 1983). Finally, the media publicizes and exploits violence. For example, television frequently emphasizes and dramatizes rough play, devastating hits, fights or brawls, and injuries from aggressive acts (Coakley, 2009). In this way, the media *models* and *legitimizes* violence, conveying "the idea that violence is acceptable, even desirable, behaviour and that violence-doers are to be admired" (Smith, 1983, p. 118).

VIOLENCE AND MASCULINITY: A HISTORICAL PERSPECTIVE

Contemporary attitudes toward violence in sport are linked to historical conceptions of violence and masculinity. During the late 19th and early 20th centuries, one of the most influential masculine ideals in North America was an aggressive version of manliness that valued combativeness, competitiveness, and toughness. For instance, Duffield Osborn, a defender of boxing, wrote in the *North American Review* in 1888, "This vaunted age needs a saving touch of honest, old fashioned barbarism, so that when we come to die, we shall die leaving men behind us, and not a race of eminently respectable female saints" (Kimmel, 1996, p. 138). Anchored in concepts of physicality, martial spirit, and primitivism, this new standard of "muscular" manhood placed a high value on bodily strength and athletic skill (Rotundo, 1993). At the same time, changes in the middle-class workplace raised questions about the ability of men in clerical, sales, business, and professional positions to fashion a masculine identity through "soft" jobs in expanding corporate and government bureaucracies. The fear that young boys were spending too much time with their mothers and female teachers also produced anxiety about weakened manhood. Capitalist production increasingly took fathers out of their homes and into factories and offices, while their sons attended elementary schools and Sunday schools. Thus, through family, educational institutions, and churches, women were frequently in charge of the socialization of the next generation of men (Burstyn, 1999; Carnes, 1989; Gorn, 1986; Howell, 1995; Kimmel, 1996; Rotundo, 1993). This "overpresence" of women in boys' lives was widely perceived as a significant problem. Michael Kimmel writes, "Men sought to rescue their sons from the feminizing clutches of mothers and teachers and create new ways to 'manufacture manhood'" (Kimmel, 1996, p. 157).

As frustrations with the new world of male white-collar work and concerns about cultural feminization and "overcivilization" spurred efforts to revitalize manhood in new ways, sport became one of the most important vehicles for countering effeminacy and conferring manliness (Burstyn, 1999; Kimmel, 1996; Rotundo, 1993). At the same time, sport was viewed as an instrument of social regeneration that would produce moral as well as physical benefits for young men (Howell, 1995). In this context, the violence and roughness of sports like boxing, football, hockey, and lacrosse were seen as acceptable—even necessary—in the building of manly character (Gorn, 1986; Lorenz & Osborne, 2009; Oriard, 1993; Wamsley & Whitson, 1998; Young, 2002). When injuries and even deaths occurred in rugged sports, supporters argued that the benefits of such activities outweighed the harmful consequences of violence.

For example, the first criminal trial involving an on-ice hockey-related death in Canada occurred in 1905 following the death of Alcide Laurin as a result of injuries sustained during a game in Maxville, Ontario (Barnes, 1990). Allan Loney, a member of the Maxville team, was arrested for striking Laurin, a member of the Alexandria Crescents, in the head with his stick following an altercation between the two players. During Loney's manslaughter trial, his lawyer claimed that "a manly nation requires manly games," and "when a life was lost by misadventure in manly sports it was excusable homicide" (Lorenz, 2004, p. A16). Similarly, *Saturday Night* magazine cautioned against overreacting to Laurin's death by curtailing participation in vigorous pastimes:

> There is little doubt that many of the qualities that have made the Anglo-Saxon race the world force that it is have been developed on the playground. It would be folly and contrary to the teachings of the past to recommend the abandonment or discouragement of strenuously contested games of athletic sport. It would be almost a national calamity if Canadian youth should discard their hockey and lacrosse sticks and puncture their footballs and grow deeply interested in croquet and "button, button, who's got the button." (*Saturday Night*, 1905, p. 1)

In other words, Laurin's death was the unfortunate price paid for forging hardy Canadian manhood through the competitive rigours of hockey. And when the jury reached a verdict of not guilty, Loney was carried through the streets of Cornwall by a jubilant group of supporters (Lorenz, 2004).

A historical examination of violence in hockey demonstrates the long-standing acceptance of a high degree of roughness and brutality in the sport. Lawrence Scanlan (2002) writes, "My overwhelming impression from reading the literature, from hearing the testimony of players from the early to mid-1900s, and from poring over news clippings, is that early hockey was very much like war. The blood flowed freely" (p. 30). The justifications for violence that were articulated during the first wave of criminal trials involving hockey players in Canada in the early 1900s are still prominent in the culture of hockey today.

In 1905, for instance, during an assault case in Brockville, Ontario, Kingston's George Vanhorn stated that in knocking an opponent unconscious with his stick during a brawl, he "only acted on the ice as an ordinary hockey player would in a strenuous game" (Lorenz, 2004). During a particularly vicious 1907 match between the Ottawa Silver Seven and the Montreal Wanderers, the Ottawa "butchers" left several Montreal men bleeding and unconscious on the ice. Although an Ottawa player was arrested for hitting a Wanderers player in the face with his stick, the judge in the case concluded that such roughness was a normal occurrence in hockey, so the attacker was discharged. As the *Montreal Star* reported, the incident happened "during a game, where all players must expect to receive their share of hard knocks, there was a scrimmage and a rough check." In addition, "no witness had shown that the blow had been delivered maliciously for the purpose of deliberately striking the opponent" (Lorenz & Osborne, 2006, p. 142).

In 1907, Charles Masson of the Ottawa Victorias was also accused of using his stick to kill Owen "Bud" McCourt of the Cornwall Hockey Club. Masson skated across the ice and, during a skirmish, struck a deliberate blow to McCourt's head. As in the 1905 Loney case, Masson was arrested but later acquitted in the courts (Lorenz, 2007). Despite the level of brutality associated with this incident, McCourt's death was widely viewed as a tragic accident. The *Ottawa Evening Journal* reported, "The general feeling in Cornwall is that the fatality is a most unfortunate affair and the result of hot-headedness and unpunished rough play rather than viciousness" (Lorenz & Osborne, 2009, p. 187). Perhaps the clearest statement of this viewpoint was offered by the judge who made the decision to reduce the charges against Masson from murder to manslaughter: "Under these circumstances, I cannot believe that any jury or any court would hold this young man guilty of murder," he concluded. "There was certainly no evidence of any intention to do anything more than the usual injury that is generally committed in this game" (Lorenz & Osborne, 2009, p. 188). Such violent and dangerous acts are still seen as "ordinary" and "usual" elements of hockey culture—and that is why it is so difficult to take violence out of the game.

Proponents of fighting in hockey argue that it decreases the level of dangerous violence in the sport.
Jay Gula/Southcreek/ZUMA Press, Inc/Alamy

CONTEMPORARY SPORTING VIOLENCE

One of the most contentious issues in modern sport is the role of fighting in hockey. Although other sports penalize fighting with ejection from the game and possible additional punishment, combatants in hockey simply receive a five-minute major penalty—served simultaneously while the teams continue to play with five skaters a side—then return to the match. Critics of fighting have become more outspoken in recent years, questioning the purpose of this practice in the modern game and calling attention to the injury risks associated with fighting. Supporters of fighting frequently argue that it is a "natural" part of the sport, emerging out of the unique mix of speed, sticks, and rugged masculinity that makes hockey distinct from other team games. Some fights develop spontaneously during the course of action, when angry or frustrated players drop their gloves and use their fists against each other. In addition, players sometimes attempt to instill a higher level of emotion in their teammates or alter the momentum of a game through fighting. Most hockey fights, however, result from the workings of an elaborate "code" that, according to its defenders, enables the players to "police" the game themselves—and ultimately to reduce the amount of violence in the sport through the strategic use of fighting (Bernstein, 2006; Proteau, 2011).

"In hockey fighting is defended as a necessary outlet for the frustrations of a high speed confrontational game," write Gruneau and Whitson (1993, p. 177). Under the "NHL theory of violence" (Dryden, 1989, p. 233), fighting functions as a "safety valve" that releases dangerous tensions among the players relatively harmlessly and prevents more serious forms of violence, such as stick attacks and overly aggressive hits (Bernstein, 2006; Dryden, 1989; Gillis, 2009; Gruneau & Whitson, 1993; Whyno, 2013). According to the unwritten "code" that governs the NHL, a player who crosses the line with excessive or unacceptable physical play must "pay the price" for his actions by fighting one of his opponents or having a teammate fight for him. Thus, fighting acts as a deterrent to potentially more vicious actions on the ice. In this way, skilled players are protected, dirty players are punished, and cheap shots are minimized. In particular, fighting is supposed to limit the way smaller "rats" and "punks" use their sticks as weapons because they will be held accountable for their choices. However, opponents of fighting argue that harmful body checks and stick work could be curtailed more effectively simply by increasing the penalties for such acts (Gruneau & Whitson, 1993). Handing out more major penalties, game misconducts, and suspensions would teach players very quickly that engaging in such behaviour will not be tolerated and would deter cheap and dirty play more effectively than fighting (Gillis, 2009; Proteau, 2011).

The "code" that governs fighting is a variation of catharsis theory—the idea that fighting safely discharges the violence inherent in the sport. NHL commissioner Gary Bettman recently likened fighting to a "thermostat" that regulates the game (Whyno, 2013). However, critics of the "code" note that catharsis theory has been discredited in many other contexts; in fact, violence generally leads to more violence, not less. Instead of preventing spearing, slashing, and dangerous hits, fighting frequently leads to more fighting or escalates into other forms of rough play. Marty McSorley's assault on Donald Brashear in February 2000 could be seen as an example of this. The two players fought earlier in the game, but McSorley was unsatisfied with the outcome—and with Brashear's taunting following the fight—so he challenged Brashear to another scrap. When Brashear refused, McSorley responded by clubbing him across the head with his stick. Similarly, Todd Bertuzzi's notorious attack on Steve Moore in March 2004 shows that fighting does not effectively "police" the sport. Three weeks earlier, Moore had hit Vancouver's Markus Näslund with a legal, but in the Canucks's judgment unacceptable, check. As a result, Moore fought Matt Cooke in the next meeting between the two teams. According to the "code," this should have resolved the issue, but Bertuzzi felt that Moore deserved further punishment and tried to entice him into yet another fight. When Moore refused, Bertuzzi punched him from behind and slammed him to the ice, giving Moore a severe concussion and breaking three vertebrae (Wamsley, 2008). Moore never played professional hockey again. Controversy followed this incident when Bertuzzi was selected to play for Team Canada in the 2006 Winter Olympic Games.

Fighting in hockey has also faced growing opposition in recent years as the long-term consequences of concussions and head injuries have become more widely understood (Arthur, 2011a). At the same time, the NHL has faced increased pressure to eliminate hits to the head, "blind-side" hits that catch players by surprise, and hits from behind into the boards. Scientists have found evidence of significant brain injury in deceased boxers, professional wrestlers, football players, and hockey players, likely as a result of repetitive head trauma. In particular, a condition known as chronic traumatic encephalopathy (CTE) has been detected in the brains of athletes who engage in these sports (Gladwell, 2009; Hruby, 2013a; King, 2010). Players suffering from CTE exhibit symptoms similar to dementia, and their brain function and capacity are severely impaired. The first NFL player diagnosed with CTE was former Pittsburgh Steelers lineman Mike Webster, and more than 40 football players—one as young as 18 years old—have been confirmed with this condition. Unfortunately, a major difficulty with assessing CTE is that the only way to detect its presence is to examine the brain tissue directly following a person's death. However, by the fall of 2012, 33 of the 34 deceased NFL players studied by researchers at Boston University had CTE (Fainaru-Wada & Fainaru, 2013, p. 8). The brains of several hockey players, including Reggie Fleming, Bob Probert, Derek Boogaard, and Richard Martin, also tested positive for CTE (Arthur, 2011a; Branch, 2011; Hruby, 2013d). As a result, the NFL and the NHL are facing difficult questions about the level of brutality in their sports. Is such violence inherent in football and hockey, or are there ways that violence can be limited in these sports to reduce the risk of head injuries (Gladwell, 2009; Hruby, 2012, 2013a, 2013b)?

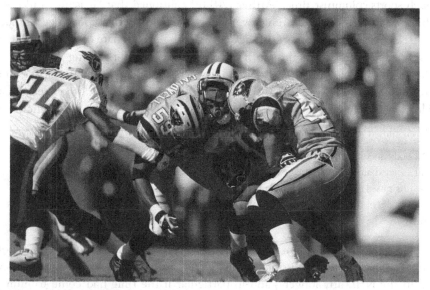

Can football be played safely, or are hits to the head a risk that players must accept as part of the sport?
Bill Frakes/Sports Illustrated/Getty Images

In December 2008, Don Sanderson, a 21-year-old university student playing senior amateur hockey for the Whitby Dunlops, hit his head on the ice after losing his balance during a fight with an opposing player. He was in a coma for three weeks before he died in January 2009. In the aftermath of Sanderson's death, his father, Michael Sanderson, spoke out against fighting in hockey. Michael Sanderson suggested that fights should lead to automatic ejections and that players should be required to keep their helmets and visors on during fights (Gillis, 2009). However, although the death of Don Sanderson triggered another round of discussion about hockey violence, the NHL made no substantial changes to curtail fighting or prevent similar incidents in the future. Commissioner Gary Bettman stated in February 2009, "I don't think there is any appetite to abolish fighting from the game. I think our fans enjoy this aspect of the game" (Gillis, 2009, p. 51).

The league had a similar response to concerns about the possible consequences of violence when three NHL players passed away under troubling circumstances during the summer of 2011. Derek Boogaard died as a result of an overdose of painkillers and alcohol, and Rick Rypien and Wade Belak committed suicide. Boogaard was a classic NHL enforcer, Belak was a journeyman defenceman who fought regularly, and Rypien was a tough, hard-working player who was willing to fight much bigger opponents when called upon. The deaths of three such players in a four-month period prompted questions about the psychological pressures and health risks of fighting, particularly the possible connections to depression, substance abuse, and brain injury (Branch, 2011):

> We just know that there aren't an awful lot of 40-goal scorers or puck-moving defencemen dying young, and that the men whose role it is to fight in the NHL are starting to vanish like professional wrestlers. This shouldn't be a political issue in the sport; it should be a human one. And at some point, some deadly serious questions have to be asked about the role of enforcers in hockey, if only to understand why these men are gone too soon. (Arthur, 2011b, p. A1)

Although sports columnist Bruce Arthur (2011c) cautioned that "it is also still possible that this is a string of tragedies strung together by a terrible sort of coincidence, as much as anything else," he added, "none of this means there isn't a legitimate debate to be had over fighting, and the effect it has on some of the people who do it for a living" (p. S1).

Did the deaths of Sanderson, Boogaard, Rypien, and Belak have an impact on attitudes toward fighting? In October 2013, when Montreal Canadiens enforcer George Parros stumbled awkwardly and hit his face on the ice during an exchange of punches with Toronto Maple Leafs heavyweight Colton Orr, Arthur (2013) observed,

> Nobody questions the courage of the men who fight. But it seems so long ago that we were all worried after the deaths of Wade Belak, of Rick Rypien, of Derek Boogaard. Their deaths raised complex issues of depression, of whether depression was linked to fighting, of suicide, of the easy access to painkillers, of overdoses, of what this thing makes some men do. The discussion flared, and . . . vanished. Nothing was resolved. (Arthur, 2013)

Nevertheless, the Parros incident and the continued presence of one-dimensional "policemen" in the game spurred discussion about whether or not such designated punchers were needed in the NHL any longer—and in particular if the time had come to eliminate "staged" fights between enforcers from the league (Duhatschek, 2013; Mirtle, 2013). At the beginning of the 2013–2014 season, the NHL finally introduced a rule requiring players to keep their helmets on during fights—a change that would reduce the chance of a player suffering a fatal head injury from a punch or, more likely, from falling to the ice.

Even though the damaging consequences of punches and checks to the head are becoming more apparent, many of the sport's most outspoken defenders, like Don Cherry, continue to glorify rough, "old-time" hockey. Cherry's "nostalgic defence" (Gillet, White, & Young, 1996, p. 67) of the game's traditional character resists any move toward a less violent and physical version of hockey. As long as fighting and aggression remain markers of masculinity— and hockey continues to be seen as a training ground for manhood—it will be difficult to remove such forms of violence from the sport. Hockey "provides a public platform for celebrating a very traditional masculine ideal" (Gruneau & Whitson, 1993, p. 190) at a time when societal roles for men and women are changing and opportunities for men to demonstrate toughness and physical prowess are diminishing. In the context of an unstable gender order, many men fear that the removal of fighting would not only jeopardize the masculine subculture of hockey, but trigger a wider erosion of manhood in society as a whole.

For example, some commentators have suggested that taking fights and hard hits out of hockey would lead to the "pansification" (Arthur, 2009) or "pussification" (Spector, 2013) of the sport. Gruneau and Whitson (1993) conclude, "The ultimate threat, the threat that produces a recalcitrance to change, is the perceived threat to the maleness of the game, and beyond this to the place of traditional masculinity in a changing economic, cultural, and gender order" (p. 192). For instance, soon after the tragic deaths of Boogaard, Rypien, and Belak, columnist Jesse Kline (2011) attributed the reduction in on-ice violence in the NHL over the past two decades to "a concerted effort on the part of soccer moms, whose post-Cold War agenda was to turn Western civilization into a politically correct snorefest" (p. A3). He added, "There is little justification for eliminating fighting from hockey, except for those who wish to see the sport emasculated even further. We've already ceded the ground on mandatory helmets and participation trophies for every kid that plays. Let's at least let the professionals play the game as it was meant to be—tough, passionate and gritty" (Kline, 2011, p. A3).

A FRAMEWORK FOR UNDERSTANDING VIOLENCE IN SPORT

Michael Messner's framework for analyzing violence related to sport is extremely useful in considering how different manifestations of violence are interconnected. Drawing upon what Michael Kaufman (1987) calls "a triad of men's violence" (p. 2), Messner (2002) suggests that male athletes commit three main forms of violence, both during and outside of their sport: violence against women, violence against other men, and violence against their own bodies. According to Messner, "Homosocial sport offers an institutional context in which boys and men learn, largely from each other, to discipline their bodies, attitudes, and feelings within the logic of the triad of men's violence" (p. 30). He argues, "Far from being an aberration perpetrated by some marginal deviants, male athletes' off-the-field violence is generated from the normal, everyday dynamics at the center of male athletic culture" (p. 28).

Messner (2002) points to the interactions and gender performances of male athlete peer groups as a crucial dimension of the triad of men's violence in sports (see Prettyman, 2006). His analysis suggests that two group-based processes underlie men's violence against women, against other men, and against their own bodies: *misogynist and homophobic talk and actions* and the *suppression of empathy* (Messner, 2002, p. 60). First, all-male groups bond through competitive, sexually aggressive talk (Curry, 1991, 2000) that "serves to forge an aggressive, even violent, hierarchical ordering of bodies, both inside the male peer group and between the male peer group and any other group" (Messner, 2002, p. 38). Misogynist and homophobic insults and banter are used to punish and police group members, as well as to distinguish the group from outsiders. Group members are aware of "an ever-present threat of demasculinization, humiliation, ostracism, and even violence that may be perpetrated against a boy or man who fails to conform with the dominant group values and practices" (Messner, 2002, p. 60). At the same time, within athlete peer groups, boys and men learn to stifle any empathy they might have for women, for other men, and even for themselves. For example, girls and women are frequently treated as potential objects of sexual conquest and as opportunities to perform heterosexual masculinity for one's male peers, rather than as equals (Lefkowitz, 1997; Messner, 2002; Pappas, McKenry, & Skilken Catlett, 2004; Robinson, 1998).

In the book *Our Guys*, Bernard Lefkowitz (1997) points to a culture of disrespect for women as one of the factors that led a group of high school athletes in Glen Ridge, New Jersey, to assault and abuse their female classmates. Growing up within "a hermetic all-male world of teams and friends and brothers and fathers," these privileged young athletes "just didn't know girls as equals, as true friends, as people you cared about" (Lefkowitz, 1997, p. 91). After several members of the Glen Ridge "jock clique" were charged with sexual assault, a father whose daughter went to the same school recalled seeing the boys "getting stronger, closer, every time they got together and humiliated a girl." He added, "My daughter would come home with stories—I'd just shake my head and wonder if they thought a girl was human" (Lefkowitz, 1997, p. 160). On the whole, there is considerable research suggesting "that the social worlds created around men's power and performance sports subvert respect for women and promote the image of women as 'game' to be pursued and conquered" (Coakley, 2009, p. 213).

Messner (2002) suggests that a lack of empathy for girls and women is one of the primary reasons that male athletes, particularly in contact sports, appear to commit acts of sexual violence against women at a higher rate than nonathletes. For example, a study of reported sexual assaults at a range of institutions with Division I sports programs indicated that male student-athletes were disproportionately involved in incidents of sexual assault on university campuses. For the years 1991 to 1993, male athletes made up 3.3% of the total male student population at these schools, yet they represented 19% of those reported to judicial affairs offices for sexual assault (Crosset, Benedict, & McDonald, 1995). However, despite the evidence of the overrepresentation of male athletes among those who engage in aggressive and violent sexual behaviour, the precise association between sports team membership and sexual assault remains unclear (Crosset, Benedict, & McDonald, 1995). In addition, disrespectful attitudes toward women are not unique to sport; the issue of men's violence against women is a broad social problem related to widely held views of women in society and culture as a whole (Coakley, 2009).

In committing violent acts against other men, male athletes are taught to objectify opponents as outsiders and enemies and to display toughness to their teammates (Messner, 2002). The following statement from a former NFL defensive back reveals how violence is rewarded and normalized in football while opposing players are eventually dehumanized:

> When I first started playing, if I would hit a guy hard and he wouldn't get up, it would bother me. [But] when I was a sophomore in high school, first game, I knocked out two quarterbacks, and people loved it. The coach loved it. Everybody loved it. You never stop feeling sorry for [your injured opponent]. If somebody doesn't get up, you want him to get up. You hope the wind's just knocked out of him or something. The more you play, though, the more you realize that it is just a part of the game—somebody's gonna

get hurt. It could be you, it could be him—most of the time it's better if it's him. So, you know, you just go out and play your game. (Messner, M. A. (2002). Taking the field: Women, men, and sports. Minneapolis and London: University of Minnesota Press.)

Another ex-NFL player said, "Anybody who tells you that they feel bad causing an injury is probably lying. How can you feel bad? . . . You're *taught* to hurt people" (Junod, 2013, p. 4). Former Dallas Cowboy John Niland adds, "We're paid to be violent. We're paid to beat up on the guy across from you" (Messner, 2002, p. 49). When the opposition becomes the enemy, inflicting pain on them becomes acceptable.

Perhaps the most innovative element of Messner's framework for understanding sporting violence is the way that he conceptualizes injury as a form of violence that athletes commit against themselves. Injuries are an expected outcome of sport, even among children. Athletes are judged on their willingness and ability to endure pain and to play hurt, even at the risk of their long-term health and well-being. Messner (2002) argues that male athletes become alienated from their own bodies to some extent: Their sense of their bodies is based on "a self-knowledge firmly bounded within an instrumental view of one's body as a machine, or a tool, to be built, disciplined, used (and, if necessary, used up) to get a job done" (p. 58). He continues:

> Boys learn that to show pain and vulnerability risks their being seen as "soft," and they know from the media, from coaches, and from their peers that this is a very bad thing. Instead, they learn that they can hope to gain access to high status, privilege, respect, and connection with others if they conform to what sociologist Don Sabo calls "the pain principle," a cultural ideal that demands a suppression of self-empathy and a willingness to take pain and take risks. (Messner, M. A. (2002). Taking the field: Women, men, and sports. Minneapolis and London: University of Minnesota Press.)

"The quickest way to earn the respect of your teammates and coaches is to play through injuries," says NFL quarterback Matt Hasselbeck. "The quickest way to lose respect is to say 'Hey, I can't go'" (Junod, 2013, p. 3).

In hockey, for instance, there is a long-standing belief that players should accept a certain degree of violence, tolerate pain and injury, and persevere through difficulty and danger. Players are expected to "take their taps like men" and to refrain from unmanly "squealing" or complaining about rough play (Lorenz & Osborne, 2009). Adam Proteau (2011) writes that today's "NHLers are instructed to use themselves as wrecking balls laying waste to the other side, regardless of the consequences for their opponents—or themselves and their own bodies" (p. 2). Similarly, Ross Bernstein (2006) asserts that "the unwritten warrior code" demands "that players must play through pain and hardship" (p. 100). He adds, "If that means playing with a broken arm, so be it. If that means getting your mouth quickly stitched up between shifts with no anesthetic, so be it. That is all part of the deal. In fact, it is not rewarded behavior, it is expected behavior" (p. 100). Former NHL player and general manager Mike Milbury even responded to the assertion that a player could die on the ice at some point by saying, "Some guy's going to die every day. It doesn't matter. If you don't want to get hurt, don't play the game" (Arthur, 2009, p. S1).

The expectation of violence committed against a male athlete's own body is upheld by the sporting peer group through the same kind of misogynist and homophobic talk and actions that support other forms of violence. If a member of the group doesn't conform to this masculine standard, he faces the threat of being labelled a girl, a coward, a queer, or a pussy—something less than a "real" man. "The boy who whines about his pain and appears not to be willing to play hurt risks being positioned by the group as the symbolic 'sissy' or 'faggot' who won't 'suck it up and take it like a man for the good of the team,'" writes Messner (2002, p. 58). At the same time, the ability to absorb pain and punishment without complaint is widely respected among players. A veteran NFL player provides an insightful example of this attitude:

> If you get hurt, you feel like you've done something *wrong*, especially if you go on injured reserve. . . . Your pain threshold is used to decide what quality of football player you are, and what quality of person. Injuries are used as a gauge. And I've done it, too. Many times, I've been battling through injuries, soreness, or pain, and I've seen a young guy come off the field for something *minute*. And I'm thinking, *What a pussy—let's get a guy in there who's tougher.* (Junod, 2013, p. 3)

Former pro football player Tim Green expresses a similar idea:

> Doctors don't coerce players into going out on the field. They don't have to. Players have been conveniently conditioned their entire lives to take the pain and put their bodies at risk. Players beg doctors for needles that numb and drugs that reduce swelling and pain. . . . Taking the needle is something NFL players are proud to have done. It is a badge of honor, not unlike the military's Purple Heart. It means you were in the middle of the action and you took a hit. Taking the needle in the NFL also lets everyone know that you'd do anything to play the game. It demonstrates a complete disregard for one's well-being that is admired in the NFL between players. (Messner, M. A. (2002). Taking the field: Women, men, and sports. Minneapolis and London: University of Minnesota Press.)

Messner (2002) concludes, "In short, in the context of the athletic team, risking one's health by playing hurt is more than a way to avoid misogynist or homophobic ridicule; it is also a way of 'performing' a highly honored form of masculinity" (p. 59).

Although this analysis of the connection between manhood and attitudes toward pain is persuasive, it does not account for female athletes' responses to injury. Charlesworth and Young (2004) found that female university athletes were willing "to place their bodies at risk by accepting injuries and tolerating pain" in ways that were "consistent with studies of male sports environments" (pp. 165–166). Similar to male athletes, these female athletes "quite frequently normalised and rationalised pain and injury as a necessary part of sport involvement" (Charlesworth & Young, 2004, p. 165). For instance, the group bonds and team commitments developed by female athletes, the pressure they felt from coaches and peers, and their acceptance of routine pain as an ordinary part of sport were comparable to the attitudes adopted by male athletes (Charlesworth & Young, 2004). Likewise, Young and White (1995) argue, "If there is a difference between the way male and female athletes in our projects appear to understand pain and injury, it is only a matter of degree" (p. 51).

As a result of these similarities in the outlook of male and female athletes, Charlesworth and Young (2004) suggest that "the data invite us to consider the fact that while pain and injury are likely to be linked to gender socialisation processes, they may also be a product of socialisation into sport culture per se" (p. 178). They add that experiences and perceptions of sports-related pain and injury "may be shaped by a distinct culture that fosters a specific attitude toward risk; a culture which may teach athletes, regardless of their gender, to tolerate pain and accept injuries" (p. 178). If such attitudes are prevalent among both male and female athletes, does "sport culture" encourage all participants to accept violence against their own bodies as a normal part of sport? And what role do gender expectations and performances play in determining responses to pain and injury? Is there a way for women to challenge or recast the ways in which sport-related injuries are addressed, or must female athletes contribute to the continuation of "a male-defined sports process replete with violent, excessive, and health-compromising characteristics" (Young & White, 1995, p. 56)? Finally, more research is needed to determine the degree to which female athlete peer groups interact in ways that are similar to Messner's description of the dynamics of male peer groups.

CROWD VIOLENCE

Another dimension of sporting violence occurs off the playing surface, in the stands and in the streets. The most thoroughly studied aspect of crowd violence is British soccer hooliganism (Young, 2000). Examinations of the forms and causes of British soccer riots have focused on the working-class background of fans, the cathartic release offered by rituals of aggression, the sense of social deprivation and alienation felt by some groups of men, the role of youth and working-class subcultures in soccer violence, and the connections between hooliganism and kinship ties, community bonds, team loyalties, and aggressive masculinities (Coakley, 2009; Smith, 1983; Young, 2000). In comparison, there has been relatively little research into sports crowd disorder in North America (Young, 2000). In addition, these theories and frameworks for understanding British and European crowd violence generally are not applicable to the North American context.

Key explanations of spectator violence include the *contagion, convergence,* and *emergent norm* theories. In the late 19th century, Gustave LeBon advanced a view of collective behaviour rooted in "the infectious spread of emotion, whereby crowd members fall under the influence of a collective mind" and individual responsibility disappears in a "sea of anonymity" (Levy, 1989, p. 70). This is the framework for contagion theory, which proposes that people in a crowd act together as one unit and frequently engage in spontaneous, impulsive, and irrational action (Levy, 1989; Wamsley, 2003). Convergence theory suggests that people "with common interests or goals come together as a crowd and use the formation for protection to engage in aggressive behaviours" (Wamsley, 2003, p. 98). According to this view, crowd violence is produced when individuals with similar inclinations converge on the same place (Levy, 1989). On the other hand, emergent norm theory questions the idea of crowd uniformity, maintaining instead that collective behaviour is uniquely produced through social interactions between individuals when they are placed in particular situations. New norms for behaviour result from exchanges of messages or cues between group members when circumstances change and, in turn, people respond to the moods and actions of those around them (Levy, 1989; Wamsley, 2003).

A more comprehensive theory of crowd violence is the *value-added* theory put forward by Neil Smelser (1962). In his work on collective behaviour, Smelser draws on the concept of "value-added" from the field of economics, noting that a finished product only emerges out of a particular combination of successive stages. For a collective event to occur, several "necessary conditions" must be present, and "these determinants must combine . . . in a definite pattern," from least to most specific (Smelser, 1962, p. 14). The first stage is *structural conduciveness.* The general social conditions that set the stage for collective violence need to be in place, although many possible outcomes remain. These conditions may include social divisions based on wealth, power, race, or ethnicity; a clear target for the outburst; an available channel to express hostility; the absence of other avenues of expression; and a means of communicating among group members. The second condition is *structural strain,* a breakdown in the social system. Several sources of strain often act simultaneously to give rise to collective violence. In sport, this conflict could develop out of pre-existing social divisions or discontents, a major dispute, or a significant defeat for a local team.

The third stage in the value-added model is the *growth and spread of a generalized belief*, which motivates potential actors. This shared belief, story, or rumour "identifies and attributes characteristics to the source(s) of strain and then determines an appropriate response" (Levy, 1989, p. 71). Fourth are *precipitating factors*, which substantiate the shared belief and intensify the determinants that have already emerged. These precipitating factors—such as a perceived bad call by an umpire or referee, or a violent act committed by a player—provide a specific context for aggression. Such trigger events may build upon existing fears, introduce a new strain to the situation, or close off an opportunity for a nonviolent outcome. The fifth stage is the *mobilization of the participants for action*, with the emergence of leadership of the group and the determination of the specific type of collective response. Finally, the sixth stage, *the operation of social control*, "arches over all the others" (Smelser, 1962, p. 17). It involves "those counter-determinants which prevent, interrupt, deflect, or inhibit the accumulation of the determinants just reviewed" (Smelser, 1962, p. 17). These social controls—including the police, the courts, the press, and community leaders—may minimize, reduce, or direct collective episodes in particular ways.

Young (2000) identifies three main themes in the study of violent sports crowds in North America. First, crowd disorder has been explained in terms of the "social and psychological conflicts taking place in society" since the mid-20th century (Young, 2000, p. 383). In an increasingly "fractured and impersonal society," frustrated spectators use sporting events to vent feelings of powerlessness, or to "re-establish forms of group identification" (Young, 2000, p. 383).

Another dimension of this approach is the idea that fan-related violence is rooted in ethnic, racial, or class conflict—what Eric Dunning (1999) calls "the major 'fault-lines' of particular countries" (p. 158). For example, one of the most significant incidents of crowd

NHL President Clarence Campbell is confronted by a fan.
Pictorial Parade/Hulton Archive/Getty Images

disorder in the history of North American sport—the "Richard Riot" in Montreal in March 1955—has been interpreted as an expression of tensions between French Canadians and English Canadians (Young, 2000). After Montreal Canadiens superstar Maurice "Rocket" Richard was involved in a violent altercation with members of the Boston Bruins, NHL president Clarence Campbell suspended him for the remainder of the 1955 season. When Campbell attended the next Canadiens game in Montreal, fans greeted him with insults and a barrage of tomatoes thrown from higher in the stands. When a tear gas bomb exploded in the Montreal Forum, the building was evacuated and a riot began on the streets outside. According to Jean Harvey (2006), "Anti-English sentiment was rampant; English-owned businesses were attacked and looted, and order was restored only through the use of riot police" (p. 38). Harvey suggests that the violence triggered by Richard's suspension "showed that French Canadians in the Quebec of the 1950s resented very keenly their status as a subordinate group, dominated and discriminated against by a wealthy and powerful English minority" (p. 38).

The second theme noted by Young (2000) is that collective violence in North American sport is linked to "the celebratory nature of sport" (Young, 2000, p. 383). The post-event riot, when fans respond to the outcome of significant sporting events, is the most common example of this type of rowdiness. As Young explains, "Combined with factors caused by aggregation (physical closeness, milling, tension, noise), sporting contests are thus characterized by emotionally charged behavior on the part of participants and spectators alike where proceedings can, under the appropriate conditions, 'get out of hand'" (p. 383). For instance, when the Montreal Canadiens won the Stanley Cup in 1986 and 1993, downtown Montreal was the scene of considerable looting, numerous arrests, and a significant number of injuries to both riot participants and police officers (Young, 2000). On the other hand, the rioting that occurred on the streets of Vancouver in 1994 and 2011 and in Edmonton in 2006 was a response to the Canucks and Oilers losing the Stanley Cup Final (Dunning, 1999).

Finally, crowd violence has been analyzed in relation to other "precipitating factors at sports events," such as player violence, unpopular decisions by officials, crowd size, or the start time of games (Young, 2000, p. 384). For instance, if fans observe or expect to see violence during the course of a contest, they are more likely to act violently themselves (Coakley, 2009; Smith, 1983). In addition, the possibility of violence may decrease or escalate depending on the composition of the audience in terms of age, gender, or social class; the amount of alcohol consumed by fans; the strategies for crowd control used by event organizers; and the power of a particular team to provide a source of identity for spectators (Coakley, 2009). For example, if the crowd at a sporting event consists predominantly of young men who have consumed large quantities of alcohol, then there is a greater likelihood of violence and confrontation, particularly if security personnel are poorly trained and the game involves a significant rivalry (Coakley, 2009). This kind of analysis fits together well with Smelser's value-added theory.

Conclusions

This chapter has provided theoretical, historical, and contemporary perspectives on violence in sport. More and more frequently, fan interest in violent sport is coming into conflict with the consequences of sporting violence for the health of participants. At the same time, questions are being raised about the responsibility of sports leagues to protect players from the damaging effects of sanctioned violence. For example, more than 4,600 former players recently sued the NFL for the way it handled the issue of concussions and head trauma, "alleging that the league not only failed to warn athletes about the long-term dangers of repetitive blows to head, but also actively hid information about the threat to their mental and neurological health" (Hruby, 2013a). The players' lawsuit claimed that the NFL distorted, dismissed, and denied evidence that football can cause long-term brain damage (Fainaru-Wada & Fainaru, 2013). In August 2013, a preliminary settlement of $765 million was reached in the NFL concussion lawsuit, although significant doubt remains about whether or not this amount of money will be sufficient to compensate all deserving players adequately (Hruby, 2013c; Zirin, 2013). A group of retired professional hockey players also launched a class-action lawsuit against the NHL in November 2013, claiming that the league neglected its responsibility to inform them of the potential dangers of concussions while promoting a culture of violence that jeopardized their long-term health (Hruby, 2013d). These lawsuits are one of the key sites where ongoing debates over sporting violence will continue as we contemplate, criticize, and celebrate the violent acts that are still central to many of our favourite sports.

Critical Thinking Questions

1. Athletes have been hurting themselves for people's amusement for centuries, going back to the *pankratiasts* of ancient Greece and the gladiators of ancient Rome. Even when fans know that players are being broken and diminished for entertainment purposes, they continue to enjoy the sport. At what point would a sport become so violent that you would stop watching it? Do you think public interest in violent sports will continue into the future?

2. As the dangers of contact sports become more apparent, the standard for what is considered "legitimate" violence appears to be changing. What are some examples of violent behaviours that were once considered acceptable within the norms of football and hockey, but which are now considered to be quasi-criminal actions deserving of significant punishment?

3. This chapter has contrasted biologically based theories of violence with socially and culturally oriented understandings of violent behaviour. Which of these models do you find most convincing in helping to explain violence in sport? Why do you find such approaches to be persuasive?

4. When punishing hits, brutal fights, or severe injuries have occurred in hockey in recent years, commentators have frequently asked the question of whether or not a player has to die as a result of such an incident for the NHL to take significant action to curtail violence in the sport. If a modern-day player was killed in one of these situations, what do you think the NHL's response would be? Would such a tragic outcome produce meaningful change in the way the league deals with illegal hits, vicious stickwork, or fighting?

5. Retired football players and hockey players have sued the NFL and NHL for failing to act properly in preventing head injuries and informing players of the potential risks of concussions over the past several decades. Do you believe these lawsuits are justified? Why or why not? What issues must be considered in assessing the extent to which sports leagues are responsible for the health of players?

6. How do you think NHL hockey would change if the league penalized fights between players with ejection from the game—and perhaps suspensions for repeated fights—in

a way that is similar to how other major team sports deal with fighting? Are you in favour of such a change? Explain your position.

7. What are the weaknesses or limitations that you see in Michael Messner's framework for analyzing violence in sport? What features of sporting violence and its consequences do not fit comfortably into Messner's descriptions of male athletes' violence against women, violence against other men, and violence against themselves?

8. Apply Smelser's *value-added* theory to the post-Stanley Cup riot that occurred in Vancouver in 2011. What other theories of crowd violence discussed in this chapter are useful in explaining violent disturbances that occur in the aftermath of important wins or losses?

Suggested Readings

Charlesworth, H., & Young, K. (2004). Why English female university athletes play with pain: Motivations and rationalisations. In K. Young (Ed.), *Sporting bodies, damaged selves: Sociological studies of sports-related injury* (pp. 163–180). Oxford: Elsevier.

Fainaru-Wada, M., & Fainaru, S. (2013). *League of denial: The NFL, concussions, and the battle for truth*. New York, NY: Crown Archetype.

Gruneau, R., & Whitson, D. (1993). Fighting, violence, and masculinity. In R. Gruneau & D. Whitson, *Hockey Night in Canada: Sport, identities, and cultural politics* (pp. 175–196). Toronto, ON: Garamond.

Lefkowitz, B. (1997). *Our guys: The Glen Ridge rape and the secret life of the perfect suburb*. Berkeley, CA: University of California Press, 1997.

Lorenz, S. L., & Osborne, G. B. (2009). Brutal butchery, strenuous spectacle: Hockey violence, manhood, and the 1907 season. In J. C.-K. Wong (Ed.), *Coast to coast: Hockey in Canada to the Second World War* (pp. 160–202). Toronto, ON: University of Toronto Press.

Proteau, A. (2011). *Fighting the good fight: Why on-ice violence is killing hockey*. Toronto, ON: John Wiley & Sons Canada.

References

Arthur, B. (2009, November 11). Winds of change a mere breeze. *National Post*, p. S1.

Arthur, B. (2011a, March 4). Probert's brain is just the start. *National Post*, p. A1.

Arthur, B. (2011b, September 1). Warriors on ice, tragedies off it. *National Post*, p. A1.

Arthur, B. (2011c, September 2). Head, not heart, must lead the way. *National Post*, p. S1.

Arthur, B. (2013, October 2). Players defend fighting after gruesome incident in Maple Leafs, Canadiens game, but there must be a better way to police the ice. *National Post*. Retrieved from http://sports.nationalpost.com/2013/10/02/george-parross-gruesome-injury-prompts-players-to-defend fighting/?utm_source=dlvr.it&utm_medium=twitter.

Bandura, A., & Walters, R. (1963). *Social learning and personality development*. New York, NY: Holt, Rinehart & Winston.

Barnes, J. (1990). Two cases of hockey homicide: The crisis of a moral ideal. Paper presented at the North American Society for Sport History, Banff, AB.

Bernstein, R. (2006). *The code: The unwritten rules of fighting and retaliation in the NHL*. Chicago, IL: Triumph Books.

Branch, J. (2011, December 6). A brain "going bad." *New York Times*, p. B13.

Burstyn, V. (1999). *The rites of men: Manhood, politics, and the culture of sport*. Toronto, ON: University of Toronto Press.

Carnes, M. C. (1989). *Secret ritual and manhood in Victorian America*. New Haven, CT: Yale University Press.

Charlesworth, H., & Young, K. (2004). Why English female university athletes play with pain: Motivations and rationalisations. In K. Young (Ed.), *Sporting bodies, damaged selves: Sociological studies of sports-related injury* (pp. 163–180). Oxford, UK: Elsevier.

Coakley, J. (2009). *Sports in society: Issues and controversies* (10th ed.). New York, NY: McGraw-Hill.

Crosset, T. W., Benedict, J. R., & McDonald, M. A. (1995). Male student-athletes reported for sexual assault: A survey of campus police departments and judicial affairs offices. *Journal of Sport & Social Issues, 19*(2), 126–140.

Curry, T. J. (1991). Fraternal bonding in the locker room: Pro-feminist analysis of talk about competition and women. *Sociology of Sport Journal, 8,* 119–135.

Curry, T. J. (2000). Booze and bar fights: A journey to the dark side of college athletics. In J. McKay, M. A. Messner, & D. Sabo (Eds.), *Masculinities, gender relations, and sport* (pp. 162–175). Thousand Oaks, CA: Sage.

Dollard, J., Doob, L., Miller, N., Mowrer, O., & Sears, R. (1939). *Frustration and aggression.* New Haven, CT: Yale University Press.

Dryden, K. (1989). *The game: A thoughtful and provocative look at a life in hockey.* Toronto, ON: Harper & Collins.

Duhatschek, E. (2013, October 2). Staged fights putting hockey's reputation in tatters. *Globe and Mail.* Retrieved from http://www.theglobeandmail.com/sports/hockey/hockeys-reputation-in-tatters-by-staged-fights/article14671271/.

Dunning, E. (1999). *Sport matters: Sociological studies of sport, violence and civilization.* New York, NY: Routledge.

Fainaru-Wada, M., & Fainaru, S. (2013). *League of denial: The NFL, concussions, and the battle for truth.* New York, NY: Crown Archetype.

Gillet, J., White, P., & Young, K. (1996). The prime minister of Saturday night: Don Cherry, the CBC, and the cultural production of intolerance. In H. Holmes & D. Taras (Eds.), *Seeing ourselves: Media power and policy in Canada* (2nd ed.) (pp. 59–72). Toronto, ON: Harcourt Brace.

Gillis, C. (2009, February 9). Can we please now ban fighting in hockey? *Maclean's, 122*(4), 48–51.

Gladwell, M. (2009, October 19). Offensive play: How different are dogfighting and football? *The New Yorker.* Retrieved from http://www.newyorker.com/reporting/2009/10/19/091019fa_fact_gladwell.

Gorn, E. J. (1986). *The manly art: Bare-knuckle prize fighting in America.* Ithaca, NY: Cornell University Press.

Gruneau, R., & Whitson, D. (1993). *Hockey night in Canada: Sport, identities, and cultural politics.* Toronto, ON: Garamond.

Hall, A., Slack, T., Smith, G., & Whitson, D. (1991). *Sport in Canadian society.* Toronto, ON: McClelland & Stewart.

Harvey, J. (2006). Whose sweater is this? The changing meanings of hockey in Quebec. In D. Whitson and R. Gruneau (Eds.), *Artificial ice: Hockey, culture, and commerce* (pp. 29–52). Toronto, ON: Garamond.

Howell, C. D. (1995). *Northern sandlots: A social history of Maritime baseball.* Toronto, ON: University of Toronto Press.

Hruby, P. (2012, December 13). Maintaining appearances. *Sports on Earth.* Retrieved from http://www.sportsonearth.com/article/40628020/.

Hruby, P. (2013a, February 8). The NFL: Forever backward. *Sports on Earth.* Retrieved from http://www.sportsonearth.com/article/41492872.

Hruby, P. (2013b, March 28). The myth of safe football. *Sports on Earth.* Retrieved from http://www.sportsonearth.com/article/43419226/.

Hruby, P. (2013c, August 30). Q&A: The NFL's concussion deal. *Sports on Earth.* Retrieved from http://therotation.sportsonearthblog.com/qa-the-nfls-concussion-deal/.

Hruby, P. (2013d, November 27). The NHL concussion lawsuit: Another league of denial? *Sports on Earth.* Retrieved from http://therotation.sportsonearthblog.com/the-nhl-concussion-lawsuit/.

Junod, T. (2013, January 18). Theater of pain. *Esquire*. Retrieved from http://www.esquire.com/features/nfl-injuries-0213-2.

Kaufman, M. (1987). The construction of masculinity and the triad of men's violence. In M. Kaufman (Ed.), *Beyond patriarchy: Essays by men on pleasure, power, and change* (pp. 1–29). Toronto, ON: Oxford University Press.

Kerr, J. H. (2005). *Rethinking aggression and violence in sport*. London, UK: Routledge.

Kimmel, M. (1996). *Manhood in America: A cultural history*. New York, NY: The Free Press.

King, P. (2010, November 1). Concussions: The hits that are changing football. *Sports Illustrated*, *110*(16), 34–40.

Kline, J. (2011, October 13). Fighting words. *National Post*, p. A3.

Kyle, D. G. (2007). *Sport and spectacle in the ancient world*. Malden, MA: Blackwell.

Lefkowitz, B. (1997). *Our guys: The Glen Ridge rape and the secret life of the perfect suburb*. Berkeley, CA: University of California Press.

Levy, L. (1989). A study of sports crowd behavior: The case of the great pumpkin incident. *Journal of Sport & Social Issues*, *13*(2), 69–91.

Lorenz, K. (2002). *On aggression*. London, UK: Routledge.

Lorenz, S. (2004, December 28). On-ice violence has been a part of hockey for almost 100 years. *Edmonton Journal*, p. A16.

Lorenz, S. (2007, October 1). Just part of the game. *Ottawa Citizen*, p. A11.

Lorenz, S. L., & Osborne, G. B. (2006). "Talk about strenuous hockey": Violence, manhood, and the 1907 Ottawa Silver Seven–Montreal Wanderer rivalry. *Journal of Canadian Studies*, *40*, 125–156.

Lorenz, S. L., & Osborne, G. B. (2009). Brutal butchery, strenuous spectacle: Hockey violence, manhood, and the 1907 season. In J. C.-K. Wong (Ed.), *Coast to coast: Hockey in Canada to the Second World War* (pp. 160–202). Toronto, ON: University of Toronto Press.

Messner, M. A. (2002). *Taking the field: Women, men, and sports*. Minneapolis, MN: University of Minnesota Press.

Mirtle, J. (2013, October 2). Hockey doesn't need designated fighters. *Globe and Mail*. Retrieved from http://www.theglobeandmail.com/sports/hockey/mirtle-hockey-doesnt-need-designated-fighters/article14654168/.

Oriard, M. (1993). *Reading football: How the popular press created an American spectacle*. Chapel Hill, NC: University of North Carolina Press.

Pappas, N. T., McKenry, P. C., & Skilken Catlett, B. (2004). Athlete aggression on the rink and off the ice: Athlete violence and aggression in hockey and interpersonal relationships. *Men and Masculinities 6*, 291–312.

Perrottet, T. (2004). *The naked Olympics: The true story of the ancient games*. New York, NY: Random House.

Prettyman, S. S. (2006). If you beat him, you own him, he's your bitch: Coaches, language, and power. In S. S. Prettyman & B. Lampman (Eds.), *Learning culture through sports: Exploring the role of sports in society* (pp. 75–88). Lanham, MD: Rowman and Littlefield.

Proteau, A. (2011). *Fighting the good fight: Why on-ice violence is killing hockey*. Toronto, ON: John Wiley & Sons Canada.

Robinson, L. (1998). *Crossing the line: Violence and sexual assault in Canada's national sport*. Toronto, ON: McClelland & Stewart.

Rotundo, E. A. (1993). *American manhood: Transformations in masculinity from the Revolution to the modern era*. New York, NY: Basic Books.

Sage, G. H., & Eitzen, D. S. (2013). *Sociology of North American sport* (9th ed.). New York, NY: Oxford University Press.

Saturday Night. (1905, April 1), p. 1.

Scanlan, L. (2002). *Grace under fire: The state of our sweet and savage game*. Toronto, ON: Penguin Canada.

Smelser, N. J. (1962). *Theory of collective behavior*. New York, NY: The Free Press.

Smith, M. D. (1983). *Violence and sport*. Toronto, ON: Butterworths.

Spector, M. (2013, October 16). The future of fighting in hockey is here, it's in the CIS. *Sportsnet*. Retrieved from http://www.sportsnet.ca/cis/the-future-of-fighting-in-hockey-is-here-its-in-the-cis/.

Wamsley, K. B. (2003). Violence and aggression in sport. In J. Crossman (Ed.), *Canadian sport sociology* (pp. 90–101). Toronto, ON: Nelson.

Wamsley, K. B. (2008). Sport and social problems. In J. Crossman (Ed.), *Canadian sport sociology* (2nd ed.) (pp. 139–157). Toronto, ON: Nelson.

Wamsley, K. B., & Whitson, D. (1998). Celebrating violent masculinities: The boxing death of Luther McCarty. *Journal of Sport History, 25*, 419–431.

Wertheim, L. J. (2007, May 28). The new main event. *Sports Illustrated, 106*(22), 52–60.

Whyno, S. (2013, November 11). NHL commissioner Gary Bettman says debate over fighting getting too much attention. *National Post*. Retrieved from http://sports.nationalpost.com/2013/11/11/nhl-commissioner-gary-bettman-says-debate-over-fighting-getting-too-much-attention/?utm_source=dlvr.it&utm_medium=twitter.

Young, K. (2000). Sport and violence. In J. Coakley & E. Dunning (Eds.), *Handbook of sports studies* (pp. 382–407). London, UK: Sage.

Young, K. (2002). From "sports violence" to "sports crime": Aspects of violence, law, and gender in the sports process. In M. Gatz, M. A. Messner, & S. J. Ball-Rokeach (Eds.), *Paradoxes of youth and sport* (pp. 207–224). New York, NY: State University of New York Press.

Young, K., & White, P. (1995). Sport, physical danger, and injury: The experiences of elite women athletes. *Journal of Sport & Social Issues, 19*(1), 45–61.

Zirin, D. (2013, August 30). The NFL concussion deal: Rotten from all sides. *The Nation*. Retrieved from http://www.thenation.com/blog/175977/nfl-concussion-deal-rotten-all-sides#.

Chapter 10

Sport and Physical Activity in Canadian Educational Systems

Tim Fletcher and Duane Bratt

Sport and physical activity represent important components of Canadian educational institutions at all levels. Early childhood facilities (both formal and informal) encourage children to learn how their bodies move through active play. Elementary and secondary schools offer formal physical education, intramural leagues, and extracurricular sport, while university and college athletic departments represent a key piece of the institutional identity of those places—whether that be for athletic participants or spectators. This is not to mention the burgeoning scholarly field of *movement studies* (which we use as a catch-all term for kinesiology, physical education, human kinetics, recreation, leisure, dance, etc.), the programs of which many readers of this textbook are likely enrolled in.

The aim of this chapter is to provide an overview of social dimensions of sport and physical activity in Canadian educational systems, identifying key themes or areas where important questions are being raised. In the first section, the current state of physical education in schools is examined using a four-dimensional framework employed in the

Physical education is most effective when teachers and students work together to develop meaningful opportunities to participate. KidStock/ Blend Images/Getty Images

Handbook of Physical Education (Kirk, Macdonald, & O'Sullivan, 2006), addressing the nature and purposes of physical education; aspects of curriculum, learners and learning, and teachers and teaching. Included in the second section is sport in universities, with a particular focus on the Canadian Interuniversity Sport system. How the history of Canadian university sport has impacted the current system, particularly in relation to gender equity, is also described. Further, the practice of hazing and doping—practices that have recently led to negative portrayals of several Canadian university sports team in the popular media—is considered. Finally, various challenges to Canadian university sports in terms of financial factors (notably scholarships and the role of alumni) and the "creeping north" of the NCAA is examined.

THE NATURE AND PURPOSES OF PHYSICAL EDUCATION IN CANADIAN SCHOOLS

What is physical education? Briefly, *physical education* is a school subject where students learn about and through movement. For the purposes of this chapter, we also ask, what *should* or *could* physical education be? And who decides? These questions are difficult to answer because of the diversity that is present in how physical education has been thought about and taught. Researchers use a wide variety of theoretical and methodological frameworks (including those described in Chapter 2), and curriculum developers and teachers similarly draw from a wide variety of theoretical and practical ideas to shape what goes on in physical education classes (Kirk et al., 2006). In addition, educational policy is governed by the provinces in Canada, which means that there is wide variability in the organization and structure of educational systems. As such, what might constitute a pressing issue in one province may not be viewed in the same way in another because of differences in culture, geography, or the political (and thus ideological) climate. These differences have significant implications for funding, policies relating to curriculum development and implementation, and the necessary conditions and requirements for excellence in teaching. Certainly the allocation of resources (financial, material, and human) to physical education in each province is discrepant due to the provincial governance of educational systems in Canada.

Despite a long history of debate about the role of physical education in schools around the world, the subject remains an important component in the education of most children. Such a view is supported internationally by the United Nations Education, Scientific and Cultural Organization (UNESCO, 1978), which identified the provision of physical education as a fundamental human right. In Canada, physical education is a required part of school life for children until at least Grade 9, with students in some provinces being required to obtain physical education credits through to Grade 12. Kilborn's (2011) comparison of physical education curricula across Canada showed the following graduation standards: in Ontario and Newfoundland and Labrador: students must attain at least one physical education credit to graduate from high school; students in British Columbia, Alberta, and Saskatchewan must complete physical education up to Grade 10 at a minimum; students in Nova Scotia are required to complete physical education in Grade 11; and Manitoba and Quebec mandate completion of physical education credits through to Grade 12.

That physical education is mandated through to completion of high school in Manitoba and Quebec may suggest that policymakers in those provinces place more value on the subject than elsewhere. However, this masks the significant issue that many students do not see enough value in physical education to choose it when it becomes an elective subject; that is, when physical education is mandatory, students may be taking it even if they do not enjoy or see value in it. To be sure, subjects such as mathematics, language (e.g., French), and science also become elective at some point in high school; yet judging by enrolment rates in these subjects, students and parents deem them to be more important than others such as physical education primarily because of their perceived value to prepare students for the "knowledge economy" of the 21st century. The declining trend in noncompulsory physical education enrolment suggests this is the case (Lodewyk & Pybus, 2013).

While there is wide variability in the language used to describe to overall aims of the subject, physical education is concerned with children learning simultaneously through movement and their bodies and about movement and their bodies. There are many reasons why this is important, but the most emphasized aspect in Canadian physical education programs is arguably to develop an appreciation of and ability to commit to a healthy, active lifestyle. Yet Canadian physical education curriculum developers are being challenged to provide students with learning experiences that teach children about things far beyond movement and healthy living. Given the growing evidence linking positive academic outcomes with participation in physical activity and physical education (Sheppard & Trudeau, 2008), physical educators appear justified to claim that the subject enables achievement of a wide range of outcomes across developmental domains. For example, Mandigo, Corlett, and Lathrop (2012) identify the potential of physical education to support cognitive and academic development, raise literacy and numeracy standards, increase school attendance, enhance school spirit and social cohesion, value diversity, and encourage attitudes of respect, fairness, and tolerance for others.

While such aims are within in the scope of what is "possible" from a quality physical education experience, there are doubts about the extent to which teachers are provided with the tools necessary to achieve these outcomes. There are many external factors that erode the quality of current physical education programs, such as reduced instructional time, the introduction of user fees, lack of specialist teachers, inadequate facilities and equipment, and an increase in standardized testing in subject areas such as literacy and numeracy. Even when one considers the added emphasis on the role of healthy lifestyles and physical activity through healthy schools policies (such as Daily Physical Activity in British Columbia, Alberta, Saskatchewan, and Ontario) or the provision of extracurricular sports programs, the existence of systemic barriers such as budget cuts, lack of professional development or planning time for teachers, or inadequate space and equipment often stand in the way of successful programming and implementation. There are also several internal barriers that are entrenched in the history and discourses of physical education (Francis & Lathrop, 2011), while others are entrenched in the institutional culture of schools in which physical education operates.

In the following pages, we outline some of the challenges that exist in overcoming these ambitious goals, while also providing some examples of promising practices that may enable these and other barriers to be overcome.

A Glimpse at the Past

Despite the emphasis on the "whole child" that is espoused in most current physical education curricula, early forms (prior to the 1950s) of physical education in Canada and elsewhere focused purely on the physical: Physical education was known as *physical training*, consisting primarily of military drills and calisthenics (Francis & Lathrop, 2011). The relationship with military practices was strong in the early days of physical education not only in terms of content and instructional styles, but also in the gendered and classed views of the overall nature and purpose of the subject.

Since that time, Kirk (2010a) has argued that "present day" physical education owes much to shifts that occurred in the 1970s, for it was during this decade that

> physical education had begun to take shape as a multi-activity, sports-based curriculum. This multi-activity form of curriculum was the outcome of a dramatic shift that took place in the years immediately following World War II, a shift that overturned some 50 years or more of domination of the curriculum of physical education by various forms of gymnastics, at least within systems of state-provided education. (p. 459)

Despite the shortfalls of the sport-based multi-activity curriculum, Kirk (2010a) describes the shift to a sports-oriented form of physical education has been identified by some as leading to a more solid justification of physical education as a school subject. For example, because sport is a significant cultural practice, initiating young people into the "institutions" of sport and physical activity was seen as a worthwhile pursuit, and schools seemed well placed to offer these experiences (Green, 2008). This is not to suggest that teaching people about and through sport and physical activity should be limited to learning the skills and techniques required to participate in, for example, basketball; it should involve learning sporting and physical culture—the customs, rituals, values, and traditions associated with these activities—as well as the practical knowledge required to participate (Siedentop, Hastie, & Van der Mars, 2004). While such a holistic view of sport and physical education has been praised by many in more rigorously justifying the place of physical education, there has been a tendency to focus only on the practical while largely ignoring the cultural aspects.

As well as general shifts in the content and pedagogy of physical education in the 1970s, it was during this time that most physical education classes became coeducational, particularly in North America after the introduction of Title IX in the United States (Vertinsky, 1992). Although this offered many girls opportunities to participate in a wider variety of activities than they previously had access to, critical theorists revealed that the "inclusive" form of physical education introduced at this time simply meant that girls now participated in boys' forms of physical education—that is, physical education that privileged forms of masculinity—with few attempts being made to tailor programs to girls' interests and needs (Lenskyj, 1986).

Those interested in the study and practice of physical education continue to wrestle with new and innovative ways to make students' experience of the subject lead to a commitment to lifelong physical activity. However, with each advance there comes the recognition that much remains contested about physical education. For example, current messages widely seen and heard in the media espouse physical education's role in trying to prevent childhood obesity, as well as the role of physical activity in providing cognitive (and therefore academic) benefits to children. Furthermore, some initiatives linked to athlete talent development also identify the role of physical education in helping foster athletic excellence. While such messages may serve to promote the role of physical education in schools, the ideological nature of such arguments has also been identified as reducing the role of physical education to a type of school-based weight-loss clinic (Sykes & McPhail, 2008) on one hand or watered-down "Institute of Sport" on the other. In addition, emphasizing the benefits of physical education for academic achievement can, in some ways, position physical education as a crutch to support excellence in other areas of schooling rather than physical education being seen as a useful, meaningful, and enjoyable part of school life in its own right. This is not to dismiss the benefits that come from participation in physical education; however, such positioning may undermine the potential of physical education subject matter and pedagogies to develop the whole child and provide experiences that help *all* students find joy and meaning in movement and develop their self-esteem.

CURRICULUM

For the purposes of this chapter we consider *curriculum* as "the social organization of knowledge for learning" encompassing the formal and informal activities that occur in schools (Kirk, et al., 2006, p. 563). When curriculum is viewed as a social undertaking, it becomes apparent that conceptualizations of physical education shift with changes in the social, cultural, and political landscape of the contexts in which curriculum is developed and implemented.

Physical education historians identify German and Swedish gymnastics as two salient forces that shaped early physical education curricula, particularly in English-speaking countries. Ennis (2006) suggests that German forms of physical education programs were predominant throughout the United States and emphasized physical and mental discipline through participation in mostly apparatus-based activities. In contrast, hybridized Swedish forms of gymnastics that consisted of calisthenics and little apparatus were favoured in the United Kingdom and its colonies, including Canada (Mandigo et al., 2012). The type of gymnastics that was favoured had important implications for how the future of physical education progressed in each context. For example, Swedish gymnastics tended to be prac-tised (and subsequently advocated) by many female physical education students (Philips & Roper, 2006). Following from this point, most countries that adopted the Swedish model tended to have more feminized forms of physical education, which included rhythmic and dance activities, in their early histories. However, this stands in contrast to what is reported to have occurred in Canada. Lenskyj (1986) suggests that the Swedish system of gymnastics was rooted in military drills and deprived many young Canadian women of any type of physical education experience until well after 1950.

The British influence on Canadian physical education programs expanded beyond gymnastics; games (usually in the form of team sports) also featured strongly in Canadian physical education curricula. The "games ethic" was a philosophical position underpin-ning many early physical education programs and stressed the important role that com-petitive team games played in developing "desirable" qualities (such as leadership, loyalty, perseverance, teamwork, etc.) in young men. This approach was reflected in the crucial role that games played in the education of many elite boys in Georgian and Victorian

Britain (Mangan, 1983). While game-playing experiences have since been offered to both males and females, some feel that such experiences still favour males, particularly those who embody "jock culture," are athletically able, and possess stereotypically masculine characteristics (Hickey, 2010).

Today, the physical education curriculum is often discussed in terms that go well beyond games and gymnastics. For example, in Canada there is currently a strong emphasis on the development of children's *physical literacy*. A physically literate individual is someone who moves with competence, confidence, and creativity in a wide variety of physical activities, and consistently develops the motivation and ability to understand, communicate, apply, and analyze different forms of movement (Whitehead, 2001). Developing these skills enables individuals to make healthy choices that are both beneficial to and respectful of themselves, others, and their environment. Tinning (2010) points out that through experience, physically literate individuals come to know themselves in a physical sense; through, for example, the joys of movement or the limits of their physical strength or endurance.

In line with the benefits of having students understand and experience a wide variety of physical activities, most current physical education programs consist of instructional units that represent sports (team and individual), physical fitness, dance, outdoor and adventure activities, aquatics, and gymnastics. This approach to teaching physical education captures Kirk's (2010a) earlier reference to a multi-activity curriculum, where the intent is to provide students with brief opportunities to sample many activities with the hope that they would find something in which they enjoy and experience success. Many physical education scholars observe that the multi-activity curriculum dominates current forms of physical education in Canada and beyond, particularly in secondary schools (Ennis, 1999). However, what is troublesome is that many problematic elements of such an approach have been identified. For example, although the multi-activity curriculum provides the scope for students to learn about a wide variety of activities, those that tend to dominate programs are competitive, "power and performance" team sports such as soccer, volleyball, basketball, or floor/ball hockey. The sporting activities that dominate these types of curriculum are not inherently problematic, but when implemented using pedagogical approaches that rely on direct instruction, the multi-activity approach (particularly when implemented in a coeducational setting) limits opportunities for participation for most girls and low-skilled boys; as such, they tend to alienate many students from physical education (Gibbons, 2009). Ennis (1999) has also highlighted the following problematic characteristics of the multi-activity curriculum:

- Short units with minimal instruction do not provide students with opportunities to learn or develop skills in any depth.
- Few educational sequences across lessons, units, and grades limit learning.
- There are few policies to equalize playing opportunities for low-skilled players.
- Public displays of ability are required.
- Class is teacher-centred and limits student ownership and leadership opportunities.

To avoid the negative aspects of the multi-activity curriculum while still providing students with opportunities to participate in a variety of activities, research on curricular models indicates their potential to promote powerful student learning by offering units that are thematically designed; enable students to develop skills in the contexts in which

Children should benefit from physical education programs that develop the whole child, incorporating physical, social, and cognitive development.
Shmel/Fotolia

they would be used; emphasize physical, social, and cognitive development; and provide teachers with a coherent set of teaching and learning features to promote positive learning (Kirk, 2013). Curricular models that have been the subject of research in physical education include Teaching Games for Understanding (TGfU), Sport Education, Teaching Personal and Social Responsibility, Co-operative Learning, and Health-Based Fitness (Metzler, 2011). Kirk (2010b) feels that a models-based approach may provide one avenue for a radical reform effort in physical education. One of the most important features underpinning the benefits of a models-based approach is the extent to which they are grounded in learning theory. Thinking about how learners and learning have been studied in physical education is addressed in the next section.

LEARNERS AND LEARNING

In the preceding section we addressed how physical education curriculum has changed over time but also acknowledged that many forms of physical education are not being taught in ways that can have a meaningful and sustainable influence on students' experiences of physical activity. Adults who have power and make decisions about physical education curricula and pedagogies should pay closer attention to what students themselves have to say about physical education. Dyson (2006) observed that, with the odd exception, there had been very little done to understand what students think and feel about their experiences in physical education. As such, it is perhaps not that difficult to see why many students find that a top-down physical education model lacks relevance or meaning in their own lives inside and outside of school (Cothran & Ennis, 1999).

Earlier in the chapter we described how the multi-activity, sports-oriented curriculum taught using direct instruction has led many students to feel isolated, marginalized, and powerless during their physical education experience. For instance, many athletic females tend to find physical education frustrating simply because the activities offered to them are largely feminized (such as rhythmic activities) and there is an assumption made that *all* girls enjoy the same types of activities. Using a similar logic, many males who do not enjoy or participate in team sports often feel isolated, because the assumption is made that *all* males enjoy body contact, competitive playing environments, and so on—that is, all males enjoy stereotypically masculine behaviours (Tischler & McCaughtry, 2010). For example, an elite male figure skater or rock climber may be disengaged from physical education programs because of the focus on team sports and pervading jock culture that tends to dominate many programs. The diverse student body that is present in Canadian schools tends to be divided into categories all too quickly, meaning that assumptions are made about the characteristics of *all* girls and boys, *all* students whose body shape is slim or not, and so on.

Several researchers have begun listening to students' opinions of physical education to stimulate change in the curriculum development process. Enright and O'Sullivan (2010) found that many adolescent females preferred activities that were individual and noncompetitive (such as boxercise, rock climbing, and dance) and could easily be undertaken outside of schools. In addition, the pedagogies used to teach these types of activities were highly varied and gave students greater roles and responsibilities. They also found that participants in their study "rose to the challenge [of reimagining physical education] and took ownership of their learning," which resulted in "a positive, energizing and exciting experience for them and one in which deep learning occurred and deep insights were produced" (Enright & O'Sullivan, 2010, p. 203). In this example, the traditional power dynamic in teaching–learning contexts was disrupted, empowering the female participants to be active constructors and agents of their own learning.

The voices of "low-skilled" students have also been studied to understand what is being done in physical education and could be done better. For example, Portman (1995) and Carlson (1995) found that physical education was a particularly unpleasant part of school for many low-skilled students, citing lack of success, little assistance to develop skills, and receiving humiliating or critical comments in the public space of the gym. Tischler and McCaughtry (2011) noted similar experiences of boys whose embodied masculinities were marginalized in physical education because they may have been, for example, slower, weaker, and the "wrong" body shape or not well coordinated—in essence they did not fit the "jock culture" typically represented in high school physical education. These boys rarely experienced success, often did not feel like they contributed to team success, and employed several strategies to remain on the margins of the physical education classroom environment.

Although Canadian schools offer strong representations of multiculturalism in action, relatively little has been done to study the experiences of Canadian students from different racial and ethnic backgrounds in "whitestream" physical education classes (see Chapter 5). One notable exception has been the work of Joannie Halas at the University of Manitoba, who has studied the physical education experiences of Aboriginal youth. Recently, Halas (2011) summarized the outcomes of her broader research program, identifying that most Aboriginal youth had a profound love of sport and physical activity, a love that was fostered and encouraged by family and friends. Yet several teachers Halas spoke to suggested "their Aboriginal students weren't taking part in gym class; some were skipping phys ed and few were trying out for teams" (p. 11). Halas (2011) suggests that most of the blame for disengagement lies not with students but in the inherent structures, patterns, and power relations of physical education programs. For example, several participants cited changing clothes for class was a tremendous source of vulnerability that can create "lots of homophobic, fatphobic, classist and racist tension" (Halas, 2011, p. 12). Moreover, students' experiences of racism (both implicit and explicit) made them feel isolated in class, in addition to feeling that their cultural beliefs were not valued or respected in the gymnasium.

So what can be learned from these disparate studies on students' experiences of learning in physical education? From our perspective, the importance of listening to students about their experiences is crucial in fostering the success and sustainability of physical education programming. When students are provided with "voice and choice" and power in their physical education program, they tend to improve in levels of motor skill proficiency, engagement in physical activity, perceived competence, and intrinsic motivation (Hastie, Rudisill, & Wadsworth, 2013). If one aim of education is to empower students to be confident and competent decision makers, involving them more intimately in the educational process seems a logical step in the right direction.

TEACHERS AND TEACHING

The role of the physical education teacher is paramount in the provision of quality physical education programs and experiences. Indeed, the role of the teacher in any subject is *the* key to student achievement, with teacher quality being a more salient factor in achievement when compared to class size or student socioeconomic status (Darling-Hammond, 2010). Despite the common public perception that teaching is often easy, teachers face mounting pressures to do their job well. This includes being asked to do more with less thanks to a combination of escalating workloads and budget cuts. As a result, at times they have withheld afterschool coaching in various labour disputes.

In contrast to the diverse group of students that enroll and participate in physical education in Canada, teachers of physical education are quite a homogeneous group. For example, Halas (2006) suggests there are few physical education teachers or teacher-educators in Canada who represent visible minorities. This lack of diversity is particularly problematic if a major goal of physical education is to build a more equitable society (Mandigo et al., 2012). The problem lies in the challenges a homogeneous teaching profession faces in fostering meaningful experiences that reflect, are relevant for, and are representative of an increasingly diverse student population (Halas, 2006). If there is some degree of truth to the saying that "teachers teach who they are," then it follows that physical education teachers teach their classes in ways that reflect the values of a mostly white, middle-class, heterosexual, athletically able population (McCullick, Lux, Belcher, & Davies, 2012). Because teachers bring their own prior experiences, values, and beliefs to their work, it is perhaps not difficult to see that tensions and struggles exist around acknowledging, respecting, and including the values and beliefs of *all* students so that they feel a sense of belonging in the gymnasium. This is not to suggest that teaching inclusively is an unattainable prospect, but rather to acknowledge the difficulties and challenges involved in "teaching well."

Examinations of the biographies of physical education teachers have revealed how personal backgrounds and experiences shape their reasons for becoming teachers and the practices they enact in schools (Green, 2008). When consideration is given to who teaches physical education, it is evident that there are two distinct groups of teachers: physical education specialists (typically found in middle and high schools) and regular classroom teachers (typically found in elementary schools). Although having a specialist does not guarantee a quality physical education program, they do tend to teach better lessons than classroom teachers. For example, specialists are more likely to have well-planned programs that consider students' development across several domains (e.g., physical and affective), individualize instruction, deliver inclusive lessons, use recommended assessment strategies, provide opportunities for skill development, have success in enhancing students' fitness levels, and have a positive impact on the overall school climate. Specialists also tend to feel better prepared to teach physical education and enjoy teaching the subject more (Mandigo et al., 2004).

It makes sense that most specialist physical education teachers tend to look back positively on their experiences of physical education when they were school students. In particular, positive experiences with sport (not necessarily physical education per se) have a profound influence on prospective physical education teachers' decisions to enter the profession. Other noted reasons why people choose to become physical education teachers include positive influences of former teachers and a desire to work with young people (McCullick et al., 2012). Because most physical education teachers enjoyed their own experiences of physical education as school students, they often see little reason or justification to change a curriculum that is, in many of their minds, a mostly "strong product." This is one of the major reasons why there has been "more of the same" in high school physical education for about the last 50 years (Kirk, 2010b):

> PE teachers are inclined towards replicating (because they feel more comfortable with) "traditional" approaches to "traditional" curricula. This is why the sport- and games-oriented PE programme associated with so-called "traditional" PE has an element of self-replication built into it and has become self-fulfilling. (Green, 2008, p. 209)

As such, unless university teacher education programs *and* the culture surrounding physical education in high schools advocates and provides support for fostering change, any type of sustainable reform in physical education becomes more difficult. Indeed, even when there are institutional cultures amenable to change, the early socialization experiences of teachers provide such strong and entrenched beliefs that they have proven to be one of the most difficult things to change (McCullick, et al., 2012).

As has been done with specialist teachers, several researchers have considered the extent to which elementary classroom teachers' biographies and identities shape their experiences of physical education. For example, Fletcher (2012) and Garrett and Wrench (2007) found that while some classroom teachers enjoyed sport, physical activity, and physical education, for many the underlying discourses within these fields served to alienate rather than encourage active participation. For instance, abilities in physical activity and physical education were often defined in terms of a dichotomous identity: "sporty" or "nonsporty." Classroom teachers often felt that individuals who participated in physical activities outside of school and held identities closely linked to the image of a "sporty" person gained the most benefits in school physical education and would make the best physical education teachers. In contrast, teachers who did not view themselves as "sporty" children believed that they lacked the abilities to adequately teach physical education (Morgan & Bourke, 2008). As such, many classroom teachers source external providers of physical activity to implement their physical education programs. What results is that students of public schools often have to pay for their physical education experience (in the form of user fees), or they are taught in ways that are not pedagogically sound or appropriate for all learners.

Understanding physical education is a complex task and there are no quick fixes that enable positive, meaningful, and sustainable change. However, what is clear is that physical education plays an important role in providing children and youth with the types of experiences that can help foster a love for being physically active and to understand how physical activity and sport can play meaningful roles in people's lives.

HISTORY OF CANADIAN UNIVERSITY SPORT

Sports have been played at Canadian universities since the 19th century. According to Canadian Interuniversity Sport (2013a), the original Canadian Interuniversity Athletic Union (CIAU) was founded in 1906 and lasted until 1955. In these initial decades, its membership comprised universities from Ontario and Quebec, and its purpose was to provide common rules and regulations. At the same time, there were multiple regional conferences across Canada, some of which were members of the national body and others that were not. There was also a parallel organization, the Women's Intercollegiate Athletic Union (WIAU), which provided athletic competitions for female students. The WIAU would broaden beyond its Ontario base and change its name to the Canadian Women's Intercollegiate Athletic Union (CWIAU) in 1969.

The modern CIAU was established in 1961 to develop national championships, coordinate common rules and regulations, and increase education and communication in the area of university sports. In addition to receiving funding from the participating universities, the Canadian government also provided money to the CIAU for the purpose of developing high-performance amateur sport at a national level. This would foreshadow the creation of Sport Canada in 1971. The CWIAU merged with the CIAU in 1978 to form one national governing body. In many respects, the changes at the CIAU reflected the wider societal changes in Canada, including expansion of the university system, efforts at gender equity, federal funding in areas of provincial jurisdiction, and the creation of national organizations (CIS, 2013a).

The CIAU changed its name to Canadian Interuniversity Sport (CIS) in 2001 (CIS, 2013b). Today, the CIS is made up of 54 member schools, 10,000 athletes, and 550 coaches. It administers 21 national championships in 12 individual and team sports: basketball, curling, cross-country, field hockey, football, hockey, rugby, soccer, swimming, track and field, volleyball, and wrestling. All sports have both men's and women's divisions with the exception of football (men's only), field hockey (women's only), and rugby (women's only). Within the CIS system there are four regional conferences: the Canada West Universities Athletic Association (CWUAA), Ontario University Athletics (OUA), Réseau du sport étudiant du Québec (RSEQ), and Atlantic University Sport (AUS). These regional conferences can sanction additional sports. For example, OUA schools also compete in badminton, fencing, figure skating, golf, and rowing, among others (Ontario University Athletics, 2013).

The remainder of this chapter analyzes the key issues and recent controversies faced by the CIS. These include gender equity, athletic scholarships, doping, hazing, the challenge presented by the National Collegiate Athletic Association (NCAA), alumni funding models, academic achievement, and student-athlete life.

Gender Equity

Women now make up the majority of Canadian university students (Turcotte, 2011). There has been a consistent improvement in the degree of gender equity in the CIS, yet there remain numerous issues. The last vestige of a parallel women's system, which was separate and unequal, finally ended when the Ontario Women's Intercollegiate Athletic Association merged with the Ontario Universities Athletic Association and jointly formed the OUA in 1997. Likewise, there are now 11 women's sports recognized by the CIS and 10 for men. Newer entrants include women's rugby (1998), hockey (1997–1998), and wrestling (1998–1999). Excluding football, there are equal amounts of opportunity for sport participation between male and female students (Donnelly, Norman, & Kidd, 2013).

Nevertheless significant gaps still exist. The first is in the recruitment and retention of female coaches. Based on 2012–2013 statistics, only 17% of all coaches in CIS sports are female. Counting only women's sports, this increases to 32% of coaches who are female (Donnelly et al., 2013, p. 33). Only field hockey has a majority of female coaches, although basketball and rugby closely follow (CIS, 2005a). A second gap is in the number of athletic directors: Only 13 of 54 athletic directors at Canadian universities are female (Donnelly et al., 2013). A third gap is in athletic scholarships. A 2005 CIS-sponsored survey on gender equity showed that only 47% of member universities had "achieved equitable allocation of athletic financial awards" (CIS, 2005b). This was exacerbated by the rise in external funding of athletic scholarships (especially in the men's football programs that are financed by alumni, as discussed below). In 2011–2012, only 42% of all external athletic scholarship dollars were awarded to women; however, when football is excluded the number rises to 49.7% (CIS, 2013c). A final gap is in the marketing and promotion of women's programs and national championships. CIS universities have acknowledged that they promote "teams with the greater probability of attracting fans" (CIS, 2005b). Yet even the presence of star players like Hayley Wickenheiser, who played hockey for the University of Calgary, was unable to shift attendance patterns. To this day, the men's teams still substantially outdraw the women's teams.

Athletic Scholarships

Athletic scholarships at Canadian universities is a heated topic because top players flee Canada for the NCAA (discussed in more detail later) and the availability of athletic scholarships. Athletic scholarships can include free tuition and fees, room and board, and required course-related books. High school athletes and Canadians outside of the university sport system may be surprised to learn that there is some financial aid available for athletes at CIS schools, although it is limited solely to tuition and compulsory fees. In 2011–2012, $12.7 million was distributed in athletic scholarships among CIS athletes (CIS, 2013d). In fact, 43% of athletes received some type of financial support (CIS, 2013c). But that aggregate number masks the low per player scholarship that most receive. The average disbursement was a little over $2,700 a year, while tuition alone averages over $5,000 a year at Canadian universities (*Maclean's*, 2013).

Athletic scholarships equivalent to tuition and compulsory fees are allowed to first-year players if they enter university with a minimum 80% average. For returning players, the requirement is a minimum 65% average. There is a more stringent athletic scholarships policy among the OUA schools. For example, athletic scholarships cannot be given to first-year players, and returning players are required to have a minimum 70% average (CIS, 2013e). The higher OUA standard has created conflict with the other divisions in the CIS. More specifically, the demand for more lucrative athletic scholarships with more lax academic requirements has pitted some large schools (e.g., Université Laval, the University of Calgary, and the University of British Columbia) against universities in Ontario and smaller schools primarily in Atlantic Canada.

This demand for athletic scholarships is fuelled by the belief that all NCAA athletes receive "full-ride" scholarships. However, this is only available in Division I and only for a few students in high-profile sports. In Division I, it is common to divide scholarships among several players that have to be renewed on a year-by-year basis. Poor athletic performance can result in a scholarship being revoked. In addition, athletes and parents who may be blinded by the allure of a "free education" sometimes forget that tuition at Canadian universities can be thousands of dollars a year less than US universities. This gap is even larger when higher out-of-state or international fees are included (CIS, 2007). Academic standards tend to be equitable across Canadian universities at the undergraduate level, but there is wide variation in the quality of the educational experience in the United States. The United States has some of the world's best universities, both private (such as those in the Ivy League, Stanford, or Duke) and public (University of Michigan, University of California at Berkeley). There are also a number of schools with much weaker academic quality. This means that graduates at some US universities received a substandard education compared to what they would have received at a Canadian university. Canadian employers have recognized this educational gap and often do not provide equal consideration for degrees from some US schools (Charbonneau, 2013). Finally, bringing in athletic scholarships to Canadian universities would require a transfer of funds from academic programs to athletic programs. It is doubtful that provincial governments (who are responsible for funding universities) or the public would support further subsidizing university athletics at the expense of academics.

Doping

Doping is discussed in greater detail in the deviance chapter (see Chapter 8), so this section concentrates on issues in the CIS. The CIS faced its own major doping scandal in 2010 when news emerged that the University of Waterloo football team was involved in the use of performance-enhancing substances, and a player was under police investigation for trafficking banned substances (human growth hormone and steroids). The university immediately asked the Canadian Centre for Ethics in Sport

(CCES) to test the entire football team (football players from McMaster University and the University of Guelph were also tested). Sixty-two Waterloo players were subsequently tested, and nine of them tested positive for performance-enhancing drugs, admitted their guilt, or refused to provide a sample (CCES, 2010a). An example of the type of prohibited substances that were found in the blood and urine samples was tamoxifen, a substance used to combat the side effects of steroids. All nine players were suspended by the CIS for one to two years. More significantly, the University of Waterloo decided to cancel its entire 2010 football season.

The scale of the Waterloo football doping scandal rocked the entire CIS. Marg McGregor, the chief executive officer of the CIS, called it "the most significant doping issue in CIS history. It illustrates that the CIS doping control program needs to be strengthened to ensure a level playing field and to protect the rights of the vast majority of student-athletes who respect the rules and compete clean" (CCES, 2010a). The Waterloo football doping scandal did lead to changes in the CIS drug-testing policies. CIS drug-testing was intended to be a year-round operation, but instead athletes supplied samples only at training camp or at the national championships. The major reason for this is that the cost is approximately $500–800 per drug test (Maki, 2012). McGregor maintained that "we want to test an athlete at any point in time and not just at the Vanier Cup. We want to be aware of performance information to look for drastic improvements in performance and weight gain" (Maki, 2010). In addition, the CIS is "going to do a complete review of [its] educational programs" (Maki, 2010).

Other measures, in conjunction with the CCES and the Canadian Football League, included hosting an anti-doping symposium at the 2010 Vanier Cup at Université Laval in Quebec City, having the CCES create an independent task force to look at performance-enhancing drugs in football, increasing the number of tests allocated to CIS football and extending testing into the offseason (seen as a more at-risk period), more extensive testing of CFL top prospects from the CIS, and a public education campaign aimed at minor football players (CCES, 2010b).[1]

Since the 1990–1991 season, the CCES has been responsible for administering drug tests to CIS student-athletes. From 1990–1991 to 2012–2013 there were 74 positive drug tests (72 men and 2 women). Football was the biggest offender with 63 positive tests, which is why approximately 40% of all players tested annually by the CCES are from football (CCES, 2010c). The top two prohibited substances that have been used are steroids (30 positive tests) and marijuana (16 positive tests) (CIS, 2013f). Considering that over 6,000 CIS student-athletes have been tested in this time period (which is about 1 in 25), it is evident that the number of athletes using drugs is small.[2] Nevertheless, every positive test is damaging not only to the individual, but also to the school and the integrity of the sport.

Hazing

Hazing has been mentioned in other chapters, so this section focuses on specific instances of hazing in the CIS. There is little societal tolerance for hazing throughout Canadian sport, and this occurs in the CIS as well. This can be demonstrated in several ways. First, there is more media attention given to alleged and actual hazing incidents. Second, many universities have been upgrading their codes of conduct for student-athletes. For example, after a 2011 hazing incident left a St. Thomas University volleyball player dead, the university toughened its code of conduct policy to include off-campus activities (Petz, 2011). Third, the penalties for hazing, as applied by both leagues and individual universities, are higher.

While incidents of hazing are being dealt with much more than in the past, they have not completely stopped. There are numerous examples of universities punishing athletes and teams for hazing. McGill suspended its football team for the rest of the 2005 season after it uncovered a serious incident during a rookie night event in August 2005. The incident involved "nudity, degrading positions and behaviours, gagging, touching in appropriate manners with a broomstick, as well as verbal and physical intimidation of rookies by a large portion of the team" (Drolet, 2006). Other examples of teams being suspended for multiple games, and even a season, included the St. Thomas University's men's volleyball team in 2010 and Wilfrid Laurier University's baseball team in 2012. Hazing is often seen as occurring primarily on male teams, but there are also examples of female teams hazing players. For example, both Carleton University's women's soccer team in 2009 and Dalhousie University's women's hockey team in 2013 suffered lengthy suspensions because of hazing incidents.

Universities have also tried to use positive measures as well as punishments. This has involved establishing new traditions that stress the importance of team building and team spirit while at the same time eliminating the degrading forms of hazing. One Canadian university encouraged its teams to participate in "ceremonies in which senior students present rookies with a team sweater" (Drolet, 2006).

Hazing is policed more rigorously in the CIS than in the Canadian Hockey League and other junior sports leagues. In 2011, the Neepawa Natives of the Manitoba Junior A Hockey League had multiple suspensions for coaches and players because of a hazing issue, but the team did not miss any games on its schedule. What explains this higher standard for CIS teams? One explanation is that universities are about education, not just sports. In addition, all universities have codes of student conduct that prohibit hazing and initiations throughout the student body, not just athletes. Finally, universities in Canada are publicly funded and therefore responsible to government. University presidents and provincial politicians have strongly objected to hazing among university students (sports teams, fraternities, residences, engineering schools, etc.) and have demanded harsh punishments for offenders (CBC News, 2011).

The Challenge of the NCAA

The NCAA in the United States represents a major challenge to the CIS. This can be shown in two ways. First is the threat of Canadian schools abandoning the CIS to join the NCAA. For example, in 2012 Simon Fraser University, after several years of probation, joined the NCAA Division II. Their motive was twofold: greater competition and saving money. Simon Fraser competes against universities in western Washington and Oregon and those schools are simply less expensive to travel to than other western Canadian provinces. Other schools, such as the University of British Columbia, have also debated leaving the CIS for the NCAA.

The second challenge for the CIS is that Canada regularly loses its top athletes to the NCAA.[3] In 2012–2013, approximately 3,500 Canadians were participating in NCAA athletics (Geiger, 2013). With the notable exception of hockey, Canadian sport has delegated its high-performance athlete development to the NCAA. For example, the 2012 training camp roster for the Canadian senior men's national basketball team had 26 of 30 players from NCAA schools and only four players who went to CIS schools (Canada Basketball, 2012a). According to Canada Basketball, more than 70 men and 80 women left Canada to play in the NCAA in the 2012–2013 season (Canada Basketball, 2012b). The 2010 Canadian senior men's field lacrosse team, meanwhile, had 13 of 22 players from NCAA schools and all four coaches had NCAA experience.[4] The Canadian women's soccer team that won bronze at the 2012 London Olympic Games had 16 of 18 players from the NCAA and only two players from CIS schools (Canada Soccer, 2013).

Players go to the NCAA because it offers a better quality of play. This is because NCAA schools have significant financial resources for large, full-time coaching staff that can develop new advanced athletic techniques. They also have state-of-the-art athletic facilities such as home rinks/fields, dressing rooms, weight rooms, specialized video rooms, and practice facilities. It is for these reasons that the NCAA is widely understood as the pathway to professional sports leagues such as the NFL and NBA.

Another reason that Canadian student-athletes decide to attend NCAA schools is to experience the sports spectacle: the attendance, media coverage, and atmosphere of big-time college sport. While there are exceptions with regard to certain sports (e.g., football at Laval), schools (e.g., New Brunswick, Acadia, or Lakehead), and national championships (e.g., football, basketball, and hockey), for the most part CIS athletes play in front of hundreds or, at most, the low thousands. In contrast, the glamour NCAA sports routinely draw sellout crowds of 60,000–100,000 (football) or 15,000–20,000 (men's basketball). Other NCAA sports such as hockey, baseball, and soccer have more spectators than their Canadian counterparts by a wide margin. For example, in 2013 the Mount Royal University Cougars played the University of Calgary Dinos at the Scotiabank Saddledome in Calgary in a special game where tickets

Action during the Crowchild Classic women's hockey game between the University of Calgary and Mount Royal University.
Megapress/Alamy

were given away. It drew over 2,000 for the women's hockey game and over 4,000 for men's hockey. Both games set CWUAA attendance records. Meanwhile, an ordinary regular season men's hockey game at the University of North Dakota, a perennial NCAA powerhouse, typically sells out its 11,889 arena.

The major NCAA sports of football and basketball are big business and are also saturated by media coverage—these sports generate billion-dollar contracts for television rights. For example, in 2010 the NCAA signed a 14-year $10.8 billion contract with CBS for the television rights of its men's basketball national tournament (Getz & Siegfried, 2010). As well, millions of viewers watch regular season televised games and there is extensive coverage of college games in national and local media. Some gamblers (legal and otherwise) bet on high-profile football bowl games and, especially, on the NCAA March Madness national basketball tournament. It is a media event where even President Barack Obama selects his annual basketball bracket; we cannot image Prime Minister Stephen Harper, a well-known hockey fan, being asked his opinion on CIS hockey.

NCAA sports are big business. In 2010, both the Big Ten and the Southeastern Conferences hit a billion dollars in athletic receipts (ticket sales, concession sales, merchandise, licensing fees, television contracts, etc.). The Ohio State University outsourced its sports merchandise to IMG College, a sports marketing firm, for a guaranteed $11 million a year. Meanwhile, EA Sports paid more than $35 million in 2010 in royalties for NCAA-based video games (Branch, 2011). Revenue is one side of the equation; the other is spending. Overall, at public universities, Division I athletic programs spent $6 billion in 2010 (Desrochers, 2013).

In contrast, CIS sport's budgets are far more modest. The CIS struggles to get games televised on sports cable stations such as TSN or Sportsnet 360. When they do, the CIS, or a regional division such as the OUA, often pay to get their games on the air and are responsible for selling their own advertising. Although there are exceptions, tickets to games at many universities are often given away. Merchandise sales of university sports paraphernalia are minute in comparison to the NCAA, especially universities with historically significant sporting legacies such as Notre Dame and Michigan.

The overall atmosphere at major US university games provides additional entertainment and excitement. There are tailgate parties, cheerleaders, marching bands, and pep rallies. Some professional sports in Canada or the United States often find it difficult to compete with the atmosphere at a big-time college game.

Alumni Funding Model

Several universities in the CIS have abandoned the traditional university sport funding model and adopted funding models for their football programs that strongly resemble the NCAA's experience with private alumni donors. Privately funded sports programs began with the Université Laval Rouge et Or, but due to its success (both on and off the field) it has been emulated by other universities (Cardwell, 2009). Laval's program was started in 1996 and is operated by a nonprofit board at arm's-length from the university. Laval has a $2 million budget, which is four or five times higher than the average school in Canada. Laval has used this money to hire five full-time coaches (most schools have two or three), establish a more sophisticated weight room, and run a spring training camp in Florida. This investment has paid off, because in the last 10 years Laval has won seven Vanier

Cups as the top university football team in Canada. It is no coincidence that Laval's program began in the same year that Quebec City lost its only professional sports team, the NHL's Quebec Nordiques. The departure of the Nordiques to Denver in 1995 meant that local businesses had money to spend on sports advertising, and the Laval Rouge et Or became the beneficiary.

The University of Regina Rams football team was once one of the most successful junior football programs in Canada, but in 1999 they began to compete in the CIS through a community partnership agreement through which the team "remains financially independent of the University and must pursue a broad range of fundraising projects and activities in order to keep the program running" (University of Regina Cougars, 2012). Similar to the Laval Rouge et Or, the Regina Rams have invested significant funds in the development of first-class training facilities. The University of Calgary Dinos, one of Canada's most successful football teams over the last three decades, is dependent on fundraising by an alumni group called the 5th Quarter (MacLeod, 2012). The 5th Quarter's role is to raise private scholarship money for football players. In 2012, 22 players received almost $100,000 in financial assistance. Many of the 5th Quarter's members are prominent businesspeople in Calgary, and they use their connections to get Dinos players careers once they graduate. The Carleton University Ravens football team, which returned to competition in 2013 after a 15-year absence, is also following the alumni funding model, as is the Lakehead University men's hockey team.

Academic Achievement

In the United States there has been significant debate about the academic achievement of student-athletes.[5] Academic achievement is typically measured in grade point averages (GPA) and graduation rates. The NCAA claims that "student-athletes annually outperform their student-body counterparts in graduation rates, and in almost all demographic categories" (2013). However, the methodology for that conclusion has been disputed by many academics precisely because the NCAA includes part-time students (who have higher dropout rates and do not include athletes) and counts athletes who transfer in good academic standing as graduates.

The adjusted graduation gap (AGG), a model that factors out part-time students, demonstrates that "in most athletic conferences, athletes graduate at rates lower than non-athletes" (Grasgreen, 2013). This gap is widest among male football and basketball players at NCAA Division I Bowl Series conferences. For example, football players in the Pacific 12 Conference have 27% fewer graduates than full-time male students. Richard Southall led the AGG study and found that the gap was highest among black football players: "It's three times more likely that black football players [in the NCAA Division I Bowl Subdivision conferences] don't graduate at the same rate" as black nonathletes (Grasgreen, 2012). This gap also exists in men's basketball, where the number of black players who do not graduate is double that of white players (Grasgreen, 2013).

Others have argued that the NCAA and its member schools manipulate graduation rates through "major clustering [of athletes in certain majors] and devalued degrees" (Grasgreen, 2012). NCAA schools offer Student-Athlete Support Service Programs that include special tutoring and advising, but it has been argued that the purpose of these programs is simply to ensure that athletes remain academically eligible to compete, rather than fostering their overall academic development and graduation rates (Geiger, 2013).

The CIS does not monitor the academic achievement of its student-athletes, and the research on graduation rates is not as extensive in Canada as it is in the United States. However, the weight of the research indicates that CIS student-athletes have both lower GPAs and lower graduation rates than non–student-athletes. Martens (1985), in an examination of University of Victoria athletes from 1970–1980, found that student-athletes had lower GPAs than the regular student body and took longer to graduate. Danylchuk (1995), in a study of male and female athletes in many different sports at a large Ontario university in the early 1990s, found that nonathletes had a higher GPA than student-athletes. McTeer and Curtis (1999), in a survey of male and female athletes at a Canadian university from 1988–1993, also showed that student-athletes had both lower GPAs and graduation rates than non–student-athletes. Finally, Miller and Kerr (2002), in a survey of male and female athletes in their fourth or fifth years at a Canadian university, argue that CIS student-athletes report lower grades in year one but showed significant improvement in years four and five as they reoriented their focus away from athletics and toward academics.

While the academic achievement of CIS student-athletes may be less than non–student-athletes, it is also clear that CIS student-athletes outperform their counterparts in the NCAA. There are a number of reasons for this. First, NCAA athletes are often given preferential access to enter university, while CIS athletes must compete with all other applicants. This means that right from entrance into university, NCAA student-athletes are often weaker academically. Second, NCAA athletics, especially in the high-profile sports of football and men's basketball, is substantially more commercial than the CIS. This means that CIS athletes have less "team events to attend per week outside of regularly scheduled training and competition, since their athletic team and league is less commercialized" (Geiger, 2013, p. 3). Third, numerous US studies have shown that there is often an "athletic subculture of low academic expectations" among NCAA student-athletes (Geiger, 2013, p. 3). Finally, these same studies have demonstrated that even some faculty members possess negative attitudes about the academic potential of NCAA student-athletes, especially black athletes (Geiger, 2013). Miller and Kerr, in contrast, found a supportive academic environment among faculty, coaches, and players for CIS student-athletes (2002).

Student-Athlete Life

How do student-athletes differ from non–student-athletes at Canadian universities? As the previous section demonstrates, there has been much research comparing student-athletes and non–student-athletes in terms of academic achievement, but what about their social experiences? There are both positive and negative features concerning the social life of student-athletes. One positive feature is that student-athletes find it easier to adjust to the loneliness that many first-year university students experience. Loneliness occurs because students have either just moved away from home or are attending a campus that is many times larger than their former high school without a developed network of friends. One of the benefits of sport participation is that fellow athletes provide an immediate social network on campus that can often alleviate "sentiments of loneliness and stress that often accompany major life changes, particularly the first year of university" (Miller & Kerr, 2002, p. 360). This social network continues throughout their university career. For example, unofficial athletic residences—off-campus housing that successive groups of student-athletes rent year after year—have sprung up at most Canadian universities (Miller & Kerr, 2002).

A negative feature is the sheer amount of time that student-athletes must spend training and competing in their sport. Miller and Kerr (2002) found that athletes spent an average of 20 hours per week in training and competition for their sport. This had an adverse effect not just on their schoolwork, but it also restricted their ability to get a part-time job, unlike most non–student-athletes (McTeer & Curtis, 1999; Miller & Kerr, 2002). Student-athletes who deal with the time pressures of combining athletics and academics often restrict their social circle to their teammates and can become isolated from the rest of the student body (Geiger, 2013; Miller & Kerr, 2002). They play together, live together, take the same classes together (a very high percentage of student-athletes are in physical education programs), and they often socialize together.

Conclusions

Given that elementary and high schools and universities are very different educational contexts, we would expect to find several differences in the ways that sport and physical activity are offered to students. School-based physical education is a compulsory requirement for the greater part of the education of Canadian children; however, participation in university sports (whether in competition, such as CIS, or intramurals) is entirely voluntary. However, most children do not experience specialized instruction in sport and physical activity (i.e., teachers and coaches) until they reach middle and high schools. There are few specialists providing movement education to small children, but at the other end of the spectrum those who educate university students in sport and physical activity contexts tend to be highly specialized.

Despite these and many other differences, there are also several common themes that are present in the two contexts. We highlighted the important role that history plays in any consideration of assessing the current "state of play" of sport and physical activity. In order to grasp the present and future, a look to the past provides important clues as to why things are the way they are and helps us identify areas where sustainable change is possible. In addition, we identified issues related to difference and diversity, particularly concerning gender, as being salient factors in understanding how sport and physical activity is offered and experienced in schools and universities. While gender equity may have improved over the years, there is still much to be done to not only understand differences between males and females, but also to understand differences among males and females. Although our analysis has indicated several changes that have been made to improve sport and physical activity provision in Canadian educational systems, students, practitioners, administrators, policymakers, and researchers have significant work ahead of them to provide high-quality opportunities for participation and engagement in sport and physical activity in Canadian educational institutions.

Critical Thinking Questions

1. Think back to your experiences of physical education in elementary and secondary school. Who tended to be successful? Why were they successful? What activities do you recall participating in most? Compare your experiences to others in a small group.

2. What role does competitive sport tend to play in secondary school physical education programs? What role *should* it play? Justify your answer by considering the experiences of many girls in sport-based physical education.

3. How can physical education programs help to develop the "whole child" (i.e., physical, social, emotional, cognitive development)? What can be done to improve how programs currently meet this aim?

4. What factors contribute to the perception that physical education is a "marginal subject" in the school curriculum?

5. Should CIS schools try to emulate NCAA schools? If so, how? If not, why not?

6. What is the biggest challenge facing the CIS: hazing, performance-enhancing drugs, gender equity, or something else?

7. How different are student-athletes in Canada when compared to students in the United States in the areas of academic performance and social experiences?

Suggested Readings

Branch, T. (2011, October). The shame of college sports. *The Atlantic*. Retrieved from http://www.theatlantic.com/magazine/archive/2011/10/the-shame-of-college-sports/308643.

Aughey, T., Danylchuk, K., & Lebel, K. (2011). The impact of the economic recession on Canadian Interuniversity Sport (CIS) programs. *Journal of Intercollegiate Sport, 4*(2), 147–157.

Donnelly, P., Norman, M., & Kidd, B. (2013). *Gender equity in Canadian interuniversity sport: A biennial report.* Toronto, ON: University of Toronto, Centre for Sport Policy Studies. Retrieved from http://physical.utoronto.ca/docs/csps-pdfs/cis-gender-equity-report---2013.pdf?sfvrsn=2.

Gibbons, S. L. (2009). Meaningful participation of girls in senior physical education courses. *Canadian Journal of Education, 32*, 222–244.

Halas, J. M. (2011). Aboriginal youth and their experiences in physical education: "This is what you've taught me." *PHEnex Journal, 3*(2). Retrieved from http://ojs.acadiau.ca/index.php/phenex/article/view/1427.

Kirk, D. (2010). *Physical education futures.* London, UK: Routledge

Quarmby, T., & Dagkas, S. (2012). Locating the place and meaning of physical activity in the lives of young people from low-income, lone-parent families. *Physical Education & Sport Pedagogy* (iFirst), 1–16.

Tischler, A., & McCaughtry, N. (2011). PE is not for me: When boys' masculinities are threatened. *Research Quarterly for Exercise and Sport, 82*, 37–48.

References

Branch, T. (2011, October). The shame of college sports. *The Atlantic*. Retrieved from http://www.theatlantic.com/magazine/archive/2011/10/the-shame-of-college-sports/308643.

Bratt, D. (in press). Different not better: Comparing Canadian and American university sport systems. In D. Taras & C. Waddell (Eds.), *How Canadians communicate V: Sport.* Edmonton, AB: Athabasca University Press.

Canada Basketball. (2012a). 2012 senior men's training camp roster. Retrieved from http://www.basketball.ca/senior-men-p148740.

Canada Basketball. (2012b). NCAA: Canadian impact. Retrieved from http://www.basketball.ca/ncaa-national-collegiate-athletic-association-s15154.

Canada Soccer. (2013). Women's national team/Olympic team. Retrieved from http://www.canadasoccer.com/index.php?t=project&sid=965.

Canadian Centre for Ethics in Sport. (2010a). Doping control test results on University of Waterloo football team announced. Retrieved from http://www.cces.ca/en/news-126-doping-control-test-results-on-university.

Canadian Centre for Ethics in Sport. (2010b). CCES, CIS and CFL announce robust anti-doping measures after more university football players test positive for banned substances. Retrieved from http://www.cces.ca/en/news-134-cces-cis-and-cfl-announce-robust-anti-doping.

Canadian Centre for Ethics in Sport. (2010c). CCES testing University of Waterloo football team. Media Backgrounder. Retrieved from http://www.cces.ca/files/pdfs/MediaBackgrounderTesting UniversityofWaterlooFootballTeam2010FINAL.pdf.

Canadian Interuniversity Sport. (2005a). Analysis of male and female coaches in CIS sports. Retrieved from http://english.cis-sic.ca/information/members_info/pdfs/pdf_research_and_stats/Analysis_of_Male_and_Female.pdf.

Canadian Interuniversity Sport. (2005b). Equity practices questionnaire: Responses of the membership. Final report. Retrieved from http://english.cis-sic.ca/information/members_info/pdfs/pdf_research_and_stats/2005_Equity_Practices_Questionnaire-CIS-Equity-Report-2005.pdf.

Canadian Interuniversity Sport. (2007). Canada vs U.S.A: The financial implications of the choice. Retrieved from http://english.cis-sic.ca/information/members_info/pdfs/pdf_research_and_stats/july2007CanadavsUSAresearchfinal.pdf.

Canadian Interuniversity Sport. (2013a). History of CIS. Retrieved from http://english.cis-sic.ca/information/about_cis/cishistory.

Canadian Interuniversity Sport. (2013b). About the CIS. Retrieved from http://english.cis-sic.ca.

Canadian Interuniversity Sport. (2013c). Athletic financial awards 2011–2012. Retrieved from http://english.cis-sic.ca/information/members_info/pdfs/pdf_research_and_stats/SportBySport AFASummary2011-12_-public-_-_english.pdf.

Canadian Interuniversity Sport. (2013d, June 20). Athletic scholarships: CIS schools provided over $12.7 M to student-athletes in 2011–12. News Release.

Canadian Interuniversity Sport. (2013e). Athlete's Guide: 2013–2014. Retrieved from http://english.cis-sic.ca/information/members_info/pdfs/pdf_elig_pack/13-14/athletes_guide.pdf.

Canadian Interuniversity Sport. (2013f). History of CIS doping violations. Retrieved from http://english.cis-sic.ca/information/members_info/pdfs/pdf_research_and_stats/Drug_stats_break-down_jan_21_2013.pdf.

Cardwell, M. (2009, November 9). Laval's field of dreams. University Affairs. Retrieved from http://www.universityaffairs.ca/laval-s-field-of-dreams.aspx.

Carlson, T. B. (1995). We hate gym: Student alienation from physical education. Journal of Teaching in Physical Education, 14, 467–477.

CBC News. (2011, November 2). N.B. student's death prompts hazing probe. Retrieved from http://www.cbc.ca/news/canada/new-brunswick/n-b-student-s-death-prompts-hazing-probe-1.887974.

Charbonneau, L. (2013, July 22). The value of a degree earned in Canada vs. one earned abroad. University Affairs. Retrieved from http://www.universityaffairs.ca/margin-notes/the-value-of-a-degree-earned-in-canada-vs-one-earned-abroad/.

Cothran, D., & Ennis, C. D. (1999). Alone in a crowd: Meeting students' needs for relevance and connection in urban high school physical education. Journal of Teaching in Physical Education, 18, 234–247.

Danylchuk, K. E. (1995). Academic performance of intercollegiate athletes at a Canadian university: Comparisons by gender, type of sport and affiliated faculty. Avante, 1(2), 78–93.

Darling-Hammond, L. (2010). *The flat world and education*. San Francisco, CA: Jossey Bass.

Desrochers, D. M. (2013). Academic spending versus athletic spending: Who wins? *Delta Cost Project*. Retrieved from http://chronicle.com/blogs/players/files/2013/01/deltacost.pdf.

Donnelly, P., Norman, M., & Kidd, B. (2013). *Gender equity in Canadian Interuniversity Sport: A biennial report*. Toronto, ON: University of Toronto, Centre for Sport Policy Studies. Retrieved from http://physical.utoronto.ca/docs/csps-pdfs/cis-gender-equity-report---2013.pdf?sfvrsn=2.

Drolet, D. (2006, January 16). University athletic departments review their hazing policies. *University Affairs*. Retrieved from http://www.universityaffairs.ca/university-athletics-departments-review-their-hazing-policies.aspx.

Dyson, B. (2006). Students' perspectives of physical education. In D. Kirk, D. Macdonald, & M. O'Sullivan (Eds.), *Handbook of physical education* (pp. 326–346). London, UK: Sage.

Ennis, C. D. (1999). Creating a culturally relevant curriculum for disengaged girls. *Sport, Education and Society, 4*, 31–49.

Ennis, C. D. (2006). Curriculum: Forming and reshaping the vision of physical education in a high need, low demand world of schools. *Quest, 58*, 41–59.

Enright, E., & O'Sullivan, M. (2010). "Can I do it in my pyjamas?" Negotiating a physical education curriculum with teenage girls. *European Physical Education Review, 16*, 203–222.

Fletcher, T. (2012). Experiences and identities: Pre-service elementary classroom teachers being and becoming teachers of physical education. *European Physical Education Review, 18*, 380–395.

Francis, N. R., & Lathrop, A. H. (2011). "Children who drill, seldom are ill." Drill, movement and sport: The rise and fall of a "female tradition" in Ontario elementary physical education—1850s to 2000. *Historical Studies in Education* (Spring), 61–80.

Garrett, R., & Wrench, A. (2007). Physical experiences: Primary student teachers' conceptions of sport and physical education. *Physical Education and Sport Pedagogy, 12*, 23–42.

Geiger, N. (2013). Intercollegiate athletics in Canada and the United States: Differences in access, quality, and funding. *College Quarterly, 16*, 3.

Getz, M., & Siegfried, J. (2010). What does intercollegiate athletics do to or for colleges and universities? Working Paper. Nashville, TN: Vanderbilt University, Department of Economics. Retrieved from http://www.accessecon.com/pubs/VUECON/vu10-w05.pdf.

Gibbons, S. L. (2009). Meaningful participation of girls in senior physical education courses. *Canadian Journal of Education, 32*, 222–244.

Grasgreen, A. (2012, September 25). Gaps in grad rates for athletes. *Inside Higher Education*. Retrieved from http://www.insidehighered.com/news/2012/09/25/report-finds-football-players-graduate-rates-lower-full-time-student-peers#sthash.ccLbD3Q9.dpbs.

Grasgreen, A. (2013, January 10). Division I basketball players graduate at lower rates than non-athletes. *Inside Higher Education*. Retrieved from http://www.insidehighered.com/quicktakes/2013/01/10/division-i-basketball-players-graduate-lower-rates-non-athletes#sthash.Nx2e7cfu.dpbs.

Green, K. (2008). *Understanding physical education*. London, UK: Sage.

Halas, J. (2006). Developing a white-race consciousness: A foundation for culturally relevant physical education for Aboriginal youth. In E. Singleton & A. Varpalotai (Eds.), *Stones in the sneaker: Active theory for secondary school physical and health educators* (pp. 155–182). London, ON: Althouse Press.

Halas, J. M. (2011). Aboriginal youth and their experiences in physical education: "This is what you've taught me." *PHEnex Journal, 3*(2). Retrieved from http://ojs.acadiau.ca/index.php/phenex/article/view/1427.

Hastie, P. A., Rudisill, M. E., & Wadsworth, D. D. (2013). Providing students with voice and choice: Lessons from intervention research on autonomy-supportive climates in physical education. *Sport, Education and Society, 18*, 38–56.

Hickey, C. (2010). Hypermasculinity in schools. In M. O'Sullivan & A. Macphail (Eds.), *Young people's voices in physical education and youth sport* (pp. 108–122). London, UK: Routledge.

Kilborn, M. (2011). Physical education curriculum across Canada. Presentation at the Canadian Society for Studies in Education Annual Conference. Fredericton, NB, May 28–June 1.

Kirk, D. (2010a). Physical education and sports. In P. Peterson, E. Baker, & B. McGaw (Eds.), *International encyclopedia of education* (pp. 459–463). Amsterdam: Elsevier.

Kirk, D. (2010b). *Physical education futures*. London, UK: Routledge.

Kirk, D. (2013). Educational value and models-based practice in physical education. *Educational Philosophy and Theory* (iFirst), 1–14.

Kirk, D., Macdonald, D., & O'Sullivan, M. (Eds.), (2006). *Handbook of physical education*. London, UK: Sage.

Lenskyj, H. (1986). *Out of bounds: Women, sport and sexuality*. Toronto, ON: Women's Press.

Lodewyk, K. R., & Pybus, C. M. (2013). Investigating factors in the retention of students in high school physical education. *Journal of Teaching in Physical Education, 32*, 61–77.

Maclean's. (2013, February 11). Sports scholarships are an expensive fix to a non-existent problem. Retrieved from http://www2.macleans.ca/2013/02/11/an-expensive-fix-to-a-non-existent-problem/.

MacLeod, R. (2012, November 16). Alumni got the Dinos' back. *Globe and*. Retrieved from http://www.theglobeandmail.com/sports/football/university-of-calgary-alumni-ensure-dinos-have-top-notch-program/article5400055/.

Maki, A. (2010, May 28). Doping common in varsity football, Waterloo player says. *Globe and Mail*. from http://www.theglobeandmail.com/sports/football/doping-common-in-varsity-football-waterloo-player-says/article4321076/.

Maki, A. (2012, September 7). Costs limit number of drug tests for football players. *Globe and Mail*. Retrieved from http://www.theglobeandmail.com/sports/football/costs-limit-number-of-drug-tests-for-football-players/article4528394/.

Mandigo, J. L., Corlett, J., & Lathrop, A. H. (2012). Physical education in the twenty-first century: To infinity and beyond? In E. Singleton & A. Varpalotai (Eds.), *Pedagogy in motion: A community of inquiry for human movement studies* (pp. 15–44). London, ON: Althouse Press.

Mandigo, J. L., Thompson, L. P., Spence, J. C., Melnychuk, N., Schwartz, M., Dunn, J. C., & Marshall, D. (2004). A descriptive profile of physical education teachers and related program characteristics in Alberta. *Alberta Journal of Educational Research, 50*, 87–102.

Mangan, J. A. (1983). Grammar schools and the games ethic in the Victorian and Edwardian eras. *Albion: A Quarterly Journal Concerned with British Studies, 15*, 313–335.

Martens, F. (1985). Academic achievement of intercollegiate athletes in physical education at the University of Victoria. *Canadian Association for Health, Physical Education and Recreation Journal, 51*, 14–22.

McCullick, B. A., Lux, K. M., Belcher, D. G., & Davies, N. (2012). A portrait of the PETE major: Re-touched for the early twenty-first century. *Physical Education & Sport Pedagogy, 17*, 177–193.

McTeer, W., & Curtis, J. (1999). Intercollegiate sport involvement and academic achievement: A follow-up study. *Avante, 5*, 39–55.

Metzler, M. W. (2011). *Instructional models in physical education* (3rd ed.). Scottsdale, AZ: Holcomb Hathaway.

Miller, P. S., & Kerr, G. (2002). The athletic, academic and social experiences of intercollegiate student-athletes. *Journal of Sport Behavior, 25*(4), 346–367.

Morgan, P., & Bourke, S. (2008). Non-specialist teachers' confidence to teach PE: The nature and influence of personal school experiences in PE. *Physical Education and Sport Pedagogy, 13*, 1–29.

National Collegiate Athletic Association. (2013). Academics. Retrieved from http://www.ncaa.org/wps/wcm/connect/public/ncaa/academics/index.html.

Ontario University Athletics. (2013). Sports. Retrieved from http://www.oua.ca.

Petz, S. (2011, September 21). Should universities punish students for off-campus behaviour? *Maclean's*. Retrieved from http://www.macleans.ca/education/uniandcollege/should-universities-punish-students-for-off-campus-behaviour/.

Philips, M. G., & Roper, A. P. (2006). History of physical education. In D. Kirk, D. Macdonald, & M. O'Sullivan (Eds.), *Handbook of physical education* (pp. 123–140). London, UK: Sage.

Portman, P. A. (1995). Who is having fun in physical education classes? Experiences of sixth-grade students in elementary and middle schools. *Journal of Teaching in Physical Education, 14*, 445–453.

Sheppard, R. J., & Trudeau, F. (2008). Research on the outcomes of elementary school physical education. *The Elementary School Journal, 108*, 251–264.

Siedentop, D., Hastie, P. A., & Van der Mars, H. (2004). *Complete guide to sport education*. Champaign, IL: Human Kinetics.

Sykes, H., & McPhail, D. (2008). Unbearable lessons: Contesting fat phobia in physical education. *Sociology of Sport Journal, 25*, 66–96.

Team Canada Lacrosse. (2013). 2010 roster. Retrieved from http://www.teamcanadalacrosse.com/team2010.aspx.

Tinning, R. (2010). *Pedagogy and human movement*. London, UK: Routledge.

Tischler, A., & McCaughtry, N. (2011). PE is not for me: When boys' masculinities are threatened. *Research Quarterly for Exercise and Sport, 82*, 37–48.

Turcotte, M. (2011). Women and education: A gender-based statistical report. Statistics Canada No 89-503-x. Retrieved from http://www.statcan.gc.ca/pub/89-503-x/2010001/article/11542-eng.pdf.

UNESCO. (1978). *The international charter of physical education and sport*. Records of the General Conference, 20th Session. Volume I: Resolutions. Paris, October 24–November 28. Retrieved from http://unesdoc.unesco.org/images/0011/001140/114032e.pdf.

University of Regina Cougars. (2012). Football: About us, club history. Retrieved from http://reginacougars.com/sports/2012/2/7/FB_0207124739.aspx?path=football.

Vertinsky, P. A. (1992). Reclaiming space, revisioning the body: The quest for gender-sensitive physical education. *Quest, 44*(3), 373–396.

Whitehead, M. (2001). The concept of physical literacy. *Physical Education and Sport Pedagogy, 6*, 127–138.

Endnotes

1. Five hundred football players were tested in 2010 because of the exposure of the Waterloo scandal, but by 2012 the number had dropped back down to 100 (out of 1,503 players) because of significant cost pressures (Maki, 2012).

2. Another possible conclusion is that athletes have become more adept at avoiding detection.

3. This section is derived from Bratt (in press).

4. Statistics for lacrosse are derived from information at Team Canada Lacrosse (2013). Field lacrosse is not one of CIS's sanctioned sports, but there is a good club league in Ontario and Quebec, plus Simon Fraser University plays in a US university league. There is also a maritime university field lacrosse league, but it is of a very poor quality.

5. This paragraph is derived from Bratt (in press).

Chapter 11
Sport, Media, and Ideology
Jay Scherer

The early days of sport on Canadian television.   AP Photo/Hans Von Nolde

The numbers and financial figures are staggering. In 2007, Rogers and CTVglobemedia (now BCE) joined forces as a multi-platform broadcasting consortium and paid the International Olympic Committee (IOC) over $150 million to secure the broadcasting rights to the 2010 Winter Olympic Games in Vancouver and the 2012 Summer Games in London. The Vancouver rights alone were more than three times what the Canadian Broadcasting Corporation (CBC) paid for the 2006 Winter Olympics in Turin ($28 million). Likewise, in December 2011, Canadian telecommunications giants BCE and Rogers paid more than $1 billion to acquire a 75% stake in Maple Leaf Sports and Entertainment (MLSE), in part, to secure the broadcasting rights to the Toronto Maple Leafs, the Toronto Raptors, and Toronto FC (Rogers also owns the Toronto Blue Jays). These sports "properties" now air on numerous Rogers-owned regional and specialty channels (Sportsnet, Sportsnet One, Sportsnet 360, Sportsnet World), BCE's TSN and TSN2, and on a host of additional platforms (radio, magazines, and the Internet) that are owned by these deep-pocketed corporations. All of these deals, of course, underscore the unprecedented value of popular, dramatic, live sports content as both BCE and Rogers battle to *secure subscribers and put together significant audiences* on their platforms and distribution outlets that can then be sold to advertisers.

The escalation of the costs of various sports broadcasting rights (see Tables 11.1 and 11.2) has also provided vast amounts of revenue and visibility for the various major leagues of North American sport and truly global sports organizations like the IOC and the Fédération Internationale de Football Association (FIFA). These are leagues and organizations that are themselves monopolies and cartels that have historically packaged and sold their exclusive sports products to various public and private networks; the ability of the major leagues to sell their products as collective entities has only been made possible thanks to their ongoing exemption from anti-trust legislation. Organized sport has, for several decades now, benefited handsomely from the substantial amount of "free" media coverage and the lucrative fees paid for the broadcast rights to their events and products. Beginning with the establishment of the first

Table 11.1 US Network Payments for Olympic Television Rights

Winter	Location	Rights	Amount	Summer	Location	Rights	Amount
1960	United States	CBS	$50,000	1960	Italy	CBS	$394,000
1964	Austria	ABC	$597,000	1964	Japan	NBC	$1.5 million
1968	France	ABC	$2.5 million	1968	Mexico	ABC	$4.5 million
1972	Japan	NBC	$6.4 million	1972	West Germany	ABC	$7.5 million
1976	Austria	ABC	$10 million	1976	Canada	ABC	$25 million
1980	United States	ABC	$15.5 million	1980	Soviet Union	NBC (cancelled)	$87 million
1984	Yugoslavia	ABC	$91.5 million	1984	United States	ABC	$225 million
1988	Canada	ABC	$309 million	1988	South Korea	NBC	$300 million
1992	France	CBS	$243 million	1992	Spain	NBC	$401 million
1994	Norway	CBS	$300 million	1996	United States	NBC	$465 million
1998	Japan	CBS	$375 million	2000	Australia	NBC	$705 million
2002	United States	NBC	$545 million	2004	Greece	NBC	$793 million
2006	Italy	NBC	$613 million	2008	China	NBC	$894 million
2010	Vancouver	NBC	$820 million	2012	United Kingdom	NBC	$1.18 billion
2014	Russia	NBC	$775 million	2016	Brazil	NBC	$1.2 billion
2018	South Korea	NBC	$963 million	2020	Japan	NBC*	$1.45 billion

*In 2014, NBC paid US$7.75 billion for the exclusive broadcast rights to the six Olympic Games from 2022–2032.

Table 11.2 Network Payments for Professional Sports Broadcasting Rights

League	Broadcasting Rights	Value	Term
CFL (Canadian Football League)	TSN (Canada)	C$43 million/year	2014–2018
EPL (English Premier League)	BSkyB, BT Group	£3 billion (US$5.1 billion)*	2013–2016
MLB (Major League Baseball)	ESPN, FOX, Turner Sports	US$12.4 billion	2014–2021
NBA (National Basketball Association)	ESPN, ABC, TNT	US$7.4 billion	2008–2016
NFL (National Football League)	CBS, NBC, FOX, ESPN	US$39.6 billion	2014–2022
NHL (National Hockey League)	Rogers (Canada)**	C$5.2 billion	2014–2026
	NBC (US)	US$2 billion	2011–2021

*Excludes hundreds of millions in broadcasting rights payments from networks in other nations.

**Largest media rights deal in NHL history, and Canada's largest sport media rights agreement.

sports section in daily newspapers and the emergence of specialist sport journalists in the 1880s, regular detailed media coverage propelled the major leagues into the mainstream of popular culture and amplified an already broadening public interest in commercial men's sport (Goldlust, 1987). To this day, for example, daily print and online newspapers provide commercial sport with an endless amount of promotional coverage, commentary, statistics and injury reports (especially for fantasy sport enthusiasts), and trade rumours on a continuous news and publicity cycle (Lowes, 1999). As the noted Canada author and sports writer Roy MacGregor remarked, the sheer ubiquity of sport in the media has been worth its weight in gold for various teams and leagues over the years: "Ever see a team advertise? Why would you advertise when you have a daily advertisement called the newspaper?" (quoted in Gilbert, 2011, p. 251).

At the same time, the creation of exciting sports "products" has, historically, provided advertisers valuable opportunities to reach significant audiences (of mostly affluent men) to market their products and brands. Indeed, in the rapidly changing digital landscape where Canadians have access to a seemingly endless flow of popular entertainment content on multiple family television sets and, increasingly, on mobile phones and tablet devices, the value of live sporting events for capturing significant and predictable audiences has never been greater; this is precisely why sponsors are willing to pay significant amounts to advertise during sports broadcasts. The "liveness" of exciting televised sport content is the crucial element in these economic calculations. That is, unlike other popular shows and films that can be recorded or purchased independently on iTunes or Netflix (allowing viewers to skip commercial messages), sporting events are generally consumed in real time and, thus, have far greater potential to expose audiences to advertising.

This latter point has only been reinforced in recent years with the price of a 30-second time slot during the Super Bowl rising to an astronomical US$4 million; in 2013, an estimated 108.4 million people watched Super Bowl XLVII in the United States alone. Likewise, in Canada the most popular sporting events continue to capture significant audiences for advertisers. In 2010, for example, an average of 16.6 million Canadians watched Canada beat the United States in overtime in the Olympic gold-medal game in Vancouver on the CTV/Rogers consortium's eight channels—an all-time viewing record in Canada. In 2013, the final game in the first round playoff series between the Toronto Maple Leafs and the Boston Bruins on CBC's *Hockey Night in Canada* (*HNIC*) set an audience record with 5.1 million viewers. Both the IOC and FIFA, meanwhile, claim to reach global audiences of billions of viewers during the Olympic Games and the World Cup, which is why television revenues have expanded significantly over the course of the last three decades (Whannel, 2005). Still, it's always important to interpret these statistics with a degree of skepticism; sport organizations (like FIFA and the IOC) report the highest audience numbers possible simply because these figures entice greater advertising revenue and, by extension, more valuable broadcasting contracts (Kuper & Szymanski, 2012).

Beyond these economic figures, there has simply never been a better time to be a sports fan: Canadians are now provided with an unprecedented amount of live sports content on television and other digital and mobile platforms that were simply unthinkable even a decade ago. Even though Canadians remain avid television watchers, in 2010 our use of the Internet for news, information, and entertainment surpassed that of television, marking a decisive shift in how we consume popular culture (Marlow, 2010). Despite the recent expansion of viewing opportunities for sports fans, though, there are now also greater costs to access digital sport content. This is particularly important in light of the power of a small number of distributors (e.g., Rogers, BCE, Shaw, and Quebecor) to bundle television channels together in expensive packages, in addition to the emergence of a wide range of expensive specialty sport channels that increasingly target niche markets and audiences of fans. As I discuss later in this chapter, there also remain significant limits in terms of the types of sports that Canadians are exposed to on a regular basis, including an ongoing lack of coverage of women's sport, Paralympic sport, and amateur sport in general.

Nonetheless, in the digital era sports fans can now follow not only the North American major leagues and the most popular sport mega-events, but a host of other competitions (such as the English Premier League and the UEFA Champions League) that were once inaccessible for Canadian audiences in an earlier analogue era. Indeed, for students born in the 1990s and who have never known a time when the Internet, Twitter, mobile handsets, and the multi-channel digital television universe did not exist, it seems unfathomable to think that there was a period when sports broadcasting and television itself were emergent phenomena in Canada and an even earlier era where live sports coverage was limited to the listening opportunities provided by another once innovative and popular form of broadcasting: radio.

Given the sheer amount of digital sports content that Canadians consume on television and increasingly online, there is little doubt that mediated sport is a "significant component of popular culture and to understand it better is to understand more about the culture in which we live" (Whannel, 1992, p. 2). In this chapter, I provide a brief review of the symbiotic and mutually beneficial multibillion dollar partnership between the media, professional sport leagues/organizations, and advertisers in Canada. By symbiotic I mean that these interest groups are now so highly intertwined and interlocked that they cannot be understood as separate entities and, crucially, they are motivated by a mutual desire for financial gain and subsequently flourish and profit by protecting and promoting each other's interests. Or, as the US communications scholar Robert McChesney (2008, p. 213) explained:

> On the one hand, the staggering popularity of sports is due, to no small extent, to the enormous amount of attention provided to it by the mass media. On the other hand, the media are able to generate enormous sales in both circulation and advertising based upon their extensive treatment of sports. Media attention fans the flames of interest in sports and increased interest in sports warrants further media attention.

Together, these institutions form the *sports-media complex* (Jhally, 1984) and share not only similar economic agendas but a host of ideological interests that set distinct limits and pressures on the production and consumption of sport content in Canada, albeit under the governance of the public regulatory agency, the Canadian Radio-television and Telecommunications Commission (CRTC). However, the Canadian sports-media complex has historically been a contested terrain, so I begin this chapter by focusing on the political, economic, and ideological struggles between various public and private networks to secure the most popular Canadian sports content, especially because telecasts of Canadian teams and athletes (amateur and professional) qualify as Canadian content (according to the CRTC, all networks must fulfill specific Canadian content requirements). These developments have, for now, culminated in an oligopoly (a market dominated by a small number of firms) controlled by vertically integrated telecommunication empires (Rogers, BCE, and Quebecor) that own and distribute vast amounts of sports content to subscribers across a host of print, radio, television, and Internet platforms.

While these broad economic dynamics and, indeed, our personal digital viewing habits may seem entirely natural and normalized—including the relatively new practice of paying for sporting and other media content—there is, in fact, a fascinating history of sports broadcasting in Canada, especially in the context of a much broader struggle between competing visions and models of broadcasting (e.g., public versus private). These struggles inevitably raise questions of cultural citizenship and whether key elements of national popular culture (such as NHL hockey games) and events of national significance (like the Olympic Games) ought to be available for all Canadians in English and French "over the air" without additional costs or fees (Scherer & Harvey, 2013).

Popular sports content distributed by various media play a critical role in organizing broader ideologies through which Canadians make sense of social relations and the ways that they see themselves and debate about society, culture, politics, and sport. The media, of course, does not sell an "innocent" product: They produce increasingly spectacular cultural sporting texts and rituals that are manufactured according to a host of economic, ideological, and institutional pressures, including widely embraced common sense understandings about what constitutes "good television" (Gruneau, 1989). Yet the sheer presence of mediated sport content—and the narrative structure of televised sport in particular—is so deeply taken for granted and familiar that we often only fully appreciate its existence as a social construction in the rare instances when the flow of sport content is significantly ruptured. This is precisely what occurred between August and October 2005 when, thanks to a Canadian Media Guild strike, CBC broadcast several CFL games with neither commentary nor additional effects (e.g., pregame profiles and storylines, instant replay, close-up images, statistical graphics, various sound effects). As such, following many of the theoretical ideas outlined in Chapter 2 on critical theories, I examine some of the ideological effects of media as sites of struggle over various meanings and cultural identities, especially those associated with the social construction of popular understandings of community/national identity, gender, race/ethnicity, and militarism within and through various mediated sport rituals (the Grey Cup and Super Bowl, the Stanley Cup, etc.).

Finally, it is also important to consider the role of sports journalists in promoting the fused economic and ideological interests of a male-dominated sports-media complex and some of the unique occupational structures that continue to set powerful limits and pressures on the agency of journalists that work to restrict a broader range of coverage (including critical commentary, coverage of female and amateur athletes, etc.). However, thanks to wider processes of convergence and concentration and the emergence of a host of technological developments (most notably Twitter), the work routines and labour practices of sports journalists have undergone substantial transformation. There is now more audience interaction than ever before between sports reporters, fans, and at times players themselves, marking a profound transformation in the way Canadians consume digital sport content.

Box 11.1

Key Terms

Mass media: The institution that produces and distributes information, interpretation, and entertainment to mass audiences.

Contribution to sport: Enhances commercial viability of sport and produces sport-specific values and ideology.

Mediamaking: A term developed to emphasize that the media produces and distributes various content just as the media are themselves being made and re-created by generations of Canadians against the backdrop of a host of political debates and cultural struggles: "[W]e must see the media and all of the relationships that the media are involved in as active relationships, producing the world at the same time that the world is producing the media. This means that the media *cannot* be studied apart from the active relationships in which they are always involved: We cannot study the media apart from the context of their economic, political, and cultural relationships" (Grossberg, Wartella, Whitney, & Wise, 2006, p. 7).

THE CANADIAN SPORTS-MEDIA COMPLEX
The Early Days of Canadian Television[1]

The era of televised sport began in Canada in 1952, when televised hockey was introduced on Canada's public broadcaster, CBC in English and Radio-Canada in French. Despite the initial trepidation of league president Clarence Campbell, who called the arrival of television "the greatest menace of the entertainment world" (Rutherford, 1990, p. 242), by the mid-1950s watching HNIC on CBC and *La soirée du hockey* on Radio-Canada had become a quintessential Canadian pastime inserted into the rhythms of the Canadian year. Pointing to the significance of the emergent medium of television in the sports-media complex, by the late 1950s revenues from *both broadcasts* had become a significant factor in the profits of the Montreal and Toronto NHL teams and in the finances of the public broadcaster itself (Rutherford, 1990). Importantly, the popularity of these hockey broadcasts also provided much needed Canadian content for CBC, which was, to the chagrin of many highbrow cultural nationalists, dependent on popular US imports to please audiences and attract advertising revenue.

The early days of Canadian television and the televised sports-media complex have been widely acknowledged as a "golden age" (Rutherford, 1990). This was an era in which CBC and Radio-Canada enjoyed a monopoly position as national broadcaster with a mandate to express and promote a separate Canadian consciousness, especially given the increasing presence and popularity of US culture and Hollywood products for Anglophone Canadians north of the border.

This was also, importantly, an era in which the ideological values of public service broadcasting were relatively dominant in Canadian society. The first of these values included *universal accessibility* and the establishment of the "viewing rights" (Rowe, 2004a) of Canadians—the ability to make television programming, to the extent that was technically possible, available "over the air" to all Canadians, including households in rural and remote areas, in both official languages on CBC and Radio-Canada. The principle of universal accessibility was clearly aligned with a broader postwar political agenda as the Canadian government sought to provide for all citizens, rich or poor, the basic economic necessities of life, but also a national standard of public cultural and leisure amenities, including access to libraries, recreation facilities, and popular television content on CBC and Radio-Canada.

The second value of the public broadcasting era was universal access to a breadth of programs that were representative of a "common culture," a notoriously difficult concept to define in light of the numerous divisions in Canadian society, most notably the enduring linguistic and regional divisions between Anglophones and Francophones. Still, the Canadian government's commitment to a split service public network in English and French made it possible to introduce a diverse and ambitious array of visual programs (musical game shows, highbrow quizzes, historical docudramas, concert music, and intellectual panel discussions) and a host of sporting events, including CFL football, wrestling, boxing, women's softball, roller derby, and of course ongoing coverage of hockey on HNIC and *La soirée du hockey*. During the 1950s, then, watching sports on CBC and Radio-Canada was quickly "naturalized" and, through all of these developments, live televised sport became understood as important components of a Canadian way of life and as a "public good" that added to the lives of many citizens in both official languages. In fact, a growing appetite for weekend sports coverage across the country prompted CBC and Radio-Canada to expand their programming to include curling, soccer, international hockey, bowling, skiing, swimming, figure skating, and golf (Rutherford, 1990), although it was nationally significant events that captured the biggest audiences. For instance, 5 million Canadians watched the 1959 Grey Cup match between the Winnipeg Blue Bombers and the Hamilton Tiger Cats—only the final game of the Stanley Cup playoffs gained a larger audience (Cavanaugh, 1992).

In the early days of television, then, the Canadian sports-media complex was both a public and a private institution—a mixture of public broadcasting, professional and amateur sport, and commercial advertising. It was a also a predominantly masculine experience, and CBC and Radio-Canada supplied an overwhelming amount of male sport that was consumed by mostly male audiences with greater levels of disposable income and influence in family households. For example, Canadian sport historian and former Olympian Bruce Kidd (1996a) has rightly argued that the partnership between CBC and the NHL distorted the development of Canadian sport and culture along two key lines. First, the sheer quantity of airtime dedicated to NHL hockey on the public broadcaster reinforced the "symbolic annihilation" of women's sport with regard to mainstream media that had "public authority" (Kidd, 1996a, p. 259). Indeed, once advertisers discovered the "remarkable ability of sports broadcasts to assemble affluent male consumers for their sponsors' appeals" (Kidd, 1996a, p. 260), the new broadcasting terrain was quickly structured to ensure that women's sport was heavily under-represented. Second, telecasts of the most popular men's sports on CBC—like NHL hockey and the CFL—were also public celebrations of hegemonic masculinity (Connell, 2005), an issue that I will return to shortly.

One of the most significant developments in the Canadian sports-media complex occurred in 1961 when CBC's dual role as national broadcaster and regulator ended thanks to the long-standing struggle by private broadcasters and their ideological allies to establish an independent broadcasting regulator, the Board of Broadcast Governors (BBG), nongovernment stations (second stations) in cities where CBC was installed and, crucially, the first national private network, CTV. Nicknamed "The Network That Means Business," CTV's emergence ran in stark contrast to the birth of CBC, which was intended to be a public instrument of nationhood. While the pursuit of profit unabashedly motivated the businessmen who invested in CTV, they also shared an ideological affinity to showcase Canadian private enterprise and to destabilize the ideological values associated with public broadcasting (Nolan, 2001).

The paramount role of sport in the establishment of CTV cannot be understated. The BBG had earlier awarded John Bassett, the owner of the CFL's Toronto Argonauts football club, the television licence for the lucrative Toronto market, and to the surprise of CBC, Bassett purchased the 1961 and 1962 rights to broadcast the Big Four (eastern CFL) games and the first right of refusal for the Grey Cup. Bassett, however, lacked the facilities and a national network to distribute his newly acquired CFL content and, as such, he was unable to provide the games with sufficient exposure for advertisers. One of Bassett's rival applicants for the television station in Toronto, Spencer Caldwell, however, had received BBG approval to form a national network in 1960, and Bassett would ultimately join with Caldwell's network to secure a distribution system for the CFL games, which were valuable Canadian content. This agreement, in turn, prompted the other seven newly licensed private stations to also sign up to the network, and ultimately secured the BBG's final approval in 1961 for CTV to begin operating. As Nolan (2001, p. 27) notes, "(w)ithout the 'Big Four' eastern conference of the CFL, CTV might never have emerged as a network."

The entrance of CTV signalled a new era of competition for sports broadcasting rights between the public and private networks, resulting in significant increases in television revenues for various sports leagues including the NHL and the CFL. Meanwhile, Canadian sports fans from coast to coast enjoyed an even greater amount of over-the-air coverage of sport on CBC and CTV. By the mid-1960s, within a climate of low unemployment, high disposable incomes, suburbanization, new levels of home and car ownership, and substantial increases in the purchase of light consumer goods, both CBC and CTV continued to stake their claims and battled to deliver significant weekend audiences for advertisers via expanded sports programming. The sport-driven audience commodity (Smythe, 1977)—a very predictable and stable demographic/market composed of mostly male viewers—was always the overriding product that these networks were putting together to sell to various advertisers and sponsors.

CTV, for example, was "highly influenced by U.S. models and the behaviour of American audiences towards sports broadcasting" (Nolan, 2001, p. 143), and the Canadian network began to show less expensive broadcasts of *Wide World of Sports* (obtained through an arrangement with the US network ABC) that blended major US and international sporting competitions and, crucially, a number of live or taped Canadian sporting events. For example, the 1964–1965 season of *Wide World of Sports* featured a mix of water skiing, softball, horse shows, wrestling, car racing, golf, soccer, and tennis. CTV, importantly, underscored the value of a combined US and Canadian sports television package for its stations across the country, which had to meet Canadian content requirements: "Self-Balancing Canadian Content" (Nolan, 2001, p. 143) that was able to deliver "the younger, larger, higher income families in CTV's ten vital marketing areas" (Nolan, 2001, p. 143). CTV also introduced new types of colourful and provocative sports-related programming such as the *Sports Hot Seat* that featured "an opinionated panel of questioners and a strong guest from the sporting world to respond to a controversial, topical issue [to] stimulate interest among viewers" (Nolan, 2001, p. 145).

Sports telecasts were thus "the lifeblood of the private broadcaster" (Nolan, 2001, p. 144) and delivered significant audiences that could be sold to advertisers. By 1965–1966, for example, sponsors were paying $1,050 for a 60-second spot during 26 consecutive weeks of CTV's *Wide World of Sports* (Nolan, 2001). CTV's executives also recognized the ability of specific sports to deliver different market segments to advertisers. For example, more affluent men watched coverage of golf and represented a valuable commodity that could be sold to more upmarket companies via advertising. Coverage of golf continues to capture a demographic of primarily affluent, middle-aged, white men, which is precisely why, to this day, BMW, Rolex, and bank and insurance companies pay significant amounts of money to advertise during the most prestigious golf events and tournaments around the world (in 2013, for example, over $1.6 billion was spent on golf sponsorship). Networks have historically used different sports to deliver specific audiences to advertisers. For example, compare the audience commodity that networks put together for advertisers during the Brier curling championship versus various World Wrestling Entertainment (WWE) events.

Still, it was the most popular sports that captured truly national audiences, and CTV continued to stake its claims in the Canadian sports-media complex by providing coverage of a succession of Winter Olympics beginning with the 1964 Games in Innsbruck, Austria. CTV also began airing NHL hockey games on Wednesday nights, capturing significant national audiences for advertisers even on weeknights. CBC and Radio-Canada, meanwhile, enjoyed a significant presence in homes across the country through telecasts of professional and amateur events, including Canadian college athletics, track and field meets, alpine skiing, and the Summer Olympic Games. However, it was the sport of hockey and weekly broadcasts of *HNIC* and *La soirée du hockey* that remained the most valuable and popular sport program for the public broadcaster. Despite the entrance of the private sector in the Canadian television sports-media complex, CTV and CBC complemented each other on a number of levels. Both networks provided a significant amount of over-the-air coverage of live US and Canadian sporting content, including joint coverage of a number of high-profile events including the 1972 Summit Series between Team Canada and the Soviet Union and the annual Grey Cup game.

A New Sport Broadcasting Order?

By the early 1960s, the entrance of cable television had already begun to radically transform the continental media landscape, thus opening the door to US television signals while siphoning audiences away from both CTV and CBC. In the context of the full emergence of cable television during the late 1960s and early 1970s, the competition between the public and private sector intensified and further escalated the cost of sports properties, and increased the pressure on CBC and CTV to retain Canadian sports content.

In an effort to meet its 80% Canadian content requirements, for example, CBC continued to expand its coverage of sport to include international hockey, the Olympic and Commonwealth Games, in addition to covering Canada's two MLB teams, the Toronto Blue Jays and the Montreal Expos. Within this context, the amount of airtime dedicated to sports on CBC emerged as the target of criticism on two widely different fronts. First, CTV's executives resented having to compete against the public broadcaster for the most popular sports broadcasting rights that captured lucrative national audiences for advertisers, especially as the emergent cable industry was gradually eroding its market share. Second, many of Canada's cultural elite openly disagreed with the significant presence of professional sport and other examples of mass/commercial entertainment (especially popular US programs) on CBC at the expense of other "highbrow programming" (i.e., the arts). In fact, CBC was actively targeted on both of these fronts during its CRTC licence renewal hearings throughout the 1970s and well into the 1980s and had to continually defend its role in providing popular sports content for all Canadians (Scherer & Harvey, 2013).

At the dawn of the 1980s, "[w]ith economic tremors from the end of the postwar boom rocking the economy and U.S. satellite signals nibbling at the edges of the broadcast system, the federal government developed a new policy vision for the communications sector" (Skinner, 2008, p. 7). Central to this new national communications agenda was an expanded subscription cable system to provide an increased range of specialty Canadian and foreign programming services to help retain Canadian audiences. Unlike CBC and CTV, which were networks that were available "over the air" for all Canadians, these new specialty channels were discretionary services to be purchased from cable distributors as part of bundled packages.

It was within the context of the expansion of cable television that another significant development in the history of the Canadian sports-media complex occurred: In 1984 the CRTC licensed the country's first 24-hour cable sports specialty channel, TSN, owned by the Labatt Brewing Company (its sister network, the all-sport French-language service RDS, was licensed in 1989). TSN was clearly established to promote the Labatt brand and products, but it was also a crucial circuit of promotion (Whitson, 1998) for the brewery to market its MLB team, the Toronto Blue Jays, to a principally male demographic that advertisers wanted to target. TSN quickly emerged as a competitor to the major national networks (Sparks, 1992) and, as a result of its sole focus on sport, the emergent cable channel was able to provide full coverage of entire tournaments, sporting events, and playoff series without disrupting regularly scheduled prime-time shows. Such a development gave TSN an immediate competitive advantage that "offered guaranteed exposure for sporting events, which in turn enticed other leagues and event organizers to side with TSN rather than any of the other 'big three' Canadian conventional broadcasters (Global, CTV, and CBC)" (Neversen, 2010, p. 37).

In addition to these developments, other political pressures were also on the horizon for CBC as the neoliberal era ascended (see Chapter 4). In 1984, a new Conservative Prime Minister Brian Mulroney declared the country to be "open for business," setting the stage for the landmark free trade agreement with the United States in 1988. Importantly, the federal government immediately directed CBC to cut its budget by 10% (Raboy, 1996) and initiated a host of market reforms that would eventually lead to the further expansion of the broadcasting system in favour of the private sector. The political and economic pressure on the public broadcaster was further heightened during the early 1990s as a result of the impacts of globalization (see Chapter 14) and the emergence of new satellite and digital technologies that were radically transforming the broadcasting and telecommunication industries. Indeed, all of these developments signalled a decisive "'power shift' towards the subordination of the public interest to private, commercial interests" (Winseck, 1995, p. 101), and the ascension of a new era of "consumer-driven" digital television characterized by unprecedented levels of consumer choice and customized channels (Skinner, 2008).

The entrance of TSN/RDS also radically heightened the competition for popular sport programming. It was at this point that private broadcasters and their ideological allies—most notably the *Globe and Mail*—stepped up their lobbying efforts to force CBC and Radio-Canada to abandon its coverage of the most lucrative and desirable sports, most notably NHL hockey and the Olympic Games (Scherer & Harvey, 2013) during an era of fiscal austerity. However, just as they had done for the past two decades, CBC and Radio-Canada executives vigorously defended the commitment they had made to *HNIC* and *La soirée du hockey* in general, and to televising the playoffs in particular, pointing to the huge audiences that hockey attracts and the advertising revenues that hockey telecasts bring to the network—revenues that subsidize other programming and Canadian content.

While the public sector was dealing with significant cutbacks, the CRTC continued to license new specialty sport channels owned by major corporate players in the broadcasting industry (e.g., Sportsnet[2]), while longstanding regulatory frameworks that kept broadcasting and telecommunications markets separate were rescinded by the federal Liberal government. Barriers that once separated print, broadcasting, telecommunications, and information/computer sectors evaporated and triggered an unprecedented acceleration of mergers and acquisitions (Mosco, 2003). In 2000, for example, BCE bought CTV (Canada's largest private television network) and with it acquired TSN/RDS. BCE then struck an alliance with the country's premier national newspaper the *Globe and Mail* and combined CTV and the Sympatico-Lycos portal (and its other content creation assets) to form Bell Globemedia. A year later, Rogers (the owner of the Toronto Blue Jays) acquired Sportsnet from CTV. Coinciding with these patterns of convergence and concentration was the entrance of digital television and, in 2001, over 200 CRTC-approved digital television channels were launched in Canada, including a host of new specialty sport channels that were financially backed by the most successful and, indeed, pre-established media players in the Canadian market (Neverson, 2010).

All of these developments heralded and encouraged tighter integration in the communications and "infotainment" industries as deep-pocketed media conglomerates like BCE and Rogers began to aggressively compete for premium sport content that could be distributed and cross-marketed to subscribers through a host of integrated digital information and entertainment service arenas. Given their size, Rogers and BCE also have the ability to overpay for various sports broadcasting rights and amortize those costs over various properties and platforms (television channels, Internet, radio, and print properties), including multiple feeds (TSN2, RDS, RDS2, Sportsnet One, etc.) and mobile phones.[3] Rogers and BCE have also joined forces as a consortium to secure broadcasting rights, just as they did to win the rights to the 2010 Winter Olympic Games in Vancouver and the 2012 Summer Games in London with an exorbitant and entirely unprofitable bid of $153 million. As such, these telecommunications giants are now able to vastly outbid CBC/Radio-Canada, which are inevitably limited by constraints on the public purse and lack similar distribution networks.[4]

The End of "Viewing Rights" for Canadians?

Predictably, in the new millennium a number of properties that had once aired on CBC (e.g., CFL football, curling, the 2010/2012 Olympic Games, the FIFA World Cup, MLS Soccer, and the Toronto Raptors) were purchased by BCE and Rogers to supply much needed popular content to their growing number of distribution networks. In 2004, moreover, RDS (and its parent company BCE) secured the exclusive rights for all French-language NHL hockey broadcasts, marking the demise of the venerable *La soirée du hockey* at Radio-Canada and the ability of French Canadians to have over-the-air access to nationally significant sporting events, including the games of the Montreal Canadiens and the Stanley Cup playoffs.

Despite widespread speculation that CBC would suffer a similar fate and lose the national broadcasting rights to NHL hockey and *HNIC*, in 2007 CBC and the NHL signed a new six-year deal rumoured to be worth $600 million—a stunning increase from the previous annual fee of $65 million. The deal was crucial for CBC, which has for many years struggled to develop genuinely popular Canadian content that consistently reaches national audiences throughout the broadcasting week, especially during prime-time hours. *HNIC* also provides CBC with an important promotional platform for the public network, and the show continues to provide a vital revenue stream (long rumoured to be half of CBC's advertising revenue) that subsidizes the wide range of other programming on the network. According to Richard Stursberg (the former head of CBC's English services), so central is *HNIC* to the financing of the public broadcaster that without the show "the CBC would fall into a grave financial crisis that would imperil its survival" (2012, p. 148). Moreover, given its current budgetary cuts, CBC simply could never afford to replace the 400+ hours of prime-time Canadian content with original dramatic programs—programs that would be expected to compete against the most popular US programs that air on CTV and Global. As Stursberg notes,

> An average one-hour drama costs the CBC between $400,000 and $450,000 per hour to commission on a total budget of $1.2–1.4 million (the rest being made up from the Canadian Media Fund and tax credits). Given their normal audiences, Canadian dramas rarely make $200,000 in advertising revenue. This means that each hour of drama commissioned by the CBC produces a loss of at least $200,000. It can be seen, then, that if four hundred hours of hockey were replaced with four hundred hours of drama, the CBC would need to find an additional $80–100 million. At the same time, the Canadian Media Fund would have to be supplemented with another $80–100 million, and the government's television production tax credits would be further drawn by a comparable amount. In other words, if the government wanted the CBC to eliminate hockey and replace it with original Canadian drama, the costs would be somewhere between $240 million and $300 million. (The Tower of Babble: Sins, Secrets and Successes Inside the CBC, Richard Stursburg, 2012, Douglas and McIntyre. Reprinted with permission from the publisher.)

By 2012, it was once again widely anticipated that the public broadcaster would be easily outbid by TSN and Rogers for the English-language hockey broadcasting rights. And in 2013,

Rogers purchased the exclusive Canadian rights to the NHL for the next 12 years at a staggering cost of $5.2 billion while also shutting out its competitor TSN. CBC did, however, manage to secure an agreement with Rogers to continue to air *HNIC* for an additional four years once the public broadcaster's contract with the NHL expires in 2014. While CBC will pay nothing for this arrangement, it will not receive a cent of revenue from the advertising that airs during *HNIC*. Rogers will also assume total editorial control over the show. Still, even without editorial control and the ability to generate advertising income, the continuation of *HNIC* in the short term will provide vital prime-time Canadian content and spare CBC from having to produce other costly original programming to fill the void left by hockey telecasts.

Canadians will have considerable choice in hockey games that will air on a number of Rogers-owned specialty channels (albeit at a cost) in addition to the Rogers-controlled *HNIC* on CBC until at least 2018 (although not in French). However, at the conclusion of that agreement, Canadians from across the country may be required to pay increasingly costly fees to access NHL content on Rogers's television channels and online platforms. These developments will signal the end of the "viewing rights" of Canadians to have access to over-the-air coverage of hockey telecasts (events of national significance), while also marking another stage in the privatization of the sports-media complex. Indeed, CBC and Canadian taxpayers have built and supported the NHL for over 50 years through extensive and high-quality coverage of the sport, although it appears that the private sector is now set to reap the substantial benefits from this historical public foundation.

All of these developments, moreover, raise important questions surrounding the institution of public broadcasting in Canada and the type of role that the public broadcaster should play in contemporary Canadian life. For example, will CBC be able to survive without NHL hockey? Or is it destined to morph into a PBS-like model (subscriber supported) that only provides content that the private networks deem to be unprofitable? What would Canada look like without the presence of a public broadcaster that has the ability to provide a wide range of content (including sport) for all Canadians, regardless of their level of income? Should there be legislation, as there is in Australia and many European countries, to enshrine the "viewing rights" of Canadians to have over-the-air access to sporting events of national significance (Scherer & Rowe, 2013)? These are not solely the private issues of hockey fans, but rather a public matter of national interest that affects all Canadians.

THE IDEOLOGICAL ROLE OF THE MEDIA

(Re)presenting Sport

I have noted throughout this chapter that the organization and structure of various sports have been profoundly transformed into increasingly exciting and dramatic spectacles that could be sold to television networks. These networks, in turn, produced entertaining sports programming to capture the imagination and attention of sizable audiences to be delivered to advertisers. Beginning in the 1960s, the imperatives of television dictated substantial changes to professional (and amateur) sport, including rescheduling game times to prime time to maximize television viewing audiences, the introduction of prearranged television timeouts for advertisers that inevitably interrupt the flow of various games, the relocation of franchises to urban centres with larger television markets (and, hence, the prospect of greater television revenue), and even the creation of entirely new sports that are supported by television revenue (e.g., most recently, Twenty20 cricket). Network executives, meanwhile, lobbied various leagues to make specific rule changes that would make sports even more exciting for television viewers. The NHL, for example, has adopted a number of rules over the years, including shorter overtime periods (with fewer players allowed on the ice) and shootouts to further dramatize the sport of hockey. The NBA implemented the three-point shot to increase scoring, and the American League in MLB approved the use of designated hitters to increase offensive production. The replacement of match play (player against player over 18 holes) for stroke play (where scores cumulate over four days of play) has heightened the drama in golf and made it more appealing to viewing audiences around the world.

As noted above, the economic pressure to cultivate larger television audiences in addition to the wide range of informational possibilities made possible by television and a host of new technologies have radically restructured the live sporting experience as a sports television program. You are likely well aware of the vast differences between attending a live sporting event and watching coverage of sport on television or on various new media devices. Or, as Richard Gruneau, David Whitson, and Hart Cantelon (1988, p. 266) have suggested, "The representation of sport on television . . . presents a different event in which the conventions of camera work and narrative combine to render ideology much more 'present' than it is when one is viewing the event live, without mediation." Rather than merely capturing and recording sporting events, television transforms those events through replays, sounds effects, graphics, close-up camera shots, commercials, and vast amounts of pre- and postgame coverage that "expert" commentators draw from selected dominant narratives and codes. To a large extent, though, it is through the live verbal commentary by the broadcasting team that the television sport narrative is constructed (Goldlust, 1987)—a narrative that privileges certain cultural identities and ideologies "while leaving others meanings and values which could be readily associated with sport very much in the background" (Gruneau et al., 1988, p. 267). In other words, both sport and the media "are important sites in the construction of a 'common sense' which makes existing social practices and social relations seem like reflections of nature rather than products of history" (Gruneau et al., 1988, p. 265).

Televised sporting events are subsequently contoured by producers and commentators according to various hierarchies. These hierarchies include the actual sport selected for television, but also the type of socially constructed content associated and prioritized with the event including personalization strategies (e.g., a focus on individual star athletes and hero-making) and various descriptive and interpretive accounts that are always contextually specific. As noted at the start of this chapter, CBC attempted to cover a CFL game with no audio (other than crowd noise) or special effects, much to the irritation of league officials who recognized that their television product was being devalued and that audiences were tuning out. Clearly, many sporting events need extensive narrative and dialogue to create appealing storylines and dramatic content to realize their potential as television spectacles. For example, the production of alpine skiing events demands considerable narrative, in part to identify individual competitors who wear similar equipment and clothing, but also to simply know who had the best run (Cantelon & Gruneau, 1988). In turn, producers of alpine skiing events work hard to manufacture and emphasize various entertainment values that focus on "spectacle, individual performance, human interest, competitive drama, uncertainty, and risk" (Gruneau, 1989, p. 148). Sports such as baseball, golf, and cricket, meanwhile, require significant amounts of narrative to heighten various dramatic elements to keep the attention of television viewers during lulls in the action (Goldlust, 1987). Other sports that have high levels of continuous drama and action (such as tennis and hockey) simply do not require as much in-game narrative.

Equally interesting is that the "style" of commentary associated with particular sports often varies tremendously and is reflective of the intended television audience:

> For example, compared to most other sports, tennis has been traditionally associated with the middle and upper-middle classes, played in well appointed tennis clubs. The style of television commentary accompanying tennis tends to reflect those social origins. At Wimbledon, the tone of the television commentators is hushed and reverent; they remain silent during the points, as the spectators are expected to do. . . . In sharp contrast, the television commentary accompanying the various codes of football—sports strongly identified with the working and lower-middle classes—tends to be loud, continuous and overly descriptive. (Goldlust, 1987, pp. 96–97)

These sentiments can easily be identified in Canada if we compare some of the commentary on Don Cherry's *Coach's Corner* to coverage of major PGA golf tournaments.

Thus, while the Canadian sports-media complex produces spectacles of accumulation and consumerism, also produced are spectacles of legitimation that socially construct and privilege certain cultural identities and ideologies over others (MacNeill, 1996). In what follows, I present a brief outline of some of the ideological meanings and themes that are prominent within sport media content in Canada. While I have addressed these issues individually, I encourage you to consider how they intersect and connect with each other to form dominant meanings and values.

Gender and Sexuality

Given their substantial investments in sports broadcasting rights and their ownership of various professional sports franchises, it is of no surprise that Rogers and BCE continue to commit significant amounts of airtime to their "properties" on a range of platforms to secure subscribers

Television transforms sport.
ALAN OLIVER/Alamy

and sizable male audiences for advertisers. The most obvious consequence of these economic dynamics is that, despite the growth in the number of girls and women playing sport across the country, coverage of sport in Canada remains almost exclusively devoted to men's professional sport, with the exception of the Olympic Games (every two years) and other sports such as figure skating, curling, golf, tennis, and increasingly coverage of the highly successful Canadian women's soccer team—a perfect example of socially constructed hierarchy. Interestingly, BCE did commit some resources to establishing a specialty digital sport channel exclusively devoted to women's sport, the Women's Sport Network (WTSN) in 2001, but the channel was ultimately abandoned in 2003 for two interrelated reasons. First, WTSN was unable to generate significant audiences to attract advertising revenue, and the executives at BCE were simply unwilling to tolerate even short-term losses to keep the channel on the air and commit to a long-term increase in the coverage of women's sport. However, according to Neversen (2010), the demise of WTSN also needs to be understood in the context of the ideological assumptions held by many of the businessmen in the sports-media complex who simply regard women's sport as an inferior "product" and not worth the airtime.

The fusion of the allied economic and ideological interests of the sports-media complex has, for some scholars, pointed to the ascendance of a "Televised Sports Manhood Formula" (Messner, Dunbar, & Hunt, 2000) as a powerful, overarching narrative that cuts across sports broadcasts and commercials. This formula celebrates popular understandings of hegemonic masculinity (that men should be tough, aggressive, stoic/unemotional, and presumably heterosexual) and consumption in ways that support and expand the economic ambitions of the sports-media complex. For the sociologist Mike Messner (2012), the cumulative impact of the "Televised Sports Manhood Formula" is that it ties many of our own sports fantasies and understandings of masculinity to our own fears, anxieties, and "failures" as men in an ever-changing gender order. The formula, for example, habitually sells boys and men "a glorified package of what masculinity is and should be, regularly nudges us with reminders that we do not measure up to this standard, and then offers compensatory products—beer, underwear, cars, shaving products and, yes, erectile dysfunction medications. . . ." (p. 115).

Male viewers are also routinely exposed to crushing hits ("legal" and otherwise), violent fights between players, and a wide range of other thundering altercations during the ever-present daily highlight shows (e.g., the "hits of the week" clips that air on TSN's *SportsCentre*, Sportsnet's *Connected*, and on weekly segments including Don Cherry's *Coach's Corner* on CBC). So too are audiences presented with a never-ending range of commercials designed to reach male audiences that celebrate and link these actions with various commodities. In fact, so naturalized and lauded is the warrior mentality and the use of men's bodies as weapons (Messner, 1990) that, even after a sequence of catastrophic injuries and the deaths of NHL enforcers Derek Boogaard, Rick Rypien and Wade Belak in 2011, sports fans were provided with only a brief critical discussion of these public issues on the major networks.[5]

Nonetheless, while the audience commodity has historically been a decidedly male one, marketers have slowly come to the realization that they have excluded a significant population of female viewers and, more recently, the lesbian, gay, bisexual, trans, queer (LGBTQ) population (Robinson, 2002). In recent years, there has been a subtle recalculation of the "Televised Sports Manhood Formula," representing a new stage in the commodification of various male athletes and an expansion of the "style" of masculinity to market and sell a wider range of products to both men and women. Recent sports stars including David Beckham, Sidney Crosby, and Dan Carter of the New Zealand All Blacks have each appeared in a variety of sexualized commercials that would have simply been unthinkable for an earlier generation of male athletes. There has certainly been more discussion about LGBTQ athletes (within definite limits) in the Canadian media than ever before, especially as more and more athletes come out (including athletes who are still in the midst of their professional careers, such as basketball player Jason Collins) and as various political projects like the You Can Play campaign gain momentum and are endorsed by high-profile athletes. Still, there is an obvious absence of LGBTQ commentators and sports writers, while old stereotypes continue to linger. During coverage of the 2010 Vancouver Olympic Games, for example, RDS commentators Alain Goldberg and Claude Mailhot engaged in the following dialogue about US figure skater Johnny Weir (Sager, 2010):

> Mailhot: This may not be politically correct, but do you think he lost points due to his costume and his body language?
>
> Goldberg: They'll think all the boys who skate will end up like him. It sets a bad example. We should make him pass a gender test on this point.

I have already discussed some of the limitations surrounding the sheer lack of coverage and systematic under-representation of female athletes and women's sport in the media, including on television and in newspapers and various magazines like *Sports Illustrated*, where female athletes remain largely ignored and silenced. In a longitudinal study of *Sports Illustrated* between 1990–1999, Lumpkin (2009) discovered that only 9.7% of feature articles were on women's sports or female athletes, and the femininity of the athletes was at times highlighted through sexist language. Women, in fact, rarely feature on the cover of *Sports Illustrated*, with the exception of the magazine's swimsuit edition. The Canadian Association for the Advancement of Women and Sport and Physical Activity (CAAWS), meanwhile, produced an annual report that detailed the newspaper coverage of women and sport. For years, the level of coverage of female athletes consistently ranged from 2% to a high of 8%, and CAAWS eventually stopped releasing their reports simply because those numbers never changed (Robinson, 2002).

In a more recent longitudinal study, Cheryl Cooky, Michael Messner, and Robin Hextrum (2013) underscored a familiar paradox: While girls and women are playing sport in greater numbers than ever before in high school, college, and at the professional level, after a brief increase in women's sport coverage between 1989–1999 (5–9%), the coverage of female athletes on US television subsequently descended to its lowest amount of 1.6% in 2009. On a more optimistic note, these researchers found that the pattern of ideological trivialization and sexualization of women in sports broadcasts has declined in recent years. They also observed, however, that female athletes were still framed in relation to four themes: (a) rare moments of respectful coverage, (b) sexualized gag stories, (c) fights, assaults, and scandals, and (d) women as wives, girlfriends, and mothers. Less hopefully, the authors acknowledged that the decline in negative portrayals of women has not "been accompanied by an increase in respectful, routine news coverage of women's sport. Instead, when the news and highlights shows ceased to portray women athletes in trivial and sexualized ways, they pretty much ceased to portray them at all" (Cooky et al., 2013, p. 223).

Despite the continued lack of coverage of female athletes, the digital era and the expansion of various sport highlight shows (e.g., TSN's *SportsCentre*, Sportsnet's *Connected*) have raised the profile of female broadcasters and a small number of reporters, although these trends have simultaneously worked to trivialize the voices of women in the sports-media complex. For the most part, women remain relegated to the role of sideline reporters or as young, sexualized sports anchors employed to seemingly capture the male audience commodity. Indeed, there are

Former gold medal Olympian, Cassie Campbell-Pascall, now commentates for NHL broadcasts to boost male audiences.
Jeff Vinnick/NHLI via Getty Images

regular online discussions about who is Canada's hottest female sportscaster and it scarcely needs stating that these predominantly young and attractive women are held to widely different standards than their male counterparts who exhibit a far greater age range and level of attractiveness (Houston, 2011). Laura Robinson (2002) has described a similar pattern as the "ponytail rule," whereby predominantly young, white, attractive, and presumably heterosexual women receive the lion's share of rare sponsorship and media opportunities in the world of sport. All of these developments, of course, speak to the extent to which the bodies of professional and amateur female athletes (who pose in various men's magazines or calendars to augment their income), in addition to popular female media commentators such as Cassie Campbell, Jennifer Hedger, and Hazel Mae now exist as commodities to attract male audiences.

Militarism and Nationalism

Since the English novelist and social critic George Orwell famously described international sport as "war minus the shooting" in 1945, sport sociologists have drawn our attention to the socially constructed links between nationalism, international sporting contests, and militarism, and how the language of sport commentators has historically been interlaced with military themes and sayings (Burstyn, 1999). Today, coverage of sport remains so heavily saturated and steeped with symbols of national identity, militarism, and hegemonic masculinity that the presence of those images and ideologies—and their seemingly "natural" link to professional men's sport in particular—are often taken for granted. Consider all of the militaristic sayings and "war-speak" that are regularly associated with sport (long-bombs, blitzes, bounties, defensive lines, battling in the trenches). Of course, our regular exposure to images of fighter jets and other military equipment, Canadian Forces personnel, and even the memorialization of fallen Canadian soldiers (e.g., on shows like *Coach's Corner*) has nothing to do with what is happening on the ice or on the football field. The television presentation of these themes, though, is usually elaborately designed and orchestrated to emphasize various dominant ideological positions and national myths (and indeed the military–industrial complex in general), overlapping and equating the context of the hypermasculine "warriors" of professional sport with military personnel and interests (Scherer & Koch, 2010).

Indeed, thanks to its representational power, sport and the media continue to serve as powerful sites through which we tell stories about ourselves, about our communities, and about what it "means to be Canadian." Sport has, of course, long provided popular and compelling spectacles to dramatize dominant national qualities, just as it has also provided occasions for public assertions of "us" versus "them," especially during international sporting competitions like the Olympic Games and other high-profile events including both the 1972 and 1974 Summit Series between Team Canada and the Soviet Union (Scherer & Cantelon, 2013; Scherer, Duquette, & Mason, 2007). In these latter contests, for example, hockey "acted as a medium not just for the expression of national identity, but also for the reaffirmation of a preferred version of 'national character': tough and hard, passionate yet determined, individualistic" (Gruneau & Whitson, 1993, p. 267).

These types of associations have played out in innumerable countries around the world and, as Jean Harvey notes in Chapter 12, various governments continue to link dominant understandings of national identity and national character with the lives of ordinary people and with widely shared popular experiences including sporting events and athletes. In other words, mediated sporting experiences that commonly feature taken-for-granted connections to other national symbols and rituals (e.g., flags, anthems, political leaders) are powerful aspects of what Michael Billig (1995) has called *banal nationalism*—the habitual, day-to-day representations of Canada that work to socially construct powerful hegemonic understandings of national identity, solidarity, and cohesiveness. Still, it's always important to question whether those visions of Canadian identity have inspired anything that even remotely approaches the imagined ideals of a unified nation, especially in light of the fact that there have always been subordinated groups (French Canadians, First Nations, working-class people, and many women) "who have been historically excluded from the process of imagining Canada as a national community" (Gruneau & Whitson, 1993, p. 273).

Race and Ethnicity

The media has significant power in socially constructing and shaping our understandings of race and ethnicity. For example, Chris Spence (1999) and Carl James (2005) have argued that the over-representation of black athletes in heavily mediated sports like basketball and football (and, conversely, the under-representation of black men in other media content and spheres of life) has naturalized a widely held belief that black men are naturally athletic—a belief that has encouraged young men to internalize a sense of biological and cultural destiny and to aspire to be professional athletes above other more "realistic" occupations. Both Chapter 5 on race and ethnicity and Chapter 8 on deviance, meanwhile, have addressed the role of the media in representing high-profile Canadian athletes such as Ben Johnson (Jackson, 1998) and NHL goalie Ray Emery (Lorenz & Murray, 2013) as racial "others," the social construction of stereotypical racial identities in the advertising associated with the Toronto Raptors (Wilson, 1999) and, controversially, the use of indigenous imagery to market and celebrate Canadian identity during the 1976 Montreal Summer Olympics, the 1988 Calgary Winter Olympics, and the 2010 Vancouver Winter Olympics (O'Bonsawin, 2013). There are significant historical antecedents to these issues. For example, Aboriginal marathoner Tom Longboat (1887–1949) was subjected to biased media coverage (see Chapter 5), while the legendary Canadian sprinter Harry Jerome (1940–1982) was the subject of racist media coverage during his athletic career (see the wonderful documentary *Mighty Jerome*). Meanwhile, hockey player Herb Carnegie (1919–2012), who was not allowed to play in the NHL simply because of the colour of his skin, remains unelected to the Hockey Hall of Fame (a form of media).

For many years, the vast majority of sports writers and commentators were, of course, white men who wielded considerable power in terms of not only representing athletes of colour but also in rendering whiteness invisible. Still, Canadian society has undergone substantive demographic change, especially as a result of unprecedented levels of immigration, and these changes have been reflected to some degree in various media content and coverage. Related to this latter point, CBC Sports extended the reach and depth of *HNIC* throughout an increasingly diverse country by providing broadcasts in Punjabi, Mandarin, and Cantonese at different points over the course of the last decade. There is also an increasingly diverse number of television anchors and on-air sports commentators, such as CBC's Kevin Weekes and David Amber, and TSN's John Lu, Farhan Lalji, Jermain Franklin, Cabral Richards, Nabil Karim, and Gurdeep Ahluwalia. However, not all Canadians have welcomed these changes. For example, in 2013 Karim and Ahluwalia were paired together as anchors on TSN's *SportsCentre* and were subjected to a number of racist comments on Twitter by various anonymous trolls (Dowbiggin, 2013). Former MLSE anchor Adnan Virk (who currently works as an anchor at ESPN) responded to the incident by noting that he had never received racist insults while working in the United States while also remarking "Canada has this pluralistic impression of itself and thinks of itself as multicultural. Maybe we're not as forward thinking as we think we are" (Dowbiggin, 2013). Finally, there remains a decisive lack of female journalists and sports commentators of colour in Canada, which may suggest that network executives do not yet regard female minorities as sellable commodities.

SPORTS JOURNALISM AND NEW MEDIA

The profession of sport journalism has been central to the growth of both newspapers and commercial sport, while various journalists have played crucial roles in the social construction of sports news and the representation of sporting events in Canada. Indeed, it is precisely because of their centrality in the sports-media complex itself that significant criticism has been levelled at sports journalists and various pundits for being little more than the "toy department" (Rowe, 2007) of the news media—unabashed promoters of sport and boosters of specific franchises, as opposed to rigorous, investigative, and critical commentators who work at a degree of distance from the sports industry.

Many of these issues have long-term historical antecedents that date back to the foundation of the sports-media complex in the latter decades of the 18th century and the early decades of the 19th century, an era of growth for the advertising-depending press and the consolidation of men's sport (Burstyn, 1999). Aided by the development of the wire telegraph and the establishment of centralized news agencies like Reuters and the American Press, central to the growth of mass newspaper circulation in this era was a "bonding process between the daily press and sport" (Burstyn, 1999, p. 105). Regular sport sections proved to be intensely popular with North American readers, including a growing middle class of mostly male readers (the audience commodity). On this note, regular and detailed newspaper coverage provided various established leagues and competitions with cultural legitimacy and visibility and helped to cultivate fans, resulting in a steady growth of paying spectators—a development that only justified more newspaper coverage and fuelled the promotional role of the press (Lowes, 1999). The early sports writers (nearly always men) "were mainly promoters for the teams and the players with whom they travelled" (Hall, Slack, Smith, & Whitson, 1991, p. 147), and helped to make heroes out of star athletes by mythologizing their athletic exploits while ignoring their private lives. Sports teams recognized the value of this publicity and granted considerable access to athletes in locker rooms (a distinctly gendered occupational structure) in addition to providing media facilities in various arenas, stadiums, and ballparks to accommodate journalists on the sports "beat" (i.e., journalists who cover a specific team throughout the season and provide regular, detailed coverage on a daily basis).

It is precisely because of the close, longstanding, mutually beneficial relationship between sport and the media that the Canadian communications scholar Mark Lowes has simply noted that "Sports journalism is an oxymoron" (quoted in Gilbert, 2011, p. 252). For Lowes, the role of sports journalists and the media in general is not simply to entertain or to provide information and stories, but to market pro franchises, their players, and the major leagues while also creating an endless flow of public buzz "that is indispensable to the franchise owners whose profits depend on filling their stands with paying customers and selling the whole spectacle to television" (quoted in Gilbert, 2011, p. 252). Lowes's point is a crucial one in light of the sheer amount of coverage of game stories, previews, and player profiles, which can all too easily slip into simple cheerleading and boosterism.

It is also important to re-emphasize the synergies between the sports media, wealthy individuals, and the concentrated group of corporations that now own various franchises and exert significant influence in the major sporting leagues. As noted earlier, there is now unprecedented ownership of sporting properties by three dominant telecommunications corporations (Rogers, BCE, and Quebecor) who, increasingly, cover their own franchises on a massive number of platforms and distribution outlets that they also own. How can we possibly expect Rogers's employees to provide substantial critical coverage of the Toronto Blue Jays or the Toronto Maple Leafs (both Rogers's properties)? Or is the main role of sports journalists and commentators to simply promote the expansive range of products and services in the Rogers empire on a continual basis?

The corollary of these ownership patterns and the dominance of this promotional ideology in the pages of the sports section is a "means not to know" about amateur sport, Paralympic sport, and women's sport in general. Indeed, it remains striking just how gendered and incestuous the sports-media complex remains. For example, it is not uncommon for former players and coaches to pursue temporary and sometimes permanent careers as media commentators on sports panel shows that, predictably, promote the economic and ideological interests of the sports-media complex as common sense. And while there have been some gains in terms of the number of female sports journalists and commentators, it will take many more substantial changes to increase the quality and quantity of the coverage of amateur and women's sport simply because of the powerful vested interests that the deeply gendered sports-media complex has in maintaining the economic and ideological status quo. As Gilbert (2011, p. 255) has noted, this is a status quo from which "others, mostly men, stand to gain: owners, management, players, players' agents, union leaders, sports equipment companies, ad agencies—everything that's integral to the professional sports behemoth, including the sports press."[6]

Nonetheless, the work routines and labour practices of sports journalists have undergone substantive changes in recent years, and it is questionable whether sport organizations remain anywhere near as dependent on sports journalists and the pages of the sports section as they were in an earlier era of commercial sport. First, a host of new media technologies have allowed various leagues and individual franchises to independently produce their own content and distribute information and commercial messages without relying on sports journalists or traditional media altogether (Scherer & Jackson, 2008). Most franchises, for example, simply post major announcements (trades, hirings, and firings) on Twitter rather than relying on press releases or individual journalists to break the news. Increasingly, sports teams and organizations are also restricting journalistic access to athletes simply because they can control the flow of information and publicity on their own networks and platforms rather than relying on traditional journalists (although as we shall see below, there have been numerous information "accidents" by both teams and players on various media platforms like Twitter).

Second, the heavily concentrated newspaper industry in Canada has been decimated thanks to declining subscription rates, substantially diminished advertising revenue, and a wide range of issues associated with the adoption of new digital platforms to accommodate new habits of media consumption. Since the 2008 economic recession, newsrooms across the country have suffered significant layoffs, and budgets to various sports departments have undergone sizable cuts as cost-saving and restructuring measures. As a result, sports journalists in Canada are now expected to simply "do more with less" (and on the same salary) and to continually produce unprecedented volumes of content for a host of online platforms (including blogs, podcasts, and various social networking sites like Twitter, let alone their "normal" stories for the newspaper) to appeal to sports fans in the digital era who demand immediate information and interaction. Traditional sports journalists must now compete with other blogs and freelance reporters, leading some observers to bemoan the lack of quality in contemporary sports journalism and the presence of even less critical commentary (Hutchins & Rowe, 2012).

While there is some substance to these claims, Canadian sports fans are far from cultural dupes who apolitically ingest and regurgitate the dominant ideologies embedded in the sports-media complex. For example, in 2000 Canadians resoundingly voiced their opposition to the federal government's proposed subsidy of Canadian NHL franchises to such an extent that Ottawa was embarrassingly forced to rescind their subsidy proposal within days of the original announcement (Scherer & Jackson, 2004). Canadians have also taken to Twitter, for example, to debate issues relating to both hockey and broader political issues during hockey telecasts (Norman, 2012), while other online forums such as sport-related blogs, message boards, YouTube, and various social networking sites (e.g., Facebook) allow for perpetual and at times politicized interaction between media producers, distributors, and users.

On this latter note, the ascension of various new media technologies in the digital era has been one of the significant developments in the formation and normalization of "networked media sport" (Hutchins & Rowe, 2012). Indeed, while an older generation of Canadians consumed sport in an era of relative scarcity of quality sport content and a limited number of analogue television channels, a digital plenitude now prevails and has become an inescapable part of the "normal" rhythm of the daily lives of most Canadians, especially for a younger generation who have grown up in an era where it is simply "natural" to access a seemingly endless amount of digital sports content on phones, tablets, and other devices. However, rather than eroding the audience for televised sport and destroying the televised sport experience, new media technologies are supplementing and enriching the experience of watching sport on television. Indeed, broadcasters like CBC are now encouraging viewers to comment on various issues and engage in discussions on Twitter and Facebook throughout broadcasts of *HNIC*. CBC has even developed a "Second Screen" option that encourages viewers to access a host of additional interactive information and experiences on their smartphones, tablets, and laptop computers in tandem with the actual hockey broadcast itself. The key idea behind these strategies, of course, is to be continually engaged with audiences and sports fans who are encouraged to personalize their experiences with various brands and commodities across as many digital platforms as possible (Scherer, 2007). And it is no surprise that the North American major leagues, the Ultimate Fighting Championship, and the most prestigious European soccer leagues are regularly the leading trending topics on Twitter each week, while television numbers (and the value of broadcasting contracts) remain significant (Hutchins & Rowe, 2012).

Still, the unprecedented level of interactivity in the digital era has also produced new challenges for various sport organizations, media, and even individual athletes who struggle to control information and images in unpredictable online environments. For example, the message boards of various sport organizations need to be continually monitored by media staff for distasteful and abusive comments, while even critical postings about sponsors are often censored and removed (Scherer, 2007). International sport organizations such as the IOC have also established blogging guidelines that contain a range of conditions, including the use of social media, to both protect the commercial interests of sponsors and to discourage athletes from making critical or politically charged comments (Hutchins & Rowe, 2012). Of course, star athletes themselves are now the subjects of an endless stream of comments on Twitter; these new conditions of digital production and consumption have resulted in a number of controversial interactions by various athletes and sport organizations. For example, after Switzerland's 2–1 loss to South Korea at the 2012 Summer Olympic Games, Swiss soccer player Michel Morganella was expelled after he tweeted that he "wanted to beat up South Koreans, that they should 'burn' and that they were a 'bunch of mongoloids'" (Saraceno, 2012). Closer to home, in 2013 Dallas Stars player Tyler Seguin posted anti-gay comments on Twitter, comments he blamed on hackers. Finally, in 2012 NFL player Chad Ochocinco updated his Twitter page during actual games—actions that earned him a $25,000 fine from the NFL (Holden, 2011).

The possibilities of the new digital sporting world seem endless, especially when we further consider the vast growth of sports games and fantasy sports leagues that point to new "transmedia" sport experiences that move between "the television, desktop, computer, tablet, and smartphone screen" (Hutchins & Rowe, 2012, p. 151). The tremendous popularity of EA Sports and the licensing of games by various leagues have resulted in billions of dollars in revenue, while the games themselves are now also important elements in the broadcast and coverage of professional sport. For example, thanks to a partnership between EA Sports and ESPN, game technology was embedded within television coverage, "which then referred back to a computer game that simulated and built upon the television experience enjoyed by both viewers and gamers" (Hutchins & Rowe, 2012, p. 160).

The tremendous popularity of the Microsoft Xbox, Sony PlayStation, and Nintendo Wii are also transforming the experience of sport, physical activity, movement, and play for young people and their families in the comfort of their own homes (Millington, 2009). Finally, fantasy sports leagues are "attention multipliers" (Hutchins & Rowe, 2012, p. 168), and millions of mostly male enthusiasts spend vast amounts of time online and watching television to take stock of injuries, player statistics, and other trends and patterns in the

Fantasy sports leagues and video games are growing in popularity.
Greg Balfour Evans/Alamy

world of professional sport, all in the name of managing "their" teams. What is clear from all of these developments, then, is that it is no longer possible to think of the interplay between these new technologies and consumption habits as "emergent" cultural phenomena, but rather as a dominant set of social relations within the digital sports-media complex.

Conclusions

In this chapter, I have emphasized a range of ideological and political struggles associated with the sports-media complex since the entrance of television in Canadian society. As the competition for sports broadcasting rights has escalated to unparalleled levels, the historical role of CBC and Radio-Canada in providing live telecasts of sporting events of national significance for all Canadians in both official languages as a right of cultural citizenship has eroded considerably. And, thanks to a number of political, economic, and technological developments—coupled with a now dominant ideology of consumer choice—the "winners" in the digital era have been an oligopoly of vertically integrated telecommunications empires (Rogers, BCE, and Quebecor) that now control significant sporting properties in addition to vast digital distribution outlets and media platforms in a near fully privatized sports-media complex. So, too, have various leagues and sport organizations profited handsomely from expansive broadcasting contracts; this is revenue that has been used to pay the increasingly high salaries of professional athletes. Canadians, meanwhile, have access to unprecedented amounts of sport content in the digital era, albeit through increasingly costly subscription packages and other associated products (mobile phones, tablets, etc.).

On this latter note, it is important to remember that one of the most significant and enduring ideological effects of the sports-media complex in Canadian society has simply been the naturalization of consumption practices and our identities as consumers. Indeed, because the dominant institutions in the sports-media complex share both ideological and commercial interests, they subsequently promote a host of cultural identities, social definitions, and ideologies as "natural" and "normal," especially to attract primarily male audiences (as subscribers to various Rogers's or BCE products and services, but also as commodities that are then sold to advertisers). As David Rowe (2004b, p. 7) reminds us, "A trained capacity to decode media sports texts and to detect the forms of ideological deployment of sport in the media, is irrespective of cultural taste, a crucial skill."

Many young Canadians are, of course, well versed in these critical capacities and they realize that the meanings audiences embrace and internalize from programs such as *HNIC* or TSN's *SportsCentre* may not be the precise meanings that were intended by producers and advertisers. Various resistant possibilities are also always present, especially in the digital era, thanks to the agency of individuals and groups with varying degrees of resources. The use of various new media devices and sites such as YouTube has, for example, allowed skateboarders, surfers, BASE jumpers, and individuals who engage in other sporting subcultures (e.g., parkour) to creatively produce alternative content and, at times, to challenge dominant definitions of sport and various social relations. Other new media technologies have allowed citizens to organize and oppose the use of public funds for the construction of arenas and stadiums for professional sports franchises, in addition to a host of other political debates (Scherer & Sam, 2008). As such, the sports-media complex in the digital era will continue to exist as a contested terrain that Canadians shape and are shaped by, albeit against the backdrop of a host of political and ideological struggles that exert powerful sets of limits and pressures on Canadian society.

Critical Thinking Questions

1. What does the term *sports-media complex* mean?
2. How has the Canadian sports-media complex changed since the entrance of television in the 1950s?
3. Why does there remain so little media attention devoted to women's sport?
4. Why has criticism been levelled at sports journalists over the years?
5. Why is sport such a valuable media property in the digital era?

Suggested Readings

Goldlust, J. (1987). *Playing for keeps: Sport, the media and society*. Melbourne, AU: Longman Cheshire.

Hutchins, B., & Rowe, D. (2012). *Sport beyond television: The Internet, digital media and the rise of networked media sport*. New York, NY: Routledge.

Jhally, S. (1984). The spectacle of accumulation: Material and cultural factors in the evolution of the sports/media complex. *Critical Sociology, 12*, 41–57.

Lowes, M. (1999). *Inside the sports pages*. Toronto, ON: University of Toronto Press.

MacNeill, M. (1996). Networks: Producing Olympic ice hockey for a national television audience. *Sociology of Sport Journal, 13*, 103–124.

Scherer, J., & Rowe, D. (Eds.). (2013). *Sport, public broadcasting, and cultural citizenship: Signal lost?* New York, NY: Routledge.

References

Billig, M. (1995). *Banal nationalism*. London, UK: Sage.

Burstyn, V. (1999). *The rites of men: Manhood, politics, and the culture of sport*. Toronto, ON: University of Toronto Press.

Cantelon, H., & Gruneau, R. (1988). The production of sport for television. In J. Harvey & H. Cantelon (Eds.), *Not just a game: Essays in Canadian sport sociology* (pp. 177–193). Ottawa, ON: University of Ottawa Press.

Cavanaugh, R. (1992). The development of Canadian sports broadcasting 1920–1978. *Canadian Journal of Communication, 17*, 301–317.

Connell, R. W. (2005). *Masculinities* (2nd ed). Cambridge, UK: Polity Press.

Cooky, C., Messner, M., & Hextrum, R. (2013). Women play sport, but not on TV: A longitudinal study of televised news media. *Communication & Sport, 1*(3), 203–230.

Dowbiggin, B. (2013). Racist tweets about TSN hosts reveal Canada's nasty side. *Globe and Mail*. Retrieved from http://www.theglobeandmail.com/sports/more-sports/racist-tweets-about-tsn-hosts-reveal-canadas-nasty-side/article9845192/#dashboard/follows.

Gilbert, R. (2011). Playing on the same page. In P. Donnelly (Ed.), *Taking sport seriously: Social issues in Canadian sport* (3rd ed., pp. 251–255). Toronto, ON: Thompson Educational Publishing.

Goldlust, J. (1987). *Playing for keeps: Sport, the media and society*. Melbourne, AU: Longman Cheshire.

Grossberg, L., Wartell, E., Whitney, D., & Wise, J. (Eds.). (2006). *Mediamaking: Mass media in a popular culture*. Thousand Oaks, CA: Sage.

Gruneau, R. (1989). Making spectacle: A case study in television sports production. In L. Wenner (Ed.), *Media, sports, and society* (pp. 134–154). Newbury Park, CA: Sage.

Gruneau, R., & Whitson, D. (1993). *Hockey Night in Canada*. Toronto, ON: Garamond Press.

Gruneau, R., Whitson, D., & Cantelon, H. (1988). Methods and media: Studying the sports/television discourse. *Society and Leisure, 11*, 265–281.

Hall, A., Slack, T., Smith, G., & Whitson, D. (1991). *Sport in Canadian society*. Toronto, ON: McClelland and Stewart.

Holden, E. (2011). The top five most controversial tweets in NFL history: A fan's view. *Yahoo! Sports*. Retrieved from http://ca.sports.yahoo.com/nfl/news?slug=ycn-10497693.

Houston, W. (2011). Women on TV: Looks first, knowledge later. In P. Donnelly (Ed.), *Taking sport seriously: Social issues in Canadian sport* (3rd ed., pp. 256–260). Toronto, ON: Thompson Educational.

Hutchins, B., & Rowe, D. (2012). *Sport beyond television: The Internet, digital media and the rise of networked media sport*. New York, NY: Routledge.

Jackson, S. (1998). A twist of race: Ben Johnson and the Canadian crisis of racial and national identity. *Sociology of Sport Journal, 15*(1), 21–40.

James, C. (2005). *Race in play: Understanding the social-cultural worlds of student athletes*. Toronto, ON: Canadian Scholars' Press.

Jhally, S. (1984). The spectacle of accumulation: Material and cultural factors in the evolution of the sports/media complex. *Critical Sociology, 12*, 41–57.

Kidd, B. (1996a). *The struggle for Canadian sport*. Toronto, ON: University of Toronto Press.

Kuper, S., & Szymanski, S. (2012). *Soccernomics*. New York, NY: Nation Books.

Lorenz, S., & Murray, R. (2013). "Goodbye to the Gangstas": The NBA dress code, Ray Emery, and the policing of blackness in basketball and hockey. *Journal of Sport and Social Issues, 38*(1), 23–50.

Lowes, M. (1999). *Inside the sports pages*. Toronto, ON: University of Toronto Press.

Lumpkin, A. (2009). Female representation in feature articles published by *Sports Illustrated* in the 1990s. *Women in Sport and Physical Activity Journal, 18*, 38–51.

MacNeill, M. (1996). Networks: Producing Olympic ice hockey for a national television audience. *Sociology of Sport Journal, 13*, 103–124.

Marlow, I. (2010). Canadians' Internet use exceeds TV time. *Globe and Mail*. Retrieved from http://www.theglobeandmail.com/technology/canadians-internet-use-exceeds-tv-time/article4352565/#dashboard/follows.

McChesney, R. (2008). *The political economy of media: Enduing issues, emerging dilemmas*. New York, NY: Monthly Review Press.

Messner, M. (1990). When bodies are weapons: Masculinity and violence in sport. *International Review for the Sociology of Sport, 25*(3), 203–320.

Messner, M. (2012). Reflections on communication and sport: On men and masculinities. *Communication & Sport, 1*(1/2), 113–124.

Messner, M., Dunbar, M., & Hunt, D. (2000). The televised manhood formula. *Journal of Sport and Social Issues, 24*(4), 380–394.

Millington, B. (2009). Wii has never been modern: Active video games and the "conduct of conduct." *New Media & Society, 11*(4), 621–640.

Mosco, V. (2003). The transformation of communication in Canada. In W. Clement & L. Vosko (Eds.), *Changing Canada: Political economy as transformation* (pp. 287–308). Montreal, QC: McGill-Queen's University Press.

Neverson, N. (2010). Build it and the women will come? WTSN and the advent of Canadian digital television. *Canadian Journal of Communication, 35,* 27–48.

Nolan, M. (2001). *CTV: The network that means business.* Edmonton, AB: University of Alberta Press.

Norman, M. (2012). Saturday night's alright for tweeting: Cultural citizenship, collective discussion, and the new media consumption/production of Hockey Day in Canada. *Sociology of Sport Journal, 29,* 306–324.

O'Bonsawin, C. (2013). Indigenous peoples and Canadian-hosted Olympic Games. In J. Forsyth & A. Giles (Eds.), *Aboriginal peoples and sport in Canada: Historical foundations and contemporary issues* (pp. 35–63). Vancouver, BC: UBC Press.

Raboy, M. (1990). *Missed opportunities: The story of Canada's broadcasting policy.* Montreal, QC: McGill-Queen's University Press.

Robinson, L. (2002). *Black tights: Women, sport and sexuality.* Toronto, ON: Harper Collins.

Rutherford, P. (1990). *When television was young: Primetime Canada (1952–1967).* Toronto, ON: University of Toronto Press.

Rowe, D. (2004a). Watching brief: Cultural citizenship and viewing rights. *Sport in Society, 7*(3), 385–402.

Rowe, D. (2004b). *Sport, culture and the media* (2nd ed.). Maidenhead, UK: Open University Press.

Rowe, D. (2007). Sports journalism: Still the "toy department" of the news media? *Journalism, 8*(4), 385–405.

Sager, N. (2010). Canadian commentators fail to cool it with Johnny Weir jokes. *Yahoo! Sports.* Retrieved from http://sports.yahoo.com/blogs/olympics-neate-sager/canadian-commentators-fail-cool-johnny-weir-jokes--olympics.html.

Saraceno, J. (2012). Swiss soccer player banned from Olympics for racist tweet. *USA Today.* Retrieved from http://usatoday30.usatoday.com/sports/olympics/london/soccer/story/2012-07-30/swiss-athlete-banned-michel-morganella-olympics/56591966/1.

Scherer, J. (2007). Globalization, promotional culture and the production/consumption of on-line games: Engaging Adidas's Beat Rugby campaign. *New Media & Society, 9*(3), 475–496.

Scherer, J., Duquette, G., & Mason, D. (2007). The Cold War and the (re)articulation of Canadian national identity: The 1972 Canada–USSR Summit Series. In D. L. Andrews & S. Wagg (Eds.), *East plays west: Essays on sport and the Cold War* (pp. 171–194). London, UK: Routledge.

Scherer, J., & Harvey, J. (2013). Televised sport and cultural citizenship in Canada: The "two solitudes" of Canadian public broadcasting? In J. Scherer & D. Rowe (Eds.), *Sport, public broadcasting, and cultural citizenship: Signal lost?* (pp. 48–73). New York, NY: Routledge.

Scherer, J., & Jackson, S. (2004). From corporate welfare to national interest: Newspaper analysis of the public subsidization of NHL hockey debate in Canada. *Sociology of Sport Journal, 21,* 36–60.

Scherer, J., & Jackson, S. (2008). Producing allblacks.com: Cultural intermediaries and the policing of electronic spaces of sporting consumption. *Sociology of Sport Journal, 25,* 243–262.

Scherer, J., & Koch, J. (2010). Living with war: Sport, citizenship, and the cultural politics of post-9/11 Canadian identity. *Sociology of Sport Journal, 27*(1), 1–29.

Scherer, J., & Rowe, D. (Eds.). (2013). *Sport, public broadcasting, and cultural citizenship: Signal lost?* New York, NY: Routledge.

Scherer, J., & Sam, M. (2010). Policing the cyber agenda: New media technologies and recycled claims in a local stadium debate. *Sport in Society, 13*(10), 1469–1485.

Scherer, J., & Cantelon, H. (2013). 1974 WHA All Stars vs. the Soviet national team: Franchise recognition and foreign diplomacy in the "forgotten series." *Journal of Canadian Studies, 47,* (2), 29–59.

Skinner, D. (2008). Television in Canada: Continuity or change? In D. Ward (Ed.), *Television public policy: Change and continuity in an era of global liberalization* (pp. 3–26). New York, NY: Lawrence Erlbaum Associates.

Smythe, D. W. (1977). Communications: Blindspot of Western Marxism. *Canadian Journal of Political and Social Theory, 1*(3), 1–27.

Sparks, R. (1992). Delivering the male: Sports, Canadian television, and the making of TSN. *Canadian Journal of Communication, 17,* 319–342.

Spence, C. (1999). *The skin I'm in: Racism, sports, and education.* Halifax. NS: Fernwood.

Stursberg, R. (2012). *The tour of babble: Sins, secrets and successes inside the CBC.* Vancouver, BC: Douglas & McIntyre.

Whannel, G. (1992). *Fields in vision: Television sport and cultural transformation.* London, UK: Routledge.

Whannel, G. (2005). The five rings and the small screen: Television, sponsorship, and new media in the Olympic movement. In K. Young & K. Wamsley (Eds.), *Global Olympics: Historical and sociological studies of the modern Games* (pp. 161–178). Amsterdam, Netherlands: Elsevier.

Whitson, D. (1998). Circuits of promotion: Media, marketing and the globalization of sport. In L. Wenner (Ed.), *MediaSport* (pp. 57–22). New York, NY: Routledge.

Wilson, B. (1999). "Cool pose" incorporated: The marketing of black masculinity in Canadian NBA coverage. In P. White & K. Young (Eds.), *Sport and gender in Canada* (pp. 232–253). Toronto, ON: Oxford University Press.

Winseck, D. (1995). Power shift? Towards a political economy of Canadian telecommunications and regulation. *Canadian Journal of Communication, 20*(1), 81–106.

Endnotes

1. The next three sections are derived from Scherer and Harvey (2013).

2. Launched in 1998 by CTV as a regional network (with four feeds for different regions), Sportsnet provided coverage of local teams, providing an important revenue stream for those franchises.

3. In a move to prevent mobile content hoarding, in 2011 the CRTC ruled that vertically integrated telecommunications companies like BCE must make their sports content available under reasonable terms (i.e., price) to competing mobile phone and Internet providers (e.g., TELUS).

4. Unlike the public broadcaster, Rogers and BCE can recover some of their costs through multiple revenue streams: ads, subscription rates, and the "fees for carriage" that they receive from other satellite and cable companies.

5. In fact, even after these tragedies Don Cherry publicly castigated those who critiqued the levels of violence and fighting in hockey as "pukes" and "hypocrites." For decades, Cherry has routinely policed the behaviour of various players—including star player Sidney Crosby and the hypermasculine style of Canadian hockey—and has, incidentally, profited handsomely from his role as an outspoken CBC commentator on *Hockey Night in Canada* and from the sales of his *Rock'Em Sock'Em* videos that have, for years, showcased and glorified violence.

6. Still, it's important to acknowledge that several Canadian sports journalists and commentators have produced a number of insightful analyses that have elevated public understandings of a range of issues (e.g., violence in sport and the changing economics of professional sport), while others, including US writer Dave Zirin, have provided consistent critical commentary on sport and social relations for many years now.

Chapter 12
Sport, Politics, and Policy

Jean Harvey

The once taken-for-granted idea that "sport doesn't mix with politics" has now vanished. For example, one of the most visible aspects of the link between sport and politics in Canada is the struggle over the allocation of scarce public resources for the funding and regulation of sport. Various groups, including national sport organizations (NSOs), provincial sport organizations (PSOs), and local sport clubs, all call on their respective levels of government to help them develop, fund, and administer competitive local, provincial, national, and international teams. Government funding is also expected for grassroots sport, high-performance sport, as well as for the construction of venues for hosting global mega-sport events such as the FIFA World Cup and the Summer and Winter Olympic Games. Regulations developed by international sport organizations such as the World Anti-Doping Agency (WADA) and the IOC not only command the attention of governments but also, to a certain degree, impose themselves on national, provincial, or territorial sport policies. Given such interrelationships, the issue is not whether the state should intervene in sport, but *where* the state "invests" in sport and

Nelson Mandela hands the 1995 Rugby World Cup to South African team captain Francois Pienaar. Mandela used the positive side of sport to unite post-apartheid South Africa, a great historical moment immortalized in the film *Invictus*. Gallo Images/Alamy

This chapter will use a number of acronyms. Here is a synopsis of the most common ones that you should be aware of.

AAP	Athlete Assistance Program
CAAWS	Canadian Association for the Advancement of Women and Sport and Physical Activity
CCES	Canadian Centre for Ethics in Sport
COC	Canadian Olympic Committee
CS4L	Canadian Sport for Life
CSP	Canadian Sport Policy
FIFA	Fédération Internationale de Football Association
IOC	International Olympic Committee
LTAD	Long-Term Athlete Development
MSO	Multi-Sport Organization
NAFTA	North American Free Trade Agreement
NSO	National Sport Organization
PSO	Provincial Sport Organization
SDRC	Sport Dispute Resolution Centre
SSP	Sport Support Program
UN	United Nations
WADA	World Anti-Doping Agency
WOG	Winter Olympic Games

what interventions and public policies become ascendant against the backdrop of a range of political struggles, debates, and competing power relations.

But fundamentally, the relationship between sport and politics is much more complex because it is deeply rooted in the social nature of sport. As noted in Chapter 1, sport is itself a contested terrain and the site of significant ideological struggle. The relationship of politics to sport prompts numerous questions: Is sport a private matter or a public good? Which social and ideological values should orient sport? Who should have access to participation in sport? How should mass and high-performance sport be funded, structured, and for what ends? Should sport be the responsibility of the state or left entirely to private organizations like PSOs? What is the role of municipalities with regard to the provision of sport facilities and programs across the country?

SPORT AS A SITE FOR POLITICAL RESISTANCE

As sport is closely entrenched in societal power relations, it has the potential to be a tool both for the reproduction of dominant power relations and for political resistance and change. For example, when governments invest heavily in high-performance sport, they hope that the victories of the athletes will bolster dominant views about national identity and raise their international profile. Conversely, high-performance sport can also be the site of resistance to dominant ideological values and various power relations. For example, at the Mexico 1968 Olympics, US athletes Tommie Smith and John Carlos raised their gloved fists as they stood on the podium; their Black Power salute was meant as an act of resistance to existing racial power relations in their country (see Zirin, 2005).

The history of the modern Olympics also provides various examples of encounters between sport and politics, through boycotts, protests, and the banning of specific

Sport can be a site of political resistance.
HANDOUT/KRT/Newscom

countries. Indeed, since their formation in Ancient Greece and their resurrection by
Pierre de Coubertin in 1894, the Olympic Games have been and are deliberately used
by nation-states for a variety of international policy purposes. For example, under the
leadership of Adolf Hitler, the 1936 Berlin Games were meant to showcase to the
world the cause of National Socialism, Nazi ideology, and the superiority of the Aryan
race. Several countries threatened to boycott the games because, initially, Hitler simply did not want Jews and black people participating. In Canada, for example, the
Workers' Sports Association, as well as religious, university, and veterans' group leaders, were in favour of boycotting the Nazi Olympics (Kidd, 1996). Eventually, Hitler
was forced to concede to international pressure and lifted some restrictions. Ironically,
his orchestrated display of white superiority was ruined by the outstanding performance
of black US athlete Jesse Owens, who won four gold medals in track and field. In
another example of the fusion between sport and politics, when the Olympics returned
to Germany in 1972, 11 Israeli athletes and trainers were tragically killed by Palestinian
extremists—an event that was explored in the documentary *One Day in September* and
the film *Munich*.

The intense public protest by various anti-racist movements, most notably the 1964
banning of South Africa by the IOC in objection to apartheid, is another strong example
of the ways in which sport has historically been used to heighten diplomatic and ideological pressure on countries. In fact, the isolation of South Africa from international
competition became almost all-encompassing after the General Assembly of the United
Nations (UN) passed a resolution in 1971 inviting countries not to participate or compete with those upholding discrimination or apartheid laws and policies. This provision

The 1936 Olympic Games in Berlin were used by Hitler as a tool for propaganda in favour of his racist political regime.
ZUMA Press, Inc/Alamy

subsequently spurred a request to ban New Zealand from the 1976 Summer Games in Montreal in protest against a series of rugby matches played between the New Zealand All Blacks and the South African Springboks. However, New Zealand was not banned, and as a result most African countries boycotted the Montreal Olympics. The next Olympic Games, held in Moscow in 1980, were also marked by a boycott, this time by the United States and several Western countries including Canada in protest against the invasion of Afghanistan by the Soviet Union. Meanwhile, communist countries from the former Eastern Bloc, with the exception of Romania, exacted their "revenge" four years later by boycotting the 1984 Los Angeles Olympic Games, alleging that the United States was simply not safe for their athletes.

Not only do governments use sport to pursue international policy, but social movements also use globally mediated sport events to persuade governments to act in favour of their political causes and ideological claims (Harvey, Horne, Safai, Darnell, & Courchesne-O'Neill, 2013). For example, the 2008 Beijing Olympic and Paralympic Games torch relay itinerary became a road paved with protests and demonstrations against the alleged Chinese occupation of Tibet and the poor record of China with regard to human rights. Prior to and during the 2010 Winter Olympic Games in Vancouver, a number of political coalitions fought for a range of issues, including the housing rights of low-income residents, the land rights of several First Nations groups, and pressing environmental issues (Boycoff, 2011). These protests are not going to fade away anytime soon. Indeed, while writing this chapter the streets of Rio de Janeiro were filled with mass demonstrations prior to the 2014 FIFA World Cup and the 2016 Olympic and Paralympic Games in protest of the rising cost of public services in the midst of massive financial investments by the state for these mega-sporting events.

GOVERNMENT INVOLVEMENT IN SPORT

Government involvement in sport in Canada is, of course, far from new. In the second half of the 19th century local governments in big cities like Montreal and Toronto created municipal parks. For several decades, these parks played a major role in preventing the working class from participating in sport through regulations that restricted the types of sports that were allowed on their grounds (Gruneau, 1983). While municipal parks were mainly conceived as peaceful and quiet retreats from the busy streets for the benefit of the urban elite, working-class sports were regularly banned from these public places. The enactment of the Lord's Day Act by the federal government in 1906, which banned the practice of sport on Sundays, was another state intervention that limited opportunities for the working class to play sports (Kidd, 1996a).

At the beginning of the 20th century, however, municipalities started to play a different role as a result of political pressure from different organizations such as the National Council of Women of Canada, which lobbied for vacation schools and supervised playgrounds as ways to prevent youth delinquency. As a result, over the last century municipalities have become increasingly involved in recreational sport through the subsidization of playground associations and local clubs, as well as through the development and maintenance of increasingly large numbers of sports fields and venues. Moreover, lobbied by the bourgeoisie to control urban masses after World War II, municipalities invested further in providing sport participation opportunities for their citizens, a role they still play today. Indeed, parks and recreation represent a significant item in current municipal budgets across the country.

The Great Depression of the 1930s prompted greater federal and provincial involvement in sport and recreation simply because of the growing numbers of unemployed youth and adults who, in their unrest, represented fertile material for leftist movements, reformist groups, and various forms of political resistance. Again, these interventions were exclusively meant as social control measures. In December 1936, the National Employment Commission of Canada prompted the Minister of Labour to establish young men's physical training centres, the goal of which was to help unemployed men develop good levels of mental and physical fitness to maintain their employability. The minister soon agreed to this recommendation and provisions were made to create training centres under the Unemployment and Agricultural Assistance Act (1937) as well as under the Youth Training Act (1939). These programs involved cost-sharing agreements with participating provinces to fund a wide variety of youth training opportunities that often involved gymnastics and other sports (Harvey, 1988). For constitutional reasons, however, not all provinces agreed to participate in these programs, a point we shall return to later on. During World War II, the federal government turned its attention to physically preparing citizens to serve in the war. To that end, the National Physical Fitness Act was passed in 1943 (and was later repealed in 1954).

The reconstruction effort at the end of World War II created a context for the transformation of the Canadian state into a welfare state (a definition of *state* is provided in the next section). A welfare state is one in which organized power is deliberately used to play a more active role in the economy and society, for example, by providing a minimum income for all as well as some state-financed social services like education and health insurance. This renewed role of the Canadian state in this era set the stage for more active involvement in sport. But according to Macintosh, Bedecki, and Franks (1987), the adoption in 1961 of Bill C-131, an act to encourage fitness and amateur sport, was predominantly the result of the government's increased preoccupation and focus on high-performance sport and the promotion of Canadian nationalism through sport.

Since the adoption of Bill C-131, the federal government has been increasingly active in the administration and governance of sport. Moreover, several historic events attracted the attention of the House of Commons, such as the 1972 Canada–USSR hockey Summit Series and the 1988 Ben Johnson doping scandal. The 1972 Summit Series was a highly volatile moment for Canadian sport and for Parliament Hill in Ottawa—not simply because it represented a symbolic confrontation between East and West, but also because the event was expected to restore Canadian nationalism via victory in its national winter sport. The Ben Johnson doping scandal at the 1988 Seoul Olympics also commanded significant political attention and intense debate in the House of Commons, and resulted in the striking of a Royal Commission, commonly referred to as the Dubin Inquiry, with a mandate to investigate the Johnson affair and the broader use of performance-enhancing drugs in Canadian sport (Dubin, 1990). The report eventually recommended that the Canadian government adopt a strict anti-doping policy and prompted the creation of the Canadian Centre for Ethics in Sport (CCES), an arm's-length organization, to control and police the use of performance-enhancing drugs in sport.

In summary, the relationship between sport and politics is complex, multifaceted, and deeply ideological and can only be understood against the backdrop of a wide range of conflicts between various social groups (with varying amounts of resources) as they struggle for power. In this chapter, I will focus specifically on an overview of current sport policies and programs in Canada, although, as we shall see, it is difficult in our globalized world to understand national policy without considering the larger international context and various global structures. I will try to answer the following questions throughout this chapter: What motivates nation-states like Canada to get involved in sport? What constitutional and political contexts at the domestic and international levels influence the development of sport policies in Canada? What are the key current sport policies in Canada? Before answering these questions, a brief review of some key concepts is in order.

DEFINING SOME KEY CONCEPTS

State, power, government, politics, policy, and programs—it is easy to become swamped and overwhelmed by political science and political sociology terminology. Anthony Giddens defines politics as "The means by which power is used to influence the nature and content of governmental activities" (1989, p. 729). This definition, by itself, speaks to the broad social reality that is covered by the word *politics*. The definition also refers to two other concepts: power and the state. In Chapter 1, power was defined as the ability of individuals or groups to use resources to secure an outcome, even in the face of opposition. For Giddens, *government* is "the process of enacting of policies and decisions on the part of officials within a political apparatus" (p. 727), while a *state* is "a political apparatus (governmental institutions, such as court, parliament, civil service, officials) ruling over a given territory, whose authority is backed by the legal system and by the capacity to use force to implement its policies" (p. 732).

The main characteristics of a modern nation-state are its sovereignty over a given territory; its monopoly of the use of force; its legitimacy, mainly provided by its democratic electoral system; and the fact that its constituents are defined as citizens who have both formal rights and duties and who generally recognize themselves as part of a given nation. A key question to ask, then, is "What is the role of the state in contemporary society?" Before attempting to answer this question, it is important to emphasize that any social institution is the product of history and the result of power relations among social classes, gender, race, and so on. This is a critical point to remember when examining theoretical traditions in political science and their differing visions of the role of the state.

For the purpose of this chapter, I will limit my discussion to the two main opposing theoretical positions. For *pluralists*, the state is a neutral referee of competing social interests. For them, in theory, no specific organized interest group has more persuasive power over others regarding the orientation or direction of state policies. For *Marxists*, meanwhile, the state needs to be understood as the instrument of the ruling capitalist class in its domination of society (refer to Chapter 2). Although many nuances have added to that bold statement, the Marxist approach is a better reflection of the unequal influence different social classes with varying resources have on the state. More specifically, the advanced capitalist state has three overall functions. The first is to adopt measures that allow the accumulation of capital including, for example, investments in transportation infrastructure, the adoption of labour laws that keep salaries at the lowest possible levels for Canadian companies to remain competitive, and policies that mandate low levels of taxation to attract private investment. The second function is to preserve social cohesion. This is achieved through measures that ease tensions between the interests of the dominant class and the dominated classes. At the minimum, the state has to give the impression that it is not the sole servant of the dominant class if it wants to keep its legitimacy. Finally, the third function of the state is one of coercion, as the state has a monopoly over the use of force to preserve social order (Harvey & Proulx, 1988).

Modern nation-states have sovereignty over a given territory but interact with other nation-states as part of their international relations. In addition, a panoply of supranational organizations, such as the United Nations, the G7, the World Trade Organization, and treaties like the North American Free Trade Agreement create a context that influences the actions and policies of individual nation-states. In the current context of globalization, many authors argue that nation-states are ceding sovereignty to these organizations (see Chapter 14 on globalization) because national policies have to be at least partially in line with the international context. For example, the Canadian sport doping policy has to follow WADA regulations in order for Canada to be able to compete in the Olympics and most amateur international sporting events.

Another example of "evasion of sovereignty" was the Olympic and Paralympic Marks Act enacted in 2008 by the federal government. This law was literally imposed on the Canadian state by the IOC as part of the hosting requirements for the 2010 Games. A third and final example that other chapters have noted was the IOC's refusal to include women's ski jumping in the program of the 2010 Games in Vancouver and the subsequent controversial court decision that ruled that the protection of the Canadian Charter of Rights and Freedom did not apply to the IOC (Barnes, 2010). In each of these examples, a nonelected international body was simply able to impose its will upon a democratically elected sovereign government—a classic example of power.

Building the concepts of politics and the state, let's explore the concepts of government, policy, and programs. Giddens (1989) states that "government refers to the regular enactment of policies and decisions on the part of officials within a political apparatus . . . we can speak of government as a process, or of *the* government, referring to the apparatus responsible for the administrative process" (p. 301). While politics is concerned with the means by which power is used, *policy* or *public policy* refers to "a course of action or inaction chosen by public authorities to address a given problem or interrelated set of problems" (Pal, 2006, p. 2). It is important to emphasize that a decision by a government not to act on a specific issue is often, by itself, a policy. Finally, there is a fine line between programs and policies. *Policies* are mostly "guides to a range of related actions in a given field" (Pal, 2006, p. 2), while *programs* are the specific courses of action taken in view of fulfilling the goals of a policy.

Governments do possess a wide variety of action tools or policy instruments for the implementation of policies and programs. Although there are a wide variety of policy instrument typologies, let's adapt Leslie Pal's (2006) classification system for the purposes of this chapter. The first broad category refers to tools of *indirect action:* Information is the first tool in this category, which can be the preferred course of action in the case of health promotion, for example. Such was the case with ParticipACTION, a social marketing program whose focus was to encourage Canadians to become more physically active. The second type of tool is expenditures, which can take several forms. Government funding as an indirect action for national, provincial, and local associations falls into this category. The third type of tool in this category relates to regulations that are explicitly made to promote or discourage certain types of behaviour, such as anti-doping policies that prohibit the use of banned performance-enhancing substances.

The second main category in Pal's classification system refers to tools of *direct action.* In this instance, state agencies are created to implement policies where the state is the delivery provider, such as the case of provincial departments of education and of health and social services. State or Crown corporations, such as Canada Post and CBC/Radio-Canada, are arm's-length agencies that offer direct public services in lieu of the state and are responsible to the House of Commons for their actions. Finally, in our neoliberal times, where state-provided public services are increasingly criticized by right-wing forces, third-party arrangements like public–private partnerships are believed within right-wing circles to be the best tool for efficient intervention. In short, tools for state intervention are numerous, but as I will outline later in the chapter, the choice of possible tools varies widely from one policy field to another as a function of the perceived overall role of the state in each of these fields.

Now that we have established a minimal basis for understanding politics and policy in our society, let's turn to the specific domain of sport and politics—which, like any other domain, has its own specificities, issues, and problems that influence and are influenced by state intervention.

REASONS FOR STATE INTERVENTION IN SPORT

At the beginning of this chapter I provided several examples of state intervention in sport. This intervention is not without issues and problems, however. One good way of getting an organized perspective of this issue is to identify what generally motivates the state to intervene in sport. Over the course of history, these motivations obviously change as new problems and issues arise, but they also change as social forces and various interest groups influence what constitutes the legitimate role of the state in society. For example, compared to the 19th century, the Canadian state is now much more interventionist in its actions. In the first known book on sport and politics, Jean Meynaud (1966) identified three major motives for public authorities to intervene in sport: (a) to safeguard public order, (b) to improve the physical fitness of the citizens, and (c) to affirm national prestige. According to Meynaud, the safeguarding of public order is an issue for the state since hosting major sporting events involves security issues and because sport is sometimes the cause of violence, on or off the field (see Chapter 9). For Meynaud, doping in sport also constitutes an issue of public order since it sometimes involves the use of banned substances. Five decades after Meynaud's work, sport has become an even more important social phenomenon, while the reasons for state intervention in sport have diversified.

I have regrouped these contemporary motives for state intervention in sport into four main categories. First, governments see sport as an ideological instrument of social cohesion. For example, high-performance sport is considered an important tool for the promotion of national unity. Governments believe that the medals and trophies earned by Canadian athletes around the globe contribute to the fostering of national pride as well as to the promotion of dominant understandings of Canadian identity. Sport is also perceived as a tool of social cohesion for at-risk populations, particularly at-risk youth, since it allegedly contributes to the prevention of delinquency. In these instances, sport also serves as a function of social control.

Second, governments increasingly use sport as an instrument of economic development (or capital accumulation). For example, hosting mega-sporting events allegedly contributes to the tourism industry by attracting athletes and visitors to the host cities. Moreover, hosting major events or having professional sport franchises is widely believed by governments to have a high economic and symbolic impact, and to help cities showcase themselves as world-class tourist destinations and ideal locations for all kinds of businesses and industries (see Chapter 13).

Third, sport is also an instrument of foreign policy. To this end, states use sport to push specific political agendas, as we have seen earlier with the international struggle against apartheid. Conversely, states also see sport as an instrument to foster international cooperation, as is the case with the Commonwealth Games and the Jeux de la Francophonie, whose functions are to increase political and economic relationships among "communities" of countries.

The fourth and final category of motivations for state intervention in sport is related to social development and the promotion of social inclusion. Sport is popularly believed to contribute to the education and health of individuals and to their participation in society as active citizens. To that end, inclusive policies are put in place by various governments to reduce social and economic barriers and to promote equity for women and men and for visible and cultural minorities.

The above description provides a wide overview of the motives of modern advanced capitalist states to deliberately intervene in sport, but not all interventions are planned or premeditated. At times, governments are forced to react and act quickly as a result of a sudden crisis, as was the case with the Ben Johnson scandal in 1988, which forced the government to create the Dubin Inquiry that investigated sport doping. Finally, the above description doesn't include the more mundane motivations of individual politicians to use sport and various athletes to boost their profile among their electorate.

THE SPORT–POLICY CONTEXT

To better understand the shape and direction of current federal sport policies and programs, I wish to return briefly to both the constitutional as well as the specific political contexts that forge sport policy in this country. First, it is of utmost importance to remember that, by its Constitution, Canada is a federal state with two major orders of government: the federal and the provincial/territorial. As such, municipalities are the creation of provinces/territories. The Constitution defines, although not always clearly, the jurisdiction of the federal government and of the provinces/territories, but there is nothing in the Constitution on sport. However, sport is generally associated with social policies, particularly education and health policy, both of which are under provincial/territorial jurisdiction. International sport is linked to Canada's foreign policy, which is clearly under federal jurisdiction. The High Performance Athlete Development in Canada agreement of 1985 and the National Recreation Statement of 1987 were passed to delineate more precisely the mutual roles of the federal and provincial/territorial governments. Similarly, in 2013 sport, physical activity, and recreation ministers agreed on an updated version of the first two agreements that further delineated each level of government's areas of responsibility. The 1985 agreement recognized the jurisdiction of the federal government on the national and international levels, while provinces and territories maintained control over and responsibility for the provincial/territorial and municipal levels of the sport system. The 1987 statement recognized the primary role of the provinces and territories in the area of recreation, including sport. Presented in this manner, the situation appeared straightforward.

Unfortunately, the outcome did not unfold as planned. For example, hosting major international sporting events primarily involves cities that orchestrate the bid process, but international sport falls under the jurisdiction of the federal government and, therefore, cities cannot bid for the event without the permission of the provinces/territories and without the financial help of the higher levels of government. Any federal government intervention in municipalities, moreover, requires provincial approval. While several provinces have a history of flexibility on these arrangements when the federal government has money to spend within their borders, other provinces are very strict in the preservation of their jurisdiction. As far as foreign policy is concerned, some provinces do request a presence on the international scene—such is the case with the Jeux de la Francophonie, where Quebec, New Brunswick, and Ontario have their own delegations in addition to a Canadian delegation (see Harvey, 2013).

The other set of considerations touches on what we call a policy field. A *policy field* is a relatively autonomous regrouping of policies related to a defined area of public policy (the field of economic policy, the field of sport policy, etc.). Each policy field has a specific culture, a set of norms and values about the general role of the state in that field at a given time in history. For each policy field, there is generally a state agency or governmental department under the responsibility of a cabinet minister that is in charge of policy development and implementation and, moreover, a specific set of social forces, power relations, or interest groups that are active. Having different agendas, these social forces constantly lobby government for their views to be considered.

Arguably, sport constitutes in itself a specific policy field, although it is related to education, health, and foreign policy. In this country, according to the current dominant neoliberal vision, the state should not intervene too directly in sport. Indeed, major interest groups like the Canadian Olympic Committee (COC) and NSOs are constantly lobbying for more funding by the federal government and, at the same time, less government control. However, other groups, such as the Canadian Association for the Advancement of Women and Sport and Physical Activity (CAAWS), are in favour of strong government regulations to force sport organizations to implement stronger gender-equity programs. As a private enterprise, professional sport does not normally want state intervention in its business affairs (unless requiring direct subsidies). Given the characteristics of the sport field, it would probably appear inappropriate for the Canadian state to take full control of the Canadian sport system through the creation of, for example, a Crown corporation (i.e., a state-owned independent corporation). Nevertheless, the Canadian government plays an increasingly prominent role in the governance of Canadian sport, namely through its imposition of strict conditions and criteria as part of the financial support it provides to NSOs and multi-sport and service organizations (MSOs), such as Commonwealth Games Canada.

The prominent role played by the federal government leads to the last set of considerations regarding the context of sport policy. It is rare that the state does not put in place a formal administrative unit in charge of the delivery of policies and programs, and sport is no exception. With the adoption of Bill C-131 in the early 1960s, a fitness and amateur sport program emerged under the Ministry of Health and Welfare. In 1971, two separate units were created under the fitness and amateur sport directorate: Sport Canada and Recreation Canada. With Sport Canada, the federal government created an administrative unit to intervene in the world of high-performance sport, until then the exclusive territory of NSOs and MSOs. Currently, two separate units in two different departments are in charge of sport and physical activity. First, Sport Canada, a branch of Canadian Heritage, remains largely in charge of high-performance sport. Second, the Healthy Living Unit is within the Centre for Health Promotion, a division of the Public Health Agency of Canada, and is in charge of promoting physical activity in its broadest sense for all Canadians. Indeed, because the federal government, starting with the government of Pierre Trudeau in 1968, has increasingly used high-performance sport as a vehicle for the promotion of national unity and international prestige on the world sporting stage, high-performance sport has become the priority over mass participation.

In summary, a complex range of constitutional, political, and administrative structures and forces, as well as pressure from organized interest groups, make up state intervention in any policy field in Canadian society. I shall return to these issues later in the next section where I describe the main policies and programs that constitute the core of Canadian sport policy.

RECENT POLICIES AND PROGRAMS

In 2002, a Canadian Sport Policy (hereafter CSP 2002) was adopted with the provision that it had a life expectancy of 10 years. Accordingly, in 2010 the federal and provincial governments undertook several initiatives to evaluate the policy and its impacts. One of the early initiatives was the commission of an evaluation report based on document analysis and interviews with key players. The commission came to the conclusion that CSP 2002 has been largely successful in achieving its goals, but that the participation pillar has been the neglected child of the family (Sutcliffe Group, 2010).

Clearly, the 2002 policy had to be revisited. Moreover, since 2002, the sport policy field had changed significantly. New players were increasingly active in the field and new trends had emerged. The Canadian Sport for Life (CS4L)/Long-Term Athlete Development (LTAD) model, for example, was becoming increasingly influential and was subsequently entrenched in Sport Canada's contributions criteria to NSO funding. Moreover, thanks to pressure by groups such as the Sport Matters Group and Sport for Development, the use of sport to reach desirable social development goals was increasingly a candidate for inclusion in the CSP. Finally, the 2010 Vancouver Olympic Games raised all kinds of questions as to what should be done next for the development of sport in Canada. It is in this context that an extensive consultation and engagement process was put in place that eventually led to a largely revised Canadian Sport Policy (hereafter CSP 2012), which was adopted by the federal, provincial, and territorial sport ministers in June 2012.

Like its predecessor, CSP 2012 reads more like a comprehensive framework to guide policy action and a "road map" in the language of the policy rather than a precise set of goals and targets, thus allowing the diverse partner governments to emphasize the aspects of the framework that better suit their needs and will. Moreover, compared to all previous policies, CSP 2012 promotes a broad definition of sport and its potential impacts on society.

Figure 12.1 illustrates the wide scope that this new policy is meant to embrace. This broad policy scope stems from an overall vision for "a dynamic and innovative culture that promotes and celebrates participation and excellence in sport" and where

> Canada is a leading sport nation where all Canadians can pursue sport to the extent of their abilities and interests . . . including performing at the highest competitive levels; and where sport delivers benefits, for increasing numbers, to individual health and well-being, and contributes to socioeconomic incomes. (Canadian Heritage, 2012)

Linked to this vision are various policy values (safety, excellence, commitment, etc.) and core policy principles (i.e., value based, inclusive, technically sound, collaborative, intentional, effective, sustainable).

Moreover, the policy framework recognizes four contexts of sport participation: high performance, competitive sport, recreational sport, and introduction to sport (as well as physical literacy). Each participation context corresponds to a broad goal. For introduction to sport, the goal is simply that "Canadians have the fundamental skills, knowledge and attitudes to participate in organized and unorganized sport" (Canadian Heritage, 2012, p. 3). For recreational sport, the broad goal is for Canadians to "have the opportunity to participate in sport for fun, health, social interaction and relaxation" (p. 3). With regard to competitive sport, the goal is for Canadians to "have the opportunity to systematically improve and measure their performance against others in competition in a safe and ethical manner" (p. 3). In high-performance sport, meanwhile, the goal is for Canadians to be "systematically achieving world-class results at the highest levels of international competition through fair and ethical means" (p. 3). Finally, CSP 2012 also addresses sport for development: "[S]port is used as a tool for social and economic development, and the promotion of positive values at home and abroad" (p. 3).

Like its predecessor, CSP 2012 is meant to be a general framework for policy action and collaboration between different levels of government, different policy fields, and the state and civil society, in partnership, with regard to the delivery of the more specific policies and programs that fall under this umbrella policy. Indeed, since the enactment of Bill C-12, several programs and policies have been redesigned and others will eventually be under review in light of CSP 2012.

Figure 12.1 Canadian Sport Policy 2012 Framework

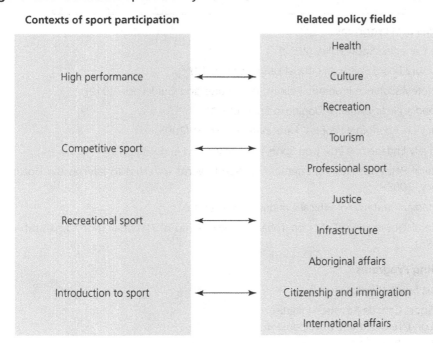

Source: Based on the Canadian Sport Policy 2012 Framework in *Canadian Sport Policy 2012*, pg. 7.

A key difference between CSP 2012 and CSP 2002 is the concept that this policy should not only benefit the development of sport per se, but also contribute to larger social goals and other policy fields. This widest scope is reflected in Figure 12.1 by arrows that point to and come from other policy fields such as infrastructure, health, culture, Aboriginal affairs, and so on.

With CSP 2012, Sport Canada's programs and policies form an intricate network of intervention mechanisms that fall mainly into the category of expenditures. Indeed, Sport Canada doesn't have its own policy and program delivery mechanisms. As stated earlier, most of the policies and programs are in fact delivered through funding to various sport organizations and athletes themselves. Even if expenditures are instruments of indirect action, the funding criteria adopted by Sport Canada over the last three decades result in an increasing indirect control over MSOs and NSOs. Indeed, more funding from the federal government means increased dependency for these organizations, which have to align their policies and programs to obtain their funding. Given the length of this chapter, it is not possible to describe and analyze in depth each aspect of these policies and programs, but Figure 12.2 provides the list of specific policies and programs (with the date of their last iteration in parenthesis) as well as the funding programs that represent the bulk of Sport Canada spending. Here, I will provide an overview of three funding programs: the Sport Support Program, the Athlete Assistance Program, and the Hosting Program.

Sport Support Program

Allegedly, the most important funding program is the Sport Support Program (SSP), which is the process by which the federal government identifies which NSOs, MSOs, and Canadian sport centres are eligible for grants by Sport Canada. SSP also determines

Figure 12.2 Federal Sport Policies, Programs, and Regulations

Policies and Programs

- The Canadian Sport Policy (2012)
- Treasury Board Policy on Official Languages (2012)
- Athlete Assistance Program: Policies, Procedures and Guidelines (2012)
- Canadian Policy Against Doping in Sport (2011)
- Policy on Aboriginal Peoples' Participation in Sport (2005)
- Actively Engaged: A Policy on Sport for Women and Girls (2009)
- Federal Policy for Hosting International Sport Events (referred to later as the Hosting Policy, 2008)
- Canadian Strategy for Ethical Conduct in Sport (2002)
- Federal Government Policy on Tobacco Sponsorship of National Sport Organizations (1985)

Funding Programs

- Sport Support Program
  - Sport Canada Research Initiative
  - Long-Term Athlete Development
  - Own the Podium
- Athlete Assistance Program
- Hosting Program

Source: Canadian Heritage, 2013a.

in what areas, at what levels, and under what conditions recognized organizations qualify for funding. Introduced in 1995, under the name Sport Funding and Accountability Framework, the SSP contains a series of criteria that determine which sport organizations should receive federal funding and at what level. With this mechanism and its accompanying contribution guidelines, Sport Canada has a tool that has significant influence on the policies and programs of each organization it provides funding to. Indeed, most of the criteria relate to commitments that sport organizations must have for several Sport Canada policies and programs. For example, an NSO must have adopted the Canadian Policy Against Doping in Sport, be committed to ethical officiating and coaching education and conduct, and have formal policies on bilingualism, access and equity, women, persons with disabilities, and Aboriginal people, as well as a policy against harassment and abuse. By attaching funding through these criteria, Sport Canada tries to ensure that all its policies, programs, and regulations are consistently implemented throughout the sport system. Thus, even if Sport Canada doesn't intervene directly in the daily life of the MSOs and NSOs, it nevertheless enforces a series of strict rules of conduct.

Through the SSP, Sport Canada also provides funding to the Sport Canada Research Initiative (a partnership with the Social Sciences and Humanities Research Council of Canada in funding independent research on sport participation), the CS4L/LTAD initiative, as well as Own the Podium (OTP), a controversial funding program targeted at NSOs and athletes most likely to earn medals at Olympics and other international games and championships.

"THEY MAY OWN THE PODIUM,
BUT IT APPEARS TO BE IN A LOW RENT DISTRICT."

The Athlete Assistance Program

The second major federal funding program is the Athlete Assistance Program (AAP). Through a carding system, the program identifies and financially supports athletes in the top 16 in the world in their sport, or those athletes who have been identified as having the potential to reach that level of performance. The program consists of a monthly living and training allowance and postsecondary tuition support, if applicable. In 2012, over 1,900 athletes in more than 80 disciplines received some funding through the AAP.

The carding system includes three major categories: the senior international cards (finished in the top eight in international competition) and the senior national cards (have the potential to reach the international criteria) both provide an allowance of $1,500 per month; development cards (has demonstrated high-performance potential) provide an allowance of $900 per month. However, the current carding system doesn't match the needs of all high-performance athletes. Athletes CAN, a lobby organization for athletes funded by Sport Canada, argues that more funding is needed and that several athletes are still living under the poverty line. This is especially the case for those who haven't yet made it to the international level and those who are unable to access the scarce private sponsorship funding and are not supported by OTP.

However, the needs of Canadian athletes are not limited to the issues of financial support. In the early 1980s an increasing number of abuses of power by coaches and NSOs was documented. A report about athlete rights in Canada argued that basic human rights, such as the right to defend oneself in the case of an alleged arbitrary decision, were often not respected in the Canadian sport system. Mechanisms were, in turn, proposed to correct these issues, but the situation didn't improve enough for athletes (Kidd & Eberts, 1982). Bill C-12 created the Sport Dispute Resolution Centre of Canada (SDRC) to provide a nonjudicial dispute resolution system to Canadian athletes and sport organizations.

As such, each NSO and MSO must adhere to the dispute resolution centre's structure and allow their athletes to access the AAP. The SDRC constitutes an improvement for athletes simply because it provides them with a tool that offers some protection from arbitrary decisions or abuse by their NSO, MSO, or coaches. Also, the SDRC offers a quicker decision process than the judicial system and has the advantage of relieving the federal authorities of the necessity to take a position on most of the controversial issues.

The Hosting Program

The third major federal funding program is the Hosting Program, which Sport Canada considers a key instrument in the government's approach to enhancing sport capacity and development. Its purpose is to assist sport organizations or organizing committees in hosting national sport events like the Canada Games or international sport events. It is widely believed in the sport community and government circles that these events produce significant sport, economic, social, and cultural benefits. The program is also seen as a contributor to other government goals, such as promoting Canadian identity and fostering the international image of Canada and Canadian cities. The current Hosting Program supports four events: international major multi-sport games, international single sport events, international multi-sport games for Aboriginal peoples and persons with a disability, and the Canada Games. Each of these components has its own set of criteria for funding; however, each project submitted must demonstrate potential for social, economic, and cultural impacts as well as the delivery of benefits or legacies for sport and the hosting communities after the events.

Other Policies, Programs, and Regulations

I will now briefly present the other policies, programs, and regulations in place, which are listed in Figure 12.2. *Actively Engaged: A Policy on Sport for Women and Girls* is a document that takes a liberal feminist approach to the issue of women in sport and was adopted by the government in 2009. The policy is mainly a series of objective statements encouraging gender equity in sports, and these objectives are operationalized in the structure of funding programs. For example, under the Sport Support Program, NSOs and MSOs have to demonstrate that they have adopted policies that commit to equity and access for women. According to the policy, Canadian Heritage is committed to a sport system that provides quality sport experiences, where women and girls are actively engaged and equitably supported in a full range of roles. Sport Canada is in partnership with organizations such as the Canadian Association for the Advancement of Women and Sport and Physical Activity (CAAWS), launched in 1981, which gets most of its funding from Sport Canada.

The Canadian Policy Against Doping in Sport originated from the recommendations of the Dubin Inquiry. Indeed, the report documented that the measures put in place by the Government of Canada (with the Canadian Council of Sports Medicine) were not sufficient and that the existing anti-doping policy had to be revised. Justice Dubin was not in favour of direct state intervention in the daily administration of sport organizations, so he suggested that a state-funded independent organization be put in place to implement an improved anti-doping policy. Currently, the organization in charge of implementing the policy, including anti-drug testing, is the CCES, which was born from the merger between the Canadian Centre for Drug-Free Sport and Fair Play Canada.

The CCES is responsible for a range of issues, including fair play, drug-free sport, equity, safety, and nonviolence in Canadian sport. Again, ethical conduct and anti-doping are among the concerns the Sport Support Program deals with. Canada is not the only country dealing with doping problems—the issue is clearly a global one. In 1999, after doping scandals in cycling, the IOC decided to convene a conference in Lausanne, Switzerland. An outcome of the conference was to recommend the creation of WADA as an independent international organization dedicated to anti-doping and equally funded by the IOC and nation-states. Housed in Lausanne, WADA moved its headquarters to Montreal in 2002 after the Canadian government lobbied to house the organization. This was seen as an opportunity for Canada to make its presence known in international sport and to foster its views on international anti-doping policies. In 2004, WADA adopted the first World Anti-Doping Code.

In addition to gender equity and doping initiatives, another important hurdle facing the Canadian sport system rests in the area of language, specifically the lack of bilingualism. Although French and English have been recognized as Canada's two official languages for decades, sport organizations continue to blame their inability to provide adequate bilingual services to their members on limited financial resources for translation and on their status as independent, not-for-profit organizations that should not be subjected to federal government legislation. Counterarguments to these claims point out that these national organizations have to adhere to the Constitution of the country if they wish to be recognized as *the* national organization in their sport. Besides, these organizations receive an increasingly important amount of public funding provided by taxpayers from both linguistic communities. Over the years, numerous complaints have been filed, mostly by French-speaking athletes, about the lack of bilingual services—for example, unilingual coaching services, the forced relocation of national-team athletes to where bilingual schooling is not available, and perceived linguistic discrimination. In 2000, the office of the Commissioner of Official Languages published a document called *The Official Languages in the Canadian Sports System*, describing these incidents and outlining the intense debates that arose over language politics in Canadian sport. Given the lack of action from the government, a follow-up report was issued by the commissioner in 2003. Now, as has been discussed, a bilingual strategy for NSOs and MSOs is a criterion under the SSP.

ISSUES AND CONTROVERSIES IN CANADIAN SPORT POLICY

In the previous section I briefly listed described the main federal-level sport policies and programs. As such, they appear as a set of different neutral administrative tools designed to efficiently and rationally manage the Canadian state interventions in sport, providing values and guidance for the Canadian sport system. In reality, these policies and programs are much-debated partial answers to a variety of issues that permeate the Canadian sport system, as well as a reflection of the status of power relations in sport politics at this time in Canada. In this section I will describe two of these issues.

The first issue is the extent the Canadian state should intervene in high-performance sport as opposed to mass participation sport. As a corollary, to what extent should the state target high-performance sport funding on Olympic medal hopefuls as opposed to providing equal funding to all high Canadian high-performance athletes in all disciplines? Since the election of the government of Pierre Trudeau (in the context of the Cold War, poor performances by Canadian athletes on the international stage, and increasing nationalism in Quebec, followed by the prospect of the Montreal Olympic Games in 1976), the federal government has increasingly considered high-performance sport as a tool to promote the image of Canada abroad as well as national unity domestically. This ideology was also reinforced by the widespread belief that great performances by high-performance athletes "trickle down" to average Canadians, inspiring them to participate in sport.

The pervasiveness of this ideology reached another level with the launch of OTP on the eve of the Vancouver Olympic Games, a controversial program targeting Canadians athletes with the highest medal potential, providing them with unprecedented resources to achieve their best performances. While this approach has literally created two classes of athletes, questions have also been raised about the impact and cost of these performances. Indeed, as shown by Donnelly (2013), since the late 1990s, while Canadian athletes have won higher numbers of medals, mass sport participation by average Canadians has been in a sharp decline. Moreover, while other countries are putting in place similar programs, the cost of winning an Olympic medal is increasingly higher. For example, Donnelly (2010) has calculated that in the four years between the Torino Games and the Vancouver Games, $94 million was spent by OTP. Yet Canadian athletes won only two more medals (n = 26) in Vancouver compared to the 24 harvested in Torino four years before, which represents an additional cost of $47 million for each of these two additional medals. How much money will Canada have to spend to continue to succeed in what is now more widely called the "global sporting arms race"?

Connected to the political decisions that have resulted in increasing resources being dedicated to the pursuit of Olympic medals is the issue of sport participation. Sport participation suffers from gross underfunding at the federal level. Despite rhetoric in CSP 2002 and CSP 2012 about the equal importance of high-performance sport and sport participation, in reality very few Sport Canada resources are devoted to the latter. Under the SSP, MSOs funding criteria related to high-performance sport account for 60% of the weighting grid, and 40% is devoted to sport participation and development. Despite these figures, it is estimated that not more than 5% of the contributions MSOs receive from Sport Canada actually go to participation (Donnelly, 2013). But one could argue that this is not the only source of funding for participation sport. Indeed, since the adoption of CSP 2002, the federal and provincial/territorial governments entered into bilateral cost-sharing agreements to support sport participation. However, at roughly $5 million in 2010–2011, for example (Harvey, 2013), when compared to the total Sport Canada contributions for that same year ($160 million), the bilateral agreements represent a modest sum in comparison to what is spent on high-performance sport.

Another source of funding to sport participation is the Children's Fitness Tax Credit introduced by the Harper government in 2007 to provide a tax credit for parents for the expenses of children under 16 years of age who are registered in sport and fitness programs. Again, this measure, this time directed at citizens/taxpayers, is highly questionable as to the extent of its impact on sport participation. First, the tax credit is a regressive tax, which means that higher income earners receive the biggest tax credit (topped at $75 for $500 in expenses for registration and membership). Yet these higher income earners are precisely the middle-class families who can already afford to register their children in sport. Moreover, the lowest income earners, those who cannot afford to register their children in sport, simply do not benefit from any tax credit. The Children's Fitness Tax Credit, moreover, does not include expenses for sport equipment and transportation costs; these are additional expenses that regularly prohibit less-affluent families from enrolling their children in sport.

Besides abysmal funding, the second problem with regard to sport participation is the bureaucratic divide between Sport Canada (in charge of sport participation) and the Healthy Living Unit within the Public Health Agency of Canada (in charge of the promotion of physical activity). Despite many attempts, there has been little meaningful dialogue and cooperation between these two administrative units. A final challenge of sport participation is the lack of community sport infrastructure. As pointed out by Donnelly (2013), if there is indeed some trickledown effect for Canadian athletes as a result of the Olympic Games, sport infrastructure has to be existing and expanded to accommodate potential new sport participants.

Conclusions

Sport, especially at the international level, has a highly metaphoric power of identification for countries and can therefore serve important political goals. High-performance sport, as well as grassroots sport, involves the distribution of collective resources and, thus, implicates the state in a wide range of power relations and struggles. In this chapter I have demonstrated that sport and politics are not mutually exclusive and that sport policy is a complex and important area of contemporary sport. Through an overview of some current policies and programs, I have shown the complexity of the federal government's intervention in sport and how private organizations like NSOs and MSOs interact with the state in the governance of Canada's sport system.

At this point I wish to underline that even if federal government funding to sport organizations is increasingly contingent on their adhesion to a vast array of precise state policies and programs, NSOs and MSOs are nevertheless organizations that still have a great deal of autonomy and often resist Sport Canada policies. Since Bill C-131, the federal government has concentrated on high-performance sport mainly for the promotion of Canada's national unity and social cohesion. But discrimination and inequalities are still thriving in Canada's sport system in terms of class, gender, race, ethnicity, and language. Only through action by citizens and organized pressure groups will the politics of sport improve in Canada.

What issues will governments face in the future? Increasing amounts of public funding will continue to be requested by sport system participants as long as the quest for Olympic medals and World Cup titles remains at the centre of state preoccupations. On the other hand, the obesity crisis, the aging population, and inequalities of access to sport participation opportunities call for more state intervention to tackle these issues. Indeed, the problem is not whether the state should intervene in sport, but rather what public policies should be adopted for the benefit of all Canadians.

Critical Thinking Questions

1. What are the main reasons why governments increasingly intervene in sport? Should that course be continued or reversed? If so, how?

2. Should the federal government continue to put the emphasis on high-performance sport or switch to improve sport participation for all?

3. What has to be done to improve current sport policies in Canada?

4. Can national sport organizations survive without state funding?

5. Should Canada play an active role on the international sport scene? If so, what should that role be?

6. Since an increasing number of athletes and sport organizations are now sponsored by private corporations, should the government reduce its funding?

Suggested Readings

Barnes, J. (2010). *The law of hockey*. Markham, ON: Lexus Nexus.

Thibault, L. & Harvey, J. (Eds.). (2013). *Sport policy in Canada*. Ottawa, ON: University of Ottawa Press.

References

Barnes, J. (2010). *The law of hockey*. Markham, ON: Lexus Nexus.

Boycoff, J. (2011). The anti-Olympics. *New Left Review, 67*, 41–59.

Canadian Heritage. (2012). Canadian Sport Policy 2012. Retrieved from http://sirc.ca/CSPRenewal/documents/CSP2012_EN.pdf.

Donnelly, P. (2010). Rent the podium revisited: Reflections on Vancouver 2010. *Policy Options, 31*(4), 84–86.

Donnelly, P. (2013). Sport participation. In L. Thibault & J. Harvey (Eds.), *Sport policy in Canada* (pp. 177–213). Ottawa, ON: University of Ottawa Press.

Dubin, C. L. (1990). *Commission of inquiry into the use of drugs and banned substances intended to increase athletic performance*. Ottawa, ON: Supply and Services Canada.

Giddens, A. (1989). *Sociology*. Oxford, UK: Polity Press.

Gruneau, R. (1983). *Class, sport and social development*. Amherst, MA: University of Massachusetts Press.

Harvey, J. (1988). Sport policy and the welfare state: An outline of the Canadian state. *Sociology of Sport Journal, 5*, 315–329.

Harvey, J. (2013). Multi-level governance and sport policy in Canada. In J. Thibault & J. Harvey (Eds.), *Sport policy in Canada*. Ottawa, ON: University of Ottawa Press.

Harvey, J., Horne, J., Safai, P., Darnell, S., & Courchesne-O'Neill, S. (2013). *Sport and social movements*. London, UK: Bloomsbury.

Harvey, J., & Proulx, R. (1988). Sport and the state in Canada. In J. Harvey & H. Cantelon (Eds.), *Not just a game: Essays in Canadian sport sociology* (pp. 93–112). Ottawa, ON: University of Ottawa Press.

Kidd, B. (1996). *The struggle for Canadian sport*. Toronto, ON: University of Toronto Press.

Kidd, B., & Eberts, M. (1982). *Athlete's rights in Canada*. Toronto, ON: Queen's Printer.

MacIntosh, D., Bedecki, T. & Franks, C. E. S. (1987). *Sport and politics in Canada: Federal government involvement since 1961*. Montreal, QC: McGill-Queen's University Press.

Meynaud, J. (1966). *Sport et politique*. Paris, FR: Payot.

Pal, L. (2006). *Beyond policy analysis: Public issue management in turbulent times*. Toronto, ON: Nelson.

Sutcliffe Group. (2010). *Interprovincial sport and recreation council: Evaluation of the Canadian Sport Policy: Final report*. Retrieved from http://www.sirc.ca/CSPRenewal/documents/CSP_Evaluation_Final_ReportEN.pdf.

Zirin, D. (2005). *What's my name, fool? Sport and resistance in the United States*. Chicago, IL: Haymarket Books.

Chapter 13

The Business of Sport

Brad R. Humphreys and Moshe Lander

"I caught a couple of hours of the supermarket employees on TV last night."

"Oh yeah? How did our guys do?"

"Terribly. A cashier mishandled an easy credit card payment and it led to a long lineup."

"They should trade him for a stock boy and future considerations."

This fictitious conversation sounds bizarre and unlikely, but fans' relationship with sports is peculiar, and this is exactly how fans talk about their teams. Fans enjoy watching games played live or on television, but to watch sport is to observe an employee earn a paycheque by performing his job at his workplace.

Before and after each contest, fans demand that athletes and coaches defend their performance and decisions, even though most fans are less informed about the intricate decisions they observe than the athletes and coaches. When a team succeeds or fails, fans speak of them as "us," "we," and "our," as if they had something to do with the outcome. Who refers to Canada Post as "ours"? Who raced out to get the newest gear when Research In Motion officially changed its name to BlackBerry? Did Montreal, the headquarters of Air Canada, celebrate the company's record third-quarter results with the same fervour it did when the Canadiens won the Stanley Cup?

More than 103,000 football fans attended Super Bowl XLV in Dallas, Texas, as the Pittsburgh Steelers defeated the Green Bay Packers.

Gary Hershorn/Reuters

The unique way in which fans approach sports is of interest to sociologists and merits the need for objective, critical analysis of sport. In this chapter, we discuss the political economy of sport that describes the study of production, consumption, and economic transactions; the distribution of wealth and income in economies; and the relationship between these economic activities and law, government, and other elements of society. We focus on a critical economic analysis of professional sports leagues in Canada and investigate the organization of these leagues, how they operate, and how they interact with fans. We also critically analyze the hosting of the Olympic Games, an event that Canada hosted in 1976 (Montreal Summer Games), 1988 (Calgary Winter Games), and most recently in 2010 (Vancouver Winter Games).

THE STRUCTURE OF PROFESSIONAL TEAM SPORTS

Professional Team Sport Leagues in Canada

Even though the presence of major league sport and various franchises is often taken for granted in our lives and simply seems "natural," it is important to note that the emergence of the major leagues was far from uncontested and followed a distinct "pattern of cartelization, stable monopoly as national institution, and the incorporation of potential competitors through mergers and/or expansions" (Gruneau & Whitson, 2001, p. 240). As we note below, while motivated first and foremost by profit, the economic structure of major league sport has a number of unique characteristics in comparison to other businesses.

The National Hockey League   The National Hockey League (NHL) is the premier hockey league in the world. It was established in 1917 out of the National Hockey Association as a four-team league consisting of two teams in Montreal, one in Toronto, and one in Ottawa.

The league was far from unique and was one of many competing hockey leagues that had varying degrees of success and failure dating back to the 1880s. For the first 25 years, the NHL experienced constant expansion, contraction, and relocation with franchises appearing in Boston, Brooklyn, Chicago, Detroit, Hamilton, Montreal, New York, Ottawa, Philadelphia, Pittsburgh, Quebec, St. Louis, and Toronto. During this time, it competed for talent with rival leagues, the Pacific Coast Hockey Association (PCHA) and the Western Canada Hockey League (WCHL).

For the first 10 years of its existence, the winner of a competition between the champions of the PCHA and WCHL would "challenge" the champion of the NHL to a contest in which the winner was awarded the Stanley Cup. Only when the PCHA and WCHL ceased operations in 1924 and 1926, respectively, did the NHL claim de facto control of the Cup, and even then it only secured exclusive control of it in 1947.

By 1942, the NHL had established itself as the monopoly provider of professional hockey in North America, a six-team league with franchises in Boston, Chicago, Detroit, Montreal, New York, and Toronto. The next 25 years (the "Original Six" era) contained no expansion, contraction, or franchise moves. A period of expansion started in 1967–1968 with the addition of six new franchises and continued with two more teams in each of 1969–1970, 1971–1972, and 1973–1974.

A challenge to its market dominance, the World Hockey Association (WHA), was eliminated with the absorption of four of the six remaining WHA teams into the NHL in 1979–1980. Further expansion brought the NHL to its current 30 teams. This last period of expansion included major markets in the western and southern United States and the relocation of the franchises in Winnipeg and Quebec City to Phoenix and Denver, respectively (although the Jets returned to Winnipeg in 2011 when the Atlanta Thrashers moved north).

The Canadian Football League The Canadian Football League (CFL) is a relative newcomer in North American professional sports leagues, but its franchises have longer histories than the league that grew out of the amateur Canadian Rugby Football Union (CRFU), founded in 1884, and a championship trophy, the Grey Cup, that is second in age only to the Stanley Cup (1909 compared to 1893).

The CFL was formed in 1958. The league expanded into the United States between 1993 and 1995, placing teams in Baltimore, Birmingham, Las Vegas, Memphis, Sacramento, and Shreveport. These US expansion teams experienced financial problems during their short existence—five folded, and the Baltimore franchise relocated to Montreal in 1996. With the exception of the US expansion in the 1990s, the league has been relatively stable at eight teams, although teams in Ottawa have periodically folded. In 2014 a ninth team was added in Ottawa, which has not had a team since 2005.

Major League Baseball Major League Baseball (MLB) consists of two leagues: the National League (NL), founded in 1876, and the American League (AL), founded in 1901. Until the late 1950s, each league contained eight teams operating in many of the largest US markets in the Northeast and Midwest. The late 1950s and 1960s saw teams moving to California and the expansion of both leagues. In 1969, MLB expanded to Montreal and in 1977 into Toronto. Further expansion resulted in MLB's current size of 30 teams. While professional baseball remains in Toronto, Montreal's team, the Expos, moved to Washington in 2005, citing financial difficulties and a bad stadium.

National Basketball Association The National Basketball Association (NBA) began in 1949 in a merger of the Basketball Association of America and the National Basketball League. The NBA started with 17 teams intended to fill NHL arenas. By 1953–1954, the league had only eight teams and the next few years saw a series of relocations. The NBA expanded in the 1960s. A rival league, the American Basketball Association (ABA), began operating in 1967, forcing the NBA to expand rapidly to compete for talent and markets; four ABA teams merged with the NBA in 1976. The NBA added four franchises in the late 1980s and two Canadian franchises in 1995: the Vancouver Grizzlies and Toronto Raptors. Professional basketball was never popular in Vancouver, and after six seasons of disastrous on-court performance the team relocated to Memphis in 2001. The NBA reached its current 30-team size in 2004.

National Football League The National Football League (NFL) was founded in 1920 with 17 teams. Only two teams remain from this league: the Chicago Bears and the Arizona Cardinals; many early teams folded. In 1933, the NFL created a two-conference structure in which the conference champions played in a championship game and expanded to a 16-team league. The NFL faced many rival leagues, including the All-America Football Conference in 1950 and the American Football League (AFL) in 1960. The NFL and AFL agreed in 1966 to a championship game, now known as the Super

Bowl, in which the champions of each league would play each other; the leagues formally merged in 1970. Since the merger, various franchises have relocated, and expansion has increased the league size to 32 teams. No Canadian teams exist in the NFL, although some regular-season games have taken place in Toronto with the Buffalo Bills as the home team.

Major League Soccer   In 1994, soccer's governing body, la Fédération Internationale de Football Association (FIFA), forced the United States Soccer Federation to establish a premier soccer league in return for awarding the United States the rights to host the World Cup. The league, now called Major League Soccer (MLS), debuted in 1996 with 10 teams; two expansion teams joined in 1998. MLS expanded to 19 teams by adding at least one expansion franchise every year after 2005, including three franchises in Canada (Toronto in 2005, Vancouver in 2011, and Montreal in 2012).

League Structure

Professional sports leagues all face a similar set of economic problems that must be solved for play to take place. They also face the unique issue of joint production: No team can operate alone, so to succeed a sports team requires competitors who can be counted on to reliably provide competition for the team. In this section, we discuss the organization of professional sports leagues in an economic context.

Cartels   A *cartel* is a group of two or more firms that formally agree to coordinate their production and pricing decisions to maximize joint profits. By acting in unison, a cartel allows a group of firms to exercise monopoly power. Some aspects of sports league behaviour can be described as cartel behaviour.

Anti-trust laws exist to prevent the formation of cartels because, in exercising monopoly power, firms engage in anti-competitive behaviour that is harmful to consumers. In particular, a monopoly firm earns excess profits by restricting output below the amount that would have been produced by competing firms and raises the price of output above the price that would have been charged by competing firms. Until recently, think of Rogers Cable in Ontario, TELUS in Alberta, or Videotron in Quebec.

How do sports leagues achieve monopoly status? First, for a cartel to be successful, it must be able to prevent new competitors from entering the market. Long-established sports leagues can do this easily. All professional sports leagues in North America have formal territorial agreements that divide up the United States and Canada into well-defined areas in which each team can act as a monopolist and prevent new teams from opening in the territory. The Toronto Maple Leafs have long exercised these territorial rights, preventing owners seeking to bring rival teams to Hamilton, Kitchener, and even to Markham. Long-term broadcasting contracts, facilities, travel costs, player development systems, brand building, and fan loyalty as well as situating franchises in densely populated areas also generate barriers to entry.

Second, cartels must be able to restrict output quantity and increase prices to earn "monopoly rents" (i.e., profits over and above what they would earn in a competitive marketplace). Sports leagues create a limited supply of franchises and restrict the length of the season that would not exist in a competitive marketplace. Absent this monopoly power, more teams would exist in every professional league and more games would be played in each season. Successful (i.e., profitable) franchises in a more conventional industry, like sports apparel, would attract new entrants, reducing prices and increasing the quantity of output produced. Sports leagues block entrants and extract rents from those seeking to enter (in the form of expansion fees), thus preventing this market mechanism from occurring.

Third, cartels must produce a reasonably homogeneous product. Sports leagues require teams to play on the same field or surface with the same dimensions, using the same rules, uniforms, and equipment. Fourth, cartels must agree how to share their monopoly power. Territorial rights, revenue sharing, restricting player movements and salaries all represent power-sharing arrangements in sports leagues. While this power is allocated to individual franchises, a governing body often enforces these agreements to ensure that cartel members do not infringe or cheat on league agreements.

In 1922, the US Supreme Court ruled that Major League Baseball was not subject to anti-trust laws because an individual baseball franchise cannot exist independently and baseball did not, according to the court, constitute interstate commerce. That is, for a team to exist there must be at least one other team to ensure some on-field competition. Up to a point, more teams means more competition, so the formation of leagues necessitates the formation of cartels. Since professional baseball could not exist otherwise, the court ruled it could not be subject to anti-trust laws. By extension, other professional sports leagues must also lend themselves to cartel behaviour.

The market power generated by professional sports leagues reduces consumer welfare. By restricting output, leagues deny access to live professional sports to fans in cities that would otherwise be able to support a team. By increasing prices, leagues force fans to pay a higher price to attend games or watch games on television than they would have to pay if leagues were subject to anti-trust laws like other businesses.

In Canada, the Competition Bureau is responsible for preventing anti-competitive business practices. However, where economic welfare and efficiency are enhanced these behaviours are permitted, regardless of whether the owner or the player is the recipient of the welfare gain. Such permissible practices include the right to collective bargaining

The Saskatchewan Roughriders won the 2013 Grey Cup, becoming the third consecutive team to win the CFL championship on their home turf.
MARK BLINCH/Reuters/Corbis

(allowing employees to form unions for the purpose of negotiating wages and other terms of employment), to forming amateur sports associations and professional sports leagues and teams, and to protecting products covered by intellectual property law, such as patents, copyrights, and trademarks.

The line between what is permitted and what is not is a fine one. For example, sharing statistics among owners and players is acceptable, but not if it leads to collusive behaviour wherein owners engage in price-fixing when setting player salaries. Another example is when a sports league has the ability to set its rules for membership or participation within the league. These rules can be used to maintain a reasonable balance among teams, but they cannot be so unreasonable that the opportunities of individual players or interested investors (i.e., new owners) to participate are severely limited.

Intellectual property rights allow league governors to "self-regulate" (i.e., to interpret and implement their own rules on the assumption that these rules are aimed at promoting the best interests of the sport or sports league that they represent). In a simple example, the league can allow each franchise to have a monopoly over its team name and to profit from it. Of course, most Canadians will be familiar with the bizarre situation in which two CFL franchises carried the name Roughriders (Saskatchewan spells it as one word while the Ottawa franchise spelled it as two).

Monopsony Power, the Reserve Clause, and Free Agency   A *monopoly* is a market with only one seller; a *monopsony* is a market with only one buyer. With the exception of the CFL and MLS, the other four major North American professional sports leagues are the premier leagues in the world in their respective sports. The world's top players in these sports have a strong preference to play in these leagues, giving teams monopsony power when negotiating player rights, salaries, contracts, and freedom of movement.

The leagues further strengthen their position through the implementation of an entry draft in which top unsigned amateur players are restricted to negotiating entry-level contracts exclusively with the team that drafted the rights to their labour services. This arrangement leaves players with little bargaining power and gives owners the potential to exploit players by paying lower salaries, benefits, or pensions and restricting the free movement and transfer of their talents to other teams. A player entering a league through the entry draft can either negotiate with the team that holds his rights or not play professionally in the league. The effect of entry drafts that assign the rights to an incoming player's labour services to a single team is a reduction in young player's salaries below what they would have earned in a competitive market where players could sell their services to the highest bidder.

Professional athletes have responded to this monopsony power by forming players' unions, like the National Hockey League Players' Association, that exert monopoly power when negotiating with franchises. Players' unions counter franchise owners' desires to exploit players by guaranteeing minimum salaries, specifying conditions under which players can move and negotiate freely with competing franchises, and developing a common set of safety standards and basic provisions such as healthcare coverage, pensions, and other rights and benefits.

Since the beginning of organized professional sports leagues in North America, team owners controlled players through an agreement under which each owner would agree not to tamper with any other owner's players by enticing a player under contract with promises of better pay, working conditions, status, and so on. This system, called the *reserve clause*, was first used by National League baseball owners in 1879 (just three years after the formation of the National League in 1876). It effectively created indentured servitude by players to their teams for as long as the player's career lasted. The reserve clause refers to an actual clause in the standard contract between each player and his team that allowed the team to "reserve" the player's services in perpetuity. A player was never allowed to sell his services to the highest bidder under the reserve clause, although teams were free to trade the contracts of players to other teams or to terminate the contract at will. Like entry drafts, the reserve clause reduced player's salaries below what they would have earned under a system where players were free to sell their services to the highest bidder. Other sports leagues incorporated varying forms of the reserve clause with differences reflecting the unique nature of their league.

Curt Flood, a defensive standout for MLB's St. Louis Cardinals, challenged the legitimacy of such an arrangement. When traded to the Philadelphia Phillies in 1969 Flood refused to report, citing racist fans and poor playing conditions. The MLB Players Association (MLBPA) offered to fund his legal options, and Flood pursued his free agency rights to the US Supreme Court, where he ultimately lost.

Nonetheless, the MLBPA secured from rattled ownership the creation of an independent arbitration panel to resolve contract disputes between owners and players. In one such ruling, the panel granted limited *free agency* to a pair of players who had played the previous season without a contract. The ability to sell one's talents competitively to the highest bidder came with restrictions, but free agency spread quickly to the other leagues. Salaries rose significantly in all professional sports leagues after the advent of free agency because the monopsony power enjoyed by teams operating under the reserve clause was significantly reduced. The last 40 years of collective bargaining agreements in each league have focused, to varying degrees, on the right balance between the owners' rights to "buy" players for their teams (i.e., the reserve system) and the players' rights to freedom of movement (i.e., free agency).

The reserve clause still exists in a limited form in all professional sports leagues in North America. Young players must play a specified number of seasons before they become eligible for free agency. From the time they are drafted until they qualify for free agency, professional athletes are still subject to the reserve clause.

League Functions

Cooperative Behaviour   In a typical industry, firms maximize profits in part by eliminating competitors. Professional sports leagues are different in that, while one team might try to defeat its competitors in on-field or on-ice competition, it does not want to eliminate its competitors from off-field operations. Without a team against which to compete, how can one team survive or be profitable?

Moreover, even in a financially viable league, if the winner of the on-field competition is a forgone conclusion, then fan interest in competitions will decline. If the outcome of a contest were certain, the result would be less opportunity to generate revenue, lower profitability, and a welfare loss for owners and consumers. Therefore, it is in each team's interest to ensure not only the financial viability of its competitors, but also their on-field competitiveness—cooperative behaviour is necessary in professional sports leagues.

Individual teams will often cede control of decisions to a coordinating body if it is more profitable than making such decisions at the team level. Examples include negotiating broadcasting agreements, joint marketing and merchandising arrangements, and revenue sharing. In circumstances where cooperative behaviour is optimal, the individual franchises benefit from the monopoly power they generate by acting collectively. This can best be accomplished when the league negotiates with an outside partner on a topic of league-wide relevance (e.g., negotiations with television networks for broadcast rights fees) and where bargaining power is essential for extracting a return in excess of the resource owner's opportunity cost. This excess return is known as *economic rent*.

In this setting, individual teams retain control over day-to-day operations subject to league-wide rules. This allows teams to maintain a vertically separated operational structure with the coordinating body acting as an intermediary. It is critical that teams retain independence or the integrity and credibility of the on-field product could be compromised. Finding the balance between cooperative behaviour and independence is essential.

Sports leagues undertake two types of cooperative actions: those that must occur for play to take place (*single-entity cooperation*) and those that are unrelated to play taking place (*joint venture cooperation*). One of the most important types of single-entity cooperation is the establishment of a league schedule. This is not as easy as it sounds. A league schedule must include all of the teams and ensure that each team plays the same number of games at home and away, that games are relatively evenly spread out over the length of the season, and that teams have roughly similar schedule strengths and opponents. This is an act that would be almost impossible, particularly as the size of the league and the length of the season increases, without cooperative behaviour. If teams decided their schedules, each team would pursue its own self-interest in trying to schedule more home games, weekend games, or games against popular or weak teams. Part of creating a league schedule is determining the optimal season length. When a league acts as a cartel, it becomes a monopolist. Monopolies, compared to competitive markets, maximize profits when they restrict output and increase prices. A league tries to establish a season length that achieves this objective, but the key point is that the season is shorter than what would exist in a competitive market.

Another important type of single-entity cooperation is establishing the rules and regulations under which teams operate and games are played. If left to their own devices, teams will try to skew the rules in their own favour to increase the probability of winning. Numerous examples of this can be found across sports. The Green Monster in Fenway Park rewards right-handed hitters; smaller ice surfaces in Buffalo or Chicago reward offence; outdoor football stadiums in frigid Green Bay or humid Miami provide these teams with advantages and affect outcomes. It also has the ability to affect attendance and, therefore, revenues and profits.

Single-entity cooperation also includes the process for determining the league champion. Some leagues, particularly in Europe, forgo a postseason, while all of the North American professional leagues do not. Even North American leagues exhibit postseason variation in terms of how many teams, how many rounds, how many games in each round, the order of home and away games, first-round byes, and even when and where the championship is played.

Playoffs are profitable; otherwise, they would not exist. By allowing more teams to play longer or simply potentially playing longer, fans remain engaged longer, creating larger revenue-generating streams from ticket sales, broadcasting rights, merchandising, concessions, and so on. Longer playoffs with more teams also decrease the chances that the team with the best regular-season record wins the championship. The more rounds of postseason play that the best team must negotiate to win the championship, the more likely they are to suffer defeat in one of those rounds. Since the team with the best record is less likely to win, teams will find it optimal to reduce their investment in talent since the direct link between talent and championships weakens. The reduced investment lowers salary expenses and increases profits.

The second type of cooperative behaviour, joint venture cooperation, involves cooperative action unrelated to making play happen. In this situation, teams surrender a portion of their autonomy to collective decision making in exchange for increased profits. Classic examples of joint venture cooperation are league-level negotiations of broadcasting rights, merchandising arrangements, revenue sharing, labour agreements, and facility development.

Entry Drafts   All professional sports leagues in North America operate some form of entry draft. In general, the system gives the worst team in the previous season the exclusive rights to negotiate with the unsigned, incoming amateur player of its choosing. The second-worst team chooses from the remaining players and so on until the best team from the previous season selects a player. All of the entry drafts held by North American sports leagues have more than one round, so the process is repeated for each round (i.e., the worst team selects first, the second-worst team second, etc.). This is called a *reverse entry draft* format. As discussed earlier, entry drafts generate monopsony power for teams and reduce the salaries of incoming players.

Because the teams gain exclusive negotiating rights with the player of their choosing, these rights have value and teams are allowed to trade these rights to other teams in exchange for compensation, financial or otherwise. Each league dictates the specific details of how this process works.

Entry drafts are intended to enhance competitive balance in leagues. If the worst teams get the best incoming talent, these teams will improve. This in turn benefits all teams because a more competitive on-field product increases fan interest and revenues. Furthermore, by granting exclusive negotiating rights to one team, the team gains leverage in negotiations because the franchise becomes a monopsony buyer. This allows the team to compensate the player at below-market value, lowering expenses. So overall, the draft increases team's profits.

Of course, the draft does not guarantee profits. Teams may lose money if they are managed badly. Granting a badly run franchise access to the player of its choosing does not mean that the team can successfully evaluate, develop, or manage talent, nor can it necessarily value it properly when using it to trade for future considerations. Additionally, even franchises with skilled management might not benefit from the draft if it is not in the franchise's best interest to win as much as fans might want. It is hard to argue that MLB's Chicago Cubs have been inept for over a century. If the ballpark sells out every game and if the fans are happy with their extracurricular activities at the game, then ownership might find it optimal to save on player development costs and keep the profit instead.

Teams

Ownership   With few exceptions, North American professional sports teams are privately owned businesses. Public share issues and stock exchange listings do not exist, in many cases because league rules prohibit this form of ownership, and as such audited financial accounts for professional sports teams are often unavailable to the public.

Some franchises are family-run affairs dating back generations, such as the Rooney family's eight-decade ownership and management of the NFL's Pittsburgh Steelers. Some franchises are community owned, such as the NFL's Green Bay Packers or the CFL's Winnipeg Blue Bombers, Edmonton Eskimos, and Saskatchewan Roughriders.

Of the 149 teams covered in this chapter, none is owned by a woman, only one has a black man as its principal owner (Michael Jordan of the Charlotte Bobcats), and only a handful of owners are non–North American, most notably Mikhail Prokorov, owner of the NBA's New Jersey Nets, and a few owners in MLS. All of them share common traits in that they are exceptionally wealthy, often worth billions of dollars, and many share a conservative viewpoint. Outspoken and flamboyant characters often struggle trying to gain ownership stakes (e.g., NBA owner Mark Cuban's failed attempt to purchase MLB's Chicago Cubs or Research In Motion's former co-CEO Jim Balsillie's failed purchase of the NHL's Pittsburgh Penguins [2006], Nashville Predators [2007], and Phoenix Coyotes [2009]). Many NHL owners also own NBA franchises (e.g., Stan Kroenke of the Avalanche/Nuggets, Ted Leonsis of the Capitals/Wizards, and Josh Harris of the Devils/76ers). Both leagues operate in the same cities and play in similar arenas, so there is room for economies of scale if the significant cost of operating the arena can be spread over two teams rather than one.

Team ownership is generally expensive but profitable. In 2013, *Forbes* magazine valued NHL franchises between US$175 million (Columbus) and US$1.15 billion (Toronto), NBA franchises between US$312 million (Milwaukee) and US$1.1 billion (New York), MLB franchises between US$451 million (Tampa) and US$2.3 billion (New York Yankees), and NFL franchises between US$823 million (Oakland) and US$2.3 billion (Dallas). MLS franchises were valued between US$26 million (San Jose) and US$137 million (Los Angeles) because of the league's shorter existence and longer history of financial troubles. Data on franchise values for the CFL is unavailable, but Table 13.1 provides the value for other Canadian professional sports franchises.

Despite news of the periodic bankruptcy or financial problems of a particular franchise, sports teams generally deliver outstanding returns. Consider, for example, the NBA's Los Angeles Clippers.

In mid-2014, the NBA forced Donald Sterling, the owner since 1981, to sell the Clippers after he made discriminatory comments. The winning bid by former Microsoft CEO Steve Ballmer valued the team at approximately US$2 billion, an impressive return for Sterling on his initial purchase price of US$12.5 million, even after accounting for inflation. And this is despite the team losing an NBA-worst two-thirds of its games over that period, making the fewest playoff appearances (seven), and setting an all-time record for longest drought between playoff appearances (15 seasons).

More astounding is the profitability of the NFL's Pittsburgh Steelers. Purchased in 1933 for US$2,500 (US$45,000 in 2013 money), the franchise remains in the ownership of the

Table 13.1 Value of Canadian Professional Sports Franchises

Franchise	Sport	League Rank (in Value)	Value (in millions of US$)
Toronto Maple Leafs	NHL	1	$1,150
Montreal Canadiens	NHL	3	$775
Vancouver Canucks	NHL	4	$700
Calgary Flames	NHL	11	$420
Edmonton Oilers	NHL	14	$400
Ottawa Senators	NHL	15	$380
Winnipeg Jets	NHL	16	$340
Toronto Blue Jays	MLB	21	$568
Toronto Raptors	NBA	21	$405

founding Rooney family and is now valued at US$1.12 billion. Since the AFL–NFL merger in 1970, the franchise has won the most regular-season games, appeared in the conference championship the most times, appeared in the Super Bowl the most times, and won the most Super Bowls.

Costs, Payroll, Salary Caps   Player salaries are the largest operating expense for each team in North American professional sports. Each league's collective bargaining agreement specifies the maximum size of each team's roster and, except for MLB, a salary cap limit, which is the total amount an owner can allocate to salaries. How strict the cap is varies from league to league and is often expressed as a percentage of total revenues and is equal for each team. The CFL "import rule" also restricts (to 19) the number of foreign-born players that can play on each team.

Philadelphia Phillies teammates Ryan Howard and Cliff Lee were the top-paid North American athletes in 2014, each earning US$25 million, with more than a dozen other players earning in excess of US$20 million. While this amount seems extremely high when compared to the average North American salary, this has not always been the case. In fact, historically professional athletes earned relatively lower salaries compared to athletes today. For example, in 1906–1908 the highest paid professional baseball player, Nap Lajoie, earned $8,500 per season, which is equivalent to about $200,000 in today's dollars.

Figure 13.1 shows the average salary of MLB players over the period 1967–2008 in inflation-adjusted 2008 dollars. In 1969 the average salary of an MLB player was just under $25,000, or about $146,000 in 2008 dollars. From the graph, MLB player salaries did not increase significantly until the late 1980s. These increases were primarily the result of collective bargaining by the MLBPA, the union representing professional baseball players, which successfully brought free agency to baseball through a lawsuit in the mid-1970s.

In some leagues, players work under a guaranteed contract (NHL, NBA, MLB, MLS) where they are paid their full salary regardless of their performance, health, or status on the team. Other leagues (CFL, NFL) pay players some guaranteed money but also nonguaranteed money that is dependent on maintaining an active roster spot. Contracts

Figure 13.1 Average Major League Baseball Salary, 2008 US Dollars

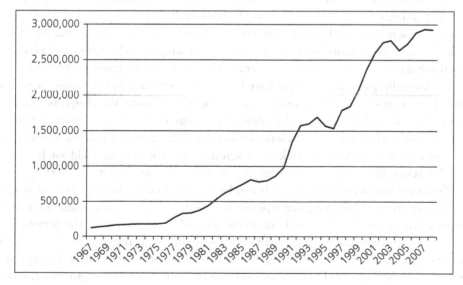

can include sweeteners such as signing bonuses and performance bonuses. The details of how much these can be and how they count against the cap are negotiated between management and labour as part of the collective bargaining process.

Upon entry into the league, a player's rights are first assigned to one team through an entry draft, at which time the team negotiates a contract with the player. During a player's employment with his team, he can be traded or waived at the team's discretion, though some players have a no-trade clause in their contract that restricts the ability of the team to act unilaterally in moving the player. Once the player's contract expires, the player becomes a free agent and can negotiate with his current team or with other teams, although the details are many and varied.

In general, NHL players can become free agents after playing seven seasons or turning 27 years of age, whichever comes first, MLB players can become free agents after playing six seasons, NBA players can become free agents after playing three or four seasons, and NFL players can become free agents after playing three seasons. While MLS does not have free agency that corresponds to the other North American leagues, it does have a variation called a *re-entry draft* that works on a similar basis for players after their third or fourth season.

In addition to player compensation, franchises incur costs related to player development (such as minor league teams), team operation costs (such as scouting, training, and facilities maintenance), day-to-day operations (such as management salaries and other business expenses), and depreciation. This last one allows firms to write down the value of their players as any other business is allowed to write down the value of its aging assets.

Salary caps, restricted free agency, and the ability to sign talent to multi-year contracts keep total player compensation costs relatively stable. Furthermore, the major North American professional sports leagues have become quite skilled at demanding and receiving subsidies from various levels of government to offset the operating and maintenance costs of their facilities. In cases where the team does not own its own facility, it is often able to negotiate steep discounts on rent, also helping to keep nonsalary costs low.

Revenues   While the mix and importance of revenue sources differs from league to league (and in some cases franchise to franchise), North American professional sports franchises generate revenues from five sources: (a) game-day revenues, including ticket sales, concessions, parking, personal seat licences, and luxury box deals; (b) local television and radio broadcasting agreements; (c) shared revenue arrangements, including league-wide broadcasting deals, merchandising, and licensing; (d) local sponsorship and advertising, including stadium naming rights and exclusivity agreements; and (e) postseason appearances revenue.

Traditionally, game-day revenues have been the biggest source of revenues for professional sports teams. Before the spread of multi-channel television and all-sports channels like RDS, TSN, and ESPN, fans could only see their teams by attending the game in person. Over the years, ticket sales became more elaborate, evolving from the single-game ticket to the season ticket to multi-game packages. High-demand facilities could add surcharges to fans who were willing to pay for the nonguaranteed right to buy a ticket or tickets.

Ticket pricing in professional sports can be described by the hedonic pricing model, which posits that a ticket to a game represents a bundle of characteristics and each characteristic has an associated price. Characteristics include proximity to the action, seat size, access to concessions, facility amenities, team quality, and other factors. The hedonic pricing model explains why premium seats cost more than other seats, since the premium seating areas have superior characteristics in terms of comfort, sightlines, proximity, access to better concessions, and other benefits compared to seats further from the action or in less desirable parts of the stadium or arena. Some teams also practise economic price discrimination by charging different prices for identical seats through student and senior citizen discounts and discounted group ticket prices. More recent developments have included differentiated pricing depending on the quality or popularity of the opposing team, the time of the season, the day of the week, or even the strength of the home team.

Secondary markets, often called "ticket scalping," have transformed from an illegal and questionable market form to a more professional and reputable market through online systems, wherein fans can purchase tickets to games posted by other fans and authenticated by reputable market makers, and even teams and leagues. Secondary ticket markets arise because of fan heterogeneity. Sports fans can be grouped into two general categories: diehard fans who plan to attend games well in advance and want to purchase tickets at the time they make these plans, and busy professionals who have the resources to pay higher ticket prices but do not know if they can attend any particular game until shortly before the contest takes place. Since the busy professionals are willing to pay a premium for tickets purchased at the last minute, arbitrage profit opportunities exist that teams cannot take advantage of because they must offer tickets early to diehard fans to obtain their patronage and cannot distinguish between diehard fans and arbitrageurs. This asymmetric information generates secondary ticket markets; the fact that teams cannot easily profit from this led to anti-scalping laws.

Over the last three decades, media broadcast rights have become a significantly more important source of revenue for professional sports teams, particularly with 24-hour sports television and radio stations chasing after content to fill out their schedules (see Chapter 11). Some franchises have even created their own networks (e.g., MSG and YES Networks) to eliminate the middleperson and capture more fully the advertising revenue generated during broadcasts.

Sponsorship has also increased in importance in the last decade or two. Naming rights for stadiums and arenas, exclusivity agreements (whereby a company can claim to be the team's exclusive and official provider of a particular good or service), advertising along the baselines, boards, playing surface, and fences have all proliferated as teams exhaust every available space to capitalize. MLS franchises have gone further than the other leagues in selling off prime space on their uniforms.

Pricing

Ticket sales represent a major source of revenue for professional sports teams in North America. All teams offer single-game tickets as well as season-ticket packages for the full slate of home games, or partial packages where the fan can select tickets to a subset of home games.

Franchises have retrofitted existing facilities or built new ones that include more expensive luxury seating nearer the game action or private suites. These premium seats often come with additional requirements, such as minimum food and drink expenditures or privileged parking fees. Because of the significant expense involved in purchasing these locations, often for the entire season, the owners of these premium seats have evolved over the years from individuals to businesses that use them as a form of entertainment expense for their employees, partners, or clients.

Attending professional sporting events is expensive. Figure 13.2 shows the *fan cost index* (FCI) of attending a game in the four prominent North American leagues from 1994

Figure 13.2 Fan Cost Index 1994–2011, MLB, NBA, NFL, NHL (2011 US Dollars)

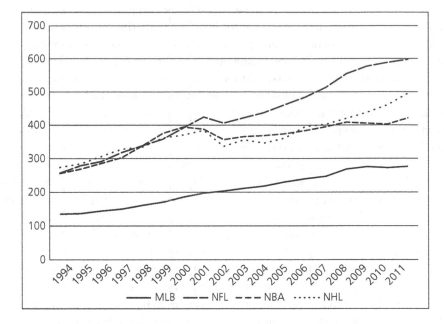

to 2011, controlling for inflation. The FCI, calculated annually by Team Marketing Report (www.teammarketing.com), reflects the total cost for a family of four to attend a game, including tickets, concessions, parking, and the purchase of licensed merchandise. In 2011 it cost a family of four between $276 and $597 to attend a pro game.

The cost of attending games has increased substantially in inflation-adjusted terms in all four leagues. From 1994 to 2011, the FCI for MLB and the NFL more than doubled and increased by 81% in the NHL and 65% in the NBA. Since the cost of attending games has increased faster than the rate of inflation, it has also exceeded the rate of increase in earnings, making attending a game increasingly difficult for individuals with lower incomes.

Attending games is also costly in relative terms. Based on the FCI, in 2011 attending 25% of the regular-season games played (40 MLB games, 10 NBA or NHL games, or 2 NFL games) would account for 9% of the median income of a Canadian household for MLB games, 4% for NHL games, 3% for NBA games, and 2% for NFL games.

The pricing of tickets to professional sports events is subject to various forms of pricing differentiation based on proximity to the action, sightlines, access to or shelter from the elements, concession stands, and other factors. *Price discrimination* occurs when a team sells identical tickets to identical seats for different prices. Examples of price discrimination include student discounts and senior citizen discounts. Not all differences in ticket prices reflect price discrimination. Some differences in ticket prices reflect seats with different characteristics, which can be thought of as differentiated products. Tickets closer to the ice in hockey arenas command higher prices because they provide proximity to the action, for which fans are willing to pay a higher price.

Many franchises have found other ways to generate revenues from ticket sales by charging fans a fee that entitles them the right to purchase tickets to home contests over the course of a season. These rights are called *personal seat licences* (PSLs). A PSL costs a predetermined price and allows the fan to reserve a specified seat location before the actual season tickets are available for purchase. Once the consumer has purchased a PSL, he or she is considered the owner of that seat and has the ability to either use it or resell it, like any other commodity. The only condition attached to the owner of the PSL is the requirement to purchase season's tickets when they become available. Failure to do so results in the loss of the rights to the specified seat and the money paid for the PSL is not refunded. The NFL's Carolina Panthers were the first North American professional franchise to make use of PSLs. When they entered the league in 1995, they played their home games at Clemson (South Carolina) University's stadium while building their own stadium in Charlotte, North Carolina. To help finance the new stadium, they sold over 61,000 PSLs, generating over US$150 million.

Labour Relations

Compensation, Risk, and Liability   In labour markets, when a union negotiates in a competitive market for labour services, the union is able to procure wages above what would prevail in the absence of the union. Similarly, when a monopsony employer negotiates in a competitive market for talent, the employer is able to obtain wages below the competitive rate. But when a monopoly union negotiates with a monopsony employer, a situation known as a *bilateral monopoly*, the equilibrium wage rate could fall anywhere between the above-average situation described in the first scenario and the below-average situation described in the second one. The relative strength of the union and the employer will determine where wages fall.

Like many industries that involve trained professionals with rare skills, the difference between the top end of the wage distribution and the bottom or middle is significant. Extraordinary talents are able to negotiate extraordinary salaries, compensation, and perks. But just as much as talent dictates compensation, risk also plays a role.

An office worker or a factory employee can expect a working life of 40 to 50 years. A professional athlete has an expected career length of a handful of seasons for a football running back and certainly no more than 20 years for an elite, healthy, and fortunate athlete. Without performance-enhancing drugs, most athletes are on the downside of their professional careers in their 30s and face an uncertain future beginning in their 40s, often with little more than a high school education, maybe a few years of college, and fleeting name recognition if they were near the top of their game.

This significant risk on the players' part often results in significant compensation in the form of high earnings over the course of their professional career and generous benefits if their career lasts beyond a certain number of games played. But even with this compensation, players face greater-than-usual health and safety risks.

Collective Bargaining and Stoppages   Negotiations between the owners and players' unions are done through a process called *collective bargaining*. This system creates a *collective bargaining agreement* (CBA) that regulates working conditions and all economic interactions between the two sides. CBAs specify salary scales, salary caps, arbitration rules and regulations, as well as other compensation such as pensions and benefits. Free agency, the draft, revenue sharing, and the division of shared revenues from merchandising and broadcasting rights are also included in the negotiations. Working conditions related to player safety, travel requirements, season length, drug testing and enforcement, and other technical issues necessary to make the league run are also part of the negotiating process.

As league revenues have increased over the last 30 years, labour relations in professional sports have become more contentious, especially as players have become more organized and unions increasingly militant. Each of the four major North American professional sports leagues have experienced multiple work stoppages, including recent extended lockouts in the NBA, NFL, and NHL.

Although often used interchangeably, there is a difference between a lockout and a strike. A *lockout* occurs when ownership does not let the players perform, even though the players are willing. A *strike* occurs when workers refuse to perform, despite the owners' willingness to allow it. The strength and resolve of each group determines the length of any work stoppage and the ultimate resolution. Despite the occasional (significant) concessions, the owners have traditionally held the upper hand in negotiations with the players.

FANS

Attendance

Figure 13.3 shows total attendance in the major North American sports leagues over the last 40 years. MLB dwarfs the other leagues because baseball teams play almost twice the number of home games as NBA and NHL teams and 10 times more than NFL teams. The NBA and NHL have roughly the same attendance level, consistent with their similar season length and venue size. Note that the NBA started from a lower level in 1970 despite having a longer season (41 homes games in the NBA versus 39 in the NHL) and despite having more teams (17 in the NBA and 12 in the NHL). Nonetheless, basketball has done a better job over the last four decades of broadening its fan base, whereas hockey has remained a niche sport, favoured primarily by Canadians and those living in the US Midwest and Northeast.

In every league total attendance has risen over time, quadrupling in the NBA, almost tripling in MLB, and more than doubling in the NHL. The smallest increases occurred in

Figure 13.3 Attendance in North American Sports Leagues

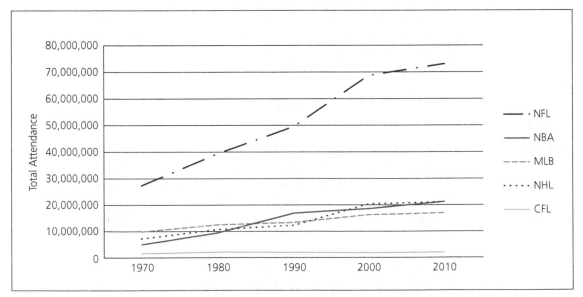

football (70 percent in the NFL and 25 percent in the CFL). Some of the increase in attendance comes from league expansion and schedule changes over that time. When compared to 1970, in 2013 the NFL schedule has expanded by 41%, the NHL by 163%, the NBA by 76%, and MLB by 25%. In terms of increased attendance per game, MLB has grown the most followed closely by the NBA with the NFL and NHL lagging far behind. The NHL's move toward a longer season (including playoffs) and expansion into the US south could explain its lagging performance.

Predicting attendance is difficult. Why a fan would want to attend a game is a function of many factors, but attendance is positively correlated with the market size of the home team. Second, good performance in the previous season, and also in the last few games, is correlated with current attendance. Finally, attendance tends to be price inflexible, meaning that higher ticket prices do not have a large impact on attendance.

SPORTS LEAGUES AND PUBLIC POLICY

Facility Subsidies

Professional sports facilities are large, highly visible structures that can be sources of civic pride. The impact that these structures and the teams that play in them have on the local economy is not lost on team owners or local politicians. In the balance of power over who receives the economic rents from the stadiums and arenas, it is all too often the franchise owners who gain the most. Again, the use of monopoly power is key.

Most cities are large enough to contain one franchise per sport. There are of course exceptions, such as metropolitan Toronto, Los Angeles, New York, and Chicago. Recall that the allocation of teams to cities also reflects the territorial rights agreements that leagues employ to provide teams with monopoly power in their local market.

As monopolies, leagues restrict output where possible. This includes limiting the season length or game time, but it also involves limiting league size. By ensuring that the number of cities capable of supporting a franchise is greater than the number of franchises in existence, leagues generate "outside options." These options are simply cities that are large enough to support a team (but do not currently have one) that can be used as leverage; owners can threaten to move their franchise to these cities unless local politicians provide strong economic incentives in the form of large public subsidies for the construction and operation of professional sports facilities. Owners extract significant economic rents by holding cities hostage and demanding sizable subsidies from state/provincial and local governments for everything from construction and operating costs to reduced rents and facility upgrades or to municipal infrastructure development and improvement. Their bargaining power lies in the threat of franchise relocation.

Politicians recognize the prestige and economic benefits that come from hosting a professional sports franchise and are loathe to be the ones that let another city enjoy those advantages. In 2013, only 11 municipal areas had an NHL, NBA, NFL and MLB franchise: Boston, Chicago, Dallas, Denver, Detroit, Miami, Minneapolis, New York, Philadelphia, Phoenix, and Washington. Although the spillover effects are less pronounced in some regions than others, Judith Long (2012) estimated that more than $22 billion in public subsidies were provided for the construction of new professional sports facilities in North America over the period 1990–2010. In cases where politicians refuse to provide subsidies, team owners sometimes move; the most recent example occurred in 2008 when the NBA's Seattle franchise relocated to Oklahoma City after Seattle would not provide public funds for the construction of a new arena.

Subsidies for Canadian Teams

Sports teams are often classified as playing in a large market or a small market; the latter group has become known as *small market franchises* (SMFs). SMFs are characterized by low revenues and are sometimes unable to generate enough revenue to cover their payroll. While it is often thought that SMFs will ultimately relocate to large market destinations, the professional sports leagues have proved a mixed bag where the direction is not always so obvious.

The NHL is most commonly associated with the idea of SMFs for several reasons. First, the NHL has the greatest number and proportion of Canadian teams in the league. Outside of Toronto, Montreal, and Vancouver, not one Canadian metropolitan area is in the US–Canada top 50 population centres. Second, hockey is the only major professional sport in North America deeply rooted in Canadian identity. In the NFL, NBA, or MLB, moving a franchise from one American city to another, or even from a Canadian city to an American city, while unfortunate for the market that loses its franchise, does not change that the game was, is, and remains American in character. But when a Canadian hockey franchise threatens to leave for the United States, its effects are not just financial but psychological too. Finally, all Canadian franchises are exposed to exchange rate risk in that their ticket revenues and local broadcasting revenues are denominated in Canadian dollars, but their biggest expense (i.e., player salaries) is paid in American dollars. Otherwise viable franchises can be harmed by unfavourable exchange rates, where a weak Canadian dollar increases salaries.

A weak Canadian dollar in the early 1990s caused financial hardship for all Canadian teams and affected the relocation of the Quebec City and Winnipeg teams to the United States. NHL commissioner Gary Bettman persuaded US-based teams to contribute to a stabilization fund to help Canadian teams hedge against unfavourable exchange rate movements, and many of the Canadian teams urged their local, provincial, and federal governments to provide financial support to prevent the relocation of their franchises (see Chapter 12 for more details about the outcome of this).

But for governments to subsidize professional sports teams, the money to finance it must come from somewhere, specifically the taxpayer. To the extent that sports teams and their facilities are public goods (i.e., goods in which one's consumption of the good is unpreventable and does not interfere with another's consumption of it), taxation is a reasonable form of ensuring that the right amount of that good is provided. Still, spending money on sports teams means less available money for the arts, education, science, and infrastructure. These are difficult and often contentious issues with which politicians must grapple.

In Canada, Edmonton has often been a battleground for this debate. Beginning with former Oilers owner Peter Pocklington in the 1980s and continuing in 2013 with current owner Daryl Katz, Oilers ownership has struggled to maintain a viable product in the sparsely populated and economically challenged area of northeast Edmonton. Edmonton city council has long supported moving the franchise to downtown, but not if it comes at a significant expense to the city. When Katz threatened to move the team to Seattle or any other bidder, city council eventually relented and controversially agreed to build a C$604.5 million arena and entertainment district. The facility, Rogers Place, is targeted to be complete in 2016.

INTERNATIONAL ISSUES: THE OLYMPIC GAMES

The Olympics and the IOC

The International Olympic Committee (IOC) is an unelected, nonprofit, nongovernmental organization (NGO) based in Switzerland. Its membership consists of representatives of national Olympic committees, international sports federations like FIFA, and Olympic athlete representatives. The IOC has a monopoly on excellence in amateur sport, promotes ethics and good governance in sport, and awards the rights to organize and host the quadrennial Summer and Winter Olympic Games.

The modern Olympic Games look very different than the original ideas promoted by Pierre de Coubertin when he revived the Games in 1894. Then, amateurism and athleticism, competition and fellowship (*le fraternité*) were guiding principles with little attention paid to the business of the Olympics. Early Olympic Games were financed entirely by de Coubertin, which contributed to his subsequent bankruptcy.

Today, the Games focus more on business. The overriding principle in much IOC decision making is maximizing profits from its key asset: the rights to host Olympic Games and its symbols. Beginning with the presidency of Juan Antonio Samaranch in 1980, the IOC transformed itself from a small organization dependent on selling broadcasting rights to US television networks into a global brand worth billions of dollars.

Samaranch appointed Canadian Richard Pound to create an integrated marketing arm known as TOP (The Olympic Program or, alternatively, The Olympic Partners) to sell corporations the exclusive rights to use the Olympic rings and other symbols associated with the Olympic Games for one four-year Olympic cycle. The rights to these symbols are sold to one company per industry and are valuable because of the global recognizability of the Olympics as well as the profitability that comes from association with the Games.

Broadcasting rights remain the biggest source of revenue, but now the IOC generally sells exclusive broadcast rights to one network per country (e.g., CTV in Canada or NBC in the United States), increasing revenue from broadcast rights significantly. Television networks spend vast amounts for the rights to broadcast the Games because of the advertising revenues that can be earned from the limited amount of commercial advertising opportunities during the broadcasts (see Chapter 11). The 2010 Vancouver Games and the 2012 London Games generated almost US$2 billion in broadcasting revenue for the IOC.

Since the IOC is a monopoly, they follow the standard profit-maximizing approach of any monopolist in restricting quantity and increasing prices above what a competitive market would generate. By holding the event quadrennially, the IOC maximizes revenues generated from billions of worldwide viewers and by TOP sponsors who themselves earn billions of dollars in revenue from their exclusiv.e (i.e., monopolistic) association agreements.

Because the potential for monopoly profits exists at every step, incentives for the ability for corruption also exist. The 2002 Salt Lake City, 2006 Nagano, and 2008 Beijing bids were all later found to involve various forms of corruption, bribery, and bid-buying by various IOC officials in attempts to influence voting and steer winning bids. Corruption over the awarding of building contracts is thought to be common and currently plagues the Rio de Janeiro 2016 process. Doha, Qatar's 2016 and 2020 unsuccessful bids for the Summer Games reportedly used its country's dominant financial position in the Middle East to try and rig the vote in its favour, an ultimately unsuccessful strategy because the games were awarded to Tokyo, Japan for 2020. While the IOC has taken steps to address these various forms of vote rigging and corruption, the chance for billions of dollars in profits continues to prove to be too attractive to resist.

Bidding and Costs

Cities and regions compete vigorously to host the Games. Each country interested in doing so creates a national organizing committee (NOC) that determines the city (or region) that will carry its bid. In some countries this is done by vote; in others it is done by the designation of its NOC. Each NOC then submits a formal bid to the IOC. Bids occur in two phases and take place years before the Games. Preparing a bid can cost tens of millions of dollars. Toronto has bid for the Summer Olympic Games twice, each time costing the taxpayers $15 million. Consequently, a group called Bread Not Circuses protested that the money would be better spent on social programs.

While bidding has become very expensive, it was not always so. Hosting the Games is also extremely expensive and can saddle a city with significant costs. The 2014 Sochi Winter Games reportedly cost US$51 billion for hosting and related infrastructure. Construction for the Montreal 1976 Summer Games was significantly behind schedule and went so far over budget that the city incurred almost C$1 billion in debt. The original price tag was $120 million. The lasting symbol of those Games was the Olympic stadium, a doughnut-shaped stadium with a retractable roof. Known affectionately as the "Big O," it is more sarcastically referred to as the "Big Owe," a reference to the financial catastrophe

The 2010 Canadian men's Olympic hockey team became only the third team to win gold on its home ice, winning in overtime in Vancouver.
Paul Kitagaki Jr./ZUMA Press/Newscom

wrought by hosting the Olympics. Only in 2006, 30 years after the Olympics ended, did the city finally retire the last of its Games-related debts.

Montreal's experience was so jarring that when bidding rights were made available in 1977 to host the 1984 Summer Olympics, only one candidate expressed an interest: Los Angeles. The Los Angeles Organizing Committee decided that its best strategy to minimize the financial risks incurred by the city of Montreal was to sell sponsorship rights on a scale that was unparalleled at the time. Television rights were sold for $240 million, an eightfold increase over the amount generated by Montreal.

Legacy Effects

These expenditures include infrastructure (e.g., transportation upgrades, facility construction, accommodation provisions), advertising, and security. As noted earlier, hosting the Games is extremely expensive. But when the Games are over and the fans and participants go home, what remains? It is hard to calculate the total net cost or benefit of hosting the Olympics for several reasons.

First, much of the infrastructure and tourism spending might be shifted forward for the Games and might have occurred on its own even without the Games. Athens was a major tourist destination before hosting the 2004 Games. New infrastructure specific to hosting the Games typically exceeds the size needed for domestic competitions, but these facilities and their associated maintenance costs remain.

Second, host-organizing committees may overstate the direct economic impact from tourism. Many host cities or regions are major tourist destinations before hosting the Games. London, Sydney, Beijing, Vancouver, and other former host cities already attracted large numbers of visitors before winning the rights to host the Games. Fans travelling to these cities to watch the Games may simply replace other tourists who would have visited if the Games were held elsewhere. If so, then the spending by hundreds of thousands of visitors touted by organizing committees must be offset by the alternative spending by the tourists who would normally have come regardless of the Games, reducing the total economic impact of the Games. Also, many locals may leave the area during the Games because of the crowds, traffic, and higher prices charged by local bars, restaurants, and shops.

Third, legacy benefits promoted before the Games, such as the increase in human capital, international recognition, and urban regeneration, might be overstated. Do international cities such as Vancouver, Sydney, London, or Beijing really gain in stature from hosting the Olympics? Do people remember Grenoble, Lake Placid, or Calgary, and even if they do, do they plan vacations based on the distant memory of Olympics past?

A study of name recognition of Canadian cities following the 1988 Calgary Games found that Europeans' recognition of Calgary was near or equal to that of Montreal, Toronto, and Quebec City only in the year the Games took place, and by the year following the Games much of that name recognition had disappeared (Ritchie & Smith, 1991). Urban regeneration, while laudable, might come at the expense of the deterioration or neglect of other needy neighbourhoods or interfere with a market mechanism that might signal the benefit of growth in other areas. In 2008, Beijing created headlines when thousands of residents were forced out of their homes and relocated to overcrowded neighbourhoods so that authorities could build the necessary infrastructure and facilities needed to host the Games. In 1996, Atlanta dismantled most of the Olympic housing facilities rather than sell them or even rent them to those in need of housing.

The economic benefits and costs might not be the deciding factor. Civic pride and unity of purpose might be reason enough to bid to host the Olympic Games. Think of the flag-waving patriotism of Norwegians in Lillehammer 1994, the reconciliation with Aboriginals in Sydney 2000, or the 2008 "coming-out party" in Beijing. Hosting the Games can provide long-lasting intangible benefits for hosts.

Benefits might also be tangible too. Vancouver benefited from improved transport links to Whistler, Calgary gained from the construction of the Saddledome, the home for the last 25 years of the NHL Calgary Flames as well as the site of numerous international skating, curling, and rodeo competitions. Calgary has also become the major training ground for many Canadian winter Olympians because of the bobsled and luge runs, the ski jumping facilities, and the proximity to the Rockies. And despite the problems with the Olympic stadium in Montreal, the Montreal subway was extended out to the Olympic park area, creating substantially improved public transportation links and thereby reducing the traffic congestion common to most big cities.

Conclusions

Irving Berlin famously wrote, "There's no business like show business," but the sports business is pretty unique in its own way. Billionaire franchise owners compete with each other over multimillionaire players to charge millions to advertisers and thousands to adoring fans. Almost every facet of sports has become commoditized and sold, from naming rights to stadiums to in-house signage to uniforms and even to the players' likeness. Even the idealistically pure Olympic Games have transformed themselves from an amateur athletic competition into a brand and identity that is sold to the highest bidder(s).

But just as sports tries to compete off the field to maximize its profits and to create opportunities to capitalize on its monopolistic position, it also creates significant costs. Players sacrifice their bodies, with careers that are often over by the time they are 40. Public funds are diverted from the arts, education, and hospitals to building arenas for modern-day gladiators and competition. Cities compete vigorously for the civic pride and tax dollars generated by hosting professional sports franchises, yet compete just as easily in giving away tax concessions, subsidies, and other sweetheart deals to wealthy owners.

The net impact of all of this is hard to measure. Professional sports teams are barely and rarely valued over US$1 billion, which is miniscule compared to Apple, Exxon Mobil, or Citibank, but the happiness and sadness that their successes and failures elicit in us, the fans, is priceless. It is for this reason that the business of sports is worthy of study and often a source of discussion in our daily lives.

Critical Thinking Questions

1. With few exceptions, professional sports leagues expand the size of their league and increase the length of their season. Why don't they ever decrease in size and length?

2. Why are some cartels successful and others unsuccessful? What conditions are needed to make their agreement to restrict output and exercise monopoly power work?

3. Aggrieved athletes often claim that they are "underpaid" or seek to renegotiate their contract after a good performance. Can an athlete be underpaid if they agree to the contract at the time that they sign it? Is it reasonable for them to seek to renegotiate when they are performing well?

4. Why are there so few women, visible minorities, and foreigners in ownership positions? Are professional sports an example of an "old boy's" club?

5. What effects do revenue sharing and salary caps have on competitive balance? Do they enhance the competitiveness of poor, small-market franchises? Do they punish rich, large-market teams?

6. Given that most players' careers are over by the time they are 35, and given that most of them lack a formal, postsecondary education, what responsibility do owners have to ensuring the long-term health and earning potential of their athletes/employees? What responsibility should the athletes themselves take?

7. Why are cities so interested in hosting a professional sports team? Is it purely an economic argument, or are there other benefits to doing so? What are the costs associated with having a professional sports team in town?

8. Municipal and state/provincial governments will often subsidize team facility construction. How can governments ensure that those that stand to benefit most from the facilities pay the taxes needed to finance these subsidies?

9. Toronto is Canada's largest city by population, but three smaller cities have already hosted Olympic Games (Vancouver 2010, Calgary 1988, and Montreal 1976). Should Toronto continue bidding for the right to host? Will it raise its international prestige if it does? Will it damage its international (or domestic) reputation if it doesn't?

10. The Olympics have evolved from a simple athletic competition among amateur athletes into a multibillion dollar global brand. Can the Olympic ideal of "higher, faster, stronger" coexist with the vast amounts of money spent on training and developing athletic skills necessary to succeed at the Olympic level? Has the amount of endorsement money available to start athletes corrupted the Olympic movement?

Suggested Readings

Fort, R. D. (2010). *Sports economics* (3rd ed.). Upper Saddle River, NJ: Prentice Hall.

Quinn, K. G. (2009). *Sports and their fans: The history, economics and culture of the relationship between spectator, and sport.* Jefferson, NC: McFarland & Company.

Zimbalist, A. (2006). *The bottom line: Observations and arguments on the sports business.* Philadelphia, PA: Temple University Press.

References

Gruneau, R., & Whitson, D. (2001). Upmarket continentalism: Major league sport, promotional culture, and corporate integration. In V. Mosco & D. Schiller (Eds.), *Continental order: Integrating North America for cybercapitalism* (pp. 235–264). Lanham: MD: Rowman & Littlefield.

Long, J. G. (2012). *Public/private partnerships for major league sports facilities.* New York, NY: Routledge.

Ritchie, J. B., & Smith, B. H. (1991). The impact of a mega-event on host region awareness: A longitudinal study. *Journal of Travel Research*, 30(1), 3–10.

Chapter 14
Globalization and Sport
David Whitson

Star Brazilian soccer player Neymar signs with Spanish powerhouse FC Barcelona.

Nippon News/Aflo Co. Ltd/Alamy

In 2004, Franklin Foer, a political journalist for the US magazine *The New Republic*, published a book called *How Soccer Explains the World: An (Unlikely) Theory of Globalization* (Foer, 2004). In a series of provocative and entertaining essays, Foer explores topics as diverse as soccer clubs' historical connections with political and regional rivalries in Spain and the former Yugoslavia; the wealth and commercial ambition that are creating new rivalries today and diminishing the meaning of traditional ones; the flood of players from Latin America and Africa to European clubs while domestic leagues in their own countries struggle to survive; and the antipathy toward the game held by some influential US sports journalists, notably ESPN radio host Jim Rome. Foer cites *New York Times* columnist Thomas Friedman (1999), who has written of globalization as a force both inevitable and beneficent, enabling historically unprecedented standards of living for many nations (China, Brazil, South Korea) and individuals. However, Foer goes on to question some of Friedman's enthusiasm for the "new world order." He argues that, in soccer at least, even though there is more money at the top, prosperity has never materialized for a great many players and clubs. On the contrary, the gap between rich and poor has widened into a chasm in soccer, just as it has in the world itself for many individuals and nations.

I introduce my own discussion of globalization with this brief overview of Foer's book because I believe that soccer offers some extraordinarily good illustrations of globalization in sport, and in the sports business.[1] In the spring of 2006, I had the pleasure of viewing several big matches from the 2006 UEFA Champions League competition on satellite TV. The Edmonton sports bar that screened the matches was packed with expatriates from England, Italy, and Latin America, but also with Canadians like myself who had not grown up with the game. I couldn't help but be struck by how satellite television has expanded the sporting horizons of the Canadian media and the sporting interests of Canadians. Canadian sportscasts and sports pages now report European soccer results and cycle races like the Giro d'Italia, where 30 years ago it was rare to find even the NBA covered in any detail in the Canadian media.

Having noted this small example of globalization, though, I should add immediately that the excitement of a small group of soccer fans in Edmonton was nothing in comparison to the passion that has gripped Canadian cities whose NHL teams have made the play-offs in recent years. In 2013, for example, when the Leafs made the playoffs and Ottawa and Montreal met in the first round, one couldn't help being reminded that hockey arouses Canada's sporting passions like no other sport and that there is no other country where hockey takes over public attention the way it does in Canada. There are limits to globalization, in other words, and even though there are many Canadians who welcome opportunities to follow other sports, there are others (almost certainly more) for whom it is our traditional sport, hockey, and our own traditional rivalries that still matter most.

GLOBALIZATION: A CONCEPTUAL OVERVIEW

The literature on globalization has grown substantially in recent years, even within the sociology of sport (see, for example, Carter, 2011; Giulianotti & Robertson, 2007; Sage, 2011; Scherer & Jackson, 2013). In fact, there has been an active debate in sport sociology about whether some of the developments often associated with the term *globalization* are better understood as *modernization*, or as the Americanization of sport in other countries (Donnelly, 1996). Even more specific discussions about particular sporting phenomena—for example, the growth of the Olympics as a television spectacle, the global appeal of Michael Jordan (Andrews, 2001), or the global manufacturing activities of Nike (Sage, 2004)—not surprisingly reflect the theoretical assumptions and research interests of their authors (see Chapter 2 for an overview of some of the most influential theoretical perspectives in sport sociology). For our purposes here, though, we will define globalization simply as a process or combination of processes through which the world is becoming a more integrated place (Robertson, 1992). As investments and goods, ideas and news, and even people (with some important qualifications) flow across international boundaries in unprecedented ways, the world is becoming one in which more people are aware of events in distant places (including sports events) and more people are affected by decisions taken in distant places—by transnational corporations or by international bodies like the World Trade Organization (WTO)—than was true for earlier generations.[2]

If our starting point, then, involves thinking about globalization as a combination of processes, it is also helpful to think of economic processes, political processes, and cultural processes—as well as the relationships among them (Short & Kim, 1999). It is beyond the scope of this chapter to depict these connections in any detail; however, some illustrations will hopefully encourage readers to think of examples in their own lives. In the economic realm, the most basic idea to grasp is that money (especially investment capital) and

Communications technologies make the world a smaller place.
Lightspring/Shutterstock

products (whether raw materials, manufactured goods, or services) now move around the world more quickly and easily than ever before. In the case of money, we now have global financial markets and a host of new financial products (like mutual funds and derivatives) that facilitate investment in other parts of the world. In addition, the concerted effort over the last quarter century to promote "freer" global trade has meant that companies can try to promote their products in other countries (whether hard goods like cars or shoes, or "soft goods" like films, sports television, or insurance products) without the tariffs or other barriers that once protected domestic products. This has led to opportunities for ambitious companies to establish themselves as global brand names (e.g., Apple, Canon, Bombardier). Meanwhile, other nationally or locally based companies (Eaton's is a good example from Canada) have disappeared because of new competition. It has also led to corporate mergers and takeovers and the phenomenon of transnational corporations (such as Nike, News Corp., and Toyota) doing business in many countries at once. None of this is unprecedented. International trade and corporate empires both date back to the days of European colonialism and (in Canada) the Hudson's Bay Company. However, computer technology has facilitated both the rapid movement of money and the management of far-flung empires, and the post-1980 period represents a new phase in the economic pressures that encourage globalization (e.g., competition and the drive for growth).

Shifting our attention to the political processes that are part of globalization, the most obvious might be the growth in importance of transnational bodies like the WTO and the International Monetary Fund (IMF), as well as regional institutions like the European Union (EU) and trade agreements like NAFTA (North American Free Trade Agreement). However, we should also recognize that much of the economic integration discussed in the previous paragraph was facilitated by the withdrawal of governments from economic functions that used to be considered essential to national autonomy. Many governments, for example, have privatized what were once publicly owned national airlines (e.g., Air Canada or Qantas) and public utilities (electricity, telephones, and sometimes water). In addition, although it may be hard for those born since 1980 to appreciate this, Canada (and other nations) once strictly regulated foreign investment in key sectors of the economy instead of welcoming it. Canada also routinely employed industrial policies including tariffs, tax incentives, and grants for Canadian companies in addition to "buy local" government procurement policies, all intended to encourage the growth of home-based industries. In the free trade agreements of the 1980s and 1990s, though, national governments signed away much of their power to "manage" their economies in return for freer access for their companies to foreign capital and foreign markets.

This was consistent with the neoliberal ideology shared by many governments in those years. Neoliberals believe that free markets—as opposed to public policy—are the most effective way of allocating resources (whether capital or labour). They also believe that the private sector can provide services more efficiently than can governments, so they have pushed for a "downsizing" of the size and scope of government. Critics of neoliberalism contend that privatization and deregulation amount to abandoning the idea of a national economy in the hope that Canadians will be "winners" in the global economy. They also contend that government cutbacks have widened the gaps between the rich and the rest (see Chapter 4). What is widely agreed is that these new restrictions on what governments can do have altered relationships between governments and investors so that governments at all levels (city and regional governments, as well as national ones) now find themselves chasing after highly mobile investment capital. We have seen this phenomenon in sports in the efforts of cities to attract or keep professional sports franchises.

In the cultural sphere, most of us—at least in the Western world—are experiencing new kinds of transnational connectedness (Hannerz, 1996). Satellite television makes possible the global broadcasting of news and sports events, while the Internet and cheaper travel enable us to connect with like-minded people in most parts of the world for purposes that vary from music to politics to sex. In these circumstances, national cultures or cultural practices once associated with particular countries—like cuisine or sports—can no longer be associated quite so closely with their places of origin. Rather, Chinese and Italian food, like soccer, have been carried to many places as people have moved around the world, taking their cultural interests and skills with them. C. L. R. James (1963) and Eduardo Galeano (1998) have described how European colonizers took the games of cricket and soccer to the West Indies and Latin America, respectively, and how new styles of play and sometimes new social meanings were developed in these "New World" societies.[3] Conversely, some recent migrants to Canada from societies where sport was not a normal part of childhood, or where sport was not encouraged among women, have feared the "Westernizing" influences of Canadian sports and worried that sports were taking their children away from the values and role models preferred in their own cultures of origin (see Chapter 5).

At another level, as some cultural practices have been turned into entertainment products—professional sports, music, and film are the best examples—they have each become big businesses that are actively marketed around the globe (Butsch, 1990). US popular culture offers the most familiar examples of the marketing of cultural products and often provokes criticism of US cultural hegemony (see Chapter 2). Yet it is simplistic to assume that US culture is spreading inexorably around the globe (Lull, 2000). Consider, for example, the global popularity of Italian and Chinese food, noted above, as well as the newer fashions for "world music" and ethnic clothing, much of which is originating in French-speaking Africa or Latin America. Consider also the ways in which cities like London or Paris are no longer English or French so much as "world cities," encompassing large communities from parts of Asia, Africa, and other parts of Europe. Finally, consider the global passion for "association football" (or soccer) everywhere outside North America, despite the US's relative indifference to the game and despite attempts by the NFL to promote US football in Europe. Ulf Hannerz (1996) thus invites us to see cultural globalization as a multi-polar process in which some regions and countries participate more actively than others and in different ways.

Each of these processes through which traditional links between culture and place are eroded—the transportation of cultural practices that follows from migration and the promotion of new cultural "products" in the popular media—are leading to unprecedented cultural heterogeneity in some places, and beyond this to cultural hybridity, which Hannerz (1996) defines as the production of *new culture*—when people and cultures blend together to produce new and original syntheses. Again, it's important to recognize that the effects of cultural globalization are not equally felt everywhere. It is the affluent countries of the global "North"—particularly Western Europe and North America—that are being transformed most visibly by immigration, and it is these same affluent countries where more homes have satellite television, multiple personal computers, and other handheld tablets. Even within Canada, moreover, evidence of cultural heterogeneity is all around us in cities like Toronto and Vancouver, but less present in rural communities that are getting older, poorer, and whiter. Thus, one visitor to Canada has remarked that while Vancouver and Toronto are among the most multicultural cities in the world, "villages only forty-five minutes away [seemed] undisturbed in their white-bread, Protestant, nineteenth century pasts" (Iyer, 2000, p. 124). Others, meanwhile, express concern that an urban/rural divide is developing in Canada that has racial and cultural overtones. In parts of the prairie provinces, northern British Columbia, northern Ontario, northern Quebec, and parts of Atlantic Canada, rural populations that include fast-growing Aboriginal communities as well as aging settler communities (farm, logging, and fishing communities)—neither of which can offer much economic future to their young—are becoming culturally and politically detached from the multicultural cities that will be the engines of economic growth (see Epp & Whitson, 2001).

What's important to emphasize here is that the processes of globalization, whether cultural or economic, are characterized by "uneven development." At one level, this refers simply to the uneven spatial distribution of the effects of globalization. Some countries, and especially cities (London and Los Angeles, Mumbai and Hong Kong, and in Canada, Vancouver and Toronto), become financial and cultural centres through which both money and ideas flow. These are the places where capital is concentrated and cultural products are produced, and where value is added to everything (not least of which is property) as a result of lucrative "new economy" activities (Short & Kim, 1999). Other countries, meanwhile, and even whole regions (parts of sub-Saharan Africa, Hannerz (1996) suggests) remain largely untouched, except insofar as they are impoverished by a steady outflow of natural resources and people. In addition, the stark contrasts associated with uneven development also invite us to see globalization as a set of processes that produces winners and losers and increases socioeconomic polarization not only between societies, but also within them. Most evidence would suggest that the affluent countries of the "North" have been net beneficiaries of globalization, as are many societies in Asia where urban standards of living are increasing rapidly. Nonetheless, both Asia and North

America have significant areas of rural poverty alongside their booming cities, while North Americans even in urban areas are all too familiar with the phenomenon of the "jobless recovery," in which more wealth is produced without producing more jobs.

Such increases in both wealth *and* poverty invite critics to ask who benefits (and who loses) from globalization, and whether more cannot be done to mitigate some of its harmful effects. Economic globalization has produced huge profits for corporations that operate successfully on a global scale (whether in mining or televised entertainment), and this translates into well-paying jobs for most of their employees. Globalization has also increased the market for various "producer services": accounting and other financial services, management consultants, and technical/scientific and advertising/marketing expertise, all providing employment for a growing cadre of educated, "knowledge economy" workers with good salaries and high standards of living (Short & Kim, 1999). Yet political integration has proceeded much more haltingly than economic integration, in the NAFTA countries as well as the European Union, and while companies can move production across borders very easily, barriers to the movement of workers and their families still remain. The debate in the United States in 2012 about immigration "amnesties" and policing along the Mexican border illustrates clearly that migrants from poor countries who try to reach countries where there are better employment prospects (whether in America or in Europe) still face many legal and political obstacles, and often grave physical dangers as well.

I cannot do justice here to what are large and ongoing debates, and I refer readers to some of the questions concerning social conflict, power, and ideology that are raised in Chapters 2 and 4. However, I want to leave readers with two ideas to consider during our subsequent discussions of globalization in sport. The first is simply that it is important to understand both the upsides and downsides of globalization, to think about who are the winners and losers, and why there are people who fiercely oppose it as well as enthusiastic advocates. The second idea, which is directly related to the first, is that some of the processes of globalization (e.g., "free trade") result from political decisions, and therefore their consequences are legitimately matters for political debate. Some of globalization's more enthusiastic cheerleaders present it as an inevitable process, a historical trend that is inexorable and therefore beyond political control (see Friedman, 1999). However, although there are new technologies that manifestly raise standards of living and that most people in most societies clearly want to incorporate into their lives (e.g., the Internet, television, sewage treatment, and safe drinking water), governments still make decisions about how we access each of these services and how much the public can be expected to pay. They can also monitor the results and hold corporate service providers accountable. These are legitimate matters of public policy, therefore, and we should not treat as inevitable any "trend" that has controversial social consequences.

THE NEW SPORTING WORLD ORDER

Conceptualizing globalization as a complex and contested process, with economic, cultural, and political dimensions, lays a foundation for exploring some of the changes we have seen in sport over the last quarter century. Some of the more significant of these changes might include the expansion of the NBA into Canada and the NHL into the southern United States; the staging of soccer's World Cup in America in 1994, in Asia in 2002, and in Africa in 2010; the growth of the Olympics into a massive media spectacle; and the migration of professional athletes from poorer countries to those where the highest salaries are paid, a phenomenon we can observe just as clearly in the NHL as we can in European soccer. This list does not pretend to be exhaustive; however, what is common to all of these examples is a search for new audiences, new markets, new jobs—in short, for opportunities to make more money from sport. This is the economic dimension, very clearly. What should become clearer, though, as we proceed is that cultural changes follow directly from these economic ambitions.

In the first two examples offered above, the pattern is clearly that the organizations and financial interests that manage each sport as a business[4] were seeking to expand the markets for their products by promoting these sports in places where they were not historically part of the local popular culture. The NHL, NBA, and FIFA each saw opportunities to dramatically "grow" their respective games, developing potentially lucrative new markets for merchandise and television packages in addition to live audiences. For this potential to be realized, though, required that NHL hockey, for example, be actively promoted in the southern United States. The same was true for NBA basketball in Canada and other nations, and for soccer in both the United States and Asia. Readers can debate how well these economic ambitions have been fulfilled (all three, arguably, remain works in progress). My point here is simply that for new sports to become popular on an enduring basis requires cultural changes in the countries and continents where sports entrepreneurs hope to promote new leisure choices. People have to get *interested* in these new activities, and if they do, this means less time and less money for the games they enjoyed before. The new cultural choices associated with globalization compete directly, in other words, for people's time and attention—and money—with the entertainment forms and spending habits that were traditional to those places. Perhaps, though, if people in Europe and Asia could afford regular access to NBA or NFL products they might flock to these US-based sports, while interest in soccer or in Asian cultural practices would decline. This is the promise—or the spectre—of "Americanization."

The Olympics, and the migration of professional athletes to North America and Western Europe, highlight slightly different dynamics. In the Olympic example, we have a global governing body—the International Olympic Committee (IOC)—that is not commercial in quite the same sense as the NBA or FIFA. However, anyone with any interest in the subject will know that the Olympic Games have become a global television extravaganza, that corporations are willing to pay higher and higher sums to be associated with the Olympics as advertisers and sponsors, and that the IOC, under the leadership of Juan Antonio Samaranch and Richard Pound, put a strategic priority on promoting the value of the Olympic "brand" (Barney, Wenn, & Martyn, 2002). Among the reasons for the global appeal of the Olympics are that they provide a global stage for many small countries that cannot support the "major leagues" and for athletes (especially women) who don't otherwise get the media exposure enjoyed by the major professional sports. The Olympic movement promotes values—internationalism, inclusiveness, excellence—that many people admire and want to be part of. The Olympic Games are a unique institution, in other words, and have a history of promoting sport around the world.

The final phenomenon flagged above, the increasingly global movement of professional athletes, will be the subject of a more extended discussion in a moment. For now, though, a striking example will suffice. Foer (2004) estimates that there are now more than 5,000 Brazilian soccer players plying their trade in other countries. Of the 22 players who represented Brazil in the 2002 World Cup, only seven still played their club soccer in Brazil. By the 2014 World Cup in Brazil, only four out of 23 players on the Brazilian team still played their club soccer in Brazil. This exodus of Brazilian soccer players is, he suggests, "one of the great migrations of talent in recent history, the sports equivalent of the post-Soviet brain drain" (Foer, 2004, p. 131). Most would agree that these Brazilian migrants have improved the standard of play—and the entertainment value—of the foreign leagues they now play in, and the economic advantage for the individual players is obvious: higher salaries than they could hope for at home, in a country whose recent economic growth still cannot support the kind of infrastructure and ticket prices that fuel the richer economy of professional sport that exists in Europe, Japan, and North America.

However, an exodus of talent on this scale has had predictable effects on the domestic game. Brazilian fans seldom get to see their top players, and the quality of Brazilian league play has suffered. For Uruguayan writer Eduardo Galeano (1998), this exodus of good players from Brazil, Argentina, and Uruguay has led to "mediocre professional leagues (at home), and ever fewer, ever less fervent fans. People desert the stadiums to watch foreign matches on television" (p. 206). It was not unusual in the late 1990s, Foer (2004) notes, for a Brazilian league match in Rio de Janeiro's famous Maracanã Stadium (with a capacity of more than 100,000) to have only a few thousand spectators. By 2013, increasing Brazilian prosperity and the hosting of the 2014 World Cup had improved this situation a little. However, Brazil's most recent young prodigy, Neymar, announced in May 2013 that he had signed to play for the next five years for Barcelona, at a salary his Brazilian club, Santos, could still never match from the gate receipts and television revenues available in Brazilian soccer.

There are many interesting examples and comparisons one could pursue—far too many to proceed in this fashion. In an effort to distill the arguments, the discussion that follows will focus on three aspects of globalization in sport, each involving phenomena that can be observed in a number of sports and in many different countries. First, we will proceed with our discussion of player migration and the globalization of the labour market in professional sports. From there, we will move to an examination of globalization in the sports business, including the growth of transnational ownership and investment, the search for global television audiences, and the experience of several sports with global marketing strategies. The final subsection will focus on fans and examine the effects of the first two changes on the ways that fans relate to teams, to players, and to sports themselves. The chapter will conclude with some observations on the extent to which sports interests have been successful in constructing the "global consumer" and enquire into the cultural implications of changes in the sports business. Returning to questions raised in our conceptual overview of globalization, we will also enquire into who wins and loses as a consequence of the increasing global integration that we find in many sports.

Professionalization and Globalization in the Sports Labour Market

We've noted above the diaspora of Brazilian soccer players now playing in better-paying leagues in Europe, and this is also true for Argentina and, to a lesser extent, other Latin American nations (e.g., Mexico, Uruguay, Colombia, and Ecuador). The rich leagues of Western Europe—Spain, England, Italy and, to a lesser extent, Germany, France, Portugal, and the Netherlands—now include substantial numbers of Latin American players as well as players from Africa and from former East Bloc countries, where player salaries also remain low. Indeed, the labour market for soccer players has now become so transnational that in the 2006 UEFA Champions League final, the English representative, Arsenal, fielded only two English players. Their starting lineup included players from France, Spain, Sweden,

Germany, Belarus, and Cote d'Ivoire. Their opponents, FC Barcelona, fielded a lineup that featured a majority of Spaniards; however, it also included star players from Brazil, Cameroon, and Mexico. This pattern has been repeated, with some variations, in every UEFA Champions League final since, and the point is simply that the wealthiest and most ambitious clubs in the major soccer nations of Western Europe can afford to buy the best players in the world.

In the North American major sports leagues, similar trends can be observed over the last quarter century. NHL teams began to employ European players in the 1970s, initially as a response to the World Hockey Association (WHA) and the competition for elite players that the new league introduced. Before 1990, though, the numbers were still fairly small, and most came from Sweden and Finland—players like Börje Salming, Mats Näslund, Jari Kurri, and Esa Tikkanen. Players from the state-supported hockey systems of Eastern Europe like Viacheslav Fetisov and Igor Larionov (from Russia) and the Stastny brothers, Anton and Peter (from Czechoslovakia), were exceptions to this pattern. With the collapse of the Soviet Union, though, and turmoil in Czechoslovakia, many players from Russia and the Czech and Slovak Republics sought their fortunes in North America, and now many NHL lineups include players from a variety of European nations, as well as increasing numbers of US players. Before 1990, the NBA was less international than the NHL, remaining overwhelmingly American. Today, there are increasing numbers of NBA players from Croatia and Serbia, from Lithuania and Italy, from Spain and Argentina, and from China (as well as Canada and Australia). Major League Baseball has had increasing numbers of players from a small core of Latin American countries (the Dominican Republic, Mexico, and Venezuela), as well as Japan and more recently South Korea, for a number of years.[5]

If a global labour market is the new "normal" in major league sports, though, why should this be an issue? To understand how globalization departs from previously established practices, and alters some of the meanings traditionally associated with intercommunity competition, requires us to look back almost a hundred years to the early days of "representative" sports. Alan Ingham has noted in an influential essay that sporting contests once provided dramatic representations of "us" and "them," and that the historical popularity of team sports derives from their capacity to dramatize communal identities and rivalries (Ingham, Howell, & Schilperoort, 1988, p. 437). In the early days of spectator sports, indeed, cheering for the home team meant cheering for teams comprising local talent, and this gave credibility to popular beliefs that sporting success reflected favourably on the community that had produced them.[6] However, as hiring a few "travelling players" to bolster the local side and then hiring whole squads of professional players became standard practice, the relationships between teams and the communities they represented began to take on a different character, which Ingham and his colleagues depict as more akin to a merchant–customer relationship. Fan support is solicited for the best team that local owners can buy. Now, though, team success no longer reflects the quality of local players, let alone the characteristics of local people. Instead, it reflects the wealth of the owners and—crucially in today's world—the wealth of a city's economy and its capacity to yield the revenues that support competitive salaries (Whitson, 2001).

For the greater part of the 20th century, then, professionalism was the norm in North American major league sports. However, although this meant that those playing for a city have very seldom been raised in that city (in 2013, for example, only one of the Vancouver Canucks was born in British Columbia, two of the Montreal Canadiens were born in Quebec, and only one of the Toronto Blue Jays is Canadian born), several factors continued to encourage fans to identify with players and to see them as local representatives. To begin with, until recent decades restrictive player contracts bound professional athletes to the teams they began their careers with, unless those teams chose to trade them or cut them. Team rosters, in these circumstances, were more stable than they are today, and fans learned to identify with players who had represented the city for many years and often had made their homes there. However, once baseball's "reserve clause" was overturned by US courts in 1976, players were no longer legally bound to their original teams, and player unions in all the North American major leagues have negotiated steadily lower barriers to free agency (see Weiler, 2000). Predictably, this has led to steadily increased player mobility.

The history of globalization in the soccer labour market, not surprisingly, is different. The most obvious difference, perhaps, is that instead of one major league in each sport, as has been the case in North America (except in those brief periods when "rival" leagues have attempted to compete), there has been financial competition among teams based in Spain, England, and Italy to sign elite players: both from each other and from anywhere else in the world. The other obvious difference is that, with soccer played on a much more global basis than any of the North American sports, the talent pool is more genuinely global, with many good players now coming from Africa and Latin America. A third important difference is that even though player associations have pushed over the years to ease restrictions on player mobility, they have been historically weaker than their North American counterparts, with the result that major change did not come until 1995 (much later than in North America), following a ruling by the European Court of Justice. The court ruled in favour of a minor league Belgian player named Jean-Marc Bosman, saying that "rules" that the major European soccer leagues had followed, which had by agreement limited teams to three foreign-born players, contravened the rights of players who were EU citizens to pursue their trade in any EU country (Ammirante, 2006). This opened the door for ambitious English teams, for example, to scout and sign players from France and Portugal, leading to the overwhelmingly foreign Arsenal and Chelsea sides that represented London in the 2006 UEFA Champions League competition. It has also encouraged many players from French- and English-speaking Africa and from Brazil and Argentina (many of whom have Spanish or Italian ancestry) to seek resident status in these EU countries.

Increased player mobility has thus led to important changes in professional sports, in both North America and Europe. On the positive side, it has led to markedly higher player salaries (though some might argue that the stars, at least, now make too much money), and it has radically altered the relationships between players and teams, undermining the absolute control that teams and managers used to have over a player's career. It has also enabled fans, at least in those countries where the top leagues play, to regularly see the world's best players and to enjoy the skills of Brazilian soccer players or Czech hockey players on a regular basis. It also speaks to ideas of human rights that wonderful players from small countries, players like Jaromir Jagr from the Czech Republic, Didier Drogba (the Cote d'Ivoire–born star who helped Chelsea win the UEFA Champions League in 2012), and Lionel Messi (three-time FIFA Player of the Year), are able to earn salaries commensurate with their abilities.[7]

On the negative side, however, we've noted that this same phenomenon has reduced the Brazilian and Argentine soccer leagues to the status of minor leagues, staffed mostly by hopefuls and has-beens, with a corresponding decline in fan interest. The same observation could fairly be made of Czech and Russian hockey in the last decade or so (Cantelon, 2006), despite the opportunities that a renewed Kontinental Hockey League (KHL) has offered to Russians and other Europeans who no longer want to play in the NHL. In the top leagues, increased player mobility has produced a situation in which good players often switch teams at the end of each contract, and players very rarely stay with the same team for their entire career. This new pattern has meant a reshaping of relationships among players, teams, and the communities they are supposed to "represent." It may also be changing the meanings of fan allegiances and loyalties, in ways we shall explore shortly.

Before leaving the phenomenon of increased player mobility behind, though, we need to reflect on the fact that globalization in the sports labour market is so far mostly a one-way street, with players from poorer countries (or at least countries where the structure of professional sport does not support "major league" salaries) migrating to those countries where the salaries are highest. There is, as yet, very little traffic in the other direction. There have always, to be sure, been some North American university hockey players and basketball players (many of them "too small" by NHL and NBA standards) who have gone on to play in Europe. However, the European leagues in these sports do not generate either the arena revenues or the television revenues (see below) that would enable them to pay North American–style salaries, even in those Western European countries (such as Germany or Italy) that support major league salaries in soccer. A further barrier to the movement of Canadian and US athletes to Europe, moreover, has been the unwillingness of many unilingual North Americans to make the sorts of cultural adjustments (including mastery of another language) that we routinely expect of European or Hispanic players coming here. Both of these issues have come to the fore during the NHL lockouts of 2004 and 2012, when some NHL athletes started to play in Europe but quickly came home, complaining of poor hotels or travel conditions, or simply the "foreignness" of the living environment (Cantelon, 2006).

Finally, however, I want to challenge one of the arguments sometimes made by advocates of globalization, namely that the increased presence of players from other cultures in our midst and the increased visibility of heroes from "other" races leads inexorably to increased tolerance, and ultimately the disappearance of racism. Even though there are bits of evidence that appear to support this thesis—the increasing number of black players in professional sports in both Europe and North America, and France's celebration of its victorious team in the 1998 World Cup (a team made up predominantly of black players from France's former colonies)—the larger picture remains discouraging. Riots in French cities in early 2006 revealed how shallow or transitory was French goodwill toward their immigrant populations and how deeply ingrained in French society were anti-black and anti-Arab attitudes. More recently, soccer matches in Spain, Italy, England, and the Ukraine have all been marred by ugly episodes of racist chanting by fans, and sometimes by racial epithets by prominent players. In some of these instances, leagues have imposed significant penalties on both clubs and players; however, the recurrence of such events only serves to demonstrate that racial prejudices persist, and legislated protection of minorities remains necessary.

In North America, the presence of black stars in professional sports is of longer standing and hence more familiar. However, the NHL and the major junior Ontario Hockey League (hockey is by far the "whitest" of the major North American sports) have both had racist incidents in recent years (Pitter, 2006). There is also a constituency in Canadian hockey that has regularly given European players (Swedes and Russians in particular) a rough reception. Examples in other professional sports are plentiful, but my point here is simply that although racism and xenophobia cannot be blamed on globalization (they clearly predate globalization by many centuries), increased player migration has led to some ugly reactions. Globalization, therefore, has not led to the tolerance that some predicted, and "global culture" is not—or not yet, at any rate—a culture in which people of all colours are readily accepted for their accomplishments (see Chapter 5).

Corporate Strategies: The Promotion of Sports "Product"

Turning from player mobility to owners, and the increasingly global horizons of professional sports entrepreneurs, we can see even greater changes in the business of sport over a period of about 40 years. The first change to note is in the kinds of people who are owners. The traditional team owner was typically a rich local businessman, for whom sports ownership was part of being a prominent local citizen or simply a prestigious hobby. From about the 1980s on, though, it became more common to find sports teams owned by corporations or by major investors from outside the community.[8] The underlying factor here is that professional sports came to be viewed as an investment that could potentially pay off in a big way. Instead of a business in which the revenues came primarily from gate receipts—and indeed from cheap seats (or, in many European soccer stadiums before the 1980s, from standing-room admissions)—leagues in all sports began to follow a business model pioneered in the NFL and the NBA, in which new "revenue streams" were actively developed. Luxury boxes, more expensive food, and new forms of electronic advertising all increased the revenues available within the stadium (or arena) itself. Of even greater potential value, though, were the revenues to be gained outside the venue: from the promotion of licensed merchandise, from the sale of television products among the much larger audiences who don't often attend live games, and from the capital gains that could be realized from increases in the values of franchises or shares (Horne, 2006; Whitson, 2001).

In the case of merchandise, of course, sports clubs have sold jerseys and other clothing bearing team insignia and colours for many years. However, most such sales were to faithful fans, and sales were mostly limited to the city or region where the team was based. The market, in other words, was local. There were a few exceptional teams that developed national followings: the New York Yankees and the Montreal Canadiens, for example. However, even for these teams, merchandise sales were a relatively small factor in team incomes. In the 1980s, though, the NBA and the NFL demonstrated that merchandise could be promoted in a much more systematic manner, and with the celebrity drawing power of Michael Jordan, Chicago Bulls gear was sold around the world, much of it to people who had never seen Jordan play. In Europe, major soccer clubs like Manchester United and Real Madrid have moved even more aggressively into the marketing of merchandise, promoting sales not only in their home countries but in the Americas and Asia, too. Real Madrid was alleged to have signed English midfielder David Beckham as much to promote merchandise sales in the Asian market as for his abilities on the field, while both Madrid and Manchester United (Beckham's former club) now regularly report higher earnings from merchandising and sponsorship than they do from gate receipts (Ammirante, 2006). In both Europe and North America, teams that once attracted national followings because of their histories of success (Barcelona FC, the Dallas Cowboys, and the Los Angeles Lakers are additional examples) now seek to establish themselves as globally recognized "brands" (Horne, 2006).

It is television, of course, that has made such commercial ambitions feasible. Satellite television has created the prospect of worldwide audiences for the most prestigious leagues (the English Premier League and Italy's Serie A in soccer, and NBA basketball), as well as for events like the Masters Golf Tournament and the Wimbledon Championships in tennis. It is satellite television, likewise, that has made possible worldwide audiences for the Olympics and the FIFA World Cup, audiences that attract rights fees now valued at well over a billion dollars. Television took these events into homes around the world, creating a version of "global culture" in which people around the world now follow the same global entertainment events and care about the fates of the same global celebrities. Television also multiplied the value of any advertising that is visible to its cameras (on team jerseys, as well as on and around the playing surfaces), thus greatly expanding the potential income from advertising and sponsorships (Bellamy, 1998; see also Chapter 13).

However, if satellite-fed broadcast television had dramatically expanded the revenues available to sports in the 1960s, both in North America and Europe, the real bonanza would not come until the late 1980s with the arrival of pay television as a commercial reality. The introduction of successive forms of pay television—cable and satellite subscriptions and later pay-per-view channels—together with the channel capacity that these technologies provide, opened up a succession of new and lucrative possibilities in the sale of televised sports entertainment. These include the now familiar sports networks (TSN and Sportsnet in Canada, ESPN in the United States, and Sky Sports in Europe), as well as more specialized channels devoted to particular sports (e.g., golf, fishing) and even particular teams (e.g., Real Madrid and the Toronto Maple Leafs). This growth of *narrow-casting*, or special-interest channels aimed at niche markets, created demand for more sports programming than the broadcast networks had ever shown and opportunities for new kinds of sports "product," notably pay-per-view channels (Bellamy, 1998). In Europe and Australia, moreover, where cable and satellite did not become established until the 1990s, having exclusive rights to televise the most popular sports (soccer in Europe and the rugby league in Australia) also proved the most effective vehicle for selling millions of satellite subscriptions and dishes (Williams, 1994). This all led to increases in the rights fees available to the most popular sports, and it illustrates the extent to which sport has become incorporated into "circuits of promotion" in a culture where the value of any event to advertisers can be calibrated according to its capacity to promote the major products and personalities associated with it (Whitson, 1998).

Ultimately, it has also led all the major sports, and the television interests now intimately connected with them, to actively seek global audiences. In both Europe and North America, the home audiences for the major sports leagues—the English and Italian soccer leagues, the NBA, the NFL—had reached saturation points, or something very close to this. Therefore, if further growth was to take place, the greatest potential clearly lay abroad, through the sale of television packages in markets that had not previously followed the English Premier League (EPL) or the NBA, for example, in any numbers. This is why EPL matches are now carried into homes around the world on television screens and new media devices throughout the season. Another innovation has seen the creation of new competitions (the UEFA Champions League soccer competition, for example, or the Rugby World Cup) that are aimed specifically at international television audiences as well as the traditional territories for these sports. Indeed, televised sport has demonstrated that, with rare exceptions, the appeal of sport crosses international boundaries more reliably than do other forms of popular entertainment—like drama or comedy—that rely more heavily on language skills and culturally specific knowledge. Specialty sports networks, and their Internet-based websites, are also popular sources of up-to-the-minute sports information.

At the same time, the optimism of some expansion-minded enthusiasts that, with the right marketing, any sport could be sold anywhere has to be viewed with some skepticism. Despite the successes of soccer's biggest clubs in promoting themselves in Asia, the world's most popular game has made only modest inroads in the United States. Likewise, despite three decades of NHL efforts to expand hockey's footprint in American popular culture, the results remain disappointing (Mason, 2006). Many US sports fans remain resistant to sports that didn't originate there—or perhaps they remain resolutely loyal to their own sporting traditions? At the same time, despite efforts by the NBA, the NFL, and MLB to establish markets for their products in Europe and other continents, these too have achieved fairly limited success. It can be hypothesized, then, that global marketing runs up against entrenched cultural tastes and loyalties everywhere.

Fans: Constructing the Global Consumer?

For many fans, though, and especially younger fans, the dynamics described above have led to a "delocalization" of sporting interests and loyalties—an idea that suggests that people are becoming less attached to the sporting practices and institutions historically associated with the cities or nations they live in (Wilson, 2006). At one level, this is illustrated in the growth of transnational television audiences for the major leagues (English and Italian soccer, as well as North American professional sports) and a corresponding decline in fan support for smaller clubs in provincial cities. It is also registered in the growth of global interest in famous teams (Manchester United, Real Madrid, the Dallas Cowboys, the Los Angeles Lakers) and a rise in "elective affinities" among young fans: supporting teams other than their local representatives on the basis of team success, "attitude," or (increasingly) celebrity players like David Beckham or LeBron James who are now extraordinarily valuable brands in their own right. Since Real Madrid signed Beckham in 2003, income from sponsorship, advertising, and merchandising has multiplied, and the club has launched its own 24-hour satellite television channel and a website in English, Japanese, and Spanish (Ammirante, 2006).

What's going on here is that fan allegiances rooted in place (the practice of rooting for the home team) and in *social* choices (class or ethnic identities, for example, or regional loyalties) are being undermined by the language of consumer choice, in which fans everywhere are encouraged to identify with "world class" teams and players (Whitson, 1998, pp. 65–66). Beckham, of course, would later sign with the Los Angeles Galaxy in 2007 in a move that paid immediate financial dividends for the club in terms of sponsorship, gate revenue, and global visibility. After being loaned to AC Milan in 2009 and 2010, Beckham eventually finished his playing career in France at Paris Saint-Germain FC in 2013.

At a deeper level, though, delocalization also means that traditional national (or regional) sports must now compete with sports imported from other countries if they are to retain their audiences and their cultural significance, especially among young people. Thus, as the major professional sports expand and go global *as businesses*, the kinds of national and regional rivalries that once defined the meanings of sports in popular culture are supplanted by the attitudes and practices of consumer choice and of global youth culture and fashion. What is emerging may be a global sporting culture in which the media industry plays a significant part, and audiences around the world (or the affluent world, at least) are invited to take an interest in the same sports events and celebrities. Canadians, for example, now have access to a wider range of sports entertainment than we had in the past, including not only NBA basketball and UEFA Champions League soccer, but also sports like cycling and rugby that were once very difficult to find on Canadian television. Canadian sports audiences, like audiences in other countries, are being addressed as free-floating consumers who might switch teams *and even develop new sporting interests* if we are given access to world-class sporting entertainment.

The claim of promoters of cultural globalization, indeed, is that "as people gain access to global information, so they develop global needs and demand global commodities, thereby becoming global citizens" (Levitt, cited in Robins, 1991, pp. 26–27). For critics of globalization, this road leads inexorably to the loss of cultural diversity, as the expensively produced cultural events that the mainstream media publicize—the major professional sports and the Olympics, Hollywood films and US television dramas, musicians on the major labels—make less well-funded cultural productions look unprofessional, even home-spun, by comparison. It should be recognized here that the purpose of marketing is precisely to create demand for new products, and that global marketing sets out to reshape patterns of cultural consumption and to "grow" the markets for the products of transnational corporations (Fawcett, 1992). However, we need to examine the rhetoric through which this is accomplished, in particular the now familiar notion of "world class" products.

I want to propose here that the label of "world class" seeks to connect global brand names with ersatz ideas of excellence, specifically the idea of being the best of its kind in the world. What global brands purport to offer—whether an event like the Olympic Games or the World Cup, or the products of the global corporations that associate themselves with such events—are famous names, state-of-the-art production values, and products that are supposed to be the best of their kind in the world. We need to carefully distinguish, though, between excellence and fame, especially where the latter is a product of expensive publicity machines. Think about how difficult it is to determine what is "the best" when considering cultural products (like films or books or sports) that may be very difficult to compare. The term *world class* was once meaningfully applied to athletics or swimming performances that were measurably the best in the world in that event in a given year. However, it is now used as a claim to superiority in so many other contexts, ranging from orchestras to universities to cities—contexts where qualitative comparisons are difficult and criteria of excellence are open to debate—that it has become devoid of concrete meaning. It can be suggested, indeed, that the label "world class" now denotes nothing but self-promotion, and indeed the status of an aspirant as opposed to an established claimant.

Conclusions

I have presented globalization as a complex set of processes that combines to make the world a more integrated place, and I have tried to distinguish, for the sake of clarity, between economic or business processes (e.g., freer trade or transnational corporate integration) and cultural processes (e.g., the spread of heterogeneity and the loosening of historical ties between cultures and places). It remains crucial, though, in thinking about globalization to remember the linkages between economic and cultural processes. For example, it is the drive on the part of sports businesses to construct global markets that has taken us some ways toward the creation of a global sporting culture. "The global expansion of the leisure and entertainment industries undoubtedly brings new opportunities to many of us—opportunities to watch or even practice sports that were once not available to us in our home countries—and this development is heralded by those who want to celebrate the benefits of increased consumer choice" (Ammirante, 2006, p. 240). However, for critics of globalization, among whom Julian Ammirante would certainly be included, this is a dubious benefit. He proceeds to point to "the metropolitan derivation of most of the cultural products (and the lifestyles) that attain worldwide promotion and distribution" (Ammirante, 2006, p. 240) and to the fact that global soccer is increasingly dominated by a handful of super-rich clubs. It is important, therefore, to understand that in the entertainment industry, globalization is an agenda promoted by the biggest of businesses, and indeed that the entertainment industry is one of globalization's most effective boosters (Fawcett, 1992).

Here we have, in capsule form, the essence of economic globalization, as well as the standard objection to it: the takeover of our most popular sports by super-rich individuals and media corporations, and their management of these popular institutions with more thought given to the bottom line than to the traditions of the team or the sport. Examples include the marketing of leagues like the English Premier League and the National Basketball Association, teams like Real Madrid and Manchester City, and celebrities like David Beckham, Kobe Bryant, and Tiger Woods.

It is also important, however, to see the continuities as well as the changes. Professional sport was a business from its inception, in both Europe and North America. However, the sports business in the United States began in the 1960s to adopt business models and practices being used with success elsewhere in US business (franchising, expansion, and branding campaigns are the best examples of this). In Europe and Australia, in contrast, teams and national governing bodies continued to operate along more traditional lines for another quarter century, and traditional ways of doing things often trumped commercial logic. Since the early 1990s, however, and the advent of pay TV, sports entrepreneurs in Europe, as well as Australia and parts of Asia, have quickly moved to adopt similar money-making strategies, and the outcome is the global spread of a more frankly commercial approach to sport (Horne, 2006, pp. 29–30). Nonetheless, globalization in the sports business has not meant the spread of US sports around the world, as some feared, so much as it has seen the spread of US business and marketing practices—practices that originated in the United States but are no longer uniquely American.

Turning to cultural globalization, it can be suggested that, as above, the threat is less the inexorable spread of US popular culture than it is the steady detachment of culture from place, as a result of a combination of migration, media, and market forces. To the extent that this continues, one might predict that some once-local cultural traditions will be commercialized and marketed around the world (West African and Cuban music might be examples of this, as is rugby in sport). Others, meanwhile, will die out, and the world's cultural diversity will be diminished. Both of these trends—that is, the commercialization of "folk" culture and the loss of cultural diversity—will be seen by some as troubling developments, and this includes not just anti-globalization activists but also some traditional "conservatives" who care about the survival of local traditions. Indeed, Foer (2004) proposes that "the innovation of the anti-globalization left is its embrace of traditionalism: its worry that global tastes and brands will steamroll indigenous cultures," and that global marketing by Real Madrid and Nike will succeed in "prying fans away from their old allegiances" (pp. 4–5).

Such fears must be credited with having some grounds, for most of us will be able to see in our own experience some evidence of cultural homogenization. However, Foer goes on to observe that in his own research into the globalization of soccer, cultural homogenization turned out to be less than he had anticipated. On the contrary, many of soccer's quirky local cultures—and blood feuds—appear to be flourishing despite globalization. And in Canada, too, we can find lots of evidence of local traditions and enthusiasms, as well as regional allegiances and rivalries that seem alive and well. All we have to do is look at the passion with which Canadians followed the fortunes of the Vancouver Canucks in the 2012 Stanley Cup playoffs and the enthusiasm for hockey that persists in many smaller cities across Canada where the junior game is thriving: places like Kamloops and Cranbrook, Red Deer and Brandon, Peterborough and London, and Rimouski and Moncton. We might also recognize the continued popularity of curling in rural Canada and in prairie cities like Edmonton (see Mott & Allardyce, 1989), as well as the revival of enthusiasm for the Canadian Football League.[9]

Foer also warns us, finally, against the temptation to see the past through highly selective glasses. He clearly enjoys many of the cultural traditions associated with soccer and regrets that in trying to move the game "up-market" soccer's new investors have destroyed some of the game's working-class traditions. Yet he also remarks that the nostalgia he encountered in some quarters for the game's good old days uncritically celebrated traditions of bigotry, drunkenness, and violence against "others" that were better left behind. It also appeared to gloss over the fact that the old-fashioned terraces where working-class male fans gathered to shout their partisan allegiances and hatreds were places where fans were often treated like cattle and where, in too many tragic instances, significant numbers of fans were injured and even killed. The cultural effects of change aren't all bad, in other words, and we should be careful about glorifying "tradition" in an uncritical way (Foer, 2004).

With these caveats—reminders that the effects of globalization may have good and bad elements and, in any event, may often be exaggerated—I want to close by returning to a point made in the introduction to this chapter, namely that both economic and cultural globalization raise issues of public policy. In our first free trade agreement with the United States in the 1980s, as well as the subsequent NAFTA, Canada did everything it could to keep culture "off the table" because the economics of cultural reproduction and distribution give enormous advantages to the US film, music, television, and publishing industries (Grant & Wood, 2004). Canada thus fought successfully for a "cultural exemption" that allowed us to continue to support our cultural industries: our music industry, our publishers, our film industry. Such policies are regularly challenged by the US cultural industries, which tend to see the Canadian market almost as an extension of their own domestic market (predominantly English-speaking and already familiar with US entertainment products and personalities). However, we need to remember that culture represents a different kind of product from wheat or auto parts. Our culture is part of our identity, and our authors and athletes and musicians and filmmakers constitute a big part of what keeps us different— from our neighbours to the south and from everyone else. This is what makes the protection of Canada's ability to produce our own culture, and of cultural diversity within Canada, matters of more than academic interest and matters of more than entertainment, too.

Critical Thinking Questions

1. Consider the popular idea that hockey is "Canada's game" in light of how many countries the game is now played in. Compare hockey and soccer as global games.

2. Is globalization leading to a greater diversity of sporting choices or to the dominance of a small handful of men's professional sports?

3. What are the differences between sports fans of 40 years ago and those of today? Is the expansion of consumer choice an important advancement? What are the limitations of consumer sovereignty?

4. What are the meanings of "world class" in relation to sports? cities? universities?

5. What does it mean to be a global citizen? How might this go beyond being a global consumer?

Suggested Readings

Foer, F. (2004). *How soccer explains the world: An (unlikely) theory of globalization*. New York, NY: Harper Perennial.

Horne, J. (2006). *Sport in consumer culture*. London, UK: Palgrave Macmilian.

King, A. (2003). *The European ritual: Football in the new Europe*. Burlington, VT: Ashgate.

Tomlinson, J. (1999). *Globalization and culture*. Chicago, IL: University of Chicago Press.

Whitson, D. (2001). *Hockey and Canadian identities: From frozen rivers to revenue streams*. In D. Taras & B. Rasporich (Eds.), *A passion for identity: Canadian studies for the 21st century*. Toronto, ON: Nelson.

Whitson, D., & Gruneau, R. (Eds.). (2006). *Artificial ice: Hockey, culture, and commerce*. Toronto, ON: University of Toronto Press.

References

Ammirante, J. (2006). Globalization in professional sport: Comparisons and contrasts between hockey and European football. In D. Whitson & R. Gruneau (Eds.), *Artificial ice: Hockey, culture, and commerce* (pp. 237–261). Toronto, ON: University of Toronto Press.

Andrews, D. (Ed.). (2001). *Micheal Jordan, Inc.: Corporate sport, media culture, and late modern America*. Albany, NY: SUNY Press.

Barney, R. K., Wenn, S., & Martyn, S. (2002). *Selling the five rings: The International Olympic Committee and the rise of Olympic commercialism*. Salt Lake City, UT: University of Utah Press.

Bellamy, R. (1998). The evolving television sports marketplace. In L. Wenner (Ed.), *MediaSport* (pp. 73–87). New York, NY: Routledge.

Butsch, R. (Ed.). (1990). *For fun and profit: The transformation of leisure into consumption*. Philadelphia, PA: Temple University Press.

Cantelon, H. (2006). Have skates, will travel: Canada, international hockey, and the changing hockey labour market. In D. Whitson & R. Gruneau (Eds.), *Artificial ice: Hockey, culture, and commerce* (pp. 215–235). Toronto, ON: University of Toronto Press.

Carter, T. (2011). *In foreign fields: The politics and experiences of transnational sports migration*. London, UK: Pluto Press.

Donnelly, P. (1996). The local and the global: Globalization in the sociology of sport. *Journal of Sport & Social Issues, 20*, 239–257.

Epp, R., & Whitson, D. (Eds.). (2001). *Writing off the rural West: Globalization, governments, and the transformation of rural communities*. Edmonton, AB: University of Alberta Press.

Fawcett, B. (1992). The trouble with globalism. In M. Wyman (Ed.), *Vancouver forum* (pp. 183–201). Vancouver, BC: Douglas & McIntyre.

Foer, F. (2004). *How soccer explains the world: An (unlikely) theory of globalization*. New York, NY: Harper Perennial.

Freidman, T. (1999). *The Lexus and the olive tree*. New York, NY: Farrar, Strauss & Giroux.

Galeano, E. (1998). *Soccer in the sun and shadow*. M. Fried (Trans.). London, UK: Verso.

Giulianotti, R., & Robertson, R. (2007). *Globalization and sport*. Oxford, UK: Blackwell Publishing.

Grant, P. & Wood, C. (2004). *Blockbusters and trade wars: Popular culture in a globalized world*. Vancouver, BC: Douglas & McIntyre.

Hannerz, U. (1996). *Transnational connections: Culture, people, places*. London, UK: Routledge.

Horne, J. (2006). *Sport in consumer culture*. London, UK: Palgrave Macmillan.

Ingham, A., Howell, J., & Schilperoort, T. (1988). Sport and community: A review and exegesis. *Exercise and Sport Science Review, 15*, 427–465.

Iyer, P. (2000). *The global soul*. New York, NY: Vintage Books.

Jamail, M. H. (2008). *Venezuelan bust, baseball boom: Andrés Reiner and scouting on the new frontier*. Lincoln, NE: University of Nebraska Press.

James, C. L. R. (1963). *Beyond a boundary*. London, UK: Hutchinson.

Klein, A. (1991). *Sugarball: The American game, the Dominican dream*. New Haven, CT: Yale University Press.

Klein, A. (1997). *The owls of the two laredos: Baseball and nationalism on the Texas–Mexican border*. Princeton, NJ: Princeton University Press.

Lull, J. (2000). *Media, commerce, culture: A global approach*. New York, NY: Columbia University Press.

Mason, D. (2006). "Expanding the footprint"? Questioning the NHL's expansion and relocation strategy. In D. Whitson & R. Gruneau (Eds.), *Artificial ice: Hockey, culture, and commerce* (pp. 181–199). Toronto, ON: University of Toronto Press.

Mott, M., & Allardyce, J. (1989). *Curling capital: Winnipeg and the roarin' game, 1876–1988*. Winnipeg, MB: University of Manitoba Press.

Pitter, R. (2006). Racialization and hockey in Canada: From personal troubles to a Canadian challenge. In D. Whitson & R. Gruneau (Eds.), *Artificial Ice: Hockey, culture, and commerce* (pp. 123–139). Toronto, ON: University of Toronto Press.

Robertson, R. (1992). *Globalization: Social theory and global culture*. New York, NY: Russell Sage.

Robins, K. (1991). Tradition and translation: National cultures in a global context. In J. Corner & S. Harvey (Eds.), *Enterprise and heritage: Crosscurrents of national culture*. London, UK: Routledge.

Sage, G. (2004). The sporting goods industry: From struggling entrepreneurs to national business to transnational corporations. In T. Slack (Ed.), *The commercialisation of sport* (pp. 29–51). London, UK: Routledge.

Sage, G. (2011). *Globalizing sport: How organizations, corporations, media, and politics are changing sports*. Boulder, CO: Paradigm Publishers.

Scherer, J., & Davidson, J. (2011). Promoting the "arriviste" city: Producing neo-liberal urban identity and communities of consumption during the Edmonton Oilers' 2006 playoff campaign. *International Review for the Sociology of Sport, 46*(2), 157–180.

Scherer, J., & Jackson, S. (2013). *The contested terrain of the New Zealand All Blacks: Rugby, commerce, and cultural politics in the age of globalization*. London, UK: Peter Lang.

Short, J. R. & Kim, Y. H. (1999). *Globalization and the city*. New York, NY: Longman.

Weiler, P. (2000). *Leveling the playing field: How the law can make sports better for fans*. Cambridge MA: Harvard University Press.

Whitson, D. (1998). Circuits of promotion: Media, marketing, and the globalization of sport. In L. Wenner (Ed.), *MediaSport* (pp. 57–72). New York, NY: Routledge.

Whitson, D. (2001). Hockey and Canadian identities: From frozen rivers to revenue streams. In D. Taras & B. Rasporich (Eds.), *A passion for identity: Canadian studies for the 21st century* (pp. 217–236). Toronto, ON: Nelson.

Williams, J. (1994). The local and the global in English soccer and the rise of satellite television. *Sociology of Sport Journal, 11*, 376–397.

Wilson, B. (2006). Selective memory in a global culture: Reconsidering links between youth, hockey, and Canadian identity. In D. Whitson & R. Gruneau (Eds.), *Artificial ice: Hockey, culture, and commerce* (pp. 53–70). Toronto, ON: University of Toronto Press.

Endnotes

1. I use *soccer* throughout this chapter, for a Canadian audience. However, readers should be aware that everywhere outside the United States and Canada the game is known as *football* (or *futbol* in Spanish-speaking nations).

2. Following Hannerz (1996), I use *international* to refer to relations or bodies that involve nation-states, and *transnational* to describe other kinds of connections (e.g., corporate or interpersonal).

3. Brazilian soccer, like West Indian cricket, is known for its offence-oriented, almost flamboyant, style of play. Both James (1963) and Galeano (1998) also relate how cricket in the West Indies and soccer in many Latin American countries (notably Brazil and Argentina) have become tied up with national identity in ways very similar to the role that hockey plays in Canada.

4. We need to understand here that sports don't have interests of their own, distinct from the interests of those who own teams, televise games, and so on. Thus, whenever we hear people talking about the "interests of the sport" (in expansion, for example, or in appearing drug free) we should recognize that this really means the interests of those who are in the business of selling that particular sport as entertainment.

5. See Alan Klein (1991, 1997) for accounts of baseball in the Dominican Republic and Mexico, respectively, and the effects of Major League Baseball on baseball in these countries. See Milton Jamail (2008) for a review of baseball in Venezuela.

6. As an example, during the Edmonton Oilers's successes in the 2006 Stanley Cup playoffs, mayor Stephen Mandel suggested that the team reflected the city itself: industrious, feisty, and with a never-say-die determination (Scherer & Davidson, 2011).

7. A qualifying note is important here. Some readers will have noticed that this discussion, which is focused on the most popular professional team sports, has said nothing about global opportunities for women athletes. This is because there are no women's professional leagues, as yet, that attract the media coverage and television audiences that would support the salary levels of the West European soccer leagues or the North American major league sports. Neither is there the competition for players described in the chapter. The Canadian and US women's soccer teams now draw substantial stadium audiences for international matches, and a very few leading athletes in some of the individual Olympic sports (notably skiing and track) can make significant prize money in international circuit competition. However, tennis and golf are still the only women's sports to have generated sufficient media audiences to support year-round circuit competition and the sorts of earnings commensurate with this.

8. English soccer in the last decade has seen several of its biggest clubs taken over by foreign tycoons: Chelsea by Russian billionaire Roman Abramovich; Manchester United by Malcolm Glazer, the US owner of the NFL's Tampa Bay Buccaneers; and more recently Manchester City by Sheikh Mansour bin Zayed Al Nahyan. On a smaller scale, the NHL's Ottawa Senators were "rescued" (i.e., taken over and kept in Ottawa) by Toronto pharmaceutical magnate Eugene Melnyk, while the Dallas Stars and the Phoenix Coyotes are each now owned by Canadian investors.

9. Curling in Canada underwent some commercialization in the 1990s with the advent of cash bonspiels that made professional careers possible for a handful of the country's leading players. It's also a sport that is now part of the Winter Olympics program and has annual World Championships (for both men and women), events at which Canada is usually a favourite but doesn't always win. The processes of commercialization and globalization are not nearly as advanced, though, as they are in the other sports that have been the focus of this chapter.

Chapter 15
Sport and the Future
Brian Wilson

Underlying the various chapters in this book—and indeed the sociology of sport field more generally—is the idea that sport is a cultural form and social practice that is rife with contradictions. Sport unites and divides people. It is healthy and injurious. It reflects and reproduces social inequalities and societal inequities, and it is a forum where social justice-oriented issues and changes are promoted (Eitzen, 2003). Put simply, sport is a contested terrain.

To identify these contradictions and explore this contested terrain, sociologists study how particular views on and features of sport came to be taken for granted and inspect the mechanisms through which they continue to be taken for granted. The idea is that by looking at the role sport plays in contemporary Canadian society—and how it came to play this role—we will be better positioned to make recommendations for changing sport (and society) for the better.

The argument that underlies this chapter is that a final analytic step is necessary to give ourselves the best chance of making recommendations for changes that are both desirable and effective. Specifically, I suggest that to respond in an informed manner to sport-related social problems we must use the information we have acquired about the processes and structures of sport and society to help us consider what the future holds—and to envision what a preferred future would look like.

This task of looking to the future requires us to consider current trends in sport and society as a way of thinking about the direction that sport is going. It also requires thinking about how this direction is influenced by (and is influencing) drivers of social change in the broader Canadian society, including all of the social institutions outlined in this book (the media, various levels of government, the economy, etc.). When we are sensitive to sport's current trajectory and the factors that influence it, we are also in a better position to assess whether aspects of sport are getting better and whether sport-related social problems seem to be intensifying. Of course, to do this type of reflection also means asking ourselves what a "better" and "worse" sport system, sport culture, and broader society look like.

This is not a straightforward task simply because views on what counts as a preferred future will vary greatly and are inevitably deeply politicized. It is well known that attempts to pursue major Utopian visions of society have led to some of the worst human rights violations imaginable (Winter, 2006). For example, the vision that guided Adolph Hitler's work in Nazi Germany leading up to and during World War II was guided by a particular understanding of an ideal society. So the question always remains, whose preferred future is being pursued?

There is agreement in the sociology of sport community that it is preferable for sport to be, for example, "more equitable and inclusive," "more democratic," "less violent," and "more environmentally friendly." Still, deciding on how to achieve these versions of sport is not straightforward. Considering what sport and society will look like in the future requires sensitivity not only to current trends in sport and society, but also to the political mechanisms and power relations that drive social change and the processes that preserve the status quo. This task requires an ability and desire to imagine what sport and society could be, and an acceptance of the fact that one can never know for sure how things will turn out. Finally, it means choosing to believe that we can use our sociological imaginations to help us improve sport and society.

In the remainder of this chapter I attempt to provoke this sort of thinking about sport and the future. I do this by first describing a set of four overarching categories that have been associated with major social changes: governance, globalization, technology, and environment. I discuss broader societal trends as they pertain to each category, and then offer a series of 11 "predictions" based on this information. Finally, I outline ways that those hoping to influence the trajectories of sport and society might use existing research and theory to inform intervention.

DRIVERS OF SOCIAL CHANGE AND IMPLICATIONS FOR THE FUTURE OF SPORT AND SOCIETY

With his 2013 book *The Future: Six Drivers of Global Change*, renowned environmentalist and former vice-president of the United States, Al Gore, identified six drivers of social change that he sees at the core of major and ongoing changes in the world around us: (a) ever-increasing economic globalization; (b) the emergence of revolutionary digital communications and new media formats that have resulted in linkages between billions of people; (c) shifts in the balance of global political, economic, and military power; (d) a deeply flawed economic compass; (e) revolutions in genomic, biotechnology, neuroscience, and life sciences; and (f) a radical disruption of the relationship between human beings and Earth's ecosystems (Gore, 2013). Gore's attempt to bring attention to some of the key trajectories of contemporary societies and offer explanations for these trajectories is part of a long tradition of futurist work that has taken place in the social sciences as well as in literature, film, and other areas of the arts.

A core assumption that underpins Gore's work that is especially useful for our purposes is that looking to the future requires sensitivity to the range of ways and reasons that societies have developed as they have. This idea is reminiscent of C. Wright Mills's argument that being sensitive to the history of particular ideologies and structures is crucial if we are to begin to see how many things we take for granted are social constructions (Mills, 1959). Of course, if ideologies and structures of society are social constructions, they can be changed by people just like they were created by people. Gore and Mills similarly remind us to remain open to the multiple directions that society could go in the future, and how particular drivers of social change might lead to outcomes that seem counterintuitive.

It is in this spirit that I have identified four overarching thematic areas and identified drivers of social change that are especially pertinent to each of these areas. These areas and drivers were chosen with the goal of capturing some of the most compelling aspects of Gore's position while at the same time illuminating major themes that have been especially pertinent for sociologists of sport. While I do not (and cannot possibly) treat these areas as comprehensive in the sense that there are so many changes associated with these broad categories—sport related and otherwise—I do see these areas as useful departure points for discussion about some current and preferred directions of sport and society. The areas and associated drivers are as follows:

1. *Governance:* The driver of social change within this area is the ongoing adoption and practice of postpolitical decision making and neoliberal governance.

2. *Globalization:* The driver of social change within this area is the ongoing development of societal changes associated with economic, social, and cultural globalization.

3. *Technology:* The driver of social change within this area is the ongoing development and effects of highly interactive and sometimes highly invasive technologies.

4. *Environment:* The driver of social change within this area is the widespread concern about the impacts of environment-related problems.

Below, I elaborate on each of these and discuss their relevance to sport and the future. As will become evident, these areas and drivers are integrally linked to one another, and for this reason should be considered holistically—as part of a shared and ever-evolving system.

Governance

In recent decades—and especially with the rise of conservative governments in Britain, Canada, and the United States in the 1980s—many social and political commentators and others observed and considered the implications of the development and implementation of what is known as neoliberal forms of governance (Brown, 2006; Harvey, 2005). While issues associated with neoliberalism in Canada are embedded in various chapters of this book (especially Chapter 4), I will offer a brief synopsis of the term and what it means for governance.

Neoliberalism, which refers to government policies as well as the ideologies that guide decisions to make these policies, is based on a belief that a "market rationality" can be used to effectively deal with social, economic, and environmental problems. To use a market rationality means being guided by the principles that private businesses use in their attempts to secure profit in the competitive corporate sector. The main incentive for businesses in this context is, of course, to secure profit—which in most cases means responding to the demands of consumers.

The ideology underlying this approach is that economic interests can be served alongside social and environmental interests—and that this competition-based model will lead to the most efficient and effective overall outcomes. Governments that are guided by neoliberal principles are, therefore, known to reduce funding for programs intended to deal with societal problems, justifying such moves by indicating that market mechanisms will lead to (a) the best service provision and (b) prosperity for businesses or nongovernmental organizations (NGOs) that provide the best services. Government-offered services have been treated similarly in the sense that reduced funding for public provisions like a municipal recreation centre requires the centre staff to be especially entrepreneurial in their attempts to stay afloat. This neoliberal-influenced approach to funding these sorts of government services is known as "new public management" (Aucoin, 1995). The idea here is that rational consumers will be able to use their purchasing power to implicitly and explicitly support prosocial societal changes by choosing the best services—decisions that, theoretically speaking, should lead to financial success and sustainability for the most effective and efficient private and public providers.

Also at neoliberalism's core is the belief that individuals/consumers are responsible for their own well-being and that external social and economic barriers can be overcome by those who are appropriately entrepreneurial. The idea is that neoliberal governments prioritize consumer choice, and therefore if one makes the wrong choices, then the consequences of these choices should not be the responsibility of the state.

Since many scholars have observed that there is a link between neoliberal forms of governance and increased inequality, it is perhaps unsurprising that critiques of neoliberalism are abundant. Health sociologist David Coburn (2004), for example, illuminates this link in an oft-quoted study he published in the journal *Social Science & Medicine*, where he concludes that

> global and national socio-political-economic trends have increased the power of business classes and lowered that of working classes. The neo-liberal policies accompanying these trends led to increased income inequality but also poverty and unequal access to many other health-relevant resources...Furthermore, countries with Social Democratic forms of welfare regimes (i.e., those that are less neo-liberal) have better health than do those that are more neo-liberal. (p. 21)

Sociologists of sport have also been highly interested in these issues and have produced a wealth of research and commentary in recent years that identifies flaws with neoliberal and new public management forms of governance (Andrews & Silk, 2012). You will have undoubtedly noted some of this work in various chapters of this book, as scholars working from a conflict perspective (concerned especially with the economic and class issues that are so central to critiques of neoliberalism) and critical perspectives (focused on how various forms of identity-based inequalities are exacerbated within particular systems) have all weighed in on this issue. Frisby and Millar (2002), for example, describe how as new public management measures have been implemented and the focus on service provision in the recreation and sport sector has shifted to efficiency and cost effectiveness in Canada, "the needs of the poor are being overlooked" (p. 217).

Instead of offering an in-depth look at these critiques, as some other authors in this book have already done, in this chapter I consider what sport and society might look like in upcoming decades if current forms of governance that are influenced by neoliberal principles continue to be dominant. The predictions I offer here pertain especially to the future of sport, recreation, and physical activity provision. The predictions are also intended to provoke thinking not only about what society will look like if public policy decisions are to be made based on neoliberal ideologies, but also about likely responses and challenges to this approach to governance. It is also worth noting here that the consequences of the rise of neoliberal forms of governance is integrally related to globalization, technology, and the environment—so governance-related themes will emerge again in each of the remaining sections.

Prediction #1: In upcoming years, access to conventional forms of participatory sport, recreation, and physical activity will continue to be highly unequal (with some variations) in Canada

Neoliberal principles have been and are continuing to influence policymaking in Canada, and it appears that these principles will increasingly find their way into government policy until an ideological shift or "evening out" takes place (Wilson, 2012a). At the same time, scholars like Donnelly and Harvey (2007) and Frisby et al. (2005) have linked neoliberal policies or the new public management approaches with unequal access to sport, leisure, and physical activity in Canada—and of course Coburn (2004) has noted (see above) that the implementation of neoliberal policies is linked with unequal access to many health-relevant resources. With these interconnected observations in mind, it is not a stretch to suggest that access to conventional (i.e., organized, often government funded) forms of participatory sport, recreation, and physical activity will remain at current levels (i.e.,they will continue to be characterized by unequal access) or become more unequal if levels of economic and social inequality continue to grow across the country.

Although much of the existing work in this area has focused on young people, this prediction is intended to account for other populations as well, especially older adults. That is to say, although it would make sense to anticipate that programs in the future will cater more to older populations, and especially the large baby boomer cohort that is entering an older age demographic, such a response would not necessarily reduce inequalities between those with more resources and those with fewer resources. Within a neoliberal model that promotes consumer-driven responses to social concerns, the target market for new and existing programs would still be those who can most readily afford user fees and thus do not need to "prove poverty" to gain reduced-fee access (Frisby, Reid, & Ponic, 2007).

Having said this, neoliberalism does offer another possible response to the problem of unequal access, which is outlined in the next prediction. As above, though, this response may help deal with some aspects of the inequality while exacerbating others.

Prediction #2: Nongovernmental organizations that use sport for development purposes will continue to—and perhaps increasingly—work to fill the gaps left by governments

In recent years, various nongovernmental organizations (NGOs) have worked to fill the gaps left by governments that have reduced their financial investment in accessible forms of physical activity, sport, and recreation programming. These groups continually face challenges to remain sustainable and serve their target populations, a point confirmed in a study Lyndsay Hayhurst and I conducted on the experiences and challenges faced by some of these NGOs in the Canadian context. We found, for example, that organizations like Vancouver-based MoreSports—a not-for-profit group mandated to provide "sustainable sport and physical activity opportunities for children and families living in Vancouver" (Wilson & Hayhurst, 2009, p. 164)—are in many cases forced to compete for resources with organizations that may also offer valuable context-specific services. These same NGOs may also be forced into partnerships that may, at times, result in compromised service provision. Of course, a shift in policymaking practices at the local, provincial, or federal levels of government away from the neoliberal practices would alter this scenario somewhat, but that is not the current trend.

So what will be the ongoing implications of this apparent trend? To answer this question, it is important to consider that such programs receive competitive government funding along with philanthropic and corporate support. This form of funding is notable here because it aligns well with a neoliberal approach to service provision where programs must appear to be a good investment to receive funding. The idea is that competition among those attempting to secure funding will lead to better programming than would be provided by organizations with ongoing and noncompetitive government funding.

Predictably, critics of neoliberal forms of service provision disagree. Instead, these critics argue that by putting these sorts of competitive pressures on organizations, an incentive system is created where those providing such services must *appear* to be a good investment. Such appearances are especially important for funders who, in many cases, are also looking to enhance their image through philanthropic work. A problematic consequence of this situation is that such organizations must consistently demonstrate the "successful" outcomes of their programs—instead, perhaps, of doing rigorous and balanced (and publicly reported) assessments that would be designed to improve programming (Wilson & Hayhurst, 2009). For example, highlighting select feel-good success stories and counting the number of people exposed to a program is quite different from assessing the quality and longer-term outcomes of a program. Organizations may also be more likely to target participants who are most likely to succeed in their program, leaving those in more difficult circumstances on the margins again. Moreover, in a competitive funding market situation, NGOs that will thrive are those that are most entrepreneurial (and perhaps the largest, with the most resources). Smaller, community-based, and grassroots organizations that are known to cater well to the context-specific needs of those in need of particular services, meanwhile, will continue to be at risk of closing down in the absence of securing competing funding (Darnell, 2012).

In sum, then, while this trend may in some ways offset the inequality problem identified in Prediction #1, there are reasons to be concerned about the quality of these programs and the unintended and intended consequences of neoliberal forms of NGO-led intervention. I would also suggest that those who are concerned first and foremost with public health—not with the survival and image of their organization—should be leading a response to the problems of unequal access to physical activity and recreational sport, problems that are themselves the public issues of social structure referred to by Mills (1959).

Prediction #3: For some young people, alternative forms of leisure and physical activity will continue to be adopted as a creative response to problems of access and ambivalence about current physical activity and sport options in formal and structured settings. Such forms of participation will become more prominent as exposure to these cultural options becomes increasingly available and prominent through the Internet

Although concerns about the more formal provision of resources that support sport, physical activity, and recreation-related practices are understandably central to many discussions about sport and society, it is also important to keep in mind that forms of physical activity also take place outside more formalized structures. This kind of sport is sometimes associated with subcultural sport-related activities (Atkinson & Young, 2008a), what some refer to as lifestyle sports (Wheaton, 2004). What is being referred to here are activities such as skateboarding, windsurfing, BASE jumping, surfing, parkour, and ultimate Frisbee that are commonly more participant-driven activities—activities that are, in some respects and contexts, intentionally oppositional to dominant aspects of mainstream (sport) culture.

We can think of this opposition in two related ways. On the one hand, this can mean opposition to the values and practices associated with mainstream, (hyper)competitive, (overly)structured, and adult-controlled sport—the power and performance model of sport. Beal (1995), for example, described how in skateboarding culture, "competitors" often actively cheer for each other to complete impressive tricks and jumps. On the other hand, *opposition* refers here to the underlying ethos of particular sport subcultural groups that are critical of many nonsport-related aspects of mainstream societies. Atkinson found this form of opposition in his research on the parkour subculture in Toronto, where he described how parkour practitioners (known as *traceurs*) equate their acrobatic movements over, through, and around various features of the urban environment as symbolic and embodied commentary on the disciplining, corporatized, and "environmentally pathological" aspects of contemporary cities (Atkinson, 2009, p. 175). Wheaton (2008), in her work on windsurfing and related lifestyle sports, refers to the activities of groups like Surfers Against Sewage that are also, in their own way, environmentalist and anti-consumerist. Referring back to Chapter 2, the perspectives of these identity-based groups—and their cultural forms of expression—would conventionally be assessed using critical cultural studies perspectives.

While it is difficult to know if more young people will be attracted to these subcultural options in the future because of feelings of disillusionment with mainstream sport and society, it seems reasonable to suggest that as more and more young people are exposed to these cultural forms—something that the dissemination of these activities through the Internet and associated new media allows—participation will also increase in Canada and globally. This final argument seems especially apropos in light of the recent publication of a study on the emergence and meaning of parkour in the Middle East (in Gaza especially), a cultural phenomenon that the authors found to be attributable to parkour's circulation through the Internet and social media (Thorpe & Ahmad, 2013).

Parkour and other alternative/lifestyle sport activities may increase in popularity in response to problems with mainstream sport and physical activity structures.
Ammentorp/Fotolia

A caveat here is that these alternative subcultures are often fairly homogenous in terms of demographic makeup and are also known at times to reflect some of the broader gendered, race and ethnicity, and ability-related exclusionary practices of the broader society (Atkinson & Young, 2008a; Beal, 1995). For example, while those involved in parkour include middle- and lower-class participants—and in some instances (but not others) there is an interethnic mix— young males are the usual participants (Kidder, 2013; Thorpe & Ahmad, 2013). It is also well documented that such subcultures are inevitably incorporated into the mainstream culture to some degree (e.g., mass-mediated "extreme" sports) when the profits associated with marketing alternative cultures are pursued (Atkinson, 2009; Wilson, 2006a).

While these caveats are important, they should not be viewed as reasons to completely dismiss the subversive potential of these groups as alternatives to mainstream sport and as conveyors of countermainstream ideologies. As I have argued elsewhere, these types of alternatives help generate new understandings of "what is possible" for participants and others (Wilson, 2012a), revealing opportunities for counterhegemonic activity. At the same time, it is known that involvement in such movements may in some cases predict future participation in more conventional politics (Staggenborg, 2008; Wilson, 2012a).

Globalization

Although globalization, the second main driver of social change, refers to various processes of change and development (see Chapter 14), sociologist Arjun Appadurdai (1996) outlines a set of five key processes (what he terms *scapes*) that have been especially useful for scholars working in this area:

1. Ideoscapes (referring to the cross-border transmission of ideas).
2. Financescapes (referring to the cross-border movement of capital).
3. Mediascapes (referring to the global influence of mass media).
4. Technoscapes (referring to the movement of technologies around the world).
5. Ethnoscapes (referring to the cross-border movement of people).

Jarvie (2006) uses these scapes to help him describe some sport-related globalization processes:

> Sporting ethnoscapes might involve the migration of professional or non-professional personnel through player, manager or coach transfers; sporting technoscapes could include sports goods, equipment…and transporting of sports technology [more generally]; sporting financescapes refer to the global flow of finance brought about through the international trade of players, prize-money, endorsements, and sporting goods; sporting mediascapes refer to the sport-media complex that transports sport across the globe [and] sporting ideoscapes are bound up with the ideologies and philosophies expressed by, in and through sport. (p. 100)

Although scholars and others have paid particular attention to these globalization-related processes in recent decades, it is worth acknowledging here that social changes associated with globalization have been at work for a long time (consider world exploration, trade, and colonization). There are, of course, particular characteristics associated with more recent iterations of globalization that will guide the discussion and predictions in this section, many of which are introduced in the above quotation from Jarvie and especially David Whitson's discussion of sport and globalization in Chapter 14.

Following Jarvie and Whitson then, we can begin to think about the range of studies pertaining to globalization and sport that might aid predictions about what sport might look like in the future. For example, some major topics pertaining especially to finance and media-related issues include ways that transnational corporations connect to and become immersed in national cultures through sport (Scherer & Jackson, 2010), the use of sweatshop labour to produce inexpensive athletic apparel (Sage, 1999), and attempts by major sports leagues to expand their global audience (Scherer & Jackson, 2010). Major sport-related peace and development programs have become a main topic of research for sociologists in recent years. In addition, a range of studies are emerging on development-related work associated with the Olympic Games and the IOC and on the emergence of international sport for development and peace (or SDP), organizations like Right to Play (formerly known as Olympic Aid, reflecting its origins as an Olympic legacy project from the Lillehammer Games in 1994). Sport-related environmental issues are cross-border issues in themselves (e.g., climate change) and have also inspired global responses (as discussed in more detail later). Many forms of social resistance also have global features and globally focused goals, as we will explore below.

Those doing the aforementioned research frequently comment on the potential impacts of globalization and debate the future of societies in an increasingly globalizing world (Maguire, 1999; Miller, Lawrence, McKay, & Rowe, 2001; Scherer & Jackson, 2010). Although these debates are long-standing and complex, suffice to say here that questions remain as to whether these trends will lead to more "homogenous" (or Americanized) global cultures, more hybridized or "glocalized" cultures (that consist of a variety of "local" and "global" features), or more intensely differentiated local cultures that are highly resistant to globalizing forces. Of course, the idea that any one of these and related perspectives on globalization is most accurate is problematic because the consequences of global–local interactions are so dependent on context. Acknowledging these complexities, there are some globalization-related trajectories that strongly suggest particular "futures." I predict a few of these below.

Prediction #4: With the growing influence of sport-related transnational corporations, national and local cultures will become less distinct and more corporatized, but not "homogenized"

As noted above, there are ongoing debates about the impacts of various forms of globalization on local and national cultures. Some scholars emphasize the cultural imperialist potential of global forces, while others celebrate the diverse and hybrid character of cultures that emerge from global–local interactions. My prediction follows the line of thinking promoted by those who "walk the middle" on these debates—who suggest that while major differences between nations and cultures will be reduced as transnational cultural entities and forces continue to circulate and be enabled by governments that increasingly defer to private interests, variations within and between national and local cultures will become increasingly evident. Maguire (1999) described this middle ground by suggesting that processes of globalization lead to "diminishing contrasts" between nations and cultures, and "increasing varieties" of global–local cultural hybrids.

An example of this was provided by Carrington, Andrews, Jackson, & Mazur, (2001) in their study on the impacts of Nike's major endorser and global icon Michael Jordan in a range of national contexts. They argued that although local cultures are certainly impacted by Nike's advances, these impacts are not uniform or predictable. The reason for this sort of variety is, in part, because shrewd global corporations commonly cater their products and advertising for particular target audiences/cultures. In a related study, Robert Sparks and I found that middle-class black adolescent males in Toronto and adolescent nonblack males in Vancouver interpreted athletic apparel commercials (and especially the celebrity black athletes featured in them) in quite distinct ways. For example, the black adolescents offered more passionate and, at the same time, more critical readings of the featured athletes (e.g., referring to the problem of race-related stereotyping in mass media), while the nonblack youth, who were also consumers of the apparel featured in the commercials and fans of the athletes endorsing the apparel, were more ambivalent and less critical in their responses to questions (Wilson & Sparks, 1999, 2001). The main point here, again, is that the impacts of cultural impositions by transnational companies are not uniform.

David Whitson's description of the increasingly diverse populations emerging in areas of Canada (see Chapter 14)—and the stark differences between many urban and rural contexts—is relevant here to thinking about the impacts of cultural messages on audiences. Whitson's point also anticipates future debates about issues raised in other sections/predictions in this chapter, such as the implications of changing demographics emerging with varying patterns of immigration and settlement. For example, our futures will include further questions about how to approach opportunities and challenges associated with emerging cultural and social differences, and with problems like the "healthy immigrant effect" (i.e., diminished health of some immigrants after spending time in Canada) (McDonald & Kennedy, 2004).

Looking to the future, then, I suspect that we will continue to see more and more cultural variations within and between nations as a result of processes of globalization. Scherer and Jackson (2010) say as much in their study of how these processes are reflected in and reinforced through Adidas, Rupert Murdoch's News Corporation, and the renowned All Blacks rugby team in New Zealand. As they suggest, although potentially homogenizing influences have increasingly circulated through New Zealand in recent years, the country is "now more diverse than ever before as a result of immigration" (Scherer & Jackson, 2010, p. xiii). This observation should remind us (as Al Gore did) of the need to be cognizant of the multiple and interacting forces of change that must be accounted for if we are to understand the social and cultural trajectories of societies.

The broader point here is that the corporatization of nations will be accompanied by the emergence of more cosmopolitan audiences that will have their own somewhat distinct sport participation and sport consumption interests and habits—interests and habits that will be increasingly difficult to predict for major sport marketers, sport leagues, and other entities thought to promote cultural homogenization. Whitson's point about immigration patterns in Canada and the implications of these patterns for sport consumption is especially relevant here (see Chapter 14).

Prediction #5: The influence of international nongovernmental "sport for development and peace" (SDP) organizations will remain strong and likely increase in upcoming years

This prediction is akin to Prediction #2 in the sense that it is based on the argument that NGOs (in this case international NGOs) are increasingly being relied upon to lead prosocial work in various regions of world, especially in areas that are experiencing high levels of poverty and are, in some cases, war-torn and in postconflict situations.

It is worth noting here (as background information for this prediction) that a rapid rise in the number of international SDP organizations since 2000 is well documented and unprecedented (Levermore & Beacom, 2009). The increase has been associated with the United Nations recognition of 2005 as the International Year of Sport and Physical Education and with the rise to prominence of international SDP leader, *Right to Play*. Hayhurst, Wilson, & Frisby, (2011) documented the ongoing use of communication technologies (e.g., the International Platform on SDP at www.sportanddev.org) to maintain and promote this SDP movement.

Although it remains to be seen whether the problems associated with having an SDP sector that is embedded in a funding culture that includes some perverse incentives outlined in Prediction #2, the involvement of those with knowledge of the enabling and constraining aspects of sport and international development could lead to some noticeable advances. This more optimistic view of the SDP movement aligns with arguments made by people such as scholar-activists Bruce Kidd (2008) and John Sugden (2010), who uniformly recognize the problems with the SDP sector while also documenting how the interventions they are involved with are thought to, in some circumstances and for some people, support reconciliation efforts or other prosocial outcomes.

It is also worth noting in this context that the IOC, a recognized "super-NGO" in its own right, has stepped up its efforts to promote development by granting the Olympics to Rio de Janeiro for the upcoming 2016 Summer Games—an act that commentators like Millington and Darnell (2012) see as part of a trend for sport mega-events to be awarded to countries of the Global South (e.g., 2010 FIFA World Cup in South Africa and the Commonwealth Games in Delhi in 2008). For Millington and Darnell, this trend speaks to the role that sport mega-events are increasingly thought to play as a form of international development for countries seen to be in need of the "most development."

Of course, the idea that holding a sport mega-event is the best avenue toward development for all citizens (including more marginalized groups) is highly controversial—as scholars like Lenskyj (2008), Hayes and Horne (2011), and several others have argued for years. Despite these debates, it is clear that the IOC has proclaimed leadership on these issues and that this leadership has been recognized by *the* key player in international development, the United Nations. I am referring here to the fact that in 2009 the IOC was given "observer status" at the United Nations—a highly significant endorsement of the IOC's work considering that this status is generally reserved for countries or for NGOs that are undisputed leaders in peace, development, and humanitarian aid (e.g., the International Red Cross/Red Crescent has this status).

Prediction #6: Ongoing and at times extreme tensions about the negative impacts of neoliberal policies will lead to local and global forms of dissent, and sport-related, Internet, and social media–enabled global movements will be part of this   In earlier sections of this chapter, I noted that current trends in governance and globalization may lead to an exacerbation of existing inequalities. The prediction offered here is intended to highlight the idea that real and perceived impacts of these trends and related problems will inspire formidable responses. The *Idle No More* movement is an example of this sort of response. While this movement was viewed by many to be an expression of dissatisfaction with a whole range of issues, *Idle No More* originated as a response to government legislation in Canada that was thought to undermine the lobbying power and rights of Aboriginal groups and to weaken environmental protection legislation. The *Occupy Wall Street* movement in 2011, meanwhile, was more broadly focused on economic inequalities associated with forms of economic

globalization and neoliberalism—and included demonstrations intended to highlight the movement's fundamental concerns with social justice and unequal power relationships (*CBC News*, 2013). Movements such as these that received support around the world would seem to be part of a developing trend toward the emergence of global social movements of all kinds—global movements that link people who are concerned about governments that implement (neoliberal) policies that seem to be directly related to increases in inequality.

As you might expect, these global developments inspired a wealth of sociological research focused on the potential implications of social resistance since the rise of the highly interactive and inexpensive Internet-related communication medium (I return to this theme later on). This research includes work by sport sociologist Jean Harvey and his colleagues, who in their 2013 book *Sport and Social Movements: From the Local to the Global* identified a range of sport-related global movements, including movements focused on the rights of workers, the rights of women, peace, and the environment. I have argued in my own research how the emergence of Internet communication offers an unprecedented platform for these sorts of sport-related social movements (Wilson, 2007). This includes resistance movements like the global anti-golf environmental movement (Stolle-McAllister, 2004), anti-Olympics movements (Lenskyj, 2008) and anti-sweatshops movements that protest poor labour conditions in factories that produce athletic apparel for companies like Nike (Sage, 1999). Increased public engagement on a local and global level by those who study sport is also likely here. Evidence of this sort of engagement includes the increasing number and prominence of blogs kept by sport scholars who have begun to respond to calls for more "public sociology" (links to such blogs can be found at http://nasssblog.blogspot.ca) (Donnelly, Atkinson, Boyle, & Szto, 2011).

In sum, it would seem that we can anticipate an increase in the number and influence of highly interconnected grassroots movements that aim to confront governments and others thought to be implicated in social injustices of all kinds.

Dissatisfaction with various forms of sport-related economic globalization may lead to further tensions and protest.
ZUMA Press, Inc./Alamy

Technology

I have alluded already to some ways that new technologies are associated with aspects of contemporary governance and globalization. Building on these arguments, in this section I outline three technology-focused predictions pertaining to the future of sport, physical activity, and society.

Prediction #7: Video games intended to promote fitness will become an increasingly important component of formal and informal physical activity programs of all kinds There is a range of video games on the market that promote activity through the use of visual simulations that require physical activity for the games' participants. These games also commonly offer users the option of measuring and monitoring aspects of the body, such as weight, body mass index, and calories burned. Although Nintendo's Wii Fit is the most prominent example of a system that runs these sorts of games, Xbox 360 and PlayStation are also in the fitness game business.

Sociologist Brad Millington (2013) and others, including the Heart and Stroke Foundation of Canada and the American Heart Association, have recognized the potential benefits of such technologies. For example, these games may support physical activity for those limited in activity by poor weather, for those with particular physical challenges (noting that some people may be able to play sports through Wii that they would be unable to play otherwise), and those who simply prefer/enjoy video game–enabled activity. Although these games are known to target young people who are thought to be the primary consumers of such games, Millington's (2013) recent research recognizes the role these games are now playing in Canadian retirement centres—and the increasingly prominent place of such video game fitness systems in health promotion plans of all kinds.

Millington (2012) also recognized some issues with having private video game companies in leadership roles around physical activity and health promotion. The most straightforward critique has to do with access to these games, precisely because not all consumers/citizens are equally positioned to purchase such health-promoting technologies. Millington's main concern, however, is with the individual-focused features of the games themselves, and especially with the ways that self-monitoring features of these games position consumers as individually responsible for their health. The point is, while individuals certainly make crucial decisions that will positively or negatively impact their health, it is also well known that environmental, economic, and social barriers to activity continue to exist, and these structural barriers are commonly deemphasized in favour of individual-focused responses. Millington suggests that this individual focus aligns well with the neoliberal "presumption that biological 'self-improvement' is achievable through the marketplace" (Millington, 2012, p. 1). By keeping the focus on the individual in these circumstances, the responsibilities that elected governments would seem to have for crucial health-related factors beyond the control of citizens are potentially overlooked.

Prediction #8: New technologies will continue to lead to new opportunities for enjoyable recreational participation in sport for some populations New technologies designed to improve the performance of competitive athletes and to enhance the experience of everyday recreational athletes have been in development and on the market for years. The previous prediction (Prediction #7) alludes to some of the benefits for recreational athletes and those interested in being physically active who may benefit from fitness-oriented video games. The development of lighter golf clubs and tennis rackets with larger "sweet spots" are examples of this. There are of course numerous other examples where new technologies have been helpful for those with disabilities, especially high-performance athletes (e.g., the blades used by Paralympic runners).

Of course, some of the same types of concerns that have been raised in previous predictions about the incentive system that underlies the development of prosocial innovations apply here as well. Marks and Michael refer to some of these issues in a 2001 *British Journal of Medicine* article entitled "Science, Medicine, and the Future: Artificial Limbs." Although the neoliberal environment is not explicitly referred to by these authors, they are clear in their suggestion that the future development of prostheses will be driven by demand (especially the demands of amputees with private funding, like highly competitive athletes)—despite the fact that prosthetics are needed by many with fewer resources, like some amputees in countries of the Global South. As they state, "one of the greatest challenges for the new millennium will be to find the will and the way to fund widespread application of prosthetic innovations" (Marks & Michael, 2001, p. 735)

Perhaps the best way to frame a prediction like this one, which speaks to the way that innovations will offer many prosocial benefits and that these benefits will be distributed unequally as long as the current incentive system remains in place, is to suggest that the future holds *promise and tensions* as battles over the social issues of prosocial new technologies would seem to be inevitable.

Prediction #9: Innovations in the field of biotechnology will lead to new ethical dilemmas in competitive sport

Many analysts—and certainly the World Anti-Doping Agency (WADA)—see "gene doping" as a main issue to be dealt with in upcoming years, as researchers begin to understand not only how particular genes may be related to athletic performance, but also how a person's genetic makeup might be altered to enhance performance. Leslie Pray (2008) describes this process as follows:

> [I]nstead of injecting DNA into a person's body for the purpose of restoring some function related to a damaged or missing gene, as in gene therapy, gene doping involves inserting DNA for the purpose of enhancing athletic performance. (p. 77)

Andy Miah, author of the 2004 book *Genetically Modified Athletes*, is a leading scholar who has weighed in on this issue and offered his own "vision of the future" on genes, sport, and society:

> I envisage a future for humanity where gene transfer—and many other forms of human enhancement—is sufficiently safe for its widespread use and where it becomes an integral part of our pursuit of good health. Indeed, undertaking such modifications would be considered as normal as body piercing or cosmetic surgery. Such attempts to promote our health will become increasingly important in an evermore-toxic world and will create a scenario where the population is, as a whole, more capable of performing in extreme conditions—such as elite sports competition. (Miah, 2010)

Miah's optimistic understanding is at odds with the near-alarmist position taken by those focused on the implications of gene doping for elite sport. It is an excellent reminder that developments that may appear to be problematic for competitive sport may, in fact, be seen as quite hopeful and enabling for the broader society. Of course, Miah is aware of the lingering implications of gene doping for sport as well:

> The challenge for the sports world is not just that gene transfer would be used to break the rules, but that the therapeutic use of gene transfer may create athletes who are even more

capable than the so-called healthy athlete. Intimations of this shift are occurring in the context of Paralympic sport, where the prosthetically enhanced athlete is beginning to surpass the so-called able-bodied athlete, as in the case of South African sprinter Oscar Pistorius. One of the big challenges that will determine whether WADA's gene doping problem can be solved is their ability to detect it. Yet, the [current] absence of detection methods, coupled with shifting social values on the morality of enhancement challenges the integrity and relevance of an anti-enhancement movement like anti-doping. (Miah, 2010)

It is obviously difficult to envision precisely how gene-doping technologies will impact competitive sport—or how gene doping and other technologies that target noncompetitive athletes and citizens might be taken up in enabling and constraining ways. What is for sure is that these and related bioethical and biotechnology issues will need to be dealt with for years to come.

Prediction #10: The experiences of sport media audiences will become increasingly fragmented, interactive, and corporatized as sport and the various forms of new media become increasingly intertwined. However, the evolution of media forms will not be accompanied by substantial changes in the types of social messages that are embedded in and imparted through media content With the range of new media technologies that have emerged in recent years, the conventional television viewing experience has been radically transformed—a point discussed in some detail by Jay Scherer in Chapter 11, and elaborated by commentators like Hutchins and Rowe (2012) and Norman (2012). While the details of this increasing fragmentation and pervasiveness of media are well documented, it is worth noting here that these developments are not necessarily accompanied by changes in the types of messages about gender, "race," and ethnicity that appear in and are reinforced through the sports-media complex, since many of the common sport media-related stereotypes and social problems found in previous studies of media still exist. A particularly provocative study that speaks to this issue is Davis and Duncan's (2006) study of fantasy sports participation. The researchers found that in the online leagues they examined, fantasy sport appeared to "reinforce hegemonic ideologies in sport spectatorship, emphasizing authority, sports knowledge, competition, male-bonding, and traditional gender roles" (p. 244). My own recent review of literature on ways that themes of war, violence, and inequality are covered in the media confirmed that trends in coverage of topics do not appear to have changed in tone in recent years (Wilson, 2012a)—although, as noted earlier, the potential for media-driven resistance to these issues is much greater.

So, while new forms of media are perhaps empowering some consumers who can now pursue sport media viewing and consumption options outside of the "old" TV-only format, thus allowing for some novel forms of sport fan communities to emerge (Norman, 2012), some "old" social problems would appear to remain unchanged, as the content of the media continues to reflect broader societal issues.

Environment

As environmental issues continue to be recognized as being among the most pressing issues of the current moment and into the future, sport managers and organizers are responding. In recent works where I wrote on the topic (Wilson, 2012a, 2012b), I identified some of the sport-related environmental problems that these managers and promoters are dealing with:

- Pollution hazards and carbon emissions from building sport venues, hosting sport events, and producing sport apparel/equipment.

- The alteration and reduction of wetland areas because of modifications to rivers and lakes for water sports like paddling and canoeing.

- The destruction of natural vegetation and erosion of soil from alpine skiing.

- Negative impacts on natural habitats and risks to the health of wildlife and humans because of golf course construction and the use of pesticides to maintain golf courses (paraphrased from Wilson, 2012a, p. 156; cf. Millington & Wilson, 2013; Wilson & Millington, 2013).

Although environmental issues are always, in essence, global issues, there are Canada-specific environmental concerns that have been studied by sociologists. For example, Whitson (2012) examined controversies and protests around the construction of a new section of highway leading up to Whistler Village in preparation for the Vancouver/Whistler 2010 Olympics—a highway plan that meant the demolition of two rare and diverse ecosystem areas. Stoddart (2012) examined links between skiing and environmental issues and explored responses by skiers and others to these issues. My own work examined sport mega-event organizers who claim to be "carbon neutral" (Wilson, 2012a, 2012b). This research included an examination of the controversial and complex carbon offsetting schemes that are commonly used to deal with the inevitable emissions associated with sport mega-events like the 2010 Olympic Games.

As those working in sport sociology have begun to engage these issues and recognize the progress that some organizations are making on environmental issues, a number of concerns have been raised about what these responses look like. Although some of these will be revealed through the prediction I offer below, suffice to say here that when organizations are left to make decisions about their environmental behaviours in response to market mechanisms, it would make sense in some cases to prioritize "appearing green" over "being green" instead of responding to stringent environmental regulations imposed from those external to industry (i.e., those who do not have a vested interest in sport events being held or cancelled).

Debates about sport's potential links with environmental and public health–related issues will undoubtedly continue into the future.
Matt Gibson

Researchers have also expressed concern that for governments mandated to both lead environmental protection work on behalf of constituents and at the same time to facilitate economic growth, compromises are commonly made that would seem to favour economic interests. Sociologist John Hannigan (2006) explained this phenomenon:

> [G]overnments often engage in a process of "environmental managerialism" in which they attempt to legislate a limited degree of protection sufficient to deflect criticism [e.g., about environmental concerns] but not significant enough to derail the engine of economic growth. By enacting environmental policies that are complex, ambiguous and open to exploitation by the forces of production and accumulations the state reaffirms its commitments to strategies for promoting economic development. (p. 21)

None of these arguments is intended to disregard or dismiss the fact that major improvements in sport and environment-related behaviour are taking place. It does seem, however, that as long as an incentive system is in place where the sport managers and organizers who are making decisions about their environment-related behaviours are mandated ultimately to make profits for their organization or make sure that the sport events are viewed positively, there will be compelling reasons to be concerned about how their leadership will, in the long run, impact public and environmental health.

It is worth emphasizing here that this exercise of looking into the future is perhaps most important for this topic because the influences of current environment-impacting behaviours will in some cases only become evident in the future when problems related to the impacts of climate change and ecosystem destruction perhaps become more obvious. This is why environmental issues are associated with a form of inequality that is rarely discussed, but is central to thinking about sport, the environment, and the future. This form of inequality is *intergeneration*, which refers to the inequality that exists between future generations that have no control over how current generations treat the natural environments that they will inherit (Maguire, Jarvie, Mansfield, & Bradley, 2002).

Prediction #11: Debates about best strategies for "greening" sport will be invigorated as existing critiques begin to take hold

In recent years, high-profile sport organizations that collectively promote the idea that sports leaders are also taking leadership on environmental issues have emerged. These networks include members of the Global Forum for Sport and Environment (www.g-forse.com) and Green Sports Alliance (http://greensportsalliance.org). Every second year many of these same organizations assemble for the World Conference on Sport and the Environment—a conference jointly organized by the United Nations Environment Programme and the local organizing committee for the Olympic Games that will be taking place in the year after the conference.

The emergence of these alliances and conferences should be unsurprising considering the attention that sport-related environmental issues have begun to receive in recent years. We should anticipate that sport leaders will continue to demonstrate proactivity on environmental issues through public relations campaigns highlighting leadership on these issues, as concerns about the environment remain in public consciousness. The fact that the IOC made the environment a third pillar of the Olympic movement, alongside sport and culture, speaks volumes to the importance that is being placed on appearing green. It is also likely that environmental performance will continue to improve as greener technologies are developed over time and as those bidding for the Olympics and other sport mega-events are required to include environmental performance strategies and measures into their bids.

Despite this apparent progress on environmental issues, there are also reasons to be cynical about current responses to environmental issues. For example, and despite the immense technology-driven progressions that have led to more sustainable sport events in recent years, sport managers ultimately have a vested interest in running the most sustainable sport event—a mandate that does not include the option of cancelling an event if it is deemed to be too unsustainable. Put another way, when sport managers are leading the regulation of their own industry's behaviours, it is unlikely that a decision to *not* hold a highly unsustainable event would ever be made, noting that sustainable sport management means balancing economic as well as environmental (and social) concerns.

However, and perhaps more optimistically, I suggest that debates about sport-related environmental issues and discussions about the best approach to dealing with sport-related environmental problems will be much richer and more nuanced in the future as people become more educated about some of the issues raised above (and perhaps the urgency of these issues becomes more evident). I suggest that some of this education will take place because the global social movements mentioned earlier (including sport-related environmental movements) will have more impact because of the power of the Internet and other new media technologies to support connections and information sharing between people. Debates will also be more likely as the public sociologists I mentioned earlier are increasingly taking their important research and arguments to blogs. Put simply, we are at a moment when there is unprecedented potential for informed sociological critique to be widely disseminated (Wilson, 2007).

While I have framed this final prediction as a likely future, it is perhaps more accurately called a preferred future—a future where sociological research is accounted for in public debates about some of the most pressing sport-related issues of our times. Given the potential implications of waiting too long to deal with environmental problems (see Foster, Clark, & York, 2010), my hope is that the future is not far off on this prediction.

HOW SOCIOLOGISTS AND OTHERS CAN DRIVE SOCIAL CHANGE

This final prediction offers a helpful segue into thinking about how sociologists and others might attempt to incite social changes and thus work toward a preferred future—one that is hopefully informed by some of the information and theories encountered in this text. I will do this first by identifying some key approaches to inciting change and linking them to some of the theoretical perspectives you have encountered in this book. Second, I will ask you to engage in an exercise of "future thinking" as a way of beginning to envision the type of sport and society you would like to see.

Strategies for Change

One of the more comprehensive lists of strategies for achieving sport-related social change was offered by Coakley and Donnelly (2009, following Hall, Slack, Smith, & Whitson, 1991), who discussed some key strategies from which social change might be instigated. One of these strategies is to work within the existing system in an attempt to create pro-social reforms. This more functionalist approach presumes that the existing system can be tweaked or altered in ways that will lead to desirable outcomes without a radical overhaul of the system. It also presumes that there is enough flexibility working within the established system to deal with the issues of concern.

Another strategy is to join a social movement that lobbies for change. Such groups can be reformist if they work closely and collaboratively with government or other decision-making entities. These groups can also be more oppositional and overtly protest oriented with their arguments and position. In this sense, the goals of social movements can be functionalist—if the aim is to be a cooperative stakeholder in discussions for change (e.g., the environmental group Greenpeace has been known to play this role when consulting with Olympic Games organizers). Other groups might be viewed as taking a critical stance because their goal is to challenge and undermine some of the basic assumptions that underlie the current system (i.e., if they are a counterhegemonic movement). For example, the anti-golf environmental movement is not interested in trying to convince members of the golf industry to improve environmental performance. Instead, they prefer to challenge the very assumption that such large tracts of golf-focused land that are often maintained through pesticide use and major water consumption should even exist.

Other critically oriented groups may not completely reject the existing system, but will attempt to transform cultures and social relations by striving to change the core values of particular organizations. This might include challenging the long-standing acceptance of fighting in hockey, the reverence for those who play when injured in many sports, or challenging sport media producers that offer objectified portrayals of women and stereotypical portrayals of race and ethnicity. The public sociologists mentioned previously commonly make contributions here through engagements with media, government, or in discussions at civic forums.

Yet another strategy is to create or join an alternative sport group that rejects the dominant power structures that underlie highly organized, competitive, and corporate forms of sport (Coakley & Donnelly, 2009). Although the activities of these groups are not always directly confrontational, the idea is that by providing cultural/symbolic alternatives to the mainstream, social and cultural change may take place (eventually) through more indirect pathways—and by promoting a personalization of politics for participants. This attempt to deal with and respond to problems with dominant power structures through participation in a cultural movement aligns well with the critical, cultural studies approach referred to in Chapter 2.

Conclusions

Ask yourself the following question: "What would an ideal sporting world look like?" The reason that a sociological imagination is useful for this sort of thinking about our preferred futures is that it helps us see sport-related problems that might otherwise fly under the radar and to ask questions that are rarely asked about what is possible. For example, could an incentive system be created that prioritizes the physical activity needs of society's marginalized groups, or could the Olympics be rethought so that environmental and social concerns take precedence over economic concerns? With the latter question in mind, scholars like Coakley and Donnelly (2009) have envisioned a situation where existing athletic facilities in different countries are used as Olympic venues (i.e., where new venues are not constructed for every Olympics) and where the Games would take place across various countries and venues (i.e., there would be multiple hosts). Sociologist Harry Edwards similarly suggested that one venue (e.g., in Greece, site of the Ancient Olympics) could be chosen as "the venue" for all future Games and that different countries could bid to organize and be the featured host of the Games in this one venue (Wilson, 2012a). This solution would reduce the environmental impacts of building new facilities while allowing for some of the tourism-related promotional and economic benefits.

Using a sociological imagination can also remind us of positive social changes that have taken place—changes that people would have considered to be unlikely at other points in time (e.g., pertaining to the integration of major sports). This is the value of using sociology as a tool to help us move in some new and preferable directions.

Critical Thinking Questions

1. What is your vision for an ideal sporting world? What are the characteristics of sport in this vision of a preferred future?

2. What aspects of the present sporting world remain unchanged in your vision of this ideal world? Why do these remain unchanged? What aspects of sport and society are taken for granted in your preferred future? What aspects of the present would you like to keep into the future?

3. What barriers do you see to some of the desirable social changes you would like to see? Why are they barriers?

4. How do sociological theories help us think about the types of changes we would like to see in the future? What theories do you find most useful for thinking about ways to change sport and society?

5. Are there strategies for social change that you find preferable to others? Explain.

6. Are there predictions offered in this chapter that you find especially compelling? Are there predictions that you take issue with? Explain your positions.

Suggested Readings

Giroux, H. (2004). When hope is subversive. *Tikkun, 19*(6), 38–39.

Gore, A. (2013). *The future: Six drivers of global change.* New York, NY: Random House.

Miah, A. (2004). *Genetically modified athletes: Biomedical ethics, gene doping and sport.* New York, NY: Routledge.

Moylan, T., & Baccolini, R. (Eds.). (2009). *Utopia method vision: The use value of social dreaming.* Bern, Switzerland: Peter Lang.

Wilson, B. (2007). New media, social movements, and global sport studies: A revolutionary moment and the sociology of sport. *Sociology of Sport Journal, 24*(4), 457–477.

References

Andrews, D., & Silk, M. (Eds.) (2012). *Sport and neo-liberalism: Politics, consumption, and culture.* Philadelphia, PA: Temple University Press.

Atkinson, M. (2009). Parkour, anarcho-environmentalism, and poiesis. *Journal of Sport and Social Issues, 33*(2), 169–194.

Atkinson, M., & Young, K. (Eds.). (2008a). *Tribal play: Subcultural journeys through sport*. Bingley, UK: Emerald Group Publishing.

Appadurai, A. (1996). *Modernity at large: Cultural dimensions of globalization*. Minneapolis, MN: University of Minnesota Press.

Aucoin, P. (1995) *The new public management: Canada in comparative perspective*. Montreal, QC: The Institute for Research on Public Policy.

Beal, B. (1995). Disqualifying the official: An exploration of social resistance through the subculture of skateboarding. *Sociology of Sport Journal, 12*, 252–267.

Brown, W. (2006). *Edgework: Critical essays on knowledge and politics*. Princeton, NJ: Princeton University Press.

Carrington, B., Andrews, D., Jackson, S., & Mazur, Z. (2001). The global Jordanscape. In D. L. Andrews (Ed.), *Michael Jordan Inc.: Corporate sport, media culture, and late modern America* (pp. 177–216). Albany, NY: SUNY Press.

CBC News. (2013, January 9). Is Idle No More the new Occupy Wall Street? Aboriginal movement compared to 2011 grassroots protests that sprang up across the globe. Retrieved from http://www.cbc.ca/news/canada/is-idle-no-more-the-new-occupy-wall-street-1.1397642.

Coakley, J., & Donnelly, P. (2009). *Sports in society: Issues and controversies* (2nd Canadian ed.). Toronto, ON: McGraw-Hill Ryerson.

Coburn, D. (2004). Beyond the income inequality hypothesis: Class, neo-liberalism, and health inequalities. *Social Science & Medicine, 58*(1), 41–56.

Darnell, S. (2012). *Sport and international development: A critical sociology*. New York, NY: Bloomsbury.

Davis, N. W., & Duncan, M. C. (2006). Sports knowledge is power: Reinforcing masculine privilege through fantasy sport league participation. *Journal of Sport & Social Issues, 30*(3), 244–264.

Donnelly, P., Atkinson, M., Boyle, S., & Szto, C. (2011). Sport for development and peace: A public sociology perspective. *Third World Quarterly, 32*, 589–601.

Donnelly, P., & Harvey, J. (2007). Social class and gender: Intersections in sport and physical activity. In P. White & K. Young (Eds.), *Sport and gender in Canada* (pp. 95–119). Toronto, ON: Oxford University Press.

Eitzen, S. (2003). *Fair and foul: Beyond the myths and paradoxes of sport*. New York, NY: Rowman & Littlefield.

Foster, J. B., Clark, B., & York, R. (2010). *The ecological rift: Capitalism's war on the earth*. New York, NY: Monthly Review Press.

Frisby, W., Alexander, T., Taylor, J., Tirone, S., Watson, C., Harvey, J., & Laplante, D. (2005). *Bridging the recreation divide: Listening to youth and parents from low income families across Canada*. Ottawa, ON: Canadian Parks and Recreation Association.

Frisby, W., & Millar, S. (2002). The actualities of doing community development to promote the inclusion of low income populations in local sport and recreation. *European Sport Management Quarterly, 2*(3), 209–233.

Frisby, W., Reid, C., & Ponic, P. (2007). Levelling the playing field: Promoting the health of poor women through a community development approach to recreation. In P. White & K. Young (Eds.), *Sport and gender in Canada* (pp. 121–136). Toronto, ON: Oxford University Press.

Gore, A. (2013). *The future: Six drivers of global change*. New York, NY: Random House.

Hall, A., Slack, T., Smith, G., & Whitson, D. (1991). *Sport in Canadian society*. Toronto, ON: McClelland and Stewart.

Hannigan, J. (2006) *Environmental sociology*. New York, NY: Routledge.

Harvey, D. (2005). *A brief history of neoliberalism*. New York, NY: Oxford University Press.

Harvey, J., Horne, J., Safai, P., Darnell, S. C., & Courchesne-O'Neill, S. (2014). *Sport and social movements: From the global to the local*. London, UK: Bloomsbury Academic.

Hayes, G., & Horne, J. (2011). Sustainable development, shock and awe? London 2012 and civil society. *Sociology, 45*(5), 749–764.

Hayhurst, L., Wilson, B., & Frisby, W. (2011). Navigating neoliberal networks: Transnational internet platforms in sport for development and peace. *International Review for the Sociology of Sport, 46*(3), 315–329.

Hutchins, B., & Rowe, D. (2012). *Sport beyond television: The internet, digital media and the rise of networked media sport.* New York, NY: Routledge.

Jarvie, G. (2006). *Sport, culture and society: An introduction.* New York, NY: Routledge.

Kidd, B. (2008). A new social movement: Sport for development and peace. *Sport in Society, 11,* 370–380.

Kidder, J. L. (2013). Parkour, masculinity, and the city. *Sociology of Sport Journal, 30*(1), 1–23.

Lenskyj, H. (2008). *Olympic industry resistance: Challenging Olympic power and propaganda.* Albany, NY: SUNY Press.

Levermore, R., & Beacom, A. (2009). Sport and development: Mapping the field. In R. Levermore & A. Beacom (Eds.), *Sport and international development* (pp. 1–25). New York, NY: Palgrave MacMillan.

Maguire, J. (1999). *Global sport: Identities, societies, civilizations.* Cambridge, UK: Polity Press.

Maguire, J., Jarvie, G., Mansfield, L., & Bradley, J. (2002). *Sport worlds: A sociological perspective.* Champaign, IL: Human Kinetics.

Marks, L. J., & Michael, J. W. (2001). Science, medicine, and the future: Artificial limbs. *British Medical Journal, 323*(7315), 732–735.

McDonald, J. T., & Kennedy, S. (2004). Insights into the "healthy immigrant effect": Health status and health service use of immigrants to Canada. *Social Science & Medicine, 59*(8), 1613–1627.

Miah, A. (2004). *Genetically modified athletes: Biomedical ethics, gene doping and sport.* New York, NY: Routledge.

Miah, A. (2010, February 5). Gene doping: A reality, but not a threat [Weblog post]. *Professor Andy Miah.* Retrieved from http://www.andymiah.net/2010/02/05/is-gene-doping-a-threat-to-sport/.

Miller, T., Lawrence, G., McKay, J., & Rowe, D. (2001). *Globalization and sport.* Thousand Oaks, CA: Sage.

Millington, B. (2012). Amusing ourselves to life: Fitness consumerism and the birth of biogames. *Journal of Sport and Social Issues.* doi:10.1177/0193723512458932.

Millington, B. (2013). Aging in the information age: An ethnographic study of video gaming in Canadian retirement centres. Paper presented at the Sport Canada Research Initiative Conference, Ottawa, ON.

Millington, B., & Wilson, B. (2013). Super intentions: Golf course management and the evolution of environmental responsibility. *The Sociological Quarterly, 54*(3), 450–475.

Millington, R., & Darnell, S. C. (2012). Constructing and contesting the Olympics online: The Internet, Rio 2016 and the politics of Brazilian development. *International Review for the Sociology of Sport.* doi: 10.1177/1012690212455374

Mills, C. W. (1959). *The sociological imagination.* London, UK: Oxford.

Norman, M. (2012). Saturday night's alright for tweeting: Cultural citizenship, collective discussion, and the new media consumption/production of Hockey Day in Canada. *Sociology of Sport Journal, 29*(3), 306–324.

Pray, L. (2008) Sports, gene doping, and WADA. *Nature Education, 1*(1), 77.

Sage, G. (1999). Justice do it! The Nike transnational advocacy network: Organization, collective action and outcomes. *Sociology of Sport Journal, 16*(3), 206–235.

Scherer, J., & Jackson, S. J. (2010). *Globalization, sport and corporate nationalism: The new cultural economy of the New Zealand All Blacks.* Oxford, UK: Peter Lang.

Staggenborg, S. (2008). *Social movements.* Toronto, ON: Oxford University Press.

Stoddart, M. (2012). *Making meaning out of mountains*. Vancouver, BC: UBC Press.

Stolle-McAllister, J. (2004). Contingent hybridity: The cultural politics of Tepoztlán's anti-golf movement. *Identities: Global Studies in Culture and Power, 11*, 195–213.

Sugden, J. (2010). Critical left-realism and sport interventions in divided societies. *International Review for the Sociology of Sport, 45*, 258–272.

Thorpe, H., & Ahmad, N. (2013). Youth, action sports and political agency in the Middle East: Lessons from a grassroots parkour group in Gaza. *International Review for the Sociology of Sport.* doi: 10.1177/1012690213490521.

Wheaton, B. (Ed.). (2004). *Understanding lifestyle sports: Consumption, identity and difference.* London, UK: Routledge.

Wheaton, B. (2008). From the pavement to the beach: Politics and identity in "Surfers Against Sewage." In M. Atkinson & K. Young (Eds.), *Tribal play: Subcultural journeys through sport* (pp. 113–134). Bingley, UK: Emerald Group Publishing.

Whitson, D. (2012). Vancouver 2010: The saga of Eagleridge Bluffs. In G. Hayes & J. Karamichas (Eds.), *Olympic Games, mega-events and civil societies: Globalization, environment, resistance* (pp. 219–235). New York, NY: Palgrave Macmillian.

Wilson, B. (2006a). *Fight, flight, or chill: Subcultures, youth, and rave into the 21st century.* Montreal, QC: McGill-Queen's University Press.

Wilson, B. (2007). New media, social movements, and global sport studies: A revolutionary moment and the sociology of sport. *Sociology of Sport Journal, 24*(4), 457–477.

Wilson, B. (2012a). *Sport & peace: A sociological perspective.* Toronto, ON: Oxford University Press.

Wilson, B. (2012b). Growth and nature: Reflections on sport, carbon neutrality, and ecological modernization. In D. Andrews & M. Silk (Eds.), *Sport and neo-liberalism: Politics, consumption, and culture* (pp. 90–108). Philadelphia, PA: Temple University Press.

Wilson, B., & Hayhurst, L. (2009). Digital activism: Neo-liberalism, the internet, and "sport for development." *Sociology of Sport Journal, 26*(1), 155–181.

Wilson, B., & Millington, B. (2013). Sport, ecological modernization, and the environment. In D. Andrews & B. Carrington (Eds.), *A companion to sport* (pp. 129–142). Malden, MA: Blackwell Publishing.

Wilson, B., & Sparks, R. (1999). Impacts of black athlete media portrayals on Canadian youth. *Canadian Journal of Communication, 24*(4), 589–627.

Wilson, B., & Sparks, R. (2001). Michael Jordan, sneaker commercials, and Canadian youth cultures. In D. Andrews (Ed.), *Michael Jordan Inc.: Corporate sport, media culture, and late modern America* (pp. 217–255). Albany, NY: SUNY Press.

Winter, J. (2006). *Dreams of peace and freedom: Utopian moments in the 20th century.* New Haven, CT: Yale University Press.

References

Aboriginal Sports/Recreation Association of BC. (1995, October). Media release on the 1997 North American Indigenous Games planned for Victoria, BC.

Active Healthy Kids Canada. (2013). Active Kids Report Card. (2013). *Are we driving our kids to unhealthy habits? Report card on physical activity for children and youth.* Retrieved Feb. 2014 from http://www.activehealthykids.ca/2013ReportCard/en/.

Adams, M. L. (2006). The game of whose lives? Gender, race, and entitlement in Canada's "national" game. In D. Whitson & R. Gruneau (Eds.), *Artificial ice: Hockey, culture and commerce* (pp. 71–84). Peterborough, ON: Broadview Press.

Adams, M. L. (2011). *Artistic impressions: Figure skating, masculinity, and the limits of sport.* Toronto, ON: University of Toronto Press.

American Alliance for Health, Physical Education, Recreation and Dance. (2013). Comprehensive school physical activity programs: Helping all students achieve 60 minutes of physical activity each day. *Journal of Physical Education, Recreation and Dance, 84*(9), 9–15.

Ammirante, J. (2006). Globalization in professional sport: Comparisons and contrasts between hockey and European football. In D. Whitson & R. Gruneau (Eds.), *Artificial ice: Hockey, culture, and commerce* (pp. 237–261). Toronto, ON: University of Toronto Press.

Anderssen, E. (2010, April 9). Game-changing sex-abuse cases mean new rules for nation's coaches. *Globe and Mail.* Retrieved from http://www.theglobeandmail.com/news/national/game-changing-sex-abuse-cases-mean-new-rules-for-nations-coaches/article4314402/#dashboard/follows/.

Andrews, D. (Ed.). (2001). *Micheal Jordan, Inc.: Corporate sport, media culture, and late modern America.* Albany, NY: SUNY Press.

Andrews, D., & Silk, M. (Eds.). (2012). *Sport and neo-liberalism: Politics, consumption, and culture.* Philadelphia, PA: Temple University Press.

Appadurai, A. (1996). *Modernity at large: Cultural dimensions of globalization.* Minneapolis, MN: University of Minnesota Press.

Arctic Winter Games. (2013). Retrieved from http://www.arcticwintergames.org.

Arthur, B. (2009, November 11). Winds of change a mere breeze. *National Post,* p. S1.

Arthur, B. (2011a, March 4). Probert's brain is just the start. *National Post,* p. A1.

Arthur, B. (2011b, September 1). Warriors on ice, tragedies off it. *National Post,* p. A1.

Arthur, B. (2011c, September 2). Head, not heart, must lead the way. *National Post,* p. S1.

Arthur, B. (2013, October 2). Players defend fighting after gruesome incident in Maple Leafs, Canadiens game, but there must be a better way to police the ice. *National Post.* Retrieved from http://sports.nationalpost.com/2013/10/02/george-parross-gruesome-injury-prompts-players-to-defend-fighting/?utm_source=dlvr.it&utm_medium=twitter.

Associated Press. (2013, June 3). Quebec soccer leaders cite safety on turban bans. *Washington Times.* Accessed from http://www.washingtontimes.com/news/2013/jun/3/quebec-soccer-leaders-cite-safety-on-turban-bans.

Associated Press. (2014, May 2). Canadiens' P. K. Subban target of racist tweets. *CBC Sports.* Retrieved from http://www.cbc.ca/sports/hockey/nhl/canadiens-p-k-subban-target-of-racist-tweets-1.2629997.

Atkinson, M. (2009). Parkour, anarcho-environmentalism, and poiesis. *Journal of Sport and Social Issues, 33*(2), 169–194.

Atkinson, M., & Young, K. (2008). *Deviance and social control in sport.* Champaign, IL: Human Kinetics.

Atkinson, M., & Young, K. (Eds.). (2008a). *Tribal play: Subcultural journeys through sport.* Bingley, UK: Emerald Group Publishing.

Aucoin, P. (1995) *The new public management: Canada in comparative perspective.* Montreal, QC: The Institute for Research on Public Policy.

Autor, D., Manning, A., & Smith, C. L. (2010). The contribution of the minimum wage to U.S. wage inequality over three decades: A reassessment. *Finance and Economics Discussion Series.* Washington, DC: Federal Reserve Board. Retrieved from http://www.federalreserve.gov/pubs/feds/2010/201060/201060pap.pdf.

Bandura, A., & Walters, R. (1963). *Social learning and personality development.* New York, NY: Holt, Rinehart & Winston.

Bannerji, H. (2000). *The dark side of the nation: Essays on multiculturalism, nationalism and gender.* Toronto, ON: Canadian Scholars Press.

Barnes, J. (1990). Two cases of hockey homicide: The crisis of a moral ideal. Paper presented at the North American Society for Sport History, Banff, AB.

Barnes, J. (2010). *The law of hockey.* Markham, ON: Lexus Nexus.

Barney, R. K., Wenn, S., & Martyn, S. (2002). *Selling the five rings: The International Olympic Committee and the rise of Olympic commercialism.* Salt Lake City, UT: University of Utah Press.

Beal, B. (1995). Disqualifying the official: An exploration of social resistance through the subculture of skateboarding. *Sociology of Sport Journal, 12,* 252–267.

Beal, B. (2002). Symbolic interactionism and cultural studies: Doing critical ethnography. In J. Maguire & K. Young (Eds.), *Theory, sport & society* (pp. 353–373). Amsterdam: JAI.

Beamish, R. (1990). The persistence of inequality: An analysis of participation among Canada's high-performance athletes. *International Review for the Sociology of Sport, 25,* 143–155.

Beamish, R. (2002). Karl Marx's enduring legacy for the sociology of sport. In J. Maguire & K. Young (Eds.), *Theory, sport & society* (pp. 25–39). Amsterdam: JAI.

Beamish, R. (2009). Marxism, alienation and Coubertin's Olympic project. In B. Carrington & I. McDonald (Eds.), *Marxism, cultural studies & sport* (pp. 88–105). London, UK: Routledge.

Beamish, R. (2010). *The promise of sociology: The classical tradition and contemporary sociological thinking.* Toronto, ON: University of Toronto Press.

Beamish, R., & Borowy, J. (1988). *Q. What do you do for a living? A. I'm an athlete.* Kingston, ON: The Sport Research Group.

Bean, D. P. (2005). *Synchronized swimming: An American history.* Jefferson, NC: McFarland.

Becket, H. W. (1882). *The Montreal snow shoe club: Its history and record.* Montreal, QC: Becket Brothers.

Bellamy, R. (1998). The evolving television sports marketplace. In L. Wenner (Ed.), *MediaSport* (pp. 73–87). New York, NY: Routledge.

Bereska, T. (2011). *Deviance, conformity, and social control in Canada* (3rd ed.). Toronto, ON: Pearson Canada.

Bernstein, R. (2006). *The code: The unwritten rules of fighting and retaliation in the NHL.* Chicago, IL: Triumph Books.

Best, C. (1987). Experience and career length in professional football: The effect of positional segregation. *Sociology of Sport Journal, 4*(4), 410–420.

Bhabha, H. K. (1994). *The location of culture.* London, UK: Routledge.

Billig, M. (1995). *Banal nationalism.* London, UK: Sage.

Birrell, S., & McDonald, M. G. (Eds.). (2000). *Reading sport: Critical essays on power and representation.* Richmond, VA: Northeastern University Press.

Bloom, M., Grant, M., & Watt, D. (2005). *Strengthening Canada: The socioeconomic benefits of sport participation in Canada.* Conference Board of Canada. Retrieved from http://www.conferenceboard.ca/e-library/abstract.aspx?did=1340.

Bompa, T. (1995). *From childhood to champion athlete*. Toronto, ON: Veritas.

Booth, D., & Tatz, C. (2000). *One-eyed: A view of Australian sport*. New South Wales, AU: Allen & Unwin.

Boudarbat, B., Lemieux, T., & Riddell, W. (2010). The evolution of the returns to human capital in Canada, 1980–2005. *Canadian Public Policy, 36*, 63–89.

Bourdieu, P. ([1972] 1977). *Outline of a theory of practice*. Cambridge, UK: Cambridge University Press.

Bourdieu, P. ([1979] 1984). *Distinction: A social critique of the judgement of taste*. Cambridge, MA: Harvard University Press.

Bourdieu, P. ([1980] 1990). *The logic of practice*. Stanford, CA: Stanford University Press.

Bourdieu, P. ([1983] 1986). The forms of capital. In J. Richardson (Ed.), *Handbook of theory and research for the sociology of education*, (pp. 241–258). New York, NY: Greenwood Press.

Bourdieu, P. (1966). Condition de classe et position de classe. *Archives Européennes de Sociologie, 7*, 201–223.

Bourdieu, P. (1973). The three forms of theoretical knowledge. *Social Science Information, 12*, 53–80.

Bourdieu, P. (1989). Social space and symbolic power. *Sociological Theory, 7*, 14–25.

Bourdieu, P. (1993). *Sociology in question*. London, UK: Sage Publications.

Bourdieu, P. (2000) *Pascalian meditations*. Stanford, CA: Stanford University Press.

Bourdieu, P., & Wacquant, L. (1992). *An invitation to reflexive sociology*. Chicago, IL: University of Chicago Press.

Boycoff, J. (2011). The anti-Olympics. *New Left Review, 67*, 41–59.

Brackenbridge, C. H. (2001). *Spoilsports: Understanding and preventing sexual exploitation in sport*. London, UK: Routledge.

Branch, J. (2011, December 6). A brain "going bad." *New York Times*, p. B13.

Branch, T. (2011, October). The shame of college sports. *The Atlantic*. Retrieved from http://www.theatlantic.com/magazine/print/2011/10/the-shame-of-college-sports/308643.

Bratt, D. (in press). Different not better: Comparing Canadian and American university sport systems. In D. Taras & C. Waddell (Eds.), *How Canadians communicate V: Sport*. Edmonton, AB: Athabasca University Press.

Braunsdorf, D. (2001, August 4). Heatstroke problem lies within athletes' mentality. *Centre Daily Times*, p. 1B.

Brenner, J. S. (2007). Overuse injuries, overtraining, and burnout in child and adolescent athletes. *Pediatrics, 119*(6), 1242–1245. doi: 10.1542/peds.2007-0887.

Breton, R. (1964). Institutional completeness of ethnic communities and personal relations of immigrants. *American Journal of Sociology, 70*, 193–205.

Brock, D., Raby, R., & Thomas, M. (2012). *Power and everyday practices*. Toronto, ON: Nelson.

Brohm J.-M. (1978). *Sport: A prison of measured time*. London, UK: Ink Links.

Brooks, E. (2007). *Unraveling the garment industry: Transnational organizing and women's work*. Minneapolis, MN: University of Minnesota Press.

Brown, A. (1980). Edward Hanlan: The world sculling champion visits Australia. *Canadian Journal of History of Sport and Physical Education, 11*, 1–44.

Brown, W. (2006). *Edgework: Critical essays on knowledge and politics*. Princeton, NJ: Princeton University Press.

Brownrigg, M. (2008). Canadian children and youth receive failing grade for physical activity levels as screen time replaces active play. Active Healthy Kids Canada. Retrieved from http://dvqdas9jty7g6.cloudfront.net/pressreleases/ahkcrelease2008-finalen.pdf.

Bryant, J. E., & McElroy, M. (1997). *Sociological dynamics of sport and exercise*. Englewood, CO: Morton Publishing Company.

Brym, R. J. (2014). *We the people: Society in question*. Toronto, ON: Nelson.

Burnaby Now. (2013, November 20). STM grad named just third CFL Canadian MVP. Accessed from http://www.burnabynow.com/sports/photo-galleries/stm-grad-named-just-third-cfl-canadian-mvp-1.708508.

Burnet, J. R., & Palmer, H. (1988). *"Coming Canadians": An introduction to a history of Canada's people*. Toronto, ON: McLelland and Stewart in association with the Multiculturalism Program, Department of the Secretary of State and the Canadian Government Publishing Centre, Supply and Services, Canada.

Burstyn, V. (1999). *The rites of men: Manhood, politics, and the culture of sport*. Toronto, ON: University of Toronto Press.

Butcher, J., Linder, K. L., & Johns, D. P. (2002). Withdrawal from competitive youth sport: A retrospective ten-year study. *Journal of Sport Behavior, 25*(2), 145–163.

Butsch, R. (Ed.). (1990). *For fun and profit: The transformation of leisure into consumption*. Philadelphia, PA: Temple University Press.

Cahn, S. K. (1995). *Coming on strong: Gender and sexuality in twentieth-century women's sport*. Boston, MA: Harvard University Press.

Canada Basketball. (2012a). 2012 senior men's training camp roster. Retrieved from http://www.basketball.ca/senior-men-p148740.

Canada Basketball. (2012b). NCAA: Canadian impact. Retrieved from http://www.basketball.ca/ncaa-national-collegiate-athletic-associations15154.

Canada Soccer. (2013). Women's national team/Olympic team. Retrieved from http://www.canadasoccer.com/index.php?t=project&sid=965.

Canadian Centre for Ethics in Sport. (2002). *Public opinion survey on youth and sport. Final Report*. Retrieved from http://www.cces.ca/files/pdfs/CCES-RPT-2002Survey-E.pdf.

Canadian Centre for Ethics in Sport. (2008). *What sport can do: The true sport report*. Ottawa, ON: True Sport. Retrieved from http://www.truesportpur.ca/files/pdfs/TS_report_EN_webdownload.pdf.

Canadian Centre for Ethics in Sport. (2010a). Doping control test results on University of Waterloo football team announced. Retrieved from http://www.cces.ca/en/news-126-doping-control-test-results-on-university.

Canadian Centre for Ethics in Sport. (2010b). CCES, CIS and CFL announce robust anti-doping measures after more university football players test positive for banned substances. Retrieved from http://www.cces.ca/en/news-134-cces-cis-and-cfl-announce-robust-anti-doping.

Canadian Centre for Ethics in Sport. (2010c). CCES testing University of Waterloo football team. Media Backgrounder. Retrieved from http://www.cces.ca/files/pdfs/MediaBackgrounderTestingUniversityofWaterlooFootballTeam2010FINAL.pdf.

Canadian Centre for Ethics in Sport. (2012). *Sport in transition: Making sport in Canada more responsible for gender inclusivity*. Ottawa, ON: Author.

Canadian Fitness and Lifestyle Research Institute. (2004). *2004 Physical activity monitor*. Ottawa, ON: Author.

Canadian Fitness and Lifestyle Research Institute. (2010). *2010 Physical activity monitor: Facts and figures*. Ottawa, ON: Author.

Canadian Heritage. (2012). Canadian Sport Policy 2012. Retrieved from http://sirc.ca/CSPRenewal/documents/CSP2012_EN.pdf.

Canadian Heritage. (2013). *Sport participation 2010: Research paper*. Retrieved from http://publications.gc.ca/collections/collection_2014/pc-ch/CH24-1-2014-eng.pdf.

Canadian Heritage. (2013a). Sport Canada policies and legislation. Retrieved from http://www.pch.gc.ca/eng/1358438405126/1358438550678.

Canadian Interuniversity Sport. (2005a). Analysis of male and female coaches in CIS sports. Retrieved from http://english.cis-sic.ca/information/members_info/pdfs/pdf_research_and_stats/Analysis_of_Male_and_Female.pdf.

Canadian Interuniversity Sport. (2005b). Equity practices questionnaire: Responses of the membership. Final report. Retrieved from http://english.cis-sic.ca/information/members_info/pdfs/pdf_research_and_stats/2005_Equity_Practices_Questionnaire-CIS-Equity-Report-2005.pdf.

Canadian Interuniversity Sport. (2007). Canada vs U.S.A: The financial implications of the choice. Retrieved from http://english.cis-sic.ca/information/members_info/pdfs/pdf_research_and_stats/july2007CanadavsUSAresearchfinal.pdf.

Canadian Interuniversity Sport. (2013a). History of CIS. Retrieved from http://english.cis-sic.ca/information/about_cis/cishistory.

Canadian Interuniversity Sport. (2013b). About the CIS. Retrieved from http://english.cis-sic.ca.

Canadian Interuniversity Sport. (2013c). Athletic financial awards 2011–2012. Retrieved from http://english.cis-sic.ca/information/members_info/pdfs/pdf_research_and_stats/SportBySportAFASummary2011-12_-public-_-_english.pdf.

Canadian Interuniversity Sport. (2013d, June 20). Athletic scholarships: CIS schools provided over $12.7 M to student-athletes in 2011–12. News Release.

Canadian Interuniversity Sport. (2013e). Athlete's Guide: 2013–2014. Retrieved from http://english.cis-sic.ca/information/members_info/pdfs/pdf_elig_pack/13-14/athletes_guide.pdf.

Canadian Interuniversity Sport. (2013f). History of CIS doping violations. Retrieved from http://english.cis-sic.ca/information/members_info/pdfs/pdf_research_and_stats/Drug_stats_breakdown_jan_21_2013.pdf.

Canadian Paediatric Society. (2006). Sport readiness in children and youth sport. *Pediatric Child Health, 10*(6), 343–344.

Canadian Press. (2011, September 23). NHL says banana-throwing incident in pre-season game is "stupid and ignorant." *The Hockey News.* Retrieved from http://www.thehockeynews.com/articles/41885-NHL-says-bananathrowing-incident-in-preseason-game-is-stupid-and-ignorant.html.

Canadian Press. (2013, June 13). NFL commissioner Goodell defends Redskins nickname, answers letter from members of Congress. *Huffington Post.* Accessed from http://www.huffingtonpost.ca/2013/06/12/nfl-commissioner-goodell-_n_3430152.html.

Canadian Soccer Association. (2012). *Canadian Soccer Association's annual report: Capturing the moment.* Ottawa, ON: Author.

Canadian Sport Centres. (2007). *Canadian sport for life: A sport parent's guide.* Ottawa, ON: Author. Retrieved from http://www.fieldhockey.ca/files/LTHD/parents_guide_eng.pdf.

Cantelon, C., & Ingham, A. G. (2002). Max Weber and the sociology of sport. In J. Maguire & K. Young (Eds.), *Theory, sport & society* (pp. 63–81). Amsterdam: JAI.

Cantelon, H. (2006). Have skates, will travel: Canada, international hockey, and the changing hockey labour market. In D. Whitson & R. Gruneau (Eds.), *Artificial ice: Hockey, culture, and commerce* (pp. 215–235). Toronto, ON: University of Toronto Press.

Cantelon, H., & Gruneau, R. (1988). The production of sport for television. In J. Harvey & H. Cantelon (Eds.), *Not just a game: Essays in Canadian sport sociology* (pp. 177–193). Ottawa, ON: University of Ottawa Press.

Card, D., Lemieux, T., & Riddell, C. (2004). Unionization and wage inequality: A comparative study of the US, UK and Canada. *Journal of Labor Research, 25,* 519–559.

Cardwell, M. (2009, November 9). Laval's field of dreams. *University Affairs.* Retrieved from http://www.universityaffairs.ca/laval-s-field-of-dreams.aspx.

Carlson, T. B. (1995). We hate gym: Student alienation from physical education. *Journal of Teaching in Physical Education, 14,* 467–477.

Carnes, M. C. (1989). *Secret ritual and manhood in Victorian America.* New Haven, CT: Yale University Press.

Carrington, B., Andrews, D., Jackson, S., & Mazur, Z. (2001). The global Jordanscape. In D. L. Andrews (Ed.), *Michael Jordan Inc.: Corporate sport, media culture, and late modern America* (pp. 177–216). Albany, NY: SUNY Press.

Carter, T. (2011). *In foreign fields: The politics and experiences of transnational sports migration.* London, UK: Pluto Press.

Cavanaugh, R. (1992). The development of Canadian sports broadcasting 1920–1978. *Canadian Journal of Communication, 17,* 301–317.

CBC News. (2011, November 2). N.B. student's death prompts hazing probe. Retrieved from http://www.cbc.ca/news/canada/new-brunswick/n-b-student-s-death-prompts-hazing-probe-1.887974.

CBC News. (2013, January 9). Is Idle No More the new Occupy Wall Street? Aboriginal movement compared to 2011 grassroots protests that sprang up across the globe. Retrieved from http://www.cbc.ca/news/canada/is-idle-no-more-the-new-occupy-wall-street-1.1397642.

CBC Sports. (2005, October 18). McGill scraps football season over hazing. Retrieved from http://www.cbc.ca/sports/football/mcgill-scraps-football-season-over-hazing-1.553792.

CBC Sports. (2009, January 31). Ron MacLean, gay-rights advocate debate the 'P-word. Retrieved from http://www.cbc.ca/sports/hockey/ron-maclean-gay-rights-advocate-debate-the-p-word-1.853760.

Centers for Disease Control. (2010). *Childhood obesity.* Retrieved from http://www.cdc.gov/Healthypeople/hp2010.htm.

Charbonneau, L. (2013, July 22). The value of a degree earned in Canada vs. one earned abroad. *University Affairs.* Retrieved from http://www.universityaffairs.ca/margin-notes/the-value-of-a-degree-earned-in-canada-vs-one-earned-abroad/.

Charlesworth, H., & Young, K. (2004). Why English female university athletes play with pain: Motivations and rationalisations. In K. Young (Ed.), *Sporting bodies, damaged selves: Sociological studies of sports-related injury* (pp. 163–180). Oxford, UK: Elsevier.

Chase, L. (2008). Running big: Clydesdale runners and technologies of the body. *Sociology of Sport Journal, 25,* 130–147.

Chiswick, B. R., & Miller, P. W. (2002). Do enclaves matter in immigrant adjustment? *Discussion paper 449.* Bonn, Germany: Institute for the Study of Labor.

Coakley, J. (2009). *Sports in society: Issues and controversies* (10th ed.). New York, NY: McGraw-Hill.

Coakley, J., & Donnelly, P. (2009). Sports and children: Are organized programs worth the effort? *Sports in society: Issues and controversies* (2nd Canadian ed., pp. 110–143). Toronto, ON: McGraw-Hill Ryerson.

Coakley, J., & Donnelly, P. (2009). *Sports in society: Issues and controversies* (2nd Canadian ed.). Toronto, ON: McGraw-Hill Ryerson.

Coburn, D. (2004). Beyond the income inequality hypothesis: Class, neoliberalism, and health inequalities. *Social Science & Medicine, 58*(1), 41–56.

Cohen, G. (1980). *Karl Marx's theory of history: A defence.* Oxford, UK: Clarendon Press.

Cohen, S. (1972). *Folk devils and moral panics: The construction of the Mods and Rockers.* London, UK: MacGibbon and Kee.

Cole, C., & Denny, H. (2004). Visualizing deviance in post-Reagan America: Magic Johnson, AIDS, and the promiscuous world of professional sport. *Critical Sociology, 20,* 123–147.

Collins, T., & Vamplew, W. (2002). *Mud, sweat and beers: A cultural history of sport and alcohol.* Oxford, UK: Berg.

Conference Board of Canada. (2012). *Canadian income inequality: Is Canada becoming more unequal?* Retrieved from http://www.conferenceboard.ca/hcp/hot-topics/caninequality.aspx.

Connell, R. W. (1990). An iron man: The body and some contradictions of hegemonic masculinity. In M. A. Messner & D. F. Sabo (Eds.), *Sport, men, and the gender order: Critical feminist perspectives* (pp. 83–114). Champaign, IL: Human Kinetics.

Connell, R. W. (1995). *Masculinities.* Berkley, CA: University of California Press.

Connell, R. W. (2005). *Masculinities* (2nd ed.). Berkeley, CA: University of California Press.

Connor, J. (2009). Towards a sociology of drugs in sport. *Sport in Society, 12,* 327–343.

Cooky, C., Messner, M., & Hextrum, R. (2013). Women play sport, but not on TV: A longitudinal study of televised news media. *Communication & Sport, 1*(3), 203–230.

Cosentino, F. (1974). Ned Hanlan—Canada's premier oarsman: A case study of nineteenth-century professionalism. *Ontario History, 66,* 241–250.

Cosentino, F. (1975). A history of the concept of professionalism in Canadian sport. *Canadian Journal of History of Sport and Physical Education, 6,* 75–81.

Cosentino, F. (1998). *Afros, Aboriginals and amateur sport in pre-World War I Canada. Canada's Ethnic Group Series,* Booklet No. 26. Ottawa, ON: The Canadian Historical Society.

Cothran, D., & Ennis, C. D. (1999). Alone in a crowd: Meeting students' needs for relevance and connection in urban high school physical education. *Journal of Teaching in Physical Education, 18,* 234–247.

Crosset, T. W., Benedict, J. R., & McDonald, M. A. (1995). Male student-athletes reported for sexual assault: A survey of campus police departments and judicial affairs offices. *Journal of Sport & Social Issues, 19*(2), 126–140.

Curry, T. J. (1991). Fraternal bonding in the locker room: Pro-feminist analysis of talk about competition and women. *Sociology of Sport Journal, 8,* 119–135.

Curry, T. J. (2000). Booze and bar fights: A journey to the dark side of college athletics. In J. McKay, M. A. Messner, & D. Sabo (Eds.), *Masculinities, gender relations, and sport* (pp. 162–175). Thousand Oaks, CA: Sage.

Dahrendorf, R. (1959). *Class and class conflict in industrial society.* Stanford CA: Stanford University Press.

Dallaire, C., & Denis, C. (2005). Asymmetric hybridities: Youths at Francophone Games in Canada. *Canadian Journal of Sociology, 30*(2), 143–169.

Daniels, D. B. (2005). You throw like a girl: Sport and misogyny on the silver screen. *Film & History: An Interdisciplinary Journal of Film and Television Studies, 35*(1), 29–38.

Danylchuk, K. E. (1995). Academic performance of intercollegiate athletes at a Canadian university: Comparisons by gender, type of sport and affiliated faculty. *Avante, 1*(2), 78–93.

Darling-Hammond, L. (2010). *The flat world and education.* San Francisco, CA: Jossey Bass.

Darnell, S. (2012). *Sport and international development: A critical sociology.* New York, NY: Bloomsbury.

Davis, K., & Moore, W. E. (1945). Some principles of stratification. *American Sociological Review, 10,* 242–249.

Davis, N. W., & Duncan, M. C. (2006). Sports knowledge is power: Reinforcing masculine privilege through fantasy sport league participation. *Journal of Sport & Social Issues, 30*(3), 244–264.

Deacon, J. (2001, March 26). Rink rage. *Maclean's,* pp. 21–24.

Deakin, J. M., & Cobley, S. (2003). A search for deliberate practice: An examination of the practice environments in figure skating and volleyball. In J. Starkes & K. A. Ericsson (Eds.), *Expert performance in sport: Recent advances in research on sport expertise* (pp. 115–135). Champaign, IL: Human Kinetics.

Demers, G. (2006). Homophobia in sport—Fact of life, taboo subject. *Canadian Journal for Women in Coaching, 6*(2). Retrieved from http:// www.coach.ca/april-2006-vol-6-no-2-p132855.

Denis, C. (1997). *We are not you: First Nations and Canadian modernity.* Peterborough, ON: Broadview Press.

Desrochers, D. M. (2013). Academic spending versus athletic spending: Who wins? *Delta Cost Project.* Retrieved from http://www.deltacostproject. org/pdfs/DeltaCostAIR_AthleticAcademic_Spending_IssueBrief.pdf.

Deutschmann, L. (2002). *Deviance and social control* (3rd ed.). Toronto, ON: Nelson Thomson.

Dimeo, P., Hunt, T., & Horbury, R. (2012). The individual and the state: A social historical analysis of the East German "doping system." *Sport in History, 31,* 218–237.

Dodd, M. (2006, April 30). Sport or not a sport? Pot is split on poker. *USA Today,* p. 13C.

Dollard, J., Doob, L., Miller, N., Mowrer, O., & Sears, R. (1939). *Frustration and aggression.* New Haven, CT: Yale University Press.

Donnelly, P. (1996). The local and the global: Globalization in the sociology of sport. *Journal of Sport & Social Issues, 20,* 239–257.

Donnelly, P. (2000). *Taking sport seriously: Social issues in Canadian sport.* Toronto, ON: Thompson Publishing, Inc.

Donnelly, P. (2002). George Herbert Mead and an interpretive sociology of sport. In J. Maguire & K. Young (Eds.), *Theory, sport & society* (pp. 83–102). Amsterdam: JAI.

Donnelly, P. (2004). Sport and risk culture. In K. Young (Ed.), *Sporting bodies, damaged selves: Sociological studies of sports-related injuries* (pp. 29–57). Oxford, UK: Elsevier.

Donnelly, P. (2010). Rent the podium revisited: Reflections on Vancouver 2010. *Policy Options, 31*(4), 84–86.

Donnelly, P. (2013). Sport participation. In L. Thibault & J. Harvey (Eds.), *Sport policy in Canada* (pp. 177–213). Ottawa, ON: University of Ottawa Press.

Donnelly, P., Atkinson, M., Boyle, S., & Szto, C. (2011). Sport for development and peace: A public sociology perspective. *Third World Quarterly, 32,* 589–601.

Donnelly, P., & Donnelly, M. K. (2013). *The London 2012 Olympics: A gender equality audit.* Toronto, ON: Centre for Sport Policy Studies.

Donnelly, P., & Harvey, J. (2007). Social class and gender: Intersections in sport and physical activity. In P. White & K. Young (Eds.), *Sport and gender in Canada* (pp. 95–119). Toronto, ON: Oxford University Press.

Donnelly, P., Norman, M., & Kidd, B. (2013). *Gender equity in Canadian inter-university sport: A biennial report* (No. 2). Toronto, ON: Centre for Sport Policy Studies. Accessed from http://physical.utoronto.ca/docs/csps-pdfs/cis-gender-equity-report---2013.pdf?sfvrsn=2.

Donnelly, P., & Sparks, R. (2000). Child sexual abuse in sport. In P. Donnelly (Ed.), *Taking sport seriously: Social issues in Canadian sport* (pp. 108–111). Toronto, ON: Thompson Educational Press.

Dos Santos, T. (1970). The concept of social classes. *Science and Society, 34,* 166–193.

Dowbiggin, B. (2013). Racist tweets about TSN hosts reveal Canada's nasty side. *Globe and Mail.* Retrieved from http://www.theglobeandmail.com/ sports/more-sports/racist-tweets-about-tsn-hosts-reveal-canadas-nasty-side/article9845192/#dashboard/follows.

Draper, H. (1978). *Karl Marx's theory of revolution: The politics of social classes.* New York, NY: Monthly Review Press.

Drolet, D. (2006, January 16). University athletic departments review their hazing policies. *University Affairs.* Retrieved from http://www. universityaffairs.ca/university-athletics-departments-review-their-hazing-policies.aspx.

Dryden, K. (1989). *The game: A thoughtful and provocative look at a life in hockey.* Toronto, ON: Harper & Collins.

Dubin, C. L. (1990). *Commission of inquiry into the use of drugs and banned substances intended to increase athletic performance.* Ottawa, ON: Supply and Services Canada.

Duhatschek, E. (2013, October 2). Staged fights putting hockey's reputation in tatters. *Globe and Mail.* Retrieved from http://www.theglobeandmail. com/sports/hockey/hockeys-reputation-in-tatters-by-staged-fights/ article14671271/.

Duncan, M. C. (2006). Gender warriors in sports: Women in the media. In A. A. Raney & J. Bryant (Eds.), *Handbook of Sports and Media* (pp. 231–252). New York, NY: Routledge.

Dunning, E. (1999). *Sport matters: Sociological studies of sport, violence and civilization.* New York, NY: Routledge.

Dunning, E., & Waddington, I. (2003). Sport as a drug and drugs in sport: Some exploratory comments. *International Review for the Sociology of Sport, 38,* 351–368.

Durant, W. (1926). *The story of philosophy*. New York, NY: Simon and Schuster.

Durkheim, É. (1951). *Suicide: A study in sociology*. New York, NY: The Free Press.

Dyson, B. (2006). Students' perspectives of physical education. In D. Kirk, D. Macdonald, & M. O'Sullivan (Eds.), *Handbook of physical education* (pp. 326–346). London, UK: Sage.

Edwards, L., Jones, C., & Weaving, C. (2013). Celebration on ice: Double standards following the Canadian women's gold medal victory and the 2010 Winter Olympics. *Sport in Society, 16*, 682–698.

Eitzen, S. (2003). *Fair and foul: Beyond the myths and paradoxes of sport*. New York, NY: Rowman & Littlefield.

EKOS Research Associates. (1992). *The status of the high-performance athlete in Canada: Final report*. Ottawa, ON: Sport Canada Directorate, Fitness and Amateur Sport.

Engels, F. ([1845] 1950). *Condition of the working class in England in 1844*. London, UK: G. Allen and Unwin.

Engh, F. (1999). *Why Johnny hates sports*. Garden City Park, NY: Avery Pub.

Ennis, C. D. (1999). Creating a culturally relevant curriculum for disengaged girls. *Sport, Education and Society, 4*, 31–49.

Ennis, C. D. (2006). Curriculum: Forming and reshaping the vision of physical education in a high need, low demand world of schools. *Quest, 58*, 41–59.

Enright, E., & O'Sullivan, M. (2010). "Can I do it in my pyjamas?" Negotiating a physical education curriculum with teenage girls. *European Physical Education Review, 16*, 203–222.

Epp, R., & Whitson, D. (Eds.). (2001). *Writing off the rural West: Globalization, governments, and the transformation of rural communities*. Edmonton, AB: University of Alberta Press.

Fainaru-Wada, M., & Fainaru, S. (2013). *League of denial: The NFL, concussions, and the battle for truth*. New York, NY: Crown Archetype.

Fawcett, B. (1992). The trouble with globalism. In M. Wyman (Ed.), *Vancouver forum* (pp. 183–201). Vancouver, BC: Douglas & McIntyre.

Fernandez, T., Berger, I., Brissette, C., O'Reilly, N., Parent, M., & Séguin, B. (2008). Sport participation in Canada: A longitudinal cohort analysis. Presented at the Administrative Sciences Association of Canada Annual Conference, Halifax. Retrieved from http://ojs.acadiau.ca/index.php/ASAC/article/view/919/802.

Figler, S. K., & Whitaker G. (1991). *Sport and play in American life*. Dubuque, IA: Wm. C. Brown.

Fletcher, T. (2012). Experiences and identities: Pre-service elementary classroom teachers being and becoming teachers of physical education. *European Physical Education Review, 18*, 380–395.

Florida, R. (2002). *The rise of the creative class: And how it's transforming work, leisure, community, and everyday life*. New York, NY: Basic Books.

Foer, F. (2004). *How soccer explains the world: An (unlikely) theory of globalization*. New York, NY: Harper Perennial.

Fortin, N., Green, D., Lemieux, T., Milligan, K., & Riddell, C. (2012). Canadian inequality: Recent developments and policy options. *Canadian Public Policy, 38*, 121–145.

Foster, J. B., Clark, B., & York, R. (2010). *The ecological rift: Capitalism's war on the earth*. New York, NY: Monthly Review Press.

Francis, N. R., & Lathrop, A. H. (2011). "Children who drill, seldom are ill." Drill, movement and sport: The rise and fall of a "female tradition" in Ontario elementary physical education—1850s to 2000. *Historical Studies in Education* (Spring), 61–80.

Fraser-Thomas, J., & Coté, J. (2009). Understanding adolescents' positive and negative developmental experiences in sport. *Sports Psychologist, 23*, 3–23.

Freidman, T. (1999). *The Lexus and the olive tree*. New York, NY: Farrar, Strauss & Giroux.

Frideres, J. S. (1988). Racism. In *The Canadian Encyclopedia* (2nd ed., Vol III, p. 1816). Edmonton, AB: Hurtig Publishers.

Frisby, W., Alexander, T., Taylor, J., Tirone, S., Watson, C., Harvey, J., & Laplante, D. (2005). *Bridging the recreation divide: Listening to youth and parents from low income families across Canada*. Ottawa, ON: Canadian Parks and Recreation Association.

Frisby, W., & Millar, S. (2002). The actualities of doing community development to promote the inclusion of low income populations in local sport and recreation. *European Sport Management Quarterly, 2*(3), 209–233.

Frisby, W., Reid, C., & Ponic, P. (2007). Levelling the playing field: Promoting the health of poor women through a community development approach to recreation. In P. White & K. Young (Eds.), *Sport and gender in Canada* (pp. 121–136). Toronto, ON: Oxford University Press.

Frye, M. (1983). *The politics of reality*. Trumansburg, NY: The Crossing Press.

Fullinwider, R. K. (2006). Sports, youth and character: A critical survey. Circle Working Paper 44, Institute for Philosophy and Public Policy, University of Maryland. Retrieved from http://www.civicyouth.org/PopUps/WorkingPapers/WP44Fullinwider.pdf.

Galeano, E. (1998). *Soccer in the sun and shadow*. M. Fried (Trans.). London, UK: Verso.

Garrett, R., & Wrench, A. (2007). Physical experiences: Primary student teachers' conceptions of sport and physical education. *Physical Education and Sport Pedagogy, 12*, 23–42.

Geiger, N. (2013). Intercollegiate athletics in Canada and the United States: Differences in access, quality, and funding. *College Quarterly, 16*, 3.

Genel, M. (2000). Gender verification no more? *Medscape Women's Health, 5*(3), E2. Retrieved from http://ai.eecs.umich.edu/people/conway/TS/OlympicGenderTesting.html.

Getz, M., & Siegfried, J. (2010). What does intercollegiate athletics do to or for colleges and universities? Working Paper. Nashville, TN: Vanderbilt University, Department of Economics. Retrieved from http://www.accessecon.com/pubs/VUECON/vu10_w05.html.

Giardina, M., & Newman, J. (2011). The physical and the possible. *Cultural Studies <=> Critical Methodologies, 11*, 392–402.

Gibbons, S. L. (2009). Meaningful participation of girls in senior physical education courses. *Canadian Journal of Education, 32*, 222–244.

Giddens, A. (1973). *The class structure of the advanced societies*. London, UK: Hutchinson.

Giddens, A. (1976). Functionalism: Après la lutte. *Social Research, 43*, 325–366.

Giddens, A. (1979). *Central problems in social theory*. London, UK: The Macmillan Press.

Giddens, A. (1984). *The constitution of society*. Berkeley, CA: University of California Press.

Giddens, A. (1987). *Social theory and modern sociology*. Palo Alto, CA: Stanford University Press.

Giddens, A. (1989). *Sociology*. Oxford, UK: Polity Press.

Gilbert, R. (2011). Playing on the same page. In P. Donnelly (Ed.), *Taking sport seriously: Social issues in Canadian sport* (3rd ed., pp. 251–255). Toronto, ON: Thompson Educational Publishing.

Gill, R., Henwood, K., & McLean, C. (2005). Body projects and the regulation of normative masculinity. *Body & society, 11*(1), 37–62.

Gillespie, G. (2002). *The imperial embrace: British sportsmen and the appropriation of landscape in nineteenth-century Canada*. Unpublished doctoral dissertation, University of Western Ontario, London, ON.

Gillet, J., White, P., & Young, K. (1996). The prime minister of Saturday night: Don Cherry, the CBC, and the cultural production of intolerance. In H. Holmes & D. Taras (Eds.), *Seeing ourselves: Media power and policy in Canada* (2nd ed., pp. 59–72). Toronto, ON: Harcourt Brace.

Gillis, C. (2009, February 9). Can we please now ban fighting in hockey? *Maclean's, 122*(4), 48–51.

Gillmor, D. (2013). Is minor hockey worth it? *Toronto Star*. Retrieved from http://www.thestar.com/news/insight/2013/01/11/is_minor_hockey_worth_it.html.

Giulianotti, R., & Robertson, R. (2007). *Globalization and sport*. Oxford, UK: Blackwell Publishing.

Gladwell, M. (2009, October 19). Offensive play: How different are dog-fighting and football? *The New Yorker*. Retrieved from http://www.newyorker.com/reporting/2009/10/19/091019fa_fact_gladwell.

Glazer, N. (1970). Ethnic groups in America: From national culture to ideology. In M. Kurokawa (Ed.), *Minority responses* (pp. 74–86). New York, NY: Random House.

Goffman, E. (1963). *Stigma: Notes on the management of spoiled identity.* Englewood Cliffs, NJ: Prentice-Hall.

Goldin, C., & Katz, L. (2008). *The race between education and technology.* Cambridge, MA: Harvard University Press.

Goldlust, J. (1987). *Playing for keeps: Sport, the media and society.* Melbourne, AU: Longman Cheshire.

Goos, M., & Manning, A. (2007). Lousy and lovely jobs: The rising polarization of work in Britain. *Review of Economics and Statistics, 89*, 118–133.

Gore, A. (2013). *The future: Six drivers of global change.* New York, NY: Random House.

Gorn, E. J. (1986). *The manly art: Bare-knuckle prize fighting in America.* Ithaca, NY: Cornell University Press.

Grabell, M. (2013). How the temp workers who power America's corporate giants are getting crushed. *Financial Post.* Retrieved from http://business.financialpost.com/2013/07/05/how-the-temp-workers-who-power-americas-corporate-giants-are-getting-crushed.

Grant, P., & Wood, C. (2004). *Blockbusters and trade wars: Popular culture in a globalized world.* Vancouver, BC: Douglas & McIntyre.

Grasgreen, A. (2012, September 25). Gaps in grad rates for athletes. *Inside Higher Education.* Retrieved from http://www.insidehighered.com/news/2012/09/25/report-finds-football-players-graduate-rates-lower-full-time-student-peers.

Grasgreen, A. (2013, January 10). Division I basketball players graduate at lower rates than non-athletes. *Inside Higher Education.* Retrieved from http://www.insidehighered.com/quicktakes/2013/01/10/division-i-basketball-players-graduate-lower-rates-non-athletes.

Green, D., & Sand, B. (2011). *Has the Canadian labour market polarized?* Ottawa, ON: Human Resources and Skills Development Canada.

Green, K. (2008). *Understanding physical education.* London, UK: Sage.

Greenberg, J. & Knight, G. (2004). Framing sweatshops: Nike, global production, and the American news media. *Communication and Critical/Cultural Studies, 1*, 151–175.

Greer, C., & Jewkes, Y. (2005). Extremes of otherness: Media images of social exclusion. *Social Justice, 32*, 20–31.

Grossberg, L., Wartell, E., Whitney, D., & Wise, J. (Eds.). (2006). *Media-making: Mass media in a popular culture.* Thousand Oaks, CA: Sage.

Gruneau, R. (1972). *An analysis of Canada Games' Athletes, 1971.* Unpublished master's thesis, University of Calgary, Calgary, AB.

Gruneau, R. (1983). *Class, sport, and social development.* Amherst, MA: University of Massachusetts Press.

Gruneau, R. (1988). Modernization and hegemony: Two views on sport and social development. In J. Harvey & H. Cantelon (Eds.), *Not just a game: Essays in Canadian sport sociology* (pp. 9–32). Ottawa, ON: University of Ottawa Press.

Gruneau, R. (1989). Making spectacle: A case study in television sports production. In L. Wenner (Ed.), *Media, sports, and society* (pp. 134–154). Newbury Park, CA: Sage.

Gruneau, R. (1999). *Class, sports, and social development.* Champaign, IL: Human Kinetics.

Gruneau, R. (in press). Goodbye Gordie Howe: Sport participation and class inequality in the "pay for play." In D. Taras & C. Wadell (Eds.), *How Canadians communicate V: Sports.* Edmonton, AB: AU Press.

Gruneau, R., & Whitson, D. (1993). *Hockey night in Canada: Sport, identities and cultural politics.* Peterborough, ON: Broadview Press.

Gruneau, R., & Whitson, D. (2001). Upmarket continentalism: Major league sport, promotional culture, and corporate integration. In V. Mosco & D. Schiller (Eds.), *Continental order: Integrating North America for cybercapitalism* (pp. 235–264). Lanham: MD: Rowman & Littlefield.

Gruneau, R., Whitson, D., & Cantelon, H. (1988). Methods and media: Studying the sports/television discourse. *Society and Leisure, 11*, 265–281.

Halas, J. (2006). Developing a white-race consciousness: A foundation for culturally relevant physical education for Aboriginal youth. In E. Singleton & A. Varpalotai (Eds.), *Stones in the sneaker: Active theory for secondary school physical and health educators* (pp. 155–182). London, ON: Althouse Press.

Halas, J. M. (2011). Aboriginal youth and their experiences in physical education: "This is what you've taught me." *PHEnex Journal, 3*(2). Retrieved from http://ojs.acadiau.ca/index.php/phenex/article/view/1427.

Hall, A. (2002). *The girl and the game: A history of women's sport in Canada.* Peterborough, ON: Broadview Press.

Hall, A. (2007). Cultural struggle and resistance: Gender, history, and Canadian sport. In K. Young & P. White (Eds.), *Sport and gender in Canada*, (pp. 56–74). Toronto, ON: Oxford University Press.

Hall, A., & Richardson, D. A. (1982). *Fair ball: Towards sex equality in Canadian sport.* Ottawa, ON: Canadian Advisory Council on the Status of Women.

Hall, A., Slack, T., Smith, G., & Whitson, D. (1991). *Sport in Canadian society.* Toronto, ON: McClelland & Stewart.

Hall, S. (2000). Racist ideologies and the media. In P. Marris & S. Thornham (Eds.), *Media studies: A reader* (pp. 271–282). New York, NY: New York University Press.

Hall, S., Critcher, C., Jefferson, T., Clarke, J., & Robert, B. (1978). *Policing the crisis: Mugging, the state and law and order.* London, UK: Macmillan.

Hannerz, U. (1996). *Transnational connections: Culture, people, places.* London, UK: Routledge.

Hannigan, J. (2006) *Environmental sociology.* New York, NY: Routledge.

Hargreaves, J., & McDonald, I. (2000). Cultural studies and the sociology of sport. In J. Coakley & E. Dunning (Eds.), *Handbook of sport studies* (pp. 48–60). London: Sage.

Harvey, D. (2005). *A brief history of neoliberalism.* New York, NY: Oxford University Press.

Harvey, D. (2007). *A brief history of neoliberalism.* Oxford, UK: Oxford University Press.

Harvey, J. (1988). Sport policy and the welfare state: An outline of the Canadian state. *Sociology of Sport Journal, 5*, 315–329.

Harvey, J. (2000). What's in a game? In P. Donnelly (Ed.), *Taking sport seriously.* Toronto, ON: Thompson Educational Publishing.

Harvey, J. (2006). Whose sweater is this? The changing meanings of hockey in Quebec. In D. Whitson & R. Gruneau (Eds.), *Artificial ice: Hockey, culture, and commerce* (pp. 29–52). Toronto, ON: Garamond.

Harvey, J. (2013). Multi-level governance and sport policy in Canada. In J. Thibault & J. Harvey (Eds.), *Sport policy in Canada.* Ottawa, ON: University of Ottawa Press.

Harvey, J., Horne, J., Safai, P., Darnell, S., & Courchesne-O'Neill, S. (2013). *Sport and social movements.* London, UK: Bloomsbury.

Harvey, J., & Proulx, R. (1988). Sport and the state in Canada. In J. Harvey & H. Cantelon (Eds.), *Not just a game: Essays in Canadian sport sociology* (pp. 93–112). Ottawa, ON: University of Ottawa Press.

Hastie, P. A., Rudisill, M. E., & Wadsworth, D. D. (2013). Providing students with voice and choice: Lessons from intervention research on autonomy-supportive climates in physical education. *Sport, Education and Society, 18*, 38–56.

Hayes, G., & Horne, J. (2011). Sustainable development, shock and awe? London 2012 and civil society. *Sociology, 45*(5), 749–764.

Hayhurst, L., Wilson, B., & Frisby, W. (2011). Navigating neoliberal networks: Transnational internet platforms in sport for development and peace. *International Review for the Sociology of Sport, 46*(3), 315–329.

Henslin, J. M., Glenday, D., Pupo, N., & Duffy, A. (2014). *Sociology: A down to earth approach* (6th Canadian ed.). Toronto, ON: Pearson Canada.

Hickey, C. (2010). Hypermasculinity in schools. In M. O'Sullivan & A. Macphail (Eds.), *Young people's voices in physical education and youth sport* (pp. 108–122). London, UK: Routledge.

Hockey Canada. (2013). *2013 Annual Report*. Ottawa, ON: Author. Retrieved from http://www.hockeycanada.ca/en-ca/Corporate/About/Basics/Downloads.

Holden, E. (2011). The top five most controversial tweets in NFL history: A fan's view. *Yahoo! Sports*. Retrieved from http://ca.sports.yahoo.com/nfl/news?slug=ycn-10497693.

Hollingshead, K. (1998). Tourism, hybridity, and ambiguity: The relevance of Bhabha's "third space" cultures. *Journal of Leisure Research, 30*(1), 121–156.

Hooks, B. (1984). *Feminist theory: From the margin to the center*. Boston, MA: South End Press.

Hooks, B. (2000). *Feminism is for everybody: Passionate politics*. Boston, MA: South End Press.

Horne, J. (2006). *Sport in consumer culture*. London, UK: Palgrave Macmillan.

Houston, W. (2011). Women on TV: Looks first, knowledge later. In P. Donnelly (Ed.), *Taking sport seriously: Social issues in Canadian sport* (3rd ed., pp. 256–260). Toronto, ON: Thompson Educational.

Howell, C. D. (1995). *Northern sandlots: A social history of Maritime baseball*. Toronto, ON: University of Toronto Press.

Hruby, P. (2012, December 13). Maintaining appearances. *Sports on Earth*. Retrieved from http://www.sportsonearth.com/article/40628020/.

Hruby, P. (2013a, February 8). The NFL: Forever backward. *Sports on Earth*. Retrieved from http://www.sportsonearth.com/article/41492872.

Hruby, P. (2013b, March 28). The myth of safe football. *Sports on Earth*. Retrieved from http://www.sportsonearth.com/article/43419226/.

Hruby, P. (2013c, August 30). Q&A: The NFL's concussion deal. *Sports on Earth*. Retrieved from http://therotation.sportsonearthblog.com/qa-the-nfls-concussion-deal/.

Hruby, P. (2013d, November 27). The NHL concussion lawsuit: Another league of denial? *Sports on Earth*. Retrieved from http://therotation.sportsonearthblog.com/the-nhl-concussion-lawsuit/.

Hughes, R., & Coakley, J. (1991). Positive deviance among athletes: The implications of overconformity to the sport ethic. *Sociology of Sport Journal, 8*, 307–325.

Hughes, T. (1904). *Tom Brown's school days by an old boy*. New York, NY: Hurst and Company.

Hunter, G., Sanchez, M., & Douglas, F. (2012). Incomes of the one per cent (and everyone else) in Canada. *Poverty Papers 5*. Regina, SK: Social Policy Research Unit, University of Regina.

Hutchins, B., & Rowe, D. (2012). *Sport beyond television: The Internet, digital media and the rise of networked media sport*. New York, NY: Routledge.

Hutchison, R. (1988). A critique of race, ethnicity, and social class in recent leisure-related research. *Journal of Leisure Research, 20*(1), 10–30.

Ifedi, F. (2008). *Sport participation in Canada, 2005*. Ottawa, ON: Statistics Canada, Culture, Tourism and the Centre for Educational Statistics.

Ingham, A. G. (2004). The sportification process: A biographical analysis framed by the work of Marx, Weber, Durkheim and Freud. In R. Giulianotti (Ed.), *Sport and modern social theorists* (pp. 11–32). London: Palgrave Macmillan.

Ingham, A., Howell, J., & Schilperoort, T. (1988). Sport and community: A review and exegesis. *Exercise and Sport Science Review, 15*, 427–465.

Institute for Diversity and Ethics in Sport. (n.d.). The Racial and Gender Report Card. Retrieved from http://www.tidesport.org/racialgenderreportcard.html.

International Olympic Committee. (2009). *Women and sport: The current situation*. Retrieved from http://www.wcse2011.qa/wp-content/uploads/2011/05/Women-and-Sport-The-Current-Situation-2009-10-eng-.pdf.

Intersex Society of North America. (n.d.). *How common is intersex?* Retrieved from http://www.isna.org/faq/frequency.

ISSA (International Sociology of Sport Association). (2005). About ISSA. Retrieved from issa.otago.ac.nz/about.html.

Iyer, P. (2000). *The global soul*. New York, NY: Vintage Books.

Jackson, S. (1998). A twist of race: Ben Johnson and the Canadian crisis of racial and national identity. *Sociology of Sport Journal, 15*(1), 21–40.

Jackson, S. (1998). A twist of race: Ben Johnson and the Canadian crisis of racial and national identity. *Sociology of Sport Journal, 15*, 21–40.

Jackson, S., & Ponic, P. (2001). Pride and prejudice: Reflecting on sport heroes, national identity, and crisis in Canada. *Culture, Sport, Society, 4*, 43–62.

Jamail, M. H. (2008). *Venezuelan bust, baseball boom: Andrés Reiner and scouting on the new frontier*. Lincoln, NE: University of Nebraska Press.

James, C. (Ed.). (1996). *Perspectives on racism and the human services sector: A case for change*. Toronto, ON: University of Toronto Press.

James, C. (2005). *Race in play: Understanding the social-cultural worlds of student athletes*. Toronto, ON: Canadian Scholars' Press.

James, C. L. R. (1963). *Beyond a Boundary*. London: Stanley Paul & Co.

Jarvie, G. (2006). *Sport, culture and society: An introduction*. New York, NY: Routledge.

Jayanthi, N. (2012). Injury risks of sport specialization and training in junior tennis players: A clinical study. Paper presented at the Society for Tennis and Medicine Science North American Regional Conference, Atlanta, GA.

Jenkins, L. (2014, May 26). All of us, not least Donald Sterling, now know this: Adam Silver, Commissioner, is his own man. *Sports Illustrated, 120*(2).

Jhally, S. (1984). The spectacle of accumulation: Material and cultural factors in the evolution of the sports/media complex. *Critical Sociology, 12*, 41–57.

Jobling, I. (1970). *Sport in nineteenth-century Canada: The effects of technological changes on its development*. Unpublished doctoral dissertation, University of Alberta, Edmonton, AB.

Johnson, J., & Holman, M. J. (2004). *Making the team: Inside the world of sport initiations and hazing*. Toronto, ON: Canadian Scholars Press.

Johnson, J., Butryn, T., & Masucci, M. (2013). A focus group analysis of the US and Canadian female triathletes' knowledge of doping. *Sport in Society, 16*, 654–671.

Junod, T. (2013, January 18). Theater of pain. *Esquire*. Retrieved from http://www.esquire.com/features/nfl-injuries-0213-2.

Kane, M. J. (1995). Resistance/transformation of the oppositional binary: Exposing sport as a continuum. *Journal of Sport and Social Issues, 19*(2), 191–218.

Kane, M. J., & Snyder, E. (1989). Sport typing: The social "containment" of women in sport. *Arena Review, 13*(2), 77–96.

Kaufman, M. (1987). The construction of masculinity and the triad of men's violence. In M. Kaufman (Ed.), *Beyond patriarchy: Essays by men on pleasure, power, and change* (pp. 1–29). Toronto, ON: Oxford University Press.

Kaufman, P., & Wolff, E. (2010). Playing and protesting: Sport as a vehicle for social change. *Journal of Sport and Social Issues, 34*, 154–175.

Kenyon, G. (1977). Factors influencing the attainment of elite track status in track and field. *Post-Olympic Conference Proceedings*. Ottawa, ON: Coaching Association of Canada.

Kenyon, G., & McPherson, B. (1973). Becoming involved in physical activity and sport: A process of socialization. In G. L. Rarick (Ed.), *Physical activity: Human growth and development*. New York, NY: Academic Press.

Kerr, J. H. (2005). *Rethinking aggression and violence in sport*. London, UK: Routledge.

Kerr, J. (2006). Examining the Bertuzzi–Moore NHL ice hockey incident: Crossing the line between sanctioned and unsanctioned violence in sport. *Aggression and Violent Behavior, 11*, 315–322.

Keynes, J. (1936). *The general theory of employment, interest and money.* New York, NY: Harcourt, Brace.

Kidd, B. (1983). In defence of Tom Longboat. *Canadian Journal of History of Sport, 14*(1), 34–63.

Kidd, B. (1984). The myth of the ancient Games. In A. Tomlinson & G. Whannel (Eds.), *Five ring circus: Money, power and politics at the Olympic Games* (pp. 71–83). London and Sydney: Pluto Press.

Kidd, B. (1996a). *The struggle for Canadian sport.* Toronto, ON: University of Toronto Press.

Kidd, B. (1996b). Worker sport in the new world: The Canadian story. In A. Kuger & J. Riordan (Eds.), *The story of worker sport* (pp. 143–156). Champaign, IL: Human Kinetics.

Kidd, B. (2008). A new social movement: Sport for development and peace. *Sport in Society, 11*, 370–380.

Kidd, B., & Eberts, M. (1982). *Athlete's rights in Canada.* Toronto, ON: Queen's Printer.

Kidder, J. L. (2013). Parkour, masculinity, and the city. *Sociology of Sport Journal, 30*(1), 1–23.

Kilborn, M. (2011). Physical education curriculum across Canada. Presentation at the Canadian Society for Studies in Education Annual Conference. Fredericton, NB, May 28–June 1.

Kimmel, M. (1996). *Manhood in America: A cultural history.* New York, NY: The Free Press.

King, P. (2010, November 1). Concussions: The hits that are changing football. *Sports Illustrated, 110*(16), 34–40.

Kirby, S., & Greaves, L. (1996, July 11–14). *Foul play: Sexual abuse and harassment in sport.* Paper presented to the Pre-Olympic Scientific Congress, Dallas, TX.

Kirk, D. (2010a). Physical education and sports. In P. Peterson, E. Baker, & B. McGaw (Eds.), *International encyclopedia of education* (pp. 459–463). Amsterdam: Elsevier.

Kirk, D. (2010b). *Physical education futures.* London, UK: Routledge.

Kirk, D. (2013). Educational value and models-based practice in physical education. *Educational Philosophy and Theory* (iFirst), 1–14.

Kirk, D., Macdonald, D., & O'Sullivan, M. (Eds.), (2006). *Handbook of physical education.* London, UK: Sage.

Klein, A. (1991). *Sugarball: The American game, the Dominican dream.* New Haven, CT: Yale University Press.

Klein, A. (1997). *The owls of the two laredos: Baseball and nationalism on the Texas–Mexican border.* Princeton, NJ: Princeton University Press.

Kline, J. (2011, October 13). Fighting words. *National Post*, p. A3.

Klingbeil, C. (2013, August 6). Pearl divers: Skyline stunt at new tower. *Edmonton Journal*, p. A1.

Koutures, C. G., Gregory, A. J., & the Council on Sport Medicine and Fitness. (2010). Injuries in youth soccer. *American Academy of Pediatrics, 125*(2), 410–414. doi: 10.1542/peds.2009-3009.

Kremer-Sadlik, T., & Kim, J. L. (2007). Lessons from sports: Children's socialization to values through family interaction during sports activities. *Discourse and Society, 18*(1), 35–52. doi: 10.1177/0957926507069456.

Krugman, P. (2009). *The conscience of a liberal.* New York, NY: W. W. Norton & Company.

Kuper, S., & Szymanski, S. (2009). *Soccernomics: Why England Loses, Why Germany and Brazil win, and why the US, Japan, Australia, Turkey—and even Iraq—are destined to become the kings of the world's most popular sport.* New York, NY: Nation Books.

Kuper, S., & Szymanski, S. (2012). *Soccernomics.* New York, NY: Nation Books.

Kyle, D. G. (2007). *Sport and spectacle in the ancient world.* Malden, MA: Blackwell.

Langford, I. (2004, February 10). Cherry's comments: Racially insensitive and nonsensical. *Toronto Observer.* Retrieved from http://observer.thecentre.centennialcollege.ca/opinion/cherry_ian021004.htm.

Laurendeau, J. (2008). "Gendered risk regimes": A theoretical consideration of edgework and gender. *Sociology of Sport Journal, 25*, 293–309.

Laurendeau, J. (2011). "If you're reading this, it's because I've died": Masculinity and relational risk in BASE jumping. *Sociology of Sport Journal, 28*, 404–420.

Laurendeau, J. (2012). *BASE jumping: The ultimate guide.* Santa Barbara, CA: ABC-CLIO.

Laurendeau, J. (2013). "Just tape it up for me, ok?": Masculinities, injury and embodied emotion. *Emotion, Space and Society.* doi: 10.1016/j.emospa.2013.03.010.

Laurendeau, J., & Adams, C. (2010). "Jumping like a girl": Discursive silences, exclusionary practices and the controversy over women's ski jumping. *Sport in Society, 13*(3), 431–447.

Laurendeau, J., & Moroz, S. (2013). Morality in the mountains: Risk, responsibility, and neoliberalism in newspaper accounts of backcountry rescue. *Communication & Sport, 1*, 382–399.

Lavallee, L. (2007). Physical activity and healing through the medicine wheel. *Social Work Publications and Research*, Paper 2. Retrieved from http://digitalcommons.ryerson.ca/socialwork/2.

LaVoi, N. M., & Stellino, M. B. (2008). The relation between perceived parent-created sport climate and competitive male youth hockey players' good and poor sport behaviours. *Journal of Psychology, 142*(5), 471–495.

Law, M., Cote, J., & Ericsson, K. A. (2007). Characteristics of expert development in rhythmic gymnastics: A retrospective study. *International Journal of Exercise and Sport Psychology, 5*(1), 82–103. doi: 10.1080/1612197X.2008.9671814.

Lefkowitz, B. (1997). *Our guys: The Glen Ridge rape and the secret life of the perfect suburb.* Berkeley, CA: University of California Press.

Lenskyj, H. (1986). *Out of bounds: Women, sport and sexuality.* Toronto, ON: Women's Press.

Lenskyj, H. (2008). *Olympic industry resistance: Challenging Olympic power and propaganda.* Albany, NY: SUNY Press.

Leonard II, W. M. (1987). Stacking in college basketball: A neglected analysis. *Sociology of Sport Journal, 4*(4), 403–409.

Levermore, R., & Beacom, A. (2009). Sport and development: Mapping the field. In R. Levermore & A. Beacom (Eds.), *Sport and international development* (pp. 1–25). New York, NY: Palgrave MacMillan.

Levine-Rasky, C. (2012). Whiteness: Normalization and the everyday practice of power. In D. Brock, R. Raby, & M. Thomas (Eds.), *Power and everyday practices* (pp. 86–109). Toronto, ON: Nelson.

Levy, L. (1989). A study of sports crowd behavior: The case of the great pumpkin incident. *Journal of Sport & Social Issues, 13*(2), 69–91.

Lewi, D. (2006, January 31). Canada's first multicultural hockey league. *Toronto Observer.* Retrieved from http://tobserver.thecentre.centennialcollege.ca/read_articles.asp?article_id=681.

Li, P. S. (1990). Race and ethnicity. In P. S. Li (Ed.), *Race and ethnic relations in Canada* (pp. 3–17). Toronto, ON: Oxford University Press.

Liazos, A. (1972). Nuts, sluts, and perverts: The poverty of the sociology of deviance. *Social Problems, 20*, 103–120.

Lindsay, C. (2008). *Are women spending more time on unpaid domestic work than men in Canada?* Statistics Canada Catalogue no. 89-630-X. Ottawa, ON: Statistics Canada.

Lindsay, P. L. (1969). *A history of sport in Canada, 1807–1867.* Unpublished doctoral dissertation, University of Alberta, Edmonton, AB.

Lindsay, P. L. (1970). The impact of military garrisons on the development of sport in British North America. *Canadian Journal of History of Sport and Physical Education, 1*, 33–44.

Lindsay, P. L. (1972). George Beers and the national game concept: A behavioural approach. In *Proceedings of the Second Canadian Symposium on the History of Sport and Physical Education* (pp. 27–44). Edmonton, AB.

Livingston, L. A., Tirone, S. C., Miller, A. J., & Smith, E. L. (2008). Participation in coaching by Canadian immigrants: Individual accommodations and sport system receptivity. *International Journal of Sports Science & Coaching, 3*, 403–415.

Lodewyk, K. R., & Pybus, C. M. (2013). Investigating factors in the retention of students in high school physical education. *Journal of Teaching in Physical Education, 32*, 61–77.

Long, J. G. (2012). *Public/private partnerships for major league sports facilities.* New York, NY: Routledge.

Longley, N. (2000). The underrepresentation of French Canadians on English Canadian NHL teams: Evidence from 1943 to 1998. *Journal of Sports Economics 1*(3): 236–256.

Lorber, J. (1994). *Paradoxes of gender.* New Haven, MA: Yale University Press.

Lorenz, K. (2002). *On aggression.* London, UK: Routledge.

Lorenz, S. (2004, December 28). On-ice violence has been a part of hockey for almost 100 years. *Edmonton Journal*, p. A16.

Lorenz, S. (2007, October 1). Just part of the game. *Ottawa Citizen*, p. A11.

Lorenz, S., & Murray, R. (2013). "Goodbye to the gangstas": The NBA dress code, Ray Emery, and the policing of blackness in basketball and hockey. *Journal of Sport & Social Issues, 38*(1), 23–50.

Lorenz, S. L., & Osborne, G. B. (2006). "Talk about strenuous hockey": Violence, manhood, and the 1907 Ottawa Silver Seven–Montreal Wanderer rivalry. *Journal of Canadian Studies, 40*, 125–156.

Lorenz, S. L., & Osborne, G. B. (2009). Brutal butchery, strenuous spectacle: Hockey violence, manhood, and the 1907 season. In J. C.-K. Wong (Ed.), *Coast to coast: Hockey in Canada to the Second World War* (pp. 160–202). Toronto, ON: University of Toronto Press.

Lowes, M. (1999). *Inside the sports pages.* Toronto, ON: University of Toronto Press.

Loy, W. J., & Booth, D. (2000). Functionalism, sport and society. In J. Coakley & E. Dunning (Eds.), *Handbook of sport studies* (pp. 8–27). London: Sage.

Loy, W. J., & Booth, D. (2002). Émile Durkheim, structural functionalism and the sociology of sport. In J. Maguire & K. Young (Eds.), *Theory, sport & society* (pp. 41–62). Amsterdam: JAI.

Lull, J. (2000). *Media, commerce, culture: A global approach.* New York, NY: Columbia University Press.

Lumpkin, A. (2005). *Physical education, exercise science, and sport studies* (5th ed.). Boston, MA: McGraw-Hill.

Lumpkin, A. (2009). Female representation in feature articles published by *Sports Illustrated* in the 1990s. *Women in Sport and Physical Activity Journal, 18*, 38–51.

Lupton, D. (1999). *Risk.* New York, NY: Routledge.

Macdonald, C. (1976). The Edmonton Grads, Canada's most successful team: A history and analysis of their success. Unpublished master's thesis, University of Windsor, Windsor, ON.

MacGregor, R. (2012). Increasingly high cost of hockey is making the game an elitist sport. *Globe and Mail.* Retrieved from http://www.theglobeandmail.com/sports/hockey/increasingly-high-cost-of-hockey-is-making-the-game-an-elitist-sport/article5864491/.

MacIntosh, D., Bedecki, T., & Franks, C. E. S. (1987). *Sport and politics in Canada: Federal government involvement since 1961.* Montreal, QC: McGill-Queen's University Press.

MacIntosh, D., & Whitson, D. (1990). *The game planners: Transforming Canada's sport system.* Montreal, QC: McGill-Queen's University Press.

Maclean's. (2012, August 14). Field of dreams: Cricket stadium proposed for Toronto. Retrieved from http://www2.macleans.ca/2012/08/14/field-of-dreams-cricket-stadium-proposed-for-toronto/.

Maclean's. (2013, February 11). Sports scholarships are an expensive fix to a non-existent problem. Retrieved from http://www2.macleans.ca/2013/02/11/an-expensive-fix-to-a-non-existent-problem/.

MacLeod, R. (2012, November 16). Alumni got the Dinos' back. *Globe and.* Retrieved from http://www.theglobeandmail.com/sports/football/university-of-calgary-alumni-ensure-dinos-have-top-notch-program/article5400055/.

MacNeill, M. (1996). Networks: Producing Olympic ice hockey for a national television audience. *Sociology of Sport Journal, 13*, 103–124.

Maguire, J. (1999). *Global sport: Identities, societies, civilizations.* Cambridge, UK: Polity Press.

Maguire, J. S. (2002). Michel Foucault: Sport, power, technologies and governmentality. In J. Maguire & K. Young (Eds.), *Theory, sport & society* (pp. 293–314). Amsterdam: JAI.

Maguire, J., Jarvie, G., Mansfield, L., & Bradley, J. (2002). *Sport worlds: A sociological perspective.* Champaign, IL: Human Kinetics.

Majors, R. (1990). Cool pose: Black masculinity and sports. In M. Messner & D. Sabo (Eds.), *Sport, men, and the gender order: Critical feminist perspectives* (pp. 109–114). Champaign, IL: Human Kinetics Press.

Maki, A. (2010, May 28). Doping common in varsity football, Waterloo player says. *Globe and Mail.* from http://www.theglobeandmail.com/sports/football/doping-common-in-varsity-football-waterloo-player-says/article4321076/.

Maki, A. (2012, September 7). Costs limit number of drug tests for football players. *Globe and Mail.* Retrieved from http://www.theglobeandmail.com/sports/football/costs-limit-number-of-drug-tests-for-football-players/article4528394/.

Mandigo, J. L., Corlett, J., & Lathrop, A. H. (2012). Physical education in the twenty-first century: To infinity and beyond? In E. Singleton & A. Varpalotai (Eds.), *Pedagogy in motion: A community of inquiry for human movement studies* (pp. 15–44). London, ON: Althouse Press.

Mandigo, J. L., Thompson, L. P., Spence, J. C., Melnychuk, N., Schwartz, M., Dunn, J. C., & Marshall, D. (2004). A descriptive profile of physical education teachers and related program characteristics in Alberta. *Alberta Journal of Educational Research, 50*, 87–102.

Mangan, J. A. (1983). Grammar schools and the games ethic in the Victorian and Edwardian eras. *Albion: A Quarterly Journal Concerned with British Studies, 15*, 313–335.

Mangan, J. A., & Walvin, J. (1987). Introduction. In J. A. Mangan & J. Walvin (Eds.), *Manliness and morality: Middle class masculinity in Britain and America, 1800–1940* (pp. 1–7). Manchester, UK: Manchester University Press.

Marchie, A., & Cusimano, M. (2003). Bodychecking and concussions in ice hockey: Should our youth pay the price? *Canadian Medical Association Journal, 169*(2), 124–128.

Marks, L. J., & Michael, J. W. (2001). Science, medicine, and the future: Artificial limbs. *British Medical Journal, 323*(7315), 732–735.

Marlow, I. (2010). Canadians' Internet use exceeds TV time. *Globe and Mail.* Retrieved from http://www.theglobeandmail.com/technology/canadians-internet-use-exceeds-tv-time/article4352565/#dashboard/follows.

Martens, F. (1985). Academic achievement of intercollegiate athletes in physical education at the University of Victoria. *Canadian Association for Health, Physical Education and Recreation Journal, 51*, 14–22.

Marx, K. ([1847] 1936). *The poverty of philosophy.* London, UK: Martin Lawrence Limited.

Marx, K. ([1852] 1935). *The eighteenth brumaire of Louis Bonaparte.* New York, NY: International Publishers.

Marx, K. ([1852]) 1934). Marx to Weydemeyer. In *Karl Marx and Friedrich Engels correspondence 1846–1895*, Marx-Engels-Lenin Institute (Ed.), (pp. 55–58). London, UK: Martin Lawrence Ltd.

Marx, K. ([1859] 1911). *A contribution to the critique of political economy.* Chicago, IL: Charles H. Kerr & Company Co-operative.

Marx, K. ([1894] 1909). *Capital: Vol. 3.* Chicago, IL: Charles H. Kerr & Company Co-operative.

Marx, K. (1963). Economic and philosophical manuscripts. In T.B. Bottomore (Ed.), *Karl Marx: Early writings.* New York, NY: McGraw-Hill.

Marx, K. (1972). Thesis on Feuerbach. In R.C. Tucker (Ed.), *The Marx-Engels reader* (pp. 107–9). New York, NY: W.W. Norton & Company.

Marx, K. (1977). *Capital: Vol. I.* New York, NY: Vintage Books.

Marx, K., & Engels, F. ([1845] 1939). *The German ideology.* New York, NY: International Publishers.

Marx, K., & Engels, F. (1948). *The communist manifesto.* New York, NY: International Publishers.

Mason, D. (2006). "Expanding the footprint"? Questioning the NHL's expansion and relocation strategy. In D. Whitson & R.Gruneau (Eds.), *Artificial ice: Hockey, culture, and commerce* (pp. 181–199). Toronto, ON: University of Toronto Press.

McBride, P. (1975). *Culture clash: Immigrants and reformers, 1880–1920.* San Francisco, CA: R & E Associates.

McChesney, R. (2008). *The political economy of media: Enduing issues, emerging dilemmas.* New York, NY: Monthly Review Press.

McCullick, B. A., Lux, K. M., Belcher, D. G., & Davies, N. (2012). A portrait of the PETE major: Re-touched for the early twenty-first century. *Physical Education & Sport Pedagogy, 17,* 177–193.

McDermott, L. (2007). Governmental analysis of children "at risk" in a world of physical activity and obesity epidemics. *Sociology of Sport Journal, 24,* 302–324.

McDonald, J. T., & Kennedy, S. (2004). Insights into the "healthy immigrant effect": Health status and health service use of immigrants to Canada. *Social Science & Medicine, 59*(8), 1613–1627.

McEwen, K., and Young, K. (2011). Ballet and pain: Reflections on a risk-dance culture. *Qualitative Research in Sport, Exercise and Health, 3,* 152–173.

McKinnon, A. (2013, May 14). Vancouver Parks Board wants to make its spaces more trans-friendly. *Xtra.* Retrieved from http://dailyxtra.com/vancouver/news/vancouver-parks-board-wants-make-spaces-trans-friendly.

McPherson, B. (1977). Factors influencing the attainment of elite hockey status. *Post-Olympic Conference Proceedings.* Ottawa, ON: Coaching Association of Canada.

McQuarie, D. (Ed.). (1995). *Readings in contemporary sociological theory: From modernity to post-modernity.* Englewood Cliffs, NJ: Prentice Hall.

McTeer, W., & Curtis, J. (1999). Intercollegiate sport involvement and academic achievement: A follow-up study. *Avante, 5,* 39–55.

Mead, G. H. (1962). *Mind, self, & society from the standpoint of a behaviorist.* Chicago, IL: The University of Chicago Press.

Messner, M. (1990). When bodies are weapons: Masculinity and violence in sport. *International Review for the Sociology of Sport, 25*(3), 203–320.

Messner, M. A. (2002). *Taking the field: Women, men, and sports.* Minneapolis, MN: University of Minnesota Press.

Messner, M. (2012). Reflections on communication and sport: On men and masculinities. *Communication & Sport, 1*(1/2), 113–124.

Messner, M., Dunbar, M., & Hunt, D. (2000). The televised manhood formula. *Journal of Sport and Social Issues, 24*(4), 380–394.

Metcalfe, A. (1970). The form and function of physical activity in New France, 1534–1759. *Canadian Journal of History of Sport and Physical Education, 1,* 45–64.

Metcalfe, A. (1987). *Canada learns to play: The emergence of organized sport, 1807–1914.* Toronto, ON: McClelland & Stewart.

Metzler, M. W. (2011). *Instructional models in physical education* (3rd ed.). Scottsdale, AZ: Holcomb Hathaway.

Meynaud, J. (1966). *Sport et politique.* Paris, FR: Payot.

Miah, A. (2004). *Genetically modified athletes: Biomedical ethics, gene doping and sport.* New York, NY: Routledge.

Miah, A. (2010, February 5). Gene doping: A reality, but not a threat [Weblog post]. *Professor Andy Miah.* Retrieved from http://www.andymiah.net/2010/02/05/is-gene-doping-a-threat-to-sport/.

Miller, P. S., & Kerr, G. (2002). The athletic, academic and social experiences of intercollegiate student-athletes. *Journal of Sport Behavior, 25*(4), 346–367.

Miller, T., Lawrence, G., McKay, J., & Rowe, D. (2001). *Globalization and sport.* Thousand Oaks, CA: Sage.

Millington, B. (2009). Wii has never been modern: Active video games and the "conduct of conduct." *New Media & Society, 11*(4), 621–640.

Millington, B. (2012). Amusing ourselves to life: Fitness consumerism and the birth of biogames. *Journal of Sport and Social Issues.* doi: 10.1177/0193723512458932.

Millington, B. (2013). Aging in the information age: An ethnographic study of video gaming in Canadian retirement centres. Paper presented at the Sport Canada Research Initiative Conference, Ottawa, ON.

Millington, B., & Wilson, B. (2013). Super intentions: Golf course management and the evolution of environmental responsibility. *The Sociological Quarterly, 54*(3), 450–475.

Millington, R., & Darnell, S. C. (2012). Constructing and contesting the Olympics online: The Internet, Rio 2016 and the politics of Brazilian development. *International Review for the Sociology of Sport.* doi: 10.1177/1012690212455374

Mills, C. W. (1959). *The sociological imagination.* London, UK: Oxford.

Mills, C. W. (1961). *The sociological imagination.* New York, NY: Grove Press.

Mirtle, J. (2013, October 2). Hockey doesn't need designated fighters. *Globe and Mail.* Retrieved from http://www.theglobeandmail.com/sports/hockey/mirtle/mirtle-hockey-doesnt-need-designated-fighters/article14654168/.

Morgan, P., & Bourke, S. (2008). Non-specialist teachers' confidence to teach PE: The nature and influence of personal school experiences in PE. *Physical Education and Sport Pedagogy, 13,* 1–29.

Morrow, D. (1979). Lionel Pretoria Conacher. *Journal of Sport History, 6,* 5–37.

Morrow, D. (1981). The powerhouse of Canadian sport: The Montreal Amateur Athletic Association, inception to 1909. *Journal of Sport History, 8,* 20–39.

Morrow, D. (1982). The Canadian image abroad: The great lacrosse tours of 1876 and 1883. In *Proceedings of the Fifth Canadian Symposium on the History of Sport and Physical Education* (pp. 11–23). London, ON.

Morrow, D. (1986). A case study in amateur conflict: The athletic war in Canada, 1906–1908. *British Journal of Sports History, 3,* 183–190.

Morrow, D. (1987). Sweetheart sport: Barbara Ann Scott and the post–World War Two image of the female athlete in Canada. *Canadian Journal of History of Sport and Physical Education, 18,* 36–54.

Morrow, D., & Leyshon, G. (1987). George Goulding: A case study in sporting excellence. *Canadian Journal of History of Sport and Physical Education, 18,* 26–51.

Morrow, D., & Wamsley, K. G. (2005). *Sport in Canada: A history.* Toronto, ON: Oxford University Press.

Morrow, D., & Wamsley, K. G. (2013). *Sport in Canada: A history* (3rd ed.). Toronto, ON: Oxford University Press.

Mosbacher, D., & Yacker, F (Producers/Directors). (2008). *Training Rules* [Documentary film]. United States: WomenVision.

Mosco, V. (2003). The transformation of communication in Canada. In W. Clement & L. Vosko (Eds.), *Changing Canada: Political economy as transformation* (pp. 287–308). Montreal, QC: McGill-Queen's University Press.

Mott, M., & Allardyce, J. (1989). *Curling capital: Winnipeg and the roarin' game, 1876–1988.* Winnipeg, MB: University of Manitoba Press.

Mullick, R. (2002, February). Warren Moon. *CFL Legends.* The Official Site of the Canadian Football League. Retrieved from http://www.cfl.ca/CFLLegends/moon.html.

Munro, J. (1970). *A proposed sports policy for Canadians.* Ottawa: Ministry of Health and Welfare.

Muslim Women in Sports. (2013, March 10). Quebec Soccer Federation finally allowing hijab on pitch. [Weblog post]. *Muslim Women in Sports.* Retrieved from http://muslimwomeninsports.blogspot.ca/2013/03/quebec-soccer-federation-finally.html.

Nack, W., & Yaeger, D. (1999, September 13). Who's coaching your kid? The frightening truth about child molestation in youth sports. *Sports Illustrated,* pp. 39–53.

Naiman, J. (2012). *How societies work: Class, power, and change.* Halifax, NS: Fernwood.

Nanda, S. (2000). *Gender diversity: Crosscultural variations*. Long Grove, IL: Waveland Press.

National Collegiate Athletic Association. (2013). Academics. Retrieved from http://www.ncaa.org/wps/wcm/connect/public/ncaa/academics/index.html.

Neverson, N. (2010). Build it and the women will come? WTSN and the advent of Canadian digital television. *Canadian Journal of Communication*, 35, 27–48.

Newman, Z. (2012). Bodies, genders, sexualities: Counting past two. In D. Brock, R. Raby, & M. Thomas (Eds.), *Power and everyday practices* (pp. 61–85). Toronto, ON: Nelson.

Nixon, H. L., & Frey, J. H. (1996). *A sociology of sport*. Belmont, CA: Wadsworth.

Nolan, M. (2001). *CTV: The network that means business*. Edmonton, AB: University of Alberta Press.

Norman, M. (2012). Saturday night's alright for tweeting: Cultural citizenship, collective discussion, and the new media consumption/production of Hockey Day in Canada. *Sociology of Sport Journal*, 29(3), 306–324.

North American Indigenous Games. (2013). Retrieved from http://www.naigcouncil.com/index.php.

O'Bonsawin, C. (2010). 'No Olympics on stolen native land': Contesting Olympic narratives and asserting indigenous rights within the discourse of the 2010 Vancouver Games. *Sport in Society*, 13, 143–156.

O'Bonsawin, C. (2013). Indigenous peoples and Canadian-hosted Olympic Games. In J. Forsyth & A. Giles (Eds.), *Aboriginal peoples and sport in Canada: Historical foundations and contemporary issues* (pp. 35–63). Vancouver, BC: UBC Press.

of the Canadian Sport Policy: Final report. Retrieved from http://www.sirc.ca/CSPRenewal/documents/CSP_Evaluation_Final_ReportEN.pdf.

Olshansky, J. S., Passaro, D. J., Ronald, C., Hershow, R., Layden, J., Carnes, B., Brody, J., Hayflick, L., Butler, R., Allison, D., & Ludwig, D. (2005). A potential decline in life expectancy in the United States in the 21st century. *New England Journal of Medicine*, 352(11), 1138–1145.

Ontario University Athletics. (2013). Sports. Retrieved from http://www.oua.ca.

Oriard, M. (1993). *Reading football: How the popular press created an American spectacle*. Chapel Hill, NC: University of North Carolina Press.

Pal, L. (2006). *Beyond policy analysis: Public issue management in turbulent times*. Toronto, ON: Nelson.

Palmer, C. (2004). Death, danger and the selling of risk in adventure sports. In B. Wheaton (Ed.), *Understanding lifestyle sports: Consumption, identity and difference* (pp. 55–69). New York, NY: Routledge.

Pappas, N. T., McKenry, P. C., & Skilken Catlett, B. (2004). Athlete aggression on the rink and off the ice: Athlete violence and aggression in hockey and interpersonal relationships. *Men and Masculinities* 6, 291–312.

Paraschak, V. (1989). Native sport history: Pitfalls and promise. *Canadian Journal of History of Sport*, 20(1), 57–68.

Paraschak, V. (1995). The Native Sport and Recreation Program, 1972–1981: Patterns of resistance, patterns of reproduction. *Canadian Journal of History of Sport*, 26(2), 1–18.

Paraschak, V. (1997). Variations in race relations: Sporting events for Native peoples in Canada. *Sociology of Sport Journal*, 14(1), 1–21.

Paraschak, V., & Thompson, K. (2013). Finding strength(s): Insights on Aboriginal physical cultural practices in Canada. *Sport in Society: Cultures, Commerce, Media, Politics*, 17(8), 1046–1060.

Parcels, J. (2002). Chances of making it in pro hockey. Retrieved from http://www.cumberlandminorhockey.ca/to_the_nhl/chances.htm.

Parcels, J. (2011). Straight facts about making it in pro hockey. In P. Donnelly (Ed.), *Taking sport seriously: Social issues in Canadian sport* (pp. 207–211). Toronto, ON: Thompson Educational Publishing.

Park, J. (2005). Doped bodies: The World Anti-Doping Agency and the global culture of surveillance. *Cultural Studies <=> Critical Methodologies*, 5, 174–188.

Parsons, T. (1961). An outline of the social system. In T. Parsons, E. Shils, K.D. Naegele, & J.R. Pitts (Eds.), *Theories of society: Foundations of modern sociological theory: Vol. I* (pp. 30–79). New York, NY: The Free Press of Glencoe.

Pascoe, C. J. (2003). Multiple masculinities? Teenage boys talk about jocks and gender. *American Behavioral Scientist*, 46(10), 1423–1438.

Peers, D. (2009). (Dis)empowering Paralympic histories: Absent athletes and disabling discourses. *Disability & Society*, 24, 653–665.

Peers, D. (2012). Interrogating disability: The (de)composition of a recovering Paralympian. *Qualitative Research in Sport and Exercise*, 4, 175–188.

Peritz, I. (2013, June 14) FIFA authorizes wearing of turbans at all levels of Canadian soccer. *Globe and Mail*. Accessed from http://www.theglobeandmail.com/sports/soccer/fifa-authorizes-wearing-of-turbans-at-all-levels-of-canadian-soccer/article12550476/.

Perrottet, T. (2004). *The naked Olympics: The true story of the ancient games*. New York, NY: Random House.

Petz, S. (2011, September 21). Should universities punish students for off-campus behaviour? *Maclean's*. Retrieved from http://www.macleans.ca/education/uniandcollege/should-universities-punish-students-for-off-campus-behaviour/.

Philips, M. G., & Roper, A. P. (2006). History of physical education. In D. Kirk, D. Macdonald, & M. O'Sullivan (Eds.), *Handbook of physical education* (pp. 123–140). London, UK: Sage.

Physical and Health and Education Canada. (2014). QDPE—The facts. Retrieved from http://www.phecanada.ca/programs/quality-daily-physical-education/facts.

Pitter, R. (2006). Racialization and hockey in Canada: From personal troubles to a Canadian challenge. In D. Whitson & R. Gruneau (Eds.), *Artificial Ice: Hockey, culture, and commerce* (pp. 123–139). Toronto, ON: University of Toronto Press.

Portman, P. A. (1995). Who is having fun in physical education classes? Experiences of sixth-grade students in elementary and middle schools. *Journal of Teaching in Physical Education*, 14, 445–453.

Pray, L. (2008) Sports, gene doping, and WADA. *Nature Education*, 1(1), 77.

Prettyman, S. S. (2006). If you beat him, you own him, he's your bitch: Coaches, language, and power. In S. S. Prettyman & B. Lampman (Eds.), *Learning culture through sports: Exploring the role of sports in society* (pp. 75–88). Lanham, MD: Rowman and Littlefield.

Proteau, A. (2011). *Fighting the good fight: Why on-ice violence is killing hockey*. Toronto, ON: John Wiley & Sons Canada.

Public Broadcasting Service. (2004). *The real Olympics: A history of the ancient and modern Olympics Games*. Alexandria, VA: PBS Home Video.

Pugliese, J., & Tinsley, B. Parental socialization of child and adolescent physical activity: A meta-analysis. *Journal of Family Psychology*, 21(3), 331–343. doi: 10.1037/0893-3200.21.3.331.

Purcell, L. K., Canadian Paediatric Society, & Healthy Active Living and Sports Medicine Committee. (2012). Evaluation and management of children and adolescents with sport-related concussion. *Paediatrics & Child Health*, 17(1), 31.

Raboy, M. (1990). *Missed opportunities: The story of Canada's broadcasting policy*. Montreal, QC: McGill-Queen's University Press.

Raedeke, T. D. (1997). Is athlete burnout more than just stress? A sport commitment perspective. *Journal of Sport and Exercise Psychology*, 19, 396–417.

Reitz, J., Zhang, H., & Hawkins, N. (2011). Comparisons of the success of racial minority immigrant offspring successes in the United States, Canada and Australia. *Social Science Research*, 40, 1051–1066.

Renold, E. (2001). Learning the 'hard' way: Boys, hegemonic masculinity and the negotiation of learner identities in the primary school. *British Journal of Sociology of Education*, 22(3), 369–385.

Riemer, B. A., & Visio, M. E. (2003). Gender typing of sports: An investigation of Metheny's classification. *Research Quarterly for Exercise and Sport*, 74(2), 193–204.

Ritchie, J. B., & Smith, B. H. (1991). The impact of a mega-event on host region awareness: A longitudinal study. *Journal of Travel Research*, 30(1), 3–10.

Robertson, R. (1992). *Globalization: Social theory and global culture*. New York, NY: Russell Sage.

Robidoux, M. A. (2001). *Men at play: A working understanding of professional hockey*. Montreal, QC: McGill-Queen's University Press.

Robidoux, M. A. (2012) *Stickhandling through the margins: First Nations hockey in Canada*. Toronto, ON; University of Toronto Press.

Robins, K. (1991). Tradition and translation: National cultures in a global context. In J. Corner & S. Harvey (Eds.), *Enterprise and heritage: Cross-currents of national culture*. London, UK: Routledge.

Robinson, L. (1998). *Crossing the line: Violence and sexual assault in Canada's national sport*. Toronto, ON: McClelland & Stewart.

Robinson, L. (2002). *Black tights: Women, sport and sexuality*. Toronto, ON: Harper Collins.

Rosenberg, D. (2003). Athletics in the Ward and beyond: Neighborhoods, Jews, and sport in Toronto, 1900–1939. In R. C. Wilcox, D. L. Andrews, R. Pitter, & R. L. Irwin, (Eds.), *Sporting dystopias: The making and meanings of urban sport cultures* (pp. 137–152). Albany, NY: State University of New York Press.

Rosenstein, J. (Producer). (1997). *In whose honor? America Indian mascots in sports*. New Jersey: New Day Films.

Rotundo, E. A. (1993). *American manhood: Transformations in masculinity from the Revolution to the modern era*. New York, NY: Basic Books.

Rowe, D. (2004a). Watching brief: Cultural citizenship and viewing rights. *Sport in Society*, 7(3), 385–402.

Rowe, D. (2004b). *Sport, culture and the media* (2nd ed.). Maidenhead, UK: Open University Press.

Rowe, D. (2007). Sports journalism: Still the "toy department" of the news media? *Journalism*, 8(4), 385–405.

Rowe, D. (2012). The bid, the lead-up, the event and the legacy: Global cultural politics and hosting the Olympics. *British Journal of Sociology*, 63, 285–305.

Royal Bank of Canada. (2011). RBC survey: 82 per cent of Canadian hockey households believe more support needed from corporate Canada. Press release. Retrieved from http://www.rbc.com/newsroom/2011/1206-grant-hockey.html.

Rushall, B., & Jones, M. (2007). Drugs in sport: A cure worse than the disease? *International Journal of Sports Science & Coaching*, 2, 335–361.

Rutherford, K. (2009). Is the cost keeping kids out of minor hockey? Absolutely, players and parents say. *CBC Sports*. Retrieved from http://www.cbc.ca/sports/hockey/ourgame/story/2009/01/16/hockey-costs-too-much.html.

Rutherford, P. (1990). *When television was young: Primetime Canada (1952–1967)*. Toronto, ON: University of Toronto Press.

Safai, P. (2013). Sports medicine, health, and the politics of risk. In D. Andrews and B. Carrington (Eds.), *A companion to sport* (pp. 112–128). Oxford, UK: Blackwell.

Sage, G. (1997). Physical education, sociology, and sociology of sport: Points of intersection. *Sociology of Sport Journal*, 14, 317–339.

Sage, G. (1999). Justice do it! The Nike transnational advocacy network: Organization, collective action and outcomes. *Sociology of Sport Journal*, 16(3), 206–235.

Sage, G. (2004). The sporting goods industry: From struggling entrepreneurs to national business to transnational corporations. In T. Slack (Ed.), *The commercialisation of sport* (pp. 29–51). London, UK: Routledge.

Sage, G. (2011). *Globalizing sport: How organizations, corporations, media, and politics are changing sports*. Boulder, CO: Paradigm Publishers.

Sage, G. & Eitzen, D. S. (2013). *Sociology of North American sport*. Madison, WI: Brown and Benchmark.

Sager, N. (2010). Canadian commentators fail to cool it with Johnny Weir jokes. *Yahoo! Sports*. Retrieved from http://sports.yahoo.com/blogs/olympics-neate-sager/canadian-commentators-fail-cool-johnny-weir-jokes--olympics.html.

Saraceno, J. (2012). Swiss soccer player banned from Olympics for racist tweet. *USA Today*. Retrieved from http://usatoday30.usatoday.com/sports/olympics/london/soccer/story/2012-07-30/swiss-athlete-banned-michel-morganella-olympics/56591966/1.

Saturday Night. (1905, April 1), p. 1.

Saunders, D. (2010). *Arrival city: The final migration and out next world*. Toronto, ON: Alfred A Knopf.

Scanlan, L. (2002). *Grace under fire: The state of our sweet and savage game*. Toronto, ON: Penguin Canada.

Scherer, J. (2007). Globalization, promotional culture and the production/consumption of on-line games: Engaging Adidas's Beat Rugby campaign. *New Media & Society*, 9(3), 475–496.

Scherer, J., & Cantelon, H. (2013). 1974 WHA All Stars vs. the Soviet national team: Franchise recognition and foreign diplomacy in the "forgotten series." *Journal of Canadian Studies*, 47(2), 29–59.

Scherer, J., & Davidson, J. (2011). Promoting the "arriviste" city: Producing neo-liberal urban identity and communities of consumption during the Edmonton Oilers' 2006 playoff campaign. *International Review for the Sociology of Sport*, 46(2), 157–180.

Scherer, J., Duquette, G., & Mason, D. (2007). The Cold War and the (re)articulation of Canadian national identity: The 1972 Canada–USSR Summit Series. In D. L. Andrews & S. Wagg (Eds.), *East plays west: Essays on sport and the Cold War* (pp. 171–194). London, UK: Routledge.

Scherer, J., & Harvey, J. (2013). Televised sport and cultural citizenship in Canada: The "two solitudes" of Canadian public broadcasting? In J. Scherer & D. Rowe (Eds.), *Sport, public broadcasting, and cultural citizenship: Signal lost?* (pp. 48–73). New York, NY: Routledge.

Scherer, J., & Jackson, S. (2004). From corporate welfare to national interest: Newspaper analysis of the public subsidization of NHL hockey debate in Canada. *Sociology of Sport Journal*, 21, 36–60.

Scherer, J., & Jackson, S. (2008). Producing allblacks.com: Cultural intermediaries and the policing of electronic spaces of sporting consumption. *Sociology of Sport Journal*, 25, 243–262.

Scherer, J., & Jackson, S. J. (2010). *Globalization, sport and corporate nationalism: The new cultural economy of the New Zealand All Blacks*. Oxford, UK: Peter Lang.

Scherer, J., & Jackson, S. (2013). *The contested terrain of the New Zealand All Blacks: Rugby, commerce, and cultural politics in the age of globalization*. London, UK: Peter Lang.

Scherer, J., & Koch, J. (2010). Living with war: Sport, citizenship, and the cultural politics of post-9/11 Canadian identity. *Sociology of Sport Journal*, 27(1), 1–29.

Scherer, J., & Rowe, D. (Eds.). (2013). *Sport, public broadcasting, and cultural citizenship: Signal lost?* New York, NY: Routledge.

Scherer, J., & Sam, M. (2010). Policing the cyber agenda: New media technologies and recycled claims in a local stadium debate. *Sport in Society*, 13(10), 1469–1485.

Scott, R. (1987). *Jackie Robinson: Baseball great*. New York, NY: Chelsea House Publishers.

Sheppard, R. J., & Trudeau, F. (2008). Research on the outcomes of elementary school physical education. *The Elementary School Journal*, 108, 251–264.

Shields, D. L., Bredemeier, B. L., LaVoi, N. M., & Power, C. F. (2005). The sport behavior of youth, parents and coaches: The good, the bad, and the ugly. *Journal of Research on Character Education*, 3(1), 43–59.

Shields, D. L., LaVoi, N. M., Bredemeier, B. L., & Power, C. F. (2007). Predictors of poor sportspersonship in youth sports: An examination of personal attitudes and social influences. *Journal of Sport and Exercise Psychology*, 29(6), 747–762.

Short, J. R. & Kim, Y. H. (1999). *Globalization and the city*. New York, NY: Longman.

Siedentop, D. (2004). *Introduction to physical education, fitness and sport* (5th ed.). Boston, MA: McGraw-Hill.

Siedentop, D., Hastie, P. A., & Van der Mars, H. (2004). *Complete guide to sport education*. Champaign, IL: Human Kinetics.

Skinner, D. (2008). Television in Canada: Continuity or change? In D. Ward (Ed.), *Television public policy: Change and continuity in an era of global liberalization* (pp. 3–26). New York, NY: Lawrence Erlbaum Associates.

Smelser, N. J. (1962). *Theory of collective behavior*. New York, NY: The Free Press.

Smith, A. L. (2003). Peer relationships in physical activity contexts: A road less traveled in youth sport and exercise psychology research. *Psychology of Sport and Exercise*, 4(1). 25–39.

Statistics Canada. (2004). Canadian Community Health Survey. Special Surveys Division. *Statistics Canada*.

Smith, M. D. (1983). *Violence and sport*. Toronto, ON: Butterworths.

Smith, M. (2006). Revisiting South Africa and the Olympic movement: The correspondence of Reginald S. Alexander and the International Olympic Committee, 1961–86. *International Journal of the History of Sport*, 23, 1193–1216.

Smythe, D. W. (1977). Communications: Blindspot of Western Marxism. *Canadian Journal of Political and Social Theory*, 1(3), 1–27.

Sparks, R. (1992). Delivering the male: Sports, Canadian television, and the making of TSN. *Canadian Journal of Communication*, 17, 319–342.

Spector, M. (2013, October 16). The future of fighting in hockey is here, it's in the CIS. *Sportsnet*. Retrieved from http://www.sportsnet.ca/cis/the-future-of-fighting-in-hockey-is-here-its-in-the-cis/.

Spence, C. (1999). *The skin I'm in: Racism, sports and education*. Halifax, NS: Fernwood.

Sport Canada. (1986). *Women in sport: A Sport Canada policy*. Ottawa, ON: Author.

Staggenborg, S. (2008). *Social movements*. Toronto, ON: Oxford University Press.

Statistics Canada. (2003). 2001 Census, Analysis series: Canada's ethnocultural portrait: The changing mosaic. Retrieved from http://www12.statcan.ca/english/census01/products/analytic/companion/etoimm/canada.cfm.

Statistics Canada. (2005, July 6). Canadian Community Health Survey: Obesity among children and adults. *The Daily*. Retrieved from http://www.statcan.gc.ca/daily-quotidien/050706/dq050706a-eng.htm.

Statistics Canada. (2009). Earnings and incomes of Canadians over the past quarter century, 2006 Census highlights. Retrieved from http://www12.statcan.gc.ca/census-recensement.

Statistics Canada. (2009). *The Canadian labour market at a glance*. Retrieved from http://www.statcan.gc.ca/pub/71-222-x/71-222-x2008001-eng.pdf.

Statistics Canada. (2011). Analytical document: Immigration and ethnocultural diversity in Canada. National Household Survey, 2011. Retrieved from http://www12.statcan.gc.ca/nhs-enm/2011/as-sa/99-010-x/99-010-x2011001-eng.cfm.

Statistics Canada. (2013a). Labour force survey estimates. Retrieved from http://www5.statcan.gc.ca/cansim/pick-choisir?lang=eng&p2=33&id=2820080.

Statistics Canada. (2013b). Time spent on various activities. Retrieved from http://www.statcan.gc.ca/tables-tableaux/sum-som/l01/cst01/famil36a-eng.htm.

Statistics Canada. (2013c). 2011 National Household Survey: Immigration, place of birth, citizenship, ethnic origin, visible minorities, language and religion. *The Daily*, May 8, 2013.

Stebbins, R. (1996). *Tolerable differences: Living with deviance* (2nd ed.). Toronto, ON: McGraw-Hill.

Steffenhagen, J. (2013, May 21). B.C.'s young athletes need protection from abusive coaches. *Vancouver Sun*. Retrieved from http://blogs.vancouversun.com/2013/05/21/b-c-s-young-athletes-need-protection-from-abusive-coaches-opinion/.

Stoddart, M. (2012). *Making meaning out of mountains*. Vancouver, BC: UBC Press.

Stodolska, M., & Jackson, E. L. (1998). Discrimination in leisure and work experienced by a white ethnic minority group. *Journal of Leisure Research*, 30(1), 23–46.

Stolle-McAllister, J. (2004). Contingent hybridity: The cultural politics of Tepoztlán's anti-golf movement. *Identities: Global Studies in Culture and Power*, 11, 195–213.

Stursberg, R. (2012). *The tour of babble: Sins, secrets and successes inside the CBC*. Vancouver, BC: Douglas & McIntyre.

Sugden, J. (2010). Critical left-realism and sport interventions in divided societies. *International Review for the Sociology of Sport*, 45, 258–272.

Sutcliffe Group. (2010). *Interprovincial sport and recreation council: Evaluation*.

Sutherland, E. (1945). Is "white collar crime" crime? *American Sociological Review*, 10, 132–139.

Suzuki, D. (2012, September 27). Get your kids away from the screen and into the green. David Suzuki Foundation. Retrieved from http://www.davidsuzuki.org/blogs/science-matters/2012/09/get-your-kids-away-from-the-screen-and-into-the-green/.

Sykes, G., & Matza, D. (1957). Techniques of neutralization: A theory of delinquency. *American Sociological Review*, 22, 664–670.

Sykes, H., & McPhail, D. (2008). Unbearable lessons: Contesting fat phobia in physical education. *Sociology of Sport Journal*, 25, 66–96.

Taylor, C., & Tracey, P., with McMinn, T. L., Elliott, T., Beldom, S., Ferry, A., Gross, Z., Paquin, S., & Schachter, K. (2011). *Every class, in every school: The final report on the first national climate survey on homophobia, biphobia, and transphobia in Canadian schools*. Toronto, ON: EGALE Canada Human Rights Trust.

Team Canada Lacrosse. (2013). 2010 roster. Retrieved from http://www.teamcanadalacrosse.com/team2010.aspx.

Teetzel, S. (2009). Sharing the blame: Complicity, conspiracy, and collective responsibility in sport. *Acta Universitatis Palackianae Olomucensis. Gymnica*, 36, 85–93.

Theberge, N. (1987). Sport and women's empowerment. *Women's Studies International Forum*, 10(4), 387–393.

Thompson, E. P. (1963). *The making of the English working class*. London, UK: V. Gollancz.

Thompson, S. T. (2002). Sport, gender, feminism. In J. Maguire & K. Young (Eds.), *Theory, sport & society* (pp. 105–127). Amsterdam: JAI.

Thorpe, H., & Ahmad, N. (2013). Youth, action sports and political agency in the Middle East: Lessons from a grassroots parkour group in Gaza. *International Review for the Sociology of Sport*. doi: 10.1177/1012690213490521.

Tinning, R. (2010). *Pedagogy and human movement*. London, UK: Routledge.

Tirone, S. (2000). Racism, indifference and the leisure experiences of South Asian Canadian teens. *Leisure: The Journal of the Canadian Association of Leisure Studies*, 24(1), 89–114.

Tirone, S. (2005). The challenges and opportunities faced by migrants and minorities in their leisure: An international perspective. Paper presented at the 10th International Metropolis Conference, Toronto, ON.

Tirone, S. (2010). Multiculturalism and leisure policy: Enhancing the delivery of leisure services and supports for immigrants and minority Canadians. In S. Arai, D. Reid, & H. Mair (Eds.), *Decentring work: Critical perspectives on leisure, development and social change* (pp. 149–174). Calgary, AB: University of Calgary Press.

Tirone, S., & Pedlar, A. (2000). Understanding the leisure experience of a minority ethnic group: South Asian teens and young adults in Canada. *Society and Leisure*, 23(1), 145–169.

Tirone, S., Livingston, L. A., Miller, A. J., & Smith, E. L. (2010). Including immigrants in elite and recreational sports: The experiences of athletes, sport providers and immigrants. *Leisure*, 34(4), 403–420.

Tischler, A., & McCaughtry, N. (2011). PE is not for me: When boys' masculinities are threatened. *Research Quarterly for Exercise and Sport*, 82, 37–48.

TMZ Sports. (2014, April 29). Donald Sterling banned for life. Retrieved from http://www.tmz.com/2014/04/29/nba-commish-adam-silver-deciding-donald-sterling-fate-livestream-l-a-clippers/.

Total Sports Management. (2013). So, you want to play pro hockey! Retrieved from http://www.totalsportsmgmt.com/pro-hockey.

Travers, A., & Deri, J. (2010). Transgender inclusion and the changing face of lesbian softball leagues. *International Review for the Sociology of Sport*, 48(6), 1–20.

Trembanis, S. (2008). Research note: Defining "Aboriginal" in a historical and sporting context. *Journal of Sport History*, 35(2), 279–283.

Turcotte, M. (2011). Women and education: A gender-based statistical report. Statistics Canada No 89-503-x. Retrieved from http://www.statcan.gc.ca/pub/89-503-x/2010001/article/11542-eng.pdf.

UNESCO. (1978). *The international charter of physical education and sport*. Records of the General Conference, 20th Session. Volume I: Resolutions. Paris, October 24–November 28. Retrieved from http://unesdoc.unesco.org/images/ 0011/001140/114032e.pdf.

United Way of Greater Toronto. (2004). *Poverty by postal code: The geography of neighbourhood poverty 1981–2001*. Prepared jointly by the United Way and Canadian Council on Social Development.

University of Regina Cougars. (2012). Football: About us, club history. Retrieved from http://reginacougars.com/sports/2012/2/7/FB_0207124739.aspx?path=football.

Vancouver 2010. (2006). *Own the Podium—2010*. Retrieved from http://www.vancouver2010.com/en/WinterGames/OwnPodium.

Vertinsky, P. A. (1992). Reclaiming space, revisioning the body: The quest for gender-sensitive physical education. *Quest*, 44(3), 373–396.

Vincent, J., & Crossman, J. (2012). "Patriots at play": Analysis of newspaper coverage of the gold medal contenders in men's and women's ice hockey at the 2010 Winter Olympic Games. *International Journal of Sport Communication*, 5, 87–108.

Von Mises, L. (1934). *The theory of money and credit*. London, UK: J. Cape.

Waddington, I. (2010). Surveillance and control in sport: A sociologist looks at the WADA whereabouts system. *International Journal of Sport Policy*, 2, 255–274.

Walvin, J. (1987). Symbols of moral superiority: Slavery, sport and the changing world order, 1800–1950. In J. A. Mangan & J. Walvin (Eds.), *Manliness and morality: Middle class masculinity in Britain and America, 1800–1940* (pp. 242–260). Manchester, UK: Manchester University Press.

Wamsley, K. B. (2003). Violence and aggression in sport. In J. Crossman (Ed.), *Canadian sport sociology* (pp. 90–101). Toronto, ON: Nelson.

Wamsley, K. B. (2008). Sport and social problems. In J. Crossman (Ed.), *Canadian sport sociology* (2nd ed.) (pp. 139–157). Toronto, ON: Nelson.

Wamsley K., & Pfister, G. (2005). Olympic men and women: The politics of gender in the modern Games. In K. Young & K. Wamsley (Eds.), *Global Olympics* (pp. 103–125). New York, NY: Elsevier.

Wamsley, K. B., & Whitson, D. (1998). Celebrating violent masculinities: The boxing death of Luther McCarty. *Journal of Sport History*, 25, 419–431.

Washburne, R. F. (1978). Black underparticipation in wildland recreation: Alternative explanations. *Leisure Sciences*, 1, 175–189.

Washington, R., & Karen, D. (2001). Sport and society. *Annual Review of Sociology*, 27, 187–212.

Weber, M. (1958). *The protestant ethic and the spirit of capitalism*. New York, NY: Charles Scribner's Sons.

Weber, M. (1968). *Economy and society*. New York, NY: Bedminster Press.

Weider, B. (1976). *The strongest man in history: Louis Cyr*. Toronto, ON: Mitchell Press.

Weiler, P. (2000). *Leveling the playing field: How the law can make sports better for fans*. Cambridge MA: Harvard University Press.

Weir, T. (2012, January 9). Hockey fan fined $200 for throwing banana at black player. *USA Today*. Retrieved from http://content.usatoday.com/communities/gameon/post/2012/01/hockey-fan-fined-200-for-throwing-banana-at-black-player/1#.UpaN6OKMmHs.

Weiss, M. R., & Fretwell, S. D. (2004). The parent-coach/child-athlete relationship in youth sport: Cordial, contentious, or conundrum? *Research Quarterly for Exercise and Sport*, 76(3), 286–305. doi: 10.1080/02701367.2005.10599300.

Wertheim, L. J. (2007, May 28). The new main event. *Sports Illustrated*, 106(22), 52–60.

West, C., & Zimmerman, D. (1987). Doing gender. *Gender & Society*, 1, 125–151.

West, C., & Zimmerman, D. (1991). Doing gender. In J. Lorber & S. Farrell (Eds), *The social construction of gender* (pp. 13–37). London, UK: Sage Publications.

Whannel, G. (1992). *Fields in vision: Television sport and cultural transformation*. London, UK: Routledge.

Whannel, G. (2005). The five rings and the small screen: Television, sponsorship, and new media in the Olympic movement. In K. Young & K. Wamsley (Eds.), *Global Olympics: Historical and sociological studies of the modern Games* (pp. 161–178). Amsterdam, Netherlands: Elsevier.

Wheaton, B. (Ed.). (2004). *Understanding lifestyle sports: Consumption, identity and difference*. London, UK: Routledge.

Wheaton, B. (2008). From the pavement to the beach: Politics and identity in "Surfers Against Sewage." In M. Atkinson & K. Young (Eds.), *Tribal play: Subcultural journeys through sport* (pp. 113–134). Bingley, UK: Emerald Group Publishing.

White, P., & Curtis, J. (1990). Participation in competitive sport among Anglophones and Francophones in Canada: Testing competing hypotheses. *International Review for the Sociology of Sport*, 25, 125–143.

White, P., & McTeer, W. (2012) Socioeconomic status and sport participation at different developmental stages during childhood and youth: Multivariate analyses using Canadian national survey data. *Sociology of Sport Journal*, 29(2), 186–209.

White, P., & Young, K. (2007). Gender, sport and the injury process. In K. Young & P. White (Eds.), *Sport and gender in Canada* (pp. 259–278). Toronto, ON: Oxford University Press.

Whitehead, M. (2001). The concept of physical literacy. *Physical Education and Sport Pedagogy*, 6, 127–138.

Whitson, D. (1998). Circuits of promotion: Media, marketing and the globalization of sport. In L. Wenner (Ed.), *MediaSport* (pp. 57–22). New York, NY: Routledge.

Whitson, D. (2001). Hockey and Canadian identities: From frozen rivers to revenue streams. In D. Taras & B. Rasporich (Eds.), *A passion for identity: Canadian studies for the 21st century* (pp. 217–236). Toronto, ON: Nelson.

Whitson, D. (2011). Changing notions of public goods: Paying for public recreation. Paper presented at the 2011 National Recreation Summit, October 23–26, Lake Louise, AB. Retrieved from http://lin.ca/sites/default/files/attachments/Whitson_Dave%5B1%5D.pdf.

Whitson, D. (2012). Vancouver 2010: The saga of Eagleridge Bluffs. In G. Hayes & J. Karamichas (Eds.), *Olympic Games, mega-events and civil societies: Globalization, environment, resistance* (pp. 219–235). New York, NY: Palgrave Macmillian.

Whyno, S. (2013, November 11). NHL commissioner Gary Bettman says debate over fighting getting too much attention. *National Post*. Retrieved from http://sports.nationalpost.com/2013/11/11/nhl-commissioner-gary-bettman-says-debate-over-fighting-getting-too-much-attention/?utm_source=dlvr.it&utm_medium=twitter.

Wickberg, E. B. (1988). Chinese. In *The Canadian Encyclopedia* (2nd ed., Vol. I, pp. 415–417). Edmonton, AB: Hurtig Publishers.

Wiersma, L. D., & Fifer, A. M. (2005). It's their turn to speak: The joys, challenges and recommendations of youth sport parents. Paper presented at the meeting for the Advancement of Applied Sport Psychology, Vancouver, BC.

Williams, J. (1994). The local and the global in English soccer and the rise of satellite television. *Sociology of Sport Journal, 11*, 376–397.

Wilson, B. (1999). 'Cool pose' incorporated: The marketing of black masculinity in Canadian NBA coverage. In P. White & K. Young (Eds.), *Sport and gender in Canada* (pp. 232–253). Toronto, ON: Oxford University Press.

Wilson, B. (2006). Selective memory in a global culture: Reconsidering links between youth, hockey, and Canadian identity. In D. Whitson & R. Gruneau (Eds.), *Artificial ice: Hockey, culture, and commerce* (pp. 53–70). Toronto, ON: University of Toronto Press.

Wilson, B. (2006a). *Fight, flight, or chill: Subcultures, youth, and rave into the 21st century.* Montreal, QC: McGill-Queen's University Press.

Wilson, B. (2007). New media, social movements, and global sport studies: A revolutionary moment and the sociology of sport. *Sociology of Sport Journal, 24*(4), 457–477.

Wilson, B. (2012a). *Sport & peace: A sociological perspective.* Toronto, ON: Oxford University Press.

Wilson, B. (2012b). Growth and nature: Reflections on sport, carbon neutrality, and ecological modernization. In D. Andrews & M. Silk (Eds.), *Sport and neo-liberalism: Politics, consumption, and culture* (pp. 90–108). Philadelphia, PA: Temple University Press.

Wilson, B., & Hayhurst, L. (2009). Digital activism: Neo-liberalism, the internet, and "sport for development." *Sociology of Sport Journal, 26*(1), 155–181.

Wilson, B., & Millington, B. (2013). Sport, ecological modernization, and the environment. In D. Andrews & B. Carrington (Eds.), *A companion to sport* (pp. 129–142). Malden, MA: Blackwell Publishing.

Wilson, B., & Sparks, R. (1999). Impacts of black athlete media portrayals on Canadian youth. *Canadian Journal of Communication, 24*(4), 589–627.

Wilson, B., & Sparks, R. (2001). Michael Jordan, sneaker commercials, and Canadian youth cultures. In D. Andrews (Ed.), *Michael Jordan Inc.: Corporate sport, media culture, and late modern America* (pp. 217–255). Albany, NY: SUNY Press.

Wilson, T. (2002). The paradox of social class and sports involvement. *International Review for the Sociology of Sport, 37*, 5–16.

Windsor Star. (2014, May 23). Senate wants Redskins renamed, p. B5.

Winseck, D. (1995). Power shift? Towards a political economy of Canadian telecommunications and regulation. *Canadian Journal of Communication, 20*(1), 81–106.

Winter, J. (2006). *Dreams of peace and freedom: Utopian moments in the 20th century.* New Haven, CT: Yale University Press.

Women's Ski Jumping USA. (n.d.), Our Olympic story. Retrieved from http://www.wsjusa.com/olympic-inclusion/.

Woolcock, M. (1998). Social capital and economic development: Toward a theoretical synthesis and policy framework. *Theory and Society, 27*, 151–208.

Wuest, D. A., & Bucher, C. A. (2003). *Foundations of physical education and sport* (42nd ed.) St. Louis, MI: McGraw-Hill.

Yalnizyan, A. (2010). *The rise of Canada's richest 1%.* Ottawa, ON: Canadian Centre for Policy Alternatives. Retrieved from http://www.policyalternatives.ca/publications/reports/rise-canadas-richest-1.

Young, A. J. (1988). *Beyond heroes: A sport history of Nova Scotia: Vol. 2.* Hantsport, NS: Lancelot Press.

Young, K. (1993). Violence, risk, and liability in male sports culture. *Sociology of Sport Journal, 10*, 373–396.

Young, K. (2000). Sport and violence. In J. Coakley & E. Dunning (Eds.), *Handbook of sports studies* (pp. 382–407). London, UK: Sage.

Young, K. (2002). From "sports violence" to "sports crime": Aspects of violence, law, and gender in the sports process. In M. Gatz, M. A. Messner, & S. J. Ball-Rokeach (Eds.), *Paradoxes of youth and sport* (pp. 207–224). New York, NY: State University of New York Press.

Young, K., & White, P. (1995). Sport, physical danger, and injury: The experiences of elite women athletes. *Journal of Sport & Social Issues, 19*(1), 45–61.

Zirin, D. (2005). *What's my name, fool? Sport and resistance in the United States.* Chicago, IL: Haymarket Books.

Zirin, D. (2013, August 30). The NFL concussion deal: Rotten from all sides. *The Nation.* Retrieved from http://www.thenation.com/blog/175977/nfl-concussion-deal-rotten-all-sides#.

Index